Critical Essays on
Ralph Waldo Emerson

Critical Essays on Ralph Waldo Emerson

Robert E. Burkholder
and
Joel Myerson

G. K. Hall & Co. • Boston, Massachusetts

Library of Congress Cataloging in Publication Data
Main entry under title:

Critical essays on Ralph Waldo Emerson.

    (Critical essays on American literature)
    Includes index.
    1. Emerson, Ralph Waldo, 1803–1882—Criticism and interpreta-
tion—Addresses, essays, lectures. I. Burkholder, Robert E.
II. Myerson, Joel. III. Series.
PS1638.C74   1983   814'.3   82-15831
ISBN 0-8161-8305-8

CRITICAL ESSAYS ON AMERICAN LITERATURE

This series seeks to collect the most important previously published criticism on writers and topics in American literature along with, in various volumes, original essays, interviews, bibliographies, letters, manuscript sections, and other materials brought to public attention for the first time. This volume on Ralph Waldo Emerson, edited by Joel Myerson and Robert E. Burkholder, is the most extensive collection of comment on this writer ever assembled. It includes, in addition to an introduction that provides an historical overview of reaction to Emerson's life and work, selections from important writers of the period, including Thomas Carlyle, Edgar Allan Poe, Margaret Fuller, Henry James, and Walt Whitman, and reprinted articles by many of the leading modern scholars, among them Perry Miller, Tony Tanner, Merton M. Sealts, Jr., Lawrence Buell, and Gay Wilson Allen. We are confident that this collection will make an important contribution to American literary study.

JAMES NAGEL, GENERAL EDITOR

Northeastern University

TO
Val *and* Greta

CONTENTS

vii

INTRODUCTION

In choosing the contents for *Critical Essays on Ralph Waldo Emerson*, we have tried to select a series of works that would accurately reflect criticism on Emerson from his beginnings as a publishing author to the present. Because nearly every book-length study of Emerson is in print or readily available in libraries, we have decided not to reprint sections from these books. We have also avoided the "standard" works—such as studies by James Elliot Cabot, Oliver Wendell Holmes, Ralph L. Rusk, Perry Miller, Stephen E. Whicher, Newton Arvin, Henry Nash Smith, and Joel Porte —because they are easily found and because they have already been quoted at length in other books on Emerson. This volume, then, complements the book-length publications on Emerson already available.

Ralph Waldo Emerson was born in Boston on 25 May 1803, the fourth child of the Reverend William and Ruth Haskins Emerson. The death of young Waldo's father in 1811, just two weeks short of his eighth birthday, left the family in financial straits. Even so, Waldo attended the Boston Latin School from 1812 to 1817, when he entered Harvard College on a scholarship. His academic progress at Harvard was, as his biographer Ralph L. Rusk phrased it, "no blaze of glory,"[1] but inwardly he began to expand, for it was during this period that Emerson started to keep his journals, which came to form a "savings bank" upon which he later drew for his writings.[2] After graduation, Emerson taught a young ladies' school until 1825, when he began studying divinity at Harvard. In 1826 Emerson was licensed to preach, but a tubercular condition forced him to travel to Charleston, South Carolina, and St. Augustine, Florida, for a rest. After returning, Emerson supplied various pulpits until 1829, when he was ordained.

Emerson's ordination on 11 March at the prestigious Second Church of Boston, where he was also to serve as associate pastor, began his career with a flourish. His good luck continued when he married Ellen Louisa Tucker in September, but their happiness was short-lived, for she died of tuberculosis in February 1831. Emerson, torn by doubts over the church and still grieving for his lost wife, resigned his pulpit in October and sailed for Europe in December. His trip in Europe, during which he visited France, Italy, and England, was a great personal success, for he

1

met most of the literary lions of the day, including Thomas Carlyle, with whom he formed a lifelong friendship.

Although following his return to Boston in October 1833 Emerson occasionally preached, his real energies went into establishing himself as a successful lecturer. This he did, and in September 1835 he married Lydia Jackson. They moved to Concord, where they lived in the house that Emerson had occupied the previous year.

The year 1836, called the "annus mirabilis" of American Transcendentalism, began a decade of hard work and wide-spread recognition for Emerson.[3] The Transcendentalists, mainly a group of Harvard-educated Unitarian ministers, expressed their disagreement with the current state of affairs on three fronts: in literature, they championed English and continental writers, such as Carlyle and Goethe; in philosophy, they followed Kant in believing that man had an innate ability to perceive that his existence transcended mere sensory experience, as opposed to the prevailing Lockean sensationalism; and in religion, they denied the existence of miracles, preferring Christianity to rest upon the spirit of Christ rather than on His supposed deeds, as was the belief of the conservative Unitarians. Emerson's first book, *Nature*, published on 9 September 1836, was a rallying cry for the Transcendentalists, espousing as it did organicism in art and viewing Nature as a divine teacher of man. Also in September, Emerson helped form the Transcendental Club, which served as a forum for the Transcendentalists over the next four years, as they met some thirty times. Emerson was also instrumental in establishing the semi-official journal of the Transcendentalists, the *Dial*, in July 1840, and edited it from July 1842 until its demise in April 1844. During this period Emerson formed friendships with the major figures of the Transcendental movement—Bronson Alcott, Margaret Fuller, Theodore Parker, Henry David Thoreau—and the lesser ones—Ellery Channing, Elizabeth Palmer Peabody, Jones Very—as well as with some of those who opposed it, such as Nathaniel Hawthorne, his neighbor in Concord for a while. Emerson rounded out his activities by delivering addresses on the "American Scholar" before the Phi Beta Kappa Society at Harvard in 1837 and on the present dangers facing the church before the Harvard Divinity School in 1838, publishing numerous articles and poems in the *Dial*, continuing his successful lecturing career, and publishing *Essays* (1841) and *Essays: Second Series* (1844).

By 1844, whatever unity that had existed among the Transcendentalists was gone, and they pursued separate careers, still tied loosely together by a belief in reform, yet differing widely on how much was needed and what means were necessary to achieve it. Emerson's own career blossomed and he was now a literary man of renown. The publication of his *Poems* (1847), *Nature; Addresses, and Lectures* (1849), and *Representative Men* (1850) helped to establish him as "the Sage of Concord." *English Traits* (1856) compared—too favorably for some—English life with American, and in *The Conduct of Life* (1860), he demonstrated a growing conservatism, balancing his earlier belief in complete Freedom with the "Beautiful Necessity" of Fate. Other successful lectures and books followed, and Emerson died, a famous and honored man, at Concord on 27 April 1882. He was buried at Sleepy Hollow Cemetery, close to the graves of Alcott, Hawthorne, and Thoreau.

During his life, Emerson had exerted great influence on his contemporaries, both by his financial support of them, as in the cases of Alcott and Ellery Channing, or by his intellectual companionship, as in the case of his Concord neighbor, Thoreau. His discussions of organic form (everything proceeds from a natural order, followed by but not imposed upon man), self-reliance, optimism (evil does not exist as an actual force, merely being the absence of good), compensation, universal unity (or the Over-Soul), and the importance of individual moral insight were all influential in forming the literature and philosophy of nineteenth-century America. In poetry too, Emerson was an important force, and his organic theory of poetry ("it is not metres, but a metre-making argument that makes a poem") and his view of poets as "liberating gods" or prophets, did much to counteract the poetic conservatism of his day, and helped lead to the experimental verse of Walt Whitman, who once hailed Emerson as his master.

As the swings in Emerson's life indicate, he was different things to different people at different times. From a beginning as a youthful divinity student and promising minister, he became, successively, an intellectually radical reformer (at the same time anathema to the religious and philosophical conservatives and an inspiration to those seeking new paths to truth), a successful lecturer, a best-selling author, and, at the end of his life, "the Sage of Concord," now beloved by all and firmly enshrined in the American pantheon. As the *Boston Transcript* put it during the many celebrations in 1903 of the centenary of his birth, "The widespread public interest in the various memorial meetings, and the expressions of gratitude and admiration made by men of varying creeds and beliefs, have shown the deep hold which Emerson's philosophy has taken on the generations succeeding him."[4] The essays reprinted in this volume also reflect these swings in Emerson's reputation.

We selected nineteenth-century reviews and criticism with the intention of providing a greater sense of the texture of Emerson's reception by contemporaries than has previously been available. For that reason, we attempted to achieve a blend of well-known, pivotal essays and reviews on Emerson and more obscure, perhaps unknown, essays and reviews that help to define how the public in general received Emerson's writings. What emerges is the impression that instead of being the beneficiary of unrestrained puffing by friends or the victim of merciless hatchet-jobs by enemies, for surely there was plenty of both, Emerson's work was often met with judicious and perceptive criticism, quite an accomplishment in a nation that supposedly lacked both a literary identity and a critical tradition at the time Emerson published his most important writings.

The reviews of *Nature* by O. A. Brownson and E. P. Peabody, and W. H. Channing's review of "The American Scholar" address are positive commentaries on Emerson's early work which suggest that not only were Emerson's friends instrumental in promoting his ideas and writing to the public, but also that his initial reception was not as negative as the many reprintings of Francis Bowen's biting criticisms would suggest.[5]

The ten considerations of Emerson's Divinity School Address represent both the diversity of the response to that controversial event and the staunch defense of Emerson's position in the face of strident and often personal attacks upon him and his views. Of course, Andrews Norton's "The New School in Literature and Religion," the opening volley in this war of words, is notable for introducing what was essentially a religious controversy into the commercial newspapers.[6] Norton's belligerent rebuke of Emerson and all the religious and literary implications of his stand was soon answered by Theophilus Parsons, who had reservations about Emerson's thought, but who protests more to the offensive manner of Norton's response;[7] G. T. Davis, who questions the tone of Norton's attack because he saw it as ultimately contributing to Emerson's growing popularity;[8] "Z.," who writes from the perspective of the small band of Boston freethinkers headed by Abner Kneeland;[9] and Chandler Robbins, who as Emerson's friend and successor in the pulpit of Boston's Second Church as well as editor of the Unitarian weekly, the *Christian Register*, demonstrates the need to protect both Emerson and the Church's official position.[10] Emerson and Boston Unitarianism not only received censure from the orthodox theologians at Princeton[11] but also from the religious conservatives at Yale, here represented by the anonymous review of Emerson's address from the *Quarterly Christian Spectator*;[12] from Southern Unitarians, notably Samuel Gilman in the *Southern Rose*, published in Charleston, South Carolina;[13] and the Boston Congregationalists who published the *Boston Recorder*, and who seem a bit incredulous in their review of the address, since they apparently assumed all along that the liberalism of Unitarianism would eventually lead to infidelity.[14] Of course, James Freeman Clarke's "R. W. Emerson and the New School" and "The New School in Literature and Religion" represent the definitive defense of Emerson's views and the definitive refutation of Norton's.[15]

The anonymous review of *Essays* from the *New York Review* continued a critical theme introduced in reviews of the Divinity School Address—that Emerson is an unsystematic fanatic preaching a godless philosophy—a far cry from Thomas Carlyle's reserved praise in his introduction to the English edition of the same work, Brownson's defense of *Essays*, or William Alfred Jones's careful consideration of Emerson's imagination, style, and voice.[16] These essays also make it apparent that the 1840s were important years for defining Emerson and the worth of his work in the minds of critics. During this decade, responses ranged from the glibly negative consideration of Emerson by Poe in his "An Appendix of Autographs," to the confusion over Emerson's value expressed by an anonymous reviewer of *The Method of Nature* in the *Monthly Miscellany of Religion and Letters*, to a strong defense of Emerson's philosophy in general and *Essays: Second Series* in particular by "A Disciple" in the pages of the *Democratic Review*, and Margaret Fuller's important but measured consideration of the same work for the *New-York Tribune*.[17] Add to this range of comment James Russell Lowell's influential portrayal of Emerson as a "Plotinus-Montaigne" in his *A Fable for Critics*, and it becomes apparent that criticism of the 1840s substantially contributed to defining Emerson for future reviewers and commentators.[18] Certainly the most elaborate praise Emerson received during this period was from an anonymous reviewer for the *Boston Post* who, in describing Emerson as a lecturer, is embarrassingly bombastic in his choice of metaphors.[19] The reviews of *Poems* by Cyrus Bartol and an anonymous critic for the *Democratic Review* represent reasonable considerations of a work not taken seriously by some reviewers, and should be compared with David Wasson's praise of Emerson's *May-Day*, a less daring and original volume than *Poems*.[20] The anonymous review of *Nature; Addresses, and Lectures* suggests that even if the Unitarians were unwilling to forgive Emerson his supposed infidelity more than a decade after his address at Divinity Hall, they were at least susceptible to being exhilarated by his work.[21] As Frederic Dan Huntington's review of *English Traits* shows, this tendency to praise Emerson's writing while at the same time lamenting his want of Christian orthodoxy was continued for many years, especially in publications representing the views of conservative denominations.[22]

The two reviews of *Representative Men* from the Amherst *Indicator* and the *Yale Literary Magazine* suggest the important influence Emerson exerted on college campuses by 1850.[23] This influence is further demonstrated in the anonymous consideration of Emerson's "shady side" in the April 1858 *Rutger's College Quarterly*.[24] Theodore Parker's definitive commentary on Emerson and his work attempts to evaluate him through a detailed examination of his writing and thought. The final section of Parker's essay, reprinted here, coalesces all of Parker's praise and blame into a final judgment that Emerson's importance lies in his goodness and humanity.[25] Two other general appraisals of Emerson from roughly the same period are George Henry Calvert's appreciative essay, which seeks to show how Emerson's originality caused him to be misunderstood, and John Custis Darby's essay, published in a religious periodical in Richmond, Virginia, which argues that Emerson would return us all to the paganism of ancient Greece.[26] The resentment of Southern critics toward Emerson, whose name was often linked with radical abolitionists like William Lloyd Garrison in the Southern press, is even more effectively illustrated in the anonymous review of *The Conduct of Life* from the *Southern Literary Messenger*, published on the eve of the attack on Fort Sumter.[27] James Russell Lowell's consideration of the same work in the *Atlantic Monthly* emphasizes the distinctly Yankee quality of Emerson's work and continues the theme of treating Emerson as a blend of practicality and mysticism that Lowell had introduced in *A Fable for Critics*. This review was later abbreviated and tacked on to a shortened version of Lowell's "Mr. Emerson's New Course of Lectures" from the *Nation* and reprinted as "Emerson, the Lecturer" in Lowell's *My Study Windows*.[28]

Two controversies that swirled around Emerson in the late 1850s are also represented by reprinted selections. The first of these involved the publication of Emerson's poem, "Brahma," in the November 1857 *Atlantic Monthly*. For the wits of 1857, the poem provided seemingly endless opportunities for parody. "Phasma," an anonymous effort published in the *New York Sun*, is only one of literally dozens of lampoons which found their way into print, and these parodies, in turn, occasioned a number of defenses of Emerson's poem, like that by Charles Godfrey Leland in *Graham's*.[29] The second controversy blossomed out of Emerson's famous congratulatory letter to Whitman following the publication of the first edition of *Leaves of Grass* in 1855.[30] When Whitman reproduced that letter in the 1856 second edition, he managed to link publicly Emerson's by-now-respected name with his own work, leaving dismayed critics, like the one in *Frank Leslie's Illustrated Newspaper*, to wonder at Emerson's motives and to denounce him along with Whitman as a pornographer.[31]

Following the Civil War, Emerson's position as the acknowledged master of American writers, even at a time when his considerable powers were on the decline, meant that he was less the focal point of attack and more the object of eulogy than ever before. For this reason, Bret Harte's appraisal of Emerson's *Society and Solitude* is all the more interesting, since it is a westerner's evaluation of the work of a man who significantly contributed to formulating America's perceptions of the West. To Harte, Emerson's notions about life on the frontier were unrealistic because they were evolved "from his moral consciousness" and not from any solid knowledge of frontier life.[32] Henry James's most famous commentary on Emerson is his review of Cabot's biography in the December 1887 *Macmillan's Magazine*, but his brief consideration of Emerson in his biography of Hawthorne is most effective in communicating to the reader the power Emerson's words held over a nation on the verge of losing its innocence.[33] As such, James's assessment of Emerson's central position in the intellectual life of his age serves as a balance to his father's curmudgeonly essay, which suggests that Emerson was completely without conscience, lacking in knowledge, and may not in fact have been real at all!

Whitman's "How I Still Get Around and Take Notes," Huntington's "Ralph Waldo Emerson," Moncure D. Conway's *Emerson and his Views of Nature*, and Christopher Pearse Cranch's "Ralph Waldo Emerson" are all pieces that appeared immediately before or after Emerson's death, but each selection offers a different perspective from which to view Emerson. As Whitman's title suggests, his essay is as much about himself as it is about Emerson; however, his accounts of visits with Emerson just six months before his death, his brief interpretation of the facts of Emerson's life, and his final tribute to Emerson's influence, make this reminiscence an important statement about the continuity of nineteenth-century American literature.[34] Conway's little-known address to the Royal Institution of Great Britain is a significant early statement of Emerson's relationship to and anticipation of the most important scientific thought of his age.[35] Huntington's assessment of Emerson caused a furor at the time of its publication because many felt it too negative a treatment of a man who deserved to be remembered in a better light.[36] It is typical of the public idolatry at the time of Emerson's death that any comment that even implied criticism of him was considerd profane. Certainly, Cranch's eulogy, although wide-ranging, substantive, and valuable because it is a tribute from a personal friend, is much more typical of appraisals of Emerson immediately following his death than Huntington's.[37] Nevertheless, this reverence afforded Emerson by the public made most substantive criticism of Emerson's work nearly impossible, as Matthew Arnold so rudely discovered when he came to Boston in December 1883 to announce that Emerson's work did not entitle him to be ranked with the great poets or philosophers.[38] Arnold's apparent perplexity over the resulting denunciation of him and his views suggests that he failed to grasp the significance of the cult of worshippers who guarded Emerson's memory and reputation as though he were a national shrine.

Such devotion, however, did not completely preempt sound criticism that is still of value today. One need only read through William Torrey Harris's discussion of the organic structure of the essay "Experience" to be convinced that not all late nineteenth-century criticism of Emerson should be dismissed as so much sentimental claptrap.[39] And the same might be said about Henry Athanasius Brann's acerbic attack on German metaphysics and Emersonian philosophy;[40] John M. Robertson's thorough and even-handed evaluation of Emerson's life, work, and philosophy;[41] Henry Demarest Lloyd's surprising argument for the importance Emerson placed upon wit and humor;[42] and George Santayana's general assessment of Emerson's significance to American and world literature and philosophy.[43] It is fitting that Santayana's dispassionate evaluation of Emerson as a thinker and writer whose importance rests on his original expression of well-worn ideas should serve as a transition to the cooler light of twentieth-century criticism, where Emerson's work would continually be the subject of analyses that would aim at casting aside the myth of the "Sage of Concord" in order to discover the substance and nature of the ideas that created the myth.

In the twentieth century, we have chosen three classes of essays:

those which deal with specific periods in Emerson's life; those which deal with general topics of interest to Emerson throughout his life; and those which place Emerson in the broad context of American literature and thought. (We have purposely not reprinted any essay which deals with only one or two works by Emerson.)

The development of Emerson's early thought, prior to the publication of his first volume of essays in 1841, can be seen by reading the articles by A. M. Baumgartner on his early lectures, Ralph C. LaRosa on his early journals, David Robinson on his early ideas about nature, and Merton M. Sealts, Jr., on his concept of the scholar.[44] Phyllis Cole deals sensitively with "Emerson, England, and Fate," as does Leonard Neufeldt on "Emerson and the Civil War."[45]

Other critics deal with specific concepts which attracted Emerson's attention: Gay Wilson Allen on Emerson and science, Robert Detweiler on the Over-Soul, Alexander Kern on Emerson and economics, Norman Miller on Emerson's each-and-all concept, Henry F. Pommer on Emerson and compensation, Robert D. Richardson, Jr., on Emerson and myth, Carl F. Strauch on Emerson's doctrine of sympathy, and Tony Tanner on Emerson's use of visionary imagery.[46] Essays by Lawrence Buell and R. A. Yoder perceptively analyze Emerson's literary method, and Joseph F. Doherty helps to explain why Emerson often appears to be standoffish in his writings.[47]

Two general essays place Emerson in a larger context. William L. Hedges discusses American thought "From Franklin to Emerson," establishing a continuity and a complementary argument to Perry Miller's famous article, "From Edwards to Emerson."[48] Miller himself examines "Emersonian Genius and American Democracy," an essay which shows Emerson's central position in the development of American thought.[49]

Because of the enormous amount of writings about Emerson (the most recent bibliography lists about 6,000 items, and it is selective), we have chosen to present in our Introduction those primary and bibliographical works with which the reader can begin a more complete study of Emerson's life, writings, and thought.

The first separate primary bibliography of Emerson was George Willis Cooke's A Bibliography of Ralph Waldo Emerson (1908).[50] Although excellent for its time, it is now outdated. The only comprehensive bibliography of Emerson's writings is Joel Myerson's Ralph Waldo Emerson: A Descriptive Bibliography (1982), which lists all editions and printings of Emerson's works in English, all foreign-language editions of his works through 1882, all collected editions and collections of Emerson's works, all first-appearance contributions to books, pamphlets, newspapers, and magazines, all books edited by Emerson, all reprinted material in books and pamphlets through 1882, and material attributed to Emerson.[51]

Cooke's book is also the first significant secondary bibliography of

Emerson. Its listing of nineteenth-century works is supplemented by William J. Sowder's list of British reviews of Emerson's works, "Emerson's Reviewers and Commentators: Nineteenth-Century Periodical Criticism" (1968).[52] Jeanetta Boswell's *Ralph Waldo Emerson and the Critics* (1979) cumulates material for the period 1900–1977, and adds a few titles to those available in earlier bibliographies, while perpetuating their errors and introducing new ones.[53] Boswell clearly has not seen most of the items she lists, resulting in numerous errors, false leads, and even non-existent works. An excellent annotated bibliography of criticism published between 1951 and 1961 is Jackson R. Bryer and Robert A. Rees's "A Checklist of Emerson Criticism, 1951–1961" (1964), and through 1976 on Emerson's prose is Annette M. Woodlief's "Emerson's Prose: An Annotated Checklist of Literary Criticism Through 1976" (1978).[54] All of these have been superseded by Robert E. Burkholder and Myerson's *Ralph Waldo Emerson: An Annotated Secondary Bibliography*, a massive, fully-annotated listing of some 6,000 works from 1816 to 1979 (forthcoming).[55]

There are a number of good bibliographical essays on Emerson. Burkholder's introduction to "Ralph Waldo Emerson's Reputation, 1831–1861: With a Secondary Bibliography" (1979) is an excellent—and the only—discussion of Emerson's contemporary reception in America during the years indicated.[56] William J. Sowder's *Emerson's Impact on the British Isles and Canada* (1966), which covers the nineteenth-century response to Emerson in those countries, focuses more on the poetry than on the prose works.[57] The bibliographical essays by Floyd Stovall in *Eight American Authors* (1956, 1971) are also useful overviews, as is the essay by Burkholder and Myerson in *The Transcendentalists: A Review of Research and Criticism*, ed. Myerson (forthcoming).[58]

Four other bibliographical works deserve mention. George Shelton Hubbell's *A Concordance to the Poems of Ralph Waldo Emerson* (1932) is restricted to those poems published in volume nine of the Centenary Edition (see below).[59] Eugene F. Irey's *Concordance to Five Essays of Ralph Waldo Emerson* (1981) arbitrarily (and despite its title) chooses *Nature*, "The American Scholar," Divinity School Address, "Self-Reliance," and "Fate," and uses the now-superseded Centenary Edition texts.[60] Mary Alice Ihrig's *Emerson's Transcendental Vocabulary* (1982) lists all appearances of certain word clusters in the first seven volumes of the Centenary Edition.[61] All three concordances list the words in context. Walter Harding's *Emerson's Library* (1967) lists all the books Emerson is known to have owned but not, as Harding acknowledges, all the ones he is known to have read or used.[62]

The standard edition of Emerson's works is *The Complete Works of Ralph Waldo Emerson*, 12 vols. (1903–1904), referred to as the Centenary Edition.[63] While the notes by Emerson's son Edward are excellent, the texts have been mangled by editing them according to turn-of-the-century standards. This edition is slowly being superseded by *The Collected*

Works of Ralph Waldo Emerson (1971–   ).[64] But some works published by Emerson will not appear in either edition, most notably his college compositions (see *Two Unpublished Essays* [1896] and *Indian Superstition* [1954]), his translation of Dante's *Vita Nuova*, and a number of periodical and giftbook contributions, some of which were slapped together as *Uncollected Writings* (1912).[65] Numerous periodical, giftbook, and pamphlet appearances still remain uncollected; for a listing, see Myerson's bibliography. Unfortunately, many works Emerson published in the last decade of his life were pieced together with the help of his daughter Ellen and James Elliot Cabot; until their role in the publication of these works (particularly *Society and Solitude* [1870], *Letters and Social Aims* [1876], and the posthumously published *Miscellanies* [1884], *Lectures and Biographical Sketches* [1884], and *Natural History of Intellect* [1893]) is clarified, the editing of them remains of doubtful value.

Some twenty-five of Emerson's 170 sermons have been edited and annotated with care in *Young Emerson Speaks: Unpublished Discourses on Many Subjects* (1938).[66] A complete edition of Emerson's sermons is a prime desideratum. Emerson's lectures have fared better. *The Early Lectures of Ralph Waldo Emerson*, 3 vols. (1959–1972), is a masterful edition from Emerson's manuscripts for the lectures given between 1833 and 1842.[67] Supplemental annotations to the first volume have been published in Kenneth Walter Cameron's *A Commentary on Emerson's Early Lectures (1833–1836) With an Index-Concordance* (1962).[68]

Editors have also done well by Emerson's journals. *Journals of Ralph Waldo Emerson*, 10 vols. (1909–1914),[69] is being superseded by *The Journals and Miscellaneous Notebooks of Ralph Waldo Emerson* (1960–1982).[70] Textually accurate (symbols allow the reader to follow the process of Emerson's writings) and fully annotated (including cross-references for journal passages that appeared in print), this edition has published sixteen volumes under its present title and will soon begin a new series, under the general editorship of Ralph H. Orth, with the publication of Emerson's poetry notebooks.

The Letters of Ralph Waldo Emerson, 6 vols. (1939), is a brilliantly edited work.[71] The texts are accurate, the annotations lengthy, and the index comprehensive. It is arguably the best edition of an American writer's letters. Still, for reasons of space and copyright, most letters that had previously appeared in print were omitted, including Emerson's correspondence with Henry David Thoreau, John Sterling, Samuel Gray Ward, Herman Grimm, William Henry Furness, and Arthur Hugh Clough.[72] Emerson's correspondence with Carlyle, first published in 1883 with a supplementary volume in 1886, was also not included, but *The Correspondence of Emerson and Carlyle*, ed. Joseph Slater (1964), edits them with care.[73] For other, uncollected letters, see Myerson's bibliography. A supplemental edition of Emerson's letters, including all the ones known but not printed by Rusk and those which have come to light since 1939, is being edited by Eleanor M. Tilton.

Mr. Burkholder has had primary responsibility for choosing the nineteenth-century materials in this volume, Mr. Myerson for the twentieth-century studies; the final selection is the choice of both editors. The introduction was written by the editors jointly. Both editors would like to thank James Nagel for his continued assistance. Mr. Burkholder would like to thank the English Department of The Pennsylvania State University and its chairman, Wendell V. Harris; Deans Thomas J. Knight and Thomas F. Magner of the College of Liberal Arts of the Pennsylvania State University; the Institute for the Arts and Humanistic Studies and its director, Stanley Weintraub; and the Scholarly Activities Committee of the Wilkes-Barre Campus and its chairman, Thomas Winter, for their support and encouragement. A debt of gratitude is also owed to Kaye Edwards, Charles Hackenberry, Loretta Ritzie, James H. Ryan, Frederick J. Stefon, Mary Thom, and especially Nils A. Parr. Mr. Myerson would like to thank the English Department of the University of South Carolina and its chairman, George L. Geckle, for support, and especially Caroline Bokinsky for helping to see the book through the press. Both editors have wisely acknowledged the sources of their most important support in the dedications of this volume.

R.E.B.

J.M.

Wilkes-Barre, Pennsylvania
Edisto Beach, South Carolina
23 April 1982

Notes

1. Ralph L. Rusk, *The Life of Ralph Waldo Emerson* (New York: Scribners, 1949), p. 86.

2. See Bliss Perry, "Emerson's Savings Bank," *In Praise of Folly and Other Papers* (Boston: Houghton Mifflin, 1923), pp. 114–29.

3. The phrase "annus mirabilis" gained popularity after Perry Miller's use of it in his edition of *The Transcendentalists: An Anthology* (Cambridge: Harvard University Press, 1950).

4. *Boston Transcript*, 29 May 1903, quoted in *The Emerson Centennial* (N.p.: n.p., 1903), p. 1.

5. [Orestes A. Brownson], [Review of *Nature*], *Boston Reformer*, 10 September 1836, p. 2; [Elizabeth Palmer Peabody], "Nature—A Prose Poem," *United States Magazine, and Democratic Review*, 1 (February 1838), 319–27; [William Henry Channing], [Review of *An Oration, Delivered Before the Phi Beta Kappa Society, at Cambridge, August 31, 1837*], *Boston Quarterly Review*, 1 (January 1838), 113–20; see F[rancis] B[owen], "Transcendentalism," *Christian Examiner*, 21 (January 1837), 371–85.

6. [Andrews Norton], "The New School in Literature and Religion," *Boston Daily Advertiser*, 27 August 1838, p. 2.

7. S. X. [Theophilus Parsons], "The New School and Its Opponents," *Boston Daily Advertiser*, 30 August 1838, p. 2.

8. [George T. Davis], [Review of *An Address Delivered Before the Senior Class in Divinity College, Cambridge . . . 15 July, 1838*], *Boston Post*, 31 August 1838, p. 1.

9. Z., "Rev. Mr. Emerson," *Boston Investigator*, 27 September 1838, p. 3.

10. [Chandler Robbins], [Mr. Emerson and the Unitarians], *Christian Register*, 17 (29 September 1838), 154–55.

11. See [J. W. Alexander, A. Dod, and Charles Hodge], "Transcendentalism," *Biblical Repertory and Princeton Review*, 11 (January 1839), 95–99.

12. [Review of *An Address Delivered Before the Senior Class in Divinity College, Cambridge . . . 15 July, 1838*], *Quarterly Christian Spectator*, 10 (November 1838), 670–74.

13. S[amuel] G[ilman], "Ralph Waldo Emerson," *Southern Rose*, 7 (24 November 1838), 100–06.

14. C., "Unitarianism," *Boston Recorder*, 24 (11 January 1839), 5.

15. [James Freeman Clarke], "R. W. Emerson and the New School" and "The New School in Literature and Religion," *Western Messenger*, 6 (November 1838), 37–42, 42–47.

16. [Review of *Essays*], *New York Review*, 8 (April 1841), 509–12; T. Carlyle, "Preface by the English Editor," in Emerson, *Essays* (London: James Fraser, 1841), pp. vii–xiii; [Orestes A. Brownson], "Emerson's *Essays*," *Boston Quarterly Review*, 4 (July 1841), 291–308; [William Alfred] J[ones], "Ralph Waldo Emerson," *Arcturus*, 1 (April 1841), 278–84.

17. E[dgar] A[llan] Poe, "An Appendix of Autographs," *Graham's Magazine*, 20 (January 1842), 48; [Review of *The Method of Nature*], *Monthly Miscellany of Religion and Letters*, 5 (December 1841), 346–47; "A Disciple," "Emerson's Essays," *United States Magazine, and Democratic Review*, 16 (June 1845), 589–602; [Margaret Fuller], [Review of *Essays: Second Series*], *New-York Daily Tribune*, 7 December 1844, p. 1.

18. See [James Russell Lowell], *A Fable for Critics* (New York: G. P. Putnam, 1848), pp. 28–32.

19. [Emerson as a Lecturer], *Boston Post*, 25 January 1849, p. 2.

20. C[yrus] A[ugustus] B[artol], "Poetry and Imagination," *Christian Examiner*, 42 (March 1847), 255–62; "New Poetry in New England," *United States Magazine, and Democratic Review*, 20 (May 1847), 392–98; D[avid] A[twood] W[asson], [Review of *May-Day and Other Poems*], *Radical*, 2 (August 1867), 760–62.

21. [Review of *Nature; Addresses, and Lectures*], *Christian Register*, 28 (29 September 1849), 155.

22. [Frederic Dan Huntington], "Editor's Collectanea," *Monthly Religious Magazine and Independent Journal*, 16 (September 1856), 214.

23. [George Gould], [Review of *Representative Men*], *Indicator* [Amherst College], 2 (February 1850), 214–20; L. W. B., "Ralph Waldo Emerson," *Yale Literary Magazine*, 15 (March 1850), 203–06.

24. "Emerson," *Rutger's College Quarterly*, 1 (April 1858), 32–38.

25. [Theodore Parker], "The Writings of Ralph Waldo Emerson," *Massachusetts Quarterly Review*, 3 (March 1850), 200–55.

26. [George Henry Calvert], "Ralph Waldo Emerson," *New York Quarterly*, 1 (January 1853), 439–46; John Custis Darby, "Ralph Waldo Emerson," *Quarterly Review of the Methodist Episcopal Church, South*, 6 (January 1852), 31–42.

27. [Review of *The Conduct of Life*], *Southern Literary Messenger*, 32 (April 1861), 326–27.

28. [James Russell Lowell], [Review of *The Conduct of Life*], *Atlantic Monthly Magazine*, 7 (February 1861), 254–55; J[ames] R[ussell] L[owell]," "Mr. Emerson's New Course of Lectures," *Nation*, 7 (12 November 1868), 389–90; both combined and reprinted as "Emerson, the Lecturer," *My Study Windows* (Boston: James R. Osgood, 1871), pp. 375–84.

29. "Phasma," *Boston Courier*, 23 November 1857, p. 2; [Charles Godfrey Leland], "Editor's Easy Talk," *Graham's Magazine*, 52 (March 1858), 272–74.

30. Whitman first published Emerson's letter, without his permission, in "Leaves of Grass," *New-York Daily Tribune*, 10 October 1855, p. 7. He again used the letter, without Emerson's permission, in the second edition of *Leaves of Grass* (Brooklyn, N.Y.: n.p., 1856), pp. 345–46, and had stamped in gold at the foot of the spine "I Greet you at the beginning of a Great Career R.W. Emerson." And, again, he printed the letter in *Leaves of Grass Imprints* (Boston: Thayer and Eldridge, 1860), p. 2.

31. [Review of *Leaves of Grass*], *Frank Leslie's Illustrated Newspaper*, 3 (20 December 1856), 42.

32. [Bret Harte], [Review of *Society and Solitude*], *Overland Monthly*, 5 (October 1870), 386–87.

33. Henry James, "Cabot's Life of Emerson," *Macmillan's Magazine*, 57 (December 1887), 86–98; rpt. in *Partial Portraits* (London: Macmillan, 1888), pp. 1–33; Henry James, *Hawthorne* (New York: Macmillan, 1879), pp. 80–84.

34. Walt Whitman, "How I Still Get Around and Take Notes. (No. 5.)," *Critic*, 1 (3 December 1881), 330–31.

35. Moncure D. Conway, *Emerson and his Views of Nature* (London: Royal Institution of Great Britain, 1883).

36. F. D. Huntington, "Ralph Waldo Emerson," *Independent*, 34 (18, 25 May 1882), 1–2, 1–2.

37. Christopher P. Cranch, "Ralph Waldo Emerson," *Unitarian Review and Religious Magazine*, 20 (July 1883), 1–19.

38. See Matthew Arnold, "Emerson," *Macmillan's Magazine*, 50 (May 1884), 1–13; rpt. in *Discourses in America* (London: Macmillan, 1885), pp. 138–207.

39. W[illiam] T[orrey] Harris, "The Dialectic Unity in Emerson's Prose," *Journal of Speculative Philosophy*, 18 (April 1884), 195–202.

40. [Henry Athanasius Brann], "Hegel and his New England Echo," *Catholic World*, 41 (April 1885), 56–61.

41. John M. Robertson, "Emerson," *Modern Humanists: Sociological Studies of Carlyle, Mill, Emerson, Arnold, Ruskin, and Spencer with an Epilogue on Social Reconstruction* (London: Swan Sonnenschein, 1891), pp. 112–36.

42. Henry Demarest Lloyd, "Emerson's Wit and Humor," *Forum*, 22 (November 1896), 346–57.

43. George Santayana, "Ralph Waldo Emerson," in *American Prose: Selections with Critical Introductions by Various Writers and a General Introduction*, ed. George Rice Carpenter (New York: Macmillan, 1898), pp. 187–93.

44. A. M. Baumgartner, " 'The Lyceum is My Pulpit': Homiletics in Emerson's Early Lectures," *American Literature*, 34 (January 1963), 477–86; Ralph C. LaRosa, "Emerson's Search for Literary Form: The Early Journals," *Modern Philology*, 69 (August 1971), 25–35; David Robinson, "Emerson's Natural Theology and the Paris Naturalists: Toward a Theory of Animated Nature," *Journal of the History of Ideas*, 41 (January-March 1980), 69–88; Merton M. Sealts, Jr., "Emerson on the Scholar, 1833–1837," *PMLA*, 85 (March 1970), 185–95.

45. Phyllis Cole, "Emerson, England, and Fate," in *Emerson: Prophecy, Metamorphosis, and Influence*, ed. David Levin (New York: Columbia University Press, 1975), pp. 83–105; Leonard Neufeldt, "Emerson and the Civil War," *Journal of English and Germanic Philology*, 71 (October 1972), 503–513.

46. Gay Wilson Allen, "A New Look at Emerson and Science," in *Literature and Ideas in America: Essays in Memory of Harry Hayden Clark*, ed. Robert Falk (Athens: Ohio University Press, 1975), pp. 58–78; Robert Detweiler, "The Over-Rated 'Over-Soul,' " *American Literature*, 36 (March 1964), 65–68; Alexander C. Kern, "Emerson and Economics," *New England Quarterly*, 13 (December 1940), 678–96; Norman Miller, "Emerson's 'Each and All' Concept: A Reexamination," *New England Quarterly*, 41 (September 1968), 381–92; Henry F. Pommer, "The Contents and Basis of Emerson's Belief in Compensation," *PMLA*, 77 (June 1962), 248–53; Robert D. Richardson, Jr., "Emerson," *Myth and Literature in the American Renaissance* (Bloomington: Indiana University Press, 1978), pp. 65–89, 245–49; Carl F. Strauch, "Emerson and the Doctrine of Sympathy," *Studies in Romanticism*, 6 (Spring 1967), 152–74; Tony Tanner, "Emerson: The Unconquered Eye and the Enchanted Circle," *Reign of Wonder: Naivety and Reality in American Literature* (Cambridge, England: Cambridge University Press, 1965), pp. 26–45, 363–64.

47. Lawrence I. Buell, "Reading Emerson for the Structures: The Coherence of the Essays," *Quarterly Journal of Speech*, 58 (February 1972), 58–69; R. A. Yoder, "Emerson's Dialectic," *Criticism*, 11 (Fall 1969), 313–28; Joseph F. Doherty, "Emerson and the Loneliness of the Gods," *Texas Studies in Literature and Language*, 16 (Spring 1974), 65–75.

48. William L. Hedges, "From Franklin to Emerson," in *The Oldest Revolutionary: Essays on Benjamin Franklin*, ed. J. A. Leo Lemay (Philadelphia: University of Pennsylvania Press, 1976), pp. 139–56; see also Perry Miller, "From Edwards to Emerson," *New England Quarterly*, 13 (December 1940), 589–617; rpt. with additional material in *Errand into the Wilderness* (Cambridge: Harvard University Press, 1956), pp. 184–203.

49. Perry Miller, "Emersonian Genius and American Democracy," *New England Quarterly*, 26 (March 1953), 27–44.

50. George Willis Cooke, *A Bibliography of Ralph Waldo Emerson* (Boston: Houghton Mifflin, 1908).

51. Joel Myerson, *Ralph Waldo Emerson: A Descriptive Bibliography* (Pittsburgh: University of Pittsburgh Press, 1982).

52. William J. Sowder, "Emerson's Reviewers and Commentators: Nineteenth-Century Periodical Criticism," *Emerson Society Quarterly*, no. 53 (4th Quarter 1968), 5–51; rpt. as *Emerson's Reviewers and Commentators* (Hartford, Conn.: Transcendental Books, 1968).

53. Jeanetta Boswell, *Ralph Waldo Emerson and the Critics* (Metuchen, N.J.: Scarecrow, 1979).

54. Jackson R. Bryer and Robert A. Rees, "A Checklist of Emerson Criticism, 1951–1961," *Emerson Society Quarterly*, no. 37 (4th Quarter 1964), 1–50; rpt. as *A Checklist of Emerson Criticism, 1951–1961* (Hartford, Conn.: Transcendental Books, 1964); Annette M. Woodlief, "Emerson's Prose: An Annotated Checklist of Literary Criticism Through 1976," in *Studies in the American Renaissance 1978*, ed. Joel Myerson (Boston: Twayne, 1978), pp. 105–60.

55. Robert E. Burkholder and Joel Myerson, *Ralph Waldo Emerson: An Annotated Secondary Bibliography* (Pittsburgh: University of Pittsburgh Press, forthcoming).

56. Robert E. Burkholder, "Ralph Waldo Emerson's Reputation, 1831–1861: With a Secondary Bibliography," Ph.D. dissertation, University of South Carolina, 1979.

57. William J. Sowder, *Emerson's Impact on the British Isles and Canada* (Charlottesville: University Press of Virginia, 1966).

58. Floyd Stovall, "Ralph Waldo Emerson," in *Eight American Authors*, ed. Stovall (New York: Modern Language Association, 1956), pp. 47–99; rev. ed., ed. James Woodress (New York: W. W. Norton, 1971), pp. 37–83; Robert E. Burkholder and Joel Myerson, "Ralph Waldo Emerson," in *The Transcendentalists: A Review of Research and Criticism*, ed. Myerson (New York: Modern Language Association, forthcoming).

59. George Shelton Hubbell, *A Concordance to the Poems of Ralph Waldo Emerson* (New York: H. W. Wilson, 1932).

60. Eugene F. Irey, *Concordance to Five Essays of Ralph Waldo Emerson* (New York: Garland, 1981).

61. Mary Alice Ihrig, *Emerson's Transdendental Vocabulary* (New York: Garland, 1982).

62. Walter Harding, *Emerson's Library* (Charlottesville: University Press of Virginia, 1967).

63. *The Complete Works of Ralph Waldo Emerson*, ed. Edward Waldo Emerson, 12 vols. (Boston: Houghton, Mifflin, 1903–1904).

64. *The Collected Works of Ralph Waldo Emerson*, ed. Alfred R. Ferguson et al., 2 vols. to date (Cambridge: Harvard University Press, 1971–   ).

65. *Two Unpublished Essays*, ed. Edward Everett Hale (Boston: Lamson, Wolffe, 1896); *Indian Superstition*, ed. Kenneth Walter Cameron (Hanover, N.H.: Dartmouth College Library, 1954); J. Chesley Mathews, "Emerson's Translation of Dante's *Vita Nuova*," *Harvard Library Bulletin*, 11 (Spring, Autumn 1957), 208–44, 346–52; rev. ed., *Dante's* Vita Nuova. *Translated by Ralph Waldo Emerson* (Chapel Hill: University of North Carolina Press, 1960); *Uncollected Writings*, ed. Charles C. Bigelow (New York: Lamb, 1912).

66. *Young Emerson Speaks: Unpublished Discourses on Many Subjects*, ed. Arthur Cushman McGiffert, Jr. (Boston: Houghton Mifflin, 1938).

67. *The Early Lectures of Ralph Waldo Emerson*, ed. Robert E. Spiller, Stephen E. Whicher, and Wallace E. Williams, 3 vols. (Cambridge: Harvard University Press, 1959–1972).

68. Kenneth Walter Cameron, *A Commentary on Emerson's Early Lectures (1833–1836) With an Index-Concordance* (Hartford, Conn.: Transcendental Books, 1962).

69. *Journals of Ralph Waldo Emerson*, ed. Edward Waldo Emerson and Waldo Emerson Forbes, 10 vols. (Boston: Houghton Mifflin, 1909–1914).

70. *The Journals and Miscellaneous Notebooks of Ralph Waldo Emerson*, ed. William H. Gilman et al., 16 vols. (Cambridge: Harvard University Press, 1960–1982).

71. *The Letters of Ralph Waldo Emerson*, ed. Ralph L. Rusk, 6 vols. (New York: Columbia University Press, 1939).

72. F. B. Sanborn, "The Emerson-Thoreau Correspondence," *Atlantic Monthly Magazine*, 69 (May, June 1892), 577–96, 736–53; *A Correspondence Between John Sterling and Ralph Waldo Emerson*, ed. Edward Waldo Emerson (Boston: Houghton, Mifflin, 1897); *Letters from Ralph Waldo Emerson to a Friend*, ed. Charles Eliot Norton (Boston: Houghton, Mifflin, 1899); *Correspondence Between Ralph Waldo Emerson and Herman Grimm*, ed. Frederick William Holls (Boston: Houghton, Mifflin, 1903); *Records of a Lifelong Friendship*, ed. Horace Howard Furness (Boston: Houghton Mifflin, 1910); *Emerson-Clough Letters*, ed. Howard F. Lowry and Ralph Leslie Rusk (Cleveland: Rowfant Club, 1934).

73. *The Correspondence of Thomas Carlyle and Ralph Waldo Emerson 1834–1872*, ed. Charles Eliot Norton, 2 vols. (Boston: Houghton, Mifflin, 1883); *The Correspondence of Thomas Carlyle and Ralph Waldo Emerson 1834–1872. Supplementary Letters*, ed. Charles Eliot Norton (Boston: Ticknor, 1886); *The Correspondence of Emerson and Carlyle*, ed. Joseph Slater (New York: Columbia University Press, 1964).

[Nature]

[Orestes Augustus Brownson]*

This is a singular book. It is the creation of a mind that lives and moves in the Beautiful, and has the power of assimilating to itself whatever it sees, hears or touches. We cannot analyze it; whoever would form an idea of it must read it.

We welcome it however as an index to the spirit which is silently at work among us, as a proof that mind is about to receive a new and a more glorious manifestation; that higher problems and holier speculations than those which have hitherto engrossed us, are to engage our attention; and that the inquiries, what is perfect in Art, and what is true in Philosophy, are to surpass in interest those which concern the best place to locate a city, construct a rail road, or become suddenly rich. We prophesy that it is the forerunner of a new class of books, the harbinger of a new Literature as much superior to whatever has been, as our political insti[t]utions are superior to those of the Old World.

This book is aesthetical rather than philosophical. It inquires what is the Beautiful rather than what is the True. Yet it touches some of the gravest problems in metaphysical science, and may perhaps be called philosophy in its poetical aspect. It uniformly subordinates nature to spirit, the understanding to the reason, and mere hand-actions to ideas, and believes that ideas are one day to disenthrall the world from the dominion of semi-shadows, and make it the abode of peace and love, a meet Temple in which to enshrine the Spirit of universal and everlasting Beauty.

The author is a genuine lover of nature, and in a few instances he carries his regard for woods and fields so far as to be in danger of forgetting his socialities, and that all nature combined is infinitely inferior to the mind that contemplates it, and invests it with all its charms. And what seems singular to us is, that with all this love for nature, with this passion for solitary woods and varied landscapes, he seems seriously to doubt the existence of the external world except as [a] picture which God stamps on the mind. He all but worships what his senses seem to present him, and yet is not certain that all that which his senses place out of him, is not after

*Reprinted from *Boston Reformer*, 10 September 1836, p. 2.

all the mere subjective laws of his own being, existing only to the eye, not of a necessary, but of an irresistible Faith.

Some great minds have, we know had this doubt. This was the case with the acute and amiable Bishop Berkeley, the audacious Fichte and several others we could mention. Taking their stand-point in the creative power of the human soul, and observing the landscape to change in its coloring as the hues of their own souls change, they have thought the landscape was nothing but themselves projected, and made an object of contemplation. The notion is easily accounted for, but we confess that we should think so accute [sic] a philosopher as our author would easily discover its fallacy.

The Reason is undoubtedly our only light, our only criterion of certainty; but we think the Reason vouches for the truth of the senses as decidedly and as immediately as it does for its own conceptions. He who denies the testimony of his senses, seems to us to have no ground for believing the apperceptions of consciousness; and to deny those is to set oneself afloat upon the ocean of universal scepticism. The whole difficulty seems to us to be in not duly understanding the report of the senses. The senses are the windows of the soul through which it looks out upon a world existing as really and as substantially as itself; but what the external world is, or what it is the senses report it to be, we do not at first understand. The result of all culture, we think will not be as our author thinks, to lead to Idealism, but to make us understand what it is we say, when we say, there is an external world.

The author calls the external world phenomenal, that is, an Appearance; but he needs not to be told that the appearance really exists, though it exists as an appearance, as that which appears, as the Absolute. Man is phenom[e]nal in the same sense as is the universe, but man exists. The author calls him "the apparition of God." The apparition exists as certainly as God exists, though it exists as an apparition, not as absolute being. God is abolute being.—Whatever is absolute is God; but God is not the universe, God is not man; man and the universe exist as manifestations of God. His existence is absolute, theirs is relative, but real.

But we are plunging too deeply into metaphysics for our readers and perhaps for ourselves.—In conclusion, we are happy to say that however the author may deviate from what we call sound philosophy, on his road, he always comes to the truth at last. In this little book he has done an important service to his fellow men.—He has clothed nature with a poetic garb, and interpenetrated her with the living spirit of Beauty and Goodness, showed us how we ought to look upon the world round and about us, set us an example of a calm, morally independent, and devout spirit discoursing on the highest and holiest topics which can occupy the human soul, and produced a book which must ever be admired as a perfect specimen of Art. We thank him for what he has done and commend his book—his poem we might say—to every lover of the True, the Beautiful and the Good.

[The American Scholar]

[William Henry Channing]*

. . . The theme proposed by the orator is the "AMERICAN SCHOLAR." Why did he not say AUTHOR? Every man is or should be a "student," "man thinking." On every mind Nature, the Past, and Action, pour their influences. Some of the most active souls—the freest, bravest thinkers of our time and country, communicate their observations, make their instincts prevalent, embody their highest spiritual vision; but it is only in their lives—their manners—their public acts—their social talk. They fill up the idea of the orator's "scholar." But they are not authors; they do not utter the spirit that is in them. They are the seers, but not the poets—the teachers, but not the artists of the time. Their influence is falling on the mountains and in the vales, instilling through the mass of the universal mind the waters of life, which one day shall well forth in crystal gleams and musical trillings to swell the stream of a truly American literature, and pour along a fertilizing stream of thought.[1] When and how shall our *Authors* be formed? They are forming. When the idea of human brotherhood, of sonship to God—of eternal reason in each human soul—of respect for man—shall be assimilated and organized in our social frame, then shall American Literature go forth in vigor, symmetry, and graceful action. Men will utter when they are filled with the spirit. Our manners, our tone of life, our habits of thought, our social garniture, are a worn out casing, and the new robes of nature's handiwork to clothe a higher form of life as yet but imperfectly grown. Many a poet is walking now our green hill sides, toiling in our mechanic shops, ay, bartering in the bustling mart, even jostling in the caucus and voting at the polls, living a poem in the round of professional duties and the ever fresh romance of quiet homes. And wherever they are, the forms—the castes—the trappings—the badges—the fashion and parade of life, are seen by them as thin disguises, and the purity and vigor of the soul in each brother, the true spiritual experiences of man beneath God's sky upon God's earth, are the only things of worth. When shall they utter the music which swells sweetly in the chambers of their own spirits? When the standard of man's measure is changed, and persons are prized for what they *are*, not for what they *have*. And whenever and however any one is filled to overflowing with this grand idea of God in the soul of man, he will utter it—he

*Reprinted in part from *Boston Quarterly Review*, 1 (January 1838), 113–20.

must utter it. He will be an American Author. He may prophesy from the pulpit, at the Lyceum, in the schoolhouse, in the daily press, in books, in public addresses. But the burden of the prophecy will be the same: "Man measures man the world over:" Man's spirit is from God: We are brethren.

In speaking therefore of the training of American authors—we should place first, second, and third, action, or rather *Life*. A man to utter the American spirit, which is now in embryo, and will sooner or later be born into life, should walk in the noonday brightness of the great Idea of our era and land, till he is quickened by its beams. The great author is he who embodies in language the spirit of his time. The great American author will be he who lives out the American idea—the Christian—the Divine idea of *Brotherhood*.

He must study "Nature." Yes! open his inmost soul to this beautiful smile of God's perfections, that the spirit of God may abide in him as a temple. But nowhere does nature respond to the call within, nowhere do the floods of being answer to the floods of will, as in the form and presence, the ways and deeds and will of man; nowhere, as in the mighty social movement, which ever sweeps along through a silent eternity the ever new present age. The nature of man, and the cycle of that nature, which even now is revolving, is God's voice to us,—a new-born creation which angels hymn.

The author must study the "Past." Yes! For every genius, every martyr, every hero, every living soul, has been a hue of promise, which Humanity has caught from the day-spring from on high. And silently through the tide of roving hordes and the storms of desolating revolutions—in calm hours of bright prosperity—and the wide hush of peaceful eras—in the uprising of down trodden millions—and the fervent hopings and prayers of philanthropy, has the present time been slowly preparing—the aloes sometime to bloom.

And the Author must "act." Yes! but chiefly, not "subordinately." He must throw himself heartily into the moving army of the time, and serve an unnoticed private or a followed leader, as his strength may be—willing to be trampled down, so the powers of good triumph. And he must go out into life too, not to build up himself and complete his being only; not to gain wisdom, to gather raw material only—not to stock a vocabulary, not to recreate only—but from a deep insight into the sublimity of daily, hourly, common life, from awe of the force of Providence stirring in the deep springs of the present generation. Not as a scholar, not with a view to literary labor, not as an artist, must he go out among men—but as a brother man, all unconscious that he has uttered any thing, all purposeless of future utterance till it is given. We rejoiced with sympathetic joy when we read that sentence in this address, "I ask not for the great, the remote, the romantic, what is doing in Italy or Arabia; what is Greek Art or Provençal Minstrelsy; I embrace the common, I explore and sit at the feet of the familiar, the low." A distinguished sculptor was asked, "where when the gods had returned to Olympus, and the iconoclastic spirit of the time had overturned the Madonnas and the martyrs, he would look for subjects for his chisel?" "To the grace and poetry of the simple acts of life," was his answer. The greatest painter of the age has breathed his purest ideal beauty through the unpicturesque attire, the easy attitude, the homely plainness, of peasant girlhood. And perfectly true is it, as our orator says, that this idea has inspired the genius of the finest authors of our day. A man must live the life of Jesus, according to his power, would he be a truly American author; yes! he must live a self-forgetting minister to men, in the charities of home and acquaintance—in thankless and unnoticed sympathy,—in painful toil amid great enterprises,—among interests of the day—sacrificing notoriety, relinquishing unfavorite tastes, penetrated through his habitual thoughts with the prayer, that the kingdom of God may come—the kingdom of truth, love, beauty, and happiness—of fresh minds and warm hearts and clear consciences, the kingdom of brother souls in their Father's mansion. And he must do this because he feels the worth of man as man—because he sees the infinite in the finite—the spiritual in the material—the eternal in the present—the divine in man. When his heart is tuned to unison with every chord that vibrates through the moral universe, and responds to the music of love through his whole being, let him pour out the joy of a spirit communing with the All Holy, of an Immortal stepping onward hand in hand with growing spirits on a brightening pathway to heaven.

All this may seem extravagant and enthusiastic. We say it with the calmest conviction. We look for a high-toned literature in this Christian, free land, where the vine of truth is not overgrown with the weeds of past civilization. We fully expect to see *American* authors. And yet more, we feel sure they will form a most numerous class, or rather be *so numerous as not to form a class*. The benefits of the existence of a literary caste have been vaunted. We have no faith in them. The change which has for years been going on, by which more and more minds have been incited to produce their store for the public good—in reviews, miscellanies, essays, fictions, lectures, is we believe auspicious. Literature has become less monkish, more manly. The days of astrology and alchemy in the world of books is over; and those of its astronomy and chemistry have come; and our bark of life will ride the safer, and our comforts be multiplied by the change. Literature should be the reflection of an age upon itself, the self-converse of the race, and the more expressions of its consciousness, the better; or again literature should be the challenge and answer of "all's well," as each generation takes its stand in time. The more minds that light up their tapers, the better. All men have genius, if they will be true to the inward voice. Let them serve God and not men, and bear what testimony they can. We cannot spare them. Literature will thus assume a more conversational, a heartier tone; and no man will be ashamed, afraid, or vain, or proud, to be an author. The age is superficial, it is said—the attention is dissipated by variety—there is a slip-shod style in vogue—thinkers are rare. We doubt much the justice of all this. The energy of the time, perhaps the genius of the time, is chiefly turned to the business of life. But never, we believe, was there a period of healthier intellectual action. The people—the public, crave thought. They passionately follow a strong man who utters his deepest self healthily, naturally; the higher, the purer his message, the better prized by them. And compare the thoughts and style of expression too of our reviews, yes even of light novels, and of newspaper pieces, dashed off as they are by ordinary minds, with what was written by the select few of earlier time, and do they not prove really a wonderful development of the thinking faculties? All writers are to some degree thinkers, if not thinking men. For their own sakes, composition is salutary; it reveals to themselves what force they have in them. The next stage will be the casting off of authority; yes, even that public opinion which now enslaves, and the rising up of an immense class of independent thinkers, to declare what they too have seen of heavenly light through the telescopes in high observatories, or with the naked eye on the bare hills. We sometimes think that the profusion, with which the knowledge of the most interesting facts, laws, and phenomena of nature, of the great miracles of art and invention, of the mighty events of history, of the original characters who have made history,—that the profusion, we say with which a knowledge of these has been diffused to readers and hearers—though done merely to amuse, will produce a fine result. Men seek novelties, something to animate and awake; where will they find them, if not in the infinity of their own spiritual natures and experiences,—in the marvels and wonders of the quite familiar and common? The crowd of authors even now has broken down the aristocracy of literature. Men are no longer notorious for being writers. Poor vanity no longer, or in a less degree, impels fools to ape sages. But yet the instinct of utterance remains. And we need not fear, that minds, which through the deep caverns of their own spirit have passed to Elysian fields, will be hindered from declaring their bright visions, because the air is full of the murmur of voices. Literature must become what it ought to be, the *best* thoughts of *all*, given out in the grand school room, debating hall, and conversazione of the world, rather let us say in the grand family group of God's children. Inspired prophets and apostles of truth will easily be recognised,—and listened to all the more eagerly by those, to whom all past utterances are familiar, and who seek something new. No Paul will be neglected at Athens. And the temptation lessens every day for a man to desert the field which heaven appointed him to till, by running into the mart to speculate in buying up popular applause. The public are tired of parrots. They want men. We feel convinced that our best minds and all minds, instead of being frittered away and dissipated by chasing the butterflies, and hunting the bright shells, and gathering the choice flowers of thoughts, to amuse or be amused with, will confine themselves more and more to laborious working in their own peculiar mines; that our public lectures will lose their desultory and take a systematic character; that private teachers will appear of higher and higher branches of knowledge. And this will prepare the way for independent, thorough, original action of the American mind. And we long to see what will be produced in that democratic age of literature, where no clan of Authors are tolerated longer as the dictators of fashion and the judges of caste in the world of books, but where appeal is only to the spirit of truth; where the court garment is always sincerity's work-day dress.

But we must bring these remarks to a close. We look, we say, for an American literature. We feel as if the old strata of thought, in the old world, had been broken up, with the old manners which clothed them and grew out from them; and as if the fused and melted mass had settled here to form a new world of higher beauty. And the rock basis of a new era will be a philosophy, which recognises the divinity of reason in every soul; which sees the identity of reason and faith, and honors common sense as the voice of truth; which feels the mystery of moral freedom in every man of that perfect liberty of the entire obedience to right, and which bows with awe before the conviction that God is in each human soul, that never is the individual so entirely himself as when at one with the indwelling Spirit. And the life, which will pervade this new world of thought, will be a poetry of love and sympathy for the commonest familiar feeling, as well as the higher and holier, and for every human tie and relation. Science is always liberal, for nature is no respecter of persons or of forms. She will speak to the humblest or highest of her children through the light which covers the heavens, as with a canopy for angels, through the swift flashes which rend the mountain, or the unseen influence which follows down the string of the paper kite. And shall not it be, is the world never to see a system of social manners too, growing out from this Christian idea of brotherhood, which shall embody the principles of this philosophy—the spirit of this poetry? Our manners will ever be the leaves to clothe with beauty the trunk and branches of our faith; but through them it must imbibe from the sun of God's love, and the atmosphere of human kindness, a purifying, a vital influence. We shall never have a healthy American Literature, unless we have an American Spirit, an American Manner of Life.

"Nature—A Prose Poem"

[Elizabeth Palmer Peabody]*

Minds of the highest order of genius draw their thoughts most immediately from the Supreme Mind, which is the fountain of all finite natures. And hence they clothe the truths they see and feel, in those forms of nature which are generally intelligible to all ages of the world. With this poetic instinct, they have a natural tendency to withdraw from the *conventions* of their own day; and strive to forget, as much as possible, the arbitrary associations created by temporary institutions and local peculiarities. Since the higher laws of suggestion operate in proportion as the lower laws are made subordinate, suggestions of thought by mere proximity of time and place must be subtracted from the habits of the mind that would cultivate the principle of analogy; and this principle of suggestion, in its turn, must be made to give place to the higher law of cause and effect; and at times even this must be set aside, and Reason, from the top of the being, look into the higher nature of original truth, by Intuition,—no unreal function of our nature:

> Nor less I deem that there are powers,
>   Which, of themselves, our minds impress;
> That we can feed these minds of ours,
>   In a wise passiveness.

But if it is precisely because the most creative minds take the symbols of their thoughts and feelings from the venerable imagery of external nature, or from that condition of society which is most transparent in its simplicity, that, when they utter themselves, they speak to all ages, it is also no less true, that this is the reason why the greatest men, those of the highest order of intellect, often do not appear very great to their contemporaries. Their most precious sayings are naked, if not invisible, to the eyes of the conventional, precisely because they are free of the thousand circumstances and fashions which interest the acting and unthinking many. The greatest minds take no cognizance of the local interests, the party spirit, and the pet subjects of the literary coteries of particular times and places. Their phraseology is pure from the ornament which is the passing fashion of the day. As, however, they do not think and speak for their own order only, as they desire to address and receive a response from the great majority of minds—even from those that doubt their own power of going into the holy of holies of thought for themselves—there is needed the office of an intermediate class of minds, which are the natural critics of the human race. For criticism, in its worthiest meaning, is not, as is too often supposed, fault-finding, but interpretation of the oracles of genius.

*Reprinted from *United States Magazine, and Democratic Review*, 1 (February 1838), 319–27. We are grateful to Margaret Neussendorfer for information attributing this article to Peabody.

Critics are the priests of literature. How often, like other priests, they abuse their place and privilege, is but too obvious. They receive into their ranks the self-interested, the partisan, the lover of power, besides the stupid and frivolous; and thus the periodical literature of the day is in the rear, rather than in advance of the public mind.

After this preamble, which we trust has suitably impressed the minds of our readers with the dignity of the critical office, we would call those together who have feared that the spirit of poetry was dead, to rejoice that such a *poem* as "Nature" is written. It grows upon us as we reperuse it. It proves to us, that the only true and perfect mind is the poetic. Other minds are not to be despised, indeed; they are germs of humanity; but the poet alone is the man—meaning by the poet, not the versifier, nor the painter of outward nature merely, but the total soul, grasping truth, and expressing it melodiously, equally to the eye and heart.

The want of apprehension with which this *poem* has been received, speaks ill for the taste of our literary priesthood. Its title seems to have suggested to many persons the notion of some elementary treatise on physics, as physics; and when it has been found that it treats of the *metaphysics* of nature—in other words, of the highest designs of God, in forming nature and man in relations with each other—it seems to have been laid down with a kind of disgust, as if it were a cheat; and some reviewers have spoken of it with a stupidity that is disgraceful alike to their sense, taste, and feeling.

It has, however, found its readers and lovers, and those not a few; the highest intellectual culture and the simplest instinctive innocence have alike received it, and felt it to be a divine Thought, borne on a stream of 'English undefiled,' such as we had almost despaired could flow in this our world of grist and saw mills, whose utilitarian din has all but drowned the melodies of nature. The time will come, when it will be more universally seen to be "a gem of purest ray serene," and be dived after, into the dark unfathomed caves of that ocean of frivolity, which the literary productions of the present age spread out to the eyes of despair.

We have said that "Nature" is a poem; but it is written in prose. The author, though "wanting the accomplishment of verse," is a devoted child of the great Mother; and comes forward bravely in the midst of the dust of business and the din of machinery; and naming her venerable name, believes that there is a reverence for it left, in the bottom of every heart, of power to check the innumerable wheels for a short Sabbath, that all may listen to her praises.

In his introduction, he expresses his purpose. He tells us, that we concede too much to the sceptic, when we allow every thing venerable in religion to belong to history. He tells us that were there no past, yet nature would tell us great truths; and, rightly read, would prove the prophecies of revelation to be "a very present God;" and also, that the past itself, involving its prophets, divine lawgivers, and the human life of Him of

Nazareth, is comparatively a dead letter to us, if we do not freshen these traditions in our souls, by opening our ears to the living nature which forevermore prepares for, and re-echoes, their sublime teachings.

"The foregoing generations," he says, "beheld God face to face: we, through their eyes. Why should not *we* also enjoy an original relation to the Universe?"

Why should we not indeed? for *we* not only have the Universe, which the foregoing generations had, but *themselves* also. Why are we less wise than they? Why has our wisdom less of the certainty of intuition than theirs? Is it because we have more channels of truth? It may be so. The garden of Eden, before the fall of man, and when God walked in its midst, was found to be a less effective school of virtue, than the workshop of a carpenter, in a miserable town of Judea, of which 'an Israelite without guile' could ask, "*Can* any good come out of Nazareth?" And is not this, by the way, a grave warning to the happily circumstanced of all time to tremble—lest they grow morally passive, just in proportion to their means of an effective activity? With the religion of history must always be combined the religion of experience, in order to a true apprehension of God. The poet of "Nature" is a preacher of the latter. Let us "hear him gladly," for such are rare.

The first Canto of this song respects the outward form of Nature. He sketches it in bold strokes. The stars of Heaven above—the landscape below—the breathing atmosphere around—and the living forms and sounds—are brought up to us, by the loving spirit of the singer; who recognizes in this drapery of the world without, the same Disposer that arranged the elements of his own conscious soul. Thus, in his first recognition of Nature's superficies, he brings us to Theism. There is a God. Our Father is the author of Nature. The brotherly "nod" of companionship assures us of it.

But wherefore is Nature? The next Canto of our Poem answers this question in the most obvious relation. It is an answer that "all men apprehend." Nature's superficies is for the well-being of man's body, and the advantage of his material interests. This part of the book requires no interpretation from the critic. Men are active enough concerning commodity, to understand whatever is addressed to them on this head. At least there is no exception but in the case of the savage of the tropics. *His* mind has not explored his wants even to the extent of his body. He does not comprehend the necessities of the narrowest civilization. But whoever reads Reviews, whoever can understand our diluted English, can understand still better this concentrated and severely correct expression of what every child of civilization experiences every day. There is but one sentence here, that the veriest materialist can mistake. He may not measure all that the poet means when he says, man is thus conveniently waited upon in order "that he may work." He may possibly think that "work" relates to the physical operations of manufacture or agriculture. But what is really meant is no less than this; "man is fed that he may work" with his mind; add to the treasures of thought; elaborate the substantial life of the spiritual world. This is a beautiful doctrine, and worthy to be sung to the harp, with a song of thanksgiving. Undoubtedly Nature, by working for man with all her elements, is adequate to supply him with so much "commodity" that the time may be anticipated when all men will have leisure to be artists, poets, philosophers,—in short, to live through life in the exercise of their proper humanity. God speed to the machinery and application of science to the arts which is to bring this about!

The third Song is of Nature's Beauty, and we only wonder why it was not sung first; for surely the singer found out that Nature was beautiful, before he discovered that it was convenient. Some children, we know, have asked what was the use of flowers, and, like little monkeys, endeavouring to imitate the grown-up, the bearings of whose movements they could not appreciate, have planted their gardens with potatoes and beans, instead of sweet-briar and cupid's-delights. But the poet never made this mistake. In the fullness of his first love for his "beautiful mother," and his "gentle nest," he did not even find out those wants, which the commodity of Nature supplies. . . .

The second passage on Beauty, is one of those which recalls the critic to the office of interpreter, for it is one which the world has called mystical. To say the same thing in worse English, the oracle here tells us, that if we look on Nature with pleasurable emotions only, and without, at the same time, exerting our moral powers, the mind grows effeminate, and thus becomes incapable of perceiving the highest beauty of whose original type the external forms are but the varied reflections or shadows. When man's moral power is in action, the mind spontaneously traces relations between itself and surrounding things, and there forms with Nature one whole, combining the moral delight which human excellence inspires, with that suggested by Nature's forms.

The next passage rises a step higher in the praise of Beauty. It recognizes the cherishing influence of Nature's forms upon the faculties. Nature not only calls out taste, not only glorifies virtue, and is in its turn by virtue glorified, but it awakens the creative impulse—God's image in man. Hence Art, or "Nature in miniature." And the works of Art lead back to Nature again. Thus Beauty circulates, and becomes an aspect of Eternity.

The next chapter, showing that Language is founded on material Nature, is quite didactic. But even here one critic[1] quotes a sentence, of which he says, he cannot understand "what it means."

> This relation between the mind and matter is not fancied by some poet, but stands in the will of God, and so is free to be known by all men. It appears to men, or it does not appear.

Where lies the obscurity? We have heard some men say that they did not believe that the forms of Nature bore any relation to the being of God, which his children could appreciate; but even these men could not understand the simple proposition of the opposite theory. Men may think that all nations, whose language has yet been discovered, have called youth *the morning of life*, by accident; but it is inconceivable that they should not understand the simple words in which other men say that there is *no accident in the world*, but all things relate to the spirit of God to which man also has relation and access. Perhaps, however, it is the second sentence which [is] unintelligible, "it appears to men, or it does not appear." In other words, *to people with open eyes there are colors; to people with shut eyes, at least, to those born blind, there are no colors.*

But having come to this fact, viz: that "the relation between mind and matter stands in the will of God," our poet grows silent with wonder and worship. The nature of this relation he acknowledges to be the yet unsolved problem. He names some of the principal men who have attempted a solution. Many readers of his book would have been glad, had he paused to tell us, in his brief comprehensive way, what was the solution of Pythagoras, and Plato, Bacon, Leibnitz, and Swedenborg, with remarks of his own upon each.

And to his own solution, some say he is unintelligible, talks darkly. They do not seem to have observed that he says nothing in the way of solution, so that nothing can be darkly said. This is what has disappointed the best lovers of his book. But if he does not give his own solution of the enigma, he does what is next best, he tells us the condition of solving it ourselves.

> A life in harmony with nature, the love of truth and virtue, will purge the eyes to understand her text. By degrees we may come to know the primitive sense of the permanent objects of Nature, so that the world shall be to us an open book, and every form significant of the hidden life and final cause.

The chapter on Discipline is still more didactic than the one on Language. The first portion treats of the formation of the Understanding by the ministry of Nature to the senses, and faculty of deduction. The second section is in a higher strain. It treats of the developement of the Reason and Conscience, by means of that relation between matter and mind, which "appears" so clearly to some men, and to all in a degree. . . .

In the last part of this chapter on Discipline, the author makes a bold sally at the cause of the analogy between the external world and the moral nature. He implies that causes (the spiritual seeds of external things) are identical with the principles that constitute our being; and that *virtues* (the creations of our own heaven-aided wills) correspond to God's creations in matter; the former being the natural growth in the moral world, the latter the natural growth in the material world; or to vary the expres-

sion once more, Goodness being the projection inward—Beauty the projection outward—of the same all-pervading Spirit.

Our author here leaves the didactic, and "the solemn harp's harmonious sound" comes full upon the ear and the heart from the next Canto of
his poem—Idealism. No part of the book has been so mistaken as this.
Some readers affect to doubt his Practical Reason, because he acknowledges, that we have no evidence of there being essential outlying beings,
to that which we certainly see, by consciousness, by looking inward, *except 'a constant faith' which God gives us of this truth*. But why should
'the noble doubt,' which marks the limit of the understanding, be so
alarming, when it is found to be but an introduction of the mind to the
superior certainty residing in that 'constant faith?' Do we not advance in
truth, when we learn to change the childish feeling by which we ascribe
reality to the 'shows of things,' for a feeling involving a sense of GOD, as
the only real—immutable—the All in All?

The theory of Idealism has doubtless been carried to absurdity by individuals who but half understood it; and has still more often been represented in a way which was not only useless but injurious to minds entirely
dependent on what others say: for, to borrow two good compounds from
Coleridge, the *half-Ideas* of many would-be Idealist writers, have passed,
perforce, into the *no-Ideas* of many would-be Idealist readers. But Mr.
Emerson has sufficiently guarded his Idealism by rigorous and careful expression, to leave little excuse for cavilling at his words or thoughts, except, indeed, by professed materialists and atheists, to whom he gives no
ground.

> "The frivolous make themselves merry," he says, "with the Ideal theory,
> as if its consequences were burlesque; as if it affected the stability of nature.
> It surely does not. God never jests with us, and will not compromise the end
> of Nature, by permitting any inconsequence in its procession. Any distrust
> of the permanence of laws, would paralyse the faculties of man. Their per-
> manence is sacredly respected, and his faith therein is perfect. The wheels
> and springs of man are all set to the hypothesis of the permanence of
> Nature. We are not built like a ship to be tossed, but like a house to stand."

He proceeds to give the progressive appearances of Nature, as the
mind advances, through the ministry of the senses, to "the best and the
happiest moments of life, those delicious awakenings of the higher
powers,—the withdrawing of Nature before its God." The means by
which Nature herself, Poetic genius, Philosophy, both natural and intellectual—and, above all, Religion and Ethics, work, to idealize our
thought and being, are then minutely pointed out. No careful thinker can
dispute a step of the process. . . .

Many philosophers have stopped at Idealism. But, as Mr. Emerson
says, this hypothesis, if it only deny, or question the existence of matter

"does not satisfy the demands of the Spirit. It leaves God out of me. It leaves me in the splendid labyrinth of my perceptions, to wander without end. Then the heart resists it, because it baulks the affections, in denying substantive being to men and women."

Mr. Emerson then proceeds to his chapter on Spirit, by which he means to suggest to us the substantial essence of which Idealism is the intellectual form. But this chapter is not full enough, for the purposes of instruction. One passage is indeed of great significance:

> But when, following the invisible steps of thought, we come to inquire, Whence is matter? and whereto?—many truths arise out of the depths of consciousness. We learn that the highest is present to the soul of man; that the great universal essence which is not wisdom, or love, or beauty, or power, but all in one and each entirely, is that for which all things exist, and that by which what they are; *that Spirit creates*; that behind Nature, throughout Nature, *Spirit is present*, that Spirit is one and not compound; that Spirit does not act upon us from without, that is, in space [or] time, but spiritually or through ourselves. Therefore, that Spirit, that is the Supreme Being, does not build up Nature around us, but puts it forth through us, as the life of the tree puts forth new branches and leaves through the pores of the old. As a plant upon the bosom of God, he is nourished by unfailing fountains, and draws at his need inexhaustible power. Who can set bounds to the possibilities of Man? Once inspire the infinite, by being admitted to behold the absolute natures of justice and truth, and we learn that man has access to the entire mind of the Creator in the finite. This view, which admonishes me where the sources of wisdom and power lie, and points to virtue as
>
> 'The golden key
> Which opes the palace of Eternity,'
>
> carries upon its face, the highest certificate of truth, because it animates me to create my own world through the purification of my soul.

This is not only of refreshing moral *aura*, but it is a passage of the highest imaginative power, (taking the word *imaginative* in that true signification which farthest removes it from *fanciful*,) the mind must become purified indeed which can take this point of view, to look at "the great shadow pointing to the sun behind us." Sitting thus at the footstool of God, it may realise that all that we see is created by the light that shines through ourselves. Not until thus purified, can it realise that those through whose being more light flows, see more than we do; and that others, who admit less light, see less. What assistance in human culture would the application of this test give us! How would our classifications of men and women be changed, did the positive pure enjoyment of Nature become the standard of judgment! But who may apply the standard? Not every mawkish raver about the moon, surely, but only a comprehender of Nature. And has there yet been any one in human form, who could be called a comprehender of Nature, save Him who had its secret, and in whose hands it was plastic, even to the raising of the dead?

Mr. Emerson must not accuse us of ingratitude, in that after he had led his readers to this high point of view, they crave more, and accuse him of stopping short, where the world most desires and needs farther guidance. We want him to write another book, in which he will give us the philosophy of his "orphic strains," whose meaning is felt, but can only be understood by glimpses.

He does, indeed, tell us that "the problem of restoring to the world original and eternal beauty," (in other words, of seeing Nature and Life in their wholeness), "is solved by the redemption of the soul." It is not unnecessary for the philosopher thus to bring his disciples round, through the highest flights of speculation, to the primitive faith of the humblest disciple, who sits, in the spirit of a child, at the feet of Jesus. But we should like to hear Mr. Emerson's philosophy of Redemption. It is very plain that it consists of broad and comprehensive views of human culture; worthy to employ the whole mind of one who seeks reproduction of Christ within himself, by such meditations as the following, which must be our last extract:

> Is not Prayer also a study of truth—a sally of the soul into the unfound infinite? No man ever prayed heartily without learning something. But when a faithful thinker, resolute to detach every object from personal relations, and see it in the light of thought, shall, at the same time, kindle science with the fire of the holiest affections, then will God go forth anew into the creation.

Note

1. Christian Examiner. [See F[rancis]. B[owen]., "Transcendentalism," *Christian Examiner*, 21 (January 1837), 371–385 (Ed.).]

"The New School in Literature and Religion"

[Andrews Norton]*

There is a strange state of things existing about us in the literary and religious world, of which none of our larger periodicals has yet taken notice. It is the result of this restless craving for notoriety and excitement, which, in one way or another, is keeping our community in a perpetual stir. It has shown itself, we think, particularly since that foolish woman, Miss Martineau, was among us, and stimulated the vanity of her flatterers by loading them in return with the copper coin of her praise, which they

*Reprinted from *Boston Daily Advertiser*, 27 August 1838, p. 2.

easily believed was as good as gold. She was accustomed to talk about her mission, as if she were a special dispensation of Providence, and they too thought that they must all have their missions, and began to "vaticinate," as one of their number has expressed it. But though her genial warmth may have caused the new school to bud and bloom, it was not planted by her.—It owes its origin in part to ill-understood notions, obtained by blundering through the crabbed and disgusting obscurity of some of the worst German speculatists, which notions, however, have been received by most of its disciples at second hand, through an interpreter. The atheist Shelley has been quoted and commended in a professedly religious work, called the Western Messenger, but he is not, we conceive, to be reckoned among the patriarchs of the sect. But this honor is due to that hasher up of German metaphysics, the Frenchman, Cousin; and, of late, that hyper-Germanized Englishman, Carlyle, has been the great object of admiration and model of style. Cousin and Carlyle indeed seem to have been transformed into idols to be publicly worshipped; the former for his philosophy, and the latter both for his philosphy and his fine writing; while the veiled image of the German pantheist, Schleiermacher, is kept in the sanctuary.

The characteristics of this school are the most extraordinary assumption, united with great ignorance, and incapacity for reasoning. There is indeed a general tendency among its disciples to disavow learning and reasoning as sources of their higher knowledge.—The mind must be its own unassisted teacher. It discerns transcendental truths by immediate vision, and these truths can no more be communicated to another by addressing his understanding, than the power of *clairvoyance* can be given to one not magnetized. They announce themselves as the prophets and priests of a new future, in which all is to be changed, all old opinions done away, and all present forms of society abolished. But by what process this joyful revolution is to be effected as are not told; nor how human happiness and virtue is to be saved from the universal wreck, and regenerated in their Medea's caldron. There are great truths with which they are laboring, but they are unutterable in words to be understood by common minds. To such minds they seem nonsense, oracles as obscure as those of Delphi.

The rejection of reasoning is accompanied with an equal contempt for good taste. All modesty is laid aside. The writer of an article for an obscure periodical, or a religious newspaper, assumes a tone as if he were one of the chosen enlighteners of a dark age.—He continually obtrudes himself upon his reader, and announces his own convictions, as if from their having that character, they were necessarily indisputable.—He floats about magnificently on bladders, which he would have it believed are swelling with ideas.—Common thoughts, sometimes true, oftener false, and "Neutral nonsense, neither false nor true," are exaggerated, and twisted out of shape, and forced into strange connexions, to make them look like some grand and new conception. To produce a more striking effect, our common language is abused; antic tricks are played with it; inversions, exclamations, anamalous combinations of words, unmeaning, but coarse and violent, metaphors abound, and withal a strong infusion of German barbarians. Such is the style of Carlyle, a writer of some talent; for his great deficiency is not in this respect, it is in good sense, good taste and soundness of principle; but a writer, who, through his talents, such as they are, through that sort of buffoonery and affectation of manner which throws the reader off his guard, through the indisputable novelty of his way of writing, and through a somewhat too prevalent taste among us for an over-excited and *convulsionary* style, which we mistake for eloquence, has obtained a degree of fame in this country, very disproportioned to what he enjoys at home, out of the Westminster Review. Carlyle, however, as an original, might be tolerated, if one could forget his admirers and imitators.

The state of things described might seem a matter of no great concern, a mere insurrection of folly, a sort of Jack Cade rebellion; which in the nature of things must soon be put down, if those engaged in it were not gathering confidence from neglect, and had not proceeded to attack principles which are the foundation of human society and human happiness. "Silly women," it has been said, and silly young men, it is to be feared, have been drawn away from their christian faith, if not divorced from all that can properly be called religion. The evil is becoming, for the time, disastrous and alarming; and of this fact there could hardly be a more extraordinary and ill boding evidence, than is afforded by a publication, which has just appeared, entitled an "Address, delivered before the Senior class in Divinity College, Cambridge," upon the occasion of that class taking leave of the Institution. "By Ralph Waldo Emerson."

It is not necessary to remark particularly on this composition. It will be sufficient to state generally, that the author professes to reject all belief in Christianity as a revelation, that he makes a general attack upon the Clergy, on the ground that they preach what he calls "Historical Christianity," and that if he believe in God in the proper sense of the term, which one passage might have led his hearers to suppose, his language elsewhere is very ill-judged and indecorous. But what *his* opinions may be is a matter of minor concern; the main question is how it has happened, that religion has been insulted by the delivery of these opinions in the Chapel of the Divinity College at Cambridge, as the last instruction which those were to receive, who were going forth from it, bearing the name of christian preachers. This is a question in which the community is deeply interested. No one can doubt for a moment of the disgust and strong disapprobation with which it must have been heard by the highly respectable officers of that Institution. They must have felt it not only as an insult to religion, but as personal insult to themselves. But this renders the fact of its having been so delivered only the more remarkable. We can proceed but a step in accounting for it. The preacher was invited to occupy the place he did, not by the officers of the Divinity College, but by the members of the graduating class. These gentlemen, therefore, have become accessories, perhaps innocent accessories, to the commission of a great offence; and the public must be desirous of learning what exculpation or excuse they can offer.

It is difficult to believe that they thought this incoherent rhapsody a specimen of fine writing, that they listened with admiration, for instance, when they were told that the religious sentiment "is myrrh, and storax and chlorine and rosemary;" or that they wondered at the profound views of their present Teacher, when he announced to them that "the new Teacher," for whom he is looking, would "see the identity of the law of gravitation with purity of heart;" or that they had not some suspicion of inconsistency, when a new Teacher was talked of, after it had been declared to them, that religious truth "is an intuition," and "cannot be received at second hand."

But the subject is to be viewed under a far more serious aspect. The words God, Religion, Christianity, have a definite meaning, well understood. They express conceptions and truths of unutterable moment to the present and future happiness of man. We well know how shamefully they have been abused in modern times by infidels and pantheists; but their meaning remains the same; the truths which they express are unchanged and unchangeable. The community know what they require when they ask for a Christian Teacher; and should any one approving the doctrines of this discourse assume that character, he would deceive his hearers; he would be guilty of a practical falsehood for the most paltry of temptations; he would consent to live, a lie, for the sake of being maintained by those whom he had cheated. It is not, however, to be supposed that his vanity would suffer him long to keep his philosophy wholly to himself. This would break out in obscure intimations, ambiguous words, and false and mischievous speculations. But should such preachers abound, and grow confident in their folly, we can hardly overestimate the disastrous effects upon the religious and moral state of the community.

"The New School and Its Opponents"

S. X. [Theophilus Parsons]*

In your paper of Monday you published an article on "The new School in Literature and Religion." The writer speaks strongly of Mr. Emerson's defects and errors; but many who agree with him in thinking these defects great and these errors dangerous, lament that they should be

*Reprinted from *Boston Daily Advertiser*, 30 August 1838, p. 2.

spoken of thus. The tone of this article is so harsh, that in many passages it seems but the outbreak of indignant contempt. It charges the objects of its rebuke with arrogance, and makes the charge with very little manifestation of humility. And while it accuses *them* of ignorance, it speaks of distinguished Europeans in a way which makes us ask with wonder, how the writer could have formed such opinions.

If it was his purpose to give to an uncomfortable feeling the relief of expression, to gratify those who were already disgusted with these "novelties," and to confirm the denial and hatred of those who already deny and hate as he does, he has written as he should. But if he wished to arrest the evil he deplores, to help the "silly women" and "silly young men" about whom the fascinations of the charmer are gathering, if he wrote in kindness and not in anger, then, and it is said with all deference, he has not written wisely.

In the fervor of his reproaches he pays Mr. Emerson and his compeers the unmerited compliment, of placing them in the same class with Cousin and Schleiermacher. But one favorable sentiment occurs in his article; and this is where he speaks of Carlyle as "an original." And this must be accidental—for that writer cannot but know, that while Carlyle *was* original, (now, long since) he was universally acknowledged as one of the most delightful writers of England; but that his admiration of Jean Paul Richter led him soon into imitation, which, in his last and largest works, he carries perhaps beyond any precedent upon the records of literature.

But there is an objection to this article which goes far deeper. The writer seems to identify the school which he attacks with all inquiry—all progress; when he objects to it that it is rhapsodical, incoherent, ignorant and presuming,—he seems to feel as if all this were expressed by calling it *new*. This is to be regretted; not merely because it is a mistake, but because it is precisely *the* mistake which the favorers of Mr. Emerson beg their opponents to make. They know and feel,—and where can he have lived who does not know,—that when the argument against them rests mainly on the supposition that they differ from the old and the past, they are placed in a position of all others the most favorable to their success. Then, all who would hope in the future, all who believe that the fountains of truth are neither sealed nor exhausted, are in fact directed to this new school as to friends who would favor their progress, while others refuse to admit its possibility.

The writer speaks of Mr. Emerson as if he were the head of this school in this country; perhaps this may be just; for his published writings, by which alone I know him, have made a stronger impression than any others of this class. In despite of peculiarities of manner, which sometime appear to go so far beyond affectation as to indicate a mind from which all discipline and order are absent,—his extraordinary brilliancy of language, his frequent beauty of imagery, and the originality of his style, which is admitted even by those who deny that this originality extends to his thoughts,—all these things have won for him decided success. But, be his faults or his mistakes what may—if they are to be encountered, by no other argument, than that they have no written precedent and were not found till the beaten pathways of thought had been deserted, they must be victorious. Nor will this argument be greatly helped, by any form or quantity of contempt or approbrium. If you say to the young students of this country, that only clouds and misty meteors will fill their field of vision, whenever they dare to look beyond the limits which satisfied the past, you tell them what is not true; and the just and prudent things you may say in connection with this untruth, will profit them the less for it.

There have been ages, and there are lands, where the human mind seeks nothing but repose. Antiquity is there the only standard of truth; and nothing is asked of the future but that it may repeat the present and the past. But not so do we live; not so can we live. The bands of all authority are relaxed; no one seeks the shelter or acknowledges the power of precedent; and if one may speak of it in figures, it might be said that the human mind is abroad upon a pathless sea, and the waves are high, the sky is dark, and the winds are loud and angry. But for all this, beyond the clouds the sun still shines; and even the pathless ocean is bounded by the steadfast land; and who can fear the triumph or perpetuity of error. And yet Error would triumph, would permanently reign, if there were nothing to resist her, but anger, derision, intolerance, and blind and fierce denunciation. He who uses only these weapons may call himself the enemy of error, but others will not call him the friend of truth. Why speak of this "School,"—which if it be a "School," embraces men among us, who, whatever be their errors, are not generally despised, and must embrace, if the words of the writer of that article have any significance whatever, some of the most distinguished men of Europe,—why speak of that "School," as if "assumption," "ignorance," "incapacity of reasoning" and whatever else is meant by "neutral nonsense,"—were their common characteristics. The reader of such an article cannot but pause, and ask, where sits the judge who passes such a sentence!

No reader can feel when a writer talks of a "Jack Cade rebellion" that he is as wise as he might be were he more temperate. Nor will it be admitted that there is any one among us authorized by his position in the world of letters, to speak of Victor Cousin as "the hasher up of German metaphysics," or of Carlyle, as a man of "some" talent. Can the writer of that article be ignorant that while Cousin is a man of remarkable originality, the views which he derives from others are drawn far more from the old philosophies than from those of any modern nation. Let his faults be pointed out, let young men be aided and protected in their study of him;—but he that can be turned from his works by this writer's contemptous sneer at "the Frenchman," may probably employ himself to more advantage than in the study of Philosophy.

The writer calls Schleiermacher a Pantheist. This may be right, but if the subject were not too weighty for the columns of a newspaper, it would be interesting to consider the grounds of this accusation, and to inquire whether it might not be brought, on very similar grounds, and with at least equal justice, against the systems of belief of some, who speak very bitterly of German metaphysics.

Let it not be supposed that we have come forward to defend Mr. Emerson; we hope that his writings will be examined and discussed. Indeed they must be so; but in this controversy we have no part to take; and if we engaged in it, certainly it would not be in their defence.

We object to his works, not because of his "antic tricks with language;" not because he talks of "myrrh and storax and chlorine and rosemary," in a way that offends our taste,—not because he is fragmentary and inconclusive and seldom communicates to the mind of the reader a clear view of any distinct and valuable principle; not even because he sometimes degrades solemn and beautiful truths by so perverting and distorting them, that they may minister to self-admiration;—but because he can find it in his heart to speak of the Bible as in the last paragraph of this Address; because he says such things as that, "if a man is at heart just, so far he is God," and thus preaches a doctrine which leads man to worship his own nature and himself;—and because I can see nowhere in his system those emotions of obedient, trustful, humble love of our Father in Heaven which lie at the root and in the heart of all religion, unless I find them laid as a sacrifice upon the altars of self-love and self-pride. But this subject is too manifestly unfit for the columns of a newspaper, to be pursued farther. And I have touched upon it only to show that I have noticed the article in your paper, not because I am unwilling to have the faults of this "New School" exposed and dealt with, but because I would have them so dealt with as to do good, and not harm.

[The Divinity School Address]

[G. T. Davis]*

We notice this address, not on account of its intrinsic merits, nor because we sympathize with the peculiar views of the author; but because it has created some little excitement in certain circles, and called forth censures, which, without a word or two of explanation, may affect the characters of some who are very far from entertaining views similar to those which Mr. Emerson is in the habit of putting forth.

We are not likely to be thought peculiarly partial to Mr. Emerson. We shall not soon forget his ill-advised letter to Mr. Van Buren concerning the Cherokees. Nevertheless, we respect Mr. Emerson, as an ac-

*Reprinted from *Boston Post*, 31 August 1838, p. 1. cols. 5–6.

complished scholar—an agreeable and entertaining lecturer—a high minded and honorable man—of a free and independent spirit, willing to utter himself and be himself, and not another. We reverence his honesty—his independence, his boldness. In this respect, we shall always be ready to enroll ourselves among his friends, and to the best of our ability defend his character.

But when it concerns Mr. Emerson's peculiar religious and philosophical views, it is quite another affair. We are not always sure that we understand him, and when we feel confident that we do catch his meaning, we do not always, by any means, approve it. But his views are his own; he has a right to entertain them, and to do his best to propagate them. All we have to do with them, is to examine them if we deem them worth examining, and to reject them, so far as they seem to us to be false or unsound. For ourselves, we have no fears that the cause of truth can be essentially injured, or retarded, by the promulgation of error. Error has always a tendency to destroy itself.

There is one thing, however, we wish to notice, and concerning which we think it desirable the public should be set in the right. There has been for sometime manifested, in certain quarters, a disposition to throw into the same category, men who have very little in common, and who entertain opinions, in philosophical and religious matters, widely different. This disposition was strikingly displayed by a writer in the Daily Advertiser of Monday last. That writer speaks of a "New School in Literature and Religion," as having lately sprung up amongst us; and he gives it, for its chiefs, the distinguished French philosopher, Victor Cousin; and the somewhat distinguished, but eccentric, Germanized-English scholar, Thomas Carlyle. He also adroitly seizes upon this address of Mr. Emerson, as a sort of exposition of the doctrines of the New School. Now in all this there is much misconception, or great disingenuousness.

There are undoubtedly, certain movements, tendencies, amongst us, which may in time, lead to the creation of a New School in Literature. A new school is certainly needed, from which may come forth a literature in perfect harmony with the higher nature of man and the democratic spirit of the institutions of this country. There are many warm hearts here craving such a school, and many noble spirits at work in earnest to create it. Nevertheless, it is hardly true to say that a New School has as yet been created.

As it concerns the movements, the tendencies, to which the writer in question alludes, it is certain that they have been much influenced by the publications of Cousin and Carlyle. But there is manifest injustice in classing the friends and admirers of one with the other. It is impossible to conceive two men more unlike than Victor Cousin and Thomas Carlyle. Cousin is a philosopher—a metaphysician—remarkable for his good taste—good sense—uncommon logical powers, and the clearness and elegance of his style. He is a rigorous logician—one of the severest reasoners that can be found. With him no proposition can be admitted till it has given an account of itself, and fully verified its claims to understanding. Carlyle, on the other hand, is no philosopher—no metaphysician. He laughs at metaphysics—at all attempts to account ourselves for ourselves—to account any phenomena of man or of nature, or to form any system of philosophy, politics, theology, or ethics. He is a poet, a seer, who has frequent and glorious glimpses of truth, and of sublime and far reaching truth, too; but one who never verifies what he sets forth as truth—who never asks how he knows what he sees is truth, or shows us how we may know that it is truth. He has genius; in many respects he is a remarkable man; and not withstanding his eccentric, and very objectionable style, he may be read with pleasure, and with profit.

Now the difference there is between these two men is still more striking between their friends in this country. The admirers of Mr. Carlyle, at the head of whom may be placed the author of the address before us, are termed, properly or improperly, Transcendentalists, and are, perhaps, in the main, correctly enough described by the correspondent of the Advertiser. But the friends of M. Cousin, ranked by the same correspondent with them, choose to be eclectics. They are a very different class of men—men of very different literary tendencies and philosophical views. The Transcendentalists, so called, are by no means philosophers; they are either dreamers, or mere speculatists, contemning logic, and holding the understanding in light esteem. The Eclectics aim to be very sober, and a very rational sort of people. They are not materialists—they do not believe John Locke finished philosophy; nevertheless, they profess to follow an experimental method of philosophizing. They differ from the Scotch school of Reid and Stewart, only in going a little further in the same route. They do not believe, indeed, that all our ideas originate in the senses; they believe that the reason furnishes from its own stores certain elements of every fact of consciousness; but at the same time they believe, with the German philosopher, Kant—"that all our knowledge begins with experience," and that the ideas or elements furnished by the reason, are developed only on occasion of experience. As philosophers, their aim is, by analysis, to separate, in the case of all the facts of consciousness, the rational elements from the sensible elements, and, by training each to their source, to determine the origin and validity of our ideas, to fix the criterion of truth, and to account for, and legitimate the universal beliefs of mankind. With the Transcendentalists, they admit Spontaneity or Instinct, the fact of primitive Intuition; but they differ from the Transcendentalists in this important particular, that whereas the Transcendentalists tell us that Instinct is to be taken as our guide without any effort to legitimate it, thereby rejecting reflection, reasoning, all philosophic thought properly so called; the Eclectics summon Instinct, Intuition itself to the bar of reason and refuse to obey it, till it has legitimated to the understanding its right to command.

To all who are competent to judge of the matter, here is surely a wide difference, and one which no man can be pardoned for overlooking. They whom we have designated as Transcendentalists, are not in the habit of speaking respectfully of Cousin. They do not study him, and we may venture to assert, that they are ignorant of both the method and spirit of his philosophy. It is wrong, altogether wrong, therefore, to represent them as the followers of Cousin. It is a wrong to them; and a still greater wrong to those individuals among us who do really study and take an interest in Cousin's system of philosophy. Honor to whom honor is due, is a good maxim; and give to every one his due, is a precept that no advocate for religion and morality has any right, on any occasion whatever, to neglect.

We have made these remarks for the sole purpose of pointing out, and requiring the public to notice an obvious, and as we regard it, a very essential difference between the two classes ranked in the same category by the correspondent of the Advertiser. For ourselves, we are not disposed to make war on either class. We say, let all opinions, all doctrines, have an "open field and fair play." We cannot, however, believe that the peculiar views set forth with so much confidence and fascination by Mr. Emerson, are likely to take a very deep root in the American heart. They are too dreamy, too misty, too vague, to have much effect except on young misses just from boarding school, or young lads, who begin to fancy themselves in love. The Americans are a sturdy race; they are reasoning people, and they will not long follow any one who cannot give to the understanding a reason for the hope that is in him.

The popularity Mr. Emerson has acquired for the moment, and which seems to have alarmed some of the grave Doctors at Cambridge, is easily accounted for, without supposing any especial regard for his peculiar notions. Something is due to his personal manners, much to the peculiar characteristics of his style as a writer and as a lecturer; but still more to his independence, to the homage he pays to the spirit of freedom. Our young men have grown weary of leading strings. They are dissatisfied with the tyranny which custom, conventionalism has exercised over them. They have felt the old formulas too straitened for them, and the air of their prison-houses too compressed, and too oppressive, and they have wished to break away, to roam at large over green fields, and to breathe the fresh air of heaven. The state of mind here described, and which we may term a craving after freedom, exists in our community to a very great extent. To this craving Mr. Emerson has spoken; this craving he has done something to satisfy; therefore, his popularity. It is as the advocate of the rights of the mind, as the defender of personal independence in the spiritual world, not as the Idealist, the Pantheist, or the Atheist, that he is run after, and all but worshipped by many young, ardent and yet noble minds. In this we see an omen of good and not of evil. It is a proof that the spirit of liberty is yet living and active in our community; that the American institutions are doing their work, and embodying their sublime Idea in literature, art, and religion. For this we are thankful, and in it we rejoice.

The Cambridge Professors who denounce Mr. Emerson, are very unwise, and seem to be verifying the old maxim, "who the Gods will to destroy they first deprive of reason." Their own sensibility to the free spirit of the age and country is the cause which leads the young men, committed to their care, to seek inspiration and instruction elsewhere. And elsewhere they will be sure to continue to go, unless their regular Professors prove themselves capable of meeting the wants of their souls. They want freedom and life, and they will go where freedom and life are to be found. Let the Professors be assured of this, and govern themselves accordingly. They must show that freedom and life can be found elsewhere than in connection with the speculations of Ralph Waldo Emerson, or to Ralph Waldo Emerson they may rest assured their pupils will resort.

"Rev. Mr. Emerson"

Z.*

The late address delivered by this individual before the divinity students at Cambridge, is talked of rather harshly by the religious, who seem to be in considerable doubt what to call it. We believe, however, that it is generally agreed to be heresy—that is, something out of the old order of things, and of course dangerous. Even the editor of the Trumpet, has caught the alarm, and, in his anxiety for Zion, says the address not only borders on infidelity, but that it is nonsensical, for he cannot understand it—an undoubted proof of Mr. Emerson's ignorance or insanity, or perhaps both.

To be serious, what an ill-natured, querulous, uncharitable set of beings our religious men are! We have an illustration of the fact in the treatment of Mr. Emerson. A man of brilliant genius and an enlarged and liberal mind, he has dared to step out of the beaten path of religious teachers, and think and preach more in conformity with reason and the spirit of the age—in a word, he has become a free enquirer. And how is he treated? How? Why, as all before him have been who have had the moral independence to broach new and unpopular doctrines. He is an infidel! cries one. An ignoramus! cries another. And so on, till he is made to run the gantlet through the whole—each sect venting its petty spleen, and all agreeing that he is either demented or foolish. Is it any wonder that bigotry and ignorance so much prevail, when, to attempt to move onward the public mind, a man is thus hooted at and vilified?

*Reprinted from *Boston Investigator*, 27 September 1838, p. 3.

[Mr. Emerson and the Unitarians]

"An Interested Christian" and Chandler Robbins*

To the Editor of the Christian Register.

Dear Sir,—I hope you will excuse me if I request you to answer this note, in the columns of your paper; not for my own satisfaction only, but to enlighten the minds of many of your readers upon a subject which causes, I am well convinced, considerable uneasiness.

The Rev. Ralph Waldo Emerson is known as a *Unitarian Minister.* He was for two or three years pastor of the same church in Boston over which you are now settled. He still, I believe, occasionally preaches. He was chosen by the class which graduated at the Cambridge Theological School, a few months ago to address and counsel them preparatory to their undertaking the solemn office of the public ministry of our holy religion. This appointment he accepted and discharged.

He is therefore identified in the public mind with Unitarianism. He is spoken of by many as a leading and eminent Unitarian. Now, I think, together with, I believe, the great majority of the community, that the sentiments advanced at various times by Mr Emerson, and especially the opinions and notions expressed in his address at the Divinity School, are at war with the distinctive features of Christianity, derogatory to the character and offices of the Savior and Mediator; tinctured with infidelity, if not with pantheism or atheism; and calculated of course, to do injury to the Church, as well as to offend the feelings of christians in general, and in particular, of the unlettered and humble.

I earnestly desire then, that you would inform myself and the public through the medium of your paper, which is rightly regarded as the organ of the Unitarian body, whether this gentleman is esteemed by you as a fair representative of the sentiments of Unitarians in New England; or what is his relation to the sect, and how you regard him.

I am well aware of the delicacy which you must feel about treating this subject in your Editorial capacity, but trust that you will not deem it proper or necessary to refuse compliance with my request, which is dictated by no personal dislike to Mr Emerson, and by no improper motives, but solely by a deep and sincere regard to the cause of Liberal Christianity, and the interests of religion.

I remain yours respectfully.

———

We shall not hesitate to comply with the request contained in the above letter. The source from which it comes, is a sufficient guaranty to us that it was prompted by the worthy and commendable motives, by

*Reprinted from *Christian Register*, 17 (29 September 1838), 154–55.

which the writer professes to be influenced. We shall answer the questions proposed with the utmost candor; and in so doing, are well assured that we shall have the approval of no one of our readers sooner than of the excellent friend of whom we speak.

Mr Emerson *has* been for several years a Unitarian Minister, and we believe *does* still occasionally preach. He is not however, and never has been a *representative* of the denomination, or of any large class of it. His sentiments on some subjects are known to have been at variance with those of a large majority of the Unitarian community. His connexion with the Second Church and society in Boston was dissolved by mutual consent, on account of some peculiarities of opinion on his part. As a serious and earnest teacher of severe and lofty morality, as an eloquent and ingenious writer of sermons, as a conspicuous exemplar and preacher of simple and unaffected piety, he has always and deservedly, occupied a high place in the esteem and love of those who have known and appreciated him best. But many of his speculations, theories and doctrines have from the first given offence to many who respect and admire him as a man. Not a few of the Unitarian Clergy and laity have always criticised and censured them.

But the circumstance of Mr Emerson having been elected to address a Graduating class at the Divinity School, seems to be considered by many as an indication that he was regarded at Cambridge as a fit Teacher and model to our young preachers, both in regard to doctrine and character. This inference, however, is a mistake. He was chosen to perform that office by the *Class* only, and not by the Government of the School, or by the voice of the Unitarian community. The class consisted only of about a half a dozen young men. Of these we have understood that Mr Emerson received the votes of a bare majority, (the rest afterwards consenting). The Professors, we believe, were surprised at the selection made by the class; and so, we know, were the great body of the Unitarian clergy. And this—for the very reason that *they did not consider Mr Emerson as a fair representative of the denomination.* Besides, he had had but a very short experience as a Pastor—was not at the time, considered as a regular Unitarian minister—was known to entertain opinions at variance with those of many of the friends and founders of the School, and was not a fit person to counsel those who were about going forth to build up or confirm the churches, and support all the ordinances of the Gospel.

The result has been what we expected. Mr Emerson was too honest to dissemble or cloak his opinions, and his convictions were too earnest to be smothered. He uttered his own word in the desk of the Cambridge Chapel, as if he had been in a Lecture room, or in his own quiet study at Concord. He published them to the world without fear, or re-coloring. They are not popular; they are denounced as heretical; they are ridiculed as mystical; they are satirized as absurd; they are protested against as profane. So it must be. So the world must clamor. So the Innovator must be buffeted. So the Theorizer must be shaken and sifted. It is his fate; and we suppose that Mr Emerson does not shrink from meeting what he has not hesitated to expose himself to. One thing is certain—if truth and purity of heart consent to him in his thinking and his uttering concerning Christ and his religion, he can no more be disturbed by the popular roar than is the evening star shaken by the ripples that trifle with its image as it is dimly and uncertainly reflected on the surface of the fickle sea—but if error and unworthy intent have influenced his opinions or their expression, there is One that judgeth and One that will condemn, whose voice shaketh the cedars, and is more awful than the tumult of the people and the thunders of the pulpit and the press.

For one, we are not yet prepared to join with those who condemn Mr Emerson; or to believe that he is either an Infidel, a Pantheist or an Atheist. We cannot indeed agree with some of his sentiments; we cannot approve of some of his speculations; we cannot always discern the exact sense of his language; we cannot always be certain that he has himself fully analysed and systematised his opinions; we cannot commend his Cambridge Address; but, that he is a highly gifted, accomplished and holy man, and at heart and in life a Christian; we shall not cease to believe and to declare, until we see the best of reasons for changing an opinion not hastily nor suddenly formed.

That however, he is to be considered as a *representative of Unitarian sentiments*, or that Liberal Christians are called upon to father and answer for all his peculiarities of opinion, this we stoutly deny; and not more stoutly, we are convinced, than would that gentleman himself.

[The Divinity School Address]

Anonymous*

There is such an obscurity in the style of this performance, that its drift and meaning are not easily perceived. On entering this labyrinth of dark words, we hoped that we possessed a clue to conduct us safely through its windings, in the fact, that this address was delivered in a Divinity College. As the audience was composed of young men about entering on the christian ministry, it seemed not unnatural to presume, that in a discourse by one, who had himself borne, and, as we understand, still bears the name of a christian preacher, some possible form of christianity was shadowed forth. As we proceeded, however, the clue, on which we relied, failed us; and if in this misty sojourn we have attained to any light, it appears rather like darkness visible. It will not be expected, therefore, that a regular analysis of this pamphlet should be here at-

*Reprinted from *Quarterly Christian Spectator*, 10 (November 1838), 670–74.

tempted. A few passages only will be noticed, where the author speaks with a little less than his usual unintelligibleness, respecting several topics of morals and religion.

"The sentiment of virtue," says Mr. Emerson, "is a reverence and delight in the presence of certain divine laws." What these laws are, which give rise to this "sentiment of virtue," he probably means to intimate, where he soon after remarks, that "the child amidst his baubles, is learning the action of light, motion, gravity, muscular force; and in the game of life, love, fear, justice, appetite, man and God interact. These *laws* refuse to be adequately stated." It is in the presence, therefore, of the laws of gravity, motion, and muscular force, if we have arrived at the meaning of the author, and which laws, we are told, refuse to be adequately stated, that the reverence and delight are excited, or exist in us, which constitute virtue. According to our notions, reverence and delight must have some object; yet no object of reverence is here presented, except these same laws. But how such reverence can be distinguished from mere wonder or admiration, is far from being apparent. It is at least certain, that such affections as respect, love, confidence, and gratitude, as usually understood, can have no place here; and the author would probably not include them in his notion of "reverence and delight,"—that is, in his notion of virtue. We find it afterwards announced, that this "sentiment of virtue," that is, this reverence in the presence of the laws of gravity, motion, muscular force, and the like, whatever else it may be, is "the essence of all religion." The religion, therefore, or the essence of the religion, which Mr. Emerson would recommend and inculcate, has, so far as we can perceive, no direct relation to God, or, indeed, any relation to him whatever. This religion, then, at least practically, must be the religion of atheism; for though the name of God is found in this address, it is so used, and apparently with especial care, as to indicate a mere abstraction;—it is a word only. We would not designedly do the author injustice; but so far as we have been able to understand his representation, the God of this discourse sinks far below the God of Epicurus.

In such a religion as this, the founder of christianity cannot be expected to hold a very high place. "Jesus Christ," we are, however, told, "belonged to the true race of prophets. He saw with open eye, the mystery of the soul." And again,—he is "the only soul in history, who has appreciated the worth of man." This looks a little like respect. But that this old-fashioned feeling towards superior excellence may not rise too high, we are soon assured that "to aim to convert a man by miracles, is a profanation of the soul." It would seem, then, that this same Jesus of Nazareth, who "belonged to the true race of prophets," who "saw with open eye the mystery of the soul," and who is "the only soul in history, who has appreciated the worth of man," and necessarily, therefore, with a full knowledge of what he was doing, has been guilty of "a profanation of the soul;" a crime which ought to subject him, according to the doctrines of this address, to the highest censure and reprobation. His guilt, in this respect, can hardly be estimated. For if any one fact is clearly stated in his history, it is this; that he professed to perform acts which were supernatural; and with an openness, distinctness and frequency, to which no parallel exists. The author has, indeed, said, what seems to amount to a denial, that the miracles of Jesus were real miracles. "He," Jesus, "spoke of miracles," observes Mr. Emerson, "for he felt that man's life was a miracle, and all that man doth, and he knew, that this daily miracle shines, as the man is divine. But the very word miracle, as pronounced by christian churches, give a false impression; it is a monster. It is not one with the blowing clover and the falling rain."

But does Mr. Emerson suppose, that the world, with the narratives of the evangelists in full view, can be persuaded into the belief, that Christ did not pretend to perform miracles out of the ordinary course of events? that he did not appeal to such miracles as proofs of his mission? and that converts were not made to his doctrines, and with his full knowledge, on the ground of the supernatural character of these miracles? Nothing can be made plainer by words, than that the miracles of the four Gospels, are not represented as "one with the blowing clover and the falling rain." The fact, that this address was delivered in a Divinity College, is not more clearly or unambiguously expressed on the title-page of the pamphlet which contains it, than is the fact in the Gospels, that the miracles there recorded, are described as real miracles, what Mr. Emerson calls "monsters," that is, events out of the common course of nature. If the miracles of Jesus, as to the manner of their performance, are to be classed with "the blowing clover and the falling rain," he who is said to have wrought them, will be viewed, by the great body of mankind, as an intentional deceiver.

But Mr. Emerson probably cares little how this question is settled. Historical christianity, that is, christianity as derived from the scriptures, he makes no account of. As actually preached, he considers it positively injurious. One great defect of historical christianity, as he represents it, is, that "it has dwelt, it dwells, with noxious exaggeration about the *person* of Jesus." "The soul," he boldly announces to his auditors, "knows no person;" that is, if we understand him, no personal God, no personal Savior, with whom we have any concern, to whom we owe any reverence, or of whose protection, guidance, or favor, we stand in any need. Still the author speaks of the "calamity of a decaying church and a wasting unbelief, which are casting malignant influences around us, and making the hearts of good men sad." Unbelief, we would ask, in what? Certainly not in the laws of gravity, motion, or muscular force. These laws, and others like them, so far as understood, are, we believe, universally admitted to exist. Who has any doubt, for instance, that action and reaction are equal? that bodies, which are said to have weight, tend towards the surface of the earth? and that in a mature and healthy body, when unrestrained, the muscles act in obedience to the will? And the same question may be asked of innumerable other truths of the same general character. Not only are the laws in question believed in, that is, believed really to exist, but they are viewed by all who have any knowledge of them, as furnishing subjects of interesting contemplation, as wonderful, and inviting the closest and most diligent investigation and inquiry. And what more than this, would Mr. Emerson include in his idea of reverence? On this scheme, an irreligious man can hardly be found; and the author, instead of mourning over a "wasting unbelief," ought, so far as we can see, to raise his voice to the highest tones of joy and gladness, for the universal prevalence of faith.

The speaker again asks, "what greater calamity can fall upon a nation than the loss of worship?" We would ask, also, the worship of what? It is here perhaps more easy to answer negatively, than positively. Certainly he cannot mean, the worship of a personal God, for "the soul knows no persons." The loss of such a worship he ought to rejoice in. Such a loss would be a real advance towards true religion. If the worship of a personal God is a delusion, the sooner it ceases the better; nor do we find any thing in this address, which would lead us to suppose, that Mr. Emerson is not of this opinion. Yet notwithstanding all this, he announces the "sad conviction," which he shares with numbers, "of the universal decay and now almost death of faith in our churches."

And here, we cannot but inquire again, what this faith is which is so near its exit? Not surely faith in the Scriptures, as the source of correct religious knowledge; for in this sense Mr. Emerson does not appear to have any faith in them himself. Nor can it be faith in Jesus Christ as the teacher of a religion binding upon the consciences of men; for this is a part of historical religion, and, therefore, according to the author of the address, of no value. Is it faith in God, as a wise preserver, a kind father, and a righteous judge? Beyond the laws of nature, as they are called, it does not appear, that the speaker, who expresses his "sad conviction" of the decay of faith, entertains any belief of a God, except in name.

But perhaps this faith, which is dying, respects the soul. The author, indeed, complains that "the soul is not preached;" and among the means for awakening "the smouldering, nigh quenched fire on the altar," he would have his auditors, if we understand him, preach, "first, soul, and second, soul, and evermore, soul." But what he means by the soul; of what benefit this faith in something or other can be to the soul; whether the soul is immortal; and if so, whether in a future life it will be the subject of rewards and punishments for actions done here, we are unable to discover the slightest intimation. The language used on this subject is everywhere indistinct and indefinite. "In how many churches," says the speaker, "by how many prophets, tell me, is man made sensible that he is an infinite soul; that the earth and heavens are passing into his mind; that he is drinking forever the soul of God." In what respect he considers the

soul infinite, we are unable, from any thing in the address, even to conjecture; and if any one can understand the concluding part of the quotation now made, we would congratulate him on his ability in interpreting
dark sayings.

The author speaks, likewise, of the "laws of the soul;" and informs
us, that these "laws execute themselves." These laws, however, he asserts,
"are out of time, out of space, and not subject to circumstance." If all this
is true of the laws of the soul, we are unable to free ourselves from the apprehension, that the soul itself, like its laws, must be also "out of time, out
of space, and not subject to circumstance;" and where either the soul, or
its laws are to be found, we are left entirely in the dark. Yet after this
flight of the soul and its laws from time, place, and circumstance, we
find, that it "invites every man to expand to the full circle of the
universe." This invitation cannot certainly be made to the body; and if
the soul itself actually swells to the proposed dimensions, as its laws must
be co-extensive with it, these laws as they pervade the universe, must
somewhere, it should seem, within the limits of time, place, and *circumstance*, have a residence. But it is no part of our intention to enter
upon a discussion of any of the topics touched upon in this address. Mr.
Emerson does not condescend to reason; he announces his dogmas in the
manner of an oracle. His description of the good and bad preacher, is at
least novel. "The true preacher," we are told, "can always be known by
this, that he deals out to the people his life—life passed through the fire of
thought. But of the bad preacher, it could not be told from his sermon,
what age of the world he fell in; whether he had a father or a child;
whether he was a freeholder or a pauper; whether he was a citizen or a
countryman; or any other fact in his biography." The author's notions of
a sermon must differ materially from those which he entertains of an address; as from the address under consideration, we are unable to ascertain
respecting himself any one of the particulars above enumerated; except
perhaps the first. Or if he has here "dealt out his life;" in passing "through
the fire of thought," it has been so sublimated, or transmuted, as to entirely elude our dull apprehension.

But we can proceed with this address no farther. In what we have
said, we may have misapprehended its meaning; but we have honestly reported our real impressions of its import. We say without hesitation, however much it may be to the discredit of our sagacity, that with no
prepossessions against the speaker, after a diligent examination of his performance, we have been able to discover in it, so far as respects opinion,
little else than impiety and nonsense; and these, in about equal quantities.
As to style, it is in the highest degree affected and obscure. This address is
said to have been delivered before the senior class in Divinity College,
Cambridge; but the public are not told, that it was either delivered or
published at the request of any one. But whether it was pronounced, and
whether it then assumed the pamphlet form, through the ordinary proc-

ess, or whether it owes its existence exclusively to the operation of some hidden law of the soul; one thing may be regarded as certain, that those who heard it were greatly benefited, though not perhaps in the way intended by the orator. If an opinion may be formed from the effect which the reading of this address produces, the hearing of it actually spoken by a living man as his own production, must have operated as an effectual antidote to any future predilection for the philosophy which it inculcates. Just as in cases of actual insanity, we sometimes look at its ravings as detailed on paper, without being greatly moved; yet to hear them proceeding from the lips of a real victim of the most deplorable of all maladies, never fails to excite in a mind not steeled against the feelings of humanity, the strongest emotions of pity and grief, accompanied with an all-pervading horror of ever becoming the subject of the same calamity.

"R. W. Emerson and the New School"

[James Freeman Clarke]*

We perceive that our friends in Boston, and its vicinity, have been a good deal roused and excited by an address, delivered by the gentleman whose name stands above. Mr. Emerson has been long known as a man of pure and noble mind, of original genius and independent thought. Formerly settled as a Unitarian Preacher over the Second Church, in Boston, he left his charge, with feelings of mutual regret, on account of his having adopted the Quaker opinion in relation to the ordinance of the Lord's Supper. Since that time he has published a small volume called "Nature," and delivered various addresses and lectures on subjects of Literature, Philosophy, and Morals. All these productions have shown a mind of extreme beauty and originality. Their style, however, has been so different from the usual one, so completely Emersonian, as to confound and puzzle some, and disgust others. Many thought too, that they detected in his thoughts and doctrines the germs of dangerous errors. On the other hand, he has been surrounded by a band of enthusiastic admirers, whom the genius, life and manliness of his thoughts attracted, and his beautiful delivery as a public speaker charmed.

Matters stood thus, when he was invited to make an address to the parting class at the Cambridge Theological School. He readily accepted their offer and the result was that they heard an address quite different, we judge, from what ever fell into the ears of a Theological class before. He told them "that the faith of Christ was not now preached, that "the Priest's Sabbath has lost the splendor of nature; it is un-holy; we are

*Reprinted from *Western Messenger*, 6 (November 1838), 37–42.

glad when it is done; we can make, we do make, even sitting in our pews, a far better, holier, sweeter for ourselves." This was not polite to the preacher's, of whom we suppose many were present, and must have been rather disagreeable to bear—especially as no exception seemed to be made in behalf of his own sect. Instead of inculcating the importance of church-going, and shewing how they ought to persuade every body to go to church, he seemed to think it better to stay at home than to listen to a formal lifeless preacher. Instead of exhorting them to be always doing the duties of a pastor, he tells them not to be too anxious, to visit periodically, each family in their parish connection. Such things as these he told them, and moreover introduced them by some general remarks, which we cannot agree with him in thinking, that "while they are general, none will contest them." Notwithstanding their generality, they seemed to excite quite as much opposition as the other part of this harrangue.

Immediately after the delivery of this address, a lively discussion and controversy sprung up with respect to its doctrines, of which the end is not yet. First, there appears an article in the Boston Daily Advertiser,[1] in which Mr. Emerson is accused of rejecting all belief in Christianity as a revelation, and as probably disbelieving in the existence of a God. The graduating class are rebuked as having become accessories to the commission of a great offence, in asking him to address them, and are called upon, in a tone of great authority, to make their exculpation or excuse before the public.

Some remarks are prefixed concerning a New School in Literature and Philosophy which we shall notice again by and by. In the same paper, there shortly appears a reply to this first attack on Mr. Emerson. This reply is well written, only a little too poetical for controversy, as his opponent observed. Its author does not, however, defend Mr. Emerson, on the whole he agrees with his opponent respecting him, but does not like the *manner* of the attack. He thinks it altogether too harsh and severe to do any good.

Then comes a good democratic article in the Morning Post, censuring Mr. Emerson for some things, and praising him for others—then follow various communications in the Courier, and in the Register, with editorials appended, lamenting that Mr. Emerson should turn out an Atheist, or enquiring whether all Unitarians think as he does? which the Editor very promptly denies. Then comes a very thorough discussion of the doctrines of the Address in the Boston Review, in which, while Mr. Emerson is treated with courtesy and respect, his supposed opinions are very sharply examined. Again, we hear that Dr. Henry Ware, Jr. has published two sermons upon the subject of this Address. We are sure that his name will never be appended to any productions not written with clear thought and in a Christian Spirit.[2]

On the whole, we think that the results of this controversy will be excellent. It will show that our Unitarian plan of church union works better in a case of real or supposed heresy, than any other. How is it in those churches where they are bound together by a minute creed? A man publishes a sermon, containing some point supposed to be objectionable; he is tried by his Presbytery, condemned, appeals to his Synod, acquitted; referred to the Assembly, and deposed. He goes on preaching, his party increases, and a rent takes place in a great church, when the entering wedge was a thin pair of volumes. In our church, on the other hand, we have no creed but the Christian Scriptures. A man proclaims some strange sounding doctrine. Whoever feels most keenly that this is an Anti-Christian one, comes out against it with severity. This brings out other opinions, already formed, of various characters. This excites the attention of others. The discussion follows, for the bitterness all dies away—but men who seriously set themselves to *thinking* are not apt to get angry. But when the business is not to think it down, but to vote it down, to get together a party, and bind them together and heat them up by party conventions—there, it seems to us, things are likely to go a little warmly, and we shall hear more denunciation than argument.

For ourselves, we are convinced that if Mr. Emerson has taught any thing very wrong, it will be found out, and then he will quietly drop out of the Unitarian church, or the Unitarian church will fall off from him. No *excommunication* is necessary. Where people are held together by no outward bond, if the inward attraction ceases, they will soon drop apart.

The question, however, is, *has* he taught any thing wrong? Is he opposed to historical Christianity? Has he given any ground for supposing that he does not believe in the God of Christianity?

To give our opinion at length, on these points is out of the question—we have neither ability nor will to do it. To confess the truth, when we received and read the Address, we did not discover anything in it objectionable at all. We were quite delighted with it. We read it, to be sure, looking for good and not evil, and we found enough that was good to satisfy us. Parts seemed somewhat obscure, and for that we were sorry—in places we felt hurt by the phraseology, but we bounded carelessly over these rocks of offence and pit-falls, enjoying the beauty, sincerity and magnanimity of the general current of the Address. As critics, we confess our fault. We should have been more on the watch, more ready to suspect our author when he left the broad road-way of common-place, and instantly snap him up when he stated any idea new to us, or differing from our pre-conceived opinions.

But we must be serious—we have already, perhaps, treated this subject too long ironically. The most serious charges that can be brought against a Christian man, have been laid against our author, founded on the contents of this discourse. He has been accused of Infidelity, disbelief in historical Christianity—and of probable Atheism or Pantheism. That charity which thinketh no evil, rejoiceth not in iniquity and hopeth all things, should induce every man most carefully to pause before he brings such charges against a brother. If Mr. Emerson maintains these sentiments, we can no longer hold any fellowship with him, for a wide chasm yawns between our sympathies. But not for an obscure passage in an address, would we believe this of a man whose course of life has been always open—whose opinions never lay hid, and who, being such an one, has preached and still preaches as a Christian Minister.

He is accused of opposing Historical Christianity, that is, we suppse, of disbelief in the historical account of the life of Jesus. Now he speaks very strongly against those whose faith is only an historical one—who believe in Jesus Christ, not feeling him in their own souls as a Savior and Friend, but only acquiescing in the fact of his past existence. He speaks very strongly—without perhaps sufficient care against misconstruction. But does he speak more strongly or unguardedly than Paul did, when he said that the *letter* of the New Testament KILLED, while the spirit gave life? (2 Cor. iii. 6.) Does not this sound like doing away entirely with the letter of the New Testament? But Paul only meant, as Mr. Emerson we suppose means, that the letter is a dead weight in the mind, if the spirit does not animate it. How many things are there in the New Testament to show that a bare historical faith in Jesus Christ is not a saving faith—that we must have the witness in our own hearts—that our faith must stand, not in the will of men but the power of God—that our Father in Heaven must reveal it to us. The true doctrine undoubtedly is, that both witnesses are necessary to believe in Christ's divinity—an outward witness, coming down through history, and an inward witness of the spirit in our heart. This is beautifully shown in John xi. 26, 27. "But when the Comforter is come, which I will send unto you from the Father, even the spirit of truth, which proceedeth from the Father, *he shall testify of me; and ye also shall bear witness* because ye have been with me from the beginning."

Now if Mr. Emerson means to deny the value of this second testimony, we think him quite wrong, but we believe he only wishes to have it, as Christ put it, *second*. The common error is to be satisfied with the historical faith, and it is this error which he thought it necessary to oppose.

If Mr. Emerson disbelieves in all our present historical Christianity, how happens it that instead of opposing it, he opposes its *defects*? "The first *defect*" says he "of historical Christianity"—"the second defect." And how happened it that in this very Address he used the strongest expression we ever met with, to show the *historical influence* of Jesus Christ? "whose name is not so much written as *ploughed into the history of the world*."

We have been taking the view of the matter, which seems to us at the same time, the most correct, and the most charitable. At the same time we freely admit that there are many expressions which we would gladly have seen altered, or not seen at all; because though not so meant, they sound like irreverence or impiety to the common ear. Thus, where he says in the passage for which he was accused of Pantheism, "If a man is at heart just, then in so far, is he God; the safety of God, the immortality of God, the majesty of God, do enter into that man with justice." Why not be satisfied with the strong language of Jesus and John, and say that if he love, God dwells *in* him, and he *in* God? or that he *partakes* of the divine nature, as Peter declares. Why go further, and seem to destroy the personality either of God or man by saying that he *is* God? The privilege of being called the *sons of God* seemed to astonish John. "Behold! what manner of love" said he "the Father has shown us, that we should be called the sons of God!" Is it not enough to dwell *in God*, and have God dwell *in us*, but that we must also aspire to *be God*?

We might go on, and find more fault with Mr. Emerson's opinions, and his expressions. But we prefer, if possible, to stand now as mediators, if it may be, to soften down a little the harshness of the attacks he has already experienced. The Unitarians have already fully vindicated themselves from the charge of agreeing with him in opinion. He has certainly been very soundly rated by them, in some instances we think with too much harshness and dogmatism. For it is too late in the day to put a man down by shouting Atheist, Infidel, Heretic. Formerly you could thus excite a prejudice against him that would prevent men from examining the truth of the charge. Not so now. Men cannot be in this day put down by denunciation. The whole religious pulpit and religious press has united for thirty or forty years in calling Unitarians, Deists. What is the result? That their principles are rapidly spreading. In view of this fact, let us lay aside prejudice and candidly examine every new thing.

Notes

1. We cannot say that we like this plan of bringing Theological disputes before the world through Political and Commercial prints. There is never space for discussion, and only room to excite prejudices in the minds of those who may be supposed to be previously ignorant of the facts of the case. We do not find that Jesus Christ commands us to tell our brother's fault to the *world*, even after telling it to himself in private. He says "tell it to the Church." He does not say "tell it to the world."

2. And lastly we perceive that some college lad, writing a class-poem, wishing to lash existing abuses, and taking his direction, like the weather-cocks, from the winds, stands up "severe in youthful wisdom," tells Mr. Emerson it is very wrong to be an Infidel, and compares him to "Gibbon and Voltaire! ! !" Ah! unfortunate Mr. Emerson! well may you say with the sad old king.

> The little dogs and all,
> Tray, Blanch, and Sweetheart, see they bark at me.

"The New School in Literature and Religion"

[James Freeman Clarke]*

The writer who first publicly attacked Mr. Emerson's Address, prefaced his remarks by observations upon what he called "the New School in Literature and Religion." Thus he speaks:—

> "There is a strange state of things existing about us in the literary and religious world, of which none of our larger periodicals have yet taken notice. It is the result of that restless craving for notoriety and excitement, which, in one way, or another, is keeping our community in a perpetual stir.   *   *   *   *   *
> "It owes its origin in part to ill-understood notions, obtained by blundering through the crabbed and disgusting obscurity of some of the worst German speculatists, which notions, however, have been received by most of its disciples at second hand, through an interpreter."

Thus far we were quite at a loss to know what this new school was. But the next sentence becomes more particular:

> "The Atheist Shelley has been quoted and commended in a professedly religious work, called the Western Messenger; but he is not, we conceive, to be reckoned among the patriarchs of the sect."

When in our simplicity, we inserted an article upon Shelley in the Western Messenger, we were not aware that because a man was an Atheist he might not be commended for writing good poetry. We lamented the nature of his opinions, we mourned over his want of faith, and expressly stated our aversion to his general views. We did not expect therefore to be accused of commending him, as though we had been praising him for his Atheism—least of all did we expect that we were to become members of "a new school" through the medium of that article. But let us hear more about this New School and its follies:

> "But this honor is due to that hasher up of German metaphysics, the Frenchman, Cousin; and, of late, that hyper-Germanized Englishman, Carlyle, has been the great object of admiration and model of style. Cousin and Carlyle indeed seem to have been transformed into idols to be publicly worshipped, the former for his philosophy, and the latter both for his philosophy and his fine writing; while the veiled image of the German pantheist, Schleiermacher, is kept in the sanctuary."

Here then we have some means given us of detecting the members of the New School. If a man praises Shelley, he is to be suspected. If he studies Cousin, the charge is almost brought home against him. But if he

*Reprinted from *Western Messenger*, 6 (November 1838), 42–47. We are grateful to Robert Habich for information attributing this article to Clarke.

admires Carlyle, and occasionally drops dark hints about Schleiermacher, he is a confirmed disciple of this new heresy.

"Hic niger est. Hunc tu, Romane, caveto.

But yet, though this seems at first an easy way of detecting these dark disorganizers, some difficulty may arise in its application. Thus, there are some who read and study Cousin, but care nothing for Carlyle, or dislike him. And again, there are admirers of Carlyle, who do not wholly admit the Eclectic philosophy. And as to the admirers of Schleiermacher, veiled or otherwise, it is rather difficult to find them. A single article on his character, translated from Dr. Lücke, appeared in the Examiner. He has been alluded to, once or twice, in the Western Messenger. One of his essays on the Trinity, translated by Moses Stuart, with copious notes of approbation, occupied several numbers of the Biblical Repository. And an essay of his upon Election, appeared in that supporter of old Calvinism, the New York Literary and Theological Review, translated by its editor, Leonard Woods, Jr., also with notes of approval. This is nearly all the notice we have seen taken of Schleiermacher in our religious periodicals. Do Professor Stuart, and the New York Calvinists, then, belong to this "New School in religion and literature?"

But our writer goes on to give some further characteristics of the New School. Let us hear:

"The characteristics of this school are the most extraordinary assumption, united with great ignorance, and incapacity for reasoning."

It is easy enough, we fear, to find men of all schools, and of no school, who would fall under this category. There is plenty of assumption, ignorance, and incapacity for reasoning, in the world. It is notorious that these traits may be found united even in those, who cherish the deadliest hostility to Transcendentalism, Carlyleism, and all new ideas. We must have some other clue then, before we can certainly distinguish this pestilent New School.

The next characteristic of the New School is thus given:—

"There is indeed a general tendency among its disciples to disavow learning and reasoning as sources of their higher knowledge. The mind must be its own unassisted teacher. It discerns transcendental truths by immediate vision, and these truths can no more be communicated to another by addressing his understanding, than the power of *clairvoyance* can be given to one not magnetized."

Now it is very true that there are those who assert that the soul is not like a sheet of white paper—that it does not acquire all knowledge by perception and reasoning, but that it is endowed by the Creator with certain ideas which arise necessarily in the mind of every sane man. The idea of cause and effect, for instance, is one—that of God another—those of time, space, infinity, and our own identity, others. We do not depend upon logic for our conviction of these things. They belong to a common sense which is back of all logic—an impartial God bestows them on all his children, and not merely on those who have been educated at Colleges and Universities.

Thus for instance, faith in God does not depend upon arguments, *a priori* or *a posteriori*, but upon a necessity of the mind. It is necessary to believe in God, just as it is necessary to believe in cause and effect, or time and space. A man may by logic so confuse himself as to think he disbelieves, but healthy minds believe by intuition, and the necessity of their own natures. To those who have never gone out of the circle of John Locke, this may seem very absurd, but it is in fact the oldest philosophy.

This belief, that all our knowledge does not come to us through the senses or from logical deduction, but that the mind itself furnishes some of the most essential convictions, as a ground-work or foundation, seems to us capable of the clearest demonstration. We know of nothing more conclusive than the train of reasoning by which Cousin establishes this, in his criticism on Locke. "Learning and reasoning," we do *not* believe to be "the sources of our higher knowledge." But observation and reasoning still have their place, though in another sphere. A man who should attempt to prove by logic his own existence, we should say, mistook the use of logic. So would every one else, yet this is all that transcendentalists say. To say that they reject *all* logic or reasoning, because they do not suffer them to be applied to those truths to which a man's own consciousness and the universal consent of the race testifies, is to mistake the matter.

This writer against the New School goes on to speak of them as announcing themselves as prophets and priests of the future—and as about to do away with old things, and abolish all the present forms of society. We do not precisely understand what this charge means. It may answer to terrify with visions of Agrarianism, respectable capitalists, but to what class of persons it applies we cannot tell. We have heard indeed of Fanny Wright and Robert Dale Owen preaching against the marriage bond, and other important institutions. The paragraph might apply to them, but then we never heard of their admiring Carlyle or Cousin, or worshipping Schleiermacher even in the most secret and veiled manner. We remain in the dark therefore as to the matter of this sentence.

This writer also says a great deal about the *bad taste* of the new school in their writings. We must remind him that *taste* is, by its nature, a very personal affair, and what to one man may seem bad taste, may appear to another very good. One man may think that good taste requires every one to write like Addison or Hume, another may think it in better taste for every man to write like himself. Bossu and Boileau thought it very bad taste to have less than five acts in a play or to violate the unities of time and space. Modern critics laugh at these rules. Voltaire used to prate about good taste perpetually, and showed his own by calling Shakespeare a barbarian. In fact, he who thinks, by rules of taste, to keep the style of writing always at one point, is as foolish as he who would hold back any other part of the great social movement.

"Labitur et labetur, in omnis volubile ævum."

From all which we have said, however, we would not have it inferred that we deny the existence of a New School in Religion and Literature; but only that the characteristics as given by the writer before, do not appear to us sufficiently descriptive. They would apply to too many sorts of schools.

The truth is, our friend has failed in his definition of the New School, because he sought it in their opinions and manners, rather than in their principles and spirit. There are many who like Mr. Emerson, but do not like Cousin. Mr. E. himself, in his Dartmouth oration, finds fault with Cousin. There are others who like Cousin, who will have nothing of Emerson or Carlyle. And the admirers of Schleiermacher, (Leo. Woods, Jr. and Moses Stuart, for example) have probably no great relish for either of the others. We cannot find any certain test in these likes and dislikes.

Yet we agree with our friend that there is a new school. Perhaps we should agree with him as to those who are its chief masters and leaders. But we should describe them quite differently. We should say—there is a large and increasing number of the clergy and laity, of thinking men and educated women, especially of the youth in our different colleges, of all sects and all professions, who are dissatisfied with the present state of religion, philosophy and literature. The common principle which binds them together and makes them if you choose a school, is a desire for more of LIFE, soul, energy, originality in these great departments of thought. If they like Carlyle, it is not that they wholly agree with his opinions, or think his style perfect, but because they find in him a genuine man, full of life and originality. If they listen with delight to Mr. Emerson, and read his works with pleasure, it is not that they agree with all his speculations, but that they sympathize with his independence, manliness, and freedom. They read Mr. Brownson's writings, and perhaps they may not admit his opinions about the sub-treasury or acquiesce in all his new views of Christianity, but they honor and esteem the free and ardent energy of thought, which every paragraph displays. In the same way they sympathize with the spirit of Mr. Furness, without accepting all his results. In a word they esteem genuine, earnest, independent thought as the one thing needful in our whole life, and where they find this in a man they are drawn toward him by strong sympathies. Wherever there is reality and not appearance, substance and not form, living energy and not hollow show, sincere conviction and not traditional cant—there they feel their chief wants met and answered. They can sympathize with orthodoxy, though holding liberal opinions, when they find orthodoxy sincere, earnest and true. They can sympathize with the doubts of those who believe less than themselves, if these doubts spring from an earnest pursuit of truth. They can join heart and hand with those who never read a page of Cousin or Carlyle, if they find them earnestly laboring by Sunday schools, city missions, and benevolent associations to put more of moral and spiritual life into society. Their sympathies embrace the secluded scholar, the active preacher, the devoted school-master, the enthusiastic artist, the true poet—every man who feels that life should not be a mechanical routine, but be filled with earnestness, soul and spiritual energy. All who look, and hope, and labor for something better than now is, who believe in progress, who trust in future improvement, and are willing to spend and be spent in bringing forward that better time; all such are members of the New School.

If we are asked who is the leader of this New School, we should not name Mr. Emerson so soon as Dr. Channing. He leads on the new school, because from him has come the strongest impulse to independent thought, to earnest self-supported activity. Dr. Channing is one of those who deeply and mournfully feel the absence of life in our religion, philosophy and literature. We know not whether or not he sympathizes with the speculations of Carlyle, Emerson and Cousin; but we know that he sympathizes with earnest sincere seeking in every shape and form. And when he might condemn the results, he would still tolerate and esteem the honest seeker. He believes in progress, he sympathizes with every effort of struggling humanity to bring on by severe thought or manly action a happier and better day. And this, we take it, is the true definition of a member of the NEW SCHOOL.

"Ralph Waldo Emerson"

S[amuel] G[ilman]*

A new comet, or rather meteor, is shooting athwart the literary sky of old Massachusetts, in the person of Ralph Waldo Emerson. He is the son of a distinguished clergyman of Boston, some time since deceased, and is now of middle age. He is attracting much public attention, and is an object of the severest reproaches from some, and the most profound admiration from others. He has delivered two or three courses of lectures in Boston, on moral and literary subjects, which have been attended by crowds. Many enthusiastic talented young people are represented to be perfectly fascinated by him. His reputation has, of late, extended so widely, that he was invited last July to deliver the Annual Addresses before the Literary Societies of Dartmouth College, and the Senior Class in the Divinity College of Harvard University. He appears to be a profound admirer, student, and imitator of Thomas Carlyle, several of whose works he has caused to be republished in this country. The character of his

*Reprinted from *Southern Rose*, 7 (24 November 1838), 100–106.

mind is poetical and imaginative, and he is strongly inclined to certain mystical and visionary habits of thought and discussion. His talents are unquestionably of a respectable order, though, as it appears to us, much inferior to the scale assigned them by his fervent admirers. The qualities, however, just mentioned, united with an irreproachable, lovely, and elevated moral character, and the graces of a commanding person and impressive elocution, go a good way to explain the effect which he has produced on a highly educated, refined, and excitable community. He delivered last winter a course of lectures on Human Culture, in which he began with Prudence, and gradually ascended to Holiness. Whatever was thought of the speculative truth, all parties allowed that the spirit was noble, and the style and manner beautiful.

From the specimens we have seen, there appears to be very little originality in his speculations,—though a youthful and miscellaneous audience might be apt to imagine quite the contrary. All his leading ideas he seems to have caught from Carlyle, who again was indebted for *his* chief resources to the modern German philosophers.[1] These ideas Mr. Emerson adorns, expands, and presents anew in a great variety of shapes, mingling them up, certainly, with much that is peculiar to himself, and occasionally yielding a profound and precious glimpse into the truth of things. At the same time, there is a good deal of mere common place in his writings, redeemed only by a quaint, fantastic, imaginative style, which deceives the young reader or hearer into the belief that it is original and valuable. Thus, instead of using the ordinary word *completed*, he talks of a thing *coming full circle*, a phrase, by the way, which seems to be a favorite one with him. He sprinkles his writings now and then with the old solemn style, as *worketh, loveth, hath*, &c. *Works, loves*, and *has*, would not so well answer his purpose. The word *forever* is too tame for him, and he employs in its stead the more sounding and poetical *forever-more*. He affects much the Saxon phraseology, as *behooted* and *behowled*, *skulks* and *sneaks*, &c. We do not find particular fault with all this. If it belongs to the man's original or acquired nature, let it come out. We only instance it, as partly explaining the cause which dazzles Mr. Emerson's admirers.

We learn that much bitterness has been expressed in the newspapers and private circles of the vicinity, in consequence of some of Mr. Emerson's recent utterances. Exposed to storms of obloquy and reproach, he stands calm and unmoved—replies to no criticisms—but meekly announces a new course of lectures in Boston, for the coming winter, and will probably have a crowded lecture-room, although we learn that the extravagances of his Cambridge Address have partially worked their own cure, and that his influence has begun to wane.

Some of his offensive doctrines, as far as we can comprehend them from his very involved and cloudy paragraphs, appear to be the following. He reduces all revelation to the level of our natural reason, maintaining, in fact, that there is a perpetual revelation going on in the soul of man, of equal authority with the Jewish or Christian. He denies the authority of miracles, or rather seems to claim them as in perpetual and present operation. He seems to represent the objects of true religious love and worship to be not any divine *person* or *persons*, but only certain abstract *qualities*, such as absolute *goodness*, *truth*, and *wisdom*. He declares that *evil* is not *positive*, but only *negative*, there being nothing positive, but *good*. From which we conclude, that *murder* is not a *positive*, but only a *negative* act. And we are still further puzzled by turning over the page, and finding the author warn us against "*absolute badness.*" His language respecting the human soul, appears to elevate it to an equality with the Supreme Being. "Man," he says, "is made a Providence to himself."—His views savour, at times, of the pantheistic doctrines of Spinoza, who is a favorite with modern German philosophers and has been charged with confounding creation with the Creator, making them both one. Others of his expressions are offensive, not from conveying any definite meaning at all, but only from apparently denying or contravening certain long-established opinions. But what is particularly remarkable, all this tissue of novel and unpopular opinions is strangely mixed in with expressions and sentiments, which imply directly the contrary, and are perfectly consistent with our old-fashioned doctrines and belief. Thus, almost the same page tells us that "God is well pleased," whenever a human spirit devotes itself to virtue, and that "if a man is at heart just, then in so far is *he* God! !" Having asserted, that "all things proceed out of the same spirit, and all things *conspire with it*," he soon after declares that sometimes men *seek* good ends, and sometimes *rove* from good ends, until they arrive at "absolute badness and absolute death."

Again, he says, it is a capital mistake in the infant man to hope to derive advantages *from another*—yet, in the next page, he allows that we can receive beneficial *provocation* from another soul, though not instruction; and further on, he acknowledges that there is a good ear, in some men, *that draws supplies to virtue out of very indifferent nutriment.* He tells us also that he loves the divine bards, because they *admonish* him—notwithstanding it is a capital mistake to hope to derive advantages from another! He also affirms that the office of a minister of religion is the first in the world, notwithstanding it is such a capital mistake for one man to hope to derive advantage from another.

Again, Mr. Emerson finds fault with preachers of modern times, because you cannot discover from any hint, or surmise in their sermons, whether they *personally* have ever "laughed or wept, were married or in love, have been commended, or cheated, or chagrined—ploughed, or planted, talked, bought and sold, read books; eaten and drunken; had the head-ache or heart-ache; smiled or suffered;"—and yet two public, solemn addresses of his own are before us, which we have studied and pondered with the utmost diligence, and we cannot for the life of us discover from them whether Mr. Emerson himself is a great laugher or weeper, or was ever married, or in love, or has ever been commended, or cheated, or chagrined, or has ever ploughed, planted, talked, bought, sold, or had the head-ache. Of the bad preacher, he declares that "it could not be told from his sermon, what age of the world he fell in; whether he had a father or a child; whether he was a freeholder or a pauper; whether he was a citizen or a countryman; or any other fact of his biography." Yet all this information respecting himself he perversely withholds from his hearers, and so far as we may dare to take *him* for authority, he is consequently a sorry teacher.

A single instance more of such unfortunate inconsistency shall complete this disagreeable portion of our task. Mr. Emerson tells us, p. 31, that "the Hebrew and Greek Scriptures contain immortal sentences, that have been bread of life to millions." Yet he has before said to us, p. 26—"Once leave *your own* knowledge of God, *your own* sentiment, and take *secondary* knowledge, as *St. Paul's*, or George Fox's, or Swedenborg's, and you *get wide from God* with every year this secondary form lasts."

We submit a few of Mr. Emerson's (*absurdities* is too harsh a word for the lips of the gentle *Rose*)—but *incomprehensibilities*, let us more reverently say. Speaking of the religious sentiment, he says, "wonderful is its power to charm and to command. It is a mountain air. It is the embalmer of the world. It is myrrh and storax, and chlorine and rosemary. It makes the sky and the hills sublime, and the silent song of the stars is it. By it, is the universe made safe and habitable, not by science or power."

"The very word Miracle, as pronounced by Christian churches, gives a false impression; it is Monster. It is not one with the blowing clover and the falling rain."

"A true conversion, a true Christ, is now, as always, to be made, by the reception of beautiful sentiments."

"The time is coming when all men will see, that the gift of God to the soul is not a vaunting, overpowering, excluding sanctity, but a sweet, natural goodness, a goodness like thine and mine, and that so invites thine and mine to be and to grow."

"In how many churches, by how many prophets, tell me, is man made sensible that he is an infinite Soul; that the earth and heavens are passing into his mind; that he is drinking forever the soul of God?"

"In one soul, in your soul, there are resources for the world. Wherever a man comes, there comes revolution. The old is for slaves. When a man comes, all books are legible, all things transparent, all religions are forms. He is religious. Man is the wonderworker. He is seen amid miracles. All men bless and curse. He saith yea and nay, only."

But the climax of the whole is the concluding sentence of the Cambridge Address:—

"I look for the new Teacher, that shall follow so far those shining laws, that he shall see them come full circle; shall see their rounding complete grace; shall see the world to be the mirror of the soul; *shall see the identity of the law of gravitation with purity of heart*; and shall show that the Ought, that Duty, is one thing with Science, with Beauty, and with Joy."

The above sentence in italics, if it have any meaning, must signify that both the law of gravitation and sincerity of heart are immediate and simultaneous manifestations of one and the same divine being. But here, the author's philosophy is more shallow and dogmatic than either he or his German masters imagine it to be. For it remains yet to be shown, that the action of gravitation *is* the immediate act of the Deity. For aught we know, it may be but the consequence of numerous other laws, of which man is perfectly ignorant. The writer might, with equal propriety, have asserted that the law of evaporation, or crystallization, or congealment, or vision, or sound, or any other of the common processes of nature, is identical with purity of heart. Or, perhaps Mr. Emerson intended boldly and undesignedly to express his belief in the identity of matter and mind. But even in that case, how the *quality* of purity of heart is identical with a *law*, surpasses our utmost powers of conjecture. If we use language at all, let us use it intelligibly.

In his Dartmouth address, Mr. E. urges on his youthful hearers the duty of assuming and maintaining forever an attitude of *inquiry*. We regret that we see little of this in his own productions. We look in vain for a truly *humble* spirit. All is dogmatism, assumption, dictation. The writer, we are sorry to say, appears to consider himself the *infallible instructer* of his age, and the idea of incurring error seems not to have entered his mind.[2] How different from this is the spirit of Channing! Channing, in the loftiest flights of speculation, and while pouring in streams of light, or stirring up torrents of feeling within the souls of his readers or hearers, rarely if ever lays aside the genuine humility of the philosophic inquirer, never assuming to be the oracle of his fellow-men, even at the moment when he most becomes so.

Mr. Emerson imagines that Christendom has degenerated from its former condition, because men have lost the spirit and the views of religion which *he* and his school entertain. But can he exhibit a single proof that the Christian Church ever approximated to such a standard?

. . . .

On the whole, we cannot help concluding, that a writer, who seems to entertain no clear and definite principles,—who bewilders his hearers amidst labyrinths of beautiful contradictions; who floats about among vague and impalpable abstractions, and who is but the second or third hand reviver of ideas and visions, that have already been more than once exploded in the course of human progress, and could never get a foothold in this matter-of-fact world—is destined to make no very deep or permanent impression on the minds of his generation. The young may be dazzled and delighted for a while—the old may tremble at seeing all they have ever held sacred, unceremoniously handled and rudely set at nought—but society will at length rigidly demand some solid and tangible platform for its belief—some practical and mighty remedy for its corruptions—and some available instrument for the development of its moral resources. Society, too, will ever instinctively feel, that all the disadvantages of the old order of things are preferable to the utter lawlessness and mistaken independence recommended in the Dartmouth Address. Say what Mr. Emerson pleases, men were made to *learn* from each other, and a certain degree of deference and dependence is necessary to the best interests of the species. Had Mr. Emerson the right control of his own powers,—did he know where to pause in the career of daring speculation,—had he the happy tact to perceive the exact needs and capabilities of our imperfect world—and especially, if instead of attempting to keep his eyes forever fixed on the too dazzling and burning luminary of abstract truth, he were contented with exploring the milder sunlight and the varying shades which rest upon the landscape of human destiny, he might be hailed as one of the benefactors of his kind. A reformer ought, indeed, to go ahead of those whom he wishes to improve. But if he rushes at one start so far in advance as altogether to lose the sight and sympathy of his fellow-men, his energies must be wasted. The most generous steed on earth could not move an ounce-weight, if his traces were ambitiously lengthened out at an immense distance from his burden, and he aspired to struggle full circle in the vague and far-off horizon. Mr. Emerson, at times, seems to be conscious of these truths. He acknowledges himself incapable of suggesting, and hopeless of seeing new forms of worship for the Christian world, and even advises that the existing ones be retained, and a new breath be breathed into them by spirits of his own stamp. One of his characteristic contradictions! For who has done more to shake men's confidence in these existing forms, though he coolly acknowledges that he has nothing to replace in their stead?

Ralph Waldo Emerson is like unto a man, who saith unto all the children and dear mid-aged people of his neighborhood, "Oh, come, let us go yonder and dance a beautiful dance at the foot of the rainbow. There, will be treasures beneath our feet, and drops of all colours over our heads, and we shall be in the very presence of the mysteries of nature, and we and the rainbow shall be one, and the drops shall be beauty, and the drops shall be usefulness, and the drops shall be righteousness and purity of heart; and mortality and immortality shall be identical; and sin and holiness, and labour and rest, and vulgarity and gentility, and study and idleness, and solitude and society, and black and white, shall all become one great commingled, homogeneous and heterogeneous spot of pure glorification, forevermore." Then all the children, and dear mid-aged people, exclaim, "Beautiful, beautiful; let us go yonder and dance beneath the foot of the rainbow." and they all go forth with Emerson at their head, and Carlyle in advance of him, and Richter and Spinoza several rods in advance of Carlyle, and they seek the foot of the rainbow, but it recedes forever from them as they proceed. But at length wearied and shattered, they will return to the humble village, and will be contented with admiring the rainbow at a distance, and will be grateful for the dark, colorless drops that come down to refresh their heads, and will permit both rainbow and drops to carry up their thoughts to the mysterious Being who created the whole together with themselves, and so continue to walk piously and practically to their graves.

Notes

1. Mr. Emerson ought to have studied the resources and habits of his own mind, before venturing on the following authoritative admonition. "The man who aims to speak *as books enable*, as synods use, as the fashion guides, and as interest commands, babbles. Let him hush." It is almost ludicrous to hear our amiable author perpetually declaiming about "independence," "standing alone," "consulting only one's soul," when, if the truth were known, there is scarcely a writer now on the stage, who has been more indebted for his lights and impulses to the inspiration of others. The only difference between him and more common-place geniuses, is, that *he* has looked for inspiration chiefly to one or two channels of thought, while other men have chosen to avoid singularity, and have endeavored to drink in the *whole spirit* of the past and present, in order that they might transmit it to the future, as much improved as their own plastic powers might permit. *Such* men, however, are regarded by Mr. Emerson as "second-hand and slavish." Is it not equally second-hand and slavish to be the quaint disciple of a quaint and narrow school?

2. We may except a sentence in the beginning of the Dartmouth Address.

"Unitarianism"

C.*

This address of Mr. Emerson's has excited no little interest among the denomination of Christians to which he belongs; it appears to have met with a prompt and decided rebuke, particularly, from the professors in the Unitarian Theological School; one of whom has published a rejoinder, entitled, "The personality of the Deity." Another professor, is said to have declared of Mr. E's address, that "what was in it which was not folly, was blasphemy."

Being of opposite religious tenets from the party most interested in this controversy, and unacquainted with the individuals concerned, moreover, judging simply from a perusal of the book, without regard to the commentaries thereupon, we claim, at least impartiality, so far as respects the two Unitarian sects, which now seem to be hotly at variance.

Why Professor Ware should term his sermon on the 'personality of the Deity,' an answer to Mr. Emerson's address, we cannot conceive, for

*Reprinted from *Boston Recorder*, 24 (11 January 1839), 5.

no where in the publication before us, does Mr. E. deny the doctrine; and we have heard, that he has expressed great astonishment that Mr. Ware should have so construed his language. The sweeping criticism, that what there is not in it of folly is blasphemy, we utterly demur. That most of the book may be so interpreted, by a large proportion of readers, we can readily conceive, but how an intelligent, unprejudiced mind can so render it, is not so clear to our vision.

Mr. Emerson, from an affectation of singularity, or from a desire to express his thoughts in their most simple and natural order, has adopted a phraseology and a style, rather out of the common course. The style is sententious, poetic and philosophical; words are fresh-coined, and others are used in new senses. Now to call a man a fool or an Atheist for these things *merely*, though it may be an easy mode of criticism, is neither wise nor honest. That serious objections, in the way of expediency, may be brought against the style and phrase of Mr. E's address, we do not doubt, but that there is some good matter in this production, and that the author has been misrepresented in various passages, we believe a few extracts from the work itself, may but support our opinion. Speaking of the Lord's Supper.

"If no heart warm this rite, the hollow, dry, creaking formality is too plain."

This from a man, who refuses to administer this rite, shows the reason why he could not do it; and however we may reverence the institution, we should at least, have candor enough to give Mr. Emerson credit for *sincerity*, and for a proper discernment of that worship which our Saviour taught to the woman of Samaria.

Who can object to the following?

"Whenever the pulpit is usurped by a formalist, then is the worshipper defrauded and disconsolate. We shrink as soon as the prayers begin, which do not uplift, but smite and offend us.

We are fain to wrap our cloak about us, and secure, as best we can, a solitude that bears not. **

A snow storm was falling around us. The snow storm was real; the preacher merely spectral; and the eye felt the sad contrast in looking at him, and then out of the window behind him, into the beautiful meteor of the snow. He had lived in vain. He had no one word intimating that he had laughed or wept, was married or in love, had been commended, or cheated or chagrined. If he had ever lived and acted, we were none the wiser for it."

The following sentiment commends itself.

"But the man who aims to speak as books enable, as Synods use, as the fashion guides, and as interest commands, babbles. Let him hush."

Whether Mr. Emerson's observation on the prevalence of formality is confined to Unitarian churches, we know not; but it is probable, that he knows but little of other denominations. Read this.

"It is time that this ill-suppressed murmur of all thoughtful men against the famine of our churches; this moaning of the heart because it is bereaved of the consolation, the hope, the grandeur, that come alone out of the culture of the moral nature, should be heard through the sleep of indolence, and over the din of routine. This great and perpetual office of the preacher is not discharged."

He seems to mourn the departure of the Puritan spirit. "The Puritans in England and America, found in the Christ of the Catholic church, and in the dogmas inherited from Rome, scope for their austere piety, and their longings for civil freedom. But their creed is passing away, and none arises in its room."

That Mr. Emerson is a 'Humanitarian,' is evident from this address; but that he is a believer in the doctrine of God's presence in the soul, as revealed by Christ, is also apparent; and to us it appears, that, the class of Unitarians to whom Mr. Emerson belongs (the Transcendental class,) are coming to the Orthodox ranks. The notorious coldness of Unitarianism, is leading men of a serious cast to a more spiritual worship; and such men must either frame a new revelation or abide under the old forms of the Puritans. That Mr. Emerson is inclined to the latter, would appear from his thoughts on the subject.

"The question returns, What shall we do? I confess, all attempts to project and establish a cultus with new rites and forms, seems to me vain. Faith makes us, and not we it, and faith makes its own forms. All attempts to contrive a system, are as cold as the new worship introduced by the French to the goddess of Reason; to-day, paste-board and fillagree, and ending tomorrow in madness and murder. Rather let the breath of new life be breathed by you through the forms already existing."

That Unitarianism, or more properly the system of negation naturally leads to infidelity, is apparent from the history of the Priestly school at Hackney; but to stigmatize those individuals as Atheists, who are sick of formality is not right. What though their flight from the Polar regions may be erratic; what though their wing be unsteady; the prompting within is right, and we should rather assist their flutterings than impede their flight.

"Preface by the English Editor"

Thomas Carlyle*

To the great reading public entering Mr. Fraser's and other shops in quest of daily provender, it may be as well to state, on the very threshold, that this little Reprint of an American Book of Essays is in no wise the

*Reprinted from Emerson, *Essays* (London: James Fraser, 1841), pp. v–xiii.

thing suited for them; that not the great reading public, but only the small thinking public, and perhaps only a portion of these, have any question to ask concerning it. No Editor or Reprinter can expect such a Book ever to become popular here. But, thank Heaven, the small thinking public has now also a visible existence among us, is visibly enlarging itself. At the present time it can be predicted, what some years ago it could not be, that a certain number of human creatures will be found extant in England to whom the words of a man speaking from the heart of him, in what fashion soever, under what obstructions soever, will be welcome;—welcome, perhaps, as a brother's voice, to 'wanderers in the labyrinthic Night!' For these, and not for any other class of persons, is this little Book reprinted and recommended. Let such read, and try; ascertain for themselves, whether this *is* a kind of articulate human voice speaking words, or only another of the thousand thousand ventriloquisms, mimetic echoes, hysteric shrieks, hollow laughters, and mere *in*articulate mechanical babblements, the soul-confusing din of which already fills all places? I will not anticipate their verdict; but I reckon it safe enough, and even a kind of duty in these circumstances, to invite them to *try*.

The name of Ralph Waldo Emerson is not entirely new in England: distinguished Travellers bring us tidings of such a man; fractions of his writings have found their way into the hands of the curious here; fitful hints that there is, in New England, some spiritual Notability called Emerson, glide through Reviews and Magazines. Whether these hints were true or not true, readers are now to judge for themselves a little better.

Emerson's writings and speakings amount to something:—and yet hitherto, as seems to me, this Emerson is perhaps far less notable for what he has spoken or done, than for the many things he has not spoken and has forborne to do. With uncommon interest I have learned that this, and in such a never-resting locomotive country too, is one of those rare men who have withal the invaluable talent of sitting still! That an educated man of good gifts and opportunities, after looking at the public arena, and even trying, not with ill success, what its tasks and its prizes might amount to, should retire for long years into rustic obscurity; and, amid the all-pervading jingle of dollars and loud chaffering of ambitions and promotions, should quietly, with cheerful deliberateness, sit down to spend *his* life not in Mammon-worship, or the hunt for reputation, influence, place or any outward advantage whatsoever: this, when we get notice of it, is a thing really worth noting. As Paul Louis Courrier said: "*Ce qui me distingue de tous mes contemporains c'est que je n'ai pas la prétention d'être roi.*" 'All my contemporaries;'—poor contemporaries! It is as if the man said: Yes, ye contemporaries, be it known to you, or let it remain unknown, There is one man who does not need to be a king; king neither of nations, nor of parishes or cliques, nor even of *cent-per-annums*; nor indeed of anything at all save of himself only. 'Realities?' Yes, your dollars are real, your cotton and molasses are real; so are Presidentships, Senatorships, celebrations, reputations, and the wealth of Rothschild: but to me, on the whole, they are not the reality that will suffice. To me, without some other reality, they are mockery, and amount to *zero*, nay to a negative quantity. ETERNITIES surround this god-given Life of mine: what will all the dollars in creation do for me? Dollars, dignities, senate-addresses, review-articles, gilt coaches or cavalcades, with world-wide huzzaings and parti-coloured beef-eaters never so many: O Heaven, what were all these? Behold, ye shall have all these, and I will endeavour for a thing other than these. Behold, we will entirely agree to differ in this matter; I to be in your eyes nothing, you to be something, to be much, to be all things:—wherefore, adieu in God's name; go ye that way, I go this!— — Pity that a man, for such cause, should be so distinguished from *all* his contemporaries! It is a misfortune partly of these our peculiar times. Times and nations of any strength have always privately held in them many such men. Times and nations that hold none or few of such, may indeed seem to themselves strong and great, but are only bulky, loud; no heart or solidity in them;—*great*, as the blown bladder is, which by and by will collapse and become small enough!

For myself I have looked over with no common feeling to this brave Emerson, seated by his rustic hearth, on the other side of the Ocean (yet not altogether parted from me either), silently communing with his own soul, and with the God's World it finds itself alive in yonder. Pleasures of Virtue, Progress of the Species, Black Emancipation, New Tarif, Eclecticism, Locofocoism, ghost of Improved-Socinianism: these with many other ghosts and substances are squeaking, jabbering, according to their capabilities, round this man; to one man among the sixteen millions their jabber is all unmusical. The silent voices of the Stars above, and of the green Earth beneath, are profitabler to him,—tell him gradually that these others are but ghosts, which will shortly have to vanish; that the Life-Fountain these proceeded out of does not vanish! The words of such a man, what words he finds good to speak, are worth attending to. By degrees a small circle of living souls eager to hear is gathered. The silence of this man has to become speech: may this too, in its due season, prosper for him!—Emerson has gone to lecture, various times, to special audiences, in Boston, and occasionally elsewhere. Three of those Lectures, already printed, are known to some here; as is the little Pamphlet called *Nature*, of somewhat earlier date. It may be said, a great meaning lies in these pieces, which as yet finds no adequate expression for itself. A noteworthy though very unattractive work, moreover, is that new Periodical they call *The Dial*, in which he occasionally writes; which appears indeed generally to be imbued with his way of thinking, and to proceed from the circle that learns of him. This present little Volume of *Essays*, printed in Boston a few months ago, is Emerson's first Book. An unpretending little Book, composed probably, in good part, from mere Lectures which already lay written. It affords us, on several sides, in such manner as it can, a direct glimpse into the man and that spiritual world of his.

Emerson, I understand, was bred to Theology; of which primary bent his latest way of thought still bears traces. In a very enigmatic way, we hear much of the 'universal soul,' of the &c. &c.: flickering like bright bodiless Northern Streamers, notions and half-notions of a metaphysic, theosophic, theologic kind are seldom long wanting in these *Essays*. I do not advise the British Public to trouble itself much with all that; still less, to take offence at it. Whether this Emerson be 'a Pantheist,' or what kind of Theist or *Ist* he may be, can perhaps as well remain undecided. If he prove a devout-minded, veritable, original man, this for the present will suffice. *Ists* and *Isms* are rather growing a weariness. Such a man does not readily range himself under *Isms*. A man to whom the 'open secret of the universe' is no longer a closed one, what can his *speech* of it be in these days? All human speech, in the best days, all human thought that can or could articulate itself in reference to such things, what is it but the eager stammering and struggling as of a wondering infant,—in view of the Unnameable! That this little Book has no 'system,' and points or stretches far beyond all systems, is one of its merits. We will call it the soliloquy of a true soul, alone under the stars, in this day. In England as elsewhere the voice of a true soul, *any* voice of such, may be welcome to some. For in England as elsewhere old dialects and formulas are mostly lying dead: some dim suspicion, or clear knowledge, indicates on all hands that they are as good as dead;—and how can the skilfullest *galvanizing* make them any more live? For they are dead: and their galvanic motions, O Heavens, are not of a pleasant sort!—That one man more, in the most modern dialect of this year 1841, recognises the oldest everlasting truths: here is a thing worth seeing, among the others. One man more who knows, and believes of very certainty, that Man's Soul is still alive, that God's Universe is still godlike, that of all Ages of Miracles ever seen, or dreamt of, by far the most miraculous is this age in this hour; and who with all these devout beliefs has dared, like a valiant man, to bid chimeras, "*Be* chimerical; disappear, and let us have an end of you!"—is not this worth something? In a word, while so many Benthamisms, Socialisms, Fourrierisms, *professing* to have no soul, go staggering and lowing like monstrous mooncalves, the product of a heavy-laden moonstruck age; and, in this same baleful 'twelfth hour of the night,' even galvanic Puseyisms, as we say, are visible, and dancings of the sheeted dead,—shall not any voice of a living man be welcome to us, even because it is alive?

For the rest, what degree of mere literary talent lies in these utterances, is but a secondary question; which every reader may gradually answer for himself. What Emerson's talent is, we will not altogether estimate by this Book. The utterance is abrupt, fitful; the great idea not yet embodied struggles towards an embodiment. Yet everywhere there is the true heart of a man; which is the parent of all talent; which without much talent cannot exist. A breath as of the green country,—all the welcomer that it is *New*-England country, not second-hand but first-hand country,—meets us wholesomely everywhere in these *Essays*: the authentic green Earth is there, with her mountains, rivers, with her mills and farms. Sharp gleams of insight arrest us by their pure intellectuality; here and there, in heroic rusticism, a tone of modest manfulness, of mild invincibility, low-voiced but lion-strong, makes us too thrill with a noble pride. Talent? Such ideas as dwell in this man, how can they ever speak themselves with *enough* of talent? The talent is not the chief question here. The idea, that is the chief question. Of the living acorn you do not ask first, How *large* an acorn art thou? The smallest living acorn is fit to be the parent of oaktrees without end,—could clothe all New England with oaktrees by and by. You ask it, first of all: Art thou a living acorn? Certain, now, that thou art not a dead mushroom, as the most are?—

But, on the whole, our Book is short; the Preface should not grow too long. Closing these questionable parables and intimations, let me in plain English recommend this little Book as the Book of an original veridical man, worthy the acquaintance of those who delight in such; and so: Welcome to it whom it may concern!

[*Essays*]

Anonymous*

This volume contains twelve essays, which are severally entitled History; Self-reliance; Compensation; Spiritual Laws; Love; Friendship; Prudence; Heroism; The Over-Soul; Circles; Intellect; Art. The substance of some, if not of all, of them has been given to select audiences in the form of lectures in Boston and its neighborhood, and it may, we think without injustice, be considered as a cause, or certainly as the type of a somewhat novel and singular species of fanaticism now prevailing more or less in that region, under the name of transcendentalism. We call it fanaticism, as being a semi-philosophical theory strangely blended with certain elementary notions of religion, making as large demands on the conduct as on the faith of those who receive it, and leading to principles and forms of social organization which have no basis in the nature of man, and which experience has already condemned as impracticable. By what right this medley of opinion and fancies has received the *sobriquet* of transcendentalism, we are at a loss to understand. Kant, and Cousin, and Coleridge, would be puzzled to recognize in it any features of the

*Reprinted from *New York Review*, 8 (April 1841), 509–12.

system they have taught, and which has passed under that name, or if it be in any way a product of their system, it is by some equivocal generation, a *lusus naturæ*, feeble, and we trust short-lived. Once the attainment of the theory of man and of the universe, that was properly styled transcendental, was the result of patient meditation for many months, and years were not thought too long to prepare the mind for a competent judgment of it. Now, it seems to be a work of moments, and for youth. Now, we judge by illapses and revelations. Now, we have but to *"live,"* and we become the arbiters of all truth, masters of all science; nay, we "judge the angels."

There are certain views, more or less fully developed in these essays, on which we think it proper briefly to remark. We do not question the purity of the author's life, the sincerity of his conviction, or the honesty of the purpose or of the means which have led him to the position which he seems to occupy in them. But we think they are essentially false, and certainly mischievous; half-truths, which will distort the character that is formed on them, and excluding negations which shut out the true life of man.

We ought to say, at the outset, that the volume contains no system, nor any attempt at one. This, in a volume of essays, we could hardly claim. But we may fairly claim that all the author's thoughts shall be parts of a system, and at least intimations of what it is. We doubt, however, whether Mr. Emerson has carefully compared his views with each other; and indeed he himself expresses the hope that he has seen "the end of consistency and conformity." We doubt, moreover, whether his thoughts and sentiments are referable to any single principle, or are properly parts of any system, so various and incongruous often are they. They are rather fragments, and glimpses, often indeed of a bright and pure meaning, than a logical or even continuous discussion.

We are disposed to censure the book, both for its theology and its philosophy. In the former respect, it is a godless book. There is evidently no recognition of the God of the Bible, a moral governor and righteous judge. The highest approach that is made to it is the doctrine, everywhere through the volume insisted on or implied, of a universal soul; which means, in our best comprehension of it, only a pervading intellect out of which, by natural genesis, all particular souls are produced and grow, and of which they are merely the organs and the manifestation, sustaining to it the same relation, and no other, that the tree does to the earth which bears it. This universal man—for such is sometimes the conception—is but the expansion and impersonality of the individual; is mere unconscious intellect, yet to man the supreme beauty, to be admired perhaps, hardly to be feared or loved. There is nowhere a recognition of sin, as actual, or even possible. In this particular, the author is rigidly systematic; for where there is no moral law but the instincts of our own being, there can be no sin. What vulgarly goes under that name, is here only infirmity and cowardice, and a fall that may hinder our progress, or may help us by a new experience. On these, and kindred topics, is shown a sturdy indifference to all established opinions, and disregard of all time-honored institutions. His spirit finds in the Bible no response to its questionings. An implicit faith is a dead faith, summarily. The Church is but a gathering of those who dare not think, to keep each other in countenance, by the bald show of knowing and seeing. Man must receive that only which his present experience affirms to him, and his own consciousness is of higher value and surer evidence than that of any and all other men.

In a work purely literary, we would not find fault with the absence of theological discussion; but in a didactic treatise, which professes to discuss problems of the highest interest to humanity, and the highest forms of human duty and attainment, we may well pause before we commend, when we find the saddest and deepest wants of our nature untouched, and the living God at once circumscribed into an universal man, and etherealised into an idea.

The philosophical aspects of the work, or the views which it presents of human life, are in like manner open to censure. It would render that life eminently unsocial. It represents every man as superior to all other men: every man as entitled to the deference of all other men; every man as utterly independent of all other men. It places each individual in a proud and selfish solitariness; ever on his guard, lest the entireness of his own being shall be in some way influenced by his fellow man; and checks kind sympathies and tender affections. But the true state of man in society is one of mutual trust, helpfulness, forbearance, patience. Isolation is not the condition of growth, whether it be a wilful separateness, or a perpetual seclusion in cell or desert; sympathy, fellowship, mutual reliance and counsel, are among the natural and appointed means of human culture. As well might an oak take root and grow in mid air, as a man attain anything truly noble by the pure doctrine of "self-reliance."

Follow nature—*naturam sequere*—as taught by Cicero, and explained by Butler, was a valuable rule in determining human duties and their proper limits. But here, this wise precept has degenerated into a vague direction—"follow your instincts,"—and what, with many cautions and much discernment, might be useful as a guide, has become the supreme law, and solves the whole problem. The revealed law has no place here. A mere conscience is quite out of date, and useless. The common sentiments of men touching right and wrong are of no authority. We may not modestly apprehend that Socrates or Paul knew more of such matters than we do. "No law can be sacred to me but that of my own nature." To a friend who suggested that his impulses might "come from below," our author records his answer—the only one, indeed, which can be made with his premises—"They do not seem to me to be such; but if I am the devil's child, I will live then from the devil;" (pp. 41, 42.) and the answer is proof enough that the rule, alone, cannot be a safe one. It makes, too, what was but one among the grounds of our moral judgments and preferences, the only one. Doubtless, we admire in a child what we might condemn in a man, and this too because the action is natural in the one and not in the other; but the beauty of right is far different from the grace of appropriateness.

Throughout the volume are scattered numberless instances of this substitution of a partial truth for the whole, and a bold statement of it as the whole; and we regret that a work, in some respects so captivating, should be so calculated to mislead the unwary. The author writes with the earnestness of a genuine enthusiasm, and fearlessly speaks out his thought. There are everywhere tokens of a clear perception, and an ardent admiration of what is noble and beautiful in man, in nature, and in art. He deals in subtle analogies, which are often of great beauty, and pictures with rare skill. In a style, which on every page delights us by its simplicity and grace, and offends us by an affected quaintness, showing brilliant fancy and curious scholarship, he has uttered many brave truths, many gross and perilous errors, hints in which the meditative and wise man may find ambrosial food, but which will prove poison to the simple and undiscerning.

"Emerson's *Essays*"

[Orestes Augustus Brownson]*

In this Journal for April last, we called attention to these Essays, and promised that we would take an early opportunity to speak of them more at large. The promise we then made, we proceed now to redeem. And yet we hardly know how to do it. The Essays are good and significant, but exceedingly troublesome to reviewers, for whose especial ease and convenience they seem by no means to have been written. They contain no doctrine or system of doctrines, logically drawn out, and presented to the understanding of the reader. They consist of detached observations, independent propositions, distinct, enigmatical, oracular sayings, each of which is to be taken by itself, and judged of by its own merits. Consequently, it is impossible to reduce their teachings to a few general propositions, and to sum up their worth in a single sentence.

To most persons, who read these Essays, they will seem to be wanting in unity and coherence. They will always strike as beautiful, often as just, and sometimes as profound; but the reader will be puzzled to round their teachings into a whole, or to discover their practical bearing on life or thought. Yet they have unity and coherence, but of the transcendental sort. The author seems to us to have taken, as far as possible, his stand in the Eternal, above time and space, and tried to present things as they appear from that point of vision,—not in their relation to each other as seen

*Reprinted from *Boston Quarterly Review*, 4 (July 1841), 291–308.

in the world of the senses, but in their relation to the spectator, who views them from above the world of the senses.

This fact should be borne in mind. Mr. Emerson, to speak scientifically, is no philosopher. He is a philosopher neither in the order of his mind, nor in his method of investigation. He explains nothing, accounts for nothing, solves no intellectual problem, and affords no practical instruction. He proposes nothing of all this, and, therefore, is not to be censured for not doing it. He is to be regarded as a Seer, who rises into the regions of the Transcendental, and reports what he sees, and in the order in which he sees it. His worth can be determined, that is, the accuracy of his reports can be properly judged of, by none except those who rise to the same regions, and behold the universe from the same point of view.

Writers like Mr. Emerson are seldom to be consulted for clear, logical, systematic expositions of any subject or doctrine, never for the purpose of taking them as teachers or guides in the formation of opinions; but for the suggestions, the incentives to thought they furnish, and the life they kindle up within us. They are thought by some to be writers without any practical value for mankind; but they have, in fact, a very high practical value; only not of the every day sort, only not that of dogmatic teachers or scientific expositors. They present new aspects of things, or at least old familiar objects in new dresses, the various subjects of thought and inquiry in new relations, break up old associations, and excite to greater and fresher mental activity. After having read them, we cannot say that we are wiser or more learned than we were before; we cannot say that we have become acquainted with any new facts in the history of man or of the universe, or that we have any new ideas in regard to the human soul or its Creator; but we feel, that somehow or other new virtue has been imparted to us, that a change has come over us, and that we are no longer what we were, but greater and better.

These are not the only writers we need; but they have their place, and one of high trust, and of no slight influence. Their influence is not sudden, noisy, obvious to all senses, but slow, silent, subtle, permanent, entering into and becoming an integrant part of the life of the age, sometimes of the ages. They live and exert a power over the souls of men, long after their names are forgotten, and their works have ceased to be read. They are never in vogue with the multitude, but they are admired in select circles, who inhale their spirit, and breathe it into other and larger circles, who in their turn breathe it into the souls of all men. Though they may seem to have no practical aim, and no reference to every-day life, they have in the end a most important practical bearing, and exert a controlling influence over even the business concerns of the world. Let no one, then, regard them as mere idle dreamers, as mere literary toys, with whose glitter we may amuse ourselves, but without significance for the world of reality. They appear always for good or evil, and their appearance usually marks an epoch.

Mr. Emerson's book is a sincere production. It could have been produced only in this community at the present moment, and only by a man who had been placed in the relations he has to society and the Church. Such a book could never have emanated from a man, who had not been bred a clergyman, nor from one, who, having been bred a clergyman, had not ceased to be one. We may also say, that it could have been produced by no man, who had not been bred in a creed, which he had found insufficient to meet the wants of his intellect and heart, and who had not, in some measure, deserted it, without having found another in all respects satisfactory. We may say again, he must have been bred a unitarian, and having found unitarianism defective in consequence of its materialism, have felt and yielded to the reaction of spiritualism, and yet not sufficiently to return to any of the standard forms of orthodoxy.

We would speak respectfully of unitarianism, as we would always of the dead. It had its mission, and it has, in the providence of God, done great good in our community. But unitarianism was not, strictly speaking, a religion, could not become a religion; and it is well known, that almost always persons brought up under its influence, desert it as soon as they become seriously impressed, and desirous of leading religious lives. Men never embraced unitarianism because they were pious, but because they would dispense with being pious. Unitarianism never spoke to the heart, to the soul; never waked any real enthusiasm, or called forth any religious energy of character. It is in its nature *un*spiritual, merely intellectual and material, a sort of baptized atheism. The same causes, at bottom, which produced deism and atheism in France, produced unitarianism in New England. If the American mind had been as consequent as the French, as bold to push a doctrine to its last results, and had the Church here been organized as it was in France, and been as oppressive, our unitarians would have been avowed deists or atheists. We can find no more to feed our piety in the *"Statement of Reasons,"* than in the *Système de la Nature."* Indeed, the author of the latter seems the more pious worshipper of the two, and betrays altogether more of peculiar religious emotion; and reverence is more readily yielded to d'Holbach's Nature than to Norton's Divinity. The one is living, plastic, active; the other is a stern, old mechanic, placed on the outside of nature, and troubling himself rarely with its operations; wrapping himself in night and silence, neither seen nor needed by men, and would be unconceived of, did he not charitably send us now and then a messenger to inform us that he really is, and no fiction,—a piece of information altogether gratuitous, as it serves no useful purpose in either the economy of nature or of salvation. With this "Statement of Reasons," unitarianism died, and there are few mourners to go about the streets, albeit there is for it no resurrection.

The old forms of faith had ceased to satisfy the minds of the generation preceding us. Calvinism could not be explained on the principles of Locke's philosophy, and the asceticism which puritanism had enjoined could not but be distasteful and offensive to the growing aristocracy of a prosperous country. Men politely educated, sumptuously clad, fond of good eating and drinking, full of hilarity and mirth, feeling in themselves an exuberance of life, and finding the world very well adapted to their tastes, and being, therefore, in no hurry to exchange it for another, were ill prepared to embrace the ascetic doctrines and practices of their stern old fathers, who never suffered their rigid features to relax with a smile, who thought to please God only by marring the beauty of his works, and by trampling under foot the choicest of his blessings. We do not blame them much. These old puritans are a very unpoetic race of beings, and neither so pious nor so ascetic, so ungiven to the flesh withal, as their admirers would fain have us believe, as may be learned by whomsoever will take the trouble to consult our old church records. They were a strong race, and able to do much; but they attempted altogether more than they could do. They undertook to demolish both the flesh and the devil, and to live on earth as they expected to live in heaven; that is, in surly communion with their own thoughts, and in singing psalms, with no better accompaniment than a jews-harp. Peace to their ashes. They were not without their mission, and have left their track on the ages. Perhaps, with less sourness, surliness, less rigidity, and with more of the amiable, the gentle, the attractive, they could not have done their work.

But the asceticism, which our puritan fathers insisted on, can be really practised by a people only while in the wilderness; while poor, exposed to a thousand hardships, and finding earth no resting place, but a weary land, from which any deliverance may be accounted a blessing. In proportion as the wilderness is peopled, the barren waste converted into the fruitful garden, as grow the ornamental shrubs, and blossoms the rose, and delights are multiplied around us, we take more cheerful views of the world, and of life, and seek not to mortify ourselves, but to enjoy. Asceticism must, then, give way in practice, if not in theory. It did give way in practice, and for years all New England presented the spectacle of a people professing one faith, and living according to another. Some saw this, and being honest, were shocked at it. These became unitarians. Unitarianism was with us a protest against asceticism, even more than against the absurdity of Calvinism, as contemplated from the point of view of the Lockian philosophy. It was an effort of those who could not live in a perpetual lie, to reconcile their theology and their religion to their philosophy and their mode of living.

For a time it could do very well; and as long as controversy could be maintained with opposing sects, it could apparently sustain some degree of intellectual life; but no longer. As soon as the orthodox ceased to controvert, threw it back on itself, left it to its own resources, it ceased to live.

Inasmuch as it was a dissent from the popular faith, unitarianism appealed to freedom of thought and inquiry. It asserted the rights of the individual reason. They who became unitarians, then, were not bound to continue such. They had a right to examine unitarianism, as well as the doctrines opposed to it. Such, again, was its own intrinsic deficiency, its utter inadequacy, as a religion, that the moment its own friends began to investigate it, they found they had outgrown it. They found elements in their nature it did not and could not accept, wants it did not and could not meet. They revolted against its materialism, its dryness, coldness, deadness. They fell back on the religious element of their natures, and sought refuge in a more spiritual philosophy. In this state of transition from materialism to spiritualism, from unitarianism to a modified orthodoxy, if we may be allowed the expression, our unitarian community now is. This transition is represented, in certain of its phases, in the book before us. It marks a movement of the unitarian mind towards a higher, a broader, a more truly religious faith and life. In this consists its significance, and if our orthodox friends were aware of this, they would read it with avidity and profit by it.

This revolt against materialism, and this return towards spiritualism, we regard as among the chief glories of our epoch, as a proof that the reign of infidelity is well nigh over, and that we are preparing a religious future. In this point of view, the men among us who represent this movement, and are for the present condemned, in no measured terms, as was to be expected, by both unitarians and the representatives of the old trinitarian asceticism, the old Calvinistic spiritualism, are the real benefactors of their age and country; the men, who, instead of abuse and discouragement, deserve honor and coöperation. But we never recognise our redeemers till we have crucified them. We cannot say of a truth, that they are sons of God, till we perceive the darkness which comes over the earth as they leave it.

These Essays mark among us the reaction of spiritualism. This constitutes their historical value. How far they represent truly the spiritualism that should become dominant, is another question, and one which can be answered only by determining their positive value. This last can be done only by entering into a critical examination of their merits, a thing which it seems to us almost sacrilegious to attempt. They do not seem to us legitimate subjects of criticism. There is a sacredness about them, a mystic divinity, a voice issuing from them, saying to critics, "Procul, O procul, este, profani." To do them justice, they should be read with reverence, with a yielding spirit, an open heart, ready to receive with thankfulness whatever meets its wants or can be appropriated to its use. The rest, what is not congenial, should be left with pious respect; perhaps there are souls which will find it wholesome food. Why should we deprive others of appropriate nutriment, because it is no nutriment to us?

But Mr. Emerson sometimes descends from the Seer, and assumes the Reasoner. He sometimes touches on dogmas and systems, and if he adopts rarely a philosophical form, a system of philosophy lies back of his poetic utterances, and constitutes even for him the ground on which they are to be legitimated. This system we may examine without profanity. It will, moreover, be ultimately drawn out and formally taught by his disciples. His book will give it currency, and be appealed to as its authority. There can, then, be no impropriety in asking if it be true or false, complete or incomplete.

This system, we say distinctly, is not scientifically taught in the book before us. We are not sure that Mr. Emerson himself is always conscious of it. We are inclined to believe, that he thinks that he eschews all systems, and entangles himself in the meshes of no theory. But every man who speaks at all implies a theory, and in general the greatest theorizers are those who profess to abjure all theory. Every man has his own point of view, from which he contemplates the universe, and whence all his reports are drawn. The question may, then, always come up, is this the true point of view, the point from which the universe may be seen as it really is, and represented in all its unity and diversity? The moment this question is asked, and we undertake to answer it, we plunge into metaphysics, and avail ourselves of system, of theory.

Mr. Emerson's point of view is, we have said, the transcendental. Can the universe, seen from this point of view alone, by truly represented? The answer to this question will enable us to determine the philosophic value of his Essays.

In the philosophy against which there is, in our times, a decided movement, there is no recognition of a transcendental world, of aught that transcends time and space. Immensity is merely space that cannot be measured; eternity is merely time without end. God, as well as man, exists in time and space, and differs from man only in the fact that he fills all space, and continues through all time. Eternal life is a life in time, but merely time endlessly continued. This philosophy never, therefore, carries us out of time and space. To all persons embracing this philosophy, transcendentalists must appear mere dreamers, endeavoring to give to airy nothing, a local habitation and a name.

Now, transcendentalism recognises a world lying back of and above the world of time and space. Time and space belong merely to the world of the senses; but the reason,—not as the principle of logic, but as the principle of intelligence,—rises immediately into a region where there is no time, no space. Immensity is not space infinitely extended, but the negation of all space; eternity is not time endlessly continued, but the negation of all time. God does not exist in space. We cannot say that he is here, there, somewhere, but that he is everywhere, which is only saying again, in other words, that he is NOWHERE. He exists not in, but out of time. We cannot say God was, God will be, but simply that he *is*, as the Hebrew name of God, I AM, plainly implies. To him there is no time. He has no past, no future. He inhabiteth eternity, dwells not in time, but in NO-time, as Watts implies, when he says, with God "all is one eternal NOW."

All our ideas of truth, justice, love, beauty, goodness, are transcendental. Truth is truth, independent of time and place. The just is the just at one epoch, in one country, as much as in another. The beautiful never varies; its laws, we all say, are eternal. Goodness is ever the same. The great principles of the Christian religion inhabit eternity. Hence Jesus says, "before Abraham was I am," and hence he is called "the Lamb slain from the foundations of the world," meaning thereby, that the principles of truth and duty he represented, and by which alone man can come into harmony with his Maker, were no principles of modern creation, but principles existing in the very Principle of things,—principles that have no dependence on time and space, but were in the beginning with God, and were God.

These remarks will help us to understand what is meant by transcendentalism. Transcendentalism, in its good sense, as used in our community, means the recognition of an order of existences, which transcend time and space, and are in no sense dependent on them, or affected by them. Transcendental means very nearly what our old writers, in Shakespeare's time, meant by the word *metaphysical*, from μετα, *beyond*, and φῦσιχος, *physical*, natural, belonging to the outward, visible, material world. Transcendentalists recognise a world lying beyond or above the world of the senses, and in man the power of seeing or knowing this transcendental world immediately, by direct cognition, or intuition.

All persons, who believe in God, in the reality of a spiritual world, and contend that their belief has any legitimate basis, are transcendentalists. Whoever is not a transcendentalist, must, if consequent, needs be a skeptic, or a materialist and an atheist. The early Christian fathers were transcendentalists, so were the distinguished English writers of the seventeenth century; so were Descartes, Malebranche, George Fox, William Penn, and our own Edwards; so were Price, and to a feeble extent, the Scottish School; so are nearly all the Germans, and the French Eclectics. Locke and his followers were not, nor were Condillac and the old French school. In fact, all real faith implies the Transcendental, and religion is an idle dream unless we admit the reality of an order of existences, a spiritual world transcending this outward, material, sensible world; and also unless we admit in man the means of attaining legitimately to faith in that reality.

Mr. Emerson, by taking his stand in this transcendental region, evidently asserts its existence, and our power to take cognizance of it. So far his philosophy is eminently religious, and as we have demonstrated over and over again in the pages of this Journal, as well as elsewhere, is sound, and worthy of all acceptation. In this consists his chief philosophical merit. In this too consists his departure from Locke and the unitarian school proper, and his approach to orthodoxy. Thus far we go with him heart and hand, and recognise him as a fellow-laborer in that school of which we profess to be a disciple, though it may be an unworthy one.

But the transcendental, or, if you please, metaphysical, or spiritual world, exists not for the senses, nor can it be inferred from data furnished by the senses. It exists only for the reason. It is ideal, as opposed to sensible, spiritual as opposed to material, but real and substantial. Its existence is indeed involved in all the perceptions of the senses, and asserted in every thought and affirmation; but we rise to the cognition of it only by means of reason, taken, as we have said, not as the principle of logic, but as the principle of intelligence.

Now, by taking our stand on the reason as the principle of intelligence, which is partly analogous to what Mr. Emerson calls the "Over-Soul," and attending exclusively to what it reveals, we are in danger of losing sight of the world of the senses, and therefore of suffering one aspect of the universe to escape us. The moment we rise into the world of reason, we find it altogether richer, sublimer, more beautiful, than this outward visible world. This outward visible world gradually loses its charms for us, disappears from the horizon of our vision, and is therefore very naturally denied to have any existence. We thus fall into Idealism.

Again; the world of the senses is manifold and diverse, while the world of the reason is one and identical. In the transcendental world we rise to the principles of things. The principle of a thing is after all, in a certain sense, the thing itself. All principles proceed from and centre in one common principle, the principle of all things,—God. The diversity noted by the senses is then no real diversity, but merely phenominal and illusory, and deserving no account from him who has risen to the perception of absolute unity, into which all is resolved at last. Diversity is therefore rejected, denied. The distinction between cause and effect ceases then to be intelligible; all difference between God and the universe to be perceptible. The universe is identical with God. God and the universe are one and the same; this is Pantheism.

Whoever then takes his stand exclusively in the Transcendental must fall into ideal Pantheism. From the transcendental point of view alone, a correct report of the universe cannot be made out, any more than from the point of view of the senses alone.

Now Mr. Emerson seems to us to verify in his own case the truth of this deduction. He falls in his philosophy, so far as philosophy he has, into ideal Pantheism. He is so charmed with the world of ideas, that he contemns the sensible, so struck with the unity and identity revealed by the reason, that he is led to overlook and occasionally to deny the manifold and the diverse, revealed by the senses. We cannot read a page of these Essays without perceiving that the tendency of his mind is to seek unity and identity. He brings together in the same sentence perpetually persons and things, events and transactions, apparently the most diverse, by a law of association which most readers are unable to discover, and the point of resemblance between which very few are able to perceive. Yet is he in general just. The resemblance, the identity he asserts is there. His power of detecting the identical in the diverse, the analogous in the dissimilar, the uniform in the manifold, the permanent in the transitory, is remarkable, and unsurpassed in any writer of our acquaintance. He is ever surprising us by unexpected resemblances. To him all things are the same. In all this he is right. He uttered a great truth when he declared the identity of the power by which Lazarus was raised from the dead, and that by which falls the rain or blows the clover; also when he so shocked some of our pious people by declaring the identity of gravitation and purity of heart. This identity does run through all nature, and he has not true insight into the universe who cannot detect it.

But diversity, dissimilarity, multiplicity, are no less obvious and real in the universe than unity and identity. They have their origin too in the same source. God, the cause and principle of the universe, is not a mere unity, but a unity that has in itself the principle of multiplicity,—not pure identity, but at once identity and diversity,—a fact shadowed forth in the doctrine of a Triune God, which runs through all religious philosophies ever promulgated. Whoever overlooks this fact must fall into Pantheism. Mr. Emerson has a tendency to overlook it; and his disciples, for disciples always exaggerate the tendencies of their masters, will most assuredly overlook it. Some of them even now avow themselves Pantheists, and most of the young men and maidens who listened with so much delight to these Essays when they were delivered as lectures, virtually run into Pantheism, whether they know it or not.

The outward visible world is not the only world into which we are admitted, but it is a real world; that is, it really exists, and is no more an illusion than the world of reason; and the idealist is as exclusive and as erroneous as the materialist. The one denies the Transcendental, the other the Sensible. Both are wrong in what they deny, both are right in what they assert; and this fact, it strikes us, does not lie at the basis of Mr. Emerson's philosophy. Hence the wrong tendency of his speculations.

We are not prone to be frightened or shocked at mere words. Thank Heaven, we have strong nerves, and can bear much; but we regard Pantheism as an error of no less magnitude than Atheism itself, and consequently must earnestly protest against every tendency to it. God and the universe are in the most intimate relation, but that relation is one of cause and effect, not of identity; and while we admit that there is this identity running through all nature, to which Mr. Emerson points us, we also contend that there is a corresponding diversity to which he does not point us. We complain not of him for not doing this, but we note the fact in order to warn our readers against taking his utterances as complete expositions of the universe. He brings up one pole of truth, the one which has been too much depressed; but in bringing up that he is not sufficiently heedful not to depress equally the other. We have revolted against exclusive materialism; let us be careful not to fall now into exclusive spiritualism; we have protested against Atheism and irreligion, or the forms of religion which were in fact no religion, and we should look to it that we do not now swallow up all diversity in unity, and man and the universe in God. The latter error would turn out to be as fatal to piety and morals as the former.

But after all, we have no serious apprehensions on this score. Ideal Pantheism, though a fatal error, is not one into which our countrymen are likely to fall, at least to any great extent. Only a few of the cultivated, the refined, the speculative, the idle, and contemplative, are exposed to it. Men in active business, taking their part in the rough and tumble of life, coming in daily contact with one another in the market, the husting, the legislative halls, scrambling for power or place, wealth or distinction, have little leisure, less inclination, and still less aptitude for that order of thought which ends in the denial of matter, and of the universe as distinguished from its Creator. The cast of their minds is too practical, and they are of too sturdy, too robust a make to find anything satisfactory in so refined a spiritualism. Their daily habits and pursuits demand a solid earth on which to work, a providence to protect them, a sovereign to rule over them, a real God to curb their headstrong violence, and to reduce them to order and peace, to chastise them for their errors, and to solace them in their afflictions. The practical tendencies of our countrymen will save them from all danger they would be likely to incur from speculative refinements like those we have pointed out; and we are not sure but Mr. Emerson's strong statements are needed to rectify their over-attachment to the material order.

As it concerns the ethical doctrines implied rather than set forth in these Essays, we have nothing to add to the remarks we have heretofore made on the same subject.[1] Mr. Emerson's moral philosophy, reduced to its systematic element, belongs to the egoistical school; but we presume, after all, that he means little more by those expressions which imply it, and which have given so much offence, than that just self-reliance, that fidelity to one's own nature and conscience, without which it is impossible to reach or maintain a true manly worth. In this view of the case, his Essay on Self-Reliance is a noble and unexceptionable performance, and inculcates a lesson, which it were well for us all to learn and practise,—a lesson which is perhaps more appropriate to the American people than to any other Christian nation, for no other Christian nation is so timid in its speculations, so afraid of solving for itself, independently, the problem of the destiny of man and society. We regard it as decidedly one of the best Essays in the collection.

We did intend to quote from the book itself, in order to justify our criticisms, but it is not a book from which quotations can be made with much satisfaction. We could not select a paragraph that would not at once confirm and refute our general criticisms. We content ourselves, therefore, with speaking merely of its dominant tendency, as it appears to us. The book cannot be judged of without being read, and the best way to read it, will be to forget its metaphysics, and to take it up as we would a collection of poems, or of proverbs.

Of the Essays we cannot speak particularly. The one on Heroism is inferior to what we expected from its author, and falls far below the general average of the book. Those on Love and Friendship are beautiful and often true, but their truth and beauty proceed from the intellect and imagination rather than the heart and soul. They read not like the confessions of a lover or a friend. There are depths in the affections, into which the author does not descend, deeper experiences than any he discloses. The Essays we have liked the best are those on the Over-Soul, Self-Reliance, and History.

These Essays are, to a certain extent, democratic; they condemn all ordinary aristocracies, and breathe much respect for labor and the laborer; but it is evident, at a single glance, that the author is at best only an amateur workingman, one who has never himself wielded spade or mattock to any great extent, and who has viewed labor with the eye of a poet, rather than with the feelings of an actual laborer. His book, though apparently radical, contains nothing more likely to give offence to the capitalist than to the proletary.

One of the most serious objections, we have to urge against these Essays, is the little importance they assign to the state, and the low rank they allow to patriotism as a virtue. This is an error of our transcendental school generally, and results, we suppose, chiefly from the fact, that its principal masters are or have been churchmen, and, therefore, not over and above acquainted with practical life. Their studies lead them to rely on preaching, persuasion, advice, appeals to the reason and conscience. Their habits and position remove them from the actual world, and its necessities, and keep them ignorant of no small part of the actual developments of human nature. Clergymen are usually able to give wholesome advice, at least, advice which will generally be regarded as canonical; but they are rarely gifted with much practical skill or sagacity. A deliberative assembly, composed entirely of clergymen, is usually a very disorderly body, and ill adapted to the speedy despatch of business. The members are all so enlightened, so wise, so good, so meek, and so conscientious, that ordinary parliamentary rules are rarely thought to be necessary; and the result is not seldom confusion, angry, disorderly debate, and no little ill feeling and ill speaking. This anti-political tendency of our transcendentalists is, therefore, easily accounted for. Nevertheless, it is a false tendency. Man, as we have endeavored to prove in a foregoing article, is to be perfected in society, and society is to be perfected by government. More, than even politicians themselves usually imagine, depends on the right organization of the commonwealth. The science of politics, when rightly viewed, is a grand and an essential science, and needs always to be held in honor. Much is lost by not making it a subject of more serious study. Everybody talks about politics, and yet there is scarcely a man among us acquainted with the simplest principles of politics, regarded as a science. The proper organization of the state, the true exposition of the constitution, and the proper administration, so as to secure the true end of government, are matters with which we, as a people, rarely trouble ourselves; and scarcely a man can be found, who can speak on them five minutes in succession, without betraying gross ignorance, both theoretical and practical. In this state of political science, our scholars are doing us great disservice by sneering at politics and the state.

As mere literary productions, these Essays must take rank with the best in the language. There is now and then an affectation of quaintness, a puerile conceit, not precisely to our taste, but it detracts not much from their general beauty. In compactness of style, in the felicitous choice of words, in variety, aptness, and wealth of illustration, they are unrivalled. They have a freshness, a vigor, a freedom from old hacknied forms of speech, and from the conventionalisms of the schools, worthy of the highest praise, and which cannot fail to exert a salutary influence on our growing literature. They often remind us of Montaigne, especially in the little personal allusions, which the author introduces with inimitable grace, delicacy, and effect.

In conclusion, we will simply add, that not withstanding the metaphysical errors to which we have referred, the Essays make up a volume unique in its character, and which all competent judges will agree in regarding as among the most creditable productions of the American press. It must secure to the author a distinguished rank among the more distinguished writers of the age. We feel ourselves deeply indebted for his present. We receive his utterances with thankfulness and reverence, and shall wait impatiently till he permits us to hear from him again. It is not often, that in our profession as a critic, we meet with a work of fewer faults, nor one that can better bear to have its faults pointed out; for it is rare that we meet with one with its positive excellencies. It is no ephemeral production; it will survive the day; for it is full of sincerity, truth, beauty. Whoso pores over its pages will find his soul quickened, his vision enlarged, his heart warmed, and his life made better.

Note

1. [Orestes Augustus Brownson], "Mr. Emerson's Address," *Boston Quarterly Review*, 1 (October 1838), 500–514.

"Ralph Waldo Emerson"

[William Alfred] J[ones]*

If the value of a writer is to be estimated not only by the number of his judicious admirers, but also, by the reputation and ability of his pupils and followers, great should be thy fame, as nobly won, O Goethe! The English Critic and expositor of the great German is Carlyle, whom Goethe speaks of in Eckermann's Conversations, as having a finer insight into German authors and as possessing higher æsthetic culture than any man in Germany—questionless, a compliment to the admiring critic of Faust and Wilhelm Meister.[1] Still, with all his crudity, his quaintness and affectation, Carlyle is a powerful thinker, and a bold writer. Often absurd, as often picturesque: frequently fantastic, and yet sometimes, really profound.

The American commentator on Goethe is R. W. Emerson, also the disciple of Carlyle, or rather, perhaps, the disciple of Goethe through Carlyle—a sort of admirer and critic, at second-hand. Mr. Emerson, we are told, travelled with Carlyle on the continent, where he studied German Literature exactly, and scanned the face of human, as well as of external nature. Some years after his return home, (meanwhile, a correspondent of his gifted fellow-traveller,) he collects his miscellaneous papers, reviews, and essays, and becomes the editor of his friend's writings.

We have thus traced the connection of Mr. Emerson with Carlyle and Goethe, to mark the resemblance between the mind of our American Mystic and the Living Lights of the old world—to show the sources of his inspiration and the origin of his doctrines. The mind of Emerson may have been naturally of a speculative cast, colored with 'figures and fantasies.' And, yet, there can be no doubt, he has derived much from the greater intellects with whom he has become familiar, both by study and personal intercourse. To employ a favorite instrument of criticism, the parallel, we may call Emerson the American Carlyle. Rather, however, from some peculiarities of style and certain doctrines, than from the general cast of his mind or the spirit of his philosophy. In this, he is a mystic—Carlyle is, no one thing and of no sect. In originality of thought, Carlyle is superior: in purity of language, Emerson has the advantage. In style, he is quaint enough at times to suit Digby himself. He has less natural fancy, perhaps, than the English writer: but more of a scholastic humor. As a scholar, we suspect his studies fall pretty much within the same circle.

Mr. Emerson is the leader of the new Boston school of philosophy—the sect of wise men from the east; a school which has a certain daring, transcendental spirit of its own, but (so far as we can discover)

*Reprinted from *Arcturus*, 1 (April 1841), 278–84.

holding no very precise doctrines, and without any one bond of union. Its sub-leaders and separate teachers, each, declare a modification of the grand doctrine for themselves, each are their own instructers. They compose an independency of opinion. They unite to differ. Referring every thing to the individual soul, they must entertain, within themselves, a contrariety of belief, a mixture of systems. They are now shrewd and practical, again absurd and visionary; at last, high and spiritual.

The tone of the sect, is at once mystical, aphoristic, oracular. They are stiff dogmatists. In treating with them, you must have a large share of faith, or rather credulity. By it they seek to move mountains of metaphysical difficulty, to unriddle the darkest problems of humanity, to disclose the secrets of the universe. Vain endeavor! to do them justice, they have high aims, spiritual views, but they rush in with boldness, where—'angels fear to tread.'

They are hardly as clear and practical, as they are daring and presumptuous. Their success is doubtful; their tendency, injurious. Injurious, especially in point of religious creed. For, the certain effect, the sure end of their philosophizing, is Pantheism. This, by making every thing God, destroys the very idea of a Deity, distinct from matter and from the creatures of his plastic hand.

The sect has a narrowing influence, not only from the very fact of its being a *sect*, but also from the reiteration of its favorite topics. These are of progress, of insight, of the individual soul. Most true and weighty are they; yet, by being eternally harped on and insulated, they lose their effect; and out of their proper place, like figures transposed, their force and complexion is entirely altered. In this way the highest truths may be converted into, may be made to assume, the appearance of the rankest falsehoods.

The style of these writers deserves to be noticed. Their favorite method of composition seems to be transposition, involution, a conciseness approaching to obscurity, and sometimes actually obscuring the thought. They are writers of maxims, thinking to make old thoughts appear new, by the striking form in which they are moulded. On the tritest topics, they are on the look-out for some grand discovery. They will not believe truth *has been* and *is*; they think it is to come. They look for a revelation. They seek a sign. But their oracles are not always veracious. There are lying prophets among them. In all probability, they employ this form to hide the truth. It is easy to speak falsely in enigmas: it is almost impossible to lie in plain phrase.

Much of this censure applies to Mr. Emerson, as the exponent and grand master of the school. He has less, however, of these defects than his friends and followers, writers in the 'Dial.'

Mr. Emerson has not published much under the sanction and with the warrant of his name;—chiefly addresses and lectures (unprinted,) papers in the Dial, and a little book, generally assigned to him—'Nature.'

His is supposed to be the spirit of the Dial.—There are *three* points, le-gally speaking, we would make in this sketch—three topics; the fancy, the style, and the voice of Mr. Emerson.

Mr. Emerson's fancy is the scholar's fancy; elaborate, quaint, ar-tificial; a little exaggerated, slightly fantastical, caught, perhaps, from foreign sources; a revival, probably, of Plato, of the poetic Neo-Platonists, strangely mingled with the dreams of Swedenborg, the reveries of the Kantian philosophy, and the noble aspirations of Goethe. Emerson's fancy is generally illustrative; sometimes, richly descriptive. Take the following picture out of 'Nature.'

'But in other hours, Nature satisfies the soul purely by its loveliness, and without any mixture of corporeal benefit. I have seen the spectacle of morning from the hill-top over against my house, from day-break to sun-rise, with emotions which an angel might share. The long slender bars of cloud float like fishes in the sea of crimson light. From the earth, as a shore, I look out into that silent sea. I seem to partake its rapid transfor-mations: the active enchantment reaches my dust, and I dilate and con-spire with the morning wind. How does Nature deify us with a few and cheap elements! Give me health and a day, and I will make the pomp of emperors ridiculous. The dawn is my Assyria; the sun-set and moon-rise my Paphos, and unimaginable realms of faerie; broad noon shall be my England of the senses and the understanding; the night shall be my Ger-many of mystic philosophy and dreams.

'Not less excellent, except for our less susceptibility in the afternoon, was the charm of a January sunset. The western clouds divided and subdi-vided themselves into pink flakes modulated with tints of unspeakable softness; and the air had so much life and sweetness, that it was a pain to come within doors. What was it that nature would say? Was there no meaning in the live repose of the valley behind the mill, and which Homer or Shakespeare could not re-form for me in words? The leafless trees be-come spires of flame in the sunset, with the blue east for their back-ground, and the stars of the dead calices of flowers, and every withered stem and stubble rimed with frost, contribute something to the mute music.'

This is what description ought to be—the actual landscape, with a coloring of reflection; in a word, a sentimental picture.

The style of Emerson is, with all its purity of mere language, in other respects, most impure.

The prevailing defect, is want of continuity. This very defect secures certain ignorant admirers, who

> Wonder with a foolish face of praise.

Yet it is startling and impressive. But it is very faulty; it discloses real weakness. It was said of Seneca, that his writings were sand without lime. This may be much more truly said of Emerson, to whom, Seneca is quite a flowing writer. It may be said, the Book of books—the words of the wise man, and the sentences of the preacher—are purely fragmentary. But they are complete in themselves, and the Book of Proverbs is literally meant to be made up of detached sayings. Emerson, however, writes an address, or delivers a lecture, which is not one and the same throughout, but made up of centos, full of scattered, heterogenous thoughts and fancies.

Emerson's voice is, in fashionable phrase, 'a magnificent organ,' full, rich, deep, with sweetness and expression. Unfortunately, it is rather monotonous. It suits his style admirably. It marks him as a sort of male sybil; with little action, and no grace of address, he is the most impressive Lecturer we have heard. He relies chiefly on a certain 'precision' stateliness of manner, and emphasis of elocution. He has somewhat the mortified look of a Puritan. But he is very far from being that.

Of his published works, his addresses, with the defect of style we have mentioned, contain, notwithstanding, pointed sentences, shrewd remarks, and occasional fullness of rich declamation. In his divinity address occurs the best definition of preaching, we can recollect. 'Preaching is the expression of the moral sentiment, in application to the duties of life.' This may be called a low view, but let us not forget that model of all preachers, the sermon on the Mount. It was, strictly, a discourse of divine morality. He notices, in a phrase, the capital secret of all preaching, 'to convert life into truth:' to import personal experience into religious doctrine.

'Nature,' is an essay descriptive, aesthetical, philological, moral, psychological, and prophetic. It is full of matter, pithy, shrewd, and often eloquent. In the chapter on 'commodity,' there is a brilliant passage on the useful arts, a part of which we quote as a fair specimen of the volume.

'Under the general name of Commodity, I rank all those advantages which our senses owe to nature. This, of course, is a benefit which is temporary and mediate, not ultimate, like its service to the soul. Yet although low, it is perfect in its kind, and is the only use of nature which all men apprehend. The misery of man appears like childish petulance, when we explore the steady and prodigal provision that has been made for his support and delight on this green ball which floats him through the heavens. What angels invented these splendid ornaments, these rich conveniences, this ocean of air above, this ocean of water beneath, this firmament of earth between? this zodiac of lights, this tent of dropping clouds, this striped coat of climates, this fourfold year? Beasts, fire, water, stones, and corn serve him. The field is at once his floor, his work-yard, his playground, his garden, and his bed.

> "More servants wait on man
> Than he'll take notice of."—

'Nature, in its ministry to man, is not only the material, but it is also the process and the result. All the parts incessantly work into each other's hands for the profit of man. The wind sows the seed; the sun evaporates the sea; the wind blows the vapor to the field; the ice, on the other side of the planet, condenses rain on this; the rain feeds the plant; the plant feeds the animal; and thus the endless circulations of the divine charity nourish man.

'The useful arts are but reproductions or new combinations by the wit of man, of the natural benefactors. He no longer waits for favoring gales, but by means of steam he realizes the fable of Æolus's bag, and carries the two and thirty winds in the boiler of his boat. To diminish friction, he paves the road with iron bars, and, mounting a coach with a ship-load of men, animals and merchandise behind him, he darts through the country, from town to town, like an eagle or a swallow through the air. By the aggregate of these aids, how is the face of the world changed from the era of Noah to that of Napoleon! The private poor man hath cities, ships, canals, bridges, built for him. He goes to the post-office, and the human race run on his errands; to the book-shop, and the human race read and write of all that happens for him; to the court-house, and nations repair his wrongs. He sets his house upon the road, and the human race go forth every morning, and shovel out the snow, and cut a path for him.'

As a thinker, we have called Emerson a mystic. Mysticism being compounded, partly, of high spiritual instincts and partly of ignorant rashness, must be a very unsafe basis for any scheme of philosophy. It must run its followers into absurdities, as well as into noble trains of thought. It is an inspired revery, and when the dreamer awakes, he awakes to ineffectual aspirations and confusion of ideas. He wants precision, even if he has power to affect any thing. Mr. Emerson is a strong man and can work himself clear of these incumbrances, but all of his admirers cannot.

As a critic, we would place Emerson high, if he gave us more criticisms like that on Goethe. We conceive him to be a man of analytical rather than creative powers. He can dissect, more easily than compose.

As a religionist, we leave his Divinity address to speak for itself.

It is very easy to see that this gentlemen is a man of theory, and not much given to practical logic. Strict argument might dispel some of those 'cobwebs of the brain' he has so industriously spun, and precipitate the downfall of those visionary notions that are even now tottering on the verge of destruction.

Note

1. The two authors corresponded with one another, and Goethe on one occasion sent to Carlyle for a drawing of his house and the localities around, that he might judge the more wisely by the knowledge of the mute companions of brick and mortar, or green fields, and share at the same time in the pleasure of his familiar associations.

[*The Method of Nature*]

Anonymous*

Two things we cannot but wonder at;—one is, that Mr. Emerson, a man of letters and of great personal excellence, should write as he does; the other, that writing as he does, he is invited by literary Societies or religious Associations to deliver what he has written. The good people at Waterville must have been sadly puzzled while listening to the Oration before us,—equally in doubt, we apprehend, in regard to his meaning and in regard to the motive which could have prompted "the Adelphi" to seek his assistance in the celebration of their anniversary. Mr. Emerson, it seems, thought it could best be "celebrated by exploring the method of nature;" his exposition of which however is such that few probably understood it any better when he closed than when he began. The doctrine on which he builds his remarks is given in the assertion, that "the spirit and peculiarity of that impression nature makes on us is this, that it does not exist to any one or to any number of particular ends, but to numberless and endless benefit, that there is in it no private will, no rebel leaf or limb, but the whole is oppressed by one superincumbent tendency, obeys that redundancy or excess of life which in conscious beings we call *ecstasy*." The description of this "ecstatical state," which "causes a regard to the whole and not to the parts, to the cause and not to the ends, to the tendency and not to the act," and the attempt to show "how far it is transferable to the literary life," occupy the Orator's attention. He says some beautiful, some strange, and some unintelligible things. "It seems" to him, he tells us, "that the wit of man, his strength, his grace, his tendency, his art, is the grace and the presence of God;" "the receiver is only the All-Giver in part and in infancy." If this language be taken literally, how can it be reconciled with the popular or the Scriptural Theism? Mr. Emerson's idea of man however is as peculiar as his idea of God. "A man should know himself for a necessary actor. A link was wanting between two craving parts of nature, and he was hurled into being as the bridge over that yawning need, the mediator betwixt two else unmarriageable facts." We give Mr. E. the credit of concealing an idea beneath these words, though it escapes our detection. We do not mean however to criticise particular passages, so much as to express our regret that this last production of Mr. Emerson's pen has fewer beauties, and certainly not less faults, than any that have preceded it.

*Reprinted from *Monthly Miscellany of Religion and Letters*, 5 (December 1841), 346–47.

[R. W. Emerson]

E[dgar] A[llan] Poe*

Mr. Ralph Waldo Emerson belongs to a class of gentlemen with whom we have no patience whatever—the mystics for mysticism's sake. Quintilian mentions a pedant who taught obscurity, and who once said to a pupil "this is excellent, for I do not understand it myself." How the good man would have chuckled over Mr. E! His present *rôle* seems to be out-Carlyling Carlyle. *Lycophron Tenebrosus* is a fool to him. The best answer to his twaddle is *cui bono?*—a very little Latin phrase very generally mistranslated and misunderstood—*cui bono?*—to whom is it a benefit? If not to Mr. Emerson individually, then surely to no man living.

His love of the obscure does not prevent him, nevertheless, from the composition of occasional poems in which beauty is apparent *by flashes*. Several of his effusions appeared in the "Western Messenger"—more in the "Dial," of which he is the soul—or the sun—or the shadow. We remember the "Sphynx," the "Problem," the "Snow Storm," and some fine old-fashioned verses entitled "Oh fair and stately maid whose eye."

His MS. is bad, sprawling, illegible and irregular—although sufficiently bold. This latter trait may be, and no doubt is, only a portion of his general affectation.

[*Essays: Second Series*]

[Margaret Fuller]*

At the distance of three years this volume follows the first series of Essays, which have already made to themselves a circle of readers, attentive, thoughtful, more and more intelligent, and this circle is a large one if we consider the circumstances of this country, and of England, also, at this time.

In England it would seem there are a larger number of persons waiting for an invitation to calm thought and sincere intercourse than among ourselves. Copies of Mr. Emerson's first published little volume called "Nature," have there been sold by thousands in a short time, while one edition has needed seven years to get circulated here. Several of his Orations and Essays from "The Dial" have also been republished there, and met with a reverent and earnest response.

We suppose that while in England the want of such a voice is as great as here, a larger number are at leisure to recognize that want; a far larger number have set foot in the speculative region and have ears refined to appreciate these melodious accents.

*Reprinted from "An Appendix of Autographs," *Graham's Magazine*, 20 (January 1842), 48.

*Reprinted from *New-York Daily Tribune*, 7 December 1844, p. 1.

Our people, heated by a partisan spirit, necessarily occupied in these first stages by bringing out the material resources of the land, not generally prepared by early training for the enjoyment of books that require attention and reflection, are still more injured by a large majority of writers and speakers, who lend all their efforts to flatter corrupt tastes and mental indolence, instead of feeling it their prerogative and their duty to admonish the community of the danger and arouse it to nobler energy. The aim of the writer or lecturer is not to say the best he knows in as few and well-chosen words as he can, making it his first aim to do justice to the subject. Rather he seeks to beat out a thought as thin as possible, and to consider what the audience will be most willing to receive.

The result of such a course is inevitable. Literature and Art must become daily more degraded; Philosophy cannot exist. A man who feels within his mind some spark of genius, or a capacity for the exercises of talent, should consider himself as endowed with a sacred commission. He is the natural priest, the shepherd of the people. He must raise his mind as high as he can toward the heaven of truth, and try to draw up with him those less gifted by nature with ethereal lightness. If he does not so, but rather employs his powers to flatter them in their poverty, and to hinder aspiration by useless words, and a mere seeming of activity, his sin is great, he is false to God, and false to man.

Much of this sin indeed is done ignorantly. The idea that literature calls men to the genuine hierarchy is almost forgotten. One, who finds himself able, uses his pen, as he might a trowel, solely to procure himself bread, without having reflected on the position in which he thereby places himself.

Apart from the troop of mercenaries, there is one, still larger, of those who use their powers merely for local and temporary ends, aiming at no excellence other than may conduce to these. Among these, rank persons of honor and the best intentions, but they neglect the lasting for the transient, as a man neglects to furnish his mind that he may provide the better for the house in which his body is to dwell for a few years.

When these sins and errors are prevalent, and threaten to become more so, how can we sufficiently prize and honor a mind which is quite pure from such? When, as in the present case, we find a man whose only aim is the discernment and interpretation of the spiritual laws by which we live and move and have our being, all whose objects are permanent, and whose every word stands for a fact.

If only as a representative of the claims of individual culture in a nation which tends to lay such stress on artificial organization and external results, Mr. Emerson would be invaluable here. History will inscribe his name as a father of the country, for he is one who pleads her cause against herself.

If New-England may be regarded as a chief mental focus to the New World, and many symptoms seem to give her this place, as to other centres the characteristics of heart and lungs to the body politic; if we may believe, as the writer does believe, that what is to be acted out in the country at large is, most frequently, first indicated there, as all the phenomena of the nervous system in the fantasies of the brain, we may hail as an auspicious omen the influence Mr. Emerson has there obtained, which is deep-rooted, increasing, and, over the younger portion of the community, far greater than that of any other person.

His books are received there with a more ready intelligence than elsewhere, partly because his range of personal experience and illustration applies to that region, partly because he has prepared the way for his books to be read by his great powers as a speaker.

The audience that waited for years upon the lectures, a part of which is incorporated into these volumes of Essays, was never large, but it was select, and it was constant. Among the hearers were some, who though, attracted by the beauty of character and manner, they were willing to hear the speaker through, always went away discontented. They were accustomed to an artificial method, whose scaffolding could easily be retraced, and desired an obvious sequence of logical inferences. They insisted there was nothing in what they had heard, because they could not give a clear account of its course and purport. They did not see that Pindar's odes might be very well arranged for their own purpose, and yet not bear translating into the methods of Mr. Locke.

Others were content to be benefitted by a good influence without a strict analysis of its means. "My wife says it is about the elevation of human nature, and so it seems to me;" was a fit reply to some of the critics. Many were satisfied to find themselves excited to congenial thought and nobler life, without an exact catalogue of the thoughts of the speaker.

Those who believed no truth could exist, unless encased by the burrs of opinion, went away utterly baffled. Sometimes they thought he was on their side, then presently would come something on the other. He really seemed to believe there were two sides to every subject, and even to intimate higher ground from which each might be seen to have an infinite number of sides or bearings, an impertinence not to be endured! The partisan heard but once and returned no more.

But some there were, simple souls, whose life had been, perhaps, without clear light, yet still a search after truth for its own sake, who were able to receive what followed on the suggestion of a subject in a natural manner, as a stream of thought. These recognized, beneath the veil of words, the still small voice of conscience, the vestal fires of lone religious hours, and the mild teachings of the summer woods.

The charm of the elocution, too, was great. His general manner was that of the reader, occasionally rising into direct address or invocation in passages where tenderness or majesty demanded more energy. At such times both eye and voice called on a remote future to give a worthy reply. A future which shall manifest more largely the universal soul as it was then manifest to this soul. The tone of the voice was a grave body tone, full and sweet rather than sonorous, yet flexible and haunted by many modulations, as even instruments of wood and brass seem to become after they have been long played on with skill and taste; how much more so the human voice! In the more expressive passages it uttered notes of silvery clearness, winning, yet still more commanding. The words uttered in those tones, floated awhile above us, then took root in the memory like winged seed.

In the union of an even rustic plainness with lyric inspirations, religious dignity with philosophic calmness, keen sagacity in details with boldness of view, we saw what brought to mind the early poets and legislators of Greece—men who taught their fellows to plow and avoid moral evil, sing hymns to the gods and watch the metamorphoses of nature. Here in civic Boston was such a man—one who could see man in his original grandeur and his original childishness, rooted in simple nature, raising to the heavens the brow and eyes of a poet.

And these lectures seemed not so much lectures as grave didactic poems, theogonies, perhaps, adorned by odes when some Power was in question whom the poet had best learned to serve, and with eclogues wisely portraying in familiar tongue the duties of man to man and "harmless animals."

Such was the attitude in which the speaker appeared to that portion of the audience who have remained permanently attached to him.—They value his words as the signets of reality; receive his influence as a help and incentive to a nobler discipline than the age, in its general aspect, appears to require; and do not fear to anticipate the verdict of posterity in claiming for him the honors of greatness, and, in some respects, of a Master.

In New-England he thus formed for himself a class of readers, who rejoice to study in his books what they already know by heart. For, though the thought has become familiar, its beautiful garb is always fresh and bright in hue.

A similar circle of like-minded the books must and do form for themselves, though with a movement less directly powerful, as more distant from its source.

The Essays have also been obnoxious to many charges. To that of obscurity, or want of perfect articulation. Of 'Euphuism,' as an excess of fancy in proportion to imagination, and an inclination, at times, to subtlety at the expense of strength, has been styled. The human heart complains of inadequacy, either in the nature or experience of the writer, to represent its full vocation and its deeper needs. Sometimes it speaks of this want as "under-development" or a want of expansion which may yet be remedied; sometimes doubts whether "in this mansion there be either hall or portal to receive the loftier of the Passions." Sometimes the soul is deified at the expense of nature, then again nature at that of man, and we are not quite sure that we can make a true harmony by balance of the statements.—This writer has never written one good work, if such a work be one where the whole commands more attention than the parts. If such an one be produced only where, after an accumulation of materials, fire enough be applied to fuse the whole into one new substance. This second series is superior in this respect to the former, yet in no one essay is the main stress so obvious as to produce on the mind the harmonious effect of a noble river or a tree in full leaf. Single passages and sentences engage our attention too much in proportion. These essays, it has been justly said, tire like a string of mosaics or a house built of medals. We miss what we expect in the work of the great poet, or the great philosopher, the liberal air of all the zones: the glow, uniform yet various in tint, which is given to a body by free circulation of the heart's blood from the hour of birth. Here is, undoubtedly, the man of ideas, but we want the ideal man also; want the heart and genius of human life to interpret it, and here our satisfaction is not so perfect. We doubt this friend raised himself too early to the perpendicular and did not lie along the ground long enough to hear the secret whispers of our parent life. We could wish he might be thrown by conflicts on the lap of mother earth, to see if he would not rise again with added powers.

All this we may say, but it cannot excuse us from benefitting by the great gifts that have been given, and assigning them their due place.

Some painters paint on a red ground. And this color may be supposed to represent the ground work most immediately congenial to most men, as it is the color of blood and represents human vitality. The figures traced upon it are instinct with life in its fulness and depth.

But other painters paint on a gold ground. And a very different, but no less natural, because also a celestial beauty, is given to their works who choose for their foundation the color of the sunbeam, which nature has preferred for her most precious product, and that which will best bear the test of purification, gold.

If another simile may be allowed, another no less apt is at hand. Wine is the most brilliant and intense expression of the powers of earth.—It is her potable fire, her answer to the sun. It exhilarates, it inspires, but then it is liable to fever and intoxicate too the careless partaker.

Mead was the chosen drink of the Northern gods. And this essence of the honey of the mountain bee was not thought unworthy to revive the souls of the valiant who had left their bodies on the fields of strife below.

Nectar should combine the virtues of the ruby wine, the golden mead, without their defects or dangers.

Two high claims our writer can vindicate on the attention of his contemporaries. One from his sincerity. You have his thought just as it found place in the life of his own soul. Thus, however near or relatively distant its approximation to absolute truth, its action on you cannot fail to be healthful. It is a part of the free air.

He belongs to that band of whom there may be found a few in every age, and who now in known human history may be counted by hundreds, who worship the one God only, the God of Truth. They worship, not saints, nor creeds, nor churches, nor reliques, nor idols in any form. The mind is kept open to truth, and life only valued as a tendency toward it. This must be illustrated by acts and words of love, purity and intelligence. Such are the salt of the earth; let the minutest crystal of that salt be willingly by us held in solution.

The other is through that part of his life, which, if sometimes obstructed or chilled by the critical intellect, is yet the prevalent and the main source of his power. It is that by which he imprisons his hearer only to free him again as a "liberating God" (to use his own words). But indeed let us use them altogether, for none other, ancient or modern, can more worthily express how, making present to us the courses and destinies of nature, he invests himself with her serenity and animates us with her joy.

"Poetry was all written before time was, and whenever we are so finely organized that we can penetrate into that region where the air is music, we hear those primal warblings, and attempt to write them down, but we lose ever and anon a word, or a verse, and substitute something of our own, and thus miswrite the poem. The men of more delicate ear write down these cadences more faithfully, and these transcripts, though imperfect, become the songs of the nations."

"As the eyes of Lyncæus were said to see through the earth, so the poet turns the world to glass, and shows us all things in their right series and procession. For, through that better perception, he stands one step nearer to things, and sees the flowing or metamorphosis; perceives that thought is multiform; that within the form of every creature is a force impelling it to ascend into a higher form; and following with his eyes the life, uses the forms which express that life, and so the speech flows with the flowing of nature."

Thus have we in a brief and unworthy manner indicated some views of these books. The only true criticism of these, or any good books, may be gained by making them the companions of our lives. Does every accession of knowledge or a juster sense of beauty make us prize them more? Then they are gôod, indeed, and more immortal than mortal. Let that test be applied to these; essays which will lead to great and complete poems—somewhere.

"Emerson's Essays"

"A Disciple"*

"The highest office of the intellect is the discovery of essential unity under the semblances of difference."—COLERIDGE.

*Reprinted from *United States Magazine, and Democratic Review*, 16 (June 1845), 589–602.

"Surprising, indeed, on whatever side we look is the revival of the individual consciousness of a living relation with the All Good. Our literature is every day more deeply tinged with a sense of the mysterious power which animates existence, and governs all events."—W. H. Channing.

It has been said that "the office of criticism is to bridge over the waters that separate the prophet from the people—to compass the distance that divides the understanding in the auditor from the intuition of the utterer,"—an office more easily indicated than fulfilled; and one which few persons have attempted to perform, for one of the most profound thinkers and inspired seers of our time: perhaps because the partition waters were too wide—the intervening gulf too deep.

Carlyle, who has lovingly unfolded to his countrymen the pure and cloistral genius of Novalis, the profound significance of Goethe and the intricate opulence of Jean Paul, has, in presenting them with the evangel of our western prophet, left them to solve the problem as they may.

His preface to the English edition of the Essays, imports that the name of Ralph Waldo Emerson is not entirely unknown in England. Distinguished travellers, he says, "have carried thither tidings of such a man—fractions of his writings have found their way into the hands of the curious: fitful hints that there is, in New England, some spiritual notability, called Emerson, glide through Reviews and Magazines." For himself, he finds that *the words of this man, such words as he finds it good to speak, are worth attending to*, and that by degrees, a small circle of living souls, eager to hear, are gathered." And in these few words, he has, perhaps, said all that the critic can effectually say in his office of Mediator between the prophet and the people. He cannot induct his readers with the "*aura*" of an author's genius, he can only point them to the source from which it emanates. He may say much that will be received with delight by those who are already the participators or recipients of the new revelation, but he cannot construct any bridge or thoroughfare by which "understanding of the populace shall pass to the intuition of the Seer." No mechanical aids can avail us here. The wings of love and faith can alone bear us to those serene heights whence the prophet overlooks the universe.

["]Authority decides in the circle of the sciences, but intuition alone, a fine inner sense assumed by all, and possessed by few, judges of the true and the beautiful, of poetry and philosophy, the two foci in the intellectual ellipse." For the highest act of philosophy also, is a divination—an intuition and not an inference.

Bulwer, in his preface to the translations from Schiller, says that the chief aim of the poet, with that of the orator on the husting, should be to make himself intelligible to the multitude; but Bulwer has little insight of the subject on which he writes; else would he know that the poet never troubles himself with thoughts like these. He sings as the bird sings, because his soul is o'erburthened with love and beauty. He casts the fertilizing flower-dust of his heart to the winds of heaven, nor asks if they have borne it to a fitting receptacle.

The most profound thinker cannot defend his faith in the inner world, nor the poet his vision thereof from the vapid gain-saying of the scoffer. Not the Seer, but the Savant is honored of the world. Spinoza had not a single follower in the age in which he lived, and it has been said that there are not at any time ten men on earth who read Plato.

The great philosopher and poet is he, who understands the spirit of his age. To do this, he must transcend the existing order of things, overlooking it from a point of view above the level of his contemporaries, and attainable as a common standpoint, only to succeeding generations; and just in proportion as he transcends the popular level, is his speech an enigma or a reproach to the multitude, who, regarding their own minds as the normal measure of human intelligence, oppose themselves with sullen determination to the new revelation, and groan, like the mandrake, when a new idea threatens to uproot them from the soil in which they vegetate.

There is no paradox so absurd, no heresy so dangerous, that men will not sooner forgive it than a truth prematurely enunciated. And no man excites such pious horror, such unmitigated reprobation, as the promulgator of such truth. The effect of a resisting medium becomes perceptible only as the planet approaches its perihelion.

The world, unwillingly aroused from its slumbers, thinks, like the silly house-maids in Æsop, by wringing the neck of poor Chanticleer to retard the dawn!

"Beware," says Emerson, "when the great God lets loose a thinker on this planet, then all things are at risk—the very hopes of man, the religion of nations, the manners and morals of mankind are all at the mercy of a new generalization. Generalization is always a new influx of the Divinity into the mind." But to see things under this new law, they must be seen from the same level, and through the same medium. The results of the synthetic intellect cannot be reached through any critical or analytical process.

A man of Emerson's large faith and intuitive reason, who has drunk deep at the fontal truths of being, and sent his plummet to the ocean-depths of thought, cannot accommodate his free unchartered utterance to the limited apprehension of men who, engrossed by the narrow arts of detail, have no capacity for the wisdom of the complex. Yet, perhaps few persons could so command the rapt attention of a popular audience, to thoughts so abstruse, expressed in language so delphic and poetic. The charm of his presence is pervasive, like music. He commands the attention of his audience, and constrains their sympathy by a power which they cannot analyze, by a spell that transcends their knowledge.

Severe truthfulness characterizes every look, tone, and gesture. He speaks from the commanding and regal attitude of one who reposes firmly on his convictions. Those earnest eyes seem to hold commune with *soul*, and regardless of the world's penalties and rewards, make their direct appeal to the inner tribunal of the conscience. Their look of profound repose, or concentrate thought deepening at times beneath a frown (severe, yet beautiful in its passionless, rebuke) which can hardly fail to remind one of the austere majesty in the countenance of the angel sent to expel Heliodorus from the temple, one of the finest of Raphael's inimitable heads. At such moments our prophet might, with Heraclitus, be compared to the Sybil, who "speaking with inspired mouth, inornate and severe, pierces through centuries by the power of the God."

The spell of his immediate influence is felt and acknowledged by the most uncultivated audience, yet we hear a constant reference to his obscurity and vagueness. Men complain that no intelligible ideas have been gained, no definite notions acquired. They were charmed while they listened, but when they seek to explain and seize the charm, its secret escapes them. They cannot analyze it—they cannot appropriate it. It is a fairy gift that turns to dross in the handling. In return for their time and money, they have brought away nothing positive and available—nothing that can be weighed and measured and turned to useful account.

But what went ye forth for to see? A partizan? a polemic? an exponent of creeds and doctrines? a propounder of articles of faith, and theories of civil polity? Verily ye have sought in vain! Yet somewhat have ye heard that stirred your stagnant souls, but what, ye know not. A wild, mysterious music, as of the winds of paradise, murmuring afar off through the Tree of Life. An improvisation, as it were, of the central laws of being. The oracular enunciation of a mystic and sublime Theosophy. Ye hear the sound thereof, yet know not whence it cometh nor whither it goeth. It is as the heavenly manna which cannot be heaped or hoarded, but which refreshes the pilgrim on his weary life-path, and imparts new strength to bear the burthen of the way.

Emerson's speech is affirmative and oracular. We must be satisfied to receive from him the enunciation of the idea, we cannot hope to hear it demonstrated, or explained. We find no attempt at a formal, scientific statement of truth, but rather an oriental dogmatism, an apostolic yea and nay. His mind betrays a quick apprehension of logical sequence, yet he renders no account of the actual process by which he arrives at results. He attacks no creed, convinces no sceptic, but he gives adequate and beautiful expression to the most profound and cherished convictions—to the most earnest and devout aspirations of the age. To some of the loftiest minds and purest spirits of the nineteenth century, his voice is as "the voice of their own souls, heard in the calm of thought."

His novel statements of the most familiar phenomena of life, have often a strange force and directness, and startle us by their simple verity, like the naive cadences of a child's voice heard amid the falsetto tones of the conventicle or the theatre.

No man is better adapted than Emerson to comprehend the spirit of the age and to interpret its mission. His insight is marvellously clear, and though less conversant than many others with concrete, special instances, he yields to none in the synthetic grasp of his intellect, and in a comprehensive and generic classification of the facts of experience. He looks not so much at that aspect of things, often partial, trivial and grotesque, which they bear to time, as at that solemn and serene, which faces eternity. The earth is to him not one of Gardiner's globes, mapped off into petty divisions of province and empire, state and territory, but one of the more recent planets of our system, moving on its destined path through space and harmoniously fulfilling its part in the grand diapason of the universe. He sees not so much the things in which man differs from man as those grand features common to humanity.

Life is viewed by him from no parish belfry, but from an "exceeding high mountain, from whence he can behold all the kingdoms of the world and the glories thereof." Seen from these serene altitudes, all conventional distinctions fade into insignificance, and Satan cannot tempt the soul even to a momentary deviation from its worship of essential truth and beauty.

With the same synthetic glance, he looks at inanimate nature; and, with Novalis, studies her not in her isolated phenomena, but in her essential unity. To him she is not the chance playmate of an hour, but the fair bride of the spirit, and its destined companion through eternity,—reflecting back from her loving and gentle eyes all that the soul hopes or fears, enjoys or suffers. He lives with her in sweet and intimate communion, as one who has won from her the "heart of her mystery," and divined the last word of her secret, or rather as one who has learned that she has no "last word," but like the fair *raconteur* of the Arabian tale, improvises from day to day, from year to year, from age to age, an interminable romance—a series of inventions, the last of which has still some mysterious connection with the first, elucidating and carrying forward but never ending her wondrous story. "To the intelligent Nature converts herself into an infinite promise."

Nor is this view of Nature, as the inseparable companion and counterpart of spirit, contradictory to the Berkeleyan idealism which frequently manifests itself in Emerson's writings, particularly in the earlier Essays. For in proportion as matter is divested of its rigid positiveness and substantial objectivity, do we the more readily conceive of it as a permanent mode of existence, capable of infinite adaptation to the wants of the spiritual intelligences that are associated with it. "The vast picture which God paints on the instant eternity of the soul." The inferences of modern science in relation to this subject are pregnant with results of the highest importance to spiritual and mental philosophy. But while science is slowly collecting facts, inducting theories and deducing results, the poet, with a surer instinct, suggests the true idea of nature, divines her mission and indicates her method. His sentient and mobile being faithfully transmits all her influences. In all her aspects and changes, he perceives a significant beauty and a mysterious sympathy with humanity. In her presence he feels not weariness, nor fears satiety: he knows that her resources are inexhaustible, and that, elastic, ductile, and permeable to spirit, she reforms herself for ever in conformity with the soul's infinitely expanding ideal.

Like Gray, Emerson delights to hear the gnarled and hoary forest-trees droning out their old stories to the storm. He listens to the song of the winds in the pine-tree and

> "Hears within their cadent pauses
> The charms of the ancient causes—
> Heeds the old oracles,—ponders the
>   spells
> Song wakes in their pinnacles when
>   the wind swells,"

and responds to these sylvan melodies in "wood-notes" not less wild and Orphic than their own.

We find in him always that uniform repose and serenity of mind that affects us somewhat like the aspect of nature itself,

> "Calm pleasures there abide, majestic
>   pains."

There is an absence of that vivid sense of personality—that intense individualism which so often manifests itself in the morbid and jealous sensitiveness, peculiar to what is called the "temperament of genius." Instead of this, we find a cheerful, inflexible courage, an Oriental quietude. We might fancy him dreaming away his life with the Sacontala, among the Lotus flowers that border the Ganges, or like the starry Magian evoking from night and silence their eternal mysteries. The words of Plotinus in relation to the supersensual portion of the triune soul, might aptly be applied to him—"Remaining free from all solicitude, not seeking to modify the world in accordance with the discursive reason, nor to transform anything in its own nature, but by the vision of that which is prior to itself informing the world with an infinite beauty."

This severity has been termed by his critics, "a vice of temperament," "an undue preponderance of the intellectual faculty," "a want of harmonious development," of "generous sympathy with humanity." I do not so understand it, nor can I assent to the criticism of a rare contemporary genius when, in speaking of these essays, he says—"They are truly noble, reporting a wisdom akin to that which the great and good of all time have lived and spoken; yet the author neither warms nor inspires me: he writes always from the intellect to the intellect, and hence some abatement from the depth of his insight, purchased always at the cost of vital integrity. But this is the tax on all pure intellect."

Can we then so separate the functions and faculties of our nature, as to believe that an intellect whose product is "a wisdom akin to that which the great and good of all times have lived and spoken," is developed at the cost of vital integrity? A sufficiency of life—a true vital integrity—would enable us to transcend these pernicious distinctions, and to see that love and wisdom are inseparable. Can the contemplation of eternal verities leave the heart cold and void? Is not the holy energy of true love ever sagacious, far-sighted and prophetic? Truth is not isolated: it is not a part, but the whole. It is love, and beauty, and joy. The wise man does not believe and opine, but he knows and *is* the very truth which he utters. His thought is action: his knowledge is love.

It is very common to hear persons speak of the mind as if reason, imagination and sensibility constituted different and distinct portions of it, though the consciousness speaks, *ex cathedra*, of a living unity. This is in part attributable to the popular empirical psychology which bears the same relation to the true, as the Grecian Theology to the Mosaic. And as the Hellenic deities make war upon each other, so in the popular psychology the faculties are represented as antagonistic, as a profound intellect and a loving heart. Yet, all great philosophers and theosophists have been devout and good men—else were their theories as profitless as their lives. Do not the bard and the prophet offer sacrifice at the same altar? Must the laurel crown extinguish the pure flame of the saintly aureole? The greatest thinker of modern Europe, who united the poetic insight of Plato with the exact method of Aristotle, says, "*Voluntas et intellectus unum idemque sunt.*" Nay, more: *that we know the right through the very attraction which it possesses for us.* "Quod quisque ex legibus naturæ suæ (rationalis) necessario appetit et adversatur id bonum vel malum hujus naturæ est."—*Spinoza, Ethic., pars II.*

This doctrine, that the soul, in its entire, unperverted action, instinctively seeks its highest good—a doctrine which lies at the foundation of all pure ethics—is held by Emerson with a cheerful, invincible faith, based on his knowledge of an infinite and divine life instant in the finite.

Of the *soul* he would say what Dr. Pusey says of the *Church*—"Our duty is not to reform it, or take away from it, but to *obey* it."

"For to the soul, in her pure action, all the virtues are natural and not painfully acquired." We want, then, not so much self-denial as self-knowledge and self-trust.

And as that friendship only is sweet to us which is won without any concession or compromise of our own individuality, so those virtues only are gracious and beautiful in which the whole nature transpires.

"People," says Emerson, "represent virtue as a struggle, and take to themselves great airs on their attainments, and the question is everywhere vexed, when a noble nature is commended, whether the man is not better who strives with temptation?" And here the most acute casuists are often at fault, and are fain to confess with honest Geoffrey Chaucer—

"For me, I cannot bolt it to the bran
As can the holy Doctor Aúgustin."

Carlyle, who, with all the dazzling lights and electric splendors of his cometic genius, seldom sees a truth with that calm and steadfast glance with which Emerson transfixes and holds it, in his review of Diderot loses himself in what he calls the "eternal ravelment" of the subject; asks if virtue is indeed synonymous with pleasure?—if Paul the apostle was not virtuous, and if virtue was its own reward when *his* approving conscience told him that he was the chief of sinners?—gets warm at the self-complacent tone in which the poor encyclopedist speaks of the delights of *"vertu, honnêteté, grandeur de l'ame,"* &c., and piously adjures him in the Devil and his grandmother's name, to *be* virtuous and say no more about it:—predicts, nevertheless, that the ascetic system will not soon recover its exclusive dominancy, and admits that the close observer may discern filaments of a nobler system, wherein this of self-denial and duty may be included as one harmonious element. Yet again relapsing into his doubts, asks how tolerance for the wrong can co-exist with an ever-present conviction that the right stands related to it as a God to a Devil?"

Here, then, lies the grand difficulty—the radical error of the popular creed—as of the Kantian ethics which closely approximate to it. Kant makes the highest morality to consist in the strength of a man's will—a power to conform his life to an idea of duty. Yet that which reason or conscience imposes as "the right" neither wins his credent love by its beauty, nor brings with it blessedness and joy. Its rewards are referred to a distant period and an exoteric source. Kant has been not unjustly charged with dislocating and sub-dividing the faculties of the human mind. He puts far apart knowledge and power, being and doing, wisdom and love. In like manner he divides the universe into antagonistic parts and principles, as matter and spirit, God and nature, good and evil, &c. Yet, not until men saw this opposition projected in a strong light, did they feel its inadequacy, and seek to restore the great idea of essential unity in a system adapted to the wants and culture of the age. Jacobi was one of the first to call attention to the vital defects of the Kantian philosophy, which sees nothing in Christianity but a code of duties, and represents the Creator of the universe as a mere Supreme Being—*"Deus extramundanus"*—apart from the creation and from man. In referring all action to a sense of obligation, in defining duty, as an antagonistic principle, Kant leaves the subject involved in that "eternal ravelment" from which few men know how to disengage it.

But these difficulties lie not in Emerson's path. He dwells ever in that clear and serene region where neither Loke nor Ahriman, Typhon nor Devil, interfere to divide with God the empire of the universe. With the great thinkers of all time, he sees that no evil is pure; that the principle of good enters into all things. "There is no pure lie, no pure malignity in

nature—the belief in depravity is the last profligacy and profanation—there is no scepticism, no atheism but that." The malevolent man is
he who holds all things as evil; and hence his destructive propensity. Sir
Thomas Brown, on the other hand, who was incapable of forming strong
conceptions of evil, says, he could never bring himself heartily to hate the
Devil. Emerson seems, with the Platonists, to regard evil as a defect, a
privation, a deviation from subsistence. He sees that God imparts to all
things good, and to each that quantity of good which it is qualified to obtain. This faith cannot subsist with any purely dualistic philosophy where
wrong stands opposed to right, as a Devil to a God rather than as Negation to Being; but in proportion as we free ourselves more and more from
a false, fragmentary and superficial life, the soul more distinctly ar-
ticulates her gospel of peace and love; we then not only believe, but know,
that all evil is relative, all being progressive, all life an emanation from
the Divine.

It is this beautiful soul-trust, and not self-trust, as some would render
it, that Emerson inculcates from a faith so sweet and inward, that the
scoffer is silenced and the caviller rebuked.

I have dwelt longer on this subject, because it forms so intimate and
essential a part of the entire view of life which I find in these volumes—a
view so pregnant and suggestive, that an expansive and liberal theory of
morals must necessarily grow out of it.

Although Emerson claims no consistency for the speculations here
presented to us, I do not find in the whole range of modern literature a
mind that overlooks life from a point of view so high and commanding—that arrives so surely, by an induction so rapid and unerring, at the
last results from the speculative reason. And moreover, notwithstanding
(or I might rather say in consequence of) the large and free scope of his intellect, I find everywhere a pervasive consistency, a living unity of
thought, which is never violated.

He has in truth no affinity with that class of thinkers described by
Novalis who construct a theory in order to free themselves from the
weariness of thought, nor, on the other hand, with that barren Eclecticism,
which, consisting only of a fortuitous collection of ideas and having no internal principle of growth, is, like fossil substances, capable of enlargement
only by accretion. For whenever thought is genuine, proceeding from a
true inner life, its most spontaneous and unpremeditated enunciation
manifests something of that formative energy, that harmonious adaptation
of parts which marks the development of organic structure.

We are told by one of Mr. Emerson's most discerning readers, that "it
may be said of him that he has never written one good work if such a work
be one where the whole commands more admiration than the parts—
where, after an accumulation of materials, fire enough be applied to fuse
the whole into one new substance." The Essays are said to resemble "a
string of mosaics, or a house built of medals."

It may be so; yet will I say of them as Andrew Marvell of his flower garden—

> "What Rome, Greece, Palestine e'er said,
> I, in this light Mosaic, read."

They are in truth Sibylline leaves, whose price decreases not with their want of completeness in number or arrangement. They have the unity of nature, where the whole reappears in all its parts.

> "Out of these scattered Sibyl leaves
> Strange prophecies my spirit weaves."

A single aphorism often suggests the whole economy of being, and unlocks to us the secret passages of things. To me they breathe a harmony so pure and responsive that I recognize therein no jarring element.

They are faithful transcripts of thought, as it evolves itself in a mind of the ripest and most harmonious development, fragmentary only in so far as the view which every man takes of life must be fragmentary, and, as are the oldest and most costly scriptures, for life itself, as read or readable by man, is but a fragment—a "*Werden*," and not a "*Seyn*."

In addition to his alleged want of unity and explicitness, we are told of his contra statements on every great question. His report is so faithful, he gives us so impartially all the aspects of things, that his meaning escapes us—"We get now one idea and then another, but seldom such a permanent and final result." Men prefer to have the bolted wheat prepared and garnered for their use. Yet always these antitheses, these apparent contradictions are coordinates of a single law, and spanned by a central principle. Through conscious dualism only do we pass to conscious unity.

The great truth to which all Emerson's affirmations point is Absolute Identity—the unity of all things in God. This is the "*mot d'enigme*" to his whole philosophy—it lies at the foundation of his entire theory of life, and is the secret alike of his singleness and his universality.

In giving such prominence to this idea he has shown himself an apt representative of the philosophical character of his age, a philosophy standing as yet far in advance of its popular and prosaic character, yet destined ultimately to determine, as it has already indicated, the point of view from which science, art, religion, law and social polity are to be contemplated.

The idea of Absolute Identity furnishes the type, in conformity with which thought develops itself in all the master spirits of the time. It suggested to Swedenborg his doctrine of correspondences—to Fourier his theory of "universal unity" and "universal analogy"—and to Schelling the parallelism that exists between the laws of nature and the laws of thought—or as Hegel has more intensively expressed it—*Die Absolute Einheit des Begriffs und der Objectivitat*—"the absolute oneness of thought and its object." It inspired St. Simon with his devout conception of the collective life of humanity, and revealed to him its harmonious and progressive development, thereby imparting to history an epic character which ennobles every phase of its progress. Under its influence science itself seems rapidly outgrowing its purely empirical limits, and approximating to a more large and poetic conception of the generic unity and dynamic power of nature. Perhaps, without falling back on the abhorrent theory of the materialists, we shall yet find that the mind has its physique and nature her Psyche. If the same law prevails in the natural as in the moral world—if the same primal energy informs them, then science becomes at once mystic and devout,—a portal through which we have access to the penetralia of that beautiful temple of nature, of which Heraclitus said, "*Enter, for here too are Gods.*"

The Pythagoreans taught that if the essence of all things admits of cognition, it is only in so far as the things of which the world consists, partake of it. With equal truth might we say, that if the things of which the world consists admit of cognition, it is only in so far as they partake of the essence of all things—"*Deus immundanus.*" Only through our oneness with actual being can we assume the possibility of actual knowledge.

An able writer in the Westminster Review, in analyzing this great doctrine of Spinoza, says, "No believer in Ontology, as a possible science, can resist the all-embracing dialectic of Spinoza, but it is our strength that we reject all metaphysics as frivolous. Men can never arrive at a knowledge of things as they are in themselves. Turn it which way you will there is nothing in the consciousness but the consciousness itself—to know more would involve the necessity to be more." Aye, verily!—but this identical fact of *being more* is that on which the believer in absolute cognition grounds his faith. No philosophy can explain the relation of thought to its object, which conceives of man as an isolated and detached particle of the great *whole* (a belief which we cannot even state without a paradox). But a more profound observation shows us the manifold, living and essential union which inwardly and invisibly unites all individuals with each other and with nature. Only through "a mystical union of all things resting in God" can we explain the most familiar facts of experience—far less the subtle mysteries of those evanescent and abnormal states in which the soul, transcending the limits of time and space, holds commune with the invisible world, recalls the past and foresees the future—moods when

> "We ebb into a former life, or seem
> To lapse far back in a confused dream
> To states of mystical similitude."

The new Platonists, who regarded this class of phenomena as a kind of natural magic or divination, based the possibility of such powers on the essential connection and dependence of all things.

The great idea then which has exercised so vast an influence on the literature of the age is the *unity of being*, or as a recent critic on the "Teutonic Metaphysics or American Transcendentalism," has satirically expressed it, "everything is everything, and everything else is everything, and everything is everything else." We cannot be surprised at the vagueness and folly which this writer finds in a Philosophy which he vainly attempts to grasp. The same plant will not grow in every soil. Yet is this "Each in all" philosophy no mere "Hall of Phantasy," no "Blind man's Holiday" or "Fool's Paradise," but a sure ground of holiest love, of sternest courage, of serenest patience, and above all of unfailing charity. Old as thought itself, it is necessarily modified by the psychical and physical culture of the ages in which it manifests itself. Dimly foreshadowed in the vast and gloomy Pantheism of India, it has shed a shimmering glory on the vistas of all the Poets of antiquity from Orpheus to Virgil. On the secret shrine of the Cabirii, it cast a lurid and fitful gleam, flashed through the night of Egyptian darkness, and shot back a pale and reflex ray from the pages of the Talmud. In the mediæval age it illumined the dream of the mystic and the theory of the naturalist, while in our own it animates and cheers with its full solar beam the whole hemisphere of thought. Receiving from the adamantine logic of Spinoza a scientific statement invulnerable to criticism, it remained for a long time without any perceptible influence on the literature and philosophy of the age. Spinoza gave to the theory of identity a complete anatomical structure, but it waited for Schelling to breathe into it the breath of life, to unfold the profound significance that was involved in it as a system that at once infused life into nature, while it recognized in humanity the control of laws as beneficent and inevitable as those which obtain in the natural world.

At the period immediately preceding his enunciation of this philosophy, society was evidently in a subversive or transition state.

Empiricism had done its work well, and proved a vigilant vassal in the temple of science, but it knew not how to avail itself of the stores it had aggregated with such tireless industry. It was overwhelmed with its own wealth, and waited for the hand of a master to dispose of its treasures. Not until philosophy had learned, like Deucalion, to cast behind it these stones of the earth could they become living forms. The Tree of Knowledge was heavy with golden fruit, but a flaming sword still barred the way to the Tree of Life.

Kant was but the precursor and not (as is sometimes thought) the founder of the recent philosophy, for he left untouched the great idea of the essential union of God with Humanity, and regarding the reason as strictly subjective, he desired all knowledge of absolute truth, and analyzed the laws of mind only as subjective phenomena. His method was therefore purely experimental. Yet it must be confessed that he gave to empiricism the noblest character of which it is susceptible, and sought to arrange for it an honorable compromise with idealism. Nor can it be denied that he proved himself an able diplomatist; but he could not succeed in satisfying the large demands of the intellect, which asks nothing less than absolute cognition.

The Manichæan hypothesis which had been reaffirmed by Bayle, and against which Leibnitz composed his Théodicée, had still many advocates. The ghost of Gnostic heresy (the belief in two principles) still walked the earth. The time was full of discord, and waited for the atonement, or reunion. The age of indeterminate although of healthful and impulsive action had long since yielded to an era of blind, unquestioning faith. With the introduction of Printing, this blind faith of the middle ages was at an end, and the sceptical, critical, self-conscious life commenced. The development of new powers and the consciousness of new wants involved the age in moral and political conflicts. With inquiry came doubt and denial, speculation and negation. All the learning and intellect of the eighteenth century was unequal to the solution of the great controversial questions that had been transmitted to it. While it examined and tested all creeds and opinions, it regarded none as worthy of belief. The work of destruction was the only work to which it seemed appointed, and faithfully did it perform its mission.

Man had eaten to satiety of the fruit of the Tree of Knowledge, and had become familiar with change and death. All things seemed shadowy and unreal. Human life was a mere point in time compared to the vast periods of history—the endless æons of science. The researches of the historian had opened interminable vistas into the twilight realms of mythical and traditionary story. Every spot of earth was hallowed by the footsteps of the departed, every city was a mausoleum of the dead.

The literature of the period, enriched with countless accessions from the distant and the past, and presenting such varied modes of apprehending life and nature, was calculated to stimulate to their highest action the reflective faculties, and particularly the faculty of comparison, thereby tending to induce that critical, self-conscious character which then began to distinguish it, and which Carlyle denounces as the unpardonable sin. Man had now learned that he must find repose in clear and adequate ideas of being, or find it not at all. Not by any grace of manner, any play of fancy, or novelty of incident, could he be lapt into forgetfulness of himself,—of his own mysterious being. For him there was no self-oblivion. He cannot be amused—he will not be deceived.

Literature was no longer an heroic song or a devotional anthem. It was introspective, self-involved, and meditative.

> "Its sweetest songs were those
> That told of saddest thought."

The poet no longer dwelt with God in the garden of innocence, where the fruits and flowers of existence proffered their willing treasures, but was driven forth to delve wearily, and often ineffectually, for the "bread of life" in the thorny fields of the intellect.

In his eloquent lament we see only the fact that an ideal was unfolding to his awakened thought, to which he could as yet in no way conform the real—the soul meanwhile awaiting in bitter travail the birth of the new conceptions that had sprung to life within it.

In reviewing this period of the history of modern literature, we seem to stand with the immortal Florentine, looking down from the brink of an abyss "that receives the thunder of infinite lamentations."

> "Vero e che in su la proda mi trovai
> Della valle d'abisso dolorosa,
> Che tuono accoglie d'infiniti quai."
>
> *Inferno, Canto IV.*

The heart of man was riven asunder with fierce conflicts; perplexed with inexplicable contradictions. The Sphinx had fixed on him her evil eye, torturing him with questions which he must answer or die. The aggregated treasures of science and learning seemed to mock the imperious demands of the restless intellect with their unavailing hoards; while History unrolled her vast scroll but to threaten or to warn, "for within and without it was written with lamentations, and mourning, and wo." From the wide Orient echoed the cry of desolation and despair—from Judea was the wail borne onward, "the wail of multitudinous Egypt"—Greece and Rome swelled with their choral voices the ancient burden, till all articulate sounds were lost in the sullen boom of a cathedral bell, heard solemnly tolling throughout the long and dismal night of the dark ages. No beneficent purpose was yet detected in the annals of the race—the development of no inherent law, either recognized or divined therein—far less that plenary inspiration now claimed for the entire record of Humanity.

The old Gods had deserted the earth—Priests and lawgivers had lost their sanctity. Man listened in vain for the spheral harmonies—no voice, no tone from those eternal depths. The song of the stars was drowned in the Babel clamor of sophists and sciolists.

At the close of the eighteenth century there was no theory too visionary, no opinion too paradoxical, to find its advocates and disciples. Pyrrhonism and Materialism, Epecurianism and Stoicism had their successive culminations. The gay and mercurial, like Diderot and Voltaire, laughed and made merry with "the great humbug of the Universe," and sought only, like Aristippus, to win from the passing hour its full complement of pleasure. Amusement was their only aim—annihilation their only hope.

The severe and saturnine, affecting the masculine virtues and indomitable volitions of the Stoics, found a congenial system in the imperious ethics of Fichte, and in his pure and proud faith in the omnipotence of the will, a pretence and a paradigm for their self-complacent egotism. Both Sybarite and Stoic expressing, under opposite forms, the extremes of sublimated self-seeking.

From this Chaos of partial and opposing systems, Schelling freed himself by a daring and sublime hypothesis, a bold affirmation of ontological truth, which affected not to justify itself by any laborious psychological analysis, but to the elucidation of which all recent discoveries in mental and physical science indubitably tend.

The fatal defect of the Kantian philosophy, the difficulty of imputing validity to our subjective conceptions, is here supplied by assuming the identity of that which knows, with that which is known; thus integrating all antagonisms, even the great antagonism of matter and spirit, the insuperable problem in every dualistic system.

In the philosophy of Schelling, the real and the ideal are equally represented. God and nature no longer appear as two conceptions fundamentally and essentially distinct, but all things are living and instinct with a divine energy. The idea of progress as the gradual development in Humanity of this inherent energy was now for the first time intelligibly and distinctly stated. Only recently have men begun to know that the destiny of the race is onward, forever onward. The successive forms, laws, creeds and institutions of society are no longer regarded as ultimate, and it is seen that any attempt to perpetuate the same beyond the time when they represent the average intelligence of society, can only lead to stagnation and paralysis. We have learned the significance of the proverb that says the new wine cannot be kept in the old bottles.

Intimately associated with the belief in progress, is that recognition of the true value of the present, which is so prominent a feature of our time.

In this despised present, men begin doubtfully to acknowledge a divinity—the last messenger of God to man—in whose bosom lies treasured the hoarded wealth of the past, and the possibilities of the infinite future.

To live well and happily in the moment is our perfect wisdom. "Five minutes to-day," says Emerson, "are as much as five minutes in the next millenium."

An abandonment to this serene, instinctive and trustful life, is a virtue of our age, and a legitimate product of its philosophy. Jesus also taught men to live in the moment without anxiety or fear, but his disciples failed to imbibe his cheerful faith.

The Greek philosophers, almost without an exception, represented life under a gloomy aspect. Endurance and submission, rather than love and joy, were the virtues of their age.

The Germans, who have been the enunciators of so many great truths, were the first to give emphasis to the idea that man's immediate duty and true mission is to conform the present to his ever expanding ideal. If God is the "Life of the world," if he is in the process as well as in the form, then is he in every phase of the process, and every moment has its message and its import.

"Surprising, indeed, on whatever side we look" (says one of the young, Heaven-taught seers of our day), "is that revival of the individual consciousness of a living relationship with the All-Good. Our literature is every day more deeply tinged with the sense of the mysterious power which animates existence and governs all events."

This philosophy of identity, under which are included all those views and opinions which are generally in New England classed under the name of Transcendentalism, perhaps we can nowhere find so pure and poetic an expression of these ideas, from which the intellect has derived at once inspiration and repose, as in the writings of Emerson. Yet, although the truths which inform his pages are essentially the same with those of the new German school, he seems to hold them rather after the manner of the Neo-Platonists than of the modern Germans. Plotinus and Proclus, Plutarch and Marcus Antoninus are evidently greater favorites with him than Schelling and Hegel. If I were inclined to look for a flaw in Emerson's crystalline intellect, I should probably find it in a want of that due appreciation of the real, the eternal and necessary correlative of the ideal, which constitutes one of the distinguishing merits of Schelling's system. Not the less true is it that the Essays contain the essential oil and expressed perfume of those truths which have infused a new spirit into the life and literature of the nineteenth century, while in their author we see a striking example of that serenity of soul which is a necessary result of his philosophy. "Beholding identity and eternal causation, the soul is raised above passion, and becomes a tranquillity out of the knowledge that all things go well."

Goethe also tells us that he derived from the theory of identity, as he obtained it from Spinoza, the serenity which pervaded his maturer life. "After seeking in vain for a means of interpreting my strange moral being, I found in the Ethics of Spinoza a calm to my passions, a wide free view over the sensuous and moral world."

By superficial observers, Emerson is often compared to Carlyle; but in Carlyle this all harmonizing sense of the unity of being (the distinguishing characteristic of Emerson's intellect), is manifestly wanting; and notwithstanding his frequent allusions to the new German philosophy, as containing the secret of a higher revelation for those who are capable of receiving it, yet it is evident that the struggle of man with destiny entirely possesses and absorbs him. The mountain of reality presses heavily on his giant heart, and its Titanic throes cannot shake off the superincumbent weight. A fierce unrest consumes him. His incessant calls to labor sound in our ears like the dismal knell of the "work-house clock" summoning a benighted race to their hopeless toil. "For, man's highest blessedness," he tells us, "is that he toil and knows not what to toil at." We recognize in him vast energies, impetuous volitions, a wit emanating from the consciousness of dissonance and disruption; a mirthfulness that makes us weep or shudder, but never do we see in him "the level glance, serene and steadfast, that marks the God."

Carlyle is still struggling with destiny, still overwhelmed and saddened by the contemplation of the "void and formless infinite," perplexed by the fearful antagonisms of good and evil, life and death, time and eternity.

The editor of the Boston Quarterly has been sometimes classed among the New England disciples or teachers of Transcendentalism, and he has, in fact, from time to time exhibited some predilections for its doctrines, as diluted by Cousin, but he has never found that point of view, from which alone these truths can be seen and comprehended as one harmonious system. He has by turns affirmed and denied the great truth of man's knowledge of the absolute, through the mystical union of God with humanity. Yesterday he believed in the impersonality of the reason; today to deny its *personality*, is to deny our own. In laboring to define human personality, and to demonstrate the exact nature and scope of its powers of cognition, will, &c., he involves himself in endless contradictions and inextricable difficulties, thus furnishing another evidence that nature abhors limitation, overflowing all our landmarks and annulling all our distinctions. In one of those aphorisms of Novalis, where a profound truth is often expressed under the form of a bold and startling paradox, he says, "men think it a vulgar error to represent God as a person, but we have yet to learn that man is not less impersonal than God." When we attempt to separate man from his life in God, we have nothing left but Mr. Brownson's "simple faculty of cognition," or the "*Tabula rasa*" of Locke. In his denial of the impersonal reason, in his review of Charles Elwood, April, 1842, Mr. Brownson seems already to have forgotten "that life which is the light of the world, and in which we live, and move, and have our being," a gospel, which in 1841, he quoted as containing the only intelligible solution of these problems.

Like a comet moving in a narrow ellipse, he sweeps athwart our hemisphere "with fear of change perplexing nations"—darts towards the central orb of truth, and is off again ere we can say "*Ecce Venit*" to the regions of outer darkness.

Carlyle, too, is to many readers but one of those nebulous meteors that hide in their rapid and eccentric course the very stars of heaven from our bewildered gaze. But with Carlyle a sincere faith lies behind this apparent scepticism—and when a calm telescopic glance is turned upon this blazing glory—this mighty mass of phosphorescent splendor, through the very centre of its burning heart, these constant stars may be seen shining afar off in the serene depths of ether.

The fact that Schelling himself has apostatized from the large faith of his philosophic creed, which has exercised so vast an influence on his age, does not in any way affect the truth of his doctrines and need not excite our surprise. Few men, says Menzel, are able to maintain themselves in a position so central, of such perfect equipoise and impartiality—and a wiser than Menzel has said an index or mercury of intellectual proficiency is the perception of identity.

Schelling's theory of a God immanent in Nature and in Humanity, on which he rested the possibility of absolute cognition, was, as we have seen, but a sublime hypothesis, and the sceptic still proposes to the idealist, although in fainter tones, the eternal question respecting the validity of his intuitions. "How will you demonstrate, how legitimate the truth of these eternal truths?"

As well might we ask the seer to demonstrate his apocalyptic vision of the future—the poet his fine sense of beauty and of love! Can a soul not beautiful, asks Plotinus, attain to an intuition of beauty?

The error seems to lie in the assumption, that all true conceptions and adequate ideas are capable of being immediately demonstrated as such to all minds. Unquestionably all the possibilities of humanity are latent in every individual of the race, but the degrees of actual development differ more than men are disposed to admit. No man can construct or accept a philosophy which transcends the level of his actual life. "The spring cannot rise higher than its source." *Alle philosophie musse geliebt und gelebt werden."*

Although true being is everywhere present, it is, as Plotinus has said, more or less present in proportion to our ability of receiving it.

According to Sir James Mackintosh, who is indeed no other than an agreeable Philistine, the theories of Fichte, Schelling, and Hegel, are so many attempts to fix the absolute as a positive in knowledge, while the absolute, like the water in the sieve of the Danaides, has run through as a negative into the abyss of nothing—

If we could arrest and appropriate it, it would no longer be the absolute. The individual intellect is in truth a sieve through which it *passes*, but in which it can never be arrested or contained.

Plato, who was disposed to seek the essence of our knowledge in ideas alone, did not attempt to enumerate these ideas, as if he shrank from subjecting them to a profane analysis. Schelling, as we have said, took his stand with Plato in the region of supra-sensible truths, where no partial results of observation could either confirm or refute him in his reasoning; yet his sublime hypothesis, in so far as it rests on the assumption of absolute identity, strictly coincides with the rigid deductions of experimental science.

Every new discovery in physics teaches that all difference is phenomenal. The integrity of being is detected under manifold disguises. The farther we push our inquiries into the different departments of science, the more obvious are the analogies subsisting between them. In nature all the lines blend and converge towards a common centre. The moment we attempt to distinguish and define, to draw lines and affix boundaries, we are perplexed and baffled by her fluidity and sameness. In the crystal we already detect a paradigm of vegetable forms, in the vegetable an approach to the sentient instinct, while sensation and volition present strange and subtle analogies with electricity.

The discovery of the dependance of the chemical affinities of bodies on their electric states—the detection of electric forces in magnetic phenomena—the close analogies subsisting between light, heat, and sound, all point to one primal energy in nature, the agent in all natural phenomena, as in the mind that perceives them—for mind itself, in so far as we are acquainted with its mode of being, is but a subtle force vibrating to the impulsion of other forces external to itself.

And what then is the omnipresent energy which determines alike the regular form of a crystal, the symmetrical structure of a flower, and the cyclic motions of a planet;—perhaps even the mysterious concords and harmonies of a human soul?—What is this invisible power, itself intangible and imponderable, from which all this bright apocalypse of visible nature is evolved?—which under certain ascertained conditions originates life in inanimate matter (see Vestiges of Creation, page 141), which dissolves into airy nothing the substance of the most solid mountains, which makes and unmakes all things.

"Nature," says Emerson, "is the incarnation of a thought and turns to a thought again." Paradoxical as this may seem, it is the affirmation of a simple fact. Berkeley, after all, was perhaps nearer the truth than has been imagined. For the question between him and his opponents was not whether the objects of perception have a *real* existence out of the mind, but simply whether they have a solid substantial existence—whether the things which affect us from without be matter or spirit?

When Berkeley says that these objects and qualities are but the immediate effects of the ever present Deity, he assumes a sublime truth in strict accordance with the results to which all modern researches into the internal structure and equilibrium of matter evidently point.

All that we know of matter may be comprised in a statement of the laws by which certain forces emanating from certain centres act upon each other. None of our senses ever go behind these forces, and we are unable to determine whether they have a substantial basis or proceed simply from an ideal centre.

Since Leibnitz rejected the Newtonian theory of hard, impenetrable, insoluble atoms, and introduced his own hypothesis of monads, or simple, spiritual, inextended units, essentially possessed of attractive and repulsive forces, science has been slowly but surely approximating to a more spiritual apprehension of the material world and of the laws by which it is governed,—to a theory which should remove the great stumbling-block of matter which has proved so formidable an obstacle in the path of the cosmogonist, and which the Manicheans and their modern disciples have elevated into the rival and adversary of Deity.

This theory of Leibnitz, when presented in a more finished state by Boscovitch, very generally superseded that of Newton. His idea that the properties of bodies depend on certain forces emanating from geometric points, or points bearing certain relations to each other in space, has subsequently received a striking confirmation from the discovery that the chemical affinities of bodies depend on their electric states; and the physical philosopher already confidently anticipates the time when the chemical problem shall be changed into a mechanical problem—a question of forces, distance and time.

"But what, then," asks the materialist, "are these ultimate atoms—these inextended points—or, as Exley has recently more correctly designated them, these 'spheres of force?'—in what do the powers and properties that pertain to them inhere?"

To this question science has returned no positive answer. All our inquiries into the laws of sensation and the phenomena which induce sensation have revealed to us only "an elastic fluid (?) vibrating to the impulsion of elastic media."

"The intellect ignores matter." "Solidity is an illusion of the senses."

May we not then reasonably assume that the latent, yet immediate and inherent principle of the forces which represent matter is the great "caused entity" of Spinoza, which manifests itself under the two modes or attributes of "extension and thought." The life of "the world?" Thus are we again brought back to the great fact of unity in diversity—to the primal manifestation of that mysterious law of polarity which comprehends all phenomena—to that absolute identity which is the starting point and result of all philosophy. And thus is the mystic God-lore of an earlier age elucidated and justified by the scientific researches of our own.

Let us not decry the age in which we live—it is rich in good gifts and instinct with an infinite hope. Though conversant in all prudential and practical arts, it is not deserted of the ancient wisdom. It is mystic and devout, yet patient and diligent in investigation and research. An age in which mighty secrets have been won from nature by the ceaseless questioning of her solitary votaries, in which science seems about to restore to us all that the imagination has from time to time surrendered to the narrow scepticism of the understanding. Already she has whispered to us the secret law of Nature's boldest miracles,—she has imparted to us a spell by which we may restore the oracles of the past, and has initiated us into the possible modes and conditions of a more spiritual and sublimated existence.

The limits of human knowledge, so accurately defined in the Augustan age of French literature, are now removed beyond even the range of conjecture.

But yesterday man pondered in blank over the origin of worlds; today we read the secrets of creation in the cavernous depths below and in the starry vaults above. We not only weigh the massive bulk of Jupiter or Saturn as in a balance with unerring precision, but by the sublime induction of La Place, we have ascended from investigations concerning the size, figure and motion of planets, to an intelligible theory of their birth. We see worlds in every stage of formation slowly evolving from an imponderable ether, and by the aid of the subtle process of analysis, invented by Newton and Leibnitz, are enabled to map out the bright pathway of the stars on the vast blank of the unrecorded past and illimitable future! Science in these latter days has wonderfully enlarged our perspective.

Our range of observation both in space and time is infinitely expanded. The reflecting man is no longer in danger of mistaking his garden wall for the boundary line of the universe, nor the nineteenth century for the hour of doom.

The old fountains from which the great and good of past ages drank wisdom and power are reopened, and their sacred and long sealed waters flow freely beside the dusty highways of life. Even the silent tombs of Etruria and the desolate temples of Egypt yield up their jealous secrets, and teach through their eloquent anaglyphs the universality of our own mythology. The torch of science gleams athwart fretted altars and graven obelisks, and the old stones become vocal beneath its ray, and pour forth a Memnonian music. Yet in the very presence of the mighty past, men aspire to a future that shall confirm the great idea of unlimited progress. Everywhere they recognize a progressive life, a beneficent law; and know that to place themselves in harmony with these laws, to "fall into the divine circuits," is to find both freedom and repose.

> "Though baffled seers cannot impart
> The secret of its laboring heart,
> Throb thine with nature's throbbing breast
> And all is clear from east to west."
>
> *Essays—2d Series.*

In asserting that the fontal idea of Emerson's writings, as of the philosophy of the age, is absolute identity, I have not been careful to avert from them the imputation of Pantheism, Platonism, Spinozism, &c., &c. It matters little how we designate this manner of interpreting the phenomena of being, since it contains an inherent vitality which alike survives neglect and defies ridicule.

Superficial and timid men may decry these ideas as unintelligible or profane; but what rational ground of faith is left to him who doubts that God is over all and in all, that evil is but the absence and privation of good, and that all apparent evil must give way before a fuller development of the life that is within us? Only when the knowledge that the highest dwells ever with us becomes "a sweet enveloping thought," shall we be enabled to lead a single and trustful life, "to live in thoughts and act with energies that are immortal."

"Poetry and Imagination"

C[yrus] A[ugustus] B[artol]*

We come now to by far the most original and peculiar of these volumes, the poems by Mr. Emerson. To his genius, considered in its peculiarity, we bow. We own the spell which, more powerfully perhaps than any other American writer, he has thrown over our fancy. We know of nothing in the whole range of modern writers superior in original merit to his productions. He is "of imagination all compact." To read his finer pieces is to our poetic feeling like receiving a succession of electric shocks; and each additional line in them, communicating subtilely with all the rest, multiplies the force of this ideal battery. He is so frugal of language, as to let no phrase stand which is not charged with meaning. His merit, however, is not uniform. He is sometimes trivial in his themes, but never weak or wordy in their treatment. He is occasionally vague and mystical, but the brilliant distinctness usual in his thoughts and illustrations we take for proof that all his sentences refer to something real in his own mind. His best strokes cut below the superficial impressions made upon us by ordinary writers, and chisel themselves in the memory; while the softest musical rhythm is often so connected with the sharply arranged parsimony of his words, that passages repeat themselves in our involuntary recollection, as in the mysteriously sounding chambers of the spirit we hear over and over again the tunes of some great master. We are always glad to confess our obligation for intellectual helps, and we have to thank Mr. Emerson for the strong flashes of wit and sense, clad in bright imagery, with which he has often waked our minds from slumber. His discernment is as keen as his invention is fruitful. No man has a finer eye than he to trace those secret lines of correspondence which run through and bind together all parts of this lower frame of things. And even when we have been in the very spot in the realms of thought where he pitches his tent, he will detect some hidden analogy, and surprise us with a new observation. We know of no compositions that surpass his in their characteristic excellence. Even his unshaped fragments are not bits of glass, but of diamond, and have always the true poetic lustre, an inward gleam like that playing amid the layers of a sea-shell. Some of his conceptions are turned into as admirable expression as we find in Milton's sonnets or Shakespeare's songs.

We have thus praised this writer, and, as some may think, overpraised him, in the sincerity of our hearts. Our reference has, we find, unconsciously included his prose as well as his poetry. But they are both of a piece, and bear alike the stamp of their author's intellectual unity. The same affluent and over-mastering imagination, the same grasp of all the powers of language, the same faithful report from sight and experience,

*Reprinted from *Christian Examiner*, 42 (March 1847), 255–62.

prevail throughout all his productions. But our criticism must find fault with the same frankness with which it bestows eulogy, and will be for that but the more prized by our friend's magnanimous spirit. He has, we think, more height than breadth. He shoots up like the pinnacle of an *aiguille* mountain into the atmosphere of the great poets, but he lacks altogether their various richness and comprehensive proportions. He is dry and cold in the comparison. The productive fields do not so spread out below the frosty cone of inaccessible sublimity which towers above. There is more of a hard, steel-like glitter than of the hue of life in his landscape. He is, in fact, rather the poet of a class than of the race. The circle of his sympathies is narrow. His intense admiration of a few forms of life and character threatens to banish the broad spirit of humanity. With all his nobleness and purity of sentiment, in the ascendency of his fancy he can hardly restrain himself from pouring contempt on most of his kind. In view of vague possibilities of achievement, he unworthily disparages actual genius and character. The heart in his poetry is less than the head, and this causes a deficiency for which nothing else can fully atone. Only a transcendent splendor and wealth of intellect could redeem many of his pieces from condemnation and forgetfulness, as being frigid and unfeeling. These are sad flaws in such noble workmanship. Did a fellow-feeling for human nature in all its varieties equal and fill out his other traits, we might think the great poet of America had been born, to bring on our flourishing Augustan age. But, as yet, our hearts acknowledge a more genial and enlivening influence from several of our other native bards. Would that one whom we unfeignedly respect might not only show his power of soaring to the empyrean, but hover with a more wide and loving interest over the lot of his fellow-men! It may be for want of this all-embracing sympathy that his flights are so infrequent, and that he can but seldom continue long on the wing. If he could but kindle his soul with some great conception of human fortunes, and write a generous epic of this our human life, including its great trials and accomplishments, its sublimer aspirations and hopes, we hazard little in predicting that it would be a production to mark the age.

And yet we hardly know how he could have the kind of human sympathy which we most value for the inspiration of such an undertaking, with his present views of religion. There is no recognition in his pages of the Christian faith, according to any, however catholic, idea of it which we are able to form. He seems to have no preference of Jesus over any other great and good man. He either does not accept the evidences authenticating a divine revelation, or they press with but little interest upon his preoccupied mind. But what we must regard as his religious unsoundness strikes still deeper. He does not even appear to own any distinction between man and Deity. He talks of "the gods" as an old Roman would do. One personal Creator is not present to his thought. He does not go for the signs of such a Being into the broad circumference of his works, but confines himself within the little rim of his own individual consciousness. He puts aside Bible and ritual, and all human speech and outward light, for the "supersolar beam." In religion he fills the whole space of thought with that mystic element, which we must perhaps admit, but should confine in a corner. He does not, with a plain trust, examine the world which God has made, but curiously inspects the inverted image of it upon his own mental retina. He does not pay to the instincts of mankind or of society the respect he would render to the peculiar instincts of the animal, the bee or the beaver. And not taking cordially to his heart the Christian doctrines of a Father and a particular Providence, how can he strongly embrace the dependent doctrine of human brotherhood, or feel the unlimited sympathy which this doctrine inspires? We speak here, of course, of his system. We doubt not the kindness of his actual relations with men. We believe a hearty historical faith in Christianity would add greatly to the power of his genius. The views we have alluded to so underlie and run through his writings, as almost to amount to the proposal of a new religious faith,—a presumption which of course astounds us, simple believers in the New Testament on what we deem irrefragable grounds. His ideas carry him wide of the humility of the Gospel,—though they give rise in his own mind not so much to personal pride as to an immense self-respect and an enormous self-reliance. He is willing to trust to or lean upon nothing but himself;—a wonderful state of feeling, when we consider our real condition of dependence in all our powers,—our bodies resting on the attractions of material nature, every vital organ in us doing its part involuntarily, and only a single silvery thread branching into various filaments of the nerves of motion being held by our own will,—our intelligence but the shadowy reflex of Divine wisdom, like the light from distant worlds in the focus of the astronomer's telescope,—and even our moral nature roused not by an internal force of conscience alone, but quickened and kept alive so greatly by instruction and example. We are made to lean, and are stronger when we lean; and, if we do not lean, we fall. Our poet is dragged by his philosophy to a lower, or at least less commanding, height than, with a better understanding on this point, he might well attain.

We ought, however, to say, that the noblest principles of conduct are often asserted in his pages. We rejoice to find instances of a truly grand morality, and surpassing expressions of a pure and beautiful spirit; but are suddenly perplexed, as we proceed, by an optimism confounding all moral distinctions. He seems, in some places, to know no difference between light and darkness, sweet and bitter. Some revelations, hinted at in one of these poems, respecting a moral indifference in all things, are represented as made by "Uriel," and as causing the older deities, who had been in the secret, to blush. Alphonso of Castile, who is said to have thought he could improve upon the world as described in the Ptolemaic system, makes a bold figure, as the *protégé* of our author's pen, entering in heaven's court a general and unqualified complaint about all things under the sun.

There is an undertone of sadness running through these rhymes, sometimes harsh and scornful, and sometimes tender and refined, like angelic melancholy. We fancy this, too, may proceed from the peculiarity of the writer's belief. Seldom do we hear from him the truly cheerful strain which an earnest faith in Christianity would prompt. In that marvellously beautiful "Threnody," near the close of the book, the sorrow at the commencement is out of all proportion to the comfort at the end. It is the song of a stricken and struggling stoicism. The note falls irresistibly into the minor key. The very voice of consolation dies away in a wail. Alas! it is a poor application here made to the heart's wounds. They still bleed into the very ointment and balm. Every stroke of genius seems but to sharpen the regret. We remember in all our reading nothing more cheerless. It is a picture we would not hang in our heart's chambers. Every touch of the pencil draws a tear. As a painting of grief it is unrivalled,—but it is of grief alone. His hand proves false to him, when he undertakes to draw the form of the angel of peace. But that the soul of the poet might be deaf to our entreaty, we would implore him to turn his eye to those fountains of comfort which God has opened in the Gospel of his Son. For nothing can be more manly than an humble reliance on the means of revival and support, in our distress, which our Father has provided. Let him in lowliness receive these, and then, for the "Threnody," and the "Dirge" which precedes it, we should hope to receive lines as highly adorned with the lights of a creative fancy, but gilded from above also by the beams of heaven. There would at least be nothing in them of the "grief whose balsam never grew."

But we must pause. The analysis of Mr. Emerson's writings is no short or easy task. We would not pretend to oversee his summit, but only to note our impressions as we stand and contemplate it. His works, on account of their peculiarity, if nothing else, will probably be among the most enduring of the present time. There is much in them to admire and be improved by. And while we must think there is much also that is unsound and must be injurious to any mind imbibing it, we intend no personal commendation in expressing our conviction that he is a true-minded and righteous man, raised above every thing unworthy, and living a blameless life according to the monitions of his own conscience. Our calling is not to speak of the man, but of the author. We think the intellectual states and tendencies which we have noted chill and cripple his genius. He would make better poetry under the sway of views and opinions which he rejects or holds slightly. Were we writing with a different design, we might state other reasons for our regret at some of the sentiments which he expresses. We have now only to say, that they have injured his book, and must restrict the width and impair the quality of its influence. Would he fetch an echo from the universal heart, as it beats in the breasts of men from generation to generation, he must add to his style a faith and fervor as signal as its brilliancy and force.

We must retire from our survey of these fruits of Mr. Emerson's labors. And as we retire, the traits we have objected to fade away from our attention, and many a melodious note from "Each in All," "The Problem," "The Humble-Bee," "Monadnoc," and "The Forerunners," lingers and renews itself pleasantly in our ear.

But having been constrained in our criticism of Mr. Emerson's volume to suggest radical objections as well as to confess strong admiration, we feel it to be right that we should here try to characterize very briefly his mind. Poetry with him is no recreation or trial of skill, but the sincerity and very substance of his soul; it shows not the passing figures of a magic-lantern, but the convictions and views of life for which he would be a martyr. What, then, is the mind that we see on his page? It is a mind subtile, brilliant, rapid, and decisive. It is a mind in which intuition takes the place of logic, and an insatiable aspiration banishes every form of philosophy. The lightning of his genius reveals the landscape of his thought, and the darkness quickly swallows it up again, till another flash reveals more or less of it. It is a mind scorning forms, conventions, and institutions, and, if it could have its way, would substitute for all this stable platform of law and custom on which we live and work the extemporaneous impulses of the spirit. It is a mind that despises all that has been done, and regards the highest and most inspired utterances of men as but "syllables" dropping carelessly from the tongue; and holds in slight esteem achievements to which even itself is not equal, except in the dreamily anticipated efforts of some distant time and unknown world to come. It sees an ideal which makes it contemn all that is actual. It draws upon the well of its own conceptions, and deems that single draught will suffice though it pass by all other fountains. It aims at a lonely, insulated being, shut up to what may come to it from the general life of the universe, and prizes all foreign helps from its fellows only in proportion to their accordance with its independent results. It weighs and oversees, in its own notion, all characters of intellect and virtue that ever were, and Jesus Christ as confidently as the rest. As we might expect, the consequence of these tendencies is much narrowness, a very partial and unfair estimate of other and differing minds, great injustice in many respects to existing arrangements and instrumentalities, and a continual rising above the useful agencies of life into an atmosphere too rarefied to support any organization less singular than his. But let us more gladly observe, in addition to these things, moral courage, fearless candor, freedom from vanity and from many false leanings, if he has not reached all that are true.

The most important effect of the intellectual habits which he indulges is seen in the aspect of his religious faith. We have barely touched on this in remarking upon the quality of his poems. We feel, however, that perfect truth to our own persuasions requires us to take here distinct notice of the point. Of the primary religious sentiment of the soul, that of reverence, we perceive, especially in his last publication which we have reviewed, but the faintest traces. The personal God of the Gospel, as well as the supernatural manifestation of that God in Christ, is in exile from all his pages. We have already alluded in another connection to this singularity. We recur to it that we may do justice to his positive faith, by noticing the substitute for an Almighty Parent which he finds in an impersonal universal essence, identical with his own spirit and with the common life of nature and of man. There is no print of kneeling on any ground he traverses, save to this vague and undefinable power. We must think his idea a poor basis for any just or truly elevated worship. We know he may think that he exalts the Deity by pantheistically making all things deity. But we affirm that he so degrades the Deity, and not only weakens the religious sentiment, but saps the foundations of good morals, though no devoted friend of his could appreciate more highly than we his personal integrity and purity of heart. So imaginative, so passionless, and so beautiful a frame of spirit as his could be left with moral safety under the influence of views which the virtue of the millions of men could not abide for an hour. If his mind were popular, we should fear that the tenor of his writings would lead multitudes away from God, and set them adrift upon the stream of their own undisciplined inclinations. We admire, nay, we will confess, in spite of all we have said, love the man, but all the more we feel it to be necessary to set up a bar against the operation of many of his sentiments upon our own minds. We wish him the largest success in all that he has done to refine and elevate the community, but we are obliged by a sense of duty to put in a protest against the soundness of much that is implied in his various publications. And may God, for him and us all, bless the truth and prosper the right!

"New Poetry in New England"

Anonymous*

From traffic to treason nothing is safe against Yankee versatility. The sons of New-England are omnipresent in every region, whether of space or thought. If you take the wings of the morning for the uttermost parts of the earth, you may expect to find that they have got there long enough before you to carry off the best bargains, and set up a newspaper: they abound in every corner, from Kamschatka to Cape Horn, and frequent the Arctic Ocean and the Great Desert with equal facility. Whether any of them might be met with by descending to certain unmentionable depths, may seem a delicate question, but we have no hesitation in

*Reprinted from *United States Magazine, and Democratic Review*, 20 (May 1847), 392–98.

answering it in the affirmative: they are not likely to neglect a locality so rich in curiosities, and so fruitful in hints for new patent cooking-stoves and hot air furnaces. Not less adventurous are they in the continents and recesses of the intellectual world. They are ready to explain all questions, and debate all difficulties. From cyphering to psychology, nothing daunts them; and it must be confessed, that they seldom attack their subject altogether in vain. Whether it be a singing book, or a new system of English grammar, they turn the matter in hand to profitable account. They are, undeniably, a nation *sui generis*—a metaphysical, machine-inventing, money-making people, that never had their like. Whatever comes they are prepared for, from making a railroad to contriving a new-fashioned pocket-comb. They are never caught napping—never are in want of resources, and always fall upon their feet. Their hands, to be sure, are very near to their heads, something nearer than to their hearts. What they think they do, with energy sharp as their own winds, and rugged as the mountains on whose barren sides they are nurtured. Thinkers and doers are they; let them have that praise; if not always the broadest and most comprehensive of thinkers, at least the most resolute, earnest and persistent of doers. They never grow weary of action, and never suffer their eyes to be seduced from their aim. If a mountain stands in their way they cut it down; if an ocean, they fill it up, or get the better of it by some shrewd stratagem. They are careful of boundary lines, and unconquerable sticklers for individual rights. They claim their due from others to the last stiver, but having got it, they are no niggards, only business is business, and generosity is another thing. If sometimes from crooked conviction they come short of the right and the wise, no capricious impulse betrays them into the wrong and the foolish. Their nature is not hot, but strong—not volcanic, but steady and sure. They go by foresight more than by hope; what they desire is the reason of the thing, and on that they will stand till doomsday or after. They know most of the force of ideas; in the power of irreflective enthusiasm, of spontaneous, unquestioning passion, they have less experience. But ideas they are convinced to be substantial and creative. They will starve for them, fight for them, die for them. They would even move the world with them, were they not sometimes too apt to take one idea for the sum of all ideas, and to urge it with such one-sided pertinacity, as to drive men from it by sheer re-action. But above all, they are men of conscience. Their great question is, "what is right?" Starting from a jealous guardianship of what they reckon to be right, as regards themselves personally, their insatiable logical faculty hastens to inquire what is right for other men, for all men, and that they are no less zealous to argue for and to work for.

Above all, like other natives of cold and sterile countries, and like all races in whom the intellect and practical faculties predominate, their's is an unconquerable love of liberty, as well as an exhaustless devotion to the common cause. They love their country, not so much because it is their birth-place, as because it is the residence of the race to which they belong. In them, what is called public spirit, is perhaps stronger than in any other branch of the Anglo-American family. The honor of New-England, of their native state or city, is never out of their minds, go where they may. A Bostonian cannot doubt that Boston is a better town than any other, though others may have some slight advantages; and if he were called to make a new map of the world, he would not fail to put Massachusetts in the centre. This too, is at the bottom, a noble feeling. It is in essence the devotion of the individual to the good of the community. What it has done for New-England would not be easy to calculate.

Next to this public spirit the Yankee character is distinguished for depth and activity of the family sentiment. The best of fathers and mothers, and brothers and sisters, are to be found in New-England. A parent there, is a providence to his children. For their education he spares neither expense nor pains; and their success in life is far dearer to him than his own. From this sentiment springs the excellent care New-England has always paid to her schools and institutions of learning, and to the maintenance of correct moral influences for the young. Indeed, these two impulses, public spirit and family affection, are the keys of New-England's history, past and present.

It is remarkable that, of the American poets whose names are at all familiar, the majority come of this stock; Bryant, Dana, Halleck, Whittier, Longfellow, and Willis,—to name no others. Their writings, through whatever personal peculiarities, all display the striking trait of New-England men—the predominance of the intellect. There is no rich southern glow about them, no exuberance of mellow, sunny, gushing enthusiasm. Of them all, Halleck, Longfellow, and Willis are the least Yankees, the most graceful and genial; the latter is also the author of more love poetry than all the others put together, though at the same time he is the least earnest and the most desultory. And now here are new names for our Olympus, also from New-England; touching them and their works, as upright and faithful critics, we have our word to offer.

First, by right undeniable, we have placed the name of RALPH WALDO EMERSON, whom there is little risk in pronouncing the most original, not only of American poets, but of living writers. He is no vendor of second-hand notions, but a man on his own account, who gives you jewels from his own mines, and of his own setting. Not that he deals in jewels only. We do not receive him as an infallible witness, are scarcely willing to reckon ourselves among his indiscriminating admirers, and have little sympathy with those who fail in the attempt to imitate his style. This class of persons is, however, too limited to be worthy of any serious notice: and as they were predestined to inanity, there is no reason why they should not take it in this way as well as any other. Certainly no disease could be more harmless to the public at large. But small as is our sympathy for these unfortunates, we confess to a feeling even less amiable towards the whipper-snappers and dilettanti who, at safe distance, presume to discharge their pop-guns at the diamond fortress of this man of genius. For the former class pity is possible, for the latter it is not.

Though we are writing under the title of New Poetry, Mr. Emerson is not altogether a new candidate for the laurel. More than ten years ago he made good his right to the name of poet, in a little book called Nature. Though wearing the guise of a philosophical essay, and written in prose, it was still a poem. You might dispute the theory which pervaded it, and find the author guilty of every heresy in the theological and metaphysical catalogue, but there was no escaping the beautiful enchantment which shone over every chapter, clear and beguiling as the aroma of woods on a May morning. Since that time, Mr. Emerson, living at Concord, Mass., upon his own fortune, (Heaven send us all that same blessed independence!) has kept good his acquaintance with the world mainly through college-orations and popular lectures, many of which have been published. Indeed, two duodecimo volumes, which he has given us as essays, and which have justly received very wide attention, were first brought out in the lecture-room. It is scarcely necessary to say, that they are all streams from the same fountain.

Those who have heard Mr. Emerson speak have enjoyed a pleasure, of which, in passing, we would fain give our readers some idea. You enter the hall, whose seats are tolerably filled with an audience motley enough. There are shrewd men of business and pale men of books, fashionable gentlemen and ladies, studious, timid youths, impassive editors, solemn clergymen, confirmed lion-hunters, skin-flint brokers, important politicians, pale mystics, oily counsellors, and fiery radicals, all waiting in peaceful contiguity for the hour that shall wrap them into an unknown world. Some maiden ladies, no strangers to the scene, are perhaps busy knitting. Precisely at the moment, the rather tall and gracefully awkward form of the orator ascends the platform. With a glance of his cool gray eye over the audience, the over-coat is laid off, and the manuscript drawn from the pocket. The man stands before you, his forehead narrow and slightly retreating, his nose prominent, all his face transparent, earnest, surcharged with thought, but yet strangely fresh and youthful, like one just from the company of those Olympian bards,

> "Who sung
> Divine ideas below,
> Which always find us young,
> And always keep us so."

With the first tones of his voice comes a new charm; rich, mellow, musical, not of great compass, but of great flexibility, managed more by impulse than by study, it is fit for its use. Mr. Emerson employs few gestures, and those wholly spontaneous. As he reads, he raises his eyes and looks straight forward, not at the audience, but beyond them. He is not aware of his listeners, or of the effect he is producing; he is occupied with his thoughts. His oratory is thus of a style peculiar to himself, but yet no speaker has more perfect possession of his audience. Even those who do not comprehend him, cannot but listen as if they did, borne along by the flow of that unique, opaline soliloquy. If he uses an illustration it is never in vain. We remember listening one night when he compared life to a wintry sea, and men to lonely barks driving over its waves, just hailing each other, and flitting past. The bleak wierdness of that moment we have never forgotten. You felt yourself out there, hurried along the cold, mountainous ocean, whence and whither, Who knows?

Mr. Emerson's humor is as happy as it is idiosyncratic. He has so much of the quality of a good joker, that sometimes you are inclined to set that down as his proper function. When you least expect it, his wit will go sparkling through half a dozen paragraphs, and you laugh not boisterously, but inwardly and unweariedly. But through the whole he is a genuine New-Englander. Everything about him is of that climate. His eloquence is the aurora borealis of the head, not the tropic warmth of the heart. The usual key-note of his music is that same Yankee public spirit; in him the love of honor, of heroism, of justice, and his unconquerable repugnance to the loss of the individual in the mass. Persons accuse him of being vague and unintelligible. To all such the old reply holds good: he is not bound to furnish them with brains also. Those who bring this charge imagine they are criticising Mr. Emerson; in fact, they are only making a confession for themselves.

We suppose that even those who are tolerably familiar with Mr. Emerson's writings are not always clear as to whether he is most of a philosopher or a poet. To our thinking, he cannot be set down distinctively as either. He is both. He poetizes philosophically, and philosophizes poetically.—To this fact we must attribute his want of perfect success in either department. His poetry is too intellectual, and his philosophy too poetic. In the one there is too much of transcendental thought, and in the other too much of personal fancy. The one lacks the heat of life, and the other still fails of that universality which belongs to the Heaven-appointed Teacher of Wisdom. In the one, to borrow the illustration a witty friend always insists on in speaking of our poet-thinker, you find a man whose blood is not red, but of a cold, moonlight whiteness, and in the other you can scarcely ever forget the Yankee propensity to urge the idea or aspect of the subject at the time apparent, as if it were the sole embracing truth of things,—defects apparently different in form, but one in essence.

But though Mr. Emerson's writings lack the human element, being mainly intellectual, devoted to the statement of those sharp intuitions and brilliant affirmations which distinguish him from other men, but which always promise more than they perform, or else to that peculiar stoicism which is his favorite ideal of conduct, the volume now in our hands has one or two poems in which a warm and more universal affection distils in strains which, to our thinking, are nowhere surpassed. We had marked extracts from them, and from other pieces, for general and particular illustration, but an implacable want of space must cheat our pages of their expected ornaments.

As a prose writer, Mr. Emerson is often the most perfect of rhetoricians. Nothing can excel the beauty of many of his periods. The very manner in which his essays are constructed favors this perfection. They are made up of detached sentences—occasional inspirations, noted down at the time. When the subject is mature, these separate stones are builded together into a whole. We believe that his poetry is written in a similar manner. A line rises in his mind to-day, or something suggests an image; it is put down, and when the next line *comes* that is put down too; thus a single piece may be months in ripening. There is no impatience about it—no desire or design to have the piece off the hands of its author. It grows up spontaneously, without being forced; as a plot of ground bears trees, flowers and herbs all at once, so this man's mind brings variety of works together towards their perfection. There is something fascinating in this, though we admire more the artist whose soul is full of his theme, who rests from it neither by day nor night, flowing, like a great swelling river, enthusiastically on to his goal.

Our author's theory of Poetry may be read in his own words in the piece called *Merlin*. That theory is a faulty though not a surprising one. Mr. Emerson speaks for himself. To borrow a musical term, he would have his poet write in the *major* mode; of the richer and more interior harmonies of the *minor* he is naturally ignorant, and wisely says nothing.

The voice of the true poet must chime not only with the grander movements of nature, but with airs of summer; with bubbling brooks and rustling flowers; not only with manly impulses, the throb of assemblies, the hum of traffic, the resolve and energy of the hero, and the ecstacy of martyrs, but with the fears and hopes of the beloved maiden, the infinite joy thrilling the heart of the young mother, the yearning aspiration and ideal sense of beauty in the artist, the generous trust of friendship, and the sacred philanthropy of the Sister of Charity. Poetry is universal, and has no narrower limits than man. Its soul is the human soul—its sphere the whole of Nature. All emotions and thoughts belong to it. It is a higher language—Speech raised to harmony. Whatever may be spoken may be poetic; and the poet is he who, in harmonious words, speaks for all men what were otherwise unsaid, or said only in meaner and ruder phrase.

Herein too, Mr. Emerson fails, as we must believe, of a thorough idea of art. He seems to regard it as something accomplished, as well as begun, solely by inspiration. According to his words—and we have elsewhere heard from him the same thing—he would have the artist ascend the skies by a leap, not by the Jacob's ladder of preparatory toil. Let him lay aside all thought of means—all coil of rhythm and of number, and make every verse a surprise—a plan which, followed by a man of less genius than the one by whom it is prepared, and sometimes even when followed by him, can make every verse a very disagreeable surprise indeed.

Doubtless the artist will not be encumbered by the means he has to use. So far as he is truly an artist, and not a dabbler or mere learner, they are become to him a subsidiary part of himself. They are a domain he long since conquered, and reclaimed to his own purposes, an extension of his native faculties and organs, which he employs without thinking of them. But there was a time when he thought much of them, and gave days and nights to their acquisition. The colors of Titian, the chisel of Michael Angelo, the rhythm and number of Dante or Milton, and the thorough bass of Beethoven and Mozart, are indeed to each a "stairway of surprise," so unconsciously and wonderfully they are employed. But those masters gained this stairway by earnest striving and seeking, and no one who would accomplish any noble work of art can hope to do otherwise. He must first subdue and appropriate the means; afterwards he may work as if he were not aware of their existence. But this is not Mr. Emerson's view of the matter. In poetry, he seems to desire not art, but undisciplined, untrimmed nature. He does not appear practically to apprehend that art is not artificiality, is only nature raised to higher and more perfect degrees. To an unfinished, off-hand composition, provided it has some gleams of sense, he will incline to give more praise than to one wrought into fine simplicity and perfect expression. Gold in the ore, with all the dross that nature in her confusion has mingled in, is more attractive to his taste than the noble metal purified and refined. Fortunately, his practice does not rely altogether upon this opinion; we notice that some of the pieces in this volume have been re-touched for the present publication.

It is plain, however, that for the merely artistic form of his poems, Mr. Emerson has little care. He lacks too much that peculiar sense which is the origin of rhythm and number, to pay much attention to either. Not endowed with the perception and love of music, he feels no need of it, and generally does not aim at it. He never sings as the wild bird sings, for the mere delight of singing, but always because he has something to communicate. The meaning and not the melody is what he thinks of. Accordingly he attempts no experiments in versification, and makes no effort for variety. The metre he most employs is monotonous to the eye, but the monotony ceases when the ear and mind are called in. Out of this hackneyed measure, Mr. Emerson makes something piquant and various. To this effect, the rough irregularities which he delights in, but which nevertheless are often no better than gross blemishes, perhaps contribute something. These irregularities are at first offensive, but the thought, which is the all-in-all, is often so keen and piercing, and the imagination which illustrates it so new, unworn and fertile, that though you begin by blaming the faults of the poet, you end by yielding to the fascinations of the writer. There is a magic in what first strikes you as rude and uncouth, that somehow compels your admiration, where your ears could scarcely conceive of tolerance, and you are vexed with yourself for consenting to what your unbiassed judgment must condemn. So genius has its own will; no matter what the metal, the royal imprint gives it currency.

But a large portion of this volume stands in need of no apology or illusion in respect of poetic structure. There are passages in every piece which approach perfection. The sculptures of the Parthenon were not chiseled into more exquisite proportions than Mr. Emerson's creations from time to time assume. It seems that his thought has now and then a proper vitality which renders language fluid to his purpose, and takes on such harmony as its natural expression. In this regard, we have been especially delighted with *Each and All, The Problem, The World-Soul, Guy, Good-Bye, The Rhodora, The Humble Bee*, and the *Ode to Beauty*. Not to speak of more positive qualities, in form these poems come little short of being faultless. Occasional strains, scattered through other pieces, are equally beautiful.

Though the substance of Mr. Emerson's poems is thought, we are not to look in them for any system of thought. The building of such systems is not an office to which their author has been appointed. He has not the constructive logical faculty necessary for such service. His sight dwells on the aspect of truth, which, at the time, presents itself to him with wonderful, sometimes with startling power. Nothing seems hidden before him; under his eye nature makes haste to lay off her disguises to the innermost. We hope that we are now to be instructed in the arcana of gods and men. But we are disappointed. We get only hints concerning them. To-morrow we shall receive other hints; it may be in apparent contradiction to those of to-day, urged likewise as if they were the sole and central truth. This makes it impossible for any but a Philistine to criticise Mr. Emerson's philosophy except in the most general manner. Like all men in whom the poetic element is active, you will often find him insisting with exaggerated emphasis on views of truth, which he knows or supposes to be neglected by persons around him. He feels that such persons are overbalanced in one direction, and by a natural love of equilibrium, goes off himself in another. Thus, there is hardly a proposition in his poems, or his prose either for that matter, which you cannot find the opposite of in some other place. This may seem a misfortune to some, and a fault to others. It may, perhaps, be wished that our poet were free from every imperfection. But the Divine Providence is not so prodigal of men of genius that the world can well afford to do injustice to one of them. As a seer of the True, and an artist of the Beautiful, what we are ready to call his deficiencies, may in some sort be to our advantage. Were he gifted with a more comprehensive, philosophic insight, we might never have had from him the immortal among these poems. Were he a man of warmer and more spontaneous nature, and more thoroughly a poet, he could hardly have opened for us so many avenues to transcendental and spiritual laws. Let us receive him, then, gratefully and friendly for what he is, and thank God, as if we are wise we shall, that we live in the age and country which have produced such a man! For ourselves, personally, we are free to confess that we owe him a debt not easy to be estimated; and we know many who have ceased to follow him as a leader, who will make the same confession.

We are not anxious to deny the errors, philosophical, theological, or human, which can be charged upon this volume, in common with every other that Mr. Emerson has put forth. We are ready to surrender them to those critics who have a special vocation for discovering such sins, and punishing the sinners. Only let them be careful that they discover the deficiencies of the poet and not their own! Some of these deficiencies we have already at least hinted at. For the rest there are truths, to us of the very highest importance, which apparently lie without the scope of Mr. Emerson's perceptions. We have a conviction that he would lose nothing could he but recognize the law of Solidarity in its extent and fulness, and the omnipresent order of ascending and descending degrees, world above world, life within life, from nature up to the infinite, or come to understand the significance of the words Divine Humanity, and see that love, and not intellect, is the vital principle of the universe. We would that he were more a Realist, and that his poems were imbued with some higher spirit than the transcendental naturalism which pervades them. But what he is, he is; a man of most original, penetrating and beautiful genius. We cannot say that he is a great poet; that title will somehow not apply. The whole tenor of our criticism must, we think, show that such distinction cannot be claimed for him. But this can be said: the whole range of our literature does not furnish his peer in depth of thought, or exhibit such ideals of beauty as can be found in this volume.

There is one other point in Mr. Emerson's writings on which we have not dwelt expressly, but which is, perhaps, sufficiently indicated by what we have said or hinted. We mean their position, and the position of their author—two inseparable things—toward the present age. Mr. Emerson is, in no sense, an actor in any branch of the great movement of the times. He is a critic, standing aloof alike from the church, the state, and society. Neither religion, politics, nor reform, counts him in its ranks, but obedient to the impulses of his own moral and intellectual constitution, he works singly at his own business. For ourselves, we do not presume to find fault with this. Every man to his post, is our motto. Still we cannot look upon a book like the one in our hands, without a regret that such talents are not enlisted more in behalf of actual interests. We would that the poet stood very near to the throbbing heart of humanity, and were wholly inspired by the high hopes with which the race is stirred. There is deep sadness in seeing a man of genius thus cold and lonely, amidst the momentous issues of an epoch like the present. Goethe has been blamed because he was silent while the whole land was rousing itself to drive forth its invaders; but what shall be said of a man, who here in America, is a cool spectator of greater struggles than the world ever saw before? We have already answered this question. We must take him and his words for what they are, and above all, beware not to measure them by our standard but by his own. In so far as he is thus isolated he is not to be envied. The icy mountain peak may glitter in the sunbeams, and be first to catch the starlight, but the hermit who climbs up to dwell in its caverns, purchases the joys of that solitude at an irreparable cost.

[Emerson]

[James Russell Lowell]*

"There comes Emerson first, whose rich words, every one,
Are like gold nails in temples to hang trophies on,
Whose prose is grand verse, while his verse, the Lord knows,
Is some of it pr————No, 'tis not even prose;
I'm speaking of metres; some poems have welled
From those rare depths of soul that have ne'er been excelled;
They're not epics, but that doesn't matter a pin,
In creating, the only hard thing's to begin;
A grass-blade 's no easier to make than an oak,
If you've once found the way, you've achieved the grand
    stroke;
In the worst of his poems are mines of rich matter,
But thrown in a heap with a crush and a clatter;
Now it is not one thing nor another alone
Makes a poem, but rather the general tone,
The something pervading, uniting the whole,
The before unconceived, unconceivable soul,
So that just in removing this trifle or that, you
Take away, as it were, a chief limb of the statue;
Roots, wood, bark, and leaves, singly perfect may be,
But, clapt hodge-podge together, they don't make a tree.

"But, to come back to Emerson, (whom by the way,
I believe we left waiting,)—his is, we may say,
A Greek head on right Yankee shoulders, whose range
Has Olympus for one pole, for t'other the Exchange;
He seems, to my thinking, (although I'm afraid
The comparison must, long ere this, have been made,)
A Plotinus-Montaigne, where the Egyptian's gold mist
And the Gascon's shrewd wit cheek-by-jowl co-exist;
All admire, and yet scarcely six converts he's got
To I don't (nor they either) exactly know what;
For though he builds glorious temples, 'tis odd
He leaves never a doorway to get in a god.

*Reprinted in part from *A Fable for Critics* (New York: G. P. Putnam, 1848), pp. 28–32.

'Tis refreshing to old-fashioned people like me,
To meet such a primitive Pagan as he,
In whose mind all creation is duly respected
As parts of himself—just a little projected;
And who's willing to worship the stars and the sun,
A convert to—nothing but Emerson.
So perfect a balance there is in his head,
That he talks of things sometimes as if they were dead;
Life, nature, love, God, and affairs of that sort,
He looks at as merely ideas; in short,
As if they were fossils stuck round in a cabinet,
Of such vast extent that our earth's a mere dab in it;
Composed just as he is inclined to conjecture her,
Namely, one part pure earth, ninety-nine parts pure
    lecturer;
You are filled with delight at his clear demonstration,
Each figure, word, gesture, just fits the occasion,
With the quiet precision of science he'll sort 'em,
But you can't help suspecting the whole a *post mortem*.

    "There are persons, mole-blind to the soul's make and
    style,
Who insist on a likeness 'twixt him and Carlyle;
To compare him with Plato would be vastly fairer,
Carlyle's the more burly, but E. is the rarer;
He sees fewer objects, but clearlier, truelier,
If C.'s as original, E.'s more peculiar;
That he's more of a man you might say of the one,
Of the other he's more of an Emerson;
C.'s the Titan, as shaggy of mind as of limb,—
E. the clear-eyed Olympian, rapid and slim;
The one's two-thirds Norseman, the other half Greek,
Where the one 's most abounding, the other 's to seek;
C.'s generals require to be seen in the mass,—
E.'s specialties gain if enlarged by the glass;
C. gives nature and God his own fits of the blues,
And rims common-sense things with mystical hues,—
E. sits in a mystery calm and intense,
And looks coolly around him with sharp common-sense;
C. shows you how every-day matters unite
With the dim transdiurnal recesses of night,—
While E., in a plain, preternatural way,
Makes mysteries matters of mere every day;
C. draws all his characters quite *à la* Fuseli,—
He don't sketch their bundles of muscles and thews illy,
But he paints with a brush so untamed and profuse,
They seem nothing but bundles of muscles and thews;
E. is rather like Flaxman, lines strait and severe,
And a colorless outline, but full, round, and clear;—

To the men he thinks worthy he frankly accords
The design of a white marble statue in words.
C. labors to get at the centre, and then
Take a reckoning from there of his actions and men;
E. calmly assumes the said centre as granted,
And, given himself, has whatever is wanted.

"He has imitators in scores, who omit
No part of the man but his wisdom and wit,—
Who go carefully o'er the sky-blue of his brain,
And when he has skimmed it once, skim it again;
If at all they resemble him, you may be sure it is
Because their shoals mirror his mists and obscurities,
As a mud-puddle seems deep as heaven for a minute,
While a cloud that floats o'er is reflected within it.

"There comes———, for instance; to see him 's rare sport,
Tread in Emerson's tracks with legs painfully short;
How he jumps, how he strains, and gets red in the face,
To keep step with the mystagogue's natural pace!
He follows as close as a stick to a rocket,
His fingers exploring the prophet's each pocket.
Fie, for shame, brother bard; with good fruit of your own,
Can't you let neighbor Emerson's orchards alone?
Besides, 'tis no use, you'll not find e'en a core,—
———has picked up all the windfalls before.
They might strip every tree, and E. never would catch 'em,
His Hesperides have no rude dragon to watch 'em;
When they send him a dishfull, and ask him to try 'em,
He never suspects how the sly rogues came by 'em;
He wonders why 'tis there are none such his trees on,
And thinks 'em the best he has tasted this season.

[Emerson as a Lecturer]

Anonymous*

We listened to Mr Ralph Waldo Emerson's second lecture on Monday evening, as we always listen to him, with admiration and delight. Yet it is quite out of character to say Mr Emerson lectures—he does no such thing. He drops nectar—he chips out sparks—he exhales odors—he lets off mental skyrockets and fireworks—he spouts fire, and conjurer like, draws ribbons out of his mouth. He smokes, he sparkles, he improvises, he shouts, he sings, he explodes like a bundle of crackers, he goes off in fiery eruptions like a volcano, but he does not lecture.

*Reprinted from *Boston Post*, 25 January 1849, p. 2.

No mere description can do Emerson justice. We think he is improving *in his line*, and everybody knows, or ought to know, what that line is, for he is, doubtless, one of the most remarkable men of the day. He is the tallest kind of "corn." He exhibited on Monday evening a wealth of imagination, an opulence of imagery, and of original and peculiar thought which amounted to a surfeit. He went swiftly over the ground of knowledge with a Damascus blade, severing every thing from its bottom, leaving one in doubt whether any thing would ever grow again. Yet he seems as innocent as a little child who goes into a garden and pulls up a whole bed of violets, laughs over their beauty, and throws them down again. So that, after all, we are inclined to think no great harm has been done. He comes and goes like a spirit of whom one just hears the rustle of his wings. He is a vitalized speculation—a talking essence—a sort of celestial emanation—a bit of transparency broken from the spheres—a spiritual prism through which we see all beautiful rays of immaterial existences. His leaping fancy mounts upward like an India rubber ball, and drifts and falls like a snow-flake, or a feather. He moves in regions of similitudes. He comes through the air like a cherubim with a golden trumpet in his mouth, out of which he blows tropes and figures and gossamer transparencies of suggestive fancies. He takes high flights, and sustains himself without ruffling a feather. He inverts the rainbow and uses it for a swing—now sweeping the earth, and now clapping his hands among the stars.

We wonder if he will ever die like other men? It seems to us he will find some way of slipping out of the world and shutting the door behind him before any body knows he is going. We cannot believe he will be *translated*, for this would be too gross a method of exit. He is more likely to be evaporated some sunshiny day, or to be exhaled like a perfume. He will certainly not be seen to *go*—he will only vanish.

[*Nature; Addresses, and Lectures*]

Anonymous*

A new volume from Mr. Emerson—and yet not entirely new; for his "Nature" was one of his earliest publications, and many of the "addresses" have appeared in the pamphlet form. But this circumstance will produce no abatement, but rather increase, in the feeling of pleasure that they are accessible in the present form, and in the desire to obtain them. "Nature," we perceive, has undergone some revision. A sentence in the early volume, which we have more than once heard fondly quoted, but which, as it seemed to us was not in very good taste, "Almost I fear to think how

*Reprinted from *Christian Register*, 28 (29 September 1849), 155.

glad I am," now reads, "I am glad to the brink of fear,"—how much improved we need not suggest.

Mr. Emerson has added to the wealth of human thought and language. We enjoy the exhilaration in reading his writings, that he speaks of in crossing, we will not say "a bare common," or "in snow puddles," but certainly "under a clouded sky." It is gladness "to the brink of fear." Or to allude to another of his illustrations—"Turn the eyes upside down, by looking at the landscape through your legs, and how agreeable is the picture, though you have seen it any time these twenty years." As we read him, *we often look at truth through the legs*. It is beautiful, enchanting, but we are not then beholding the REALITY of things—and to remain too long in that position would produce congestion of the brain. It has been said that Mr. Emerson does not manifest much feeling. If so, it is because the "over-soul" for him has pressed down his particular soul. His imagination, his idealism, his speculative reason, have been exercised, perhaps, more than his heart. Would that he could always have spoken in a form so harmonizing with Christianity, as in the following words,—(and in spirit we confess he often leads us quite to the verge of this,)—"The best moments of life are those delicious awakenings of the higher powers, and the reverential withdrawing of nature before its God."

[*Representative Men*]

[George Gould]*

In the common phrase of the reviewers, Mr. Emerson would not be called a popular writer. His sentences are thrown off with such a want of logical affinity, and his ideas are so deeply imbedded in a mystic phraseology, that he can hardly become a universal favorite with those who at this day form the mass of the literary public; yet so long as intellect shall command homage, and men retain their partiality for erratic genius and brilliant oddity, there will not be found a lack of readers for this High Priest of strange sayings.

It has come to be the fashion of late, to discuss abstract principles in morals and mind, by the use of some historic personage as a type; and while nominally treating of individual character, to indulge in the widest range of generalization. Such is the nature of the book before us. It consists of a series of lectures on, Plato, or the Philosopher; Swedenborg, or the Mystic; Montaigne, or the Skeptic; Shakspeare, or the Poet; Napoleon, or the Man of the World; Goethe, or the Writer. We took up the volume, expecting to find it like the author's previous writings, a strange medley of dark and

*Reprinted from *Indicator* [Amherst College], 2 (February 1850), 214–20.

wayward sentences, from which at times, would gleam a brilliant thought the common eye might catch, but oftener presenting only a dreamy haze impervious to common sense and common interpretation. In this we were in a good degree disappointed. The book reads the most like plain English of anything we have yet seen from the author's pen; and though by no means free from much of his usual obscurity of expression, and want of logical connection, yet the general scope of his argument is tolerably easy of comprehension. An exception to this remark is the introductory chapter, on "The Uses of Great Men," which for vagueness, extravagance, and refined mysticism would have rivalled the ancient Sybil herself. We can have no patience with such a spirit of non-committal of ideas. If a man writes for the public, let him write so the public can understand him, and not wrap himself up in a cold and unbending self-sufficiency, and tantalize his readers with now and then a glimpse of an idea, as though every un-equivocal sentence he penned, was the surrender of an intellectual vantage-ground, which he must hasten to re-occupy by writing the dozen following in just the blindest jargon imaginable. We have not the presumption to charge our author with a want of a clear and definite comprehension in his own mind, of what he would express to others; although we confess he ap-pears to us, occasionally, to chase an idea into rather a thin atmosphere; nor would we assert that he is not in some measure necessitated to such a style by the peculiar subtility and range of his thoughts; yet that he has not been wholly free from a species of affectation of the mysterious and pro-found, we are the more inclined to suspect since reading this last volume. To say the least, it proves him to possess the power, when thus disposed, to write intelligibly.

We shall not attempt an extended notice of its contents. The book is eminently philosophical. With but few biographical incidents, each lec-ture, with one or two exceptions, is only the generalization of certain psychological phenomena into some fundamental law of human conduct. The first lecture presents Plato as the great representative, or prototype of all philosophy. All philosophy has two cardinal facts at its base, *amity* and *variety*. "These two principles re-appear and interpenetrate all things, all thought; the one, the many. One, is being; the other, intellect: one is necessity; the other, freedom: one, rest; the other, motion: one, power; the other, distribution: one, strength; the other, pleasure: one, con-sciousness; the other, definition: one, genius; the other, talent: one, earnestness; the other, knowledge: one, possession; the other, trade: one, caste; the other, culture: one, king; the other, democracy: and, if we dare carry these generalizations a step higher, and name the last tendency of both, we might say, that the end of the one is to escape from organization,—pure science; and the end of the other is the highest in-strumentality, or use of means, or executive deity." Plato was a balanced soul, perceptive of the two elements. A remarkable occurrance in this world of "one idea," a man was born who could see two sides of a thing. "Plato is philosophy, and philosophy is Plato."

The second lecture treats of Mysticism, in the person of Swedenborg; a man, "who appeared to his contemporaries, a visionary and elixir of moonbeams," but in the opinion of Mr. Emerson "led the most real life of any man then in the world." Swedenborg was a model saint. The problem he strove to solve was the Whence and What and Whither of life. Nature was to him, the "picture-language" of the Ideal and Spiritual. His peculiar views were set forth in his doctrine of "Series and Degrees" and "Correspondence." He saw nature "wreathing through an everlasting spiral, with wheels that never dry, on axles that never creak." But he ascended the series too high and stepped off into the invisible, thinking to unlock the meaning of the world! The popular objection against his system is its want of life and poetic expression.

Skepticism, according to our author, is running a middle course between the Infinite and Finite; the Relative and Absolute. All men are born with a predisposition to one or the other of these sides of nature—men of action and men of faith and philosophy. Montaigne is a man who avoids extremes, keeps cool, and is not ready to believe a thing until pretty satisfactorily proved. "He talks with shrewdness, knows the world, and books, and himself and uses the positive degree: never shrinks or protests or prays; no weakness, convulsion, no superlative: does not wish to jump out of his skin, or play any antics, or annihilate space or time; but is stout and solid; tastes every moment of the day; likes pain because it makes him feel himself, and realize things; as we pinch ourselves to know that we are awake."

Shakespeare was the type of Intellect. His greatness was rather that of the mass than of the individual. "Great men," says our author, "are more distinguished by range and extent than by originality. The Genius of our life is jealous of individuals, and will not have any individual great, except through the general." "Men, nations, poets, artisans, women, all have worked for him, and he enters into their labors." "A good reader can, in a sort, nestle into Plato's brain, and think from thence; but not into Shakespeare's. We are still out of doors. For executive faculty, for creation, Shakespeare is unique." Napoleon, Mr. Emerson styles the "incarnate Democrat." "He was the idol of common men, because he had in transcendent degree, the qualities and powers of common men. He came unto his own, and his own received him." But Bonaparte fell, for his life was "an experiment of intellect without conscience."

Goethe was the reporter of nature—the universal writer, "the philosopher of multiplicity, hundred-handed, Argus-eyed, able and happy to cope with the rolling miscellany of facts and sciences." "He has one test for all men—*What can you teach me?*" ["]I dare not say that Goethe has ascended to the highest grounds from which genius has spoken. He has not worshipped the highest unity; he is incapable of self-surrender to the moral sentiment. There are nobler strains in poetry than any he has sounded. There are writers poorer in talent, whose tone is purer, and more touches the heart. Goethe can never be dear to men. His is not even the devotion to pure truth; but to truth for the sake of culture."

Our limits have forbidden more extended extracts from these lectures, though we should have been glad to have enriched our columns more freely. They abound in many shrewd hits on ways and things, and some fine delineations of character. Particularly of the portrait of Socrates, in the first lecture, is admirably drawn. Of the whole series, we think the lecture upon Napoleon is the best, because it is the most popular; being in an unusual degree, free from that *subjective* mode of treatment, which the author is so much inclined to adopt, upon whatever theme he touches. On the whole, we think the book a great advance, in the way of clearness, coherence of ideas, and a practical aim, upon anything the author has yet published. We cannot but hope that Mr. Emerson is beginning to be convinced that the public are better pleased with what they can comprehend, than with what they can only stare at as mysterious and profoundly queer;—and that men like a little mixture of common sense in what they read, better than to witness the author's feats of "grand and lofty tumbling," as the play-bills have it, on an arena of fog and moonbeams. His style is better adapted for speaking, than for essay reading. There is such a precision in his use of words, and such a condensation of thought in his sentences, that his full meaning often escapes the reader, without a somewhat tedious process of perusal. The author's peculiar manner and accent in public address, is admirably calculated to remedy this defect, and bring out the key-words of an abstruse sentence with a tact and impressiveness that reveals much of what would otherwise be overlooked as impertinent and mystical. His conciseness in the use of language, is remarkable. There is not a superfluous word in all his works. In short, his writings present a most marked contrast between a style of almost mathematical brevity and precision, and ideas of such volatile and evaporative tendency, as hardly to come within the domain of sober reflection.

His style is poetic; but it is the poetry of intellect, rather than of the fancy. He has little to do with painting fine landscapes, and listening to the music of running brooks. His soul is wrapt in the great problem of Being. He gazes into the awful depths of his own nature, and culls the flowers of poetry that spring by the way-side of Life, and drinks in the harmonies that roll in upon his soul from the great ocean of the Universal Spirit. And yet, he betrays no enthusiasm, and never for once loses his cool self-possession. He never condescends to the maneuver of startling his readers with a sudden flash, but lies back on his dignity, and announces his truths with the quiet and collected air of a man who is conscious of dealing with great thoughts, and is more disposed to puzzle, than to make himself intelligible to, those whose understandings are too earth-wed to appreciate them.

Mr. Emerson's peculiar theological notions run through all his writings; evidently having a powerful influence in shaping his topics and style. We are at a loss whether his theology has done more toward molding the man, or the man his theology; but true it is, he has come to act in most wonderful harmony with his teachings. One could hardly reconcile such stoical self-reliance, and such a cool and studied irreverence toward all that is great and holy, with any thing else than the most ultra stage of pantheism. He virtually recognizes no higher Deity than himself. The very essence of his religion and philosophy is self-worship. With his standard of virtue, taken in the abstract, we have no fault to find; but it has little to do with the guilt or innocence of men. It is at most, but the virtue of fatalism, and not of choice. Every man is a law unto himself. To act out his own nature, good or bad, is each man's great life-work. To this strange conclusion his premises must inevitably drive him. He has had the candor to recognize the deduction in the following passage, in his lecture on Napoleon, after speaking of the causes of his inglorious end. "But it was not Bonaparte's fault. He did all that in him lay to live and thrive without moral principle. It was the nature of things, the eternal law of man and of the world, which baulked and ruined him." It is unnecessary to remark the tendency of such a philosophy to subvert the principles of a sound morality, and its complete antagonism to the spirit and teachings of Christianity.

In reading this book, we have been led to compare it with Carlyle's Hero Worship; both from the similarity of their design, and that they set forth perhaps in a clearer contrast, than any of their other writings, the peculiar tenets and characteristics of these two leaders of a new school of philosophy, in Europe and America. In these two books both write of great men; and yet their views are widely different. Indeed, their very titles indicate the distinction. Carlyle treats of Heroes: Emerson of Representative Men; for strictly speaking, he acknowledges no great men. Every man is great so far as he acts himself. Men differ not in degree but in kind; and are to be judged of, not by others, but by themselves. Carlyle believes in a royal line of Great Souls, which alone can penetrate into the Divine significance of Life. His great men are few, but universal in their genius; each Great Soul can be Prophet, Poet, Priest, or King, with equal readiness, according as outward circumstances may dictate. Carlyle's hero is the embodiment of earnestness; Emerson's of individuality. Carlyle's hobby is Insight; Emerson's, Self-reliance.

As a writer and thinker, Carlyle is the more intense and practical; but Emerson the more original and comprehensive. Carlyle's innovations on the common ways of thinking, are more apparent than real. The novelty of his words, and the fiery emphasis with which he utters them, often give to a very harmless idea, the semblance of a profound truth. Carlyle often passes for more than he is worth; Emerson as often for less. The ostentatious style, and oracular bearing of the former catch the eye at once; but time and thought are needed to measure the strength of the latter. Carlyle delights in a startling hyperbole; Emerson in a quiet paradox. Carlyle offends our taste; Emerson our common sense. The one will leave his impress on our style of writing: the other on our mode of thinking. In their moral tendency, we think the writings of Carlyle far less objectionable than those of Emerson. Emerson is the better philosopher; but Carlyle the better philanthropist. The mind of Emerson instinctively *generalizes* all the phenomena of society; and loses its interest in particulars, in striving to grasp the universal law of man and the world. The mind of Carlyle is narrow, powerful, concentrative and earnest; looks at sin and popular abuses in the concrete, and hurls the thunders of his invective at all their canonized Forms.

We will trace the comparison a step farther, and say we think Carlyle is on the retrograde, and Emerson on the advance, as a popular writer. Whoever will compare the essays on Burns, Voltaire and Schiller, with the monotonous and spasmodic cant of the Hero Worship, will not be long in discovering the marks of degeneracy; while he who, after losing himself amid the jargon of the essays on Circles and The Over-Soul, will turn to the volume now before us, will be equally expeditious in noting the evidences of a pleasing and decided improvement. All that Emerson needs to be universally read and relished, is to stoop to the common modes of expressing thought. Although we lament his errors, we must admire his genius. Whoever reads him, must think—think vigorously—think for himself; and though at times, his brilliant and wayward thoughts only dazzle and bewilder, we always rise from his perusal, with the consciousness that our intellects have been quickened and strengthened by communion with a master-mind.

[*Representative Men*]

L. W. B.*

The appearance of a new book from the pen of Mr. Emerson is an event of no little interest and importance in the literary world. We say this with confidence, notwithstanding the sneers and deprecations of many excellent people who are ignorant of his productions, and of a few who are not. It is a matter of fact that Mr. Emerson has numerous readers and warm admirers, and with these the cry of Nonsense! Absurdity! Blasphemy! will be of little avail. Since it can not be denied that he possesses a singular power of attraction and fascination over some minds, would it not be more just and philosophical to search for the elements of this power, than to decry and ridicule its effects?

*Reprinted from *Yale Literary Magazine*, 15 (March 1850), 203–06.

We can not believe, as some would fain have us, that his power is merely that of obscurity and mystery,—a sort of Masonic profundity, into the dark emptiness of which many spend time and toil to penetrate, and then care not to confess that they have laid out a fool's labor. We have too much faith in human nature to admit it; besides this our own reading has convinced us that the judgment of his admirers here, and the almost universal voice of foreign criticism is not false in awarding to him at least the merit of great brilliancy and attractiveness of style and abundant originality and richness of thought. The grace and fitness of his metaphors, the freshness of his expressions, the poetic and truthful originality of his descriptions, in which by the introduction of new items and new facts, unknown to the common-place book of the poet, he re-creates old scenes of which the eye was tired, and restores to them more than their primitive interest,—all these rare qualities it would be an easy task to illustrate from the volume before us; but they are so evident to the eye of the reader that we need not specify them particularly. Another and more important element of Mr. Emerson's power is an earnest and genial manliness. With this his writings are quickened and flushed as with a heart-blood. His reverence for virtue, his love of man, his hopeful faith in progress, his religious care for the spiritual above the material, and his unrestrained freedom of thought and speculation, must and do make him many friends among a class whom mere genius and intellect fail to conciliate. We think it no arrogance, if, in this place, we assume to represent the class of young men; and we may not believe that any cry of blasphemy or impiety, or any frightful exhibition of consequences, will ever convince the consciences of young men of the sinfulness of free-thought. The sin of blasphemy lies as we think, not in opinion, but in language. In the present instance, however Mr. Emerson's carelessness of other people's opinions, or rather his desire of irritating their ideas, may have led him into startling expressions, we are not ready to believe him guilty of intentional impiety.

We come now to speak of the substance of intellectual opinions which underlies the qualities we have described above. And we say in the outset that we speak of these with no favorable feelings. Mr. Emerson, both in his manner of life and manner of writing, seems to hold himself in a sphere beyond the weaknesses and limitations of ordinary humanity. Secluded in his cottage at Concord, he spends his time in rapt communion with Nature and with "the Spirit" only interrupting his meditations to make his annual journey to Boston, where his Egerian revelations are communicated to wondering disciples in lectures whose spiritual contents are afterwards set forth to the less appreciating vulgar by means of the material types of Monroe & Co. Now an oracular and exclusive style like this does not commend Mr. Emerson to the favor of this puritanic and democratic community. We feel toward him as toward those fantastic itinerant prophets, hatless and bearded, who sometimes attempt to enlighten our incredulous ears with a new apocalypse,—that is, we take pleasure in seeing him contradicted and "*snubbed*." But we have always noticed that the most effectual method to pursue toward these characters is not a course of dispute and argument, but one of concession and respect; to receive their disturbing novelties as if they were the most unquestioned, old-fashioned, matter-of-course orthodoxy; or (when this is impossible) as if they were at least nothing but very old and commonplace error. Then, certainly, if not before, will the unentertained angels be persuaded to shake off the dust of their feet, and leave the light-haters in peace and darkness. Thus we wish to show that the sublimated Emerson is much such an one as ourselves, that his oddities and peculiarities rise from very human causes, and that his oracular sayings find their proper category in some of the various "isms" known to the dictionary.

Perhaps the characteristic by which Mr. Emerson is best known is his obscurity. This we do not ascribe to affectation, though if we did there would be few to deny it. Neither is it due entirely to the abstract nature of his subjects, and the ethereal and spiritual substance of his thoughts, as his friends would fain persuade us. There is another cause, quite sufficient to account for it, and which is very well known to exist—*his excessive horror of cant*. This he learned in his early training as an Unitarian minister, and soon bettered his instruction so that his teachers discarded him. His hatred of cant has now risen to such a pitch that it has become a moral principle with him never to call a thing twice by the same name: we verily believe he would deny the Deity of Reason or his own inspiration, if it were offered to him in a formula and mentioned as "the same" and "the aforesaid," we only wonder that he has not conscientious scruples against the use of the personal pronouns. The obscurity that must result from the want of a nomenclature is too obvious to need further words.

Mr. Emerson's ostentation of universal learning has become in his later works, and particularly in this his last, so striking as to be a marked characteristic of his style. It is difficult to charge a character of such beauty and nobleness with the attempt to impose upon his reader's admiration; still we can not but think that this feature in his writing is some little relic of human weakness. We do not allude so much to his quotations from unused and unknown authorities, and his display of Chinese and Hindoo lore, as to the long and strangely diversified lists of names with which he continually decorates his pages, and which, however they may illustrate his meaning, excite an inward suspicion that they have a second object—to display the author's reading. His writings in this respect remind us strongly of compositions for the Piano-Forte, "arranged for the left hand only," instead of carrying his theme plainly along, with an explanatory counterpoint, he flies off in a celestial rhapsody of spiritual analogies, occasionally fetching in his harmony by sweeping up an arpeggio of great names, in incongruous juxtaposition, from Adam to the Poughkeepsie prophet,—the object being "to show the skill of the performer."

To leave these mere externals: in speaking of Mr. Emerson's

philosophical opinions it will be our chief end to assign him his proper place among philosophers. And first, he is *not* an Idealist,—at least in the sense in which the critics are pleased to consider him so.[1] That is, he believes in the reality of matter, in contradiction to the Ideal Theory of Berkeley. We are aware that in his essay on "Idealism" ("Nature," p. 59) he exhibits the nature and grounds of this theory in his most beautiful and eloquent manner, and it is from this, doubtless, that the critics have formed their opinion. Yet in the very next essay, he discards it expressly, in terms like the following. . . . "if it only deny the existence of matter, it does not satisfy the demands of the spirit. . . . The heart resists it, because it baulks the affections" p. 78. And again: "Let it stand then, in the present state of our knowledge, *merely* as a useful introductory hypothesis," p. 79. Will not this clear him from the charge of "Idealism," which most of the critics seem to take for granted?

Mr. Emerson *is* a mystic. His belief that the soul is a member of God, is perhaps the most prominent feature of his philosophy. We say "a *member* of God," for to say an *emanation* would not express the whole of his meaning. His ideas on this point he has so often and so variously expressed, that there can be no mistake about them. His first volume of Essays opens with the following proposition—an intuitive one, we suppose, or a special revelation, for he does not attempt to prove it. "There is one mind common to all individual minds. Every man is an inlet to the same, and to all of the same. He that is once admitted to the right of reason is made a freeman of the whole estate. . . . Who hath access to this universal mind is a party to all that is or can be done, for this is the *only and sovereign agent*." So elsewhere, "man is conscious of a universal soul within or behind his individual life. . . . This universal soul he calls Reason. . . . That which intellectually considered, we call Reason, considered in relation to nature, we call spirit. Spirit is the Creator." (Nature, p. 34). Not only does he consider himself in direct communication and connection with God, but he would fain have us believe that he is "in some degree divine." We know not just what he would think to be his share of Omnipotence. We have not yet heard of his attempting to show or lighten. He claims indeed to be the author of "Nature," and Mr. Thoreau quite worships him: but Mr. Emerson defines his own position more exactly in the following precise and philosophical terms. "Standing on the bare ground,—my head bathed by the blithe air, and uplifted into infinite space,—all mean egotism vanishes. I become a transparent eyeball. I am nothing, I see all. The currents of the Universal Being circulate through me; I am part or particle of God."

Mr. Emerson would apparently be glad to be considered an eclectic. He displays great liberality and catholicity in examining the doctrines of all schools except the materialists; for these he has no mercy. His eclecticism, however, seems more like the easy yielding of an amiable reader to what is said last, than the candid discrimination of a careful inquirer. We imagine that he justifies this style of criticism from some peculiar views of Universal Truth; he doubtless supposes that, as "all evil is good in the making," so all error may be undeveloped Truth—a truly transcendental conclusion.

After all, it is a very difficult task to say with certainty of Mr. Emerson, what he is, except that he is a poet. His opinions are set forth not in a system, nor with the clear and exact expressions of the philosopher, but in the unconstrained and brilliant diction of the poet. He mingles in a splendid medley, the spiritual deductions of philosophy, and the graceful analogies of poetry, with the effect, if not with the intention, of making it extremely difficult for the mind to discriminate between the two. His pages appear in the dangerous disguise of simple prose; half their harmfulness would be prevented by the introduction of those warning capital letters which stand uttering their continual *caveat* along the pages of Bailey's Festus, and Pollok's Course of Time. It is by the grandness of his imagination, the brilliancy and beauty of his language, and the genial enthusiasm of the manner, rather than by logical power and the force of argument, that he succeeds in impressing opinions, from the plain statement of which, however true they may appear to himself, the minds of most of his readers would shrink in horror.

It only remains for us to say a word on the character of the work whose title stands at the head of this article. It exhibits in a high degree the beauty and strength of Mr. Emerson's style, at the same time presenting a practical and earthy character very unusual in his writings. Even had we room, it would not be easy to give a satisfactory account of it, for its beauties lie more in the execution than in the plan. It is sufficient to commend it as a "book to be chewed," but not to be swallowed.

Note

1. See, for example, Westminster Review, vol. xxxiii, Blackwood, for Jan. 1848. [The articles referred to are probably R[ichard]. M[onckton]. M[ilnes]., "American Philosophy—Emerson's Works," *Westminster and Foreign Quarterly Review*, 33 (March 1840): 345–372, and [William Henry Smith], "Emerson," *Blackwood's Edinburgh Magazine*, 62 (December 1847), 643–657 (Ed.).]

"The Writings of Ralph Waldo Emerson"

[Theodore Parker]*

From what has been said, notwithstanding the faults we have found in Emerson, it is plain that we assign him a very high rank in the literature of mankind. He is a very extraordinary man. To no English

*Reprinted in part from *Massachusetts Quarterly Review*, 3 (March 1850), 252–55.

writer since Milton can we assign so high a place; even Milton himself, great genius though he was, and great architect of beauty, has not added so many thoughts to the treasury of the race; no, nor been the author of so much loveliness. Emerson is a man of genius such as does not often appear, such as has never appeared before in America, and but seldom in the world. He learns from all sorts of men, but no English writer, we think, is so original. We sincerely lament the want of logic in his method, and his exaggeration of the intuitive powers, the unhappy consequences of which we see in some of his followers and admirers. They will be more faithful than he to the false principle which he lays down, and will think themselves wise because they do not study, learned because they are ignorant of books, and inspired because they say what outrages common sense. In Emerson's poetry there is often a raggedness and want of finish which seems wilful in a man like him. This fault is very obvious in those pieces he has put before his several essays. Sometimes there is a seed-corn of thought in the piece, but the piece itself seems like a pile of rubbish shot out of a cart which hinders the seed from germinating. His admirers and imitators not unfrequently give us only the rubbish and probably justify themselves by the example of their master. Spite of these defects, Mr. Emerson, on the whole, speaks with a holy power which no other man possesses who now writes the English tongue. Others have more readers, are never sneered at by respectable men, are oftener praised in the Journals, have greater weight in the pulpits, the cabinets and the councils of the nation; but there is none whose words sink into the mind and heart of young men and maids; none who work so powerfully to fashion the character of the coming age. Seeing the power which he exercises, and the influence he is likely to have on generations to come, we are jealous of any fault in his matter, or its form, and have allowed no private and foolish friendship to hinder us from speaking of his faults.

This is his source of strength: his intellectual and moral sincerity. He looks after Truth, Justice, and Beauty. He has not uttered a word that is false to his own mind or conscience; he has not suppressed a word because he thought it too dangerous to the repose of men. He never compromises. He sees the chasm between the ideas which come of man's nature and the institutions which represent only his history; he does not seek to cover up the chasm, which daily grows wider between Truth and Public Opinion, between Justice and the State, between Christianity and the Church; he does not seek to fill it up, but he asks men to step over and build institutions commensurate with their ideas. He trusts himself, trusts man, and trusts God. He has confidence in all the attributes of infinity. Hence he is serene; nothing disturbs the even poise of his character, and he walks erect. Nothing impedes him in his search for the true, the lovely and the good; no private hope, no private fear, no love of wife or child, of gold, or ease, or fame. He never seeks his own reputation; he takes care of his Being, and leaves his seeming to take care of itself. Fame may seek him; he never goes out of his way a single inch for her.

He has not written a line which is not considered in the interest of mankind. He never writes in the interest of a section, of a party, of a church, of a man, always in the interest of mankind. Hence comes the ennobling influence of his works. Most of the literary men of America, most of the men of superior education, represent the ideas and interests of some party; in all that concerns the welfare of the Human Race, they are proportionably behind the mass who have only the common culture; so while the thought of the people is democratic, putting man before the accidents of man, the literature of the nation is aristocratic, and opposed to the welfare of mankind. Emerson belongs to the exceptional literature of the times—and while his culture joins him to the history of man, his ideas and his whole life enable him to represent also the nature of man, and so to write for the future. He is one of the rare exceptions amongst our educated men, and helps redeem American literature from the reproach of imitation, conformity, meanness of aim, and hostility to the progress of mankind. No faithful man is too low for his approval and encouragement; no faithless man too high and popular for his rebuke.

A good test of the comparative value of books, is the state they leave you in. Emerson leaves you tranquil, resolved on noble manhood, fearless of the consequences; he gives men to mankind, and mankind to the laws of God. His position is a striking one. Eminently a child of Christianity and of the American idea, he is out of the Church and out of the State. In the midst of Calvinistic and Unitarian superstition, he does not fear God, but loves and trusts Him. He does not worship the idols of our time—Wealth and Respectability, the two calves set up by our modern Jeroboam. He fears not the damnation these idols have the power to inflict—neither poverty nor social disgrace. In busy and bustling New England comes out this man serene and beautiful as a star, and shining like "a good deed in a naughty world." Reproached as an idler, he is active as the sun, and pours out his radiant truth on Lyceums at Chelmsford, at Waltham, at Lowell, and all over the land. Out of a cold Unitarian Church rose this most lovely light. Here is Boston, perhaps the most humane city in America, with its few noble men and women, its beautiful charities, its material vigor, and its hardy enterprise; commercial Boston, where honor is weighed in the public scales, and justice reckoned by the dollars it brings; conservative Boston, the grave of the Revolution, wallowing in its wealth, yet grovelling for more, seeking only money, careless of justice, stuffed with cotton yet hungry for tariffs, sick with the greedy worm of avarice, loving money as the end of life, and bigots as the means of preserving it; Boston, with toryism in its parlors, toryism in its pulpits, toryism in its press, itself a tory town, preferring the accidents of man to man himself—and amidst it all there comes Emerson, graceful as Phoebus-Apollo, fearless and tranquil as the sun he was supposed to guide, and pours down the enchantment of his light, which falls where'er it may, on dust, on diamonds, on decaying heaps to hasten their rapid rot, on seeds new sown to quicken their ambitious germ, on virgin minds of youth and maids to waken the natural seed of nobleness therein, and make it grow to beauty and to manliness. Such is the beauty of his speech, such the majesty of his ideas, such the power of the moral sentiment in men, and such the impression which his whole character makes on them, that they lend him, everywhere, their ears, and thousands bless his manly thoughts.

"Ralph Waldo Emerson"

John Custis Darby*

Who is this man, and whence his philosophy? He is the Carlyle of America, answer some. He is the great American thinker say others. He is the product of Cambridge philosophy and of Boston religion, say we. He talks about Egypt, and Socrates and Plato for the one time; and about Montaigne, and Rousseau, and Voltaire, and Shakspeare, and Goethe for another time. The difference between him and the former, is this; they wrote by the light of the morning dawn; they were sincere men; they thought what they wrote; they produced the philosophy of their day; they had faith according to the light that was given them. The light of revelation, so far as any distant glimmerings of it had penetrated the age in which they lived, illumined their minds. The divine light which they saw, was as a star seen at noon-day. It was because the sunlight was dim, that they saw the star at all; but the star was only dimly seen. Its place in the Heavens could not be defined.

It has been permitted to man to find out many things; to comprehend many things by the natural powers God has given him. What has been recently done in science and in the arts, those old sages did in mental and moral philosophy. They comprehended themselves, and the principles and springs of human action, as fully and as clearly as human nature, *per se*, can comprehend itself. If they wanted faith, it was because they wanted the revelation upon which faith rests. Mr. Emerson is a man who flees from the burning, dazzling light of the noon-day sun, into a hall hung round with gas lights. Socrates and Plato and Cicero and Virgil, may be compared to the simple hearted child, who said to a man who had become impatient, waiting for his father, running again to the door he exclaimed, I can almost see father coming. If they ever lost sight of the star in the east, whose distant twinkle had once appeared, they felt that they

*Reprinted from *Quarterly Review of the Methodist Episcopal Church, South*, 6 (January 1852), 31–42.

could *almost* see it, and hoped that it would soon appear again to shine more brightly. Mr. Emerson, on the other hand, would hide himself from the light of the sun in an Egyptian temple, irradiated only with the light of torches.

Mr. Emerson's thoughts appear new, and striking, and truthful, because of their great antiquity. He takes us back to old Egypt, where men were polytheists or to Athens, where the wisest worshiped at the shrine of "the unknown God." He draws from modern science illustrations to present truths and doctrines which Socrates and Plato much better understood. Diogenes in his tub, when asked by Alexander what he could do for him, answered, get out of my light. Mr. Emerson turns his back to the sun, and his own shadow darkens the small spot of earth at which he looks. We understand what Socrates, and Plato, and Cicero said; their doctrines are clear and perfectly intelligible. They had not studied grammar nor logic in the schools, yet their thoughts are as household words; we know them to be human thoughts, and we feel them to be full of love and truth. But Mr. Emerson writes in a language which even his own children cannot understand. We have sometimes thought, that perhaps, it is not possible for man to utter an articulate sound which is not a word in some human language. Mr. Emerson's thoughts are like these strange sounds; they were all, no doubt, ideas at some period of the earth's history, though perhaps never well understood. Some of them at one time may have arrested the attentive ear in old Thebes or Nineveh; and some of them may now be considered wonderful truths among the Brahmins. If some one should ask the mysterious knockers in New York to call up Pythagoras, and Inquire of the old sage who he is at this time, he would no doubt answer, I am Ralph Waldo Emerson.

But Mr. Emerson differs no less from the great infidels of the last century, than he does from the old philosophers of Greece and Rome. Gibbon and Hume and Rousseau and Voltaire, and many more that might be named, believed that Jesus Christ lived in the time of Tiberius Cæsar; that he in person founded the Christian religion. The German doctrine of myths had not then been conceived. No Strauss or Taylor had then appeared. "We know thee that thou art the Christ, the son of the living God, but trouble us not," applied to many of them. The new school of infidelity, which would destroy Christianity by praising its beauties and its truths, had not then started. Voltaire, (says Mr. Emerson,) said, I pray you let me never hear that man's name (Jesus) again: and even Montaigne, "the skeptic," had mass said in his room at the hour of death: so says Mr. Emerson. These men, all, would as soon have tried to prove from astronomical principles, that the sun could have been set back on the dial of Ahas, as to have carried back the world to Egypt or to Athens, to learn new truths in mental and moral science. If they were hardened as the clay, and not softened as the wax by the sun of Righteousness, still they did not turn their backs upon the sun light of revelation, and see nought but in their own shadow.

Mr. Emerson speaks of the church of Rome, of Geneva, of England, and of Boston. He is a product of Boston theology, as much so as one of Bigelow's carpets is a product of the Lowell mills. He is a fine pattern we admit; he is adorned with gorgeous colors; but much more truly may it be said, that each and every of his doctrines may be heard under some form or other in hundreds of New England pulpits, than he can say that the rosettes and scrolls of the carpets may be found engraven or painted in the temples of old Thebes. When "the author of the Moral Science" said that the doctrines and principles of the New Testament were designed to be extended and improved upon or advanced, as civilization progressed, he gave to Mr. Emerson what Archimedes so much wanted. He may overturn the doctrine of the children of the Pilgrim fathers; he may carry back the people of New England to Germany to learn a new religion, or he may carry them back to believe with Mirabeau, that it is impossible for the human mind to conceive of God at all; he may do all this, though he may at last find, as we trust, that many thousands will be left, who will never forget the principles of him who planted the old elm at Northampton; but when he has done all this, he may then as soon undertake to set back the sun so that he shall not shine on Bunker Hill, as expect to carry back the American mind from the noon-day light of Gospel truth, and of Anglo-Saxon thought, to the mysteries of Egypt, the naturalism of Germany and the Fourrierism of France.

It may be true that the doctrines of Plato and of Aristotle are still potent in the philosophy and dialectics of men. Perhaps it is as true of all other great men in proportion to their greatness. But it is no less true, that the living writer is the representative of the doctrines and philosophy of the people and of the age in which he lives; and of no period of the world's history is this more emphatically the case, than of the present. A man has not the power to separate himself altogether from any of the great doctrines taught during his life-time; but he may elect which he will embrace, advocate and defend. Mr. Emerson is the representative of the New England infidelity; at the head of which form of doctrines, stands Strauss of Germany. The practical honesty of the English mind, would not allow Mr. Taylor, the author of "The Diegesis," to pretend to fall in love with Bible truths. He made an effort to convince the world, that all that was good and great in Bible doctrines and precepts, was taken from some one of the old philosophers who lived in some age and some country of the world; he cannot tell where; but yet he does not pretend to conceal his hatred of Christianity. Like Mr. Emerson, Mr. Taylor had once been a teacher of Christianity. Strauss and his school start out with the doctrine of myths; a thing so vague, that if they themselves understand what they mean, they cannot make one in a thousand of their readers comprehend them: which is, perhaps, a thing desirable with them, as it allows an ampler field for their unintelligible speculations. But Strauss *loves mythical Christianity*. The Boston opinion is this; they believe the Bible, they greatly admire its wholesome truths and its flowery beauties, but they cannot receive the Mosaic history, nor subscribe to the deity of Christ; nor will they allow Paul to interpret the meaning of the Gospel. Mr. Gilfillan says in his notice of Carlyle, that the hostility which had formerly existed between literature and religion has ceased; and that on the one part at least, there is a disposition to be on good terms. *Timeo Danaos et dona ferentes*, is perhaps as applicable in this instance, as it was in old Troy. Mr. Theodore Parker, and we take it, Mr. Emerson, believe in a God in the same sense that Strauss and his disciples believe in what are considered the great truths of the Bible; that is, in a mythical sense. A myth, according to Strauss, is not a fable, but the gradual and imperceptible personification of an idea. A fable, we understand to be an immediate personification of an idea; it is not a thing made by piece-meal, but is the direct and immediate production of the intellect of the man who presents it. A myth is another thing altogether. Paul says, "by faith Abraham when he was tried offered by Isaac, and he that had received the promises, offered up his only begotten son." Now the meaning of a myth, says Strauss, is this; no such man as the Abraham here spoken of ever lived, and no such sacrifice or trial of faith was ever made. It is a myth. The subject of the myth is faith and a reliance upon a full promise; it matters not in the present inquiry, whether the promise was made by God or by man. In the lapse of ages, after the idea of faith and reliable promise, had, for a long time found an abode in the minds and the affections of men, it was thought well to give it an apotheosis; or at any rate, to personify this beautiful truth. Hence the story of Abraham and his son Isaac. Strauss receives the truth, but denies the record as genuine, authentic history. In the same sense does the modern school of Infidelity, at the head of which in this country stands Mr. Emerson, believe in a God. There is no God; it is all a myth. But inasmuch as the idea of a God has somehow entered the world, it must be accounted for. The idea of a superintending Providence, the author and creator of all things, had by little and little presented itself to the minds of men as they rose from the level of the brute, and begun to turn *vultus ad astra*. After cycles of ages, running back through the centuries upon centuries which preceded the building of the first Egyptian pyramid, ("which is more than ten thousand years old,") some greater man than Moses, who lived long before him, but whose name, unfortunately, has not come down to us, personified what had so long been vaguely floating through the visions of men, and made a God! In a very short time, the world became full of Gods, until Juvenal could say of old Egypt:

"Religious nation, sure and blest abodes,
Where every garden is o'errun with Gods."

But the time of this ignorance, philosophy winked at, until some wise man arose among the Hindoos, some several thousand years before the reign of Tiberius Cæsar, and personified God in the person of an Immanuel or God-man; who was variously called Chrisna, Christ, Mahomet, and may be now, Joe Smith. This is the God of Mr. Emerson.

One of the most remarkable passages perhaps, in the Mosaic history is the following: "and Moses and Aaron went in unto Pharaoh, and they did as the Lord had commanded; and Aaron cast down his rod before Pharaoh, and before his servants, and it became a serpent. Then Pharaoh called the wise men and the sorcerers; now the magicians of Egypt, they also did in like manner with their enchantments: for they cast down every man his rod, and they became serpents." This same power of the wise men and sorcerers of old Egypt has never ceased to operate. Pharaoh had contended long and powerfully with Moses and Aaron, before his Magicians began to weaken their power, by performing as great miracles as they could perform. But the age of miracles has passed by, (though Mr. T. Parker thinks not,) and a new power has been brought to bear upon the minds of men, more influential for good or evil than miracles ever were. It was a saying of Jean Paul Richter, that while the French have the dominion of the land, and the English of the sea, to the Germans belong the empire of the air; cloud-land, gorgeous land. We will venture to add, that it is mental power, intellectual and moral power, which now governs French, English, Germans, and the world besides. Physical forces and the physical senses may be the proximate causes of what is done, and seen, and heard in this world; but this does not satisfy the man of the 19th century. It is in the cloud-land that we delight to dwell; in the region of thought. Hence it is, that the infidels of the present day are evoking from "the vasty deep" of ancient days, what they are pleased to call the myths of the Egyptians, and the philosophy of Plato. Many are willing and ready to accept the Bible in the same sense; for they perceive that its (sacred truths) myths are the most beautiful, and by far the most powerful. Mr. Emerson is forced to admit this, even in regard to his favorite Plato; but he does it, we might almost say, in a very devilish manner. "It is," (he says,) "almost the sole deduction from the merit of Plato, that his writings have not, what is no doubt incident to the regnancy of intellect in his work; the vital authority which the screams of prophets and the sermons of unlettered Arabs and Jews possess." Modern infidels agree with John James Rousseau in one thing; that mankind must have a religion, and they all would have their rods to be turned into serpents. Many of them praise Christianity without stint, and have some soft and easy way to get round and over what they are not willing to receive. But Mr. Emerson is more bold. It is a favorite doctrine with him to praise and admire the doctrines and excellencies of all religions except Christianity; and if he name the latter, to disparage it by a comparison with the doctrines of Vishnu and the philosophy of Plato. Among his representative men, the only Christian he has chosen to introduce, is the good and the learned, but the deranged Swedenborg. Let us hear what Mr. Emerson has to say.

We have said that Mr. Emerson is the American representative of the new school of infidelity, at the head of which stands Strauss of Germany. But Mr. Emerson does not even comprehend Strauss. We have referred to Mirabeau. It was from Strauss's "Life of Chirst," that we learned the doctrine of Mirabeau. Strauss says that Mirabeau gave expression to the greatest, that is, the largest truth that has ever been advanced in modern times. It was this; "that it is impossible for the human intellect to conceive of or have any idea whatever of Spiritual existences: of God." And why, because all human knowledge is derivable directly or indirectly through the senses. This is the primary source and the only source of all knowledge. All reasoning, and all imagining, go back to things which have been seen, heard, smelt, tasted, touched or felt. Mirabeau does not say that there is no God, but only that man cannot be informed of the fact, if there be. Man is precluded, shut out from all such knowledge, as the man born blind, is shut out from the idea of colors. You cannot make the blind man comprehend colors, because there is no sense through which you can convey the idea. Now Mirabeau was right so far as he went. Such is the state of man. This is the narrow circle of his natural faculties. But some how, the idea of God has entered the human mind. The philosophers do not lay claim to the discovery, for Mirabeau says, it was not possible for them to have discovered it; and Gibbon says, of the religions of the ancients, that the philosophers believed them all to be equally false, while the magistrates believed them all to be equally useful, (an admission pregnant with significant meaning;) but the people, aye, the great body of the uneducated millions, believed them all to be equally true. Now, what say the people? They answer, we got our knowledge from above; the power which conferred upon us this knowledge, gave us the faculty to receive it. So stood the world till the time of Jesus Christ. Since then there have been added to the unnamed millions, the names of Paul, Augustine, Wickliffe, Luther, Calvin, Pascal, Bacon, Milton, Newton, Bunyan, Kant, Wesley, Robert Hall. These men say, and these men (viri) have a right to be heard; we believe that there is a God. But ask them whence their belief? They answer, "through faith, we understand that the worlds were framed by the word of God, so that the things which are seen were not made of things which do appear." Through faith we understand that God made man in his own image, and after his own likeness: now faith is the evidence of things not seen, (Kant's doctrine.) These men not only placed themselves in the category of "the people," of whom Gibbon so sneeringly spoke, but they all recognized the doctrine of Mirabeau, that without faith we know nothing and can know nothing of things spiritual: of God. But faith is the gift of God, and all divine knowledge is from above. Here is the faculty with the knowledge which Mirabeau says man wants. Now if the philosophers of Greece and Rome, as Gibbon asserts, all believed all religions to be equally false, how comes it that our philosophers believed no such thing? Are not St. Paul, Augustine, Wickliffe, Luther, Calvin, Pascal, Bacon, Milton, Newton, Bunyan, Kant, Wesley and Robert Hall, equal to the philosophers of Greece and Rome?

But let us see how this knowledge advanced. In the fullness of time, God was made flesh, and Immanuel dwelt among men. Out of Christ, God is a consuming fire, and he is equally inconceivable and incomprehensible. It is in a personal Deity that the men of whom we spoke, believed. It is in a Divine Redeemer that they believed. It is in a God who so loved the world, that he gave his only begotten son that whosoever believed in him might not perish, but have everlasting life, that they believed. It was in a God, who said that except a man be born again, he cannot see the kingdom of Heaven, that they believed.

Now how stands Mr. Emerson. He believes in religion; but he hardly ever quotes from the Bible. He finds a richer field of truer wisdom in the writings of the Hindoos and of Mahomet. Here is a quotation: "That is actual duty, say the Hindoos, which is for our liberation: all other duty is good only unto weariness." Of Swedenborg, he says: "under the same theological cramp, many of his dogmas are bound. His cardinal position in morals is, that evils should be shunned as sins; but he does not know what evil is, or what good is, who thinks any ground remains to be occupied, after saying that evil is to be shunned as evil. I doubt not he was led by the desire to insert the element of personality of deity. But nothing is added." Now perhaps Swedenborg, being a pious Christian, full of faith and of good works, might have added, that he so much believed in the personality of Deity, as to receive the Sermon on the Mount as the words of Him by whom the worlds were made; while Mr. Emerson believes with Mr. Theodore Parker, that God is nothing more nor less than the great law which includes all other laws; as gravitation may be said to include all the laws which govern the solar system; and that all else is the stuff that dreams are made of. Again, "another dogma," says Mr. Emerson, "growing out of this pernicious theologic limitation is this inferno. Swedenborg had devils." Was, or was not, the doctrine of devils taught by Christ? Our philosophers say yes. "Evil, according to the old philosophers," (those of whom Gibbon speak,) "is good in the making. To what a painful perversion had Gothic theology arrived, that Swedenborg admitted no conversion for evil spirits. But the divine effort is never relaxed; the carrion in the sun, will convert itself into grass and flowers" (equivocal generation) "and man, though in brothels or jails, or on gibbets, is on his way to all that is good and true, i.e. grass and flowers. Burns, with the wild humor of his apostrophe to "Poor old Nickie Ben,"

"O, wad ye take a thought and mend,"

has the advantage of the vindictive theologian. The largest is always the truest sentiment, and we feel the more generous spirit of the Indian

Vishnu; 'I am the same to all mankind. There is not one who is worthy of my love or hatred. They who serve me with adoration, I am in them and they in me. If one whose ways are altogether evil serve me alone, he is as respectable as the just man; he is altogether well employed; he soon becometh a virtuous spirit, and obtaineth eternal happiness.' " Mr. Emerson could not more pointedly express his opinion of Jesus Christ than by endorsing Grotius. He says "Grotius makes the like remark in respect to the Lord's Prayer, (Mr. E. has just been speaking of the Bible and the Liturgy,) that the single clauses of which it is composed were already in use in the time of Christ, in the rabinical forms; he picked out the grains of gold." Perhaps Mr. Emerson picked this blasphemy out of Taylor's Diegesis. He quotes more than once from the Koran in the following glowing terms. "One remembers again the trumpet text in the Koran; The heavens and the earth and all that is between them, think ye, we have created them in jest." The moral teaching of this sage of modern times may be presented in a single extract. He adopts the Fourrier and Eugene Sue doctrine of marriage. He says, "Swedenborg pinned his theory to a temporary form. He exaggerates the circumstance of marriage; and though he finds false marriages on earth, fancies a wiser choice in heaven. But of progressive souls, all loves and friendships are momentary. Do you love me? means do you see the same truth? If you do, we are happy with the same happiness; but presently one of us passes into the perception of new truth; we are divorced, and no tension in nature can hold us to each other. I know how delicious is this cup of love. I existing for you, and you existing for me; but it is a child's clinging to his toy; an attempt to eternize the fire-side and nuptial chamber."

Such is Ralph Waldo Emerson. This is the bright star of the East; of the Land which is one hundred years in advance of the entire South and West. But let us endeavor to find his place in the moral heavens; let us tell, if we can, where he stands. The great principles of his philosophy and of his logic, even Plato's principles, must govern him and fix him somewhere. Where is it?

Well we have seen that he denies a personal Deity, and *a fortiori*, an Incarnate God. He denies the fall of man with all its consequences; and he denies the redemption of Christ with all its consequences. In a word, he denies altogether a Divine Revelation, and if there be a Heaven or a Hell, he knows not of it. If there be a God even in the sense in which Moses and Paul, Augustine, Luther, Calvin, Newton, Bacon and Milton believed that there is a God, he knows not of it. But still he believed in a God, in religion, in eternal happiness. He first shuts himself out from the light of revelation, from the influence of the Power which gives the faculty to believe, while it gives the knowledge, and finds himself placed back in the category of Mirabeau; and then lo! and behold! preaches of God, of religion, and of eternal happiness.

"Ralph Waldo Emerson"

[George Henry Calvert]*

An original man is not foreshadowed. Though born of the times, the times announce him not. He has to announce himself. He arrives suddenly without herald. Like an unbidden guest, at his entrance he is not welcomed; he is coldly and haughtily scanned. The company who have possession of the floor, scowl on him as an intruder, and justly too, for he is that and more; he not only thrusts himself in, but he comes to thrust out to the kitchen some who have been pranking it in the parlor.

The original man brings the newest intelligence. He is the last comer from the lands of thought. Once found out that he is charged with fresh reports, and men eagerly hearken to him. From those who have never been in person to that spirit-governed realm, but speak from hearsay, they turn aside, valuing them now no more than a pile of old newspapers after that of to-day has come to hand.

The dealers in the old stock of thought, discredited by him who arrives with a fresh store, at first deny, ridicule, slander him, and only then acknowledge him, when he has been acknowledged by the public. Mr. Carlyle, we have heard, had nearly written himself out of the British Quarterly Reviews about the time that appeared his French Revolution. Some of those great papers, which, collected now in five volumes, form the best body of criticism, from one hand, in the English language, were deemed unsuitable. They were so, just as it is unsuitable to put a sovereign into the same purse with a dozen shillings. In England, at this moment, how much bigger men would not the Broughams, the Jeffreys, the Macaulays seem, did no Carlyle hold before the public mind the dimensions of a genuine thinker.

With Mr. Emerson it has fared in New England somewhat as with his friend Mr. Carlyle in Old England. Here too are handy manufacturers, in whom ambition strives to do the work of genius. Up through these Mr. Emerson lift himself, like a granite peak through secondary conglomerates. His foundations begin where theirs end. Those first academical addresses of his, how they must have fluttered the elders of his auditory, sleek unquestioning plodders, who had long lived, and wished to die, in the belief, that learning rests most securely on fat "foundations," and draws its best nourishment from tradition! Or, were they too deeply bemired in the old to be at all shaken by the new? Did it even reach them through apoplectic ears, which, like ophthalmic eyes against a sudden gush of light, instinctively close against newness. But in some ears those wise fresh words did not sleep. The few, not yet fully encircled in the Circean arms of the past, who looked eagerly forward with hope, upward

*Reprinted from *New York Quarterly*, 1 (January 1853), 439–46.

with aspiration—the strongest of the young—to them there was that in the utterances of this new man, that moved their spirits to unwonted agitation, and filled them with ennobling consciousness of manhood. Higher spiritual vistas opened to them. Lights that they had trustingly steered by began to wax dim; men, hitherto held substantial, grew hollow; pages, that they had been taught to believe full, became suddenly empty. Certain critical journals—that have ever, with a jealous pertinacity, hugged dullness as though it were a privilege—became suspected, and were then discovered to be unfaithful buoys, timidly moored too far landward, midst shallows and shoals, to denote truly the channels of literature.

In a spirited, sagacious note to his admirable translation of Goethe's Essays on Art, Mr. S. G. Ward, of Boston, says, "nearly all our literature falls within Goethe's definition of Dilettanteism." That is, it is secondary, imitative, the product of culture, not of creative warmth. Admiration of genius, tasteful aspiration, love of fame, are the parents of our books. If this is more the case here than in Europe, the cause is in our newness. Our peculiar life has not heretofore had breadth and depth enough to be a soil for fresh, strong growths in literature. Our politics are American, our libraries are British. Scholars, too, are prone to conservatism. An adventurous democrat shall be a strict conformist in matters literary. Invention in the separate departments of politics and letters, requires quite different powers. Dilettanteism fosters and maintains mediocrity. It seeks amusement, enjoyment, intellectual luxury, not truth. It is content with old truth: new truth tasks, strains, disturbs it.

When, therefore, an earnest mind has the power and the purity to free itself from the bands and gyves of contemporary interests and opinions, to earn for itself, by resolute self-dependence and up-stretching will, a clean bold stand-point; and thence, calmly surveying the universe, has, through pious meditation, through cordial communings with the great thinkers of all times, through manly penetrating self-search, matured in the shelter of a sunny solitude a work as rich as it is fresh, weighty with the gold of original thought, and buoyant with beauty; and then, with coy solicitude, with solemn hope, casts his volume upon the world, the world receives it more as an enemy than as a friend, with more of fear than of hope. Such a work, so received, was Mr. Emerson's first little book, called "Nature"—the best book America had yet produced.

It was a work built on an eminence, high above the common level of accepted books. To get up to it, was a steep ascent. Many who tried grew dizzy; others stood at the base and gazed up indolently or hopelessly; to some, the summit was shrouded in mist; to the most, the whole was obscure, enigmatical.

Mr. Emerson dwells in an altitude whence the finite and temporary are looked down upon. People without power of ascent, having no experience of his point of view, find him trivial or hieroglyphical. Barren to them are his most pregnant pages. His bodiless thoughts, glancing with the lights of that high sphere, are enigmas, as futile as they are ingenious, or the fleeting bubbles of a sportful fancy. When now and then, in one dazzling stream, he flashes down into the heart of some practical matter, they guess not whence comes the oak-cleaving power. Materialized by gross habits, they will not believe what they cannot finger. Like children, they must touch everything; but not with the wise seeking of children, who would thus find out what a thing is; they would handle it, to assure themselves that it is. The little thinker breaks his drum, to get at the mystery of its sound; they are not troubled about mysteries. A play of imagination baffles, irritates them. They are like the Scotchmen, whom Charles Lamb told of with humorous complaint. Lamb was one of a dinner-company invited to meet a son of Burns. While waiting for his arrival, "I happened to remark," says Lamb, "in my foolish way, that I wished it was the father instead of the son; whereupon three Scotchmen started up together to assure me, that was impossible, as he had been dead more than thirty years."

Mr. Emerson traces an humble thought back to a lofty source; he reveals high pedigrees. He transfigures a common-place into a spirituality. This disturbs common-place readers. It dazzles them, as when from a mirror the sun's rays are cast upon their eyes. Mr. Emerson throws mental light in too concentrated a volume for weak intellectual vision. His essays have page after page of intellectual poetry.

He deals in fine-spun thought; he works with the original filaments of mental products. And well is it that he and a few others do. Could you have ropes without threads? A frigate's cable is spun from gossamer-like fibres, and all firmest opinions and practical judgments are wrought at last from perceptions so delicate as to be transcendental; that is, they transcend the apprehension of the sensuous intellect. See that mechanic at work. He is suddenly balked in his expectation; his calculations and contrivances fail of their promise. He stops; bethinks him; then gives another turn to the process; the obstruction is removed; the work goes smoothly forward again. While he stops to think, he is a transcendentalist; he rests his senses and executive faculties, to busy his creative. He has sought counsel of the higher powers of thought, the regents of life. Whoever thinks, is thereby a transcendentalist; the height to which he transcends beyond sensuous perception being gauged by the subject and his own strength. He who concerns himself with the moral or the intellectual nature, must at once rise to a high range; and the more shrewdly he plies his theme, the more transcendental does he become. Thus, all great thinking Poets are eminently transcendental; in our own language, Wordsworth, Milton, Shakespeare. In Hamlet, his greatest poem, Shakespeare is most transcendental. The Prince of transcendentalists is St. Paul.

Let not our ears be deafened by outcries. Hate and derision, backed by the times, could cry down an angel. What a reproach it was in the beginning to be called a Christian, and is still in many lands. The shallow and the contemptuous are ever ready with the finger of derision; and writers whose darkness is made visible by the light of Mr. Emerson's genius and style, have sought to discredit him, by pointing it at him as a transcendentalist. In his highest moods (if he be capable of high moods,) every man is a transcendentalist—the more so, the higher the mood. Christianity is the essence of transcendentalism.

The man of meditation is mostly by natural endowment inapt for didactic minuteness. He trusts us with the applications and construction. If he furnishes good brick, surely we can supply the mortar. He has misgivings about specific embodiments of his airy imaginations. He dreads lest, giving them form, they become mortal, these offspring of the immortal soul. He draws back from schemes; they are too positive, too definite. He wishes all good to all men, but he has no calling for co-operation. Like Hamlet, he is fond of soliloquy. His business is, to think; and a productive business it is; it brings up thoughts in other minds. To keep him company, you must think closely; and when you quit him, you are still kept thinking.

But Mr. Emerson is one-sided. So is Byron one-sided, so is Wordsworth. Mr. Emerson is not one-sided in that he takes a partial or a contracted view of things. He takes a wide, liberal view, and he handles divers themes with equal keenness. But his point of view is always from the heights of thoughtful speculation. His one-sidedness is on the upper side. Would you not rather have an hour of Paganini's one string than a dozen ordinary concerts?

Were the warmth and breadth of his affective nature equal to his subtlety and reach of thought, Mr. Emerson would, with his sensibility to the beautiful, be one of the richest and completest of poets. His moral nature, upright, aspiring, void of impurity, has yet not volume enough to flow into the widest channels of human wants and capabilities. In his soaring, his intellect is busier than his feeling. His mind is not equally open on both sides; he is more perceptive than susceptive. In passion and human sensibilities, he is not an uncommon man; in intellect, in love of beauty, in gifts of expression, he is an uncommon man. This inequality of his equipment explains some characteristics of his writings, much of their quaintness and captivating contrasts. Hence the mild audacities; the modest self-complacency; the conscious dreaminess; the poetic chilliness; the keen edges of thought that flash before your mind, like brightest Damascene blades without handles; the auroral light that comes out of the North instead of the East, and casts no shadow. Hence, his thoughts are often ghost-like; they have form and shape, but when you would lay hold on them they escape you. So purged are they of passionate alloy that they do not intertwine and uphold one the other. They lack the amalgam of heating sympathies. They are not linked together in warming proximity, but stand apart, self-subsistent, and even defiant, like a man living in a proud and impoverishing isolation. We follow his flight with high intellectual zest. He enchants us in the ascent; but his voice rings not always cheerily from the upper sphere; it sometimes grows thinner instead of stronger as it mounts. Like the lark's, while sweetly sounding, it loses itself in the clouds. It brings not back the richest messages from heaven. While discoursing with angels, he has been too curious in scanning their qualities to imbibe fully of their fragrant effluence.

His sympathies are refined and pure, rather than broad and ardent. The wants of the time do not knock piteously at his heart; the moan of manifold misery racks not his ear; the contortions of brutalized millions glaze not his eye. One readily figures him in the solitude of the woods, with visage uplifted, radiant with captivating visions; not as gazing on a group of sportive children, with brow darkened by the shadows of vice and agony that lower over them.

He puts his elaborated thought for universal fact, and depicts the rapt mental state of a cultivated tranquil thinker, as though it could be the daily condition of the turbid multitude; as if the unschooled, hungry laborer, without opportunities or leisure, could, by effort of will, lift himself into that serene sphere. The incongruity is almost comic. It sounds like the words of the high lady, who lived so aloof from the doings and sufferings of the crowd, that on hearing the poor had no bread, asked, "Why then do they not eat pastry?"

His mind is not plastic; it is not apt at construction; it does not take hold of large masses, but deals with their subtlest elements, such as will not hinder arbitrary flights. In a region above the concrete lie his joy and his strength. Hence, he is greater in the Essay than the Poem. A slight bond will hold together the parts of the Essay, (if strictly it can be said to have parts,) so feeble is its organization. But a poem must be energetically organized; it must have beginning, middle, and end; a symmetrical, subservient body. It is a celestial spirit that puts on flesh, and to secure its inviolability, the incarnation must be compact and solid, as well as flexible and transparent. The waters that flow from the sacred fountain of poetry should be gathered through separate channels into limpid pools, where all reflecting alike the far heaven that beautifies all, each one, bordered by its chosen attendants of flower, turf, rock, tree, reflects thus at the same time a distinct and unique circle of the near earth, that with exclusive affection embosoms it. With Mr. Emerson the streams often run waste, or intersect one the other, or dissipate themselves in spray; and thus each one impairs its vitality, and comes short of its full purpose and effect. Most of his poems want body and rotundity.

Nature never contradicts herself; the over-subjective mind, like Mr. Emerson's, does; its judgments depending much on its moods and a confident will. But Nature resents willfulness. The instant the individual will grows officious, objective truth—that is, universal truth—recedes, and eludes it. By too strong subjectivity—that is, personality—the beautiful equilibrium between the inward and the outward, between the human mind and the universe, is shaken. No longer on the same level, the communication between them becomes unsteady, circuitous. Who may say— "My thought, that is the Universe," should have such depth and universality of sensibility, such keenness of insight, that for him objective and subjective are dissolved into unity. Unless he have this Shakspearean myriad mindedness, the universe will throw his thought back on him a carcass.

In his great Essay on Self-Reliance, Mr. Emerson celebrates with most emphasis what is at bottom the theme of nearly all his writings, the immeasurable innate resources, the all-sufficient energy, the ineffable grandeur of the human soul; and towards the end, he exclaims,—"Ask nothing of men, and in the endless mutation, thou only firm column must appear the upholder of all that surrounds thee." Whoso asks nothing of men, takes without asking; for consciously or unconsciously, voluntarily or involuntarily, every man owes much, owes infinitely to other men. In isolated independence, the innate energy of the soul expands not, its grandeur remains a dream. Absolute solitude soon grows dark, and the soul shrivels, as flowers do, banished from the sun. A man cannot be a man by himself; his fellow-men are necessary compliments to his being. Alone, he is but an unattempted possibility, a potential man; he unfolds not, but remains a moral embryo. The richer his nature, the more urgently will he seek communion with men; and the more numerous his points of contact, the stronger and fuller will be his own development. At once self-centered and dependent, he is like a deep spring, which, ever receiving from the clouds above it, from the earth beneath it, from the trees above it, ceases to give when it ceases to receive. Man is both a beneficiary and a benefactor, and his moral health much depends on the equilibrium between his gifts and his obligations. By taking in, through cordial participation, through warm daily sympathies, the most gifted of mortals, the great poets and the creative thinkers, feed their generous natures, their large faculty of giving. This hospitality of the soul makes the best great men; through this, they grow like unto angels.

The precept of proud independence, of defiant individualism, reiterated through Mr. Emerson's Essays, is but a momentary balm to pains, which in the end they aggravate. It is like swallowing pills to cure a disease these same pills have helped to cause. There is here more of desperation than of hope. It is the effort of a pure manly nature, to protect itself against infection from the putridities of custom. Disgusted with the servility of men to effete forms and unsanctified authorities, with the soul-sapping hypocrisies, with the heart-hardening antagonisms and belittling selfishness engendered by unjust economical relations and a false social organization, a nature like his, too genuine and religious for misanthropy, seeks refuge in personal will and self-sustaining pride. But there is no healing virtue in pride; and the strength of will that isolates, neutralizes. By excess, its strength turns to weakness.

Comments like these, Mr. Emerson invites, challenges, teaches. In him there is so much life, so much truth, such pregnant depths, such shining heights, that in studying him we grow discerning, expansive, creative. We are borne away to the great neighborhood of primary questions. Not writing for temporary purposes, but from inward urgency, and the high joy of mental elaboration, he imparts to the reader somewhat of his depurated intellectual activity, No thinker of these times but comes under obligations to him, so fresh and so strong is his thinking. By the vigor of his intellect and the chasteness of his desires, he ascends towards the Empyrean centre, where truth is ever evolving. There, with self-renewing power, he sustains himself, shooting forth words that are luminous with a biblical wisdom. They go beyond eloquence, some of his utterances. They have the still depth and fascination of midnight stars. So deep, so full are they, that one desires for them even a more solemn tone, a more oracular emphasis.

Have no misgiving about the uttered thought of a pure man of genius. It *must* tell healthily. Surrender yourself, for the time, to his dominion. He will not lead you, like Dante, through Purgatory and Hell, but into calm Elysian Fields of contemplation. But mistake not Mr. Emerson's high thoughts for what, thank God, they are not, viz., stout ready-furnished guides. This they are not, nor pretend to be. They are subtle hints, delicate remembrancers. By subtilizing, they reveal the essence of things, but in too unmixed a condition for instant use. They have not sinew enough for coarse work; they are, rather, nervous conductors of force. Yet, reproach him not with supersubtlety. High mental play cannot but have its profit. It makes the intellect prompt, elastic, penetrative. No man mounts into these electrified clouds without imbibing the fertilizing fluid. It re-issues from Mr. Emerson in beautiful flashes, and blind are they who see them not. Whoever can reach these rarified heights, gets, moreover, clear, piercing views below; and so, Mr. Emerson, with all his transcendental subtlety, and somewhat through that, abounds in common sense, in homely wisdom. Gifted is he too, with the blessed gifts of cheerfulness and admiration; and his thoughts are as clear and sweet as healthiest childhood.

For this, especially, should Mr. Emerson be prized, that all themes and opinions he treats with the directness and openness of a man who feels that most sacred in the world is the mind and its action upon all things. Other sacrednesses give place to this one. And, in truth, how do things grow to be sacred but by the will of the mind? This made them, this can un-make them; to this they must submit themselves. Thence, of dogmas and creeds, Mr. Emerson speaks with a plainness which, to the liveried retainers of custom, seems audacity. In him it is not even effort, but the unforced step of an upright mind that goeth where it listeth, without boldness and without fear.

A word, before closing, about Mr. Emerson's words. For giving body to his high-born thoughts, he is opulently endowed. His diction—nervous, select, vernacular, ever vivified by the breath of thought—is joyous with felicities. His style is fresh, compact, springy. Its clean Muscle, firm as that of an athlete, lifts the thought up into the sunshine. Many of his paragraphs are winged Mercuries, with a foot on the earth, bounding gracefully skyward.

[*English Traits*]

[Frederic Dan Huntington]*

For the most part, Mr. Emerson has written this volume in a very direct, straightforward style. It has less of his distinguishing peculiarities of expression than his other productions, and, in this respect, stands in somewhat the same relation to them that Carlyle's "Life of Schiller" does to what came after. But these judgments on the national life of England bear frequent marks of their author's own philosophy and genius. Showing something more of common-sense reflection and practical observation than is generally looked for in him by those who know him least, they discover also his special views of the highest subjects,—life, society, duty, religion. To say that the book abounds in wit, insight, originality, learned allusion, profound thought, is to say only what everybody would expect. To say that there are to be found in it occasional exaggerations, paradoxes, one-sided opinions, and criticisms too unqualified for justice, is to say what the author would not probably himself contradict. Mr. Emerson, in his boundless catholicity, does not ask people to accept his conclusions: he is content, as he is sure, to stir their brains and quicken their perceptions. From all ordinary records of travel, his work stands wide apart. If he received more of what we receive as of the Christian faith, we should find his chapters as genial, encouraging, and true, as we now find them racy, entertaining, and brilliant.

[*Leaves of Grass*]

Anonymous*

We find upon our table (and shall put into the fire) a thin octavo volume, handsomely printed and bound, with the above curious title. We shall not aid in extending the sale of this intensely vulgar, nay, absolutely *beastly* book, by telling our readers where it may be purchased. The only

*Reprinted from *Monthly Religious Magazine and Independent Journal*, 16 (September 1856), 214.

*Reprinted from *Frank Leslie's Illustrated Newspaper*, 3 (20 December 1856), 42.

review we shall attempt of it, will be to thus publicly call the attention of the grand jury to a matter that needs presentment by them, and to mildly suggest that the author should be sent to a lunatic asylum, and the mercenary publishers to the penitentiary for pandering to the prurient tastes of morbid sensualists. Ralph W. Emerson's name appears as an indorser of these (so-called) poems (?)—God save the mark! We can only account for this strange fatuity upon the supposition that the letter is a forgery, that Mr. Emerson has not read *some* passages in the book, or that he lends his name to this vile production of a vitiated nature or diseased imagination, because the author is an imitator of his style, and apes him occasionally in his transcendentalisms. Affectation is as pitiful an ambition in literature as alliteration, and never has it been more fully exhibited during the present century than in the case of Thomas Carlyle, a man with an order of intellect approaching genius, but who for a distinguishing mark to point like a finger-board to himself, left a very terse and effective style of writing to adopt a jargon filled with new-fangled phrases and ungrammatical super-superlative adjectives—Mr. Carlyle buried himself for a long time in German universities and German philosophy and came forth clothed in a full "old clothes" suit of transcendentalism worthy of the Chatham street embodiments of that pseudo-philosophy, Kant and Spinosa—Carlyle by this operation became a full-fledged Psyche from the chrysalis, and sported in the sunshine of popularity, whereupon a young gentleman ambitious of making New England an umbra of Scottish-Germanic glory, one Ralph Waldo Emerson, suddenly transforms himself into a metaphysical transcendentalist and begins talking about "Objective and Subjective," the "Inner and Outer," the "Real and Ideal," the "God-heads and God-tails," "Planes," "Spheres," "Finite, Infinite," "Unities," and "Dualities," "Squills, Ipecac," "Cascading and Cavorting," &c., &c. And lo! another appeared after this Mr. Emerson, one Walt Whitman, who kicked over the whole bucket of the Milky Way, and deluged the world with the whey, curds and bonny-clabber of Brooklyn—which has resulted from the turning of the milk of human kindness in a "b'hoy's" brains to the cream of Tartar—and a delicious dish of the same is furnished under cover of Leaves of Grass, and indorsed by the said Emerson, who swallows down Whitman's vulgarity and beastliness as if they were curds and whey. No wonder the Boston female schools are demoralized when Emerson, the head of the moral and solid people of Boston, indorses Whitman, and thus drags his slimy work into the sanctum of New England firesides.

"Phasma"

Anonymous*

If the big boy think tops he spins,
　　Or the dead top think it is spun,
They know not where the maze begins,
　　Or ends, when I have once begun.

Syntax and sense from me are far,
　　Pease-pods and cobwebs are the same;
To me old tracks of giants are
　　Alike, if made by whole or lame.

Ill-reckoners must their ledgers shut,
　　When I the balance-sheet make wrong,
I am the nut-cracker and nut,
　　The simpering miss's Orphic song.

Odd men with beards whose senses veer,
　　Bloomers, more odd, my temples cram,
But thou, whose mother-wit is clear,
　　Find me the Mab-struck thing I am!

[A Defense of "Brahma"]

[Charles Godfrey Leland]*

. . . . . . It may be a little late in the day to speak of the subject, but as we intended to discuss it two or three months ago, our readers may pardon us a few remarks on Emerson's Brahma, which, appearing first in the Atlantic, has since been so extensively be-parodied and be-quizzed. We believe, in sober truth and fairness, that no poem of equal merit was ever so absurdly misunderstood, or outrageously misrepresented. When we remember that it sets forth, if nothing more, at least the sublimest and most poetic form of the oldest philosophy in the world, and the one which gave to the world endless phases of art and song, we must admit that it is at least entitled to respect, while if it be borne in mind on the other hand, that "Brahma" consists almost entirely of the characteristic and leading points of a poem which the clear-headed and common-sensible Warren Hastings could not sufficiently praise, it may certainly be admitted that there are some persons in existence who may claim to *understand* it. The original poem to which we refer is the Bhagavat-Geeta, or dialogues of

*Reprinted from *Boston Courier*, 23 November 1857, p. 1.

*Reprinted from *Graham's Magazine*, 52 (March 1858), 272–274.

Kreesha and Arjoon, forming a portion of the Mahabahrata—the great original epic of the Eastern world, to which both Homer's Iliad and the Nibelungen Lied are under distinctly-marked and separate obligations. So much for the origin of Mr. Emerson's poem, which those, who have laughed at it, may, perhaps acknowledge, is at least *respectable*.

As regards its meaning, it is briefly given in the formula of pantheism—God is all things, one being, and one substance, or *all* beings and *all* substances. Pantheism is the antithesis of atheism, as reducing all things to spirit, just as the latter reduces every thing to matter. Brahma is an attempt to set this forth by giving pictures of opposites, and declaring them to be identical. The accusation of plagiarism cannot lie in the poem—it is the most atrocious of donkey-isms. The very name and nature and esthetic harmony of the poem would require that it borrow Sanscrit forms, since it merely professes, according to conception and exertion, to re-produce what Brahma is represented to have said of himself. But to the poem. In the first verse we have:

> "If the red slayer thinks he slays,
>   Or if the slain thinks he is slain,
> They know not well the subtle ways,
>   I keep and pass and turn again.

In the Sanscrit poem, Arjoon, the hero is shocked at the idea of going to a battle in which his nearest relations are opposed to him, and in which thousands must inevitably be slain. But Brahma, under the form of Kreeshna or Chrishna, tells him that it is of no consequence, since the soul is immortal.

"The man who believeth that it is the soul which killeth, and he who thinketh that the soul is killed, are both alike deceived. . . . The ignorant being unacquainted with my supreme nature, which is superior to all things, and exempt from decay; believe me who am invisible to exist in the visible form, under which they see me. The ignorant world do not discover this, that I am not subject to birth or decay. I know, oh! Arjoon, all the beings that have passed, all that are present, and all that shall hereafter be; but there is not one amongst them who knoweth me."

This concluding paragraph is, indeed, essentially the same with the first line of the second verse:

> "Far or forgot to me is near."

As also "It standeth at a distance, yet is present," and, "From me proceed memory, knowledge, and the loss of both."

As regards the next line:

> "Shadow or sunlight are the same."

We find in the same poem the expression, "These two, light and darkness, are esteemed the world's eternal ways." In Henry's History of Philosophy, we are told that "Brahma existed eternally in luminous shadows; shadows, because Brahma was a being indeterminate, in whom nothing distinct had yet appeared, but these shadows were luminous, because being is itself light."

> "The vanished gods to me appear,
> And one to me are shame or fame."

In the Bhagvat-Geeta, we find, as regards the first line of this couplet, that Brahma declares himself to be *all* the other gods. "They also serve other gods with a firm belief, in doing so, involuntarily worship even me. I am he who partaketh of all worship, and I am their reward." As for the second line, in the tenth lecture of the same poem, Chrishna says, "renown and infamy all distinctly come from me," and in another passage, "I am fame."

> "They reckon ill who leave me out,
>   When me they fly, I am the wings,
> I am the doubter and the doubt,
>   And I the hymn the Brahmin sings."

"He who beholdeth no other agent than himself," speaking of those who acknowledge no divine agency, says Chrishna, "is an evil thinker, *and seeth not* at all." We cannot recall distinctly a Brahminic assertion that God is wings to those who fly from him, but we find Chrishna speaking of himself as the journey from himself, and assuring Arjoon that he will be sure to fly to battle in trying to avoid it. "Thou wilt involuntarily do that from necessity, which thou wantest through ignorance to avoid."

Of the doubter and the doubt, he asserts that the greatest doubt is, not to decide whether wisdom (*i.e.* faith) or works are of most avail, and that "they are but one, for both obtain the self-same end." As regards being the hymn the Brahmin sings, we find an approach to it in the following: "I am the sacrifice, I am the worship, I am the spices, I am the invocation, I am the ceremony to the manes of the ancestors; I am the provisions, I am the fire, and I am the victim."

> "The strong gods pine for my abode,
> And pine in vain the sacred seven."

Kreeshna says in the tenth lecture, "Neither the hosts of Soors, nor the Maharshees know of my birth; because I am before all." The *Soors* are the good angels, while the *Maharshees* are emphatically the sacred Seven, or "the great saints, of whom there are reckoned seven, who were, at the creation, produced from the mind of Brahma." To know Brahma means to attain him or his abode. While in one sentence we are told that the great and good deities, "the strong gods," and the sacred Seven do *not* know him, we are, however, told in the next, that whatever man "free from folly, *knoweth me* to be without birth, before all things, and the mighty ruler of the universe, he shall amongst mortals be saved, with all his trangressions."

> "But thou, meek lover of the good,
> Find me and turn thy back on heaven."

Nothing is so strongly insisted on, or so frequently repeated in the Bhagvat-Geeta, as that the perfectly pure should not be influenced by the mere hope of heaven, as by the desire to attain to God the pure source of goodness in himself, and for himself alone. Thus, in speaking of mere literal followers of the law of the selfish sort, he says that they "being purified of their offences, address me in sacrifices, and petition for heaven. These obtain the regions of Indra, the prince of celestial beings, in which heaven they feast upon celestial food and divine enjoyments; and when they have partaken of that spacious heaven for awhile, in propor-tion to their virtues, they sink again into this mortal life as soon as their stock of virtue is expended. . . . But he who findeth me, returneth not again to mortal birth." That the man who is thus to "find Brahma," and turn his back on heaven, must be a *meek* lover of the good, is declared a score of times. "A man indued with a purified understanding, having humbled his spirit by resolution, and abandoned the objects of the organs; who hath freed himself from passion and dislike, who worshipeth with discrimination, eateth with moderation, and is humble of speech, of body, and of mind; who preferreth the devotion of meditation, and who constantly placeth his confidence in dispassion; who is freed from ostenta-tion, tyrannic strength, vain-glory, lust, anger, and avarice; and who is exempt from selfishness, and in all the things temperate, is formed for be-ing Brahma."

To get to heaven, is but a small affair in the stupendous theology of Hindustan—to get to God is all in all. There is, however, a wild legend of the Puranas, which, while giving the same idea as this, in the last verse of Emerson's "Brahma," is infinitely superior to it in force, or poetic beauty. The three great members of the Hindu trinity, Brahma, Vishnu, and Siva, once disputed as to which of the three precedence belonged.

> "Then Vishnu said, 'if one of you uprising fleet,
>   Can soar to where my head extends in regions dim,
> Or dive so far as to discern my feet,
>   At once I will the palm of greatness yield to him.'
>
> For fifty million years, like lightning, Braham soared;
>   For fifty million years, like lightning, Siva dived,
> But Siva could not reach where Vishnu's were lowered,
>   And Brahma could not reach where Vishnu's head was
>   hived."

But a very inferior spirit, by a simple wish inspired by a good motive, reached the highest presence of the Preserver in an instant. Southey has embodied this beautiful myth in his Kehama. Surely, employing the second and third persons of the Trinity, is a far bolder flight than evoking the strong gods, or even the sacred Seven. But Mr. Emerson always had a peculiar affection for the theosophic-astrologic-Trismegistic-Behmenish seven.

> "I am the owner of the sphere,
> Of the seven stars, and the solar year."

Very solemn it used to sound in the cloud-compelling days of the Dial. "For the Mind being God; Male and Female, Life and Lighte, brought forth by his Word; another Minde, the Workman. Which being God of the Fire and the Spirit, fashioned and formed Seven other Governors, which, in their Circles, contain the Sensible World, whose Government or Disposition is called Fate or Destiny."

. . . . . . Tol-de-rol de riddle lari fari. *Nous avons changé tout cela!* And here is the one fault we have to complain of. Eighteen or twenty years ago, it was all very pretty to go Neo-Platonizing, Schellingizing, Taulerizing and mysticizing about in literature. Some of us have learned since then that the root of the sacred lotus is a good substitute for potatoes, (they sell them two for a cent in Canton,) while the best thing that one can do with the flower, is to crown with it a pretty woman. Unfortunately for Mr. Emerson, he was selected High Grand Gooroo of the order, and has had no chance to resign ever since. And he abides by the Mighty Mother, and Schelling, and Spinoza, and he has traveled to the East—but it has always been Germany and Pantheism—*c'est toujours l'Allemagne*—and he gives us Brahma—a splendid institution, doubtless—and it is still Schelling and the Absolute world without end.

> "First in England—then 'mid Spaniards—then where Brahma's darkness scatters.
> Everywhere the same old story—*German coat and shoes in tatters!*"

That's Heine. So is the following:

> "At old Saadi's imitators *tout le monde* just now are wondering.
> Seems to me the same old story, if we east or west go blundering.
> Of the rat-catcher of Hameln, ancient poet, you remind me,
> Whistling eastward, while the little singers follow close behind thee."

Well, the transcendentalists made us read some fine books in their day—(many pretty light poetic trifles, such as Hegel's *Encyclopædie der Wissenchaften,*) and it is the blackest ingratitude to depreciate the bridge which took us over. But such is life,

"Passato il ponte gabbato il santo."

There is, however—we must say it—one point in the Brahminic pantheism, which Mr. Emerson has not touched on, yet which the *Puranas* teach us lies at the bottom of all the mystic identities, and cuts and come again of the old gentlemen on the lotus leaf—it is the Sacred Maya, or Illusion, or Bosh, in which it all ends. That we miss. And yet we appeal to any Orientalist to tell us if that was not the upshot of the illimitable machinery, and if Brahma is really a fair *resumé* of Hindu theology, without a small touch of it? That's all!

"Emerson"

Anonymous*

"And when the fit was on him I did mark
How he did shake: 't is true this god did shake!"

   *   *   *   *   *

"And that same eye whose bend doth awe the world,
Did lose its lustre."

The bravery of Hotspur converted his thick-tongued vice into a perfection ardently imitated by polished courtiers. Like a showman's lens, which gives to a coarse lithograph the appearance of a superb steel plate, a great man's virtues refine his faults into attractions. The people shout for Cæsar as for a god, and a Cassius is rare with pluck enough to maintain, that Cæsar, like other mortals, is liable to a rush of blood to the head, and cramp in the leg. It is natural, therefore, that so great a genius as Ralph Waldo Emerson should have wholesale worshipers, and of them some doubtless belong to the "mutual admiration society." But we remember how human it is for the wisest of men to fall into the gravest of error; how proverbial that men through excess of wisdom become fools; how Schiller, the pride of Germany, could not write well, except under the inspiration of the fragrance of rotten apples; how the splendid Burke propounded a theory of the sublime, in some respects too obviously defective to stand against the common sense of the common school-boy; how the scientific Goethe, after a life of vain experiment, ludicruously persisted in glorifying himself upon having overthrown Newton's theory of light; and so we do not hesitate to question the conclusions of the "American Plato," as Lola Montes, in a silly mood, calls Mr. Emerson. In a just judgment, it is difficult to praise, too highly, his merits, but more difficult to handle too severely his defects. No language could more aptly describe him, than that which Shelly, with so much truth, applied to

*Reprinted from *Rutgers College Quarterly*, 1 (April 1858), 32–38.

himself, "*a power girt round with weakness.*" Mr. Emerson is a profound thinker, and investigates from the beginning. He accepts nothing on trust, and hence deals largely in first principles. His own brain is the crucible where, with the fire of earnestness, he tests the metal of every dogma. With keenest precision, he dissects mental states, to arrive, if possible, at a clearer apprehension of truth, by seeing its skeleton; and with solemn energy seeks in consciousness to perceive ultimate truth. With great depth of thought, he combines vast and curious learning, very odd wit, and always the charming paradox of the utmost faith in the wildest of skepticism. His style is a word, victory, unique and singularly strong, perhaps because close in extreme. But while terseness is its peculiarity, yet it is adorned most richly with illustration and quaint allusion and beautiful tropes. Every word is chosen with reference to its exact meaning, and the language is of such compass that an attached glossary, or a Webster's unabridged, is absolutely necessary for its full comprehension. In regard to style, Lola Montes might, with some propriety, have called him the American Tacitus, for whom he has a warm admiration, and whose style, rather than that of Carlyle, he imitates. Strong thought and strong composition render his writings peculiarly fascinating in an age when the facility of publishing deluges the world with weak thought doubly weakened by imperfect expression. But alas! Zeus, "greatest and best," when stripped of mythologic halo does not, Proteus-like, change from the sublimest of gods into the meanest of scamps, more quickly than Mr. Emerson, upon a faithful scrutiny of his subtleties, descends from the sacred tripod of a truth-revealer to the common level of a mystico-spiritualistic-seer. It avails nothing to insist that the scamp is still Zeus, and the seer Mr. Emerson; for the God is emphatically human, and our truth-seeker not less so an errorist. The key to his errors is found in his own words, "Congratulate yourself, if you have done something strange, and extravagant, and broken the monotony of a decorous age." It is not strange that such "vaulting ambition" should "O'er leap itself." Accordingly the first paradox with which he startles is the production of so much thought with so little method. This want of system is sadly apparent. It gives to his ideas, and sentences the appearance of fitfulness, obscurity, and incoherency.

He has energy enough to chisel thoughts of all shades for a mosaic, but not patience enough to accomplish the design, which in its symmetry and beauty, as a whole, might give to the worthless fragment a diamond like preciousness. Serious as is this failing, it is slight compared with many false views, which Mr. Emerson with dangerous vigor maintains. That some of his views must be false might be argued a priori from three causes;

1st. A *hugely* egotistical self-reliance,

2ndly. A superficial habit of accepting an illustration as an argument,

3rdly. A belief that knowledge obtained from consciousness is a revelation from God.

Now self-reliance is a rare, and commendable virtue, but with Mr. Emerson it means little more than universal non-conformity. "Whoso" says he "would be a MAN must be a *non-conformist.*" In the extreme of this spirit he abominates all authority, all dogmas, all systems, all conventionalities, all creeds, and at last his own consistency, which he sneeringly calls the "HOBGOBLIN of little minds," and a thing "with which a great soul has simply nothing to do." That the self of one moment should thus be allowed to contradict the accumulated wisdom of mankind, embodied in institutions, and the former experiences of that same self, perhaps in strong hours, is the very foolhardiness of self-reliance. And to this degree of folly our author has been driven by the excessive application of a good principle. No self-reliance can dispense with the benefits which accrue from associations. But Mr. Emerson in the presumption of self-dependence cries "trust thyself," and then in a transcendental ecstacy over "NATURE" declares that "our Sunday schools, churches, and pauper societies are a yoke to the neck," nay even inveighs against catechising children, if not agreeable to their will. Now there is no guide for the future, but the past, and is there anything in the past to justify such absolute independence? A re-perusal of Robinson Crusoe would be worth more to our mystic philosopher than "new readings," of Plato; and what is meant by "NATURE," and "NATURAL WAYS," whose operation would "ARRIVE AT" what associations simply "AIM?" If the history of the world proves anything, does it not prove it NATURAL for men to form conventions, or associations, permanent and temporary, for the purpose of carrying forward the great ends of life? Could there be a *truer* manifestation of *nature* than these very institutions which Mr. Emerson would have "nature" overthrow? Verily, to cast out a devil he summons Beelzebub, the prince of devils. Again, can it be possible that our author has so entirely forgotten his childish experience, as not to know that a child left to the control of an unguided will, can not by any possibility escape becoming a slave to its passions, and a moral ruin? A self-reliance that rejects creeds simply is dangerous.

A Titanic intellect like that of Mr. Emerson, or that of Mr. Channing may not perhaps need such aids. But even their reach of thought alone is not sufficiently comprehensive to grasp with ease, and rightly balance the multifarious parts of an extensive system. With minds of less sweep the part would, from narrowness of vision, be magnified so as to distort, or to become greater than the whole. What the systematic text book is to the student, a creed is to the believer.

The truths of geometry might have been left scattered in unconnected, and apparently unrelated fragments. But surely the student would then have been liable to fall short of one truth for want of another. So the truths of the Bible might be left spread out from Genesis to Revelation. If so, is it not evident that particular texts would engross the minds of many to the exclusion of other vital texts, and the result be confusion, and perversion? A creed therefore, which consists of the largest experience of the most searching minds, is in any case a great help, and in most cases an imperative, absolute necessity. The licentiousness of speculation, in which Mr. Emerson has indulged until he "hopes he has heard the last of conformity, consistency," and restraint is terribly rebuked in the warning lesson, which Baron Trench draws from the etymology of the word "libertine." It signified according to its earliest use in French, and in English, a speculative free-thinker in matters of religion, and in the theory of morals, or it might be of government. But as by a *sure process, free-thinking* does, and will end in *free-acting*, as he who has cast off the one yoke will cast off the other, so a "libertine" came in two or three generations to signify a profligate, especially in relation to women, a licentious and debauched person. Experience, and reason prove that a speculative intellect, unchecked by a simple faith in the sublime truths of Christianity, will wander lost in mazy error as certainly as unrestrained passion will fill the body with disease, and death. However the wrong views necessary to Mr. Emerson's ambition for free-thinking are multiplied by a fallacious process of reasoning. From pretty analogies, which might serve to illustrate an argument he deduces a conclusion as from substantial proofs. This superficial logic is not uncommon to errorists. The Hindoo pantheist reasons thus, "as one diffusive air, passing through the perforations of a flute is distinguished as the notes of a scale, so the nature of the *Great Spirit is single*, though its forms be *manifold*." This simple illustration of unity in variety is the basis for the stupendous conclusion that the substance of *all* variety is identical, and God. Of such miserable sophistry is made Hindoo theology, and Swedenborgian nonsense, and much of Mr. Emerson's famous "orginality." For how exactly he follows the Hindoo, his own language is proof. "Genius detects through the fly, through the caterpillar, through the grub, through the egg, the constant individual; through countless individuals the fixed species; through many species the genus? through all genera the steadfast type; through all kindoms of organized life the ETERNAL UNITY." Nothing is easier to an imaginative mind than to find illustrations, and even for the wildest and absurdest of theories. It is natural therefore that Mr. Emerson, with a powerful imagination should discover many such as the above, and giving them the weight of arguments should be inevitably led into pantheism. Fact sustains the inference. Pantheism is the doctrine that the substance or essence, underlying all things, is God. It maintains that God is identical with nature, which is a cunning Proteus to day in one form, tomorrow in another, yet always the same, living, and intelligent. In the following quotations from his works this identity is clearly advocated. "*Compound it how she (i.e. nature) will, star, sand, fire, water, tree, man, it is all one stuff.*" "*This is the ultimate fact, which we so quickly reach on this as on*

every other topic, the resolution of ALL *into the ever blessed* ONE."
["]*Everything is made of one hidden stuff, as the naturalist sees one type
under every metamorphosis, and regards a horse as a running man, a bird
as a flying man, a fish as a swimming man, and a tree as a rooted man.
Under all this running sea of circumstance, whose waters ebb and flow
with perfect balance, lies the aboriginal abyss of real Being, Essence, or*
GOD, *not a relation or a part; but a* WHOLE." "*There is a soul at the center
of nature.*" "*Jesus and Shakspeare are fragments of the soul.*" "*The consciousness in each man is a sliding scale, which identifies him now with
the First Cause, and now with the flesh of his body.*" "*Plants are the
young of the world, vessels of health, and vigor: but they grope ever
upward toward* CONSCIOUSNESS; *the trees are imperfect men, and seem to
bemoan their imprisonment, rooted in the ground.*" "*Nature is the incarnation of thought, and turns to thought again, as ice becomes water and
gas. Man imprisoned, man crystalized, man vegetative, speaks to man im-
personated.*" "*The maples and ferns are still uncorrupt, yet no doubt
when they come to consciousness they will curse, and swear.*" "*Great
dangers undoubtedly accrue from this incarnation and distribution of the
Godhead.*" Quotations of this kind might be multiplied, but these are
more than sufficient to show, what many are slow to believe, that Mr.
Emerson is a genuine pantheist. It is sad to think that a mind so powerful
and cultivated should be overshadowed with this heathenish belief. Like a
renowned errorist, who dwelt in truth's heaven, he seems to have been
"blasted with excess of light."

It is not our intention to attempt a refutation of any pantheistic
theory. Pythagoras may dream out one, the Brahmin may repeat the
dream, and Mr. Emerson may dream again what they dreamt, and
glorify the triple dream with the splendor of learning, still the solid sense
of the world replies not, except by a smile or an impatient "pshaw!" We
are content with the judgment. But error is twin born. As an outgrowth of
the above, our author claims the capability of perceiving truth by intuition, which is the same as the inspiration of the prophets and apostles.
"The elements," says he, "exist in many minds around you, of a doctrine
of life, which shall *transcend any written record we have.*" "NOR CAN THE
BIBLE BE CLOSED UNTIL THE LAST GREAT MAN IS BORN." He regards the Holy
Scriptures as a revelation from God, and so also the Koran and the sacred
books of India. For the world's Redeemer he has reverence of the same
kind as for Plato, Menu, Behemen, Swedenborg and other mystics. These
abominable sentiments are uttered so slyly, and interwoven so skilfully
with weighty truths, as almost to find an unconscious lodgment in the
reader's mind. But the infidel sword occasionally gleams through the fog
of mysticism. Here is an audacious thrust: "*Jesus would absorb the race;
but Tom Paine, or the coarsest blasphemer, helps humanity by resisting
this exuberance of power.*" This stab, at the very heart of Christianity,
causes a shudder. The open blow, however, can be parried. Not so the

TONE of his writings, which insinuates a pious poison into the soul, and deadens its sensibilities as gently as carbonic acid drops death into the lungs. Other idiosyncracies, not less hurtful, might be mentioned, but space will not permit, and we pass to notice his imagination only. It is not fiery, but calm and strong; not meteoric in its movement, but regular, sweeping an incalculable curve. No faculty of his mind seems to be under more perfect control, and yet none is more supremely unbridled. As the crafty politician, who apparently follows, but really leads his constituents; so his imagination seems to obey, while it actually sways all the other faculties. The possession of this faculty is a precious endowment, and its right use prolific of the highest blessings; but its tyranny is fearful, and it becomes the father of every mental delusion. It was imagination that agitated Mohammed with false inspiration; that bound Joan of Arc in trances of heavenly vision; that conjured up the devil, at whom Luther leveled his inkstand; and who pulled at Bunyan's coat; that summoned good and evil spirits with whom Swedenborg held communion; that tricks Mr. Emerson into believing that he can perceive divine truth by an unexplainable process—called intuition.

This review was designed to show the shady side of Mr. Emerson's character. It has also its sunny side, which shines out in many high-toned thoughts and unforgetable sentences. We sympathize with his deep and beautiful love of nature; admire his strict enjoinment of rectitude; wonder at the feats of his lofty intellect, and always feel the strength of a power colossal. But alas! what with reckless speculation, what with false reasonings, with an imagination unrestrained, his mind is

> "A dark
> Illimitable ocean, without bound,
> Without dimension; whose length, breadth and hight,
> And time, and place are lost; where eldest night
> And Chaos, ancestors of *Nature*, hold
> Eternal anarchy."

[*The Conduct of Life*]

[James Russell Lowell]*

It is a singular fact, that Mr. Emerson is the most steadily attractive lecturer in America. Into that somewhat cold-waterish region adventurers of the sensation kind come down now and then with a splash, to become disregarded King Logs before the next season. But Mr. Emerson always draws. A lecturer now for something like a quarter of a century,

*Reprinted from *Atlantic Monthly Magazine*, 7 (February 1861), 254–55.

one of the pioneers of the lecturing system, the charm of his voice, his manner, and his matter has never lost its power over his earlier hearers, and continually winds new ones in its enchanting meshes. What they do not fully understand they take on trust, and listen, saying to themselves, as the old poet of Sir Philip Sidney,—

> "A sweet, attractive, kind of grace,
>   A full assurance given by looks,
> Continual comfort in a face,
>   The lineaments of gospel books."

We call it a singular fact, because we Yankees are thought to be fond of the spread-eagle style, and nothing can be more remote from that than his. We are reckoned a practical folk, who would rather hear about a new air-tight stove than about Plato; yet our favorite teacher's practicality is not in the least of the Poor Richard variety. If he have any Buncombe constituency, it is that unrealized commonwealth of philosophers which Plotinus proposed to establish; and if he were to make an almanac, his directions to farmers would be something like this:—"OCTOBER: *Indian Summer*; now is the time to get in your early Vedas." What, then, is his secret? Is it not that he out-Yankees us all? that his range includes us all? that he is equally at home with the potato-disease and original sin, with pegging shoes and the Over-soul? that, as we try all trades, so has he tried all cultures? and above all, that his mysticism gives us a counterpoise to our super-practicality?

There is no man living to whom, as a writer, so many of us feel and thankfully acknowledge so great an indebtedness for ennobling impulses,—none whom so many cannot abide. What does he mean? ask these last. Where is his system? What is the use of it all? What the deuse have we to do with Brahma? Well, we do not propose to write an essay on Emerson at the fag-end of a February "Atlantic," with Secession longing for somebody to hold it, and Chaos come again in the South Carolina teapot. We will only say that we have found grandeur and consolation in a starlit night without caring to ask what it meant, save grandeur and consolation; we have liked Montaigne, as some ten generations before us have done, without thinking him so systematic as some more eminently tedious (or shall we say tediously eminent?) authors; we have thought roses as good in their way as cabbages, though the latter would have made a better show in the witness-box, if cross-examined as to their usefulness; and as for Brahma, why, he can take care of himself, and won't bite us at any rate.

The bother with Mr. Emerson is, that, though he writes in prose, he is essentially a poet. If you undertake to paraphrase what he says, and to reduce it to words of one syllable for infant minds, you will make as sad work of it as the good monk with his analysis of Homer in the "Epistolæ Obscurorum Virorum." We look upon him as one of the few men of genius whom our age has produced, and there needs no better proof of it

than his masculine faculty of fecundating other minds. Search for his eloquence in his books and you will perchance miss it, but meanwhile you
will find that it has kindled all your thoughts. For choice and pith of
language he belongs to a better age than ours, and might rub shoulders
with Fuller and Browne,—though he does use that abominable word,
reliable. His eye for a fine, telling phrase that will carry true is like that of
a backwoodsman for a rifle; and he will dredge you up a choice word
from the ooze of Cotton Mather himself. A diction at once so rich and so
homely as his we know not where to match in these days of writing by the
page; it is like homespun cloth-of-gold. The many cannot miss his meaning, and only the few can find it. It is the open secret of all true genius.
What does he mean, quotha? He means inspiring hints, a divining-rod to
your deeper nature, "plain living and high thinking."

We meant only to welcome this book, and not to review it. Doubtless
we might pick our quarrel with it here and there; but all that our readers
care to know is, that it contains essays on Fate, Power, Wealth, Culture,
Behavior, Worship, Considerations by the Way, Beauty, and Illusions.
They need no invitation to Emerson. "Would you know," says Goethe,
"the ripest cherries? Ask the boys and the blackbirds." He does not advise
you to inquire of the crows.

[*The Conduct of Life*]

Anonymous*

Whoever undertakes to conduct his life according to the precepts (if
there be any) inculcated in this book, will find himself in a worse labyrinth than that of Crete. EMERSON never had a fixed opinion about anything. His mind is like a rag-picker's basket—full of all manner of trash.
His books are valuable, however, for the very reason that they are of no
earthly account. They illustrate the utter worthlessness of the philosophy
of free society. Egoism, or rather Manism, (if we may coin a word,) propounded in short scraps, tags, and shreds of sentences, may do very well
for a people who have no settled opinions in politics, religion or morals,
and have lived for forty years on pure fanaticisms. We of the South require something better than this no-system system. Your fragmentary
philosopher, of the EMERSON stamp, who disturbs the beliefs of common
folk, without again composing or attempting to compose them with a
higher and purer faith, is a curse to society. Such a man ought to be sub-
jected to the mild punishment of perpetual confinement, with plenty of
pens, ink and paper. Burn his writings as fast as they come from his table,
and bury the writer quietly in the back yard of the prison as soon as he is

*Reprinted from *Southern Literary Messenger*, 32 (April 1861), 326–27.

dead. If, in early life, the speculative lobes of his brain had been eaten out with a nitric acid, EMERSON would have made a better poet than any New England has yet given us. As it is, he is a moral nuisance. He ought to be abated by act of Congress, and his works suppressed.

[May-Day and Other Pieces]

D[avid] A[twood] W[asson]*

Mr. Emerson's prose style and that of his poetry have been moving in opposite directions. In prose we find of late years less color, and a more determinate form, less imagination and more reason, less of gleaming suggestion, more of steady light. He has applied the telescope, and resolved star-dust and shining nebulæ into definite stars, and he has learned to make his expression a telescope for the eye of the reader,—though the lens is so transparent, and the mechanism so withdrawn from view, that the beholder may think himself looking with the naked eye. Or to change the figure, and suggest better certain qualities in his later prose, he has acquired at once more precision of aim and more projectile force. It is a telescope *rifle* that he uses. In the "Conduct of Life" the sentences go off like minie bullets. We remember to have been exceedingly impressed in reading that work by an intensity of projectile power fitted to cause some shrinking in sensitive nerves. One was half inclined to desire a little more of lambent luminous play, and to spare here and there a jet of searching flame. "Speak softly," we could have said, "electricity, they tell us, is necessary to life, but lightning kills."

The first poem, particularly, in the present volume shows, on the contrary, a richness of color and a fine flow of movement which he has never elsewhere attained. There does indeed appear the art of a master, the precision and governed expression which his prose has acquired; but it is shown rather by ease than by demonstrative force, and rather by the ability to reconcile high color with delicacy of tint than by the emphasis of form and content in distinction from color. It is Tarneresque. There is a diffused auroral glow and blush throughout the poem; dews sparkle, birds sing, there is the joy of opening blossoms, the love-whisper of young leaves and silent hilarity of springing blades. It is a poem which could have come only from the New World,—such a song of the morning, such a gush of exuberant young life, with no graves under its feet, its possibilities as yet infinite, no blight nor canker-worm, with untimely falling of fruit, as yet thought of. If there is any meditation upon the past, this appears only as longing for that future which has now become present. This is signified in a passage wherein we know not whether to admire more the

*Reprinted from *Radical*, 2 (August 1867), 760–762.

fine observation on which it is based or the freshness of spirit which converts it to such a use.

> "See every *patriot* oak-leaf throws
> His elfin length upon the snows,
> Not idle, since the leaf all day
> Draws to the spot the solar ray,
> Ere sunset quarrying inches down,
> And half-way to the mosses brown."

As if they fell, and with joy sacrificed themselves, only out of love and desire towards the grass, which beneath the snow

> "Has hints of the propitious time."

In other poems, as in the "Boston Hymn" and "Terminus," there is a simplicity as of primitive men, innocent of literature, and sublime without knowing it. Has this man read any books? Does he know that there are books? He is as aboriginal as Walt Whitman; nay, more so, for Walt has only taken the fig leaves, and in somewhat marked manner, but the nakedness is here only that of a noble spirit, clothed upon with the grace of self-forgetfulness. Was there ever a purer pathos, more hidden in lofty cheer, than that of "Terminus"?

A critic in the *North American Review*, says of Mr. Emerson, "His poems are for the most part more fitted to invigorate the moral sense than to delight the artistic." There is truth in this, but it hardly seems discriminating enough. The fact, as it appears to us, is that in the moral sense, or as we prefer to say in the moral intelligence, he is whole, but in the artistic sense he is broken. His artistic whole is a paragraph, it may be only a sentence or a line, while his moral intelligence is true to the centre. This is so of his prose and poetry alike, but less so of the latter, for in some poems, as in the "Humble Bee," for example, there is the unity of a perfect crystal. But in the faculty of intellectual as of artistic construction he is more deficient than any other writer we know, whose thought keeps the axis so surely, and whose esthetic feeling and beauty of expression are so rare.

"Mr. Emerson's New Course of Lectures"

J[ames] R[ussell] L[owell]*

The readers of the *Nation*, who are interested in all good things, will perhaps like to hear a word of Mr. Emerson's new course of lectures now going on in Boston. The announcement that such a pleasure is coming, to people as old as I am, is something like those forebodings of spring that

*Reprinted from *Nation*, 7 (12 November 1868), 389–90.

prepare us every year for a familiar novelty, none the less novel, when it arrives, because it is familiar. We know perfectly well what we are to expect from Mr. Emerson, and yet what he says always penetrates and stirs us, as is apt to be the case with genius, in a very unlooked-for fashion. Perhaps genius is one of the few things which we gladly allow to repeat itself—one of the few that accumulate rather than weaken the force of their impression by iteration? Perhaps some of us hear more than the mere words, are moved by something deeper than the thoughts? If it be so, we are quite right, for it is thirty years and more of "plain living and high thinking" that speak to us in this altogether unique lay-preacher. We have shared in the beneficence of this varied culture, this fearless impartiality in criticism and speculation, this masculine sincerity, this sweetness of nature which rather stimulates than cloys, for a generation long. At sixty-five (or two years beyond his grand climacteric, as he would prefer to call it) he has that privilege of soul which abolishes the calendar, and presents him to us always the unwasted contemporary of his own prime. I do not know if he seem old to his younger hearers, but we who have known him so long wonder at the tenacity with which he maintains himself even in the outposts of youth. I suppose it is not the Emerson of 1868 to whom we listen. For us the whole life of the man is distilled in the clear drop of every sentence, and behind each word we divine the force of a noble character, the weight of a large capital of thinking and being. We do not go to hear what Emerson says so much as to hear Emerson. Not that we perceive any falling-off in anything that ever was essential to the charm of Mr. Emerson's peculiar style of thought or phrase. The first lecture, to be sure, was more disjointed even than common. It was as if, after vainly trying to get his paragraphs into sequence and order, he had at last tried the desperate expedient of *shuffling* them. It was chaos come again, but it was a chaos full of shooting-stars, a jumble of creative forces. The second lecture, on "Criticism and Poetry," was quite up to the level of old times, full of that power of strangely-subtle association whose indirect approaches startle the mind into almost painful attention, of those flashes of mutual understanding between speaker and hearer that are gone ere one can say it lightens. The vice of Emerson's criticism seems to be, that while no man is so sensitive to what is poetical, few men are less sensible than he of what makes a poem. Of the third lecture (and I have heard but three) I shall say something by-and-by.

To be young is surely the best, if the most precarious, gift of life; yet there are some of us who would hardly consent to be young again, if it were at the cost of our recollection of Mr. Emerson's first lectures during the consulate of Tyler. We used to walk in from the country to the Masonic Temple (I think it was), through the crisp winter night, and listen to that thrilling voice of his, so charged with subtle meaning and subtle music, as shipwrecked men on a raft to the hail of a ship that came with unhoped-for food and rescue. Cynics might say what they liked. Did our own imaginations transfigure dry remainder-biscuit into ambrosia? At any rate, he brought us *life*, which, on the whole, is no bad thing. Was it all transcendentalism? magic-lantern pictures, on mist? As you will. Those, then, were just what we wanted. But it was not so. The delight and the benefit were that he put us in communication with a larger style of thought, sharpened our wits with a more pungent phrase, gave us ravishing glimpses of an ideal under the dry husk of our New England; made us conscious of the supreme and everlasting originality of whatever bit of soul might be in any of us; freed us, in short, from the stocks of prose in which we had sate so long that we had grown well-nigh contented in our cramps. And who that saw the audience will ever forget it, where every one still capable of fire, or longing to renew in them the half-forgotten sense of it, was gathered? Those faces, young and old, a-gleam with pale intellectual light, eager with pleased attention, flash upon me once more from the deep recesses of the years with an exquisite pathos. I hear again that rustle of sensation, as they turned to exchange glances over some pithier thought, some keener flash of that humor which always played about the horizon of his mind like heat-lightning, and it seems now like the sad stir of the autumn leaves that are whirling around me. To some of us that long-past experience remains as the most marvellous and fruitful we have ever had. Emerson awakened us, saved us from the body of this death. It is the sound of the trumpet that the young soul longs for, careless what breath may fill it. Sidney heard it in the ballad of "Chevy Chase," and we in Emerson. Nor did it blow retreat, but called to us with assurance of victory. Did they say he was disconnected? So were the stars, that seemed larger to our eyes, still keen with that excitement, as we walked homeward with prouder stride over the creaking snow. And were *they* not knit together by a higher logic than our mere sense could master? Were we enthusiasts? I hope and believe we were, and am thankful to the man who made us worth something for once in our lives. If asked what was left? what we carried home? we should not have been careful for an answer. It would have been enough if we had said that something beautiful had passed that way. Or we might have asked in return what one brought away from a symphony of Beethoven? Enough that he had set that ferment of wholesome discontent at work in us. There is one, at least, of those old hearers, so many of whom are now in the fruition of that intellectual beauty of which Emerson gave them both the desire and the foretaste, who will always love to repeat—

> "Che in la mente m'è fitta, ed or m'accuora
> La cara e buona immagine paterna
> Di voi, quando nel mondo ad ora ad ora
> M'insegnavati come l'uom s'eterna."

I am unconsciously thinking as I write of the third lecture of the present course, in which Mr. Emerson gave some delightful reminiscences of the intellectual influences in whose movement he had shared. It was like hearing Goethe read some passages of the "Wahrheit aus seinem Leben." Not that there was not a little *Dichtung*, too, here and there, as the lecturer built up so lofty a pedestal under certain figures as to lift them into a prominence of obscurity, and seem to masthead them there. Everybody was asking his neighbor who this or that recondite great man was, in the faint hope that somebody might once have heard of him. There are those who call Mr. Emerson cold. Let them revise their judgment in presence of this loyalty of his that can keep warm for half a century, that never forgets a friendship, or fails to pay even a fancied obligation to the utter-most farthing. This substantiation of shadows was but incidental, and pleasantly characteristic of the man to those who know and love him. The greater part of the lecture was devoted to reminiscences of things substantial in themselves. He spoke of Everett, fresh from Greece and Germany; of Channing; of the translations of Margaret Fuller, Ripley, and Dwight; of the *Dial* and Brook Farm. To what he said of the latter an undertone of good-humored irony gave special zest. But what every one of his hearers felt was that the protagonist in the drama was left out. The lecturer was no Æneas to babble the *quorum magna pars fui*, and, as one of his listeners, I cannot help wishing to say how each of them was commenting the story as it went along, and filling up the necessary gaps in it from his own private store of memories. His younger hearers could not know how much they owed to the benign impersonality, the quiet scorn of everything ignoble, the never-sated hunger of self-culture, that were personified in the man before them. But the older knew how much the country's intellectual emancipation was due to the stimulus of his teaching and example, how constantly he had kept burning the beacon of an ideal life above our lower region of turmoil. To him more than to all other causes together did the young martyrs of our civil war owe the sustaining strength of thoughtful heroism that is so touching in every record of their lives. Those who are grateful to Mr. Emerson, as many of us are, for what they feel to be most valuable in their culture, or perhaps I should say their impulse, are grateful not so much for any direct teachings of his as for that inspiring lift which only genius can give, and without which all doctrine is chaff.

This was something like the *caret* which some of us older boys wished to fill up on the margin of the master's lecture. Few men have been so much to so many, and through so large a range of aptitudes and temperaments, and this simply because all of us value manhood beyond any or all other qualities of character. We may suspect in him, here and there, a certain thinness and vagueness of quality, but let the waters go over him, as they list, this masculine fibre of his will keep its lively color and its toughness of texture. I can never help applying to him what Ben Jonson said of Bacon: "There happened in my time one noble speaker, who was full of gravity in his speaking. His language was nobly censorious. No man ever spake more neatly, more pressly, more weightily, or suffered less emptiness, less idleness, in what he uttered. No member of his speech but consisted of his own graces. His hearers could not cough, or look aside from him, without loss. He commanded where he spoke." Those who heard him while their natures were yet plastic, and their mental nerves trembled under the slightest breath of divine air, will never cease to feel and say—

> "Was never eye did see that face,
>   Was never ear did hear that tongue,
> Was never mind did mind his grace,
>   That ever thought the travail long;
> But eyes, and ears, and every thought,
> Were with his sweet perfections caught."

[Society and Solitude]

[Bret Harte]*

Perhaps there is little in this volume that will strike Mr. Emerson's admirers as being new, although there is undoubtedly much that is fine, and nothing that is not characteristic. Yet to most of us who rejoice and believe in him, will recur the suspicion that we entertained long ago, that the wonderful essay on "Compensation" comprised the substance of his philosophy. At least we feel that, given the theories of "Compensation," we can readily forecast what Mr. Emerson would say on any other subject. How he would say it—with what felicity of epithet or illustration—is another matter. "The orator possesses no information which his hearers have not, yet he teaches them to see the thing with his own eyes," is what Mr. Emerson says of the Orator, and is very possibly what the Orator might say of Mr. Emerson. Our disappointment comes perhaps from the tendency of all belief to get into condensed and epigrammatic statement. After a man has told us he is a pessimist or an optimist, he has nothing novel to say. And knowing that Mr. Emerson believes in a kind of Infinite Adjustment, his results no longer astonish us, although we are always entertained with his processes. We come to listen to the pleadings, without caring for the verdict.

Besides the titular essay, this volume contains, "Art," "Domestic Life," "Works and Days," "Eloquence," "Books," "Old Age," and others of less moment—but all characterized by the old aphoristic directness; by the old, familiar completeness of phrase, but incompleteness of sequence, and by the old audacity that would be French but that it is free of levity, and has an Anglo-Saxon dignity and reliance on fact, peculiar to Mr. Emerson's thought. There is perhaps more of the latter quality in "Works

*Reprinted from *Overland Monthly*, 5 (October 1870), 386–87.

and Days"—which we confess to admire beyond the other essays; a quality which is quite American in its practical boldness, and yet calmer,
finer, and more subdued by a sense of equity and breadth than is usual to
American picturesque statement and prophetic extravagance. Mr. Emerson is one of the few Americans who can talk appreciatively and even
picturesquely of such things as "manifest destiny," "progress," and
"invention," and yet be willing to admit that the millennium is not to be
brought about by "steam" or "electricity."

All this is, perhaps, the more praiseworthy from the fact that he has a
tendency to an extravagant appreciation of the power of progress, and is
often tempted to utter such absurdity as the following:

> "Tis wonderful how soon a piano gets into a log-hut on the frontier.
> You would think they found it under a pine stump. With it comes a Latin
> grammar—and one of those tow-headed boys has written a hymn on Sun-
> day. Now let colleges, now let Senates take heed! for here is one who,
> opening these fine tastes as the basis of the pioneer's iron constitution, will
> gather all their laurels in his strong hands."

If Mr. Emerson had been an observer instead of a philosopher; if he
had ever studied the frontier and not evolved it from his moral consciousness, he would know that the piano appears first in the saloon and
gambling house; that the elegancies and refinements of civilization are
brought into barbarism with the first civilized idlers, who are generally
vicious; that the proprietor of the "log-hut" and the "tow-headed" boys
will be found holding out against pianos and Latin grammars until he is
obliged to emigrate. Romance like this would undoubtedly provoke the
applause of lyceum halls in the wild fastnesses of Roxbury (Mass.), or on
the savage frontiers of Brooklyn (N.Y.), but a philosopher ought to know
that, usually, only civilization begets civilization, and that the pioneer is
apt to be always the pioneer. So, too, we think should he, in speaking of
"books," study his subject a little less abstractly than he does when he
speaks of the "novel" as a "juggle;" as only "confectionery, not the raising
of new corn;" as containing "no new element, no power, no
furtherance"—in brief, when he exhibits that complete ignorance of its
functions which makes his abuse of it solemnly ludicrous even in its
earnestness. It is surely no way to make us in love with Plotinus, Por-
phyry, Proclus, Synesius, or even the excellent Jamblichus—"of whom the
Emperor Julian" spoke so enthusiastically—to allude to the "great poverty of invention" in Dickens and Thackeray, and to sum up their theses in
the formula, "She was beautiful, and he fell in love." "The colleges," says
Mr. Emerson, "furnish no Professor of Books; and, I think, no chair is so
much wanted." If the professor should also be a philosopher—and that is
undoubtedly the suggestion of the above—perhaps it is well for literature
that there is none. But these are not functions of the philosopher, who accepts and finds the true office of even those things he can not understand;

and we are constrained to find Mr. Emerson's teachings at variance here with his philosophy.

In the essay on "Old Age" we expected more than we have got. Not, indeed, that we did not look for quotations from Cicero—for who has written on this subject without borrowing from *De Senectute*—but that we looked for more from Mr. Emerson, and of a better quality. His twenty pages, we fear, do not compare with the playful wisdom and tender humor with which Oliver Wendell Holmes has in a few paragraphs in the *Autocrat* adorned this theme, and who, if we except Bacon, has said the best that has been said since Cicero wrote.

There is no philosophy that will suit all the occasions of taste, prejudice, and habit. There are some things we all know, or believe we know, better than our advisors. But there remains to Mr. Emerson, we think, the praise of doing more than any other American thinker to voice the best philosophic conclusions of American life and experience. And it would be well for those who affect to regard him as a harmless mystic, to know that no other man, for years, has left such an impress upon the young collegiate mind of America; that his style and thought go far to form the philosophic pothooks of many a Freshman's thesis; that from a secular pulpit he preaches better practical sermons on the conduct of life than is heard from two-thirds of the Christian pulpits of America; and that, what is rare on many a platform and pulpit, he believes what he says.

[Emerson and His Age]

Henry James*

A biographer of Hawthorne might well regret that his hero had not been more mixed up with the reforming and free-thinking class, so that he might find a pretext for writing a chapter upon the state of Boston society forty years ago. A needful warrant for such regret should be, properly, that the biographer's own personal reminiscences should stretch back to that period and to the persons who animated it. This would be a guarantee of fulness of knowledge and, presumably, of kindness of tone. It is difficult to see, indeed, how the generation of which Hawthorne has given us, in *Blithedale*, a few portraits, should not, at this time of day, be spoken of very tenderly and sympathetically. If irony enter into the allusion, it should be of the lightest and gentlest. Certainly, for a brief and imperfect chronicler of these things, a writer just touching them as he passes, and who has not the advantage of having been a contemporary, there is only one possible tone. The compiler of these pages, though his recollections date only from a later period, has a memory of a certain

*From Henry James, *Hawthorne* (New York: Macmillan, 1879), pp. 80–84.

number of persons who had been intimately connected, as Hawthorne was not, with the agitations of that interesting time. Something of its interest adhered to them still—something of its aroma clung to their garments; there was something about them which seemed to say that when they were young and enthusiastic, they had been initiated into moral mysteries, they had played at a wonderful game. Their usual mark (it is true I can think of exceptions) was that they seemed excellently good. They appeared unstained by the world, unfamiliar with worldly desires and standards, and with those various forms of human depravity which flourish in some high phases of civilisation; inclined to simple and democratic ways, destitute of pretensions and affectations, of jealousies, of cynicisms, of snobbishness. This little epoch of fermentation has three or four drawbacks for the critics—drawbacks, however, that may be overlooked by a person for whom it has an interest of association. It bore, intellectually, the stamp of provincialism; it was a beginning without a fruition, a dawn without a noon; and it produced, with a single exception, no great talents. It produced a great deal of writing, but (always putting Hawthorne aside, as a contemporary but not a sharer) only one writer in whom the world at large has interested itself. The situation was summed up and transfigured in the admirable and exquisite Emerson. He expressed all that it contained, and a good deal more, doubtless, besides; he was the man of genius of the moment; he was the Transcendentalist *par excellence*. Emerson expressed, before all things, as was extremely natural at the hour and in the place, the value and importance of the individual, the duty of making the most of one's self, of living by one's own personal light, and carrying out one's own disposition. He reflected with beautiful irony upon the exquisite impudence of those institutions which claim to have appropriated the truth and to dole it out, in proportionate morsels, in exchange for a subscription. He talked about the beauty and dignity of life, and about every one who is born into the world being born to the whole, having an interest and a stake in the whole. He said "all that is clearly due to-day is not to lie," and a great many other things which it would be still easier to present in a ridiculous light. He insisted upon sincerity and independence and spontaneity, upon acting in harmony with one's nature, and not conforming and compromising for the sake of being more comfortable. He urged that a man should await his call, his finding the thing to do which he should really believe in doing, and not be urged by the world's opinion to do simply the world's work. "If no call should come for years, for centuries, then I know that the want of the Universe is the attestation of faith by my abstinence. . . . If I cannot work, at least I need not lie." The doctrine of the supremacy of the individual to himself, of his originality, and, as regards his own character, *unique* quality, must have had a great charm for people living in a society in which introspection—thanks to the want of other entertainment—played almost the part of a social resource.

In the United States, in those days, there were no great things to look out at (save forests and rivers); life was not in the least spectacular; society was not brilliant; the country was given up to a great material prosperity, a homely *bourgeois* activity, a diffusion of primary education and the common luxuries. There was, therefore, among the cultivated classes, much relish for the utterances of a writer who would help one to take a picturesque view of one's internal responsibilities, and to find in the land-scape of the soul all sorts of fine sun-rise and moonlight effects. "Mean-time, while the doors of the temple stand open, night and day, before every man, and the oracles of this truth cease never, it is guarded by one stern condition; this, namely—it is an intuition. It cannot be received at second hand. Truly speaking, it is not instruction but provocation that I can receive from another soul." To make one's self so much more interest-ing would help to make life interesting, and life was probably, to many of this aspiring congregation, a dream of freedom and fortitude. There were faulty parts in the Emersonian philosophy; but the general tone was magnificent; and I can easily believe that, coming when it did and where it did, it should have been drunk in by a great many fine moral appetites with a sense of intoxication. One envies, even, I will not say the illusions, of that keenly sentient period, but the convictions and interests—the moral passion. One certainly envies the privilege of having heard the finest of Emerson's orations poured forth in their early newness. They were the most poetical, the most beautiful productions of the American mind, and they were thoroughly local and national. They had a music and a magic, and when one remembers the remarkable charm of the speaker, the beautiful modulation of his utterance, one regrets in especial that one might not have been present on a certain occasion which made a sensation, an era—the delivery of an address to the Divinity School of Harvard University, on a summer evening in 1838. In the light, fresh American air, unthickened and undarkened by customs and institutions established, these things, as the phrase is, told.

"How I Still Get Around and Take Notes. (No. 5.)"

Walt Whitman*

Camden, N. J., Dec. 1, '81—During my late three or four months' jaunt to Boston and through New England, I spent such good days at Con-cord, and with Emerson, seeing him under such propitious circumstances, in the calm, peaceful, but most radiant, twilight of his old age (nothing in the height of his literary action and expression so becoming and im-

*Reprinted from *Critic*, 1 (3 December 1881), 330–31.

pressive), that I must give a few impromptu notes of it all. So I devote this cluster entirely to the man, to the place, the past, and all leading up to, and forming, that memorable and peculiar Personality, now near his 80th year—as I have just seen him there, in his home, silent, sunny, surrounded by a beautiful family.

AN EARLY AUTUMN SIDE-BIT.

Concord, Mass., Sept. 17.—Out here on a visit—elastic, mellow, Indian-summery weather. Came to-day from Boston (a pleasant ride of 40 minutes by steam, through Somerville, Belmont, Waltham, Stony Brook, and other lively towns), convoyed by my friend F. B. Sanborn, and to his ample house, and the kindness and hospitality of Mrs. S. and their fine family. Am writing this under the shade of some old hickories and elms, just after 4 P.M., on the porch, within stone's throw of the Concord river. Off against me, across stream, on a meadow and side-hill, haymakers are gathering and wagoning-in probably their second or third crop. The spread of emerald-green and brown, the knolls, the score or two of little hay-cocks dotting the meadow, the loaded-up wagons, the patient horses, the slow-strong action of the men and pitch-forks—all in the just-waning afternoon, with patches of yellow sun-sheen, mottled by long shadows—a cricket shrilly chirping, herald of the dusk—a boat with two figures noiselessly gliding along the little river, passing under the stone bridge-arch—the slight settling haze of aerial moisture, the sky and the peacefulness expanding in all directions, and overhead—fill and soothe me.

EMERSON AS HE LOOKS TO-DAY.

Same Evening.—Never had I a better piece of luck befall me: a long and blessed evening with Emerson, in a way I couldn't have wished better or different. For nearly two hours he has been placidly sitting where I could see his face in the best light near me. Mrs. S.'s back parlor well fill'd with people, neighbors, many fresh and charming faces, women, mostly young, but some old. My friend A. B. Alcott and his daughter Louisa were there early. A good deal of talk, the subject Henry Thoreau—some new glints of his life and fortunes, with letters to and from him—one of the best by Margaret Fuller, others by Horace Greeley, Channing, etc.—one from Thoreau himself, most quaint and interesting. (No doubt I seemed very stupid to the room-full of company, taking hardly any part in the conversation; but I had "my own pail to milk in," as the Swiss proverb puts it.) My seat and the relative arrangement were such that, without being rude or anything of the kind, I could just look squarely at E., which I did a good part of the two hours. On entering he had spoken very briefly, easily and politely to several of the company, then settled himself in his chair, a trifle pushed back, and, though a listener and apparently an alert one, remained silent through the whole talk and discussion. A lady friend quietly took a seat next him to give special attention.

And so, there Emerson sat, and I looking at him. A good color in his face, eyes clear, with the well-known expression of sweetness and the old clear-peering aspect quite the same.

Next Day.—Several hours at E.'s house, and dinner there. An old familiar house (he has been in it thirty-five years), with the surroundings furnishment, roominess, and plain elegance and fulness signifying democratic ease, sufficient opulence, and an admirable old-fashioned simplicity—modern luxury, with its mere sumptuousness and affectation, either touched lightly upon, or ignored altogether. Dinner the same. (It was not my first dinner with Emerson. In 1857, and along there, when he came to New York to lecture, we two would dine together at the Astor House. And some years after, I living for a while in Boston, we would occasionally meet for the same purpose at the American or Parker's. Before I get through these notes I will allude to one of our dinners, following a pretty vehement discussion.)

Of course the best of the present occasion (Sunday, September 18, '81) was the sight of E. himself. As just said, a healthy color in the cheeks and good light in the eyes, cheery expression, and just the amount of talking that best suited, namely, a word or short phrase only where needed, and almost always with a smile. Besides Emerson himself, Mrs. E., with their daughter Ellen, the son Edward and his wife, with my friend F. S. and Mrs. S., and others, relatives and intimates. Mrs. Emerson, resuming the subject of the evening before (I sat next to her), gave me further and fuller information about Thoreau, who years ago, during Mr. E.'s absence in Europe, had lived for some time in the family, by invitation.

But I suppose I must glide lightly over these interiors. (Some will say I ought to have skipped them entirely.) It is certain that E. does not like his friends to make him and his the subjects of publication-gossip. I write as I do because I feel that what I say is justified not only in itself, and my own respect and love, but by the fact that thousands of good men and women, here and abroad, have a right to know it, and that it will comfort them to know it. Besides, why should the finest critic of our land condemn the last best means and finish of criticism?

FINALES OF LITERATURE.

If Taine, the French critic, had done no other good, it would be enough that he has brought to the fore the first, last, and all-illuminating point, with respect to any grand production of literature, that the only way to finally understand it is to minutely study the personality of the one who shaped it—his origin, times, surroundings, and his actual fortunes, life, and ways. All this supplies not only the glass through which to look, but is the atmosphere, the very light itself. Who can profoundly get at Byron or Burns without such help? Would I apply the rule to Shakspere? Yes, unhesitatingly; the plays of the great poet are not only the concentration of all that lambently played in the best fancies of those times—not only the gathered sunset of the stirring days of feudalism, but the particular life that the poet led, the kind of man he was, and what his individual experience absorbed. I don't wonder the theory is broached that other brains and fingers (Bacon's, Raleigh's, and more,) had to do with the Shaksperian work—planned main parts of it, and built it. The singular absence of information about the *person* Shakspere leaves unsolved many a riddle, and prevents the last and dearest descriptive touches and dicta of criticism.

Accordingly, I doubt whether general readers and students of Emerson will get the innermost flavor and appositeness of his utterances, as not only precious in the abstract, but needing (to scientific taste and inquiry, and complete appreciation), those hereditary, local, biographic, even domestic statements and items he is so shy of having any one print. Probably no man lives too, who could so well bear such inquiry and statement to the minutest and fullest degree. This is all just as it must be—and the paradox is that that is the worst of it.

A LIFE-OUTLINE.

Emerson, born May 25, 1803, and now of course in his 79th year, is the native and raised fruit of New England Puritanism, and the fullest justification of it I know. His ancestry on both sides forms an indispensable explanation and background of every page of his writings. "The Emerson family," says his latest biographer, speaking of his father, "were intellectual, eloquent, with a strong individuality of character, robust and vigorous in their thinking—practical and philanthropic. His mother (Ruth Haskins her maiden name) was a woman of great sensibility, modest, serene, and very devout. She was possessed of a thoroughly sincere nature, devoid of all sentimentalism, and of a temper the most even and placid—(one of her sons said that in his boyhood, when she came from her room in the morning, it seemed to him as if she always came from communion with God)—knew how to guide the affairs of her house, of the sweetest authority—always manners of natural grace and dignity. Her dark, liquid eyes, from which old age did not take away the expression, were among the remembrances of all on whom they ever rested."

As lad and young man his teachers were Channing, Ticknor, Everett, President Kirkland of Harvard, and Caleb Cushing. His favorite study was Greek; and his chosen readings, as he grew to manhood, were Montaigne, Shakspere, and old poets and dramatists. He assisted his brother William at school-teaching. Soon he studied theology. In 1826 he was "approbated to preach"—failed in strength and health—went south

to Florida and South Carolina—preached in Charleston several times—
returned to New England—seems to have had some pensive and even
sombre times—wrote

"Good bye proud world, I'm going home,"

—in 1829 was married, ordained, and called to the Second Unitarian
Church of Boston—was acceptable, yet in 1832 resigned his post (the immediate cause was his repugnance to serving the conventional communion service)—his wife died this year—he went off on a European tour,
and saw Coleridge, Wordsworth, and Carlyle, the latter quite intimately—back home—in 1834 had a call to settle as pastor in New Bed-
ford, but declined—in 1835 began lecturing in Boston (themes, Luther,
Milton, Burke, Michel Angelo, and George Fox)—married the present
Mrs. E. this year—absorbed Plotinus and the mystics and (under the
influence of them, but living at the Old Manse, and in the midst of New
England landscape and life), wrote and launched out "Nature" as his formal entrance into highest authorship—(with poor publishing success,
however, only about 500 copies being sold or got rid of in twelve years).

Soon afterward he entered the regular lecture field, and with
speeches, poems, essays and books, began, matured, and duly maintained
for forty years, and holds to this hour, and in my opinion, fully deserves,
the first literary and critical reputation in America.

OTHER CONCORD NOTATIONS.

Though the evening at Mr. and Mrs. Sanborn's, and the memorable
family dinner at Mr. and Mrs. Emerson's, have most pleasantly and permanently filled my memory, I must not slight other notations of Concord.
I went to the Old Manse, walked through the ancient garden, and entered
the rooms. Here Emerson wrote his principal poems. (The spot, I see as I
look around, serves the understanding of them like a frame does a picture.
The same of Hawthorne's "Mosses".) One notes the quaintness, the
unkempt grass and bushes, the little panes in the windows, the low ceil-
ings, the spicy smell, the creepers embowering the light, a certain severity, precision, and melancholy, even a *twist* to all, notwithstanding the
pervading calmness and normality of the scene. The house, too, gives out
the aroma of generations of buried New England Puritanism and its
ministers.

I went to the Concord Battle Ground, which is close by, scanned
French's statue, "the Minute Man," read Emerson's poetic inscription on
the base, lingered a long while on the Bridge, and stopt by the grave of the
unnamed British soldiers buried there the day after the fight in April, '75.

Then riding on, (thanks to my friend Miss M. and her spirited white
ponies, she driving them), a half hour at Hawthorne's and Thoreau's
graves. I got out and went up of course on foot, and stood a long while and

pondered. They lay close together in a pleasant wooded spot well up the Cemetery Hill, "Sleepy Hollow." The flat surface of the first was densely covered by myrtle, with a border of arbor-vitæ, and the other had a brown head-stone, moderately elaborate, with inscriptions. By Henry's side lies his brother John, of whom much was expected, but he died young.

Also to Walden Pond, that beautifully embowered sheet of water, and spent over an hour there. On the spot in the woods where Thoreau had his solitary house is now quite a cairn of stones, to mark the place; I too carried one and deposited on the heap. As we drove back, saw the "School of Philosophy," but it was shut up, and I would not have it opened for me. Near by stopped at the house of W. T. Harris, the Hegelian, who came out, and we had a pleasant chat while I sat in the wagon.

I shall not soon forget my Concord drives, and especially that charming Sunday forenoon one with my friend Miss M., and the white ponies. The town deserves its name, has nothing stunning about it, no mountains, and I should think no malaria—ample in fields, grass, grain, orchards, shade trees—comfortable, roomy, opulent-enough houses in all directions—but I saw neither any thing very ambitious indeed, nor any low quarter; reminiscences of '76, the cemeteries, sturdy old names, brown and mossy stone fences, lanes and linings and clumps of oaks, sunny areas of land, everywhere signs of thrift, comfort, ease—with the locomotives and trains of the Fitchburg road rolling and piercingly whistling every hour through the whole scene. I dwell on it here because I couldn't better suggest the background atmospheres and influences of the Emerson cultus than by Concord town itself, its past for several generations, what it has been our time, and what it is to-day.

BOSTON COMMON—MORE OF EMERSON.

Oct. 10–13, '81.—I spend a good deal of time on the Common, these delicious days and nights—every mid-day from 11.30 to about 1—and almost every sunset another hour. I know all the big trees, especially, the old elms along Tremont and Beacon Streets, and have come to a sociable-silent understanding with most of them, in the sunlit air (yet crispy-cool enough); as I saunter along the wide unpaved walks.

Up and down this breadth by Beacon Street, between these same old elms, I walked for two hours, of a bright sharp February midday twenty-one years ago, with Emerson, then in his prime, keen, physically and morally magnetic, armed at every point, and when he chose, wielding the emotional just as well as the intellectual. During those two hours, he was the talker and I the listener. It was an argument-statement, reconnoit-ering, review, attack, and pressing home (like an army corps, in order, artillery, cavalry, infantry), of all that could be said against that part (and a main part) in the construction of my poems, "Children of Adam." More precious than gold to me that dissertation—(I only wish I had it now, verbatim). It afforded me, ever after, this strange and paradoxical lesson; each point of E.'s statement was unanswerable, no judge's charge ever more complete or convincing. I could never hear the points better put—and then I felt down in my soul the clear and unmistakable conviction to disobey all, and pursue my own way. "What have you to say then to such things?" said E., pausing in conclusion. "Only that while I can't answer them at all, I feel more settled than ever to adhere to my own theory, and exemplify it," was my candid response. Whereupon we went and had a good dinner at the American House.

And thenceforward I never wavered or was touched with qualms, (as I confess I had been two or three times before).

A CONCLUDING THOUGHT.

Which hurried notes, scribbled off here at the eleventh hour, let me conclude by the thought, after all the rest is said, that most impresses me about Emerson. Amid the utter delirium-disease called book-making, its feverish cohorts filling our world with every form of dislocation, morbidity, and special type of anemia or exceptionalism (with the propelling idea of getting the most possible money, first of all), how comforting to know of an author who has, through a long life, and in spirit, written as honestly, spontaneously and innocently, as the sun shines or the wheat grows—the truest, sanest, most moral, sweetest literary man on record— unsoiled by pecuniary or any other warp—ever teaching the law within—ever loyally outcropping his own self only—his own poetic and devout soul! If there be a Spirit above that looks down and scans authors, here is one at least in whom It might be well pleased.

"Ralph Waldo Emerson"

F[rederic] D[an] Huntington

I.

Mr. Emerson's withdrawal from the pastorship of the Unitarian Congregational Society, in Boston, where he was colleague with the younger Henry Ware, after a ministry of only three years, marked as distinctly as any other event a transition period in what has been called the Liberal Religious Movement in New England. It attracted little attention at the time and made no profound impression on the public mind. The young preacher, then less than thirty years of age, had not been greatly distinguished in the pulpit, being less fervent and less practical

*Reprinted from *Independent*, 34 (18, 25 May 1882), 1–2, 1–2.

than Dr. Ware and less commanding in eloquence than Channing or Buckminster, or Dewey or Kirkland. He was known as a young student of retiring habits, good scholarship, and uncommon skill and taste as a writer. Averse to popular notoriety, he made as little parade as possible of his disagreement with his people; and when he went away, instead of being exalted by his heresy, as has sometimes happened, to a more conspicuous theater, he passed quietly to a small farm in Concord, the country village of his ancestors. Nothing could have looked less like the putting on of armor or the seizing of a trumpet for the tumultuous career of a great reformer. He avowed it as his intention to divide his time between some light agricultural employment and study; but it was not long before he confessed that, in any attempt to combine practical husbandry with success in literature, one or the other must presently succumb. As the world very well knows, however, this hiding of a lofty head in a rural homestead turned out to be only a signal step in a sure ascent to a lofty place among the intellectual masters of his age.

It was characteristic of the man's mind that he broke with his denomination not over any doctrinal system or ecclesiastical law; but over a single ceremony, scarcely belonging, where he found and left it, to any ritual at all and not significant of any particular theological belief. The general view of the Lord's Supper taken by the Unitarianism of that day was essentially Zwinglian; certainly not higher than that; but the minister, with his keen perception and honest conscience, saw that the rite meant something to the worshipers which it did not mean to him, and that was enough. Instead of compromising and parleying and twisting about to find new meanings for old religious words, he took his leave. It must be owned that there was a certain moral dignity in the act. It was in wholesome and handsome contrast with those unmanly devices whereby incumbents, here or there, have gained or kept their stations and salaries through the trickery of a double sense. And this quality of candor, this standing squarely at all hazards on the fact, let it be said, was as obvious in the man as any other trait, to the end. This does not require us to conclude, however, that all his reasons for abandoning his profession and quitting his sect were proclaimed.

Up to that time the Unitarians were generally of one mind. Their negations and affirmations were pretty well understood. They denied the generally accepted doctrines of the Trinity, the Incarnation, the Personality of the Holy Spirit, Salvation only by the sufferings of Christ, native depravity, with the absolute need of Regeneration by Divine Grace, and all the Calvinistic points. They preached personal righteousness, the virtues, the Christian graces, the Fatherhood of God, and the Perfect Example of individual holiness in Jesus Christ. As to Christ's nature, they differed widely, their opinions ranging all the way down from high Arianism to the profane theory that the Son of Mary was fallible and peccable. Some were Socinians. Some were Sabellians. A few were Deists. All were Arminians. A

Quaker estimate of the Sacraments was not usual, and yet was not altogether unknown. But what will strike those who have observed the Denomination only within the thirty years last passed as most remarkable is that, even for sometime after Emerson threw off his gown in the vestry of the "Second Church," the Holy Scriptures were constantly appealed to as a final authority in religious faith and practice. There were various theories of inspiration; there were sharp exegetical contests over a dozen or twenty passages in the English Version. The Old Testament was sometimes disparaged in comparison with the New. The Gospels were more highly valued than the Epistles. Nevertheless, in all the controversial war, well fought on both sides, from 1810 to 1840, between the Unitarian and the Trinitarian Congregationalists, it was assumed by both parties that when the meaning of Scripture was found out it was binding upon the Christian mind. The Bible was the rule of belief, "the Religion of Protestants." Worcester and Channing and Whitman and Norton and the Wares held to this just as explicitly as Stuart and Woods and Adams and Beecher and the "Panoplist." Among historical lapses from Orthodoxy there has hardly been an instance of swifter decline than this.

A new Unitarian school appeared in Boston and the neighborhood, just before the death of Dr. Channing, in 1842. It was not precisely identical with the transcendental coterie of that period; but it was largely influenced by it. It was partly a philosophy, partly a scheme of interpretation, and partly a social assertion of the liberty of human thought in matters of religious belief. It was not an organization. Its spirit was too diffuse, its aims were too indefinite, and on many points its leaders were too inharmonious with one another to admit of that. It sat in parlors and private libraries. It was often found at Concord. It held many an earnest and entertaining symposium at the West End of Boston. Its chiefs were Theodore Parker, George Ripley, Hedge, Francis, Stetson, and Bartol. Parker came into Boston about ten years after Emerson went out. A contest which had no charms to the calm and contemplative scholar was fascinating and inspiring to the sanguine and self-confident iconoclast. In his suburban parish, in West Roxbury, a delighted and credulous reader of the modern German Rationalists of all varieties, Parker had gone much further than his rationalizing American brethren. To a large majority of the Unitarian people he seemed little better than an Infidel. So, for a time, his fight was as much with the then surviving Conservatives and Supernaturalists—like Gannet and Norton and the elder Frothingham and Putnam—as with the Puritans. Gradually the lines shifted their place. Rationalism gained; Conservatism and Supernaturalism lost. The appeal to Revelation became indecisive and nugatory. The foundations sank away. At his death, if not before, Parker was recognized as a Unitarian preacher, on the whole, sound enough for the congregations. King's Chapel and a few other cautious sanctuaries were never opened to him and there are Unitarians to-day who disown most of his irreverent and desperate denials, finding in them neither power nor peace. But the drift has been steadily and rapidly the other way; men of Mr. Parker's opinion stand well in ministerial circles. It has been freely discussed in denominational circles whether Unitarians ought to be requried to call Christ Lord and Master; to a considerable extent, even the forms of baptism and the Lord's Supper are disused; and Dr. James Freeman Clarke, who has generally been upborne by both wings of the descending body, eulogized Mr. Emerson, at his funeral, the other day, without stint or qualification, as a Christian thinker and teacher.

Had Mr. Emerson anything to do with this extraordinary shifting of the denominational landscape? Very much. Personally and visibly, the enchanter was not much on the scene, with his wand; but he was never far absent, and, though to most observers he might seem to be only a reserved, careless, or smiling spectator, his potent spirit was always silently at work, creating or energizing these changes, and the incisive strokes of his genius were felt everywhere, smiting the old fabric and cutting to pieces the voluntary compact which had hitherto held the scattered Liberal Flocks together. Without the slightest concern or conscious effort to achieve a revolution, he was really undermining the cause for which he tried to keep up a qualified respect and making its inconsistencies ridiculous. His methods were as unlike those of his friend, Mr. Parker, as possible; not from policy, but because their mental and moral constitutions, like their faces, were of opposite types. One was a man of solitude, thought, ideas. The other was a man of society, objects, reading, and passions. Emerson served his intuitions. Parker served specific ends and his emotions. Both had a high moral sense and meant to be of use to mankind, especially to the abused and oppressed classes; but Emerson wrought with his brain, Parker with his nerves and blood. Neither really cared much for theology; neither had the theological instinct or talent; but both were fond of dealing in a certain fashion with those subjects which theology handles scientifically. Emerson used to go to hear Parker preach occasionally. It must have been because he relished his cleverness; because they were both in an attitude of repugnance toward the accepted orthodoxy and were together under suspicion, accordingly; and because they were both enemies and assailants of the same great social wrongs, the one as a prophet and the other as a crusader. Mr. Parker used to go to hear Mr. Emerson lecture, because he admired his singular gifts, recognized his elevation, and was thankful for his friendship and support.

It was not long after the Transcendental irruption when those minds in the movement which cared more for philosophy and poetry than for any religious creed or cultus drew gently apart from the Unitarian pulpits and pews and arranged themselves in an informal club. To be sure, they left behind them a great deal that went to modify and disintegrate the former substance of the sect; a great deal that has tended and must tend more and more to unsettle the traditions of a religious movement which, we must acknowledge, in its earlier period produced noble specimens of manhood and womanhood; held up an exalted standard of personal character, and, in fact, was a well-nigh unavoidable reaction from some intolerable dogmatic errors and bigotries which had long held in fee simple the Puritan soil. Transcendentalism in itself, however, divested of all ecclesiastical sympathies, took a course of its own, not destined to be very much prolonged, but picturesque and entertaining while it lasted. Through the wit and culture of a brilliant though slightly sentimental circle, having Concord for its first Delphi, with Emerson and Margaret Fuller for its foremost oracles, it presently grouped a community of hierophants and sibyls at Brook Farm, issued the "Dial," put into it a large number of scholarly and striking articles, but made haste to spoil and kill it by the infusion of much laughable and unintelligible orphic nonsense, of which the responsible conductors were in due time, no doubt, heartily ashamed. Community, "Dial," shrine, and oracle have vanished. Exotics wonderful to see and not without interest to the social and critical botanist, they struck no root, whatever indirect influences they may have shed upon the manifold growth and mixed composition of American life.

II.

Beneath the surface of society, trade, politics, and education, and, to a great extent, independent of all modern religious combinations, a great movement has been going on within the last two generations of momentous interest to reflective and studious minds. It is really a continuation of the ancient struggle between the world of spirit and the world of matter. The conflicts of Platonist and Aristotelian, Oriental and Roman, Realist and Nominalist, Mystic and Experimentalist are only side issues in this long contention. The immediate descendants of the Massachusetts colonists and Harvard College were not much concerned about this immense problem. They were planting and building—planting practical institutions and building a free commonweath. In religion they were, for the most part, satisfied with a Genevan doctrine and discipline. This is not the place for us to say what, in our judgment, they had forgotten or forsaken, to their own loss or that of their children. We speak now of a spiritual philosophy, not of an ecclesiastical economy.

Till about the time of Emerson's graduation the College at Cambridge followed, as its masters in psychology and ethics, Locke and Priestley and Paley, rather than Cudworth and More and their Continental companions. The systems of expediency, empiricism, and common sense, so-called, ruled without much question. There were always exceptions, and even those who held to those systems failed to see by what easy steps their disciples might be led into sheer materialism and the worship of the senses. So far as that danger was avoided it was largely by an escape from philosophic thought into the regions of an intense dogmatical or emotional evangelical piety. More than any other one man, Mr. Emerson, in his thinking, writing, and lecturing, faced this downward, sensuous tendency, exposed its hollowness and barrenness, and resisted it. Asserting the value of man's moral and spiritual intuitions, drawing largely upon Kant's "*Critique*," looking steadily into his own clear soul, and by no means disinheriting himself of the ancestral devotion which had burned in the hearts of eight generations of godly ministers in his own family, he reported what he saw and spoke what he believed. To the end of his earthly days he delivered unceasingly and eloquently his message of anti-materialism. Through all his utterances, on all platforms, as the speaker at numberless anniversaries and celebrations there runs this fine vein of serene spirituality. It required no special courage. Nobody disputed or hindered him. His fidelity to his convictions cost him few sacrifices. Of course, there were those who suspected or feared him, on grounds which we shall presently notice; but, on the whole, his path was open, he was greeted with words of cheer, and his journey was prosperous. His audience was always made up from the brightest and best class of listeners. Aspiring young men from seats of learning and the scholarly professions were constantly resorting to his house, and he was always awake to the stirring of any intellectual life in persons or communities. His fame reached out more and more on both sides of the sea. His classical features were in fine keeping with the high tone of his discourse, and his epigrammatic, paradoxical, illogical style, with flashes and fragments of truth tossed out with careless lavishness, had the effect of a perpetual surprise, a propounding and answering of riddles. His home was happy. If he was not in the strict sense popular, his audience was sufficient to give him the means of comfortable living.

These were the fair and honorable aspects of his literary life through half a century. What now were the principal limitations? Indiscriminate eulogy is here out of place. It certainly would be out of keeping with his own impartial, unprejudiced, unexaggerating mind. An intellectual nature, so royally endowed as his, could well afford to be weighed in the scales of truth. It is well understood that not a blemish was ever supposed to disfigure the beauty of his moral life: that he was free from the jealousies, meannesses, and petty competitions of authors; that he was kind to the poor, just to those from whom he differed, patient toward his critics, almost passionless in his purity, and temperate in all things. Considering the coolness of his natural temperament, the reserve of manners by which he half removed himself from those to whom he spoke, and the fact that he lacked all that sympathetic or magnetic power which belongs to those who give an impression of having suffered, it is remarkable how many about him regarded him not only with confidence and admiration, but with affection. It was so not only with his village neighbors, but with persons of all classes whom he met casually and infrequently, though he rarely inspired personal enthusiasm and was without those qualities which make men leaders of their fellows. All this being gratefully granted, it must, in judicial fairness, be said that there was nothing in Mr. Emerson's everyday character to distinguish him above a thousand unnoticed Christians in every Christian community. Not a few of his virtues were those of a Greek Stoic. As his ethical teaching was cosmopolitan and ethnic and not avowedly due to Christianity, so his temper and conduct were molded upon principles belonging to universal morality, and not distinctively to the Gospel or Kingdom of Christ. It seems to us a grievous defect in the generosity of his spirit that he did not with emphasis acknowledge his own indebtedness and that of the world to the supreme and sole moral perfection of Jesus, Son of God and Son of Man.

A grave fault in Mr. Emerson's moral teachings was found in his superficial theory of sin. As he appeared before the world, vice of all sorts was alien to his nature. Perhaps it was for that very reason that he had an inadequate conception of its wickedness. His optimism ran to that extent that it would not be difficult to collect from his writings a formidable array of passages which look very much as if he regarded transgressions of the moral law as small matters, accidents of an unfortunate constitution, inconvenient idiosyncrasies, or awkward though necessary stages in the onward progress of the race. Some sentences of that sort might be quoted which would shock the conscience of an upright and chaste heathen. It is not imagined that they were meant to bear any such construction; but they are very dangerous combustibles for a severe moralist to throw about promiscuously in the open magazine of youthful appetites or among all sorts of temptations. Very likely this loose conception of moral opposites was one of the bad fruits of Mr. Emerson's weak hold, at least, through a large part of his public career, of the truth of the Personality of God. Unless we see, what the Bible shows us, the willfully sinning soul in direct and rebellious hostility to a Personal God its Father, from which it is rescued only through the grace of a Personal Saviour, we shall have a feeble appreciation either of iniquity itself or of its penalties. Whether the Pantheism so commonly charged upon Mr. Emerson sometimes lurked in his mind or not, he evidently entertained at intervals a theory of a universal Soul, which though far from Materialism, was equally far from the Christian Theism of the Bible.

To a degree, Mr. Emerson's aberrations in religious thought were due to his inaptitude for thinking consecutively and logically on any abstract subject. Seers are not expected to be reasoners, and very commonly are not capable of being such. This particular Seer's mental activities were not in a process or chain, but in leaps and separate strokes. It has been observed that the order of his sentences is immaterial. The signs of this incapacity run all through what he did and wrote. He flouted consistency as mental servility, refusing to give any account of his self-contradictions. It was forces, facts, and men that interested him; not organizations. Everywhere acknowledged as a peer among scholars, he was not learned in any science, language, period of history, or department of letters. The scientific method was alien to his habits. His genius had no sympathy with the historic spirit. Statesmanship, institutions, systems of philosophy were objects of poetic observation to him and formed the subject-matter of witty aphorisms; but it would be absurd to class him under the name of any system-builder and his quotations were chiefly from poets, proverbialists, conversations, and biographies. We do not recollect anything like an argument in all his volumes. Nothing could be more natural than that he should fail to connect himself with any kind of institutional usefulness, or to appreciate the majestic sweep of organic power, or a historic and successive life in the corporate constitution of the Church. The individualism of democratic societies found in him a very persuasive and celebrated mouthpiece. He might be caught now and then at a popular meeting; but he stuck to no platform, signed no articles, swore to no compact, joined no church. He was never weary of the assertion of his independent personality; and, if there was any affectation in his style, it arose from his persistent determination to be unlike anybody else. Whoever thus isolates and distinguishes himself may, by the virtue of genius, become famous; he may stimulate, arouse, dazzle, or expand innumerable minds, especially the minds of the young, as Mr. Emerson did; but to those grand forms and consolidated agencies of thought and life which accumulate and transmit the treasures of ages he can make only an insignificant contribution. How, then, did this original man's influence stand related to what the world has for several centuries agreed to call Christianity? If that word means a voluntary aggregation of people agreed in promoting love to God and love to man, he undoubtedly, belonged to the company and was a great voice in its behalf. If it means a visible society, drawing all its vitality from the person of Jesus Christ, adored as the only Son of God and Saviour of mankind, forever rooted and centered in Him, a Spiritual Kingdom, having a constitution, laws, and officers of administration, held together by definable principles or a creed, then the case appears to be otherwise. It is rather childish for any set of men to cry or scold because their favorite is refused a title which signifies a believing discipleship and loyal obedience toward a Personage avowing himself to be in a special sense the Son of God and Redeemer of Men; but who, by that favorite, is supposed to have been ignorant of his own nature and position and to have put forth preposterous, if not blasphemous claims to homage. It is easy enough to make the term *Christianity* synonymous with general goodness, and then to affirm that every good man is a Christian believer, and to whimper or groan if everybody does not assent to this confusion of ideas and abuse of language. It will be quite safe for Mr. Emerson's admirers, and we rank ourselves among them, to challenge in his behalf what he challenged for himself, applying to him such terms of distinction as he clearly most valued. His ponderous blows at the hollow fabrics of expediency, utilitarianism, and materialism would have fallen with far greater weight if his spirituality had been that of St. John the divine or if his doctrine of the two worlds had been that of evangelists and apostles. His sharp thrusts at vulgar wealth and a corrupt civilization would have told with double effect if his supersensuous scheme had been the revealed supernaturalism of the New Testament. His ingenious and fine-drawn treatise on the "Over-Soul" would have brought ten-fold more consolation to desolate hearts, solace to mourners, joy to the disappointed and forsaken, strength to the tempted, and peace to "those whose consciences by sin are accused"; in short, it would have been more like glad tidings to souls bewildered and lost if he had spoken out clearly and with holy confidence the name of the God and Father of Jesus Christ our Lord.

We have desired without presumption to submit these imperfect and unworthy notices of a luminous mind, with a grateful confession of intellectual obligations which cannot be repaid.

Emerson and his Views of Nature

Moncure D[aniel] Conway*

When the statue of Carlyle was unveiled, the speaker on that occasion (Dr. Tyndall) expressed the hope that some day a memorial of Ralph Waldo Emerson might be placed beside it. The long friendship between those men, which defied dissimilarities and differences to sunder their hearts, was due to their profound moral relationship. They were children of the Human Age of Literature. Indeed Literature is hardly a large enough word to describe the works of men whose words were "half-battles" and victories. The artist of the Carlyle memorial has significantly piled Carlyle's books beneath his chair. For Emerson, however, the intellectual and poetic life and work were precisely those which circumstances made the most practical and humane. Although, by moral and humane aims, the descendant of the Puritans and the descendant of the Covenanters were brothers, the chief influence on the intellect of Emerson was rather that of Wordsworth, whose poetry raised in him the vision of a loving life with nature. When Emerson visited Rydal Mount in 1833, Wordsworth warmly advised him against too much intellectual culture. He may have recognised the fact that Emerson was at that time chiefly interested in the discussions which had followed the controversy between Geoffroy St. Hilaire and Cuvier. Of all that literature which prepared the way for Charles Darwin's great generalisation, in French, Ger-

*Reprint of *Emerson and his Views of Nature* (London: Royal Institution of Great Britain, 1883).

man, and English, Emerson was an assiduous student. Perhaps his first lecture was one given in the Winter of 1833–34, on 'The Relation of Man to the Globe.' It has not been published or reported, but Dr. Emerson has explored it for me, and it contains passages showing elation at meeting the dawn of a great truth. "By the study of the globe in very recent times we have become acquainted with a fact the most surprising—I may say, the most sublime—to wit, that man, who stands in the globe so proud and powerful, is no upstart in the creation, but has been prophesied in nature for a thousand, thousand ages before he appeared; that from times incalculably remote there has been a progressive preparation for him, an effort (as physiologists say,) to produce him: the meaner creatures, the primeval sauri, containing the elements of his structure and pointing at it on every side, whilst the world was at the same time preparing to be habitable by him. He was not made sooner because his house was not ready." "Man is made, the creature who seems a refinement on the form of all who went before him, and more perfect in the image of his Maker by the gift of moral nature; but his limbs are only a more exquisite organization,—say, rather, the finish of the rudimental forms that have been already sweeping the sea and creeping in the mud: the brother of his hand is even now cleaving the Arctic sea in the fin of the whale, and innumerable ages since was pawing the marsh in the flipper of the saurus." It is in a sense studying the law of evolution itself to study the impression it made upon the mind of Emerson, as a law of which he was absolutely convinced in the beginning of his career. His first book *Nature* (1836) is a Vedas of the scientific age, in which instead of man's ancient worship of sun, cloud, star, these glorious objects unite in celebration of Man. The development of man is the spiritualization of nature. The course of man's culture turns nature to a kingdom of Use, translates its laws into ethics, its aspects into language, its facts and phenomena into science, builds its sublimities into a temple. Man is what nature means. The only break in the radiant optimism of the book is a complaint that Science had not explained the relationship of man to the forms around him, the unity of things; and almost at the very moment when that book appeared (Sept., 1836) young Charles Darwin landed from the *Beagle* with tidings of the new intellectual world for which the new world thinker was calling. It was to be twenty-two years yet before Darwin was prepared to announce his theory, but meanwhile Emerson had gained some farther light in that direction. It came to him while exploring an unpromising region,—the works of John Hunter. In an essay he speaks of an "electric word" of Hunter's on development. I can find but one reference to development in Hunter's works. Palmer's Hunter appeared in 1835, while Emerson was writing his *Nature*, and its reference to development is in Vol. I., a footnote to p. 265:—"If we were capable of following the progress of increase of number of the parts of the most perfect animal, as they formed in succession, from the very first to its state of full perfection, we should probably be able to compare it to some of the incomplete animals themselves of every order of animals in the creation, being at no stage different from some of those inferior orders; or in other words, if we were to take a series of animals, from the more imperfect to the perfect, we should probably find an imperfect animal corresponding with some stage of the most perfect."

The fact that each animal passes in the course of its development through stages comparable to those of adult animals of lower organization is now explained by evolution; to Emerson it was itself a partial explanation, bringing order into phenomena which traditional theories left chaotic. His second essay on Nature (1844) shows him realising how vast may be the function of a small agency working in boundless time and boundless space. Geology, he says, has taught us to disuse our dameschool measures. "We know nothing rightly for want of perspective. Now we learn what patient periods must round themselves before the rock is formed, then before the rock is broken, and the first lichen race has disintegrated the thinnest external plate into soil, and opened the door for the remote flora, Ceres and Pomona, to come in. How far off yet is trilobite! how far the quadruped! how inconceivably remote is man! All duly arrive, and then race after race of men. It is a long way from granite to oyster; farther yet to Plato and the preaching of the immortality of the soul. Yet all must come as surely as the atom has two sides." Simultaneously with the appearance of this essay in America, the 'Vestiges of Creation' appeared in England. Agassiz sought to persuade Emerson that these relations and degrees of forms were only ideal; but Emerson's idealism was too wide to admit of any dualism in nature. In the order of thought he read the order of nature, before it was proved. "Development" was the religion of Emerson before it was the discovery of science. It was the vision of his poetic genius, the affirmation of his moral enthusiasm, the hope of his humanity. He founded his life and work upon it long before Darwin proved that he had founded on a rock. Whenever he touched the theme he broke forth into song. In his poem "Musketaquid" his view of natural evolution is exquisitely humanised.

The charm which Emerson's writings have for scientific men is partly due to the nature in them; but also to the fact that in them is foreshadowed the kind of character, sentiment, religion, legitimately related to the scientific generalisations which have alarmed many worthy people, not unnaturally solicitous for the spiritual beauty of life. When others were alarmed at this or that new statement, Emerson said: "Fear not the new generalisation. Does the fact look crass and material, threatening to degrade thy theory of Spirit? Resist it not; it goes to refine thy theory of matter just as much." This is from his 'First Series of Essays,' a volume which closes with this pregnant sentence:—"When Science is learned in love, and its powers are wielded by love, they will appear the supplements and continuations of the material creation." Whatever his audience, Emerson always did his best; he never put out his talent to work for him, reserving his genius. In America Emerson's life and spirit were always the strongest argument on the progressive side. When his house was burned down in 1872, persons of different parties and beliefs insisted, despite his deprecations, on rebuilding what had been a home for many minds.

"Ralph Waldo Emerson"

Christopher P[earse] Cranch

For many years, it has seemed to me that the writings of Emerson, highly as they are prized by a large number of the best minds of America and England, and steadily on the increase as his fame is, are not yet rated at their worth, nor as they will inevitably be rated in the ages to come. That there has been a marked increase in his value among American readers since his first appearance before the public nearly a half-century ago, there is no question. But I think that he is far from occupying that undisputed position that will be his in future times, when he will rank as one of the great minds of the ages, and take his place by the side of some of his own representative men.

This might once have seemed extravagant praise. But to-day, the most cultivated minds are beginning to wake to a conviction of its simple truth. If we rightly recall the comparative barrenness of that region of thought among us, which Emerson almost alone tilled and brought into efflorescence and fruit, and trace the remarkable influence his books have had in elevating the standard of our higher literature, we must regard the advent of so rare a genius in the New England of 1835 as a phenomenon so remarkable that it stands entirely alone. In comparison with the intellectual lights of the time, he seemed almost like a mind out of another planet,—so original, so fearlessly transcendental, yet in the highest sense so practical. And America at least has been more enriched by the new mines he opened to her higher life than she ever was in material prosperity by the ores of Colorado and California.

I think we are apt to forget our debt to this remarkable genius for his fresh currents of intuitive thought when conventional views of nature and life were so prevalent. At the present day we have grown accustomed to his voice. His style and modes of thought no longer startle and tantalize us as they did once. For he has left his stamp upon other minds who have followed his leading and imbibed his spirit. We must remember that it is quite within the memory of many of us, when the name of Emerson stood for all that was visionary in philosophy and heretical in religion, when

*Reprinted from *Unitarian Review and Religious Magazine*, 20 (July 1883), 1–19.

there were few who believed in him as the inaugurator of a newer, healthier, larger era of thought. It was necessary that he should have lived and written to a ripe old age, illustrating his books by his life, with time and opportunity to impress himself upon the younger generations that grew up around him, before the world's opinion of him could ripen into its present prospect of maturity.

If the enthusiasm with which his early lectures in Boston and his first books were greeted by a few of the younger minds of the time has seemed to diminish since his first appearance before the public, it is only because it has developed and broadened into a life of thought, faith, and conduct with many cultivated men and women, who hardly know how much they have owed to this once almost isolated thinker. The seed he planted has sunk out of sight, but into congenial soil, and has sprouted, budded, and borne fruit far and wide through the country; for large numbers of cultivated and spiritually-minded people now require that their intellectual food should at least be flavored with the rich and fragrant juices condensed in his books. But, in enjoying our inheritance, we are somewhat too forgetful of its testator; and perhaps we are a little too near him to measure his height.

Like all the greatest minds, Emerson has been known by a minority of readers. Outside of America and England, he is little known. It seems strange that even Victor Hugo should have asked, "And who is Emerson?" Or at least it would seem strange, were it not known how superciliously indifferent France is about all great men except her own.

Though some of his sentences have got to be household words as those of few other modern writers have among us, and though we have Emerson Birthday Books, and stick up an Emerson Calendar on our walls, yet it goes without saying that, except in some of the lecture-rooms of New England, what is called popularity could not reasonably have been expected for essays like his. The highest intellectual genius may become famous, but is not likely to be popular. Shakspeare is more famous than popular. Most of his plays are, to be sure, well known, so far as the plot and story go; but his golden passages are for the cultured few. And I think it is chiefly in the last hundred years that many of these have been quoted as exceptionally fine. And his sonnets seem to have received little attention till a recent period, and even now are a treasure to the poets chiefly.

It may be said that Emerson was always popular as a lecturer. I do not deny that there was an element, in most of his lectures, which struck here and there the popular mind. There was a charm to his audiences in his originality of diction, in his occasional wit and humor, in his touches of poetry, his surprising flashes of intuitive vision, his quaint and condensed apothegms, his illustrations of practical life, and (what went very far with his audiences) his rich musical voice and his earnest and impressive delivery. And those who were so fortunate as to hear him in his prime cannot forget that rapt expression of his eye, as he sometimes followed the conclusion of a sentence with a long look toward his audience, as if to enforce it with all his own grand conviction of its truth. There was something that lifted his hearers in spite of their lack of entire appreciation,—just as it is with the mixed audiences who listen to a symphony of Beethoven. Nobody believes that all concert-goers really feel the music of this grand master, except distantly, and in "the suburbs of his graces." In their hearts, the majority of listeners prefer something less transcendental. A thorough appreciation is reserved for those only who have a fine and cultivated musical sense. So I suppose it was with Emerson's audiences. There was a vague sense of being floated into a higher region, even when they could not follow the speaker into the profounder recesses of his thought, or make out the connection of all his sentences. And often, when their attention flagged in the effort, he would flash upon them with some metaphor or illustration from common life, which kept alive their interest and stimulated their expectation of more good things to come. This was undoubtedly the charm his lectures had for the people. It was that, however vague and idealistic he may have seemed, he touched so originally upon life and history, and made his hearers feel the practical side of his genius, and the bearing of the actual upon the spiritual. And one is reminded of the passages of bewitching melody in the work of some great composer, that cheer so many listeners to whom the grand movements of pure harmony are unintelligible. There was always *something* they could understand; and this was presented in a way that excited anticipation, and kept them at least in a lofty intellectual mood.

The aspects in which we may consider the writings of Mr. Emerson will readily suggest themselves.

Take him first as an observer of nature and of man, and we are struck with the variety, the freshness, the accuracy of his observation. He uses his eyes well, and gives us brief, vivid touches like a painter's out-of-door sketches. And these are not the less realistic, that he passes from them to the subject he illustrates, holding the outer world to be always symbolic of the inner. A poet by nature as well as a deep thinker, he is spontaneously alive to the beauty and order of the universe, yet always looks to analogies and correspondences between material and spiritual facts. An eager hunter after facts as the raw material of truths, yet a literal fact is of no importance standing by itself. It must be related to an intellectual or moral meaning. The universe is a symbol of the soul. Such is the theme of his first essay "Nature,"—the admirable overture to his later music, remarkable for the poetic beauty of its style no less than for its subtle thought, its masterly arrangement, sequence, and development of ideas. Yet he is no mystic in the ordinary sense. He must enter the great temple of the invisible and spiritual through the door of the visible.

Hence, he read every book, ancient and modern, which could help him to a knowledge of nature and man. He was indefatigable in pursuing facts that looked fertile in suggestion: he would know all that science, history, and society could teach him. He not only dips into all sorts of books, and observes all that surrounds him, in nature and in human life: he must see Europe, Egypt, California. He was greatly drawn to England. He has written an almost exhaustive book on English Traits. He studies the character of the British race from its root to its flower and seed. He sees the English virtues and vices side by side, or strangely mixed up, tracing them all from one ethnic origin. His praise and his blame rise and fall like a necessary *systole* and *diastole* pulsing through every chapter. He swings incense under the olfactories of these British with one hand, while in the other he holds a rod to chastise them. His criticism is like fate. The highest dignitaries and institutions of the realm are attacked on one side and defended on another. The lowest exhibitions of mob violence are held to be of the same genesis as the most chivalrous examples of nobility. Every witness is brought into court, the high and the low, the evil and the good, to testify; and the judge sums up the evidence impartially and without heat, for the consideration of a world-wide jury.

Thus, the old saying, "History is Philosophy teaching by example," finds continually new and original illustration in his writings. One of his most instructive books is his "Representative Men," opening with an essay on the uses of great men, and then taking up Plato, or the Philosopher; Swedenborg, or the Mystic; Montaigne, or the Sceptic; Shakspeare, or the Poet; Napoleon, or the Man of the World; and Goethe, or the Writer. Each chapter of this book is a masterpiece, for observation, for comprehensive grasp of his subject, for profound and subtle analysis, for expression of the predominant character and genius of each of his representative men, and for a rich, picturesque, and incomparable style.

I mention these two facinating books in this connection, because they show his powers of observation and biographical knowledge united with those of the thinker, which we proceed to consider more fully.

It is through this perception of the intimate correspondence of the outward to the inward, of nature to the soul, of historical characters to the principles they illustrate, that Emerson is to us the profound philosopher or seer. But he is the philosopher of no one special school. He belongs to no known sect of thinkers. He has no method but that of nature. He does not argue, but he affirms—out of an intuition which he assumes is or should be shared by all rational minds. He writes as the seer,—as one standing on a hill only a little higher up, who beckons his friends to come up and see with him what cannot be seen in the dim and obstructed valleys. And so his writings are of the quality of the great scriptures of all times and peoples. And though he never drops into the fashion of the old Hebrew formula, "Thus saith the Lord," he never lets us doubt that he speaks with authority, because from a conviction he shares with the wisest of all time. He believes that you and I say the same thing he does, in our better and wiser moods.

If we were particularly desirous to classify him, we might call him the Affirmative philosopher,—that is, as opposed to the speculative, the tentative, the sceptical. He is far enough away from what is rather too much talked about and prescribed nowadays as the only solid ground and method of thought,—I mean the scientific. And the purists of science can find very little in him to interest them. Let Prof. John Tyndall, however, stand as an exception, than whom probably few have a higher admiration of his genius. I suppose the metaphysicians also are rather disposed to let his books lie on the their shelves. But can they afford to do so, unless so incorrigibly bent on evolving abstractions out of their interior consciousness that nature and history and the lessons of life beat up against their bleak and barren formulas as ineffectually as the sea beats on the rocks? The time, I think, must come, when broader methods, larger affirmation of instinctive and universal truths, comprehensive estimates of all the qualities of men, perceptive, aesthetic, intellectual, moral, social, imaginative, religious, will press in and demand recognition in the professors' closet and the students' class-room, as in the public places of life; and when the books of this teacher will shine with a light which philosophers and scientists of this time fail to notice.

If it is asked what new truths does Emerson tell us, it may be answered: the province of the thinker is to illustrate and emphasize old rather than reveal new truths; to speak the truth as *he* sees it out of his freshest and most interior thought; to settle things on their right foundations; to detach the true from the half-true; to build on the sure basis of undisputed ideas and principles, and so to keep on affirming, affirming, out of his deathless conviction and insight, that scepticism will fade out in the fulness of the light he turns upon all subjects of thought.

It is here that Emerson stands pre-eminent. His themes are by no means new. But take his writings from first to last, and there is not a single one of his essays that does not sparkle and glow with fresh statement and original illustration, commanding repeated perusal and consideration. New vistas are continually opened before us. See how old and hackneyed are his themes,—Nature, Art, History, Spiritual Laws, Compensation, Love, Friendship, Prudence, Heroism, Poetry, Experience, Character, Manners, Politics, Farming, Domestic Life, and so on. There are no sensational titles. There is no rhetorical flourish, no struggle for effect. But every sentence reveals the keen observer, the ripe scholar, the original thinker, the master of language and style. Hardly a page but furnishes something strikingly quotable and memorable. His statements of ideas and principles are profounder and his illustrations of them more pertinent and picturesque than any writer of modern times, Carlyle excepted. But he has a calm depth which Carlyle only occasionally reaches.

Other thinkers draw their circles of statement; but they are almost all included in his, although concentric. He touches no subject without opening new reaches of thought, or at least suggesting them. "The lesson of life," he tells us, "is practically to generalize: to believe what the years and the centuries say against the hours; to resist the usurpation of particulars, to penetrate to their catholic sense." "Things seem to say one thing, and say the reverse."

A broad, wholesome vein of common sense is everywhere apparent. His most original statements are supported by the experience of ages. No essayist draws more frequently on past histories and biographies, but every citation is made in the interests of some commanding principle. He is wonderfully clear-eyed and alert in his application of essential meanings to facts. He has also a delicate and quiet humor at times, which adds variety and grace. His originality bears out his own definition of the word,—"being one's self and reporting accurately what we see and are."

Whatever subject he took up he treated from within outward. The structure and habit of his mind was such that he could not content himself with surfaces, but must penetrate to its central significance. Thus, he always leads his reader within door after door, till he has him seated in his private *sanctum* of thought, showing a princely hospitality which only the master and lord of himself has a right to exercise,—entertaining us with apt illustration of his theme, and so opening to our eyes the profoundest aspects of all that occupies his mind. In this deep interior sphere of thought, he rarely misses the right solution of things, his essay on the Comic being almost the only instance I remember where he fails to define with complete satisfaction.

But still it is true that some of his essays are much clearer, more continuous, keeping before the reader a more definite line of thought than others. The essay on Experience, for example, is a succession of subtle but rather evasive ideas; and the effect of the whole is vague. But take him at his best, as in that on Character which follows it, and the impression is one of wholeness and continuity that should satisfy the most superficial readers.

In a word, we might briefly define his intellectual superiority to be that he discerns as few philosophers have done the Duality that runs through the universe; touching with one hand the apparent, with the other the unapparent world, and delighting to find in the one a significant symbol of the other. His range is so wide that he swings easily from the most matter-of-fact things and events of the day to the very verge of mysticism, and seems as much at home in one extreme as in the other. Lowell calls him "a Greek head upon Yankee shoulders, a Plotinus-Montaigne," and compares his style to "home-spun cloth of gold."

It is not easy to consider the scholar and thinker apart from the ethical and spiritual guide. His lessons point always to the highest ideal of life. Every thought is the thought of a sage to whom truth is utterly empty and vain, if not moral and spiritual. This runs like a thread of gold through every line he has written. If not expressed, it is implied. His doctrine of self-reliance is one with obedience to the divine law. He is more tonic and inspiring, more full of faith and hope in the great laws of the universe than any other ethical teacher of the day. Indeed, I think many readers value him more for this quality than for anything else. In his "Conduct of Life," he shows a wonderful knowledge of the various phases of practical life, and an exuberant power of applying to them the doctrines of common sense and of the higher ethics. The style of these chapters is in unison with his theme. In the three first chapters, Fate, Power, Wealth, see the impetuous vigor of his thoughts, leaping into pithy, nervous, full-armed sentences; the acceptance of the rough, tyrannical powers of fate and circumstance; the almost extravagant generalizations in extolling the value of human power of whatever sort; the belief in the great compensations and balancing of all things and events; and the assurance of the satisfactions of wisdom and of high moral and spiritual standards. Illustrations from the latest discoveries in science abound, as well as from daily life. So that I am almost inclined to qualify what I have before said as to the essayist's probable lack of interest to the scientist. This is a book the most practical minds may enjoy. But it is the prose of life irradiated by the highest ideas and principles.

Between the time when he wrote "Nature" and "The Conduct of Life," he had read and observed extensively; and these pages abound with the most pertinent and varied illustrations. As he grows older, his horizon of facts enlarges, and makes him appear as if dealing more in detail with them, but always the same serene sky of idealistic thought bends over and harmonizes all. It is noteworthy that Carlyle (in the Carlyle and Emerson Correspondence) praises this book with special emphasis for its practical character. "I read it," he says, "with a satisfaction given me by the books of no other living mortal, . . . the best of all your books." "You have grown older, more pungent, piercing. I never read from you before such lightning gleams of meaning as are to be found here."

We must regard Emerson as not only the great ethical teacher of the age, but one of our profoundest and most earnest religious teachers. I am at a loss to understand how there should be any doubt on this point to any thorough reader of his books. It seems to have been the province of some sectarians to put in queries about Emerson's religion, because they cannot make it coincide with theirs; because they have not been able to classify and label him as belonging to any Christian sect, if even in any way Christian. Mr. Joseph Cook seems to have experienced this difficulty, and was obliged to call in Mr. Emerson's old friend and neighbor, Mr. Alcott, to help him to a classification and a name. Whereupon, Mr. Alcott calls him a Christian Theist. But it is found that even this convenient label will not stick. Mr. Emerson could not and did not wish to classify himself, or furnish the least hint toward a denominational name. For he was of the broadest church of God and Humanity; and his spiritual sympathies reached back to the oldest seers of divine truth of all races, and took in Hindu, Chinese, Persian, Greek, and Judean scriptures, as all, when at their best, proclaiming one central essential idea of the relations of man to God. Shall we say he is pagan or Christian, Pantheist or Theist? He has intuitions which include them all. It is sufficient that he emphatically declares as well as currently implies his profound belief that all that is flows from a supreme and infinite Source; that religion is not confined to one time or people; that it is a life, and not a creed,—the highest, divinest life of which man is capable.

It is only the sectarians who are puzzled to find a label for his religion. His creed escapes from their fingering like impalpable air, takes as many forms as Proteus, swims, dives, soars, hides in secular crowds or lonely solitudes, as suits its convenience, never dogmatizes, never attaches itself to one exclusive symbol, yet to the sympathetic reader brings an ever-present conviction of its uncompromising reality. It has too much mystery and grandeur for verbal self-definition. It finds an echo in the scriptures of Persia and Hindustan, as well as in those of the Hebrews and Christians. Its fullest expression is found in his essay on the Over-Soul, his chapter on Worship, and his celebrated Divinity School Address. But, in whatever class of religious thinkers he may be placed, we can never forget that Emerson was the great pioneer of liberal Christianity in this country; we can never compute our debt to him for having broken through the jungle and malarial swamps which for so many centuries obstructed the growth of a free, generous, and humane religion.

But there is one predominating characteristic of Emerson's thought, and therefore of his style, which it is time to consider, though I have unavoidably alluded to it; and that is that, though a prose essayist, he is essentially a poet. His pages are tinged through with his symbolizing imagination. Underneath the prose, you feel the poet, both in the structure of his sentences and his modes of thought, in which the facts must lead out from an imprisoning foreground of literal truth into the large aerial horizon of the ideal. What Aristotle said of the style of Plato might be said of Emerson's, that "it was a medium between poetry and prose." Herein, he is alone and original among modern thinkers, and recalls the Platonists and some of the Elizabethan writers. What we call logic does not appear in him. He has a vision of a truth, and utters it in a quaintly compact or fluently lyric sentence. He is not over-anxious about its sequence, if it is in the main line of his theme. This lack of apparent continuity baffles ordinary readers. And the prosaic minds find him wide of their mark. I have known even some persons of fine intellect and not without imagination who could never arrive at any lively interest in him.

Perhaps the fault is sometimes the writer's as well as the reader's. For his sentences are often like stepping-stones over a broad stream, and puzzle the demand for continuity and connection, though they all lead in one direction. A certain vigorous and determined foothold is required, and a steadiness of vision toward the main idea, to carry us along over the deep, wide waters of his subject. His illustrations and metaphors often have the same disjointed look, and you may be at a loss to see their precise application, until you compare one with another, as the naturalist constructs an animal out of scattered vertebræ. It is quite natural that most readers should prefer a continuous bridge through a book than to leap from one stone to another.

This peculiarity of style arises, I suppose, partly from his habit of writing his thoughts day by day as they occur, without any idea at the time of stringing his pearls on a connecting thread. It is hardly strange that, when afterward brought into an essay, they should sometimes have a mosaic-work appearance. Thoughtful readers have now grown accustomed to this peculiarity, but forty years ago he puzzled some very wise heads. When as a lecturer in Boston he charmed so many young persons of both sexes, there were, of course, many who could not share their enthusiasm; for they were not in his magnetic current, and failed to make the connections of his thought. The Rev. Dr. Channing could not see much profoundly valuable thought in him. "What was it all about?" I once heard him ask. "What definite thought or principle have you brought away from hearing him?" Jonathan Mason, the distinguished Boston lawyer, when asked if he understood Emerson, replied, "No, but I have a daughter who does,"—a saying which used to raise a laugh at the young lady's expense, but *why* the laughers never condescended to explain. These hearers and the lecturer failed to meet on a common ground. His symbolism submerged the facts they were so eager for. As Emerson himself says, "A man is like a bit of Labrador spar, which has no lustre as you turn it in your hand until you come to a particular angle, then it shows deep and beautiful colors." Those who most appreciated Emerson's early lectures in Boston were not always of the highest education and culture. I know a simple-minded man, a tailor, who always attended and always took notes, and who really enjoyed and understood him. And it is well known how the simple farmers of Lexington claimed to understand him better than they did any one else among their preachers and lecturers.

In his metrical poetry, Emerson is fresh, sparkling, tonic; and his verses are like jets of cold mineral water. His lines are packed with original thought, and glow with images drawn at first hand from nature. There is nothing in them that has been trailed through the conventional avenues of books. In his best poems, he is terse, apt, noble. And, though his style is evidently founded on the old Elizabethan, he is always original. None of our poets have described winter and snow-storm with such a free, swift, and realistic brush; or the hazy horizon of a New England May day; or the green silences and the perfumes of the pine woods. No American verse has so immortalized a flower as his lines on the Rhodora; none has so spiritualized the beauty of gems as have his three stanzas entitled "Rubies"; none has treated so graphically the sunshine on the seashore and the roar of the surf as his "Each and All." And, in his purely subjective themes, he has the charm of a subtile and mystic attraction. In many of his poems occur lines and passages as rare as some of the golden lines of Shakspeare.

But, with all these high qualities, there is in most of his verse a general lack of rhythmic and artistic form. Emerson's ideal of poetry was so high that it o'erleaped itself. In exalting the substance and spirit of Poetry, he underrated the form. Though in theory he was logically bound to appreciate form, in practice he slighted it. Sometimes, his theory would slight it, as in this passage from "Merlin":

> "Great is the art,
> Great be the manners, of the bard.
> He shall not his brain encumber
> With the coil of rhythm and number;
> But, leaving rule and pale forethought,
> He shall aye climb
> For his rhyme.
> 'Pass in, pass in,' the angels say,
> 'In to the upper doors,
> Nor count compartments of the floors,
> But mount to Paradise
> By the stairway of surprise.' "

And this Mr. Emerson certainly does, whatever else he fails in. But something more than "surprise" is necessary, whether it be to enter Paradise or Parnassus.

The mysticism and obscurity of some of his poems is faulty, and seems unnecessary, though great allowance should always be made for the peculiarity of the poet's mood, inspiration, and intention.

He is imperfect in rhythm and rhyme. Imperfect rhymes are sometimes found in the best poetry, and sometimes, though rarely, imperfect metre. But the poems of Emerson that approach completeness in the union of thought and form may almost be counted on the fingers. These are all admirable, some of them nearly perfect, which only makes us regret the deficiencies of the rest. The poet, when he once chooses rhythm and rhyme for the expression of his thought, is bound to see that the form of the expression is as perfect as the thought and feeling. For the poet must be the artist. Poetry must have a beautiful body as well as a beautiful soul. The poet deals not only with thoughts, feelings, and imaginations, but with language that may best embody them. He is free, of course, to choose his form of utterance, and may pour himself out quite unconfined by rhythm and rhyme. But, then, it is true that these are to writers of a delicately poetical nature natural and spontaneous moulds into which their poetry tends to run. And, if they elect this form, they should aim to make it worthy of its spiritual mate. It is a marriage, and should be as perfect a marriage as possible.

There are sometimes fits of quaint caprice, delicate but wilful whims of expression, in Mr. Emerson's prose sentences. But, in his verses, these are still more apparent. His lines seem sometimes bewitched, like dancing dervishes, as if tipsy with a nitrous oxide of fancy. Though their intention is genuine, they seem playing antics and attitudinizing, and make one smile where the theme is serious. While endeavoring to express a thought vividly and concisely, he adds an element of half-sportive wit,—a mental quality not very distantly related to humor, and striking for audacity and surprise. In his prose, this often tends to make him brilliant and fresh. But there he has elbow-room for self-explanation and expansion, which he cannot find in the close quarters of rhymed verse. The result is an appearance of obscurity and oddity mingled with much that is expressive and beautiful. Add to this a harsh, halting, irregular metre, continually violating rule, and the *ensemble* is more quaint than pleasing or inspiring. In these respects, he sometimes sins beyond all absolution; and we often find his prose more poetical than his verse.

But, if he has written verses that are not poems, he has also written some of the best that have been done in this country. Besides the splendid lines, couplets, quatrains, and passages scattered through his verse, like well-cut and well-set diamonds in a pile of rough ones, there are entire poems of exceptional beauty, such as "Each and All," "The Problem," "Good-by, Proud World," "The Rhodora," "The Humblebee," "The Snow-storm," "Woodnotes," "Forerunners," "The Amulet," "Threnody," "Rubies," "Days," "The Titmouse," "Nemesis," etc. Such poems as these make us forget his many failures, and are enough to rank him high, if not the highest, among American poets. But we sometimes ask if this title is not due as much to his prose as to his verse?

I have begun several times to write about Emerson, and each time, on reviewing what I had written, found it cold and inadequate. His books are so alive with suggestion that there seems to be always something omitted in whatever we say of him.

In summing up his characteristics, I run some risk of repetition, but important omission would be worse.

We are struck with his wide range of subjects. But he enters upon all with the same sympathy and power. Little escapes his vision that can furnish symbol, relation, analogy. His sentinel-like intellect stands day and night on the alert, on its watch-tower, noting the heavens and the earth, the signs of the times and the eternal verities. I have said that he writes from within outward, but it is as true that only nature and human life are his stand-point. All truth is authenticated to him by a perception of reality. If he inclines to mysticism, it is only because he has intimations of mysteries insoluble and beyond sense and the literal understanding.

He has no dealings with metaphysics. His mind seemed to shed Kant and Hegel as a duck sheds water. But he thought greatly of Goethe, for *he* harmonized the material and spiritual worlds. These two poles of the universe co-existed in perfect accord for Emerson. He valued the affirmations of Plato and the scepticism of Montaigne. He was drawn to books of travels, history, biography, natural science, as to the thinkers, poets, saints, and mystics. But he was fascinated by the least hint of correspondence between natural and spiritual. Whatever practical subject he touches, before he is done with it he glides into deeper relations underlying it. If it is politics, an ideal government is suggested; if it is manners, he sees always beneath it a substratum of character; if it is art, he has the key to its essential meaning and origin. The wildest sort of power in Southern, Western, or Irish communities, has its place and use, or at least its compensations. What he tried to express was the essence of things. He is never drawn out of his track by confusing side-lights, but moves directly toward the centre of his theme.

No one so harmonizes facts and ideas, and brings into view the underlying unity of Oriental and Occidental thought. His sublime optimism is not born of mood and temperament, but of broad intellectual insight. For he is aware of the great laws which govern mind as clearly as of those that govern matter; and there is no essential break or discord in the vast forces of the universe.

His self-sustainedness—if such a word is allowable—was a characteristic. Amid the various intellects and characters with which he came into contact, he was always unbiassed and original. He looks into his heart, and writes. Day by day, he records his most intimate thoughts, and weaves them into his public lectures. He trusts to memory as little as the artist with his pictures. I don't know any instance of his entire truth to himself, while absorbing from without all that was related to him, more remarkable than his complete immersion in the theology of Swedenborg without losing his foothold and being swept away by the New Jerusalem Church. And the result was that no writer has given us such a fair and full estimate of the great Swedish seer as he has. This, of course, is not admitted by the disciples of the New Church, to whom Swedenborg's unique system of theology is absolutely without flaw.

It ought to be an encouraging sign that, whether he has many readers or few, Mr. Emerson's fame has grown immensely. I look back to the time when his little book "Nature" appeared. Where the American mind noticed it at all, it was as a strange and visionary production. But there were those who hailed it as a contribution to a new gospel. If I may be pardoned for mentioning the influence it had on the present writer, in common with several of his contemporaries, it was like a breath of morning and a vision of sunrise. It was profound, poetic, full of suggestion of larger and more beautiful horizons than the youth of that day were accustomed to have opened to them. (Carlyle's immortal *Sartor Resartus* was its only peer.) But those who shared the enthusiasm awakened by this, or that grand lyric poem the Divinity School Address, were comparatively few. And the extreme heterodoxy, hinted or expressed, was perhaps the head and front of their offending.

To-day, the intellect of America and of England entertains these "new views" as almost orthodox; while the beauty, the profoundness, and subtile force of the Emersonian ideas are indorsed by almost all right-minded readers. At any rate, the rare genius of this scholar, thinker, and poet, has not only maintained its stand among us, but has survived in spite of sectarians, literalists, and advocates of the "scientific method," until even these must admit it among their illustrations of the "Survival of the Fittest." Whether from the prevalence of this scientific method there are as many eager readers of Emerson now as in the days of the Transcendental Movement in New England, we cannot tell without statistics. But we can be sure that, if not, there will be a reaction in the direction of his line of thought, which will give him an even more enduring fame than he has already acquired.

"The Dialectic Unity in Emerson's Prose"

W[illiam] T[orrey] Harris*

It has often been said that there is no unity in Emerson's prose essays, and, that they consist of a vast number of brilliant statements, loosely connected and bound into paragraphs, with only such unity as is given by the lids of the volume. We hear it said that the experiment has been tried of reading an entire essay, sentence by sentence, backward from the end, without injury to the sense. This lack of order and connection has even been praised as giving variety of form and freshness of style.

While it is true that there is no parading of syllogistic reasoning in Emerson's essays, and no ratiocination, there is quite sufficient unity of a higher kind if one will but once comprehend the thoughts with any degree of clearness.

In a work of literary art, such as a drama or a novel, we expect organic unity as well as logical unity. There must be a beginning, in which we form our acquaintance with the persons, their surroundings, and the peculiarities of character and situation; then a middle, in which character and situation develop into collisions as a natural result; then a solution of

*Reprinted from *Journal of Speculative Philosophy*, 18 (April 1884), 195–202.

the collision by one mode or another, restoring the equilibrium in the social whole.

In the prose essay we cannot expect organic unity, but we may expect rhetorical unity and logical unity.

There need be no formal syllogisms; the closest unity of the logical kind is the dialectic unity that begins with the simplest and most obvious phase of the subject, and discovers by investigation the next phase that naturally follows. It is an unfolding of the subject according to its natural growth in experience. Starting with this view, we shall discover this and that defect, this and that necessary correction, and in the end we shall reach a better insight, which, of course, will be the second step in our treatise, and must be followed out in the same way as before. Such development of a theme exhibits and expounds the genesis of conviction, and is the farthest removed from mere dogmatism. We pass through all shades of opinion, adopting and rejecting them in succession, on our way to the true final conclusion.

There is no logical method equal to this dialectic one that expounds the genesis of the subject. When we have reached the conclusion we have exhausted the subject, and seen the necessity of our result. Such is the method that Plato describes and indorses in the seventh book of his "Republic." To be sure, the untrained intellect will often get confused amid the labyrinth of conflicting opinions, just as the callow young men did when Socrates applied his method to their theories. The reader is apt to expect a consistency of opinion from the beginning to the end. Difference of views bewilders him.

Emerson has furnished us many very wonderful examples of dialectic treatment of his subject. But he has been very careful to avoid the show of ratiocination and the parade of proof-making. The object of his writing was to present truth, and to produce insight, and not to make proselytes.

The student of literature who wishes to learn the dialectic art, and, at the same time, to become acquainted with the genesis of Emerson's view of the world, should study the essay on "Experience" in the second series of essays. In this wonderful piece of writing we have a compend of his insights into life and nature arranged in dialectic order. Master his treatment of the topics, and you will discover what constitute real steps of progress in experience, and at the same time you will learn how the first grows into the second and that into the next, and so on to the highest view of the world that he has attained, or to the final view reached by men of deepest insight, called seers. He names these steps or stadia in experience, (1) illusion, (2) temperament, (3) succession, (4) surface, (5) surprise, (6) reality, and (7) subjectiveness.

(1) The first phase of experience, according to him, brings us to the consciousness of illusion. This is a great step. The *naïve* man without culture of any sort has not reflected enough to reach this point. He rests in the conviction that all about him is really just what he sees it. He does not

perceive the relativity of things. But at the first start in culture, long since begun even among the lowest savages, there appears the conviction that there is more in things than appears at first sight. Things are fragments of larger things; facts are fragments of larger facts. Change of the totality of conditions changes the thing or fact that is before us. Things escape us, and thus "dream delivers us to dream, and there is no end to illusion. Life is a train of moods like a string of beads, and, as we pass through them, they prove to be many-colored lenses which paint the world their own hue, and each shows only what lies in its focus."

What experience comes next after this one of illusion? Evidently the perception of conditioning circumstance, the perception of fate or external influence, which may be called temperament. (2) Structure or temperament "prevails over everything of time, place, and condition, and is inconsumable in the flames of religion." When experience has exhausted the view of temperament it finds that it has learned the necessity of succession in objects. For there is a process underlying things, and we see that what made us explain illusion by temperament was the discovery that things changed through external influences. Now we see a little better, and understand that there is succession—one phase giving way to another, and thus exhibiting a series of influences instead of one final result. Temperament therefore, is no finality, for it produces no ultimate state or condition, but succeeds only in making a transitory impression.

(3) We pass out of this stadium of experience and enter on the theory of the world that sees change and succession according to some law or other. We look now for that law. When see the law we shall understand the order of sequence, and can map out the orbit of life and of things. We shall see the true order of genesis.

This view of the necessary order of sequence is no longer a view of mere change, but a view of the whole, and hence a view of the fixed and stable. The orbit remains though the planet wanders perpetually.

(4) Emerson calls the view of the law of change "surface," as if the seeing of a line as a whole were the seeing of a surface. Various tadia of opinion there might be on this plane of experience. As very narrow orbit or a very wide one might be computed for the cycle of succession. The progress of experience will correct the narrow view. We think to-day that we have taken in all the metamorphoses of the object of investigation, but to-morrow we discover new ones and have to enlarge our description. "Surface" expands and we make new theories of the law. We are, however, dealing with the law of cause and effect, and cannot formulate the whole under it, for the whole cannot be cause of something else or the effect of some other being.

(5) Emerson calls the next form of experience "surprise," because it begins with the insight made in some high moment of life, when for the first time one gets a glimpse of the form of the whole. What must be the form of the whole, you ask? The whole does not admit of such predicates

as we apply to the part or fragment. The dependent has one law, and the independent has another. The dependent presupposes something, it is a relative existence and its being is in another. The independent is self-contained, self-active, self-determined, *causa sui*. The first insight is a "surprise," and so is the second insight; all of the high moments of experience admit us to "surprises," for we see the fountain of pure energy and self-determination, in place of the limitations of things, and the derivative quality of objects which receive only their allotted measures of being. The soul opens into the sea of creative energy, inexhaustible and ever-imparting.

By these moments of "surprise," therefore, we ascend to a new place of experience, no longer haunted by these dismal spectres of illusion, temperament, change, and surface or mechanic fixed laws. Things are not fragments of a vast machine, nor are men links in a cosmic process that first develops and then crushes them. Things do not exist in succession, as it before seemed to us, but the true, real existence that we have found is always the same.

(6) We enter through the moments of surprise into the realm of insight into reality, hence *reality* is Emerson's sixth category of experience. "By persisting to read or think, this region gives further sign of itself, as it were, in flashes of light, in sudden discoveries of its profound beauty and repose, as if the clouds that covered it parted at intervals and showed the approaching traveller the inland mountains, with the tranquil eternal meadows spread at their base, whereon flocks graze and shepherds pipe and dance."

(7) One more step experience takes—it identifies the deepest reality as of one nature with itself. The absolute is mind. Emerson names this step of insight subjectiveness, because in it we arrive at the conviction that the absolute is subject and not merely unconscious law or power. At this highest point of experience we reach the station of the seer, the culmination of human experience. The seer as philosopher sees the highest principle to be reason; the poet sees the world to be the expression of reason; the prophet and law-giver sees reason as the authoritative, regulative principle of life; the hero sees reason as a concrete guiding force in society.

In a certain sense all of Emerson's writings are expansions and confirmations of some one of these phases of experience. The essay on the "Over-Soul" treats of surprise and reality; that on Circles treats of succession, surface, and reality, under other names; that on Spiritual Laws on reality and subjectiveness; that on Fate treats of temperament and succession; those on Worship, History, Gifts, Heroism, Love and such titles, treat of subjectiveness. His treatises on concrete themes use these insights perpetually as solvent principles—but always with fresh statement and new resources of poetic expression.

There is nowhere in all literature such sustained flight toward the sun—"a flight," as Plotinus calls it, "of the alone to the alone"—as that in the essay on Over-Soul, wherein Emerson, at great length, unfolds the insights, briefly but inadequately explained under the topic of "surprise" in the essay on experience. It would seem as if each paragraph stated the idea of the whole, and then again that each sentence in each paragraph reflected entire the same idea.

Where there is no genesis there can be no dialectic unity. The absolute is not a becoming but a self-identical activity. In those essays in which Emerson has celebrated this doctrine of the highest reality, and its subjectivity or rational nature, and its revelation to us, he writes in a style elevated above dialectic unity. These essays do not have dialectic unity only because they have a higher form of unity—that of absolute identity. Each is in all and all is in each.

To give one specimen of this I offer a very short analysis of the contents of the essay on "The Over-Soul." He says in substance that man has some moments in his life when he sees deeply into reality; what he sees then has authority over the other parts of his life. He sees principles of justice, love, freedom, and power—attributes of God. This seeing is the common element in all minds, and transcendent of the limitations of particular individuals. Just as events flow down from a hidden source, so these ideas and insights descend into the mind. He calls this the "over-soul," "a unity within which every man's being is contained and made one with every other. Although we live in division and succession, and see the world piece by piece, yet the soul is the whole, and this is the highest law." These glimpses of the eternal verity come on occasions of conversation, reverie, remorse, dreams, and times of passion. We learn that the soul is not an organ, but that which animates all organs; not a faculty, but a light, and the master of the intellect and will. Individual man is only the organ of the soul. These deeps of the spiritual nature are accessible to all men at some time. The sovereignty of the over-soul is shown by its independence of all limitation. Time, space, and circumstance do not change its attributes. Its presence does not make a progress measurable by time, but it produces metamorphoses causing us to ascend from one plane of experience to the next—as great a change as from egg to worm, or from worm to fly. Society and institutions reveal this common nature or the higher person, or impersonal one—for, in order to prevent the confusion of attributing to the over-soul the passions and imperfections of human personality, Emerson sometimes speaks of Him as impersonal (using Cousin's expression). This revelation of the divine is a disclosure of what is universal, and not the telling of fortunes. There is no concealment when in the presence of its light; the reality appears through all its disguises. The growth of the intellect as well as of the character obeys the same law. The emotion of the sublime accompanies the influx of its light. Its presence distinguishes genius and talent. Faith, worthy of the name, is faith in these transcendent affirmations of the soul. Thus revering the soul, man "will calmly front the morrow in the negligency of that trust which carries God with it, and so hath already the whole future in the bottom of the heart."

In his book on "Nature," his first published work, Emerson developed substantially the same views, with a system of classification much like that in the essay on experience, and showing a genesis in the same dialectic form. (1) Nature for use or "commodity," as he calls it, is the first aspect recognized. After food, clothing, and shelter comes next nature's service to man in satisfying the spiritual want of the (2) beautiful. Then through this comes the symbolic expression of human nature through its correspondence with material nature, and thus arises (3) language. Fourthly, nature is a (4) discipline, educating understanding and the reason, and also the will and conscience. Then the transition to (5) idealism is easy. Nature is for the education of man, and this lesson is taught us in five distinct ways. Sixthly, we arrive at the knowledge of the (6) one spirit that originates both nature and man, and reveals its nature in the ethical and intellectual constitution of the mind and its correspondences in nature. Thus from nature we come to the over-soul, or what was called reality and subjectivity in the essay on experience. The eighth and final chapter of Nature draws practical conclusions, making application of the doctrine to life: "The problem of restoring to the world original and eternal beauty is solved by the redemption of the soul. The ruin or blank that we see when we look at nature is in our own eye. The axis of vision is not coincident with the axis of things, and so they appear not transparent, but opaque. Build, then, your own world. As fast as you conform your life to the pure idea in your mind, the world will unfold its great proportions."

Emerson looks on the world of nature and man as the revelation that the over-soul makes to him, and accordingly looks reverently toward it, and through it, to the great soul of souls, and always sees, under whatever guise, some good. He finds help in everything. He helps every one, too, most by teaching to them the significance of the world as he has found it.

This thought of the revelation of the soul in man and nature is the idea that forms the unity of all that he has written, whether it be in essays like the "Over-Soul," or in historical and critical studies like "English Traits and Representative Men," or in poems of nature like "Monadnoc." One will find everywhere, though under slightly differing names, the elements of experience described in this sublime poem prefixed to the essay on Experience:

> "The lords of life, the lords of life,
> I saw them pass
> In their own guise,
> Like and unlike,
> Portly and grim,
> Use and surprise,
> Surface and dream,
> Succession swift and spectral wrong

Temperament without a tongue,
And the inventor of the game,
Omnipresent without name;
Some to see, some to be guessed,
They marched from east to west:
Little man, least of all,
Among the legs of his guardians tall,
Walked about with puzzled look.
Him by the hand dear nature took,
Dearest nature, strong and kind,
Whispered 'Darling, never mind!
To-morrow they will wear another face,
The founder thou; these are thy race!'

"Mr. Emerson"

Henry James, Sr.*

At all events, if we are still to go on cherishing any such luxury as a private conscience towards God, I greatly prefer for my own part that it should be an evil conscience. Conscience was always intended as a rebuke and never as an exhilaration to the private citizen; and so let it flourish till the end of our wearisome civilization. There are many signs, however, that this end is near. My recently deceased friend Mr. Emerson, for example, was all his days an arch traitor to our existing civilized regimen, inasmuch as he unconsciously managed to set aside its fundamental principle in doing without conscience, which was the entire secret of his very exceptional interest to men's speculation. He betrayed it to be sure without being at all aware of what he was doing; but this was really all that he distinctively did to my observation. His nature had always been so innocent, so unaffectedly innocent, that when in later life he began to cultivate a club consciousness, and to sip a glass of wine or smoke a cigar, I felt very much outraged by it. I felt very much as if some renowned Boston belle had suddenly collapsed and undertaken to sell newspapers at a street corner. "Why, Emerson, is this *you* doing such things?" I exclaimed. "What profanation! Do throw the unclean things behind your back!" But, no; he was actually proud of his accomplishments! This came from his never knowing (intellectually) what he stood for in the evolution of New England life. He was lineally descended to begin with, from a half-score of comatose New England clergymen, in whose behalf probably the religious instinct had been used up. Or, what to their experience had been religion, became in that of their descendant *life*. The actual

*Reprinted from *The Literary Remains of the Late Henry James*, ed. William James (Boston: James R. Osgood, 1885), pp. 293–302.

truth, at any rate, was that he never felt a movement of the life of conscience from the day of his birth till that of his death. I could never see
any signs of such a life in him. I remember, to be sure, that he had a great
gift of friendship, and that he was very plucky in behalf of his friends
whenever they felt themselves assailed—as plucky as a woman. For instance, whenever Wendell Phillips ventilated his not untimely wit at the
expense of our club-house politicians, Emerson, hearing his friends among
these latter complain, grew indignant, and for several days you would
hear nothing from his lips but excessive eulogies of Mr. Garrison, which
sounded like nothing else in the world but revilings of Mr. Phillips. But,
bless your heart! there was not a bit of conscience in a bushel of such experiences, but only wounded friendship, which is a totally different and
much lower thing.

The infallible mark of conscience is that it is always a subjective
judgment couched in some such language as this: "God be merciful to *me*
a sinner!" and never an objective judgment such as this: *God damn Wendell Phillips, or some other of my friends!* This latter judgment is always
an outbreak of ungovernable temper on our part, and was never known to
reach the ear of God save in this guise: *God* BLESS *W.P. or any other
friend implicated!* Now Emerson was seriously incapable of a subjective
judgment upon himself; he did not know the inward difference between
good and evil, so far as he was himself concerned. No doubt he perfectly
comprehended the outward or moral difference between these things; but
I insist upon it that he never so much as dreamed of any inward or
spiritual difference between them. For this difference is vitally seen only
when oneself seems unchangeably evil to his own sight, and one's neighbor unchangeably good in the comparison. How could Emerson ever have
known this difference? I am satisfied that he never in his life had felt a temptation *to bear false-witness* against his neighbor, *to steal, to commit adultery,
or to murder*; how then should he have ever experienced what is technically called a conviction of sin?—that is, a conviction of himself as *evil*
before God, and all other men as *good*. One gets a conviction of the evil
that attaches to the natural selfhood in man in no other way than—as I can
myself attest—by this growing acquaintance with his own moral infirmity, and the consequent gradual decline of his self-respect. For I myself
had known all these temptations—in forms of course more or less
modified—by the time I was fourteen or fifteen years old; so that by the
time I had got to be twenty-five or thirty (which was the date of my first
acquaintance with Emerson) I was saturated with a sense of spiritual
evil—no man ever more so possibly, since I felt thoroughly *self*-con-
demned before God. Good heavens! how soothed and comforted I was by
the innocent lovely look of my new acquaintance, by his tender courtesy,
his generous laudatory appreciation of my crude literary ventures! and
how I used to lock myself up with him in his bed-room, swearing that
before the door was opened I would arrive at the secret of his immense

superiority to the common herd of literary men! I might just as well have locked myself up with a handful of diamonds, so far as any capacity of self-cognizance existed in him. I found in fact, before I had been with him a week, that the immense superiority I ascribed to him was altogether personal or practical—by no means intellectual; that it came to him by birth or genius like a woman's beauty or charm of manners; that no other account was to be given of it in truth than that Emerson himself was an unsexed woman, a veritable fruit of almighty power in the sphere of our *nature*.

This after a while grew to be a great discovery to me; but I was always more or less provoked to think that Emerson himself should take no intellectual stock in it. On the whole I may say that at first I was greatly disappointed in him, because his intellect never kept the promise which his lovely face and manners held out to me. He was to my senses a literal divine presence in the house with me; and we cannot recognize literal divine presences in our houses without feeling sure that they will be able to say something of critical importance to one's intellect. It turned out that any average old dame in a horse-car would have satisfied my intellectual rapacity just as well as Emerson. My standing intellectual embarrassment for years had been to get at the bottom of the difference between law and gospel in humanity—between the head and the heart of things—between the great God almighty, in short, and the intensely wooden and ridiculous gods of the nations. Emerson, I discovered immediately, had never been the least of an expert in this sort of knowledge; and though his immense personal fascination always kept up, he at once lost all intellectual prestige to my regard. I even thought that I had never seen a man more profoundly devoid of spiritual understanding. This prejudice grew, of course, out of my having inherited an altogether narrow ecclesiastical notion of what spiritual understanding was. I supposed it consisted unmistakably in some doctrinal lore concerning man's regeneration, to which, however, my new friend was plainly and signally incompetent. Emerson, in fact, derided this doctrine, smiling benignly whenever it was mentioned. I could make neither head nor tail of him according to men's ordinary standards—the only thing that I was sure of being that he, like Christ, was somehow divinely begotten. He seemed to me unmistakably virgin-born whenever I looked at him, and reminded me of nothing so much as of those persons dear to Christ's heart who should come after him professing no allegiance to him—having never heard his name pronounced, and yet perfectly fulfilling his will. He never seemed for a moment to antagonize the church of his own consent, but only out of condescension to his interlocutor's weakness. In fact he was to all appearance entirely ignorant of the church's existence until you recalled it to his imagination; and even then I never knew anything so implacably and uniformly mild as his judgments of it were. He had apparently lived all his life in a world where it was only subterraneously known; and, try as you would, you could never persuade him that any the least living power attached to it. The same profound incredulity characterized him in regard to the State; and it was only in his enfeebled later years that he ever lent himself to the idea of society as its destined divine form. I am not sure indeed that the lending was ever very serious. But he was always greedy, with all a Yankee's greediness, after facts, and would at least appear to listen to you with earnest respect and sympathy whenever you plead for society as the redeemed form of our nature.

In short he was, as I have said before, fundamentally treacherous to civilization, without being at all aware himself of the fact. He himself, I venture to say, was peculiarly unaware of the fact. He appeared to me utterly unconscious of himself as either good or evil. He had no conscience, in fact, and lived by perception, which is an altogether lower or less spiritual faculty. The more universalized a man is by genius or natural birth, the less is he spiritually individualized, making up in breadth of endowment what he lacks in depth. This was remarkably the case with Emerson. In his books or public capacity he was constantly electrifying you by sayings full of divine inspiration. In his talk or private capacity he was one of the least remunerative men I ever encountered. No man could look at him speaking (or when he was silent either, for that matter) without having a vision of the divinest beauty. But when you went to him to hold discourse about the wondrous phenomenon, you found him absolutely destitute of reflective power. He had apparently no private personality; and if any visitor thought he discerned traces of such a thing, you may take for granted that the visitor himself was a man of large imaginative resources. He was nothing else than a show-figure of almighty power in our nature; and that he was destitute of all the apparatus of humbuggery that goes to eke out more or less the private pretension in humanity, only completed and confirmed the extraordinary fascination that belonged to him. He was full of living inspiration to me whenever I saw him; and yet I could find in him no trivial sign of the selfhood which I found in other men. He was like a vestal virgin, indeed, always in ministry upon the altar; but the vestal virgin had doubtless a prosaic side also, which related her to commonplace people. Now Emerson was so far *unlike* the virgin: he had no prosaic side relating him to ordinary people. Judge Hoar and Mr. John Forbes constituted his spontaneous political conscience; and his domestic one (equally spontaneous) was supplied by loving members of his own family—so that he only connected with the race at second-hand, and found all the material business of life such as voting and the payment of taxes transacted for *him* with marvellous lack of friction.

Incontestably the main thing about him, however, as I have already said, was that he unconsciously brought you face to face with the infinite in humanity. When I looked upon myself, or upon the ordinary rabble of ecclesiastics and politicians, everything in us seemed ridiculously undivine. When I looked upon Emerson, these same undivine things were what gave *him* his manifest divine charm. The reason was that in him everything seemed innocent by the transparent absence of selfhood, and in us everything seemed foul and false by its preternatural activity. The difference between us was made by innocence altogether. I never thought it was a real or spiritual difference, but only a natural or apparent one. But such as it was, it gave me my first living impression of the great God almighty who alone is at work in human affairs, avouching his awful and adorable spiritual infinitude only through the death and hell wrapped up in our finite experience. This was Emerson's incontestable virtue to every one who appreciated him, that he recognized no God outside of himself and his interlocutor, and recognized him there only as the *liaison* between the two, taking care that all their intercourse should be holy with a holiness undreamed of before by man or angel. For it is not a holiness taught by books or the example of tiresome, diseased, self-conscious saints, but simply by one's own redeemed flesh and blood. In short, the only holiness which Emerson recognized, and for which he consistently lived, was innocence. And innocence—glory be to God's spiritual incarnation in our nature!—has no other root in us than our unconscious flesh and bones. That is to say, it attaches only to what is definitively universal or natural in our experience, and hence appropriates itself to individuals only in so far as they learn to denude themselves of personality or self-consciousness; which reminds one of Christ's mystical saying: *He that findeth his life (in himself) shall lose it, and he that loseth his life for my sake shall find it.*

"Hegel and his New England Echo"

[Henry Athanasius Brann]*

The rarest quality in this world is what theologians call "prudence,"[1] or counsel, or judgment, and what ordinary people call "common sense." Its deficiency is often most marked in men otherwise most gifted. Great orators and great poets, even great statesmen, sometimes show a lamentable lack of it; but great metaphysicians most frequently lead the vanguard in the army of fools. We are not surprised to miss it in poetic characters in which imagination and passion predominate; but it is astonishing to find it lacking in men gifted with logical powers of extraordinary force. These are the thoughts that come naturally into the mind of one who reads George William Frederick Hegel's *Propädeutik*, in which he explains his theory of the "Logic of Being." The coolness with which this wonderfully gifted man wades through page upon page of serried argument to expound a system repugnant to the common sense of the

*Reprinted from *Catholic World*, 41 (April 1885), 56–61.

average child, is but one instance of the imperturbable gravity with which other metaphysicians propound equally absurd systems of philosophy. He is the most logical and consequently the most absurd of the modern German metaphysicians.

Starting out with the admission of Kant's false assertion that it is impossible to get from the subject to the object in the realm of thought, like Fichte and Schelling, Hegel holds to the universal identity of all things. Kant would not concede that the mind apprehends any real object, or that there is a bridge uniting the subject and the object in thought, and consequently he led logically to scepticism, although he was not willing to admit the conclusion of his own premises. He spurred his reason to the dividing line, to the abyss which he said separated the thinking subject from its object; and then, balking at the imaginary chasm, he applied the whip of a *dictamen practicum rationis* to his intellect, and made it bound to the other side instead of walking along the straight road and the safe bridge pointed out to him by homely common sense and self-consciousness.

Fichte, shutting his ears to the voice of the same monitors, and not willing to admit the "practical dictate" of reason, to get from subject to object identified them both, and made them mere forms or modifications of his own personality. For him there is nothing in the universe but one large capital I, to which everything physical, intellectual, and moral is referable. Schelling advanced a step farther in the direction of silly systematization. Fichte considered everything objective a mere form of the I; Schelling made all things mere forms of the *absolute*. This *absolute* destroys the personal in nature and develops itself in the real order in the forms of weight, of light, motion, life, and organization, and in the ideal order produces virtue and science, goodness and religion, beauty and art. The absolute, personal I, of which all things are forms with Fichte, becomes the absolute, impersonal *not-I* of Schelling. Yet his conscience gave the lie to his theory.

Farther onward marched Hegel with a theory of his own which he intended to be an improvement on the two preceding ones. He built all things on what he calls the *idea*. Its object is being, which is found by analysis in all our conceptions. This being is conceived with various and often contradictory attributes. It is one, it is multiple; it is material, it is spiritual; it is absolute yet it is relative, it is finite and yet it is infinite. These attributes of being suppose one another at the same time that they destroy one another. Thus the finite supposes the infinite, and the infinite supposes the finite, as they are correlative terms; yet they destroy each other, for what is finite cannot be infinite, nor can what is infinite be finite. Therefore beyond the finite and the infinite we must look for a term common to both, a term neither finite nor infinite, yet which can be either. Such a term is *being*, taken in its most general sense—that is, being without any properties, modes, or determinations. This idea of indeterminate, abstract *being* supposes another idea—namely, the idea of *nothing*. We cannot conceive being without thinking of its opposite, no-being; nor can we think of no-being, or *nothing*, without thinking of be-ing, its contrary. The ideas of being and nothing are therefore correlative ideas. But these ideas do not differ like those of the different beings already mentioned. For the being of which Hegel speaks is the same in all things and entirely destitute of properties, and, since no form or modifica-tion can be apprehended in it, it does not really differ from nothing. Hence the fundamental principle of Hegel's system—*nothing and being are identical*. Yet this *being-nothing* is not the same as absolute nothing. Being-nothing is a medium between being, properly so-called, and ab-solute nothing. This medium is the *becoming das Werden*: because, although it is nothing real, it may become so. This *becoming*, in develop-ing itself, produces logic, nature, and the human race! Such is the pan-theistic nightmare begotten of this great man's mind in the full possession of his mental powers, and such is the system now in vogue even among hard-headed and practical New England thinkers.

"Τέκτει πρώτιστον ὑπηνέμιον Νὺξ ἡ μελανόπτερος α ὁν."[2]

The "wind-egg" has burst, and out of it a high-soaring transcendental fledgling has sprung into existence in New England, in the character of Ralph Waldo Emerson. Hegel's pupils, young and intelligent Germans, used to listen in raptures to his vagaries, and go into ecstasy over his high-sounding phrases about the *idea*, which is ever producing God and the universe, the chimeras of human intelligence. In like manner the "Con-cord School of Philosophy" in Massachusetts has been, season after season, dilating on the Emersonian philosophy and writing essays on the words of the "master," as they love to call him. Clever men like Oliver Wendell Holmes blasphemously compare him to the Messiah and write his life as that of an original genius and a saint. Professor W. T. Harris and F. B. Sanborn extol him as a new Plato or a Socrates, and would have us take his poetry and prose as the great masterpieces of the age. And yet Emerson is purely a plagiarist. There is hardly an original thought in his works. There are odd forms of expression, conceits of thought, and striking peculiarities of style, a crispness and brilliancy peculiarly his own; but the matter, the ground-work, the ideas are all stolen. He read almost every volume of Goethe—fifty-five of them at least, according to his own testimony[3]—and the pantheism of the German poet impregnates his whole mind. In his essay on *Books* Emerson himself confesses that his learning is second-hand. A hundred passages in his works point to the Hegelian sources from which he drew his inspiration. "The receiver," the human mind, "is only the All-Giver in part and in infancy." Again he writes: "We can point nowhere to anything final but tendency; but ten-dency appears on all hands." This is Hegel's eternal *Werden*. Nothing is. Everything is only becoming or going to be. Such is the teaching. But how nonsensical it is! We know that things are fixed in existence and we see them. There are real trees and animals around us, fixed in their nature, their life, and their death. There is in them a tendency to death; they are going to die, if you will; but there is no indefinite tendency and nothing of the infinite in them. "The true Christianity is a faith in the *infinitude* of man." Humbug! Man is not infinite, and he knows it. Mr. Emerson knew that even he, great as his followers thought him, was limited on every side, physically, mentally, and morally. Why, then, this twaddle about the "infinitude of man"?

"The idealist takes his departure from his consciousness, and reckons the world an appearance. His thought—that is the universe." Here is another Hegelian aphorism in New England clothes. Now, if the "idealist"—that is, the transcendentalist—takes his departure from his consciousness and he is not crazy, he knows that he is a distinct, finite existence; and that the universe, the trees, flowers, birds, stars around and above him, are realities and not appearances. Botany is as much a science of reality as astronomy; and the transcendentalist who asserts that their objects are only appearances and not realities deserves only to be laughed at. "His thought" is not "the universe," and he knows it. His thought is his mental act; the universe is external to him and not identified with his personality. He surely ought to know it, for every child does. A hot stove is a part of the universe, and when the child burns his fingers by touching it he knows that the stove is not in his head nor a part of himself. Mr. Emerson knew that the cabbages in his garden were not a part of himself. Then why pretend to believe that they were? And why should sensible men call such raving by the dignified name of philosophy? "The mind is one, and nature is its correlative," and in the light of these two facts "history is to be read and written."[4] This man expects every one to accept his assertions as gospel. The Concord School of Philosophy may do so, but we cannot. Nature is not the correlative of the mind; there is no essential connection between them; the one is conceivable as existing without the other, and their relation is purely accidental. History written from Emerson's standpoint is simply fiction and imagination. It cannot be written *à priori*. If it is a science at all, or if there is anything scientific in it, it is all *à posteriori*. It is a statement of facts, of the acts of free agents governed by an all-wise Providence, and not a development of the *me* or the *absolute* or the *idea*. Ordinary people think so and know so, and so did Emerson before he got moonstruck by reading Goethe, the German pantheist, and Swedenborg's dreams. Emerson shows evidence of insanity in some of his expressions. Thus he says, "I become a transparent eyeball," in his essay on *Nature*. We wonder, when he wrote that, whether he was not bilious and his "eyeball" bloodshot as he looked at it in the glass? How can the practical and usually sensible New-Englander be enchanted by such crazy poetry as the following?

> "The clouds are rich and dark, the air serene
> So like the soul of me, *what if 'twere me?*"

Was Emerson drinking when he thus could not tell whether the clouds and the air were himself or not? No, he was a sober man. Was he insane, or was he merely writing this transcendental stuff to make a name as an original thinker? We know that Seneca says, "Nullum magnum ingenium sine quadam mixtura insaniæ." We know that men have burned temples and leaped into volcanoes, impelled by a desire for notoriety, the morganatic sister of fame. Has the New-Englander been copying Hegel for the same motive?

> "Saying, Sweetheart! the old mystery remains
> *If I am I; thou, thou or thou art I?*"

If Emerson could not really tell the difference between himself and his sweetheart, she should have boxed his ears to bring him back to his senses and a knowledge of his distinct personality. He should have taken counsel with his dog to get proof of the identity about which he is always in doubt:

> "If it be I, he'll wag his little tail;
> And if it be not I, he'll loudly bark and wail."

The dog might be a better authority than the "clouds" or the "sweetheart."

The fact is, the New-Englander out-Hegels Hegel in fantastic expressions. Hegel is dry and logical. His style is sober, his opinions themselves are the monstrosities of his system; but his argumentation is consecutive, and he insists on convincing his audience. Emerson disclaims any such purpose. "Do not set the least value on what I do, or the least discredit on what I do not, as if I pretended to settle anything as true or false. I unsettle all things. No facts are to me sacred; none are profane: I simply experiment, an endless seeker, with no Past at my back."[5] Here is a confession for a pretended philosopher to make! He has nothing to give to hungering humanity. He means to unsettle convictions, disturb the peace and happiness of minds, and give nothing in return. He has no reverence for the hoary and venerable past with its creeds and churches, some of which have done so much good for the moral regeneration of mankind; no veneration for the Mosaic laws which, given from Sinai, are the perfection of reason in the government of human morals; none for the Christian Church, which abolished paganism, barbarism, and their atrocities, and is still engaged, like its divine Founder, in "going about doing good." What is the use of such a man, of such a seeker, who upsets all that men hold dear, burns their homes and temples over their heads, and sends them adrift in the cold, bleak world of doubt and uncertainty? To borrow his own expression, he has been engaged in "tapping the tempest for a little side-wind"; and he has filled himself with the wind! Sensible people, however, will follow his advice. They will not "set the least value" on what he says or does. They will hold to the teaching of inner consciousness and continue to believe in their distinct personalities. The transcendental lover may believe, if he pleases, that his sweetheart is himself; but the common-sense Yankee farmer will believe no such rubbish, nor will he give up his reason to believe that he is the "cloud" or the "breeze," or the west wind or the south wind, though the "Concord School of Philosophy" may consider themselves the whole cave of Æolus, if they please.

Notes

1. *Recta ratio agibilium*, St. Thomas calls it. Plato names it φρονήδις.

2. Aristophanes Ορνιθες, v. 695.

3. Oliver Wendell Holmes, *Ralph Waldo Emerson* (Boston: Houghton, Mifflin, 1883), p. 380.

4. Emerson's *Essay on History*.

5. Essay on *Circles*.

"Emerson"

John M. Robertson*

I.

It is an instructive fact in the history of culture that the English-speaking population of North America, while considerably out-numbering for some time back that of the old country, has thus far contributed but a small part of the permanently important literature of the language. Save for the very notable works of Jonathan Edwards, which bring such remarkable reasoning power to the demonstration of the incredible, and for the vigorous rationality of Franklin, American authorship only began to exist for English readers within the present century; and only in the latter half of it have American books begun to get any cordial recognition. The novels of Fenimore Cooper represented no original or enduring culture force; and the pleasing works of Washington Irving were rather an assimilation of previous English culture than an addition to it. It is with Emerson that a visibly important American factor first appears in our higher literature; and while in Emerson's first generation there were at least two other American figures in the front literary rank, the number to-day is certainly no greater absolutely, and is smaller proportionally.

*Reprinted from *Modern Humanists: Sociological Studies of Carlyle, Mill, Emerson, Arnold, Ruskin, and Spencer with an Epilogue on Social Reconstruction* (London: Swan Sonnenschein, 1891), pp. 112–136.

Contemporary with the young Emerson were Edgar Poe, that singular apparition of pure intellect in the literature of imagination; and Hawthorne, nearly the first great novelist of the psychological school, and still the most individual. Longfellow, of course, has been much more popular than either of these, as Dr. Holmes has perhaps been more popular than Emerson, but these beloved writers hardly count as first-rate literary influences. And whereas the strangeness and subtlety of Hawthorne keep him the favourite of only a minority, and the electric light of Poe's intellect is too cold and unearthly to please average human nature, Emerson remains, of that group, the one who will be most generally recognised as an important writer on this side of the Atlantic. Since Emerson's rise to fame, again, we have Mr. Lowell, happily still alive, and still in general power second to no critic of his time; and among the younger men, two highly accomplished novelists, at the very top of the second rank, Mr. James and Mr. Howells, of whom the former is even more gifted as a critic than as a fictionist. Further, we have Walt Whitman, who in some respects has influenced men's minds in this country more forcibly than any of his now surviving contemporaries, by virtue rather of his spirit and message than of his literary performance. That short list exhausts the foremost names in American literature for fifty years back; and if at this moment we in England seem to flag in the production of first-rate writers and thinkers, the ebb is still more obvious in the United States, since here several men of the first degree of reputation still survive. A few able scholars there are in the great Republic, and a number of more or less capable writers on sociology and philosophy, of whom Mr. Lester Ward and Mr. Daniel Greenleaf Thompson deserve special mention. But these writers have still to conquer a British or European fame; and the fact remains that the great American population yields a very small crop of eminent writers.

The fact cannot be faced without some casting-about for an explanation, and that is not easy to formulate. It cannot be merely that the limited development of university life in the States is unfavourable to literature, for the majority of our own leading writers of the past hundred years owe little or nothing to universities. The younger Mill, Ricardo, Grote, Scott, Dickens, Lewes, Spencer, Huxley, Tyndall, George Eliot, Mrs. Browning, Charlotte Brontë, Jane Austen—these men and women represent no university training; and though our poets generally do, still Browning might conceivably have had as much importance without attending London University, and Thackeray's work savours little of his university preparation. And the same with Darwin, not to speak of Carlyle. Nor can the discrepancy be wholly due to the commercial conditions of American literature, which go to starve out the native author by the unlimited reproduction of books imported from England;[1] for the majority of the English writers I have named do not represent life conditions peculiar to this country. Apparently we must allow something for both these causes, operating directly and indirectly, and add the inference that a productive intellectual soil takes a long time to develop even in a receptive community. America has produced one of the very greatest of inventors, Edison, and a perfect multitude of lesser inventors; but her literature is still indigent in point of quality relatively to her civilisation. In fine, the general civilisation has not yet been overtaken by the thought of the literary class; and the chances are that important social readjustments will take place before that happens.

II.

Emerson then represents for us the most conspicuous American influence on modern English culture. Before him, as Mr. Lowell says, his countrymen were "still socially and intellectually moored to English thought": it was he who "cut the cable" and gave them "a chance at the dangers and the glories of blue water."[2] And though Emerson's main lines of thought were not new, and not peculiar to him, his was essentially an independent development. Mr. John Burroughs has said of him that his culture was "ante-natal,"[3] this by way of summing-up the remarkably copious clerical ancestry of which he came on both sides of the house. If the effect of many generations of clergymen were to produce Emersons, human prospects would in general be brighter; but we must continue to surmise that Emerson owed rather more to the culture he imbibed after birth than to what he inherited. What he did inherit—and this is sometimes overlooked—was a faculty for rhetoric, in the best meaning of the term, both on the side of the literary sense and the necessary physical equipments. At school the future lecturer asserted himself not in any noteworthy intellectuality, such as might have been looked for in the scion of a clerical line, but in a turn for recitation—certainly of his own verses.[4] What is more, the terse effective style of his mature writing is evidently formed on the model of the epistolary and conversational manner of that very remarkable woman, his aunt, whose style we know he greatly admired,[5] and whose influence on the formation of his character he has emphatically acknowledged.[6] I see the Puritan moral heredity much more in her than in him. Passionately attached to her nephews, she yet was capable of absolutely breaking with Ralph Waldo in later life, despite his continued affection, simply because she could not tolerate his "airy speculations."[7] Not that she was an orthodox Puritan. Her nephew has told us[8] how, with a strong constitutional clinging to the old Calvinism, she was in spite of herself a reasoner and a sceptic, and so always divided against herself. In her, a strenuous intelligence was welded to a passionate and headstrong character; in her nephew, whose mother was of a stable and undemonstrative temperament,"[9] the inherited leanings were modified by a serene temper and a turn for what Walt Whitman points to when he says, "I loafe and invite my soul." There is small trace of the

Puritan in that; and though Emerson drew back after his first praise of the "Leaves of Grass," he was always something of a Greek, composed in the presence of the primary human instincts.

Mr. Lowell would seem to make out that the trace was obvious, but it is all a matter of the use of terms. "The Puritanism of the past," he says, "found its unwilling poet in Hawthorne, the rarest creative imagination of the century, the rarest in some ideal respects since Shakspere; but the Puritanism that cannot die, the Puritanism that made New England what it is, and is destined to make America what it should be, found its voice in Emerson."[10] And he further says: "The truth is, that both Scotch Presbyterianism and New England Puritanism made their new avatar in Carlyle and Emerson, the heralds of their formal decease; and the tendency of the one towards Authority and of the other towards Independency might have been prophesied by whoever had studied history." Well, on that plan you might prove that anything came of any one thing that preceded it. To say that Carlyle grows out of Scotch Presbyterianism, and that, as Mr. Lowell further puts it, "the Transcendental Movement was the Protestant spirit of Puritanism seeking a new outlet," is much the same as it would be to say that Protestantism grew out of Catholicism, and Christianity out of Paganism, and so on for ever. There is a positive truth in each of these propositions, but only the general truth of evolutionary change. James Mill came of Scotch Presbyterianism just as much as Carlyle did; and he tended not towards Authority but towards Independency. And unless I am mistaken, New England Puritanism to this day would stand upon Authority pretty often if it could, as it certainly did in the past, no less than Scotch Presbyterianism. No: if Protestantism or Puritanism is to be credited with the Transcendental movement, it is also to be credited with Atheism, which, as Mr. Lowell would admit, must have descended from something.

I prefer to say that Emerson, brought up in New England Unitarianism, and coming early under the influence of Channing, as well as of European Transcendentalists, gradually let go the last remnants of definite dogma that he had inherited, and professed a Theism which he never took any logical trouble to distinguish from Pantheism.[11] The successive stages of Unitarianism, of which he thus exhibited the last, are perfectly intelligible, so much so that one's only puzzle is as to how so much of the old Unitarianism still survives. It does so, I suppose, as a result of the continued movement of reluctant Christians along the line of least resistance to their emotions. I always think, though Unitarians do not seem ever to admit it, that the sect owed a good deal last century to the movement of the Deists, as it was modified by the criticism of Butler. Logical Deists, met by that criticism, would answer that it clearly gave no more voucher for Christianity than for Mohammedanism, and that the final position of reason must be Atheism, or what some now call Agnosticism. Less logical Deists, unable however to accept all the extravagances of Christism, would be disposed to range themselves with Priestley. However that may be, Unitarianism has at no time presented itself as a movement that fostered perfectly consistent or penetrating thought. Good service it has rendered in detail scholarship, from Lardner down to Samuel Sharpe, but never, I think, any notable help to accurate reasoning; though of course the admirers of Dr. Martineau will give a very different judgment. And in Emerson, the literary flower of the movement in America, we see just the kind of development that remained possible after the old spirit of cautious rationalism had played itself out, and the system was left to the influences of vaguely catholic emotion. Some would gravitate to orthodoxy; others would pass into poetic pantheism.

Emerson's withdrawal from his ministerial charge represents the strength of the orthodox bias among the Unitarians of his day. There was no precise conflict of nominal belief between him and his flock; only Emerson was averse to keeping up the institution of the Communion, as being irrelevant and of too much impaired significance, while the congregation, true to the religious idiosyncrasy, did not see why he should abandon a venerable practice. He was really asking them to go back to the position from which the early Unitarians of Poland had been persuaded away by Sozzini; but they, grown fixed in Socinian orthodoxy, would not follow him. He was disappointed, but quietly withdrew, and the world gained an essayist and lecturer, while the sect lost a preacher always a little too essayish and secular for its taste. His gift of elocution and phrase and charm of presence had given him his main hold; and we learn that he "won his first admirers in the pulpit," while he shocked or disturbed others.[12] On the merits of his withdrawal one can say that if he was willing to keep up the assumption of the Bible being a special revelation, he might as well have held by the bread and wine Communion. As he himself argued later against other people: "What is the use of going about setting up a flag of negation?"[13] The bread and wine Communion is a venerable usage, which was old in Mithraism before it was adopted by the Christians. But your eclectic is always liable to caprices.

III.

Emerson's recoil from the orthodoxies of Dissent must needs have been strengthened by that early visit to Europe, in the course of which he saw Italy and Landor, and England and Coleridge, Wordsworth and Carlyle. His instinct for distinction and the refinement of cultured life was reinforced, and his leanings took him in the way of men who would encourage his Transcendentalism without pressing him to cultivate his deficient logic. For he himself early recognised his complete lack of the power of continuous reasoning; and, as human nature is apt to do, he sought to make out to himself that his defect was rather an advantage. In his journal, at the age of 21, we find him writing of his love of poetry, with the addition: "My reasoning faculty is proportionally weak; nor can I ever hope to write a Butler's 'Analogy,' or an 'Essay' of Hume." And then he goes on to plume himself with the reflection that "the highest species of reasoning upon divine subjects is rather the fruit of a sort of moral imagination than of the reasoning machines, such as Locke, and Clarke, and David Hume."[14] Now, that doctrine, which is not peculiar to Emerson, brings us to close quarters with what we may term the practical side of his Transcendentalism. His views on this head, as on all other points of his philosophy, were very loosely held; and against such a deliverance as the fore-going, you may find in his works plenty of a contrary tone. Nor is this surprising when we realise that Emerson had fallen into a mere empirical confusion, which, however, has ensnared many harder reasoners than he. No concrete issue comes up oftener in modern philosophy than this as to how men come by what we call original ideas, by new generalisations, or flashes of perception which seem to have no derivation from previous knowledge. Kant, I am much inclined to believe, was led to his special theory of Reason by way of accounting for his own intellectual experiences in the course of those earlier scientific speculations of his which the students of his philosophy, as a rule, so strangely ignore. Again and again others have insisted on that progressive element in the human understanding which so constantly exhibits itself in hypothesis; and men have frequently been led to suppose that this progressive element is something wholly unconnected with what we call the reasoning faculty, or at least with the process of reasoning, commonly so called.[15] You will find this attitude partly assumed by Edgar Poe.[16] Goethe appears to have adopted it when he found that the scientists would not accept his theory of colours;[17] and Schopenhauer, whose philosophy ran so much to the personal equation, repeatedly affirmed the position,[18] which he found lying ready to his hands in previous Romanticism and Transcendentalism. He too uses language which amounts to calling previous philosophers reasoning machines; and though he would have made short work of Emerson's philosophisings, he might have said with him: "I believe that nothing great and lasting can be done except by inspiration, by leaning on the secret augury."[19]

Now, the whole question is, what is this secret augury? Is it something which the reasoners never have? On the contrary, it is the condition precedent of all their work. It shows how narrow and how superficial a would-be profound and really catholic Transcendentalist can be, that Emerson should never have suspected that the analytic ideas of Locke and Hume are just as much inspirations, or secret auguries, as his own. There can be no greater blunder than to suppose that men who use the analytic method begin to get notions by analysing mechanically. The act of analysis is itself a reaching-forward identical in character with what Emerson called the secret augury. People who object to consequent literary criticism tell you that true appreciation is for them a matter of spontaneous judgment. But so it is for the critic. Always the impression comes first and the analysis and the reasoning after. I have heard a Wagnerian attempt to disparage the late Edmund Gurney's criticism of Wagner, by saying that Gurney had a feeling against that music and sat down to find reasons for it. Now, as that Wagnerian ought to have known from his own experience, that is the formula of all criticism. The whole question is whether your subsequent reasoning does or does not prove your particular impression to be consistent with all your other impressions; and the advantage of the reasoner, the analyst, over other people is that he applies this test, which is at bottom the only way of distinguishing truth from error, while the mere impressionist has no test, and rests in his secret augury as he began. The formula of all error is just Incomplete Thought; and he insists on keeping his thought as incomplete as possible. Inspiration is "as plentiful as blackberries." Coleridge told an inquiring lady that he did not believe in ghosts because he had seen too many. So the circumspect rationalist does not believe in inspirations because he has had too many. He knows that while the test of reasoning, the test of universal consistency, verifies some of his inspirations, it discredits many more; and he knows better than to bow before a notion merely because it came into his head, when he knows there was no other way that an error could come. That he should ever have new ideas may be to him a mystery; but not more of a mystery[20] than the fact that his muscles grow stronger with using. Any fairly intelligent person can have fifty inspirations in a morning walk; and if he uses Emerson's literary method, and has a touch of Emerson's literary genius, he may soon make books of them. But even if he has unquestioned genius, he will, I fear, be preparing a good deal of matter for the dustbins of posterity.

Emerson's genius is certainly beyond question. Such a gift of luminous and stimulant speech, in single dicta, you shall not readily parallel in all literature. And, be it said at once, multitudes of the sayings are as true and valuable as they are brilliant. But we are dealing for the moment with that Emersonian principle of the secret augury, considered as an asserted truth. It is just as much a counsel of darkness as a counsel of perfection. Act on it, and you can as well be a bigot and a crank as a liberal and a sane citizen. What else did all those fanatics and enthusiasts do, at whom Emerson smiled or shrugged his shoulders? At times he would answer, no doubt, that it was well they should be what they were; but in that case all his counsels to mankind were strictlly gratuitous—that is, if you were to allow yourself to reason on the matter.

IV.

This weak place in Emerson's doctrine is sufficiently obvious to his more intelligent disciples; and when I speak of disciples, I should still wish to be ranked as, at least, an ex-pupil. Emerson helps you, half the time, to anti-Emersonise. But still there are always the idolators, or the lovers, who are fain to deny or palliate the obvious. Emerson in effect teaches a hundred times over that truth is just how you happen to feel; and plain people on this observe that that is a very good gospel for self-conceit. And in point of fact, while Emerson is in the main one of the most likeable and modest of men, this very foible of committing himself to every "inspiration" that struck him, makes him often utter what amounts to idle arrogance. What name but conceit can we give to that phrase about Locke and Hume being mere reasoning machines—as if it were any better to be an imagining machine? His later depreciation of the masterly Hume as a man who was not deep, and who won his reputation by a single keen observation,[21] taken with the further facile depreciation of so many powerful faculties, as those of Scott and Gibbon,[22] goes to convince us that only the habit of connected reasoning, resting on a favourable temperament, will ever make a thoroughly catholic mind. Emerson's temperament was in itself admirable: his natural gift of amenity and catholicity is always shining through even his dogmatism; but still the narrowness and the dogmatism are there, because he must needs book all his "inspirations." As if all our prejudices and unjust caprices were not such!

On the question of the philosophic and practical bearing of this doctrine, as put in the phrases, "Revere your intuitions," "To the involuntary perception a perfect faith is due," and so on, Mr. Cabot, in his "Memoir of Emerson," observes that "nothing was more foreign to him than idolatry of his opinions or his moods."[23] Now, that is quite true in the sense that in Emerson one mood readily drove out another, and an inspiration of arrogance was soon checked by an inspiration of humility. But is not this claim an admission that Emerson abounds in contradictions, and that some of his most characteristic doctrines are not to be taken as if he fully or constantly meant them, but only as rash indications of one of his prevailing mental habits? The best that can be made of the matter is Mr. Cabot's proposition[24] that "reverence for intuitions meant to Emerson resistance to the sleep that is apt to come over our spiritual faculties." No doubt Emerson does help much to dispel that sleep; but it is also true that he often promotes it, or a trance that is singularly like it in results, by encouraging superficial people to worship their prejudices, and those habit-born notions which get to feel like necessary truths.

The flaw in the matter is really that kind of mental indolence in Emerson which consists with, or consists in, the incapacity for the drudgery work of thinking. That stamps all his writings regarded as literary compositions, and all his verse, regarded as a set of artistic performances. What is it in his poetry that baffles and repels so many friendly readers, and all his best critics? The constant lapsing from metre and rhythm, the frequent hiatus in music and flow, which is, in the last analysis, the result of sheer want of taking pains, since no man capable of verse at all could commit such offences in pure blindness. It is "the unlit lamp and the ungirt loin" that make all these racking gaps and fissures in the texture of Emerson's verse, supremely fortunate as it so often is in detached inspirations. He knew it himself: again and again he confesses to a "vast debility,"[25] to an inveterate indolence. In his heart he knew that great and enduring books could not well be made as his were, by the process of jotting down all random ideas in note-books, indexing them, and then just collecting them under headings, in essays or lectures, eked out as need might be.[26] Carlyle, in all friendliness, early compared the essays to bags of shot,[27] and Emerson himself, in a letter to Carlyle, spoke of his manner of composition as one which made "each sentence an infinitely repellent particle."[28] "He was well aware," says Mr. Cabot, "of the inconsecutiveness that came from his way of writing, and liked it as little as anybody:—

> "(Journal, 1854)—'If Minerva offered me a gift and an option, I would say, give me continuity. I am tired of scraps. I do not wish to be a literary or intellectual *chiffonnier*. Away with this Jew's rag-bag of ends and tufts of brocade, velvet, and cloth-of-gold; and let me spin some yards or miles of helpful twine; a clue to lead to one kingly truth; a cord to bind some wholesome and belonging facts.' "

Such directness of self-criticism is startling and pathetic; for the moment it disarms our criticism, especially by being so well phrased. But it was only a passing mood, as Mr. Cabot goes on to show:—

> "But it was contrary to his literary creed to aim at completeness of statement:—
> " 'I would not degrade myself by casting about for a thought, nor by waiting for one. If the thought come, I would give it entertainment; but if it comes not spontaneously, it comes not rightly at all.' "[29]

Thus does self-will send self-criticism packing. But indeed this too is pathetic. How easily can the wisest of us, as here, cajole ourselves into feeling that our foible is our *forte*, and our indolence the choice of our enlightenment. For all which, Time will bring us into judgment, if we be writers of books. Those of us who have most ingenuously delighted in Emerson feel at times the chill of a coming indifference. Everybody knows the story of the effect of his lecture on Plato:—"Can you tell me," asked one of his neighbours, while Emerson was lecturing, "what connection there is between that last sentence and the one that went before, and what connection it all has with Plato?" "None, my friend, save in God!" One reads with regret Walt Whitman's disdainful remark that he had called Emerson Master for a month in his youth; this after he had availed himself of, and gained so much by, Emerson's cordial praise of his first book. But it must be admitted that that Master's dignity is insecure, of whom his disciples come to feel that his lamp to their path may at any moment be a will-o'-the-wisp for all they can tell beforehand. As he himself said, Even a wise man speaks three times without his full understanding for once that he speaks with it. And he was unduly adventurous in the face of his confessed risks.

V.

If our explanation be the right one, that he did not think hard enough in proportion to his gift of crystallising and phrasing his impressions, our negative criticism may soon be ended as regards his so-called philosophy, which was produced under the same conditions as his every-day aphroisms. By this time, indeed, all his leading exponents have admitted that he is not to be looked to for philosophy properly so-called.[30] He was a poet, giving voice to those pantheistic impressions which have come to poets in all ages and in all civilisations, Hindu, Greek, Egyptian, Teutonic. Poetry, if you like, is primeval philosophy. The more need that we should be clear as to the philosophic inadequacy of the poetic method in the age of science and prose, which is such a much more resourceful thing. Like his predecessors and contemporaries in the intuitive faith, Emerson had ever and anon an exalted perception of the unity of the universe, which in his poetic exaltation he must needs call God; and like them, he proceeded with fatal unconsciousness in every other mood to repudiate his generalisation and reduce the unity to duality, to multiplicity, to the terms of the perceptions of the people who do not generalise at all. "Transcendentalism was to him," says Mr. Cabot, "not a particular set of doctrines, but a state of mind."[31] Say an occasional state of mind, and you have complete accuracy. Mr. Cabot himself thus states Emerson's doctrine as to the relation of man to the all-pervading energy:—"When he *submits his will to the Divine inspiration*, he becomes a creator in the finite. *If he is disobedient*, if he would be something in himself, he finds all things hostile and incomprehensible." What girlish inconsistency is this? How in the name of reason can a human phenomenon be disobedient to the universal Will? Is not even Madness as truly Nature as Sanity? To this dilemma must always come the would-be Seer who persists in formulating the Universe in terms of his own transient soul, and making its measureless energy a God in his own image.

Emerson talking on Atheism is as conventional, as inanely clerical, as Carlyle. Hear him in a late tractate, fittingly entitled "The Preacher:"—

"Unlovely, nay frightful, is the solitude of the soul which is without God in the world. To wander all day in the sunlight among the tribes of animals, unrelated to anything better, to behold the horse, cow, and bird—no, the bird, as it hurried by with its bold and perfect flight, would disclaim his sympathy, and declare him an outcast. To see man pursuing in faith their varied action, warm-hearted, providing for their children, loving their friends, performing their promises—what are they to this chill, houseless, fatherless, aimless Cain, the man who hears only the sound of his own footsteps in God's resplendent creation? To him, it is no creation; to him, these fair creatures are hapless spectres; he knows not what to make of it; to him, heaven and earth have lost their beauty."[32]

The hand is the hand of Emerson, though the voice is the voice of Talmage. Every phrase is a negation of the principle of the Over-Soul, of the Universal Spirit, of the Unity of Nature, of the law of Compensations, of all the doctrines in which Emerson rises above conventionality. The bird relates providentially to the Universe; but the heretical man does not. And the end of it all is that the Over-Soul animates all things, except those which it doesn't. Let the preacher be answered by a stave of his own song of Brahma, in which, echoing the philosophy of ancient India, he comes almost within sight of a consistent Pantheism:—

> "They reckon ill who leave me out;
>   When me they fly, I am the wings;
> *I am the doubter and the doubt,*
>   And I the hymn the Brahmin sings."

After the prose, certainly, Emersonians may with much plausibility deny that Emerson was a Pantheist. Theodore Parker denied it indignantly "He has been foolishly accused of Pantheism, which sinks God in nature; but no man is further from it. He never sinks God in man."[33] Here, again, we are reading the language of one who, though a moralist and a scholar, cannot properly philosophise. To say that Pantheism "sinks" God in Nature, when it says God *is* Nature, is the merest hiding behind words; and to say that "no man is further" from Pantheism than Emerson is to be very reckless indeed. Others of his admirers admit that Emerson "will always doubtless be open to the charge of Pantheism;" and they can only urge that where his phraseology is "undoubtedly pantheistic," it is "poetical, not to be read literally."[34] The simple truth is, as we have seen, that Emerson was sometimes pantheistic and sometimes not, because of his fortuitous method of thinking and composing. "He ignores," says one of his best expositors, "those sharp distinctions and definitions which would have saved him from the charge of Pantheism."[35] He "ignored" them because he could not make them. "The children of the gods," he declared, "never argue."[36] No; not if they cannot, which would seem to be the nature of that family.

Now, we cannot say that all this fallacy and contradiction is a light matter: we cannot dismiss it with the Emersonian aphorism that "a foolish consistency is the hobgoblin of little minds," and that "with consistency a great soul has simply nothing to do." When great or other souls apply that principle to commercial morals, they are apt to get into jail; and if they habitually act on it in didactics they are likely to be confined one day to the second-hand bookstalls. Rational men will never be bounced out of common sense by bravado of that sort. Happily for Emerson, he could not be consistent in inconsistency, though he flaunted the flag of chaos. Some harm, however, must have been done by his bravado

among the weaker heads; and we shall perhaps not be wrong in laying at
his door the condition of subsequent American literature in the matter of
religious flatulence. These school-girl philosophemes of his are grown
fatally popular in the country which he taught to be proud of him. We
have enough of irrational Theism in these islands in all conscience; but
American Theism is a product so copious, so spontaneous, as to deserve a
separate label in literary commerce. You splash into it everywhere, in Mr.
Howell[s]'s charming novels, in Mr. Lowell's admirable criticisms, in the
novels and criticisms which are neither admirable nor charming. It
reaches at times an astonishing degree of gaseousness. Mr. O. B. Frothingham, who has written an interesting and useful history of New England
Transcendentalism, writes of the phenomenon, with apparent rationality, as "a wave of sentiment" which elated and transported a few people,
and passed on. With probable truth he declares that it had a powerful influence on character. But beyond that point he becomes incoherent.
"New England character," he affirms in one breath, "received from it an
impetus that never will be spent." In the next, we learn that "transcendentalism as a special phase of thought and feeling was of necessity
transient—having done its work it terminated its existence." It is not now
surprising to learn that a "phase of thought" "did its work, and its work
was glorious."[37] And after that we can turn back with a scientific interest
to the proposition that, in the Hegelianism of Bruno Bauer and Strauss,
"by being adopted into the line of the intellectual development of
mankind, Christianity, though dethroned and disenchanted, was
dignified as a supreme moment in the autobiography of God."[38] Comment here would not be superfluous, but I find it impossible. All I can
manage to say is, that you need only give a Theist rope enough if you
desire to see his philosophic existence violently curtailed.

VI.

It is a relief to turn from these phases of a state of mind which Emerson unluckily fostered, to others which can be contemplated with very
different feelings. Taking his books in the mass, we may say of them that
if his moonshine is much the same as other people's, his sunshine is
peculiarly his own, and very much above the average. Matthew Arnold,
after going in his gracefully incisive way over the points of Emerson's
work, and settling that he is not a great writer of prose, because his style
"wants the requisite wholeness of good tissue," and that he is not a great
poet because he lacks plainness and concreteness and the power of evolution, finally decides that, nevertheless, "as Wordsworth's poetry is in my
judgment the most important work done in verse, in our language, during
the present century, so Emerson's *Essays* are, I think, the most important
work done in prose. His work is more important than Carlyle's."[39] He is
not a great writer or man of letters in the sense that Cicero and Swift and

Plato and Bacon and Pascal and Voltaire are great writers; but still, in that he "holds fast to happiness and hope" as he does, he is the most important English prose writer of the century. That verdict is very characteristic of Arnold, in its suave arbitrariness; and of course his "most important" cannot be taken as final for Emerson any more than for Wordsworth. Arnold had not the means or the method of finding out what is really "most important" in the literature of a century. He would pass over all Spencer with a graceful wave of the hand and the handkerchief, and sum up in a limpid phrase the heavy volumes he had not read. It would not occur to him to ask how it was, precisely, that George Eliot, or Mill, was less "important" than Emerson; or wherein importance chiefly consisted, and why. But if we take the generalisation with the discount which is proper for Arnold's "paper," we shall find ourselves directed to a reasonably just conclusion. Emerson's hold of "happiness and hope" is not quite the most important thing in our nineteenth century English prose, because these are not the things of which we stand in the most pressing need; but when all is said, his gift to us in that regard is a splendid one. Certainly no one stimulates as he does. The morality of George Eliot has invalid airs and an indoors odour in comparison; and the thinkers, while they instruct, exhaust us somewhat. But in Emerson you have ever the air of the Concord woods and plains, the air that Thoreau breathed by Walden Lake. His very foible of booking all his inspirations has given us a multitude of tonic sentences, of exhilarations that pulse as if from the veins of spring. Arnold, and everybody else, has remembered how the young heart responds to some of his unmatchable phrases. "Trust thyself: every heart vibrates to that iron string. Whoso would be a man must be a nonconformist.[40] He who would gather immortal palms must not be hindered by the name of goodness, but must explore if it be goodness. Nothing is at last sacred but the integrity of your own mind. Absolve you to yourself, and you shall have the suffrage of the world."[41] There is the pure note of the moral truth in the doctrine of the secret augury and the inward voice: the true note, neither sharp nor flat, concordant with all the master notes of human science. Again and again comes in that vibration, which is the breath in the nostrils of democracy:—

> "Zoologists may deny that horsehairs in the water change to worms; but I find that whatever is old corrupts, and the past turns to snakes. The reverence for the deeds of our ancestors is a treacherous sentiment. *Their* merit was not to reverence the old, but to honour the present moment; and we falsely make them the excuses of the very habit which they hated and defied."[42] "The reliance on property, including the reliance on governments which protect it, is the want of self-reliance. Men have looked away from themselves and at things so long, that they have come to esteem the religious, learned, and civil institutions as guards of property, and they deprecate assaults on these because they feel them to be

assaults on property. They measure their esteem of each other by what each has and not by what each is. But a cultivated man becomes ashamed of his property, out of new respect for his nature. Especially he hates what he has, if he see that it is accidental—came to him by inheritance, or gift, of crime; then he feels that it is not having; it does not belong to him, has no root in him, and merely lies there because no revolution or no robber takes it away."[43]

These maxims of his on politics are certainly worth many treatises as stimulants to what is best in men; and though States cannot any more than men live on stimulants, they may at times escape death or prostration by them. When I think of the resonant nobleness of some of his didactic verse I forgive its unfiled rudeness; and in the end I decline to subscribe to Arnold's dictum that a smoothly musical performance of Longfellow or Whittier is worth all Emerson's poetry. His song is short-breathed and soon broken, but he has caught notes of Apollo that they have never heard. His poetic teaching has a quintessential quality that is to theirs what Milton is to Cowper; and at times it only needs the last magic of finish to compare with the noblest song in Goethe:—

> "Nor kind nor coinage buys
>   Aught above its rate.
> Fear, Craft, and Avarice
>   Cannot rear a State.
> Out of dust to build
>   What is more than dust—
> Walls Amphion piled
>   Phœbus stablish must.
> When the Muses nine
>   With the Virtues meet,
> Find to their design
>   An Atlantic seat,
> By green orchard boughs
>   Fended from the heat,
> Where the statesman ploughs
>   Furrow for the wheat,—
> When the church is social worth,
> When the state-house is the hearth,
> Then the perfect state is come,
> The republican at home."[44]

In other keys and measures he can attain to radiances of phrase and thought that are not for the Longfellows at their luckiest. And when we are dissecting, as we must, the fibre of his teaching, and rigorously weighing his message, even as he himself fully authorised us to do, we can hardly refuse to bow at least for a moment under the melodious rebuke which in one of his moods he passed on a friend:—

"Set not thy foot on graves;
    Nor seek to unwind the shroud
Which charitable Time
    And Nature have allowed
To wrap the errors of a sage sublime.

"Set not thy foot on graves;
Care not to strip the dead
Of his sad ornament,
His myrrh, and wine, and rings,
His sheet of lead,
And trophies burièd:
Go, get them where he earned them when alive;
As resolutely dig and dive.

"Life is too short to waste
    In critic peep or cynic bark,
Quarrel or reprimand;
    'Twill soon be dark;
Up! mind thine own aim, and
    God speed the mark!"[45]

But, indeed, there is small suggestion of the grave as yet about Emerson's teaching; nor will there soon be. He is the very poet of optimism, which it is not an easy thing to be: prosperity is prosaic, and the poetic instinct turns most spontaneously to shadow. It is his glory, and a glory not easily won, to have convinced men that every age must find its highest inspiration in itself if it is ever to be capable of giving inspiration to others. Before Walt Whitman, though Whitman seems to have forgotten it, he taught the people of America to frame a literature for themselves:—[46]

"The test or measure of poetic genius is the power to read the poetry of affairs—to fuse the circumstance of to-day; not to use Scott's antique superstitions, or Shakespeare's, but to convert those of the nineteenth century and of the existing nations into universal symbols. 'Tis easy to repaint the mythology of the Greeks or of the Catholic Church, the feudal castle, the crusade, the martyrdoms of mediæval Europe; but to point out where the same creative force is now working in our own houses and public assemblies, to convert the vivid energies working at this hour into universal symbols, requries a subtle and commanding thought. . . . Every man would be a poet if his intellectual digestion were perfect. The test of the poet is the power to take the passing day, with its news, its cares, its fears, as he shares them, and hold it up to a divine reason till he sees it to have a purpose and beauty, and to be related to astronomy and history and the eternal order of the world. There is no subject that does not belong to him—politics, economy, manufactures, and stock-brokerage—as much as sunsets and souls; only these things, placed in their true order, are poetry; displaced or put in kitchen order, they are unpoetic."[47]

These are the words of a man who lived his life genuinely and with genius; and if they and others of his doctrines are found to expand some that are associated with the name of Carlyle, nothing can be idler than to repeat the vacuous old epigram that he was but a pocket edition of his friend.[48] Carlyle himself seems to have thought that Emerson was in a measure a "spiritual son" of his; but it would be hard to lay the finger on a passage in Emerson, good or bad, wise or unwise, which he could not conceivably have come by if Carlyle had never lived. That he himself was a magnetic and commanding personality is shown by his marked influence on Thoreau,[49] who, however, made the Emersonian style as much his own as Emerson did when he developed it from that of his aunt. Thoreau, I take it, repaid the debt when he gave Emerson the right lead on the slavery question. Not that Emerson could, under any conceivable circumstances, have gone wrong on that as Carlyle went wrong; but that it did not come quite naturally to him to cleave to the right side in the face of all its extravagances and fanaticisms. At first he was not hearty against slavery; and he blamed the Abolitionists for their "impatience of discipline" and "haste to rule before we have served."[50] But his "unhappy conscience" respected them; and he went straight. By degrees he warmed to the great issue. From the first he spoke well: no man better; but he writes of it in his journal as "stirring in philanthropical mud," and adds:—"I fully sympathise, be sure, with the sentiment I write; but I accept it rather from my friends than dictate it. It is not my impulse to say it."[51] At an earlier stage he had sophisticated himself out of doing anything by means of his all-accommodating Theism. In 1852 he wrote in his journal:—

> "I waked last night and bemoaned myself because I had not thrown myself into the deplorable question of slavery, which seems to want nothing so much as a few assured voices. But then, in hours of sanity, I recover myself and say, God must govern his own world, and knows his way out of this pit without my desertion of my post, which has none to guard it but me. I have quite other slaves to free than those negroes, to wit, imprisoned spirits, imprisoned thoughts, far back in the brain of man—far retired in the heaven of invention, and which, important to the republic of man, have no watchman, or lover, or defender but I."[52]

On that reasoning no man need ever move, since God could always find his way out of the pit if he wanted; and if he did not go, why then it was best so. But when the crisis came, Emerson's manhood pushed his theistic sophistry aside, and in the fiery trial of the war his heart did not falter or change, seeming indeed to find there, as others found, the rectification of many moral confusions.

But his service to mankind is wider than the example of his own conduct in any one conjuncture; and it is wider, too, than his mere optimism, bracing as that is. Arnold, estimating in his facile way the value of the

English Traits, decides that that book misses permanent value because it is the "observation of a man systematically benevolent," as Hawthorne's *Our Old Home* fails because it is "the work of a man chagrined."[53] That is a singular misfit in criticism. Emerson was indeed benevolent, but Arnold's criticism is meaningless unless it signify that his benevolence blinded him to English defects. Now, it did no such thing. The weakness of that book is not systematic benevolence, though it is undoubtedly over-benevolent to Anglo-Saxonism in the lump. Its weakness is that which always inheres in Emerson's method, unresolved contradiction and unabashed inconsistency. If you analyse it you find that, as usual, he has booked every generalisation that occurred to him day by day, and made no attempt to correct one by another, though in the nature of the case each is a generalisation from a few particulars. But take the book as you find it, and you have a series of the most brilliant characterisations of English defects and limitations, so much to Arnold's own purpose, many of them, that you can hardly avoid concluding that he had only skimmed the book or had mostly forgotten it when he spoke of its systematic benevolence.

But Arnold himself goes on to avow that, "Strong as was Emerson's optimism, and unconquerable as was his belief in a good result to emerge from all which he saw going on around him, no misanthropical satirist ever saw shortcomings and absurdities more clearly than he did, or expressed them more courageously."[54] That is true of his criticism alike of English and American life and institutions; and his general social doctrine, at its best, is medicinal for all civilisation:—

> " 'Tis pedantry to estimate nations by the census, or by square miles of land, or other than by their importance to the mind of the time. Leave this hypocritical prating about the masses. Masses are rude, lame, unmade, pernicious in their demands and influence, and need not to be flattered but to be schooled. I wish not to concede anything to them, but to tame, drill, divide, and break them up, and draw individuals out of them. The worst of charity is, that the lives you are asked to preserve are not worth preserving. Masses! the calamity *is* the masses. I do not wish any mass at all, but honest men only; lovely, sweet, accomplished women only; and no shovel-handed, narrow-brained, gin-drinking million stockingers or lazzaroni at all. If Government knew how, I should like to see it check, not multiply, the population. When it reaches its true law of action, every man that is born will be hailed as essential."

These are the words, remember, of a republican of republicans, not merely the friend but spiritually the representative of the temper of democracy. They are not a call for a stoppage of progress, but an earnest incitation to progress of a better kind. "We think our civilisation," he writes again, "near its meridian, but we are yet only at the cock-crowing and the morning star."[55] That is a protest and a prediction in one. And if he who delivered it did not also give the science by which the prediction should be realised, none the less is he to be honoured and laurelled for that he brought to bear on all who could share his ideal the compulsion of his noble aspiration and his beautiful speech.

Notes

1. The new copyright law will modify this tendency.

2. Essay on Thoreau in *My Study Windows*.

3. *Birds and Poets*, English ed. p. 223.

4. Cabot's *Memoir*, English ed. i. 44.

5. *Ib*. i. 58.

6. *Ib*. i. 30.

7. *Ib*.

8. *Ib*. p. 31.

9. *Ib*. pp. 35, 37.

10. Essay cited.

11. "Emerson might, in his 'metaphysics' [*Collected Writings*, ii, 58], deny personality to God; but he never gave much attention to his metaphysics, and what he means by personality seems to be nothing more than limitation to an individual." Cabot, i., 340.

12. Cabot, i., 150.

13. Said to one who objected to be called a Christian. J. B. Thayer, *A Western Journey with Mr. Emerson*, p. 18.

14. Cabot, i, 100–1.

15. It was contemned by Bacon. On this compare the criticisms of Jevons (*Principles of Science*, p. 576), and Bagehot (*Postulates of English Pol. Ec.*, pp. 17–19), and Mill (*Logic*, B. vi., ch. 5 § 5).

16. In the *Eureka*.

17. See Professor Wallace's *Life of Schopenhauer*, p. 83.

18. *Ib*. pp. 82, 87, 96–97, &c.

19. *Letters and Social Aims: Inspiration*.

20. On this compare again Mill's *Autobiography*, p. 180, and Todhunter's *Conflict of Studies*, p. 15.

21. *English Traits*, ch. xiv.

22. For Emerson, "Poe was merely 'the man who jingles.' " Conway, *R. W. Emerson*, p. 292. After this it is well to know that "Of himself he said once, when forced to speak, 'My reputation, such as it is, will be one day cited to prove the poverty of this time.' "

23. Cabot, *Memoir of Emerson*, i., p. 251.

24. p. 252.

25. Letter to Carlyle, *Correspondence*, ii., 334. Also pp. 59, 326, etc.

26. Cabot, i. 294.

27. *Correspondence*, ii., 82.

28. *Correspondence*, i., 161.

29. Cabot, i. 295.

30. "Mr. Emerson's place is among poetic, not among philosophic minds." Frothingham, *Transcendentalism in New England*, p. 236.

31. Cabot, ii 39.

32. Essay on *The Preacher*, in *Unitarian Review*, Jan. 1880; cited by G. W. Cooke, *R. W. Emerson*, p. 289.

33. Cited by Cooke, p. 290.

34. *Ib*. p. 291.

35. *Ib*.

36. Mr. Conway's *R. W. Emerson*, p. 272.

37. *Transcendentalism in New England*, pp. 355–6.

38. p. 186.

39. *Discourses in America*, p. 196.

40. Naturally Mr. Arnold did not quote this clause.

41. *Self-Reliance*.

42. *Works and Days*.

43. *Self-Reliance*.

44. *Prelude to Essay on Politics*.

45. "To J. W."

46. As did Poe, *Marginalia*, vii.; Ingram's ed. of *Works*, iii., 351.

47. *Letters and Social Aims: Poetry and Imagination*.

48. That this view was shared by Poe is one of the heaviest critical charges against that great critic. (*Works*, iii. 378.)

49. Described in Cabot's *Memoir*.

50. Cabot, ii. 45.

51. Cabot, pp. 51–2.

52. *Emerson in Concord*, by Edward W. Emerson, p. 78.

53. *Discourses in America*, p. 173.

54. Pp. 189, 190.

55. *Politics*.

"Emerson's Wit and Humor"

Henry Demarest Lloyd*

On the Pacific coast in 1871 Emerson met John Muir, who has since written "The Mountains of California," every leaf of it a leaf of nature. Muir had read the rocks, streams, and forests of his Eldorado, as Emerson the leaves in the libraries of Boston. He led Emerson as no one else could have done through the valley of the Yosemite and the passes of the Sierras. The two guides—such both were—explored each other as well as the scenes through which they were going. Emerson said that Muir was another Thoreau. Muir was felicitous in replying with an inspiration caught from the grandest trees of the grandest flora in the world. "Emerson," he said, "is the Sequoia of mankind." Speaking of these forest sublimities in his book, Muir points out that the beauty of their propor-

*Reprinted from *Forum*, 22 (November 1896), 346–57.

tions is so perfect that the onlooker finds it impossible to realize the size of their different parts, except by actual measurements. Certainly nothing is farther from the common idea of Emerson than that he was a wit and humorist. This part of our "Sequoia" is a limb which, to be seen for what it is, needs to be separated from a whole too great and harmonious for partial effects. But his audiences followed his lectures with laughter and smiles. Apt quotations from him get quick recognition of the same kind to-day from public and private gatherings.

Oliver Wendell Holmes recognized in Emerson a brother wit of the first water. No one who is not sensitive to humor should venture on Emerson, he says. "If not laughter, there is," thinks Morley, "at least gaiety in every piece." "His fine humor," says Conway. Lowell, in "My Study Windows," commemorates Emerson's "glance of humor"; his biographer Cooke, "his keen and ready wit"; F. B. Sanborn, "the salt of his wit"; Harriet Martineau, "his exquisite sense of humor." Tyndall found "immortal laughter" in his poetry—"in his case Poetry with the joy of a Bacchanal takes her graver brother Science by the hand, and cheers him with immortal laughter." This enthusiastic language might well apply to the last two lines of the famous prelude to Emerson's essay on "Nature," published in 1836, twenty-three years before Darwin's "Origin of Species": —

> "And striving to be man the worm
> Mounts through all the spires of form."

In the shrewd face which looks upon us out of his portraits we see that there is that sense—that saving sense—which can detect the ridiculous side—the other side—of anybody or anything. None of their commemorators has said more reverential words of the Puritans than he. But he passes in one sentence from an almost choral admiration of the religious pleasure with which they read for daily food such authors as Milton, Flavel, Bunyan, to the anti-climax of the remark of an old lady who remembered them as being so pious that "they had to hold on hard to the hucklebery bushes to hinder themselves from being translated." He could illuminate the subject of religion as well by a stroke of wit as by the solemn and tender passages of his "Divinity School Address." "All the religions," he held, "are one wine in different colored glasses." In the same manner, he said: "There is but one standard English novel, like the one orthodox sermon which with slight variation is repeated every Sunday from so many pulpits." Cabot quotes him as writing about "the prevailing Boston beverage of Channing and water." "The Church"—he is speaking of the English Church—"has nothing left but possession. If a bishop meets an intelligent gentleman, and reads fatal interrogation in his eyes, he has no resource but to take wine with him." "The clergyman who would live in the city *may* have piety, but he *must* have taste."

On a certain Sunday morning which he spent in Stratford Church,

Emerson remained beside Shakespeare's grave throughout the service. The English friend who went with him was ashamed of the sermon, which was very poor. He was relieved when Emerson asked quaintly, "Did he preach?" Happily perceiving what Emerson meant he replied, "Who? Shakespeare?" "Yes," replied Emerson. Pope taught that "discord" was "harmony not understood." Emerson was of this philosophy, which is older than Pope. He called the devil "the great second best." "If Emerson went to hell," said his friend Father Taylor, of the Sailor Mission, "the devil would not know what to do with him. The climate would change and emigration would set that way."

Disraeli, Sir William Fraser tells us in his gossipy reminiscences, had an elaborate code of signals to give notice to his audience that a joke was coming. His well-trained hearers in the House of Commons would begin to laugh in anticipation as they saw his handkerchief travel, stage by stage, from his pocket to the tip of his nose, where he kept the point of his witticisms, as Herrmann, the magician, uses the same organ as a never-failing fountain of eggs, watches, playing-cards, and rabbits. But in the best wit it is always the unexpected that happens. Emerson gives no notice, does not affect to be a wit, and slips from grave to gay and back again in a flash. He begins solemnly, "The mysteries of creation";— "known only to the pious," he concludes. He made merry with Swedenborg's intimate knowledge of these "mysteries" and declared that his carefully elaborated angels looked as stiff as country parsons. There were other things more important than angels. "An actually-existent fly is more important than a possibly-existent angel." His scepticism about angels extended to the plans of aërial navigators that men should imitate angelic methods of locomotion. "We are not yet ripe," he said, "to be birds."

The wit is even more judicial than the judge who knows neither friends nor enemies. The wit must know both his friends and enemies, and himself who is of both these. Emerson said of himself, "I am always insincere as always knowing that there are other moods." He did not spare himself. He did not spare his own craft. "There is indeed this vice about men of thought, that you cannot quite trust them. . . . They have a hankering to play Providence, and make a distinction in favor of themselves from the rules they apply to the human race." We can see what he meant when we open our Renan, and read where, under the certainly inapt title, "Intellectual and Moral Reform," Renan says in substance to the Church: Leave us literary men alone and we will leave you alone with the people—a passage not too sharply criticized by Mazzini as the most singular and the most immoral compromise that could enter into the brain of a thinker.

In the eye twinkling through Emerson's pages we get the clue which many of his would-be critics have missed. Having no sense of humor concealed about their persons, as he had, they did not detect that he was laughing, if not at them, at their kind. Expressions at which they brayed in terror were not the extravagancies they took them to be, but the broad strokes of an imagination translucent with the inner flames of wit. His one subject, as he put it, was, in all his lectures, "the infinitude of the private man." He has uttered this thought of the partnership of man in the creative power in many inspired passages which have become familiar quotations. But he had more than one way of expressing this thought. Looking out of a window at a winter storm, he once said, as a friend of his told me, "I snow."

Emerson's utterances on Immortality have taken their place among the litanies of sacred anthology. A well-known literary woman of Chicago having heard the reports, current some years ago, of a reaction in his opinions said to him, "Mr. Emerson, you do believe in the immortality of the soul, do you not?" In his essay, whose sentences go sounding on like organ chords, Emerson makes Yama, the Hindoo god of Death, say: "The soul is not born, it does not die; . . . unborn, eternal, it is not slain, though the body is slain; subtler than what is subtle, greater than what is great, sitting it goes far, sleeping it goes everywhere." It had been with such majestic notes that she had been filling her ears. It may well be believed that she was unprepared for the rapid transition in the tone of her oracle, who parried her with, "Madam, we are not swill." For he was no *poseur*; he would not "show off," nor act the augur, and he would take any liberty with words that his audacity or wit or gaiety might prompt. His mind was not only original but, as E. P. Whipple said of it, "aboriginal." Alternation of the currents in the brain as in the dynamo is the invariable accompaniment of power. The great orator swings his audience from tears to laughter, not from the calculated use of contrasts but in obedience to a law of emotion which rules him as he rules his audience.

It was the heat of his high combustion that condensed Emerson's sentences, as he described them, into paragraphs infinitely repellent, "incompressible." It is this which makes him the most quotable of writers. You can find in him the philosophies packed into phrases. We are not in the habit of thinking of scholars and poets as men of high vitality. Rather they have the reputation of being of a low tone physically. But performance is the nigh horse of power, and this low tone of a great author usually evidences not a lack of physical power, but diversion of energy to inner channels. "Health is the first wealth," Emerson said, and one of the secrets of his style is the exuberant spring that rose within him, and overflowed in an affluent stream. It was from this he got the joy of life that bubbled up in his deportment in a perpetual serenity, in his philosophy in common sense, and in his working power in an affluence which had no thought of an eight-hour day but produced during almost every waking moment. "Every man would be a poet," he says, "if his digestion were perfect," and again, "The work of the writer needs a frolic health." Emerson, delicate as he seemed, could eat pie every day, having it always for the first thing at breakfast, and he never had indigestion. To most of us this would be a frolic health indeed.

"How can Mr. Emerson," said one of the younger members of the party with which he made the trip in California, "be so agreeable all the time without getting tired?" His balance was moral as well as physical and mental. It is quite scientific to attribute his goodness as also his good humor largely to the same health which gave him the power of continuous literary production and made him equal at an advanced age to arduous journeys in snow and ice in Michigan and Illinois to fulfil lecture engagements. Health is not only the first wealth, as he says, but the first piety. His sanity or soundness ran through his whole nature. His too brief Boswell, Mr. Woodberry, is not afraid to say that Emerson probably did not know in his own experience what sin was as other men know it. If we pass that by as the admiration of the worshipper, we find the critical Henry James the elder, in his "Literary Remains," drawing the portrait with the same halo. Carlyle must have felt the same thing, for on one occasion he refused to precede Emerson to the dinner-table. "I am too wicked," he said. This is but to say that in his case sanity, or soundness, had evolved itself up to sanc-tity, and it would not be easy to see why it should not have done so in his case, or why we should not all believe that to be the common destiny. "What one is why may not millions be?" asks Wordsworth. Emerson felt the sickness and wickedness were one and the same. "One sometimes suspects," he put it, "that outer have something to do with inner com-plaints, and, when one is ill, something the devil 's the matter." No machinery could throw him out of employment. He would come back from a walk with a pocket full of little bits of paper on which he had jotted down things that had come to him, as Sir Walter Scott used to return from an ex-pedition in the Highlands quizzing lairds or picking up ballads with a handful of twigs whose notches and crooks were memoranda to be transcribed into a "Waverly," or some "Canto of the Lakes."

The gaiety of health and strength which expressed itself in other men in exuberance of spirits came out in Emerson in exuberance of phrase. The feeble pulse of the didactic exhorter says, "Aim high," but Emerson, the earth light under his happy feet, cries, "Hitch your wagon to a star." So in another address he says the time will come when "we shall be willing to sow the sun and the moon for seeds." He was almost French in his dislike of dull expression. For commonplace phrase about the "Unity of Nature," he substitutes, "The tree is rooted man," or, "The musk-rat is man modified to live in a mud-bank," or, "Yonder mountain must migrate into your mind." When he wants to tell what *Podsnap* would wave away as, "The universal social unrest," he says: "Nowadays every man carries a revolution in his vest-pocket." "The transfusion of the blood," he says, "it is claimed in Paris, will enable a man to change his blood as often as his linen." He quotes another Parisian fancy that by electro-magnetism our salads shall be grown from the seeds while our fowl is roasting, and dismisses it thus, "Nothing is gained, nature cannot be cheated. Man's life is but seventy salads long, grow they swift or grow they slow." Speaking of the resistance of the party of property to every progressive step, he said: "They would nail the stars to the sky." To make the living virtue of his beloved Montaigne's style comprehended, he says: "Cut these words and they would bleed." Many writers have described the insularity of the English. He brings the metaphor buried in that word to life again. "Every one of these islanders is an island himself." He contrasts French love of display with English love of reality. "A Frenchman invented the dickey, an Englishman added the shirt." It was his frolic health of mind, or, as he said of his friend Carlyle, "this glad and needful venting of his redundant spirits," from which came the felicities, paradoxes, contradictions, he revelled in. "Consistency" he thought to be "the bugbear of small minds." He would say on one page, "Solitude is impracticable, and society fatal," and on another, "He only who is able to stand alone is fit for society." He saw everything in flight, even truth. "The truest state of mind, rested in, becomes false."

Emerson, the reformer, descendant of reformers, inspiring spirit of reform, shot some of his sharpest shafts at reformers. He was a reformer, but he was also a wit. All great wits, from Aristophanes to "Mark Twain," have been reformers, but alas! all reformers are not wits. Emerson had that love of fun, that insight into the absurd, that sharp ear for the other side, that detective eye for humbug, which makes the wit, and makes the wit the most dangerous enemy of the wrong-doer. In his day in New England the air fairly sizzled with unrest. Every accepted idea, every established institution, every conventionality, had its assailant. It was a time when, as he puts it, "The young men seemed to have been born with knives in their brains." Through this whirl of agitation Emerson held his way, sympathetic but smiling, never off his feet or out of his head. Morley thinks that in him was realized Hawthorne's hope in the "Blithedale Romance" that "out of the very thoughts that were wildest and most destructive might grow a wisdom holy, calm, and pure, and that should incarnate itself with the substance of a noble and happy life." "In the person of Emerson," declares Morley, "this ferment and dissolvency of thought worked itself out in a strain of wisdom of the highest and purest." Emerson was able to run these intellectual rapids without slipping back into the doubt, aversion, and reaction that caught Burke, Wordsworth, and Tennyson.

Speaking of the enthusiasts who were then discussing the plans that ended in Brook Farm, Emerson wrote to Carlyle: "One man renounced the use of animal food, another of coin, another of domestic hired service, and another of the state, and on the whole we have a commendable share of reason and hope." "I am," he says, "gently mad myself, and am resolved to live cleanly." We recognize his pen in the description in "The

Dial" of one of the characteristic conventions of that period, one of many then meeting in Boston. This gathering of 1840 called itself the "Friends of Universal Progress." "There were in it," says Emerson," many persons whose church was a church of one member only." "Madmen, madwomen, men with beards, Dunkers, Muggletonians, Come-Outers, Groaners, Agrarians, Seventh-Day Baptists, Quakers, Abolitionists, Calvinists, Unitarians, and philosophers all came successively to the top, and seized their moment, if not their hour, wherein to chide, or pray, or preach, or protest." One woman, who was always jumping up with a roll of manuscript in these conventions, he styles "that flea of conventions." "Even the insect world was to be defended. That had been too long neglected, and a society for the protection of ground-worms, slugs, and mosquitoes was to be incorporated without delay." Reporting upon these swimmers—these fellow-swimmers—in "the storm-engendering sea of liberty," Emerson made the remark: "There is nothing a reformer hates so much as—another reformer." And with quite as much pungency, he laid it down that "Society gains nothing whilst a man not himself renovated attempts to renovate things around him." He gives a related idea an equally felicitous expression, when he says, "There can be no concert in two, where there is no concert in one." "I go to a convention of philanthropists. Do what I will, I cannot keep my eyes off the clock." "The reformers," he said, "bite us and we run mad too."

These gentle recalls to reason are the notes of a friend, not of an enemy. The reformers smiled at themselves with their critic, a privileged character, for he had been the first American scholar of his generation to thrust his pen into the heart of slavery.

What Holmes so happily calls the inward inaudible laughter of Emerson, "more refreshing than the explosion of our noisiest humorists," is to be seen in his account of Brook Farm. "The married women were against the community. . . . The Common School was well enough, but to the common nursery they have grave objections. Eggs might be hatched in ovens, but the hen on her own account much preferred the old way." He describes the community as "a perpetual picnic, a French Revolution in small, an Age of Reason in a patty-pan." It was a paradise of shepherds and shepherdesses, but, "The ladies took cold on washing-day, and it was ordained that the gentlemen-shepherds should hang out the clothes, but—in the evening when they began to dance the clothes-pins dropped from their pockets."

No weapons have cut deeper into the public enemy than those of the leaders who know how to make the people smile while kindling their wrath. In his speech on affairs in Kansas, Emerson fetched one of these strokes. "The President says, 'Let the complainants go to the Courts.' He knows that when the poor plundered farmer comes to the court, he finds the ringleader who has robbed him, dismounting from his horse, and unbuckling his knife to sit as his judge." He could turn on the farmer too.

Writing to Carlyle of the "honest solid farmers" of America, he said, "Horace Greeley does their thinking for them at a dollar a head."

When Choate belittled the Declaration of Independence as made up of "glittering generalities," Emerson retorted, "I call them, rather, blazing ubiquities." Mrs. Carlyle said that Carlyle's love of silence was entirely Platonic. But there was no lack of performance in Emerson's love of utterance. He smote, when need was, with a hammer as heavy as Thor's. He loved Webster, and no finer characterizations than his have been made of the great man, all whose dimensions, as Emerson put it, were such as to make him the personification of the American continent. But when Webster voted for the Fugitive Slave Bill, Emerson spoke in words that still bite. "Every drop of Webster's blood," he said, "has eyes that look downward." Such fierceness is rare in his humor. One more instance of it is in "English Traits," where the rampant and couchant glories of the coats-of-arms of the English nobility are given a turn not to be found in the philosophy of the Heralds' College. After describing "the twenty thousand thieves who landed at Hastings" with William the Conqueror "as greedy and ferocious pirates," who "burned, harried, violated, tortured, and killed," he turns his pen in the wound he has made. "Such however is the illusion of antiquity and wealth that decent and dignified men now existing boast their descent from these filthy thieves, who showed a far juster conviction of their own merits by assuming for their types the swine, goat, jackal, leopard, wolf, and snake, which they severally resembled."

Emerson was so far from seeking effect that, as Conway found, in printing his essays he would omit passages which when spoken had made a laugh. Thus he left out of his paper on "Superlatives" a remark about oaths which had greatly entertained his audience, to the effect that the oath could be used by a thinking man only in some great moral emergency. He meant his wit to be the sauce, not the roast; a touch of nature, not the intellectual elephantiasis of the professional. His opinion of the class known as "men of wit" is given in his new book, "The Natural History of the Intellect." "There is really a grievous amount of unavailableness about men of wit. A plain man finds them so heavy, dull, and oppressive with bad jokes, and conceit, and stupefying individualism that he comes to write in his tablets." He gives another slap at this class in his essay on "Clubs." "Things are in pairs. . . . A story is matched by another story, and that may be the reason why when a gentleman has told a good thing, he immediately tells it again." This was not the Puritan in him preferring the frown to the laugh. He never frowned; he was, as Mr. Mangasarian has so well said, "the smile of the century." He believed that "a rogue alive to the ludicrous is still convertible." He called "the perception of the comic a balance-wheel in our metaphysical structure." Nothing in Carlyle appeals more to Emerson than his wit—his "playing of tunes," as this fellow-wit most keenly characterized it, "with a whip-lash like some renowned charioteer." "We have had nothing in literature so like earthquakes," he says, "as the laughter of Carlyle. . . . These jokes shake down Parliament House and Windsor Castle, Temple and Tower, and the future shall echo the dangerous peals."

With the same feeling that led him to strike out some of the laughable passages, and made him unwilling to play the man of wit, he always used a quiet note in referring to his own work. When he speaks of giving a course of lectures, he calls it beginning to "sell tickets again," or going "peddling with my literary pack of notions." One reason perhaps why Emerson was so agreeable was this reserve and refinement of his humor. He disliked loud laughter. He came to have a great friendship for Margaret Fuller, but it had to conquer a strong feeling he at first had against her because she made him laugh more than he liked. He was very seldom heard to laugh. His laugh, as Prof. Thayer describes it, was "a quiet ground-swell." To force a laugh from his readers would have been not to be Emerson. "True wit," he said, "never made us laugh." His sparks fly only when his mind is working at a high heat. His letters seldom reach this level, unlike Lowell's which bubble and sparkle at every turn with fun which sometimes is all the more agreeable because so obviously produced like ice at New Orleans, artificially, and with the set purpose to be agreeable.

Similarly there was little drollery in Emerson's conversation, though it had a sweetness which the testimony of a cloud of witnesses makes it not extravagant to call ineffable. But we get a touch of fun once in a while. A pleasantry recorded of him is a story he told of a friend who carried a horse-chestnut to protect him from rheumatism. "He has never had it since he began to carry it, and indeed it appears to have had a retrospective operation, for he never had it before." An English friend tells me that while with Mr. Emerson in his garden discussing some problem of life, Mrs. Emerson called to him for some wood. Emerson went to the wood-pile; when he came back he said, with his wonderful smile, "Now we will return to the real things." When Oliver Wendell Holmes asked him if he had any manual dexterity, he illustrated his want of it by replying, that he could split a shingle four ways with one nail. "Which," says Dr. Holmes, "as the intention is not to split it at all in fastening it to the roof, I took to be a confession of inaptitude for mechanical work." In later years he lost his memory of the names of things. Once he wanted his umbrella, but could not recall the word. But he got around the difficulty. "I can't tell its name, but I can tell its history. Strangers take it away." His daughter ran in one day to ask who should be invited to join their berry-picking party. "All the children," he said, "from six years to sixty." Equally tender is the humor of this in the essay on "Illusions": "When the boys come into my yard for leave to gather horse-chestnuts, I enter into nature's game, and affect to grant the permission reluctantly, fearing that any moment they will find out the imposture. . . . But this tenderness is quite unnecessary; the enchantments are laid on very thick."

This recluse could sit in his garden at Concord or wander along the shores of Walden and see into the penetralia of Vanity Fair quite as keenly as the clubmen of Michigan Avenue or Piccadilly. He was once asked if he approved of Platonic friendship between men and women. "Yes," he said, "but—hands off!" Once when Emerson was in Chicago to lecture to its Fortnightly Club of women, its president said to him, "It is too bad you were not here last week, Mr. Emerson. We were discussing Goethe's 'Elective Affinities,' and would have been so glad to get your views." Emerson bowed with gracious silence. "What would you have said to us about it?" the lady persisted. "Madam," he replied, "I have never felt that I had attained to the purity of mind that qualified me to read that book."

We all know the kind of men he described as those who "seem to steal their own dividends," and the kind of girl like *Lillian* who "began the world with a cold in her head and has been adding to it ever since." Of the type Disraeli chose for the hero of "Vivian Grey," Emerson said: "They never sleep, go nowhere, stay nowhere, eat nothing, and know nobody, but are up to anything though it were the genesis of nature or the last cataclysm. Festus-like, Faust-like, Jove-like, they could write an Iliad any rainy morning if fame were not such a bore." Very delicate but very penetrating is his characterization of a certain class of the American youth, who are "converted into pale caryatides to uphold the temple of conventions."

He did not care much for metaphysics. "Who has not looked into a metaphysical book, and what sensible man ever looked twice?" He wanted only a teaspoonful a year of its crop of pepper, and he added, "I admire the Dutch who burned half the harvest to enhance the price of the remainder."

There has already come to be an Emerson legend, like the Lincoln legend, grave and gay. This legend is the repository of the familiar story that having gone together to see Fanny Elssler dance, Margaret Fuller said to Emerson, "This is poetry!" and he replied, "It is religion!" Legend also attributes to Emerson the maxim that the consciousness of being well-dressed gives one a moral support greater than the consolations of religion. But it was not his own but a quotation he gives from the talk of a bright woman. Conway tells this story as current about Emerson, though he does not pretend that it is true. Wishing to know Bowery life at its roughest, Emerson mussed his hat, turned up his coat collar, and going to the bar of a saloon called for a glass of grog. The barkeeper took a glance at his visitor, and said, "Lemonade will do for you." This must be classed with the legend that when Emerson visited Egypt the Sphinx said to him, "You're another!" Among the traditions of Emerson is that one night in the small hours his wife was wakened by hearing him stir about the room.

"Are you sick?" she asked anxiously. "No, only an idea." But Cabot spoils this story by saying, evidently with direct reference to it, that Emerson never got up at night, as some one has fancied, to jot down thoughts. In Boston a story is current which is well found, even if it is not true. A believer in the immediate second coming of Christ went about warning people that the end of the world was at hand. Emerson heard him serenely, and only said, "We can do without it." The Emerson legend is as good a place as any in which to put the Concord witticism about his relations with one of its philosophers. Emerson somewhere says that no one can easily be a good judge of his own admirers. Many of his friends thought there was no better exemplification of this than the, as it seemed to them, extravagant estimation in which he held this neighbor. They said this assimilating brother would repeat to Emerson on Tuesday the good things Emerson had said to him on Monday, and Emerson would marvel at the felicities of his inspired friend. The wits of Concord said that Emerson was a seer and his friend a seer-sucker.

Emerson styles himself a reporter merely, a suburban kind of man. He tried to see, he said, and to tell what he saw. To round a sentence or play the oracle was not possible to his integrity and sanity. In Arthur Hugh Clough's phrase, he "wholly declined roaring." When he speaks in the accents of the solemn, the grand, the beautiful, it is because his soul found itself in these deep waters. But if in the next moment the transition to comic or satiric came within, it would be given free speech, without. Wit shading down at one end of its spectrum to the merely comic brightens at the other into celestial radiations of wisdom too strong for laughter, as Wordsworth's thoughts were too deep for tears. From this sublimer wit came the illuminated vision with which Emerson saw and reported realities where others saw only mysteries, and mysteries where others thought they saw realities. Along his whole range from the essay on the "Oversoul" to that on the "Comic," this power of surprising the truth in front and rear is Emerson.

"Ralph Waldo Emerson"

George Santayana*

Those who knew Emerson, or who stood so near to his time and to his circle that they caught some echo of his personal influence, did not judge of him merely as a poet and philosopher, nor identify his efficacy with that of his writings. His friends and neighbors, the congregations he preached to in his younger days, the audiences that afterwards listened to

*Reprinted from *American Prose: Selections with Critical Introductions by Various Writers and a General Introduction*, ed. George Rice Carpenter (New York: Macmillan, 1898), pp. 187–93.

his lectures, all agreed in a veneration for his person that had nothing to do with their understanding or acceptance of his opinions. They flocked to him and listened to his word, not so much for the sake of its absolute meaning as for the atmosphere of candor, purity, and serenity that hung about it, as about a sort of sacred music. They felt themselves in the presence of a rare and beautiful spirit, who was in communication with a higher world. More than the truth his teaching might express, they valued the sense it gave them of a truth that was inexpressible. They became aware, if we may say so, of the ultra-violet rays of his spectrum, of the inaudible highest notes of his gamut, too pure and thin for common ears.

Yet the personal impression Emerson may have produced is but a small part of his claim to general recognition. This must ultimately rest on his published works, on his collected essays and poems. His method of composition was to gather miscellaneous thoughts together in note-books and journals, and then, as occasion offered, to cull those that bore on the same subject or could serve to illustrate the same general train of thought, and to piece a lecture out of them. This method has the important advantage of packing the page with thought and observation, so that it deserves to be reread and pondered; but it is incompatible with continuity of thought or unity and permanence of impression. A style of point and counterpoint, where the emphasis attained by condensation and epigram is not reserved for the leading ideas, but gives an artificial vividness to every part, must tend to make the whole indistinct and inconclusive. The fact that the essays were lectures led to another characteristic which is now to be regretted. They are peppered by local allusions and illustrations drawn from the literary or scientific novelties of the hour. These devices may have served to keep an audience awake, but they were always unworthy of the subject, and they now distract the reader, who loses the perennial interest of the thought in the quaintness or obscurity of the expression. Yet, in spite of faults, Emerson's style is well fitted to his purpose and genius: it has precision, picturesqueness, often a great poetic beauty and charm, with the eloquence that comes of ingenuous conviction and of dwelling habitually among high things. The very element of oddity, the arbitrary choice of quotations and illustrations, is not without its charm, suggesting, as it does, the author's provincial solitude and personal savor. Taken separately, and with the sympathetic coöperation of the reader's fancy, his pages are inspiring and eloquent in a high degree, the best paragraphs being sublime without obscurity, and convincing without argumentation.

The themes treated seem at first various—biography, literary criticism, natural science, morals, and metaphysics. But the initiated reader will find that the same topics and turns of thought recur under every title: we may expect under "Friendship," as much moral cosmology as under "Fate," and under "Science" as many oriental anecdotes as under "Worship." The real subject is everywhere the same. As a preacher might under every text enforce the same lessons of the gospel, so Emerson traces in every sphere the same spiritual laws of experience—compensation, continuity, the self-expression of the soul in the forms of nature and of society, until she finally recognizes herself in her own work, and sees its beneficence and beauty. The power of thought, or rather, perhaps, of imagination, is his single theme: its power first to make the world, then to understand it, and finally to rise above it. All nature is an embodiment of our native fancy, and all history a drama, in which the innate possibilities of our spirit are enacted and realized. While the conflict of life and the shocks of experience seem to bring us face to face with an alien and overwhelming power, reflection can humanize and rationalize the power by discovering its laws; and with this recognition of the rationality of all things comes the sense of their beauty and order. The very destruction which nature seems to prepare for our special hopes is thus seen to be the victory of our deeper and impersonal interests. To awaken in us this spiritual insight, an elevation of mind which is an act at once of comprehension and of worship, to substitute it for lower passions and more servile forms of intelligence—that is Emerson's constant effort. All his resources of illustration, of observation, rhetoric, and paradox, are used to deepen and clarify this sort of wisdom.

Such thought is essentially the same that is found in the German romantic or idealistic philosophers, with whom Emerson's affinity is remarkable, all the more as he seems to have borrowed little or nothing from their works. The resemblance may be accounted for, perhaps, by the similar conditions that existed in the religious thought of that time in Germany and in New England. In both countries the abandonment, on the part of the new school of philosophy, of all allegiance to the traditional theology, coincided with a vague enthusiasm for science and with a quickening of national and humanitarian hopes. The critics of human nature, during the eighteenth century, had shown how much men's ideas of things depended on their natural predispositions, on the character of their senses, and the habits of their intelligence. Seizing upon this thought, and exaggerating it, the romantic philosophers attributed to the spirit of man that omnipotence which had belonged to God, and felt that in this way they were reasserting the supremacy of mind over matter and establishing it upon a safe and rational basis. The Germans were great system-makers, and Emerson cannot rival them in the sustained effort of thought by which they sought to reinterpret every sphere of being according to their chosen principles. On the other hand, those who are distrustful of a too systematic and complete philosophy, especially of this transcendental sort, will regard it as a fortunate incapacity in Emerson that he was never able to trace out and defend the universal implications of any of his ideas, and never wrote, for instance, the book he had once planned on the law of compensation. A happy instinct made him always prefer a fresh statement on a fresh subject, and deterred him from repeating or defending his trains of thought. A suggestion once given, the spirit once aroused to speculation, a glimpse once gained of some ideal harmony, he preferred to descend again to common sense and to touch the earth for a moment before another flight. The faculty of idealization was in itself what he valued. Philosophy for him was rather a moral energy flowering into sprightliness of thought than a body of serious and defensible doctrines. And in practising transcendental speculation only in this poetic and sporadic fashion, Emerson was perhaps retaining its truest value and avoiding its greatest danger. He secured the freedom and fertility of his intelligence, and did not allow one conception of law or one hint of harmony to sterilize the mind and prevent the subsequent birth of other ideas, no less just and inspiring than itself. For we are not dealing at all in such a philosophy with matters of facts, or with such verifiable truths as exclude their opposites, but only with the art of conception and the various forms in which reflection, like a poet, can compose and recompose human experience.

If we ask ourselves what was Emerson's relation to the scientific and religious movements of his time, and what place he may claim in the history of opinion, we must answer that he belonged very little to the past, very little to the present, and almost wholly to that abstract sphere into which mystical and philosophic aspiration has carried a few men in all ages. The religious tradition in which he was reared was that of Puritanism, but of a Puritanism which, retaining its moral intensity and metaphysical abstractness, had minimized its doctrinal expression and become Unitarian. Emerson was indeed the Psyche of Puritanism, "the latest born and fairest vision far" of all that "faded hierarchy." A Puritan whose religion was all poetry, a poet whose only pleasure was thought, he showed in his life and personality the meagreness, the constraint, the conscious aloofness and consecration which belonged to his clerical ancestors, while his personal spirit ranged abroad over the fields of history and nature, gathering what ideas it might, and singing its little snatches of inspired song.

The traditional element was thus rather an external and unessential contribution to Emerson's mind; he had the professional tinge, the decorum, and the distinction of an old-fashioned divine; he had also the habit of writing sermons, and he had the national pride and hope of a religious people that felt itself providentially chosen to establish a free and godly commonwealth in a new world. For the rest he separated himself from the ancient creed of the community with a sense rather of relief than of regret. A literal belief in Christian doctrines repelled him as unspiritual, as manifesting no understanding of the meaning which, as allegories, those doctrines might have to a philosophic and poetical spirit. Although as a clergyman he was at first in the habit of referring to the Bible and its lessons as to a supreme authority, he had no instinctive sympathy with the inspiration of either the Old or the New Testament; in

Hafiz or Plutarch, in Plato or Shakspere, he found more congenial stuff. To reject tradition and think as one might have thought if no man had ever existed before was indeed the aspiration of the Transcendentalists, and although Emerson hardly regarded himself as a member of that school, he largely shared its tendency and passed for its spokesman. Both by temperament and conviction he was ready to open his mind to all philosophic influences, from whatever quarter they might blow; the lessons of science and the divinations of poetry could work themselves out in him into a free and personal religion.

The most important part of Emerson's Puritan heritage was the habit of worship which was innate in him, the ingrained tendency to revere the Power that works in the world, whatever might appear to be the character of its operation. This pious attitude was originally justified by the belief in a personal God and in a providential government of human affairs, but survives as a religious instinct after those positive beliefs had faded away into a recognition of "spiritual laws." The spirit of conformity, the unction, and the loyalty even unto death inspired by the religion of Jehovah, were dispositions acquired by too long a discipline, and rooted in too many forms of speech, of thought, and of worship for a man like Emerson, who had felt their full force, ever to be able to lose them. The evolutions of his abstract opinions left that habit undistrubed. Unless we keep this circumstance in mind, we shall not understand the kind of elation and sacred joy, so characteristic of his eloquence, with which he propounds laws of nature, and aspects of experience which, viewed in themselves, often afford but an equivocal support to moral enthusiasm. An optimism so persistent and unclouded as his will seem at variance with the description he himself gives of human life, a description colored by a poetic idealism, but hardly by an optimistic bias. We must remember, therefore, that Calvinism had known how to combine an awestruck devotion to the supreme being with no very roseate picture of the destinies of mankind, and for more than two hundred years had been breeding in the stock from which Emerson came a willingness to be "damned for the glory of God." What wonder, then, that when for the former inexorable dispensation of Providence, Emerson substituted his general spiritual and natural laws he should not have felt the spirit of worship fail within him? On the contrary, his thought moved in the presence of moral harmonies which seemed to him truer, more beautiful, and more beneficent than those of the old theology; and although an independent philosopher might not have seen in those harmonies an object of worship or a sufficient basis for optimism, he who was not primarily a philosopher but a Puritan mystic with a poetic fancy and a gift for observation and epigram, saw in them only a more intelligible form of the divinity he had always recognized and adored. His was not a philosophy passing into religion, but a religion expressing itself as a philosophy, and veiled as it descended the heavens in various tints of poetry and reason.

While Emerson thus preferred to withdraw, without rancor and without contempt, from the ancient fellowship of the church, he assumed an attitude hardly less cool and deprecatory towards the enthusiasms of the new era. The national idea of democracy and freedom had his complete sympathy; he allowed himself to be drawn into the movement against slavery; he took a curious and smiling interest in the discoveries of natural science, and in the material progress of the age. But he could go no farther. His contemplative nature, his religious training, his dispersed reading, made him stand aside from the life of the world, even while he studied it with benevolent attention. His heart was fixed on eternal things, and he was in no sense a prophet for his age and country. He belongs by nature to that mystical company of devout souls that recognize no particular home, and are dispersed throughout history, although not without intercommunication. He felt his affinity with the Hindoos and the Persians, with the Platonists and the Stoics. Like them he remains "a friend and aider of those who would live in the spirit." If not a star of the first magnitude, he is certainly a fixed star in the firmament of philosophy. Alone as yet among Americans, he may be said to have won a place there, if not by the originality of his thought, at least by the originality and beauty of expression he gave to thoughts that are old and imperishable.

"Emerson and Economics"

Alexander C. Kern*

It makes a difference whether a man is called a materialist or an idealist, yet within the province of economics Emerson has been called both. This sharp clash of critical opinion perhaps indicates that Emerson's economic thought has not been sufficiently examined. Although he was not an economist, not even primarily interested in economics, he so frequently touched the subject that an understanding of his economic ideas is a prerequisite to the evaluation of his entire thought on any relative or absolute scale. Even those critics who disagree as to the nature of his economic thought acknowledge its importance as a symptom of the times or as a motivating force. While the subject of Emerson's influence remains to be explored, it is certain that his lectures must in some way have expressed, if they did not mold, the hopes and ideals of a generation of Americans. Beyond this, there is no agreement.

The variety of interpretation is explicable enough, for it is not easy to understand Emerson, and this is equally true of his economic thought. What he said is much more easily determined than what he most deeply,

*Reprinted from *New England Quarterly*, 13 (December 1940): 678–96

most constantly, thought or felt. Emerson has an unequalled lubricity. His disregard of foolish consistency means that he is all things to all men. They can see in him what they wish to see, for the difficulty lies precisely in the fact that Emerson contains fragments of every type of view. The task of ascertaining his economic position is, however, far from hopeless, if his major principles are constantly kept in mind.

For Emerson does show, I boldly assert, a consistency which transcends any number of conflicting judgments—a consistency which is produced by his steady adherence to a small number of fixed principles—and herein lies the importance of his thinking. The bases on which he built the structure of his thought were the principles of correspondence, melioration, individualism, and, to a lesser extent, compensation. When these principles are used to explain his economic theories, some of the apparent inconsistencies will vanish.

Perhaps it will be most useful to go at once to the central snarl of the problem and there attempt to unwind the threads of Emerson's thinking. The tangle is this: On the one hand Lucy Hazard calls Emerson the spokesman of frontier individualism and optimism, the friend "of those who want to annex a territory or corner a market,"[1] and V. F. Calverton assigns him a petty bourgeois philosophy.[2] On the other hand, Vernon L. Parrington describes Emerson as the most searching critic of contemporary American materialism,[3] and Matthew Arnold, who could recognize a Philistine, thought of Emerson as "the friend and aider of those who would live in the spirit." More recently he has been pictured as an opponent of "a rising materialistic middle class without education and tradition, who were winning cultural and economic power and changing the tone of American life."[4] Where does the truth lie? While there is evidence for both sides, I contend that a complete understanding of Emerson will dictate a decision in favor of the more idealistic thread. For as Hamilton's approach to economic problems was political, and Jefferson's approach was sociological, so Emerson's approach was moral.

First let me unwind the skein of materialism. It is clear that the frontier required, if it did not engender, optimism and individualism, qualities which were also emphasized by the middle class. These same qualities are to be found in Emerson, and it is therefore contended that he was merely rationalizing American materialism in his philosophy. But this is not true in any simple sense.

Emerson was an optimist. In so far as he believed that evil was not real, he was influenced by the Neo-Platonists, but he more emphatically asserted that the cosmos was animated by a beneficent tendency or melioration in nature which would alone permit amelioration in mankind.[5] Society was likewise progressive, since the ideals and aspirations of one century become the code of the next. Emerson did not, however, accept the ordinary form of the idea of progress. Rather, he felt that the individual advanced, while social change came only through those few whose example modified the aspirations of the group.[6]

Emerson's belief in an immanent, conscious law of beneficent force has a number of sources. Professor Harry Hayden Clark has convincingly traced this idea to Emerson's knowledge of Newtonian and Lamarckian science.[7] Stoicism and the French meliorists might also be pointed out as sources. It would, however, be foolish to deny that Emerson's optimism was reenforced by his consciousness of the youth, size, and future of his country.[8] For decades he celebrated the prospects of America because of the greatness of its material basis. In 1844 he said, "An unlooked for consequence of the railroad is the increased acquaintance it has given the American people with the boundless resources of their own soil. . . . The bountiful continent is ours, state on state, and territory on territory to the waves of the Pacific sea." "We cannot look on the freedom of this country . . . without a presentiment that here shall laws and institutions exist on some scale of proportion to the majesty of nature." America was "another word for opportunity," and "manifest destiny" signified "the sense all men have of the prodigious energy and opportunity lying idle here."[9]

He saw in commerce, too, another sign of beneficence, another mark of melioration. The rise of trade produced the breakdown of feudalism at the same time that it expanded man's power over the resources of his country. Even the rise of the exploiting class into an aristocracy of wealth was desirable, for such a group did much material good and could, in any case, not last long. Since he was unfortunately wrong in this prophecy, it is not surprising that his optimism has been thought a tragic illusion,[10] or that Carlyle is said to have taken Emerson through the slums of London and then asked, "Well, do ye believe in a devil noo?"[11]

This was optimism enough, and optimism which found reenforcement in the frontier, but more damagingly serious is the contention that Emerson advocated what is now called "rugged individualism," a grasping, predatory, and exploiting bourgeois materialism. Individualism was certainly one of the fundamentals of Emerson's thought, and self-reliance was one of his primary principles. But the relation of this self-reliance to "rugged individualism" needs examination. There are certain points of contact, for Emerson's doctrine that riches are both the deserved product of character, fore-sight, and thrift and also a sign of man's domination over nature, links with the ruthless cruelty and exploitation of nineteenth-century America. But this was not the whole of Emerson's opinion.

Emerson believed that man could come into contact with the conscious law, higher law, or Over-Soul by intuition. It was upon the view that all men were capable of this direct contact with God that Emerson's rather temperate belief in democracy was based. Thus self-reliance became reliance upon God or upon the common mind of man. His individualism was, then, less materialistic than moral, less romantic than ethical in its nature. And while he did admire the sturdy independence of the farmers around Concord, this independence was not so much frontier as agrarian, a distinction which is sometimes forgotten by the Turnerites.

Nevertheless, Emerson's individualistic theory of wealth must have tickled the ears of the materialists to whom he lectured, for he did contend that the attainment of worldly possessions was not accidental. There was "always a reason *in the man*, for his good or bad fortune, and so in making money."[12] The application of mind to the material world, to achieve harmony with the laws of nature, was most important, for it was the ability to forecast what would be valuable in the future that made men rich.[13] Thus, as he maintained, wealth was mental and moral; it resulted from close application "to the laws of the world, and since those laws are intellectual and moral, an intellectual and moral obedience." To him the "counting room maxims liberally expounded" were "laws of the Universe," and great fortune, far from being evil, was a certificate of ability and "of virtues of a certain sort."[14]

Thrift and industry were likewise important to the financially successful man. Since Emerson felt that financial attainment was within the reach of man's insight and will, he emphasized a wise frugality which adjusted wants to income, so that each man could feed himself. And besides thrift he advocated work as a salutary influence, whether educative and strengthening, or so fatiguing as to render violence impossible. Worldly failure, then, was due to lack of these virtues, and the proper treatment for poverty was not charity but moral education.

The influence of Emerson's puritan New England background upon this crass portion of his thought seems to have escaped notice, despite the fact that since the publication of Max Weber's brilliant studies of religion and economics, for which the writings of Benjamin Franklin were an inspiration,[15] the relation of puritan ethics and economic individualism has been recognized. R. H. Tawney, the leading English exponent of this general view, states the elements of the case very simply. The business virtues of thrift and industry become Christian virtues; "practical success is at once the sign and reward of ethical superiority"; and since the poor are sinners, charity becomes less important than moral reform.[16] There is ample evidence to indicate that this belief was common in New England, and I suggest that Emerson's doctrine of wealth was to a considerable extent the product of his puritan background. And though he may not have seen it in himself, he recognized a mixture of religion in the English worship of property.

Besides the belief that wealth was earned by ability, Emerson also saw wealth as a sign of man's domination over the material world. He had never seen "a man as rich as all men ought to be, or with an adequate command of nature."[17] Consequently Emerson appeared to justify both increased mechanization and the exploitation of natural resources. The railroads, he thought, hastened by fifty years the settlement and cultivation of land and the working of mines. Man had wonderful power in steam and electricity, and although there was some danger that they could master man, in the right place they were good.

> 'Tis fit the forest fall,
> The steep be graded. . . .

Emerson did not, to be sure, foresee the dust bowl which was to be born of ruthless, unintelligent deforestation and of over-extensive cultivation of submarginal land. But neither did other Americans of Emerson's day. Orestes Brownson alone among New Englanders recognized that the frontier would pass,[18] yet not even he could prophesy the havoc that would be wrought.

Up to this point the case for Emerson's materialism looks rather strong; the middle-class individualism and optimism seem dominant. To begin unraveling the other thread, I cannot do better than quote Bronson Alcott, who had just heard Emerson deliver a lecture on wealth. "Emerson said fine things last night about 'Wealth,' but there are finer things far to be said in praise of Poverty. . . . Eloquent, wise, and witty as were the orator's praises of Gold . . . still the moral laws were too faintly implied. . . . But there are more lectures to come on 'Culture' and 'Worship' to soften and set things in their proper lights, doubtless, and justify the whole to the conscience and intellect of good men of all times."[19]

Emerson could and did talk well about poverty, as will be seen, but the second of Alcott's points is the more immediately significant. People who accepted Emerson's encomiums of wealth were not taking into account all of his thought. Emerson had a habit in an essay or lecture series of using a rising scale, beginning on a mundane plane and ending on a spiritual. Consequently a refusal to accept his highest thought makes him sound like a Babbitt, a Rotarian, or a Dale Carnegie. Materialists should not, perhaps, be blamed for taking what they want from Emerson's lectures, but it is only by disregarding what Emerson himself deemed most important that he can be made out a vulgar bourgeois apologist.[20]

Behind Emerson's thought lies the assumption that there are layers of law which roughly correspond. Lowest on the scale are the physical laws, the laws for things. Since each law in nature has a counterpart in the intellect, there is a set of intellectual laws also, but over all is the moral or spiritual law. This law pervades everything, for "All things are moral," and betray their source in a "Universal Spirit."[21] Thus material organization exists to a moral end, and this end is cultivated man. As Emerson said, "The true test of civilization is, not the census, nor the size of cities, nor the crops—no, but the kind of man a country turns out."[22] When used for the advancement of human culture, wealth and mechanization were not to be condemned, since they increased man's power and command over nature and forced her to disgorge her treasures. But when these means became ends, they deserved utter condemnation.

This ambivalent view is compactly stated in the "Ode to W. H. Channing":

> There are two discrete,
> Not reconciled,—
> Law for man, and law for thing;
> The last builds town and fleet,
> But it runs wild,
> And doth the man unking. . . .
> Let man serve law for man.

First, then, man ought not to serve the law for thing. Gaining wealth for its own sake is absurd and self-defeating. The miner is not rich. Spurious "prudence," Emerson said, that makes "the senses final, is the god of sots and cowards, and is the subject of all comedy. It is nature's joke." And again, "No land is bad, but land is worse. If a man own land, the land owns him." Nor is it wiser to seek too strenuously to obtain opulence; "in getting wealth the man is generally sacrificed, and often is sacrificed without acquiring wealth at last." Society too turns ends to means, and Emerson saw, as did Arnold later, that the present generation is sacrificed to the future.[23]

On the other hand, poverty is not necessarily a detriment. "The greatest man in history was the poorest,"[24] Emerson points out, and Socrates, Paul, and John were far from rich. There is after all no need for wealth. If a man cannot make what he needs for himself with his own hands, then he can go without. "Immense wisdom and riches are in that." It is better to go without than to have "at too great a cost."[25]

Here lies the answer to the frequently put question whether Emerson thought that people received the income they deserved. A categorical yes or no is insufficient, because Emerson judged on two different planes. In so far as individuals work for material ends they earn their rewards. Wealth is the product of intelligence and virtue, but wealth alone is useless; its advantages are "in the skin or not much deeper." "For he is the rich man in whom the people are rich, and he is the poor man in whom the people are poor; and how to give all access to the masterpieces of art and nature is the problem of civilization." Wealth thus carries with it responsibilities, and to "live without duties is obscene."[26] Napoleon, of the materialist type, received his material reward. As opposed to him there are the idealists whose wants transcend money, and Emerson knew and admired many of them. Thoreau and Alcott were not poor through lack of ability; Emerson realized, at least part of the time, that their objectives were higher. It was easy, he thought, "for the philosophic class to be poor,"[27] since its aims are lofty, and he had a soft spot in his heart for idealistic reformers,[28] who were fighting, or trying to fight, on Emerson's side. Their lack of wealth was an ornament, a sign of superior ability, rather than a stigma. In this judgment Emerson was showing the influence of another side of puritanism, a side typified by Mary Moody Emerson's statement, "My grandfather prayed every night that none of his descendants might ever be rich."[29]

Though he may not himself have lived up to these principles of poverty, Emerson became increasingly aware of the materialism of the rich. While, as he became more prosperous, he more frequently praised the benefits of wealth, he also more and more sharply criticized the tendency to make property the ultimate goal. At first he concentrated his attack on the vulgar and uneducated masses who supported Jackson and Van Buren,[30] but by 1840 he began to show doubts about the integrity of the wealthy groups as well. He then decided that the Democratic party had the best cause and the Whig party the best men.[31] At that time his social prejudice tilted the balance against Van Buren, probably because he realized that both parties had the same aims. The Whigs were "merely defensive of property," but the poor Democrats attacked the capitalists only in the hope of themselves becoming rich.[32]

When, however, New England financiers and cotton manufacturers championed slavery to protect their investments, Emerson waxed indignant about the "cotton Whigs." The money power was perpetrating a great wrong, which was finally unmasked. The effect of this group was so strong that "fine gentlemen, clergymen, college presidents and professors . . . will of course go for safe degrees of liberty—that is, will side with property against the Spirit."[33] Thus the taint of materialism was corrupting even those groups who should remain free from bias.

As he brooded over the situation, he decided that "The lesson of these days is the vulgarity of wealth. . . . Wealth will vote for rum, will vote for tyranny, will vote for slavery, will vote against the ballot, will vote against international copy-right, will vote against schools, colleges, or any high direction of public money." Later he wrote, "The obstacle the philanthropic movements meet is the invincible depravity of the virtuous classes."[34] In such strong terms as these Emerson unburdened his mind of the oppression by the middle- and upper-class materialism which developed with industrialism.

Unlike the typical American liberal who is the champion of the underdog, Emerson did not express any very great sympathy for the laboring man, whose lot was steadily growing worse during the decades of the eighteen-forties and fifties. The factory operatives had at first found their work more lucrative than it had previously been on their farms. But as work was speeded up and earnings were decreased, a large number of laborers were depressed to the point of destitution. Emerson's reaction to this situation was less sensitive than that of John Greenleaf Whittier, for example, who supported a strike for the ten-hour day, or that of Orestes Brownson,[35] who for a time took an active part in the labor movement.

When, during the panic of 1837, the discharge of sixty thousand workers was threatened, Emerson worried that these men might "make a formidable mob to break open banks and rob the rich,"[36] rather than that the laborers themselves might suffer. In the later depression of 1857 his immediate reaction was one of anger at the loss of his investments in railroad stocks, although a later result was his fine essay "Works and Days."

If he was not especially concerned with the lot of the common laborer, the evils of extreme specialization were, however, more evident to him. "A man should not be a silk-worm," he said, "nor a nation a tent of caterpillars. . . . The incessant repetition of the same hand-work dwarfs the man, robs him of his strength, wit, and versatility . . . and presently, in a change of industry, whole towns are sacrificed like ant hills when the fashion of shoe-strings supersedes buckles. . . ." It is perhaps significant that this passage continues with the remark that "in these crises all are ruined except such as are proper individuals, capable of thought and of new choice and the application of their talents to a new labor." It is the individual who counts, and it is the individual whom industrialism stultifies. "The machine unmakes the man." "The weaver becomes a web, the machinist a machine."[37]

It should be evident by this time, I think, that Emerson was far from a simple materialist, trumpeting the pecuniary virtues. While it is true that he recognized the utility of wealth, it is no less true that he attacked the cupidity, the foolishness, and the conservatism of the middle classes both in England and in America. In an industrial society the individual was disregarded, and that Emerson deplored. He felt that moral progress had not kept pace with material power and that industrialism was, therefore, not a judicious investment.[38]

After the problem of Emerson's economic attitudes has been discussed, the problem of his economic theory still remains. Here too, his basic concept of the correspondence of layers of law must be kept constantly in mind, or a distorted image will result. On its level the law for things will operate, and cannot with impunity be broken. On the higher level man must follow the superior validity of the spiritual law, obedience to which will break the chain of determinism. In the case of the state Emerson's view was the same. For the time being, government must of necessity follow the law for things, but as moral education produces a superior citizenry, the higher law will operate to an ever-increasing extent. Following Emerson's upward course will, I think, make his economic theory sufficiently clear.

To begin on the material level, necessity demands obedience to material laws. Emerson maintained that property would always write the laws of property, and thus expressed the Hamiltonian and also the Marxian view that to insure stability, the dominant economic group of a country must control the government. This he saw to be true even in case the rich lost control, for then the joint treasury of the poor would exceed the holdings of the wealthy. Emerson also recognized the corollary that political parties follow necessary economic laws; even when a party member could not give a logical account of his position, it was clear that he had unconsciously joined the group which defended his economic interests.[39]

This doctrine cannot be represented as economic determinism, for on its own plane the law for things can be broken, and on the higher plane, as I shall point out later, the moral law supersedes the material law when and if they come into conflict. Time after time Emerson made the point that economic laws *should* be obeyed, an indication that he thought they were not being obeyed in the United States. If, as Emerson also believed, the operation of the natural laws produced a beneficent tendency characterized by a slight plus or balance of good in the outcome, then man could not do better than to adhere to the processes of nature. Any factitious interference on the part of man or government could only result in harm.

Consistently with these ideas, Emerson staunchly believed in the doctrine of *laissez faire*. He maintained:

> The basis of political economy is non-interference. The only safe rule is found in the self-adjusting meter of demand and supply. Do not legislate. Meddle, and you snap the sinews with your sumptuary laws. Give no bounties, make equal laws, secure life and property, and you need not give alms. Open the doors of opportunity to talent and virtue and they will do themselves justice, and property will not be in bad hands.[40]

If man tries to meddle or to help, the serene Power resists.

> We devise sumptuary and relief laws, but the principle of population is always reducing wages to the lowest pittance on which human life can be sustained. We legislate against forestalling and monopoly; . . . but the selfishness which hoards the corn for high prices is the preventive of famine; and the law of self-reservation is surer policy than any legislation can be. We concoct eleemosinary systems, and it turns out that our charity increases pauperism. We inflate our paper currency, we repair commerce with unlimited credit, and are presently visited with unlimited bankruptcy.[41]

His *laissez faire* doctrine made Emerson a steady opponent of the protective tariff, the most prominent American example of nonconformity to natural economic laws. He recognized that free trade was "certainly the interest of nations, but by no means the interest of certain towns and districts, which tariff feeds fat."[42] Free trade, he felt, would produce more desirable economic results than any statutes which only interfered with the operations of natural law. Free trade, for example, had been obtained in substance among the thirty states in 1851, and it had greatly increased the production of iron. Thus Emerson desired, if he could have it, "free trade with all the world, without toll or custom-house."[43]

Such ideas indicate a certain acquaintance with the English *laissez faire* economists, and it is true that he knew the writings of Adam Smith, Ricardo, Bentham, and especially Malthus. But Emerson rejected their materialism. Utilitarianism he called a "stinking philosophy." "I know nothing," he said, "which induces so base and forlorn a feeling as when we are treated for our utilities, as economists do."[44] By rejecting their doctrine of the economic man, he escaped the contradiction of the utilitarian school and brought himself closer to the position of Jefferson, though Emerson was at once the more complete Utopian and the less thorough-going agrarian.

The ideal state, according to Emerson's theories, was that which gave the individual the most freedom for self-development. Like Jefferson, he felt that the best government was that which governed least. Indeed, he maintained that when wise men came, the state would cease to exist: when people were morally educated, no government would be required. Emerson extended this not uncommon form of intellectual anarchism equally to economics: in the present half-fledged state the economic services of the government were essential, but in the ideal future these functions could be carried on by individuals. "Governments of nations of shop-keepers must keep shop also," he wrote, and

> there will always be a government of force where men are selfish; and when they are pure enough to abjure the code of force they will be wise enough to see how these public ends of the post-office, of the highway, of commerce and the exchange of property, of museums and libraries, of institutions of art and science can be answered.[45]

Emerson was forced, like all others, to face the gap between his ideal state and the one which actually existed. Society was barbarous, he thought, until every industrious man could earn an honest living,[46] but not every one could in Emerson's day. How could he bridge to the new order? Whether logically or not, he decided that the government must perform certain necessary functions during the intermediate period; it must "instruct the ignorant," "supply the poor with work," mediate between "want and supply," and furnish "good guidance."[47] Just what, beyond education, Emerson meant by his solution is not at once clear. It has been asserted that his view tended "perhaps toward socialism,"[48] which I doubt, or toward paternalism,[49] which is much more probable, since the idea seems to have grown out of a conversation with Carlyle.[50] This aid to the poor, however, was only temporary in nature, until society should improve. But how would it advance?

Emerson thought that institutions were a mere expression of the culture which existed in a state, and furthermore that the laws were usually behind the present because they reflected the time when they were passed.[51] Thus the laws would change to conform with a society which itself slowly changes under the influence of individual leaders. Consequently all history shows the power of minorities of one, and the "institution is the lengthening shadow of one man."[52] It is not surprising that Emerson, with such a theory, should place his emphasis upon education rather than upon legal reform. He did not think that all societal restraints should be cast off, nor did he feel it worth while to attack institutions. As indicated by his refusal to vote against required chapel at Harvard, Emerson seemed on the whole to have been cautious about abandoning institutions until they had been thoroughly tested, and, in practice, to have favored retaining the *status quo*.[53]

Nevertheless Emerson always faced the future and took the advanced side of the question; he stood for possibilities rather than necessities, and as would be expected of a social critic, he took a sympathetic interest in attempts to advance society. He lived in an age of reforms and was consequently influenced by them. A few minor ones such as manual labor and vegetarianism he tried himself with ill success, but the attempts show his spirit. Much more important was his regard for the various types of communistic experiments which were designed to solve the problems of industrial urbanization and the need for education. He was perhaps most closely related to Brook Farm, where he was asked to become a member. He was a constant visitor and retained his interest in the experiment even after the colony adopted Fourier principles in 1845. The Socialists had his admiration for "the magnificence of their theories and the enthusiasm with which they had been urged. They appeared the inspired men of their time." But their plans seemed defective to Emerson. "Fourier had skipped no fact but one, namely life." Emerson felt further that individualism had never really been tried, thought all that was valuable in the phalanstery, the individual Fourier unit, came of individualism.[54]

While he examined agricultural units like Brook Farm and Fruitlands with a critical eye, he was himself interested in agrarianism. It is difficult to pin him down to any theory or program, for nowhere is he any more slippery than on this subject. He had no complete agrarian theory like Jefferson, who believed that cities produced corruption. Emerson merely thought that everyone should get into primary relationship with the work of the world, and that this could best be accomplished in farming.[55] While he recognized that agricultural work might dull the wits, at the same time he praised it because it developed an all-round man in a world of specialists.[56] The fact is, I think, that Emerson liked small-town life, where he was freed of the constant bustle of the larger city, had ready access to the natural beauties of the country-side, and could know upright men like Hosmer and Minot. But it seems to me impossible to tie Emerson's vague ideas with the Physiocratic movement or with the Southern Agrarians.

Emerson was not a reformer, just as Socrates was not a reformer. He was content to confine himself to what was for him a proper realm of intellectual and moral education. Except in the case of slavery, which struck him as an ethical rather than as an economic issue, he never mounted the platform with the specific intention of changing an institution. His interest was in the individual rather than in the group. He himself wrote, "Let me embark in political economy and I am soon run aground," but not so in the "law of laws."[57] This must be admitted, I think. The *laissez faire* idea in which he believed has never dominated American thought[58] and is not of immediate use today. Furthermore, as an economic thinker Emerson is much too general to meet practical problems. But on the moral plane his ideas are as important today as they ever were. The materialism which he opposed deserves just as much criticism now as it did in his time, and his example, is heartening and inspiring.

So, at least, Emerson appears to me. A reflector of his times, he combined elements of puritanism and Transcendentalism. If he seems to have advocated thrift, industry, and even exploitation, I maintain that this is Emerson's lower truth. I read the essay, not the excerpt only, and detect a higher law, a law which proclaims that "cultivated man, wise to know and bold to perform, is the end to which nature works."[59]

Notes

1. *The Frontier in American Literature* (New York: Thomas Y. Crowell, 1927), p. 152.

2. *The Liberation of American Literature* (New York: Scribners, 1932), p. 248.

3. *The Romantic Revolution in America* (New York: Harcourt, Brace, 1927), pp. 386–387.

4. William Charvat, "Romanticism and the Panic of 1837," *Science and Society*, 2 (Winter 1937): 80.

5. *The Complete Works of Ralph Waldo Emerson*, ed. Edward Waldo Emerson (Boston: Houghton, Mifflin, 1903–1904), Centenary Edition, I, 372. This edition will hereinafter be referred to as "*Works*."

6. Mildred Silver, "Emerson and the Idea of Progress," *American Literature*, 13 (March 1940): 19.

7. "Emerson and Science," *Philological Quarterly*, 10 (July 1931): 247.

8. See Ernest Marchand, "Emerson and the Frontier," *American Literature*, 3 (May 1931): 149–174. Arthur I. Ladu, "Emerson: Whig or Democrat," *New England Quarterly*, 13 (September 1940): 434–437, clarifies the question of frontier influence.

9. *Works*, I, 364, 370; XI, 299. See also *Journals of Ralph Waldo Emerson*, ed. Edward Waldo Emerson and Waldo Emerson Forbes (Boston: Houghton Mifflin, 1909–1914), X, 106.

10. James Truslow Adams, "Emerson Re-read," *Atlantic Monthly*, 146 (October 1930): 492.

11. Townsend Scudder, *The Lonely Wayfaring Man* (London: Oxford University Press, 1936), p. 148.

12. *Works*, VI, 100.

13. *Works*, X, 46.

14. *Works*, VI, 101, 125; *Journals*, IV, 217.

15. Max Weber, *The Protestant Ethic and the Spirit of Capitalism*, trans. Talcot Parsons (London: G. Allen and Unwin, 1930), pp. 48–50. This work first appeared in German in 1904–1905). Cf. H. M. Robertson, *Aspects of the Rise of Economic Individualism* (Cambridge, England: Cambridge University Press, 1933), p. 161.

16. R. H. Tawney, *Religion and the Rise of Capitalism* (New York: Harcourt, Brace, 1926), pp. 266–267.

17. *Works*, VI, 95.

18. Arthur M. Schlesinger, Jr., *Orestes Brownson* (Boston: Little, Brown, 1939), p. 92.

19. *The Journals of Bronson Alcott*, ed. Odell Shepard (Boston: Little, Brown, 1938), p. 261.

20. Certain American scholars and critics, while recognizing the idealistic element in Emerson, contend that it merely cloaks a basic materialism. Miss Hazard asserts that "This incorrigible optimism which was a psychological necessity of frontier life, was given a philosophical rationalization by transcendentalism. Its most familiar literary expression is found in the dogmatic optimism of Emerson's essays" (*The Frontier in American Literature*, p.150). "With Emerson," she continues, "as with the lesser transcendentalists, the basic materialism was so subtly interfused into the very substance of their gospel, that from Carlyle to Macy, critics have denied that transcendentalism had any vital connection with the actual life of the nineteenth century" (pp. 161–162). Mr. Calverton says, "In a word, the philosophic idealism embodied in the doctrine of self-reliance was but a subtle camouflage, however unconscious, for the petty bourgeois materialism which was concealed beneath its inspiration" (*The Liberation of American Literature*, p. 254). These statements go farther, I think, than the facts will warrant.

21. *Works*, I, 40, 44.

22. *Works*, VII, 31.

23. *Works*, II, 224; VI, 115; VII, 114; I, 374.

24. *Works*, VII, 115–116.

25. *Works*, I, 245.

26. *Journals*, IV, 409; *Works*, VI, 97; X, 52.

27. *Journals*, IV, 244.

28. Edward Waldo Emerson, *Emerson in Concord* (Boston: Houghton, Mifflin, 1889), p. 201.

29. James Elliot Cabot, *A Memoir of Ralph Waldo Emerson* (Boston: Houghton, Mifflin, 1887), I, 9.

30. *Journals*, III, 356–357; VII, 12.

31. *Works*, III, 209. Emerson greatly admired strength of will and character, and later appreciated Jackson's rugged individualism (*Works*, XI, 521). Nevertheless, Emerson did not adopt any set principle of voting for the man of force, since he might be wrong in his convictions. This he felt to be true of the Southern representatives in Congress during the slavery controversy (*Journals*, VIII, 323, 340).

32. *Works*, III, 210; I, 388.

33. *Journals*, VIII, 164. The conservative and effectually pro-slavery Union party he called a "shoptill party" (*Journals*, VIII, 213).

34. *Journals*, VIII, 532; X, 5.

35. T. F. Currier, "Whittier and the Amesbury-Salisbury Strike," *New England Quarterly*, 8 (March 1935): 109–110; Schlesinger, *Brownson*, pp. 97–98.

36. *Journals*, IV, 210. Cf. *The Letters of Ralph Waldo Emerson*, ed. Ralph L. Rusk (New York: Columbia University Press, 1939), II, 52–53, 65–66, 68–69, 89–90, and 92–93,

which cast some light on the complexity of Emerson's financial arrangements, especially in 1837, when his brother Edward was in embarrassed straits.

37. *Works*, V, 167; VII, 165, 164.

38. *Works*, VII, 166.

39. *Works*, III, 205–208.

40. *Works*, VI, 105–106.

41. *Works*, I, 374.

42. *Works*, XI, 301.

43. *Journals*, VIII, 233–234; X, 228. Cf. *Uncollected Lectures of Ralph Waldo Emerson*, ed. Clarence Gohdes (New York: William Edwin Rudge, 1932), p. 6; E. W. Emerson, *Emerson in Concord*, p. 83.

44. *Journals*, II, 455; *Works*, X, 56.

45. *Journals*, IX, 364–365; *Works*, III, 220.

46. *Works*, VI, 85.

47. *Works*, I, 381–385.

48. *Ralph Waldo Emerson: Representative Selections*, ed. Frederic Ives Carpenter (New York: American Book Co., 1934), p. xlvi.

49. George E. Woodberry, *Ralph Waldo Emerson* (New York: Macmillan, 1914), p. 144.

50. Carlyle told Emerson on his first voyage to England, that "Government should direct poor men what to do. Poor Irish folk come wandering over the moors . . . [where there] are thousands of acres which might give them all meat, and nobody to bid these poor Irish to go to the moor and till it. They burned haystacks and found a way to force the rich to attend to them" (see *Works*, V, 17–18).

51. *Works*, III, 200.

52. *Works*, II, 61.

53. O. W. Firkins, *Ralph Waldo Emerson* (Boston: Houghton Mifflin, 1915), p. 22; Raymer McQuiston, *The Relation of Ralph Waldo Emerson to Public Affairs* (Lawrence: University of Kansas, 1923), p. 9.

54. *Works*, X, 347, 352; *Journals*, VII, 323.

55. *Works*, I, 240–241.

56. *Journals*, VII, 63–64.

57. *Journals*, II, 426.

58. Charles A. Beard, "The Idea of Let Us Alone," *Virginia Quarterly Review*, 15 (Autumn 1939): 501.

59. *Works*, VI, 53–54.

"Emersonian Genius and the American Democracy"

Perry Miller[*]

Ralph Waldo Emerson was a poor boy, but in his community his kind of poverty mattered little. Few of his classmates at Harvard had

*Reprinted from *New England Quarterly*, 26 (March 1953), 27–44.

more money than he did, and they made no such splurge as would cause him to feel inferior or outcast. His name was as good as, if not better than, anybody else's. At reunions of the class of 1821, Emerson and his fellows, without embarrassment, quietly took up a collection for their one insolvent member. In the logic of the situation, Emerson should have received the stamp and have embraced the opinions of this group—self-consciously aristocratic, not because of their wealth but because of their names and heritage, at that moment moving easily from the Federalist to the Whig party. In 1821 there could hardly be found a group of young Americans more numb to the notion than there were any stirring implications in the word "democracy."

Actually, Emerson did take their stamp and did imbibe their opinion. We know, or ought to know, that to the end of his days he remained the child of Boston: he might well have lived out his time like Dr. Holmes (whom he admired), secure in his provincial superiority, voting Whig and Republican, associating the idea of the Democratic party with vulgarity, with General Jackson and tobacco-chewing. In great part he did exactly that; for this reason he poses difficult problems for those who would see in him America's classic sage.

For reasons which only a sociological investigation might uncover, youths at Harvard College after the War of 1812 began to exhibit a weariness with life such as they fancied might become a Rochefoucauld, which, assuredly, was nothing like what the college in its Puritan days had expected of sons of the prophets. Perhaps this was their way of declaring their independence of Puritan tradition. At any rate it is exactly here that the pose of indifference commenced to be a Harvard tradition and to take its toll. But in the first days it was difficult to maintain; only a few resolute spirits really carried it off, and Emerson, of course, lost much of Prufrock-ism in the enthusiasm of Transcendentalism. Yet not all of it—he never got rid of the fascination he early felt for this first, faint glimmer of an American sophistication; unless we remember it, we shall not understand his essays on "Culture," "Manners," "Aristocracy," or the bitterness of those who, like Parker and Ripley, had to look upon him as their leader even while hating just these aspects of him.

At the age of eighteen, in July, 1822, Emerson was bored with the prospect of another Independence Day. (At this time he also found Wordsworth crude, and what he heard of German philosophy absurd.) We Americans, he wrote his friend Hill, have marched since the Revolution "to strength, to honour, & at last to ennui." There is something immensely comic—and sad—in this spectacle of a young American of intelligence and good family, in 1822, already overcome with lassitude. Suppose the event should prove—the disdainful youth continued—that the American experiment has rashly assumed that men can govern themselves, that it demonstrates instead "that too much knowledge, & too much liberty makes them mad?" He was alrady determined to flee from the oratory of the Fourth of July to the serenity of cherry trees: "I shall expend my patriotism in banqueting upon Mother Nature."

However, events and ideas in Europe were already indicating that nature was a dangerous refuge for a nice young Bostonian. In America they were soon to demonstrate just how dangerous: the crisis in Emerson's intellectual life, which he endured for the next several years, coincided with those in which the natural politician—General Andrew Jackson—rose by nature's means, certainly not those of culture, to the Democratic Presidency.

With part of his brain—a good part—Emerson reacted to the triumph of Jackson as did any Bostonian or Harvard man. He informed his new friend, Carlyle, on May 14, 1834, that government in America was becoming a "job"—he could think of no more contemptuous word—because "a most unfit person in the Presidency has been doing the worst things; and the worse he grew, the more popular." Nothing would be easier than to collect from the *Journals* enough passages about the Democratic party to form a manual of Boston snobbery. In 1868, for instance, meditating upon the already stale Transcendental thesis that beauty consists largely in expression, he thus annotated it: "I noticed, the other day, that when a man whom I had always remarked as a handsome person was venting Democratic politics, his whole expression changed, and became mean and paltry."

This was the Emerson who, in his last years, escaped as often as he could from Concord to the Saturday Club. I believe that students of Emerson get nowhere unless they realize how often Emerson wished that the cup of Transcendentalism had not been pressed to his lips. Had he been spared that, he might comfortably have regarded the Democratic party as a rabble of Irish and other unwashed immigrants, and could have refused, as for long he did refuse, to find any special virtue in democracy as a slogan.

But he could not thus protect himself; other ideas forced themselves upon him, and he was doomed to respond. He lacked the imperviousness that armored State Street and Beacon Street; intellectually he was too thin-skinned. To the friends about him, and I dare say also to himself, the reason was obvious: he was a genius. This was his burden, his fate, and the measure of his disseverance from the ethos of his clan.

He emerged into literature as the castigator of the genteel, the proper, the self-satisfied; he aligned himself with forces as disruptive of the Whig world as Jacksonianism was of the world of John Quincy Adams. He called for a stinging oath in the mouth of the teamster instead of the mincing rhetoric of Harvard and Yale graduates, who stumbled and halted and began every sentence over again. He called the scholar decent, indolent, complacent. When he cried that the spirit of the American freeman was timid, imitative, tame, he did not aim at Democrats but at the fastidious spirits who made up Boston society. He meant the corpse-cold Unitarianism of Harvard College and Brattle Street. Or at least he said that is what he meant (whether he really did or not may be argued), wherefore he seemed to uphold standards as uncouth as those of that Democrat in the White House.

The first of these, notoriously, was the standard of self-reliance, but behind it and sustaining it was the even more disturbing one of genius. Emerson had to have a flail for beating those who stammered and stuttered, and he found it in the conception of genius; he pounced upon it, and spent the rest of his life vainly struggling with its political consequences.

It is a commonplace of literary history that the cult of genius came to a special flowering in the early nineteenth century. (We cannot possibly employ the word today with a like solemnity; half the time we use it as an insult.) Wherever it prospered—whether with the Schlegels and Tieck in Germany, with Hugo and George Sand in France, with Byron and Coleridge in England—it meant revolt against convention, especially the kind of social convention that made up Harvard and Boston. "If there is any period one would desire to be born in," Emerson asked the Harvard Phi Beta Kappa, "is it not the age of Revolution?" This was precisely the sort of period many of his listeners did not want to be born in, for revolution meant Old Hickory. But to some Emerson opened alluring prospects which, he appeared to say and they wanted to hope, would have nothing to do with politics; leaving the political revolution aside, they responded to his exhortation and became, over-night if necessary, geniuses. The works of Emerson served them as a handbook; with him in one hand they learned to practice with the other the requisite gestures, much as a bride holds the cookbook while stirring the broth. But his own *Journals* show him as never quite so certain as he appeared from the outside, never entirely sure as to just what constituted genius or just how politically healthy it actually was.

Genius, he would write, consists in a trueness of sight, in such a use of words "as shows that the man was eye-witness, and not a reporter of what was told." (The early lectures are full of this idea.) Still, he had to admit at the beginning—and even more as he thought about it—that genius has methods of its own which to others may seem shocking or incoherent or pernicious. "Genius is a character of illimitable freedom." It can make greatness out of trivial material: well, Jacksonian America was trivial enough; would genius make it great? Genius unsettles routine: "Make a new rule, my dear, can you not? and tomorrow Genius shall stamp on it with starry sandal." Year after year, Emerson would tell himself—coming as near to stridency as he was capable—"To Genius everything is permitted, and not only that, but it enters into all other men's labors." Or again, he would reassure himself: "I pardon everything to it; everything is trifling before it; I will wait for it for years, and sit in contempt before the doors of that inexhaustible blessing." He was always on the lookout for genius; wherefore he sweetly greeted Whitman at the dawn of a great career, and was dismayed when this genius—who assumed that to him everything was permitted, including, the attempt to make greatness out of a trivial democracy—used Emerson's endorsement in letters of gold on the back cover of the second edition of *Leaves of Grass*.

There the problem lay: it was pleasant to appeal to nature against formality, to identify religion with the blowing clover, the meteor, and the falling rain—to challenge the spectral convention in the name of the genius who lives spontaneously from nature, who has been commended, cheated, and chagrined. But who was this genius—if he wasn't Andrew Jackson, was he then Walt Whitman? Was he, whichever he was, to be permitted *everything*? An inability to spell or parse might, as in the case of genius Jones Very, be amusing; but suppose genius should find permissible or actually congenial sexual abberation or potential domination? If before it all convention is trifling, must genius flaunt both monogamy and the social hierarchy? Suppose the youth did learn to affirm that a popgun is a popgun, in defiance of the ancient and honorable of the earth—and then chose as his guide to genius not the reserved sage of Concord but the indisputably greatest literary genius of the age, Goethe, or the outstanding genius in politics, Napoleon?

There were other dangerous geniuses, of course—above all, Lord Byron. He, said Andrews Norton (who clearly thought Emerson no better), was a corrupter of youth, violator of "the unalterable principles of taste, founded in the nature of man, and the eternal truths of morality and religion." But Emerson and the New England geniuses were not too perturbed by Byron; he did indeed exhibit that love of the vast which they thought the primary discovery of their times, but, as Emerson said, in him "it is blind, it sees not its true end—an infinite good, alive and beautiful, a life nourished on absolute beatitudes, descending into nature to behold itself reflected there." The moral imperfections of geniuses—including the obscenities of Shakespeare—could likewise be exculpated. But the early nineteenth century, more acutely conscious of its peculiar identity than any age yet recorded in history, could not permit itself to tame the two greatest geniuses it had produced, the two who above all others, in the power of nature and of instinct, shattered the "over-civilized" palace of artifice. An ethic of self-reliance could not pretend that such reliers upon self as Goethe and Napoleon were blind. They were the twin "representatives of the impatience and reaction of nature against the *morgue* of conventions,—two stern realists, who, with the scholars, have severally set the axe at the root of the tree of cant and seeming, for this time, and for all time." But the point Emerson had to make, obstinately, was that if Napoleon incarnated "the popular external life and aims of the nineteenth century," then by the same token Goethe was its other half, "a man quite domesticated in the century,"—in fact, "the soul of his century."

The story of Emerson's lifelong struggle with Goethe has been often recounted. He could not give over the contest, for if Goethe had to be pronounced wicked, Emerson would become what Norton called him, an infidel. "All conventions, all tradition he rejected," says Emerson, in order to add that thus Goethe uttered "the best things about Nature that ever were said." The ancient and honorable of the earth—well, of Boston's earth—sneered that the man was immoral, but the New England geniuses dug in their heels and insisted with Margaret Fuller that Goethe was "the highest form of Nature, and conscious of the meaning she has been striving successively to unfold through those below him." Those below were demonstrably (like Andrews Norton) non-geniuses.

Life for geniuses would have been simpler could Goethe have been separated from Napoleon. But the two giants met at Erfurt—and recognized each other. (Emerson punctiliously copied into his *Journals* what Goethe said about Napoleon: it was as though he kept hitting himself with a hammer.) Emerson came back from Europe to start his brave adventure as a free-lance lecturer with a series entitled "Tests of Great Men." To judge from the notes, he spent much time explaining that Napoleon was beneath contempt: he was "the very bully of the common, & knocked down most indubitably his antagonists; he was as heavy as any six of them." Measure him against any of the tests young Emerson proposed, and Napoleon failed on every count. One test was whether a man has a good aim: "Well, Napoleon had an Aim & a Bad one." Another was whether he be in earnest: "Napoleon was no more a believer than a grocer who disposes his shop-window invitingly." The lectures held up to American admiration Luther, Washington, Lafayette, Michelangelo, Burke, Milton, Fox, but the constant moral was this (Emerson came back to it from every angle): "Of Napoloen, the strength consisted in his renunciation of all conscience. The Devil helps him." Emerson delivered this statement on January 29, 1835—eleven months after he had assured Carlyle that "a most unfit person" was President of the United States, when that person was still in office.

There is no better gauge of Emerson's progress into sophistication than the contrast between this moralistic lecture and the chapter published in 1850 in *Representative Men*—although that too has its ambiguities. No one would call it a paean of praise to Bonaparte, but still, the conscienceless devil of 1835 has become one who "respected the power of nature and fortune, and ascribed to it his superiority, instead of valuing himself, like inferior men, on his opinionativeness, and waging war with nature." But if Napoleon was now on the side of the meteor, against the timidity of scholars, what of the democracy in America? What of our own Napoleons—Jackson and Van Buren? Neither Napoleon nor they could be consigned to the Devil, for in that case there would exist in the universe of the Over-Soul a foreign, an extraneous, element, something uncontrollable; in that case, for children of the Devil to live from the Devil would be really demonic, really unnatural—as it often did seem to cultured New Englanders that Democrats lived.

There was a great temptation to identify this upsurging of democracy with nature. (Brownson was willing to risk it, but not for long; except Bancroft, hardly an American before Whitman dared—that is, after Jefferson's nature became "romantic" nature.) If the stinging clarity of a teamster's oath was worth paragraphs of Harvard prose, was not Jackson a rod of nature reproving the timid, the imitative and tame? Emerson sometimes made this identification, or almost made it; but he was still the Bostonian, ninth in a line of ministers, and by no stretching of his conception of nature could he learn to look upon the naturals who composed the Jacksonian rabble with anything but loathing. The soliloquy—the endless debate with himself—runs throughout the *Journals*; it turns upon a triangle of counterstatement: democracy raises the problem of genius; genius the problem of Napoleon and the American politician: they in turn raise the problem of democracy and of America. The pattern is not always quite so explicit, but over and over again any mention of genius is sure to be followed, within an entry or two, by a passage on democracy, the Democratic party, Napoleon. The inconclusiveness of the inner meditations makes a striking contrast to the seeming serenity of the published oracles. The art—or should we call it the artfulness?—of Emerson is nowhere more charmingly revealed than in the fashion in which he managed to separate in the *Essays* the three themes that in the *Journals* were constantly intertwined. Yet even his great ingenuity could not keep genius, Napoleon, and democracy from coming together and forming knotty passages in the *Essays*, and especially in *Representative Men*.

Surely he ought, did he respect logic, to have been like Whitman a democrat, and therefore a Democrat. Returning from Europe in 1834, having seen how monarchy and aristocracy degrade mankind, he could write:

> The root and seed of democracy is the doctrine, Judge for yourself. Reverence thyself. It is the inevitable effect of that doctrine, where it has any effect (which is rare), to insulate the partisan, to make each man a state. At the same time it replaces the dead with a living check in a true, delicate reverence for superior, congenial minds. "How is the king greater than I, if he is not more just."

But the fact remained that, in the America of Jackson or of Polk, democracy in the abstract could not be dissociated from the gang of hoodlums who showed nothing more, to Emerson's view, than withering selfishness and impudent vulgarity. The boy had fled from the ranting of orators to the cherry trees; the man of 1834 sought the same comfort: "In the hush of these woods I find no Jackson placards affixed to the trees."

Yet, the literature of the new age, the revolt against, "upholstery," gave a hollow sound to the names of king and lord because it voiced the forces "which have unfolded every day with a rapidity sometimes terrific, the democratic element." Today "the Universal Man is now as real an ex-

istence as the Devil was then." At the mention of the Devil, if not of the
king, Emerson must recollect himself: "I do not mean that ill thing, vain
and loud, which writes lying newspapers, spouts at caucuses, and sells its
lies for gold." He meant only "that spirit of love for the general good
whose name this assumes." A man need not be a Transcendentalist to find
this ill thing disgusting: he need only to have gone to Harvard. Viewed
from this angle, there was nothing to be preferred in Abraham Lincoln
over General Jackson. After the assassination, Emerson tried to atone; but
in 1863 the President caused him to reflect that people of culture should
not expect anything better out of the operations of universal suffrage:

> You cannot refine Mr. Lincoln's taste, extend his horizon, or clear his
> judgment; he will not walk dignifiedly through the traditional part of the
> President of America, but will pop out his head at each railroad station and
> make a little speech, and get into an argument with Squire A. and Judge B.
> He will write letters to Horace Greeley, and any editor or reporter or saucy
> party committee that writes to him, and cheapen himself.

In the clutch of such reflections, Emerson was frequently on the
point of making democratic naturalism signify an open, irreconcilable
war between genius and democracy. Genius, he said in 1847, is an-
thropomorphist and makes human form out of material, but
America—"eager, solicitous, hungry, rabid, busy-bodied"—is without
form, "has no terrible and no beautiful condensation." Had he let himself
go in that direction, we could summarize him in a sentence: America's
philosopher condemned America's democracy as something unnatural.

He came perilously close to this way out: he dallied with the solution
that was always available for romantic theorists, that some great and
natural genius, out of contempt for the herds might master them. A man
of strong will "may suddenly become the center of the movement, and
compel the system to gyrate round it." Cromwell was never out of Emerson's mind. Such an actor would settle the problem, would redeem both
nature and the ideal, the stability and the security of the commonwealth:

> We believe that there may be a man who is a match for events,—one
> who never found his match—against whom other men being dashed are
> broken,—one of inexhaustible personal resources, who can give you odds,
> and beat you.

The rest of us could even tell ourselves that we did not abdicate self-
reliance should we follow such a genius: "We feed on genius."

Still, Emerson had to add, we "have a half-belief." There was always
the danger that a resolution of the political question into the personality of
the great man would be like trying to resolve the poetic problem into the
personality of Byron. Genius has laws of its own, but in the workings of a
commonwealth neither whim nor demonism should be permitted. "Politics
rest on necessary foundations, and cannot be treated with levity."

Levity! There was indeed the devil. It would be levity to give way to looking down one's nose at Jackson and Lincoln, to turn from them to the great man who promised to bring mediocrity to heel. For suppose this genius should prove a demon of the only plausible devil, of levity?

Here Emerson was back again with Napoleon. Upon his mind, upon the mind of his generation, was indelibly impressed the spectacle of that meeting in Erfurt. The Goethean genius met with and subscribed to the Napoleonic. Henceforth it was impossible to lift the standard of the epicurean, civilized Goethe against the leveling thrust of Napoleon, or to rally around him against Jackson. Assuredly Napoloen was unscrupulous, selfish, perfidious, a prodigious gossip: "his manners were coarse." So was Jackson, so was Lincoln. But Napoleon fought against the enemies of Goethe: timidity, complacence, etc., etc. If Goethe had sided with Bonaparte, how then ought an American intellectual act toward the Democratic party? After all, as Emerson in "Politics," was obliged to say, "Democracy is better for us, because the religious sentiment of the present time accords better with it."

He hoped that the rhetorical balance of his famous sentence would remove his anxiety, that while the Whigs had the best men, the Democrats had the best cause. The scholar, philosopher, the man of religion, will want to vote with the Democrats, "but he can rarely accept the persons whom the so-called popular party propose to him as representatives of these liberalities." On the other hand, the conservative party was indeed timid, "merely defensive of property." No wonder that men came to think meanly of government and to object to paying their taxes: "Everywhere they think they get their money's worth, except for these."

This was a miserable prospect, an intolerable dilemma, for the author of *Nature*. Yet Emerson was never more the spokesman for nature, and never more the American, than when he added, "I do not for these defects despair of our republic." He might have mourned with Henry Adams and every disillusioned liberal, with every disgruntled businessman, that the country was going to the dogs, that there was no hope left (there being no longer hope in a compensatory Christian heaven) except in the great man, the political genius, the dictator. There was everything in Emerson's philosophy to turn him like Carlyle into a prophet of reaction and the leader-principle.

But he did not go with Carlyle; and he meant what he said, that he did not despair of the republic. Why not? Was it merely that he was stupid, or mild-mannered, or temperamentally sanguine? Was it dogmatic optimism for the sake of optimism? Perhaps it was partly for these reasons, but the play of his mind kept hope alive and vigorous by circling round and round, by drawing sustenance from the inexhaustible power of genius. However odd, fantastic, or brutal might be the conduct of genius, it does submit to laws. Levity gets ironed out. So in society: "No forms can have any dangerous importance whilst we are befriended by the laws of things." Emerson's historical perspective was deeper, richer than that of a Cooper—great historical novelist though he was. Cooper had Natty Bumppo to give grandeur to the sordid scene of *The Pioneers*, but no philosophy of genius to sustain him once he entered into conflict with *Home as Found*. Cooper let himself dream of violent catastrophe, a devastating judgment not of Jehovah but of nature, as an ultimate solution to the ills of democracy, and prophesied it in *The Crater*. But Emerson could comprehend democracy in a larger frame of reference, as a phase of western society, and see its connection, where the *rentier* could not, with the new kind of property. Emerson could point out that it was not something a gentleman could afford to despise and then expect still to have the refuge of being a gentleman. In other words, Emerson understood the portent not alone of Goethe but of Napoleon.

For this reason, Napoleon figures in the carefully planned structure of *Representative Men* as a prologue to Goethe, as the next-to-the-last. There is some perversity—one might say almost levity—in the other choices (Swedenborg most obviously) or in the arrangement, but Emerson was pushing his way through the book to the two problems which, his genius informed him, constituted one problem: that of genius in modern society, where the bad manners of democrats would not be sufficient reason for consigning them, on that ground alone, to the limbo of levity.

Representative Men had its origins in a few simple ideas which took hold of Emerson in the 1830's, of which he was the prisoner but which, for as long as possible, he held off from publishing. The secret record of his life with these ideas is the *Journals*, but there was a public record before his fellow countrymen: the lectures, those discourses he gave for audiences and for money, out of which he mined paragraphs for what became *Essays* but which, guided by some obscure impulse, he never translated directly from the platform to the page. (From the beginning of his career as a lecturer down to his last series at Harvard in 1871, there was always a discourse on "Genius"; materials from one or another recasting of this draft found their way into "Self-Reliance," "Art," "Intellect,"—but never into a full-dress essay on genius.) With the lecture of January, 1837 (entitled "Society"), Emerson had already gone so far beyond 1835 that he could define the genius as one who has access to the universal mind and who receives its influx in wise passivity. He could employ terms he was to use throughout many subsequent lectures, but which, at least in this same and revealing language, he would never print:

> Genius is never anomalous. The greatest genius is he in whom other men own the presence of a larger portion of their common nature than is in them. And this I believe is the secret of the joy which genius gives us. Whatever men of genius say, becomes forthwith the common property of all. Why? Because the man of genius apprises us not so much of his wealth as of the commonwealth. Are his illustrations happy? So feel we [that] not *his* mind but *the* mind illustrate[s] its thoughts. A sort of higher patriotism

warms us, as if one should say, "That's the way they do things in my country."

Thus early the problem took shape in his mind—never to leave it—of genius and "my country." All men share in "*the* mind," and all men are the democracy; genius must be, in some sense, a patriotic triumph. But Napoleon was a threat to the conception of a "good" genius; his American aliases, Jackson and the Democrats, were a threat to State Street. Writers are often obliged to ask themselves exactly who they are, and fear to find out that they may be the most evil of their creations. Was Emerson, in his heart of hearts, a Napoleon? If not, were the Over-Soul and all its spokesmen, all the geniuses, to be counted in the Whig column? Obviously Whiggery was no home for genius. Maybe one would have to admit that Jackson was a genius? Maybe one would have to confess—as the easiest way out—that Lincoln was a genius? Lincoln was, nominally, a Republican, but before 1865, Emerson saw him only as the creature of universal suffrage: the assassination and the rapid canonization undoubtedly helped, but Emerson was still feeling his own way and not merely moving with the times when in 1871 he told his Harvard audience, "John Brown and Abraham Lincoln were both men of genius, and have obtained this simple grandeur of utterance."

Years before he was thus able to reconcile himself to Lincoln, Emerson tried to reconcile himself to the whole panoply of genius, and the result was *Representative Men*. The value of the book is not that it invents a way out of the quandary which we now confront as terribly as did Emerson. It is not a guide for the preserving of personality against mass pressures. Too many of his terms are altered; few of us can accept his metaphysics, and many of the geniuses we admire do not seem so clearly to contribute wealth to any commonwealth. But the exhilaration of the book consists in the fact that Emerson here got his many-sided perplexity in hand, sacrificed no one aspect to any other, and wrote a book not about heroes and how to worship them, but about how an intelligent and sensitive man lives, or must learn to live, in a democratic society and era.

By calling great men not heroes but representatives, Emerson, in the most American of fashions, put them to work; the first chapter is slyly entitled "Uses of Great Men." He divides geniuses as a genus into subordinate species, whereupon for each type a specific set of laws can be worked out. Thus the individual genius, even when seemingly lawless, adheres to a pattern of coherence in relation to the sum total of the parts. If it be necessary—as we are compelled to recognize—that all sides of life be expressed, then each genius has a function, be he good or evil; what each incarnates we recognize as an accentuated part of ourselves—because all men are one, and any one man is all men.

Likewise, genius is fragmentary, and so deficient on several sides. Sometimes the moralizing Emerson appears to line up his great men like naughty children and to tell them wherein they all fall lamentably short of what teacher expects of them. But you forgive him some (although not all) of this didacticism not so much because he was a New Englander but because behind it lay the intense moments recorded in the *Journals*, such as that in which he had taken the very existence of such a person as the Democrat Hawthorne to signify "that in democratic America, she [nature] will not be democratized." Therefore in this book Emerson can go far—as far as clear sight can see—toward making genius democratic. The genius is great not because he surpasses but because he represents his constituency. His crimes and foibles are as much a part of the record as his triumphs and nobilities; Napoleon belongs to genius not as a child of the historical Devil whom Emerson foolishly invoked in 1835, and not even as a creation of the metaphorical devil, levity, but as a serious, real, and terrifying power in modern western civilization.

Wherefore something more should be required of the scholar, the poet, the man of religion, than timid antipathy to a blatant democracy. Napoleon was "the agent or attorney of the middle class of modern society"—of those in shops, banks, and factories who want to get rich. He represents "the Democrat, or the party of men of business, against the stationary or conservative party." And—Emerson here plunges to the bottom of his insight—"as long as our civilization is essentially one of property, of fences, of exclusiveness, it will be mocked by delusions"—against which some Bonaparte is bound to raise the cry of revolt, for which men again will die.

What Emerson most gained, I believe, by this analysis was an ability to comprehend, even while never quite reconciling himself to, the vices of democracy—whether with a small "d" or a capital "D." He did not need to blind himself by patriotic fanaticism; by the same token he did not need to despair. He could confess his mistake about Lincoln without retracting his contempt for Franklin Pierce. He could criticize his country without committing treason, without having to demand, as did an irate Cooper, that they become like himself or else go to hell. The example and the laws of genius might work, would work, even in the ranks of the Democratic party.

Of course, Emerson trusted the self-operating force of moral law more than do most of us today. Napoleon (for him read Jackson, Lincoln, the boss, the district leader) did everything a man could do to thrive by intellect without conscience. "It was the nature of things, the eternal law of the man and the world, which balked and ruined him; and the result, in a million experiments, would be the same." Emerson was fully aware of what the lesson cost: "immense armies, burned cities, squandered treasures, immolated millions of men, . . . this demoralized Europe." He did, we must confess, look upon the desolation with what seems to us smugness, we who have seen Europe infinitely more burned and demoralized; but these things are relative, and he was happy to note that out of the destruction arose a universal cry, "assez de Bonaparte."

Emerson was too often chilly. But had he been only that, *Representative Men* would have been for him the end of a theme, would have put a period to a chapter in his *Journals*. It was nothing of the sort. No sooner was it published than the debate was resumed, and many of the most fascinating combinations of the triple meditation on genius, Napoleon, and democracy occur in later entries. The Civil War was for him as for others an excruciating ordeal, the more so as during the worst years he believed Lincoln the example of democratic incompetence. But in the darkest moments he never quite lost his bearings. The sanity (the chilly sanity, if you will) that sustains the essay on "Politics" and informs *Representative Men* never deserted him—the levelheadedness which is his most precious bequest to a posterity that is understandably exasperated by his unction. In 1862, although not yet respecting the President, he was able to keep the personality from obscuring the issue:

> A movement in an aristocratic state does not argue a deep cause. A dozen good fellows may have had a supper and warmed each other's blood to some act of spite or arrogance, which they talk up and carry out the next month; or one man, Calhoun or Rhett, may have grown bilious, and his grumble and fury are making themselves felt at the legislature. But in a Democracy, every movement has a deep-seated cause.

This was written by no flag-waving, tub-thumping patriot shouting, "My country right or wrong." This is no campaign orator mouthing the word "democracy" even while desecrating it by his deeds. It was written by a great American, a serious man who could finally run down the devil of politics and declare that his name is levity, who understood as well as any in what the difficult ordeal consists, that magnificent but agonizing experience of what it is to be, or to try to be, an American.[1]

Note

1. Materials from the unpublished lectures are used with the permission of the Ralph Waldo Emerson Memorial Association.

"The Contents and Basis of Emerson's Belief in Compensation"

Henry F. Pommer*

Despite reservations we may have about Emerson's theory of Compensation, it was fundamental to his philosophy. Nor was its truth or falsity settled by Stephen Whicher's assertion that "the notion of an

*Reprinted from *PMLA*, 77 (June 1962), 248–53.

automatic moral compensation . . . is without question the most unacceptable of Emerson's truths, and a major cause of his present decline of reputation."[1] As Emerson himself said, "the great questions affecting our spiritual nature are not one of them decided. . . . The system of Compensations in moral and material nature, and a hundred other questions of primary concernment to the state of man, are all open to discussion."[2]

Emerson began his essay, "Compensation," by recognizing the difficulty of the topic: he would be "happy beyond . . . expectation" if he could "truly draw the smallest arc" of the subject.[3] In the same year he wrote in his journal that he knew only "three persons who seem to me fully to see this law . . . [Thoreau,] Alcott, and myself."[4] He made the topic more difficult for his readers by sometimes altering his vocabulary and writing of Reciprocity, Contrast, Repairs, or Off-sets.[5] Sometimes he used the doctrine as a truth of theology, of natural science, or of psychology. But its most important function was as a theory of morals, not in the sense of stating how one ought to behave, but of stating how values are distributed.

Nowhere did Emerson state the theory with methodical precision, but in a mass of quotations covering forty-five years of his life he left the materials for a systematic definition of Compensation and of its relations with other of his theories.

His earliest known statement of the principle is a journal entry of 1820.[6] During his decade of sermon-writing (1826–36) he never devoted an entire discourse to it, though the subject was important in many sermons from his fourth onward,[7] and in his journals, letters, and lectures. In 1831, for example, he wrote to his brother Edward, "I am trying to learn the ethical truths that always allure me from my cradle till now & yet how slowly disclosed! That word *Compensations* is one of the watchwords of my spiritual world—& time & chance & sorrow & hope do not by their revelations abate my curiosity" (*Letters*, I, 330). Four years later he wrote that "in this age of seeming, nothing can be more important than the opening and promulgation of the gospel of Compensations to save the land" (*Journals*, III, 486). By at least 1839 he was drafting the work which appeared two years later in *Essays, First Series* with the title "Compensation" (*Letters*, II, 201). The chapter which immediately followed, "Spiritual Laws," he regarded as part of his attempt to do justice to the subject (*Works*, II, 96). Indeed, hardly any of his essays and poems, no matter how short, avoids some use of the doctrine. And when he was sixty-two he told a group of women who had been his students when he was scarcely out of his teens, "I was at that very time already writing every night in my chamber my first thoughts on morals and the beautiful laws of Compensation and of individual genius, which to observe and illustrate have given sweetness to my life" (*Works*, II, 395–396).

We read in his journal this dialogue between Emerson and himself:

> Is not the law of compensation perfect? . . . Different gifts to different in-
> dividuals, but with a mortgage of responsibility on every one. . . . Well,
> old man, hast got no farther? Why, this was taught thee months and years
> ago. It was writ on the autumn leaves at Roxbury in keep-school days; it
> sounded in . . . [your] ear at Cambridge. . . . I can't help it. . . . I have
> nothing charactered in my brain that outlives this word Compensation.
> (*Journals*, II, 389)

Emerson wrote the dialogue in 1831. He could just as well have written it
in '61. Compensation lived essentially unchanged through years of stress
and of calm because its roots went down to the very foundation of Emerson's thought and personality.

Within Emerson's thought, compensations of value and disvalue may
appear in any of four guises: definitional characteristics, external circumstances, pleasure or pain, and knowledge. The definitional characteristics
appear whenever Emerson asserts that certain types of action bring the
compensation of advancing a man towards his true nature or of
withdrawing him from it. This kind of reasoning seems to underlie Emerson's writing in the margin of his Bible, "What is the reward of virtue?
Virtue."[8] A man may accept a definition of ideal character, and then as
compensations develop within him, measure his progress or regress. This
is "the view of individual, unconnected character, . . . [of] having duties
to fulfil and a character to earn in the sight of God." As to whether certain
acts impoverish or enrich me, "myself—the man within the breast—am
the sole judge" (*Journals*, II, 75–76). The social dimension of this type of
compensation is achieved by ceasing to think of the differences between
His and *Mine*; the heart and soul of all men are then seen to be one, and
all "inequalities of condition" are dissolved by love (*Works*, II, 123).
Perhaps Emerson's most clear-cut statement of compensation by definition is that "casual retribution is . . . seen by the soul. . . . Inasmuch as
. . . [a criminal] carries the malignity and the lie with him he so far
deceases from nature."[9] It is not difficult to imagine a criminal's retorting
that to seek present and future pleasure is *his* true nature, and that Emerson was simply mistaken in asserting that the true nature of all men involves a divine Reason which permits God-reliance.

On occasions when Emerson was not arguing by definition he sometimes asserted that compensations come through outward circumstances.
At one point in his journal, having argued from definition that Compensation is true "in the aspect of *self*," he went on to assert that it "is no less
true, no less important in its respect to our social nature. If a man steals, is
it not known?"[10] In a sermon he stated that "God enables us to be of use to
our fellow men . . . and rewards our goodness by making us see often the
fruits of our exertions."[11] "The retribution in the circumstance is seen by
the understanding; it is inseparable from the thing, but is often spread
over a long time and so does not become distinct until after many
years. . . . The martyr [for example] cannot be dishonored. Every lash

inflicted is a tongue of fame; every prison a more illustrious abode; every burned book or house enlightens the world" (*Works*, ii, 103, 120).

But Emerson reasoned in this way only rarely; compensation through external events could not be long maintained by anyone who believed, as he sometimes did, in the amorality of objects and events, in "the indifferency of circumstances." If "every thing has two sides, a good and an evil,"[12] outward circumstances need not be a compensation of any sort.

So we are to expect compensation not so much in our purses and dinner guests as in the third guise of pleasant or painful states of mind. When he was a Unitarian minister Emerson preached that a sufficiently long course of observation would show virtue "to produce happiness, and the want of virtue to inflict woe, as undeniably as the sun produces light and the absence of sun produces darkness."[13] As a Transcendentalist lecturer he spoke about pain and satisfaction.[14]

But in both parts of his career Emerson's dominant emphasis was on a fourth type of compensation—increased knowledge of how life is regulated.

> The pure and the wise who leave this world receive . . . [their] natural reward . . . in the removal of all doubt as to the course and the end of their secret journey. (*Young Emerson*, p. 140)

> A great man is always willing to be little. Whilst he sits on the cushion of advantages, he goes to sleep. When he is pushed, tormented, defeated, he has a chance to learn something; he has been put on his wits, on his manhood; he has gained facts; learns his ignorance; is cured of the insanity of conceit; has got moderation and real skill. (*Works*, ii, 117–118)

When Emerson said "It is better to fail in our efforts in a good cause, then not to have striven in it" (*Young Emerson*, p. 30), he probably had in mind the wisdom and courage which can come even from unsuccessful effort.

Compensation may, then, be a matter of definition, of outward circumstances, of pleasure competing with pain, of knowledge—or a combination of these. Furthermore, it can flow from one to another time of an individual's life, from an individual to society, and vice versa. Compensations to an individual for his own past have already been cited. But

> a man must ride alternately on the horses of his private and his public nature. . . . So when a man is the victim of his fate, has sciatica in his loins and cramp in his mind; a club-foot and a club in his wit; . . . or is ground to powder by the vice of his race;—he is to rally on his relation to the Universe, which his ruin benefits. Leaving the daemon who suffers, he is to take sides with the Deity who secures universal benefit by his pain.[15]

Maria Moravsky in a slashing attack on the doctrine of Compensation complains that "if we lived on compensation only . . . we should be deprived of sacrifice."[16] Some of Emerson's statements bear her out: for example, "If in the hours of clear reason we should speak the severest truth, we should say that we had never made a sacrifice."[17] Here and elsewhere, however, he is in part reporting that *he* never had to give up anything for which he did not eventually feel there had been repayment—to himself or the public. Yet the belief that repayment is sometimes to the public rather than to oneself is all the assurance necessary to make sacrifice possible.

These are all the kinds and distributions of compensation that Emerson mentions. How, in his view, are they brought about?

Most of the time he writes of automatic compensation. In such passages he is sometimes considering compensation by definition; more frequently he is saying that outward circumstances, pleasure, pain, and knowledge are justly distributed by powers of nature and of human psychology which are either an expression of God or a part of God.

An anti-Emersonian of the twentieth century might say that compensation is obviously assured for a manic-depressive but not for a stock market investor. Emerson would say it is assured for both. If the investor loses his money and even after many years observes no compensation, any of several situations may exist: He may have failed to see benefits which flowed to other men from his loss; he may not yet have watched long enough;[18] he may be paying for some defect in his own character (*Young Emerson*, p. 106).

Emerson would also say that within the limits of automatic compensation brought about by human psychology, various relations between one period and another are possible. In particular, the form which tomorrow's compensation will take depends less on the nature of today's experience than on the intelligence and emotion of one's response. With respect to that response Emerson advises,

> Let it . . . be felt by us that we exist wholly in the mind; that all happiness is there, and all unhappiness; that the present condition and appearance is nothing. (*Journals*, ii, 249–250)

> Let us take refuge in . . . applying ourselves to an active interest in the welfare of those persons who have the nearest claims upon us. . . . It will bring courage and conscience and God to our aid. (*Young Emerson*, p. 127)

> Keep the habit of the observer, and, as fast as you can, break off your association with your personality and identify yourself with the Universe. (*Journals*, iv, 315–316)

In our own words we might say that the way a man looks at an experience often determines whether he will find for it a good or evil compensation. If on the one hand the experience was happy, then expecting to have to pay for it may create—psychologically or psychosomatically—the unhappiness which will "prove" the truth of Compensation. If, on the other hand, the experience was unhappy, then actively looking for a compensatory happiness or insight will often create a good which would otherwise not exist. One possibility for controlling the kind of compensation one receives lies, therefore, in man's great capacity for deriving happiness and unhappiness from the most curious and seemingly inappropriate circumstances. A part of this capacity permits man to transcend himself either by accepting a state of mind in lieu of a state of outward affairs or by accepting a gain to society as compensation for a personal loss.

Whether we want compensation to take the form of happiness or of knowledge, reason (or what Emerson might have called *understanding*) is the capacity most useful in creating it. Reason can bring us joy and insight out of sorrow and error. It can even prevent undesirable compensations of the evil we do, for instead of permitting evil to be punished by evil, reason can make evil produce good (*Young Emerson*, p. 211).

And what will make a man use his reason to follow Emerson's advice? Emerson might have answered that if his advice *is* followed, the wisdom to follow it is a reward for earlier virtues and will produce further rewards; if the advice is neglected, that folly is a punishment for earlier vices and will garner its own retribution. Such an answer is obviously related philosophically to some of the problems besetting determinism.

When Emerson asserted the existence of various types of compensation—compensations sometimes automatic but sometimes to be won by keeping the habit of the observer—he did so on the basis of his personal experience, his theology, and his observation of nature, men, literature, and history. The most important of these was his own experience: the response of his emotions to the circumstances of his life. Here was the real foundation for his typical generalizations about all men's lives: as with many of us, the foundation of his beliefs seems to have lain much more in his temperament than in his intellect.

Whicher would have it that Emerson's "serenity was a not unconscious *answer* to his experience of life, rather than an inference from it. . . . It was an act of faith, forced on him by what he once called 'the ghastly reality of things'."[19] The statement may have to be modified from the record of Emerson's experienced compensations.

Occasionally Emerson asked himself why he believed in Compensation, and left us his answer. In 1822,

> The principle of . . . [Compensation] which we find engraven within—
> . . . how came it there, whence did we derive it? Either the Deity has
> written it as one of his laws upon the human mind, or we have derived it
> from an observation of the invariable course of human affairs. (*Journals*,
> I, 96)

Twelve years later he asserted that a man can learn the nature of laws such as Compensation "only by *acting*, and observing how they determine and reward every action."[20] But most interesting of all is this journal entry:

> Why do I believe in a perfect system of compensations, that exact justice is done? Certainly not upon a narrow experience of a score, or a hundred instances. For I boldly affirm and believe the universality of the law. But simply that is better in the view of the mind than any other way, therefore must be the true way. Whatever is better must be the truer way. (*Journals*, ii, 447)

The theory of truth implied by this passage is interesting, but more immediately relevant is the implication that Emerson had observed in his own life "a score, or a hundred instances" of compensation.

Some of these instances we know about. In 1828, for example, one of Emerson's brilliant younger brothers, Edward, suffered temporary insanity. In his journal Ralph Waldo objectively analyzed how compensations would protect him against a similar attack:

> I have so much mixture of *silliness* in my intellectual frame that I think Providence has tempered me against this. My brother lived and acted and spoke with preternatural energy. My own manner is sluggish; my speech sometimes flippant, sometimes embarrassed and ragged; my actions . . . are of a passive kind. Edward had always great power of face. I have none. I laugh; I blush; I look ill-tempered; against my will and against my interest. But all this imperfection, as it appears to me, is a . . . ballast—as things go, is a defence.[21]

A little later the young preacher whose conversation was often "embarrassed and ragged" confided to his journal, "It is a curious compensation to be noticed of such as I, that those who talk when everybody else is silent are forced to be silent when everybody else talks."[22] When he had reached thirty-one, he believed "My entire success, such as it is, is composed wholly of particular failures" (*Journals*, iii, 334).

But whether the doctrine of Compensation accurately reflected Emerson's personal experience depends not only on these rather minor instances but also on certain major ones: his responses to the deaths of those near him. All of Emerson's strongest attachments ended in the premature death of the person he loved: his first wife, Ellen; his two favorite brothers, Edward and Charles;[23] his first child.

None of his reactions was marked by a Dostoievskyan anguish, but each was strongly marked by gloom. Two days before the first of these deaths, that of Mrs. Emerson, and when it was apparent that she would soon die, Charles wrote to William Emerson that their brother was "as one over whom the waters have gone."[24] A month later Waldo wrote to William "I did not feel my solitude when all spoke & tho't of nothing else as now I feel it when I come home and all have forgotten it —& the common things go on and she is not here" (*Letters*, i, 319). Shortly after his son, Waldo, had died not yet six years old, the father wrote,

> this losing is true dying;
> This is lordly man's down-lying,

> This his slow but sure reclining,
> Star by star his world resigning. (*Works*, IX, 153)

There is abundant additional evidence of the intensity of Emerson's griefs.[25] But there is also evidence of his feeling some of the widespread compensations of humanity: that the deceased is free of pain;[26] that the hope of reunion in an after life makes death not just less fearful, but even attractive (*Letters*, I, 330); that although no broken attachment is ever precisely replaced, rough equivalents do come (*Works*, XII, 414); that intellect and art can alter the bitterness of loss into "tuneful tragedy."[27]

Of all the compensations he records, however, the most striking is that of his own spiritual growth. Because of his losses he became greater. The boldest statement of this response came after Ellen, Edward, and Charles had all died:

> The death of a dear friend, wife, brother, lover, which seemed nothing but privation, somewhat later assumes the aspect of a guide or genius; for it commonly operates revolutions in our way of life, terminates an epoch of infancy or of youth which was waiting to be closed, breaks up a wonted occupation, or a household, or style of living, and allows the formation of new ones more friendly to the growth of character.[28]

Or, more succinctly, "We cannot let our angels go. We do not see that they only go out that archangels may come in."[29] The record of his life shows that in these statements Emerson was honestly recording his personal long-range experience.[30]

But the emotional basis of Emerson's belief in Compensation was not a matter simply of feeling short-range griefs followed by abundant consolations. Those fluctuations existed, one might say, like sometimes raging, sometimes glassy seas surrounding a tranquil island. The very day of Ellen's death was a day of compensations. He wrote to his aunt,

> My angel is gone to heaven this morning & I am alone in the world & strangely happy. . . . I see it plainly that things & duties will look coarse & vulgar enough to me when I find the romance of her presence . . . withdrawn from them all. But now the fulness of joy occasioned by things said by her in the last week & by this eternal deliverance [from pain] is in my heart. . . .
>
>   The past days the most eventful of my life are all a dim confusion & now the pall is drawn over them, yet do they shine brilliantly in my spiritual world. (*Letters*, I, 318)

The coarseness and vulgarity of days without Ellen did come during the six months that followed, but three years later Emerson recorded in his journal "I am born tranquil . . . never a keen sufferer. I will not affect to suffer. Be my life then a long gratitude."[31] Even more striking is a passage written after three and a half more years—after his second marriage and the birth of Waldo:

I told Jones Very that I had never suffered, that I could scarce bring myself to feel a concern for the safety and life of my nearest friends that would satisfy them; that I saw clearly that if my wife, my child, my mother, should be taken from me, I should still remain whole, with the same capacity of cheap enjoyment from all things. I should not grieve enough, although I love them. But could I make them feel what I feel,—the boundless resources of the soul,—remaining entire when particular threads of relation are snapped,—I should then dismiss forever the little remains of uneasiness I have in regard to them. (*Journals*, v, 114–115)

In these and other passages Emerson seems to reveal an imperviousness to grief such that no death is so saddening as to call for compensation. Yet the evidences of his having grieved still stand, and one wonders what paradox or contradiction lies here. A partial solution has been offered by McGiffert: "In neither the earlier nor later period of his life did . . . [Emerson] fail to encounter evil. He felt its knife in protracted personal illness, bereavement and vocational frustration, although he never had to face long periods of pain, hunger, and economic insecurity, nor a social situation which made his ideals seem utterly impossible of realization" (*Young Emerson*, p. 258). A further solution of the problem recognizes that statements that Emerson suffered and that he never suffered are contradictory only if *he* and *suffered* mean the same in both clauses. But *he* may refer to different levels of his self, and *suffered* to different qualities of consciousness. Melville provides a parallel when he says, "Even so, amid the tornadoed Atlantic of my being, do I myself still for ever centrally disport in mute calm; and while ponderous planets of unwaning woe revolve round me, deep down and deep inland there I still bathe me in eternal mildness of joy."[32]

Even though we may reject some of the generalizations which Emerson drew from his personal experiences and other sources, many of us will envy his capacity to respond to hardship elastically. He lived his deepest life on an "insular Tahiti, full of peace and joy, but encompassed by all the horrors of the half known life."[33]

To most of us, the notion that automatic compensation inheres in the nature of the universe is more credible than that all good and evil comes from God's hands to serve his purposes of punishing, rewarding, warning, or tempting his people. And many of us go so far as to wonder whether there is any rational distribution of values; perhaps the only patterns which really hold are of similar events, not of values.

In the Pilgrim world of William Bradford, a profane sailor who was the first person to die on the *Mayflower*'s famous voyage had been punished by a just and interposing God.[34] In the naturalistic world of Stephen Crane, a deserving sailor is drowned by the chances of man's existence.[35] Standing between those two worlds, Emerson agreed with Crane in denying the existence of an interposing God, but elevated justice to a self-administering principle of the universe. His doctrine of the Pervasiveness of Compensation was part of the transition from the Providence of God to the Predominance of Chance.[36]

Notes

1. Stephen E. Whicher, *Freedom and Fate: An Inner Life of Ralph Waldo Emerson* (Phildelphia: University of Pennsylvania Press, 1953), p. 36.

2. *The Early Lectures of Ralph Waldo Emerson*, ed. Stephen E. Whicher and Robert E. Spiller (Cambridge: Harvard University Press, 1959-), I, 383-384.

3. *The Complete Works of Ralph Waldo Emerson*, ed. Edward Waldo Emerson, Centenary Edition, 12 vols. (Boston: Houghton, Mifflin, 1903-1904), II, 96.

4. *Journals of Ralph Waldo Emerson*, ed. Edward Waldo Emerson and Waldo Emerson Forbes, 10 vols. (Boston: Houghton Mifflin, 1909-1914), VI, 74.

5. *Journals*, VI, 74; I, 96; II, 502; *The Letters of Ralph Waldo Emerson*, ed. Ralph L. Rusk, 6 vols. (New York: Columbia University Press, 1939), II, 201.

6. *The Journals and Miscellaneous Notebooks of Ralph Waldo Emerson*, ed. William H. Gilman et al. (Cambridge: Harvard University Press, 1960-), I, 19. Some anticipations of Compensation appeared in correspondence of 1817-1818 (*Letters*, I, 43, 45, 59).

7. *Young Emerson Speaks*, ed. Arthur Cushman McGiffert, Jr. (Boston: Houghton Mifflin, 1938), p. 235; Ralph L. Rusk, *The Life of Ralph Waldo Emerson* (New York: Scribners, 1949), p. 123.

8. Rusk, *Emerson*, p. 111. Also *Young Emerson Speaks*, pp. 101-102, 210.

9. *Works*, II, 103, 121. Also *Journals*, II, 75, 201-202.

10. *Journals*, II, 76 (italics in original).

11. *Young Emerson Speaks*, p. 68. Also p. 104.

12. *Works*, II, 120. Also II, 124-125.

13. *Young Emerson Speaks*, p. 35. Also pp. 104, 160, 210; *Journals*, II, 202.

14. *Works*, XII, 415; II, 98, 104, 123.

15. *Works*, VI, 47. Also *Young Emerson Speaks*, p. 186.

16. Maria Moravsky, "The Idol of Compensation," *Nation*, 108 (28 June 1919): 1005.

17. *Works*, II, 131. Also *Journals*, II, 72; III, 453-454.

18. See the previous page.

19. Stephen E. Whicher, "Emerson's Tragic Sense," *American Scholar*, 22 (Summer 1953): 290 (italics in original).

20. *Young Emerson Speaks*, p. 209 (italics in original).

21. *Journals*, II, 245 (italics in original).

22. *Journals*, II, 432. Also the second stanza of "Compensation," *Works*, IX, 83; *Journals*, X, 98-99.

23. Evidence of Charles Emerson's belief in some aspects of Compensation appears in five of his letters to his brother William: 12 April 1831, 9 May 1831, 1 October 1831, 7 July 1835, 29 August 1835 (all owned by Dr. Ethel Wortis and temporarily deposited in the Reis Library of Allegheny College).

24. Charles Chauncy Emerson to William Emerson, 2 June 1831 (owned by Dr. Ethel Wortis). Printed with a slight misreading in *Letters*, I, 318.

25. Charles Chauncy Emerson to Edward Bliss Emerson, 12 March 1831 (Houghton Library, Harvard University); Rusk, *Emerson*, pp. 230-231 (1835); *Letters*, II, 117 (1838);

Ralph L. Rusk, "Emerson and the Stream of Experience," *College English*, 14 (April 1953): 378.

26. Ruth Haskins Emerson to Edward Bliss Emerson, 1 March 1831 (Houghton Library); *Letters*, I, 318.

27. *Works*, XII, 416. Also II, 131; *Journals*, III, 563.

28. *Works*, II, 126. Also X, 129–130; XII, 102.

29. *Works*, II, 125. Also IX, 92.

30. Phillips Russell, *Emerson: The Wisest American* (New York: Brentano's, 1929), p. 81.

31. *Journals*, III, 298–299. Also III, 454.

32. *Moby-Dick*, ch. lxxxvii. Also Newton Arvin, "The House of Pain: Emerson and the Tragic Sense," *Hudson Review*, 12 (Spring 1959): 37–53.

33. *Moby-Dick*, ch. lviii.

34. *Of Plymouth Plantation*, ch. ix.

35. "The Open Boat."

36. Whicher, *Freedom and Fate*, pp. 36–37.

" 'The Lyceum Is My Pulpit': Homiletics in Emerson's Early Lectures"

A. M. Baumgartner*

The publication of the first volume of Emerson's early lectures evidenced the need for a re-evaluation of his later works.[1] The volume has done more than fill a gap in Emerson's thinking and writing; it has shown how much of an effect Emerson's lyceum experience had on the writing of his later works. Though Emerson formally resigned the ministry of the Second Church, the experience he gained there and at the Harvard Divinity School was indelibly stamped on his mind and his work. His success in the lyceum was not unrelated to his success in the pulpit. The answer to the question of why he was the most popular figure in the lyceum of his day, I suggest, may be found in a study of his homiletical training, thence of the survival of homiletical techniques in the early lectures.

Unfortunately for us, there is very little evidence of Emerson's formal training during his years at the Divinity School. But in 1825, his first year there, Henry Ware, Sr., was in charge of homiletical instruction and was to be relieved in a few years by his son. Emerson was "approbated" to preach in 1826; presumably his training was conducted in those two years. Ware's course report states that "during the Autumnal term [1825] H. Ware met on Saturday evening of each week the whole theological school in an exercise in preaching."[2] On Wednesday evenings of the sec-

*Reprinted from *American Literature*, 34 (January 1963), 477–86.

ond term, "extemporaneous voluntary discussion" was conducted, and on Saturday evenings the whole school was led "in an exercise in preaching, after which a Lecture and an exercise with the Senior Class of Theol. Students on pastoral duty." Rusk comments, "It seems that he at least went now and then to hear the students preach their practice sermons."[3] It is possible that these exercises were connected with the Society for Extemporaneous Speaking, which was founded in 1825. The records of the society contain the only mention of Emerson officially while he was studying at the school: "Subject selected for the next meeting, 'Is it expedient, in consideration of the spirit of the age, that a minister should be a profound theologian?' This question was proposed by Brother Emerson."[4]

However, the content of the instruction proves to be more useful for our purposes. In 1825, students at the Divinity School were directed to consult the following works for their studies in homiletics: Jeremy Taylor's *Holy Living and Dying* (which is surprising in view of the fact that metaphysical preaching was not fashionable), Coppe's *Sermons*, Paley's *Sermons*, Campbell's *Lecture on Pulpit Oratory*, and Robinson's "Note on the Composition of Sermons." William Ellery Channing, who gave the directions, added, "Let him [the student] follow the dictates of Blair, Campbell, Claude."[5] We also are fortunate to have the lecture notes of Henry Ware, Jr., which he used in 1830, in which he quotes frequently from these three writers.[6] Emerson at one time had a copy of Hugh Blair's *Lectures on Rhetoric* in his library.[7] In the *Journals* (1827) he mentions Taylor's *Holy Living* and sermons by Channing and Buckminster. In 1823 he had withdrawn from the Harvard Library all five volumes of South's sermons, and later, the *Works* of Tillotson (father of the modern style of preaching) and *Sermons* of Butler.[8] At the Divinity Library he withdrew the works of Jeremy Taylor with great frequency (which leads me to believe that it was from Taylor that Emerson developed his interest in the rich imagery that was incorporated into the early lectures and occasionally into the sermons.[9]

It seems reasonable to conclude, therefore, that Emerson had access to and made frequent use of the work of these writers. Basing my examination mainly upon the techniques discussed in Blair's *Lectures*, I have found six respects in which Emerson's rhetorical methods correspond to those discussed by Blair and fellow commentators.

1. Emerson's subjects are common rather than novel, but he succeeds because of his fresh and vigorous treatment of them. Blair regards this as the distinguishing characteristic of the sermon. "Nothing within the reach of art is more difficult, than to bestow, on what is common, the grace of novelty, . . . dressing truths which they [the listeners] knew, and of which were before convinced, in such colours as may most forcibly affect their imagination and heart."[10] "Topics are the masters of the preacher," Emerson wrote, but he knew how to make that master serve his ends.[11] In his sermons "he draws richly from astronomy, geology, chemistry, and biology

for his illustrations, astronomy leading the others. A study of his analogies especially shows his indebtedness to natural philosophy."[12] Such an approach as this was rarely found in Emerson's contemporaries; only a few English clergymen were then aware of its importance. Claude, though fairly dogmatic in his own views, writes: "I would not blame a man who should use them discreetly [examples from non-Biblical sources]. A quotation not common, and properly made, has very good effect."[13]

Similarly, in the early lectures, the subjects are "Home," "School," "Genius," "Tragedy," "Comedy," "Duty." These contrast with other lyceum topics of a more parochial sort: "Causes of the American Revolution," "The Sun," "The Sources of National Wealth," "Common School Education," "The Honey Bee," and many others.[14] "Instinct" was the topic of Henry Ware, Jr., whose background was homiletical. In his lecture notes to the Divinity pupils, he warned against certain topics—"the millenium" and matters superhuman, matters of curiosity, mere "natural religion," proofs of God, and the intricacies of metaphysical speculation.[15] In his lecture on Edmund Burke, Emerson carefully avoids discussion of Burke's political ideas. He did not hold the superficialities of his fellow lecturers in very high regard, as he remarks, to George F. Moore:

> I remarked to Mr. Emerson that I had often thought that this Lyceum system would be a temporary affair,—that is was calculated to give superficial views.
> This, he said, probably would be the result of many of our common lyceums, if carried on the way they have been for there is too much of manufacturing. Men write lectures, in order to contribute their share towards carrying on the Lyceum. The consequence is that they take that subject upon which they think they can write the easiest. Now, men . . . must write upon a subject that the time, the age, calls forth. . . . they must treat it in a new way.[16]

When, in his later years, Emerson preached his last sermons at the East Lexington Church, he used many of the early lectures.[17]

What "new ways" did Emerson discover for giving novelty to the common? He achieved this partly through the unconventional structure of these lectures (see my sixth point) and partly through the judicious use of metaphorical detail. References were made where they would serve a definite function—and not, certainly, as a vain show of knowledge. On some occasions he would substitute a metaphorical concrete reference for a more abstract summarizing statement:

> Composition is more important than the elegance of individual forms. . . . The smell of a field surpasses the scent of any flower and the selection of the prism is not comparable to the confusion of a sunset. A hillside expresses what has never been written down.[18]

Often an idea was developed with the linking quotation:

There is deep reason for the love of nature that has characterized the highest minds. The soul and the body of things are harmonized; therefore the deeper is a man's insight into the spiritual laws the more intense will be his love of the works of nature.

"The smallest production of nature," says Goethe, "has the circle of its completeness within itself. . . . A work of art, on the other hand, has its completeness out of itself. The Best lies in the idea of the artist which he seldom or never reaches. . . . In works of art there is much that is traditional; the works of nature are ever a freshly uttered Word of God." Perhaps it is the province of poetry rather than prose to describe the effect upon the mind and heart of these nameless influences.[19]

2. Emerson is especially attentive to the individuals in his audience, their backgrounds and their interests. Blair comments:

Study above all things to render your instructions interesting to the hearers. . . . A dry sermon can never be a good one. . . . The great secret lies in bringing home all that is spoken to the hearts of the hearers, so as to make every man think that the preacher is addressing him in particular. . . . It will be of advantage to keep always in view the different ages, characters, and conditions of men. . . . Hence, examples founded on historical facts, and drawn from real life . . . when they are well chosen, command high attention. No favourable opportunity of introducing these should be omitted.[20]

Mr. McGiffert observes this in Emerson's sermons, where the remarks were often addressed to "unnamed, but particular" persons who he knew would be present. He even added bits of dialogue, dramatizing the conversation of these persons.[21]

The same concern is found in the early lectures. In illustrating the character of Edmund Burke, Emerson took examples from rural life:

It is said that he had on his estate among his cattle some favorite cows, and an affecting incident has been preserved that after the death of his son he gave orders that an old horse formerly much used by his son should be turned out to feed at will and should not be worked or molested. One day walking in his grounds this horse approached him and after looking at him a moment put its head on his breast. Mr. Burke was so much affected that he put his arms round the animal's neck and hugged and kissed it, with tears.[22]

A historian speaking on the same topic surely would have chosen some famous historical incident to dramatize Burke's character and beliefs. Emerson chose similar references when seeking to express the long process which prepared the world for human habitation:

Man is made; and really when you come to see the minuteness of the adaptation in him to the present earth, it suggests forcibly the familiar fact of a father setting up his children at housekeeping, building them a house, laying out the grounds, curing the chimney, and stocking the cellar.[23]

One can imagine the magnificent effect the following passage must have had upon the listeners, with its short, dramatic sentences:

> But go out into the woods, break your hours, carry your biscuit in your pocket, and you shall see a day as an astronomical phenomenon. You shall forget your near and petty relations to Boston and Cambridge and see nothing but the noble earth on which you were born and the great star which enlightened and warms it. The contented clouds shall be to you an image of peace. The pines glittering with their innumerable green needles in the light every breath of air will make audible. "It is Day. It is Day." That is all which Heaven saith. Then look about you and see the manifold works of which day is the occasion. At first all is solitary. You think nothing lives there. But wait a little. Hundreds of eyes and ears watched your approach. The rabbit bounded away as you entered the field. The snake glided off at the noise of your approach from the very rock on which you stand, the bee flew from the neighboring shrub, the titmouse has only taken the next pinetree, and listen a moment, and you shall hear the ground robin scratching the leaves at the side of the brook.[24]

3. "The end of all preaching is to persuade men to become good," argues Blair, and all the commentators agree on this.[25] Ware sees enlightenment as the *means* to the end—persuasion to Christian conduct.[26] Technically the preacher may apply each point to the conduct of the listeners, or he may develop a chain of reasoning with a concluding moral. The latter method is used by Emerson in his lecture on Michelangelo, as it is frequently in many of the lectures in the "Human Culture" and "Human Life" series. Emerson's interest in Michelangelo as a person is quite secondary to his ultimate purpose: to prove that "perfect beauty and perfect goodness are One." Having done this by a subtle and interesting method, he urges his audience to "acknowledge the beauty that beams in external nature" and "seek by labor and denial to approach its source in Perfect Goodness."[27] In his first lecture on Shakespeare, his interest again centers on moral values: ". . . that every man finds in him [Shakespeare] what delights and what instructs him and the most enlarged mind learns that the dominion of human nature is broader than it knew whilst a spirit of beauty and of joy broods over it from side to side."[28] Sometimes this moralizing becomes painful when Emerson inveighs against the immorality of the Elizabethan drama.[29] "Helps he not me? . . . The moral of M. Angelo," he broods in his notes on Michelangelo.[30]

4. A preacher attempts to be at all times *positive* rather than negative in his views. The negative views in a sermon, Henry Ware points out, should be omitted or else used to support more positive views.[31] To a rationalist, a lecturer, a scholar, this is embarrassing; we all feel that we are the custodians of objectivity. So it was to those who wrote about sermons, and they make little mention of it. But it stands to reason that if one is trying chiefly to persuade others, he will not proceed by considering the

negative aspects of the subject. "I think it the main guard to a correct judgment, not to accept degrading views. It is a primal instinct and duty of the human mind to look with a sovereign eye of hope on all things."[32] Such were the remarks of Emerson prefacing a series of negative views in one of his lectures. Mr. McGiffert has observed this at work in his sermons—"For the most part his homiletical strategy seems to be to state the positive principles of his thought rather than to attack or criticise the views he has abandoned."[33] In "The Naturalist" Emerson twice wrote out several objections to his propositions, but in the final version both sets of objections were crossed out.[34] There are other examples too numerous to include here.

5. Whereas most lecturers or speakers need concern themselves only slightly with the problem of economy (i.e., limitation in use of words, ideas, time), the preacher must be very seriously aware of these problems. He must succeed, if only in a limited sense. Thus Emerson often wrote on the manuscript the number of minutes which each sermon required.[35] The early lectures in print are mostly of the same length, none exceeding thirteen pages.

In discussing various aspects of the subject, Emerson obviously was tempted to include as much material as possible. That he fought this temptation is evident from his comment after giving five uses of natural history and discussing each. Before briefly slipping in a sixth, he writes, "But I am already trespassing on your time."[36] A preacher, wrote Blair, "must never study to say all that can be said upon a subject; no error is greater than this."[37] The best sermons, he notes, have between three and five divisions.

In a similar fashion did Emerson demonstrate his concern for economy in language. In "The Naturalist," he composed two passages on the same theme. The second was used in the final version.

> [1] To know a robin or a titmouse intimately, would make us acquainted with its cries of affectation, fear, complaint, hunger, would show us the different months the manners . . . & (as we say) the morals of the bird. Would it not greatly inhance the expression of these natural signs We should understand the meaning of signs in the wood that now convey quite no meaning to us. Well then here poetry & fact meet The Arabian Nights said they understood what the birds said.[38]
> [2] I fully believe in both, in the poetry and in the dissection. I believe that we shall by and by know as the Arabian nights tell us what the social birds say when they sit in the autumn in council chattering upon the tree, the caprices of the cat-bird, the affectation of the titmouse.[39]

Emerson's ability to reduce his reasoning to one controlling idea or thought here becomes very evident. The words are much fewer; the effect is far greater.

6. In theory at least, the structure of a sermon differs markedly from the structure of a lecture or a similar address. This seems logical if we

keep in mind the five points above concerning the sermon as a distinct type of discourse. What seeks to convince rather than to prove is automatically going to require a different type of structure. None of the homiletical writers, with the exception of Claude, gives much consideration to the structure of the sermon. Claude was a strict conservative who provided an exact outline of the perfect sermon with all the divisions, subdivisions and their technical names. But the

> formal division, designed to focus the attention of the hearers, dropped slowly out of use. The basic principle that the sermon ought to have an outline, and the notion that it ought normally to be divided into three parts sandwiched between an introduction and an application, persisted throughout the nineteenth century, and are still persistent.[40]

William Ellery Channing, perhaps the most lively and convincing preacher of his day, used the divisions of the formal sermon to a limited extent. Emerson, of course, hallowed Channing above all, but there are few cases in Emerson's lectures at least, of formalized homiletical structure. One exception is "The Uses of Natural History," which has the introduction, the five divisions, and the summary. Here and there in the other lectures there are traces of this organization.

But if we are to establish any sort of relationship which is crucial to an understanding of Emerson's later thinking and writing, we must find a more general and essential difference in the structure of these forms of address. The first thing we notice in Blair's essay is his distrust of traditional logic—"to be an accurate reasoner will be small praise if he [the preacher] be not a persuasive speaker also."[41] Ware suggests that the idea be developed through implication, allusion, "indirect directness."[42] This is observed by Mr. McGiffert in Emerson's sermons, where he seems to be thinking out loud in the pulpit, "as though he were endeavoring to share with his congregation the process by which he has reached his conclusions, instead of preaching them the conclusions alone with no clues as to how he reached them."[43]

Emerson, therefore, did not force into an artificial logical pattern the concepts which he wished to convey to his listeners. Why? Not only because he had been trained in homiletics, but because he understood and had to appeal persuasively to what Mr. McGill has called "the common mind."[44] His approach was similar in theory to what has come to be known as "the stream of consciousness" or the multiple point of view—Gertrude Stein, Faulkner, Richardson, Joyce, Virginia Woolf. Emerson understood that people do not like to be "preached at." At the same time they must be persuaded of something in a distinctly natural and individual way—the way of the man who is doing the talking.

Thus, if I were asked to distinguish between the sermon and the lecture in a symbolic way, I should refer to the distinction between a tree and a building. With the tree one needs only the seed, the root or shrub; with the building, one needs a framework of sorts, with the limits and dimensions established in advance, so the whole is evident from a glance at the plans. Not so with the tree: from a root various branches extend in unforeseen directions. The beauty and naturalness of the tree is in the challenge it makes to the imagination. The results convince because they are natural and have little to do with logic.

In practice this theory takes the form of a pyramid or a circle with a central point. Ware suggests this more directly when he writes—the preacher must "see the object from many sides, parts."[45] Thus several chains of thought are established, each beginning at the periphery of a circle and working toward a central point. At times they are joined to one another, forming some sort of network. But ultimately they will culminate in the major idea which the sermon seeks to establish. If one thinks in terms of a pyramid or a spiraling figure, one has, in miniature, Emerson's philosophy of life as well. His habit of thinking and writing in these terms may well have prepared the ground for his maturing philosophy of Transcendentalism. But that is someone else's story.

Walter Blair and Clarence Faust argue that Emerson's literary method was parallel to that of Plato, and they imply that it was derived from Plato.[46] But Emerson had little literary acquaintance with Plato at the time that he was writing sermons and the early lectures. It seems to me that his training in homiletics had more influence in this respect than any other factor. Surely, as he began to read Plato, his ideas and his writing became more sophisticated. But one thing seems evident: had Emerson gone the way of his fellow lecturers, James Russell Lowell might never have said: "Those faces, young and old, agleam with pale intellectual light, eager with pleased attention, flash upon me once more from the deep recesses of the years."[47]

Notes

1. *The Early Lectures of Ralph Waldo Emerson*, ed. Stephen E. Whicher and Robert E. Spiller (Cambridge: Harvard University Press, 1959–), I.

2. *Reports to the Overseers of Harvard College*, 1 (1761–1825), 179.

3. Ralph L. Rusk, *The Life of Ralph Waldo Emerson* (New York: Scribners, 1949), p. 129.

4. Conrad Wright, "The Early Years," *The Harvard Divinity School*, ed. George H. Williams (Boston: Beacon, 1954), p. 63.

5. Kenneth Walter Cameron, *The Transcendentalists and Minerva* (Hartford, Conn.: Transcendental Books, 1958), III, 1017.

6. Rev. Henry Ware, Jr., outline notes for "A Course on the Composition of Sermons (1835–41)." These can be obtained in the Harvard Archives, HUC 8839.318.

7. Cameron, *Minerva*, III, 856.

8. Kenneth Walter Cameron, *Emerson's Reading* (Raleigh, N.C.: Thistle Press, 1941), pp. 45–47.

9. Cameron, *Emerson's Reading*, p. 45.

10. Rev. Hugh Blair, *Lectures on Rhetoric and Belles Lettres* (New York: E. Duyckinck, 1817), p. 280.

11. See the unpublished Ph.D. dissertation by Robert A. McGill, "Emerson and His Audience" (University of Pennsylvania, 1959), p. 54.

12. Kenneth Walter Cameron, "History and Biography in Emerson's Unpublished Sermons," *Emerson Society Quarterly*, no. 12 (3rd Quarter 1958), 2–9.

13. Jean Claude, "Essay on the Composition of a Sermon," in Rev. Charles Simeon, *Claude's Essay on the Composition of a Sermon and 100 Sketches of Sermons* (London: J. Cornish, 1853), p. 8.

14. Carl Bode, *The American Lyceum* (New York: Oxford University Press, 1956), p. 48.

15. Ware, outline notes, p. 24.

16. Cameron, *Minerva*, II, 464–465.

17. *Young Emerson Speaks*, ed. Arthur Cushman McGiffert, Jr. (Boston: Houghton Mifflin, 1938), p. xxxviii.

18. *Early Lectures*, I, 73–74.

19. *Early Lectures*, I, 72.

20. Blair, *Rhetoric*, p. 285.

21. *Young Emerson Speaks*, p. xviii.

22. *Early Lectures*, I, 192.

23. *Early Lectures*, I, 32.

24. *Early Lectures*, I, 77.

25. Blair, *Rhetoric*, p. 282.

26. Ware, outline notes, p. 15.

27. *Early Lectures*, I, 100, 117.

28. *Early Lectures*, I, 304.

29. *Early Lectures*, I, 355.

30. *Early Lectures*, I, 433.

31. Ware, outline notes, p. 37.

32. Introductory lecture on "The Philosophy of History." This excerpt is taken from the typescripts of the second volume of early lectures (in preparation), collection of Robert E. Spiller, University of Pennsylvania.

33. *Young Emerson Speaks*, p. xx.

34. See textual variants for "The Naturalist," in *Early Lectures*, I, 413, 416.

35. *Young Emerson Speaks*, p. xxvii.

36. *Early Lectures*, I, 23.

37. Blair, *Rhetoric*, p. 284.

38. *Early Lectures*, I, 418.

39. *Early Lectures*, I, 79.

40. Charles Smyth, *The Art of Preaching* (London, 1940), p. 207.

41. Blair, *Rhetoric*, p. 282.

42. Ware, outline notes, p. 23.

43. *Young Emerson Speaks*, p. xx.

44. McGill, "Emerson and His Audience," p. 30.

45. Ware, outline notes, p. 78.

46. "Emerson's Literary Method," *Modern Philology*, 42 (November 1944), 79–95.

47. James Russell Lowell, "Ralph Waldo Emerson," in *Great Teachers*, ed. Houston Peterson (New Brunswick, N.J.: Rutgers University Press, 1946), p. 335.

"The Over-Rated 'Over-Soul' "

Robert Detweiler*

An often unavoidable part of the critical process, in the necessary dependence upon previous research, is the perpetration of errors along with the exposition of truth. Some of the errors become classic; a minor one may be the persistent use of *Over-Soul* as a central concept in Ralph Waldo Emerson's philosophy. It comes as something of a shock to learn that Emerson himself used the term only twice in his complete essays and never in his poetry, sermons, or journals.[1] "The Over-Soul" serves as the title of the ninth essay in the *First Series* and occurs in a passage within that essay. He did not employ the term until 1840 (the year of the composition of the essay), at which time the main lines of his philosophy had already been established. Yet in spite of Emerson's own lack of emphasis upon the word, scholarship has adopted it as the focal point and epitomizing metaphor of the Transcendental ontology.

Emerson's son, in annotating the essays, initiated the erroneous stress upon the term. In commenting on "Worship" he speaks of "the Universal Mind or Over-Soul of which each human being is a channel," and in a note to "Illusions" he refers to his father's "doctrine of the Over-Soul."[2] Other interpreters have followed his lead ever since. George Woodberry tried to improve on the terminology by discussing not only *Over-Soul* but *Over-Will* as well; Mildred Silver employed "the doctrine of the Over-Soul" to explain Emerson's philosophy; and Perry Miller treated "the metaphysic of the Over-Soul."[3] Although the word is a handy one for labeling Emerson's thought, it is also dangerous, not only because it implies an accent that Emerson never had but also because it leads to fruitless speculation. There is little point in arguing about the source of the term, as Harrison, Christy, and Carpenter have done. More important, accepting the concept of the Over-Soul as the main expression of Emerson's thought imparts an unnecessary vagueness to him—the very aura that one tries to overcome in interpreting him.

What is the actual meaning of *Over-Soul*, and what is its place in the Emersonian system? It must be understood in its proper perspective as only a small part of the whole picture, as a single concept which together with other equally important concepts reveals a basic insight into Emerson's idea of God and man. An examination of the only passage in which the word appears yields information regarding his own usage. He writes:

> The Supreme Critic on the errors of the past and the present, and the only prophet of that which must be, is that great nature in which we rest as the earth lies in the soft arms of the atmosphere; that Unity, that Over-Soul, within which every man's particular being is contained and made one

*Reprinted from *American Literature*, 36 (March 1964), 65–68.

with all other; that common heart of which all sincere conversation is the worship, to which all right action is submission; that over-powering reality which confutes our tricks and talents, and contrains every one to pass for what he is, and to speak from his character and not from his tongue, and which evermore tends to pass into our thought and hand and become wisdom and virtue and power and beauty. We live in succession, in division, in parts, in particles. Meantime within man is the soul of the whole; the wise silence; the universal beauty, to which every part and particle is equally related; the eternal ONE.[4]

There is little doubt that *Over-Soul* is a synonym among other synonyms for God. *Supreme Critic, prophet, wise silence*, and *universal beauty*, for example, are diverse ways of designating the deity. However, each of these synonyms is specialized and says something specific about the Emersonian divinity. If Emerson wishes to make a general statement about God he uses a general term, such as *deity* or *divinity* or even *being* or *essence*. Sometimes he is ambiguous and will employ *spirit* or *soul*, which can mean either *universal* or *individual* spirit and soul, depending upon the context. The underlying difficulty is in Emerson's insistence upon a "panentheistic" view of deity, which understands God as both transcendent and immanent, as inhabiting—in fact, constituting—the universe yet also existing (nonspatially) "outside" it. When terms like *soul* or *spirit* fail to convey enough of his intended meaning, Emerson's strategy is to turn to analogy and a succession of semipoetic synonyms which will appeal to the imagination as well as to the reason of the reader.

Emerson's struggle to communicate his experience of God in the passage cited is indicated by the wealth of synonyms. Examining *Over-Soul* in relation to the other terms, one discovers that it has three fairly distinct connotations. First, it can be understood in the sense of "over-the-soul," as representing a quantitative contrast to the individual soul, since it is more than and therefore greater than the individual soul which man possesses. Thus the individual soul responds to the "that great nature," to "the overpowering reality" somehow outside of itself. Second, the Over-Soul is the "super-soul" (the Germans, if they translate it at all, render *Over-Soul* as *Überseele*, thereby giving the *super-soul* connotation), which indicates a qualitative difference. The Over-Soul is greater than the individual soul because it is not infected by the material qualities of mortality. In its purity and absoluteness, it stands as the model and ultimate goal of the individual soul. The idea corresponds to the Neo-Platonic view of the *One* as first member of the divine triad, through which all emanations begin, and Emerson reveals his indebtedness to that view by referring to "the eternal ONE" as the culminating synonym of the passage. Third, Over-Soul means *general soul*, the all-prevading soul, the principle of divine immanence in man and the world. In spite of the differences in quantity and quality between the individual soul and the universal soul, they are the same in origin and ultimate destination. Emerson's concern is to inform the individual of his present godliness and thus aid him in assimilating his soul to God. His emphasis is therefore on the "Unity" and the "common heart" which man can now experience. Through the word *Over-Soul*, then, Emerson attempts to say that 1) God is different from and more than worldly existence (transcendence); 2) God pervades and forms worldly existence (immanence); 3) man can become one with God even in worldly existence simply by realizing his own divine potential (unity). *Over-Soul* emerges as an imaginative name which combines two aspects of the divine nature, usually thought of as mutually exclusive, while inviting man to share in them.

Far from developing a doctrine of the Over-Soul, Emerson used the word as a description among others for a troublesome, even paradoxical series of concepts about God and man that he explained, both in earlier and later essays, in other terms. As the term *Over-Soul* stands, it is neither very clear nor very valuable as a representative label. If we continue to use it as a convenient catch-all for Emerson's brand of Transcendentalism, we should be aware that we are radically oversimplifying and at once obscuring his thought.

Notes

1. Besides examining all the published works of Emerson, I looked for the term "Over-Soul" in his unpublished sermons and journals in the Houghton Library collection and was unable to discover it there.

2. *The Complete Works of Ralph Waldo Emerson*, ed. Edward Waldo Emerson, Centenary Edition (Boston: Houghton, Mifflin, 1903–1904), VI, 388, 425.

3. George E. Woodberry, *Ralph Waldo Emerson* (New York: Macmillan, 1926), p. 118; Mildred Silver, "Emerson and the Idea of Progress," *American Literature*, 12 (March 1940), 10–11; Perry Miller, "From Edwards to Emerson," *Interpretations of American Literature*, ed. Charles Feidelson, Jr., and Paul Brodtkorb, Jr. (New York: Oxford University Press, 1959), p. 116.

4. Emerson, *Works*, II, 268–269.

"Emerson: The Unconquered Eye and the Enchanted Circle"

Tony Tanner*

Emerson unquestionably played a key role in the shaping of the American imagination, and yet he seems to have had some trouble in defining his own role in his own times. Once he ceased to be a minister he did not start to become an artist; his work has neither the intense passion or still serenity of the true mystic nor the intellectual rigour of the philosopher. He experimented with various characters or projections of parts of his own uncommitted imagination—the Scholar, the Seer, the Man of Genius, the Contemplative Man, the Student, the Transcendentalist, even the Reformer and the Hero. Professor Henry Nash Smith is surely correct in referring to these as 'a collection of embryos' and in going on to suggest that we should understand the essays and addresses in which Emerson deploys these characters as 'rudimentary narratives rather than as structures of discursive reasoning'.[1] In his work, therefore, it is wiser to seek the suggestive drift of the whole than to attempt to establish a consistently developed system of thought. In his many characters he canvassed many problems, but recurringly, insistently, he returned to the discussion of the relationship between man and nature, 'the marriage of thought and things'. He saw no basic hostilities in nature and no radical evil in man. When he does turn his attention to the problem of pain and suffering his tone remains suspiciously bland.[2] It is hard to feel that he has deeply registered some of the more rigorous paradoxes of existence; hard to feel that he ever experienced the chaos within. Evil was neither lasting nor real to Emerson. Thus the problem he addresses himself to is not how to restrain what is dark in man, but rather how to maintain a sense of the enveloping, involving divinity of the world. 'What is life but the angle of vision'[3] he asserts, and much of his work is occupied with attempts to define the appropriate angle of vision. He felt that one of America's deepest needs was a 'general education of the eye'[4] and it was just such an education that many of his essays and addresses attempted to give. I want to suggest that in the course of his 'education' he procured special prestige for the angle of vision of the child.

In his diagnosis of what was wrong with contemporary attitudes towards the world, Emerson insisted that the fault was not in the world itself so much as in man's manner of regarding it. 'The ruin or the blank that we see when we look at nature, is in our own eye. The axis of vision is not coincident with the axis of things, and so they appear not transparent but opaque. The reason why the world lacks unity, and lies broken and in heaps, is because man is disunited with himself.'[5] If things appeared to

*Reprinted from *The Reign of Wonder: Naivety and Reality in American Literature* (Cambridge, England: Cambridge University Press, 1965), pp. 26–45, 363–64.

lack unity that was because of some disorder in the eye: a new eye would unify the world in a new way—salvation is visual. Emerson shifts attention from environment to spectator. In one way he was merely continuing the tradition of neo-platonic thought among the romantics. When he writes: 'Not in nature but in man is all the beauty and worth he sees'[6] we hear echoes of Blake and Goethe, and Coleridge. But in emphasizing the responsibilities and creative powers of 'the eye of the beholder' he had a motive which the European romantics could not have had. For, as long as the interest of a locale was considered to be inherent in the place rather than the viewer, then Americans would be forever looking to Europe. By denying a hierarchy of significance among external objects he not only eliminated the special prestige of Europe (since everywhere is equally significant), he confronts the eye with an enormous, if exciting, task.

In the introduction to his earliest work he had written: 'Why should not we also enjoy an original relation to the universe?'[7] and he had started out with the resolution: 'Let us interrogate the great apparition that shines so peacefully around us.'[8] Emerson wanted the eye to see the world from scratch, wanted to inculcate 'the habit of fronting the fact, and not dealing with it at second hand, through the perceptions of somebody else'.[9] But from the start we should alert ourselves to a doubleness which is inherent in almost everything Emerson says about man's visual relationship with nature. Briefly this doubleness consists of an emphasis which points both to the importance of particulars *and* the unmistakable presence of general truths. The world is full of isolated details which should command our equal attention and reverence, and yet ultimately it is all one vast simple truth: the world is both a mosaic *and* a unified picture which admits of no fragmentation. To pick up his own words the world is both opaque and transparent—it both resists and invites visual penetration. His complaint is that 'as the high ends of being fade out of sight, man becomes near-sighted, and can only attend to what addresses the senses.'[10] The senses bring us indispensable particulars but to limit knowledge to the 'sensuous fact' is to be a Materialist: the Idealist, by a deliberate 'retirement from the senses',[11] will discern truths of which material things are mere representatives, truths of 'the high ends of being'.

> We live in succession, in division, in parts, in particles. Meantime within man is the soul of the whole; the wise silence, the universal beauty, to which every part and particle is equally related; the eternal ONE. . . . We see the world piece by piece, as the sun, the moon, the animal, the tree; but the whole, of which these are the shining parts, is the soul.[12]

Man must see all the shining parts of the world anew, as for the first time with his own uninstructed eye: but this is merely the prelude to his discerning 'the ONE'. Emerson's work would seem to prescribe an ascent from materialism to idealism and thence to mysticism—a passionate scrutiny of the minute particulars of a world which suddenly turns transparent and gives us an insight into 'the background of being', 'the Over-Soul', 'the ONE'. This duality of vision Emerson himself recognized, noting in his journal: 'Our little circles absorb us and occupy us as fully as the heavens; we can minimize as infinitely as maximize, and the only way out of it is (to use a country phrase) to kick the pail over, and accept the horizon instead of the pail, with celestial attractions and influences, instead of worms and mud pies.'[13] Emerson is not consistent in his advice for he is quite as likely to recommend that a man should scrutinize the pail rather than kick it over. But the passage describes very graphically one of his own habitual practices; for both visually and stylistically he moves from the pail (the discrete detail) to the horizon (the embracing generalization). Sherman Paul, who has written so well on Emerson, shrewdly adopts an idea from the work of Ortega y Gasset, and makes a similar point about Emerson. 'The eye brought him two perceptions of nature—nature ensphered and nature atomized—which corresponded to the distant and proximate visual powers of the eye.'[14] Emerson, seeking a sense of the unity and inter-involvement of all things, felt there was a great value in focusing the eye on 'an unbroken horizon':[15] not only because the unbroken horizon offers an image of an unbroken circle, not only because at the horizon different elements meet and marry, but also because when the eye pitches its focus thus far, all things between it and the horizon fall into what Paul calls 'a blur of relatedness'.[16] Seen thus, individual things seem not to be discrete and unrelated but rather a part of one vast unifying process. The world appears as a concave container. On the other hand, when the eye fastens on to one single detail the rest of the world falls away and one is only conscious of the separateness and isolation of the thing: there is no hazy unity but only the encroaching fragment. The world becomes convex, thrusting out its differentiated particulars. The dangers of the close scrutinizing vision were clear to Emerson: 'If you bury the natural eye too exclusively on minute objects it gradually loses its powers of distant vision.'[17] The paradox is, I think, that Emerson himself effectively, if unintentionally, stressed the value of the close scrutinizing vision. In his case, of course, the detail seldom failed to reveal the divine spirit which rolls through all things. But Thoreau developed a habit of close scrutiny, a reverence for details, which occupied itself with 'minute objects' to a degree never intended by Emerson. Thoreau was convinced that every fact, no matter how small, would flower into a truth, conveying to him a sense of the whole, the unity which maintained the details. Yet he seems to bear out Emerson's warning in a late melancholy complaint: 'I see details, not wholes nor the shadow of the whole.'[18] In such a phrase he seems to anticipate what could, and I think did, happen to subsequent writers. For many of them the eye got stuck at the surface, it was arrested among particulars. The mosaic stayed illegible with no overall, or underall, pattern discernible. Emerson himself gives intimations of such a possibility. 'Nature hates peeping'[19] and, more forcefully, 'Nature will not be a Buddhist: she resents generalizing, and insults the philosopher in every moment with a million of fresh particulars'.[20] One of Emerson's natures is one divine unbroken process wherein all the teeming, tumbling details are seen as part of a flowing Unity, a Unity not described so much as felt, passionately, ubiquitously, emphathetically. This is the nature that Whitman was to celebrate. But the other nature described by Emerson is a mass of discrete, clearly defined objects, a recession of endless amazing particulars—particulars which seem to quiver with hidden meanings but which never afford us the revealing transparency. This nature of clear contours and suggestive details is the nature of Anderson, Stein, Hemingway and many others.

As we noticed, the threat to the Transcendentalist lay precisely in the extreme generality of his assertions, his reliance on the all-explaining presence. For without a final mystical concept of nature Emerson confesses that he is left 'in the splendid labyrinth of my perceptions, to wander without end'.[21] Without the affirmed presence of the Over-Soul the world becomes a labyrinthine maze of perceptions which do not add up. The only way out of the maze was to look at it in a different way: this is why Emerson continually raises the question of how man should look at the world.

'Make the aged eye sun-clear'[22]—so Emerson appeals to Spring in one of his poems: it is an appeal which follows logically from his constant complaint that 'we are immersed in beauty, but our eyes have no clear vision'.[23] The age of an eye is presumably its sum of acquired habits, its interpretative predispositions, its chosen filter through which it sieves the world even while regarding it. Emerson thought that a person could become fixed in his ways of looking just as we talk of people getting fixed in their ways of thinking. Consequently he wants the eye to be washed clear of those selective and interpretative schemata which prevent us from 'an original relation to the universe'. As we now think, without these acquired schemata vision would be impossible: we have to learn to see and a 'washed' eye would be an eye blinded by undifferentiated confusion. But the important thing is not that Emerson did not understand the mechanics of sight but that he thought it possible and desirable to start looking at the world as though one had never seen or heard of it before. What Emerson wanted from man was a renewed faculty of wonder. 'All around us what powers are wrapped up under the coarse mattings of custom, and all wonder prevented . . . the wise man wonders at the usual.'[24] 'The invariable mark of wisdom is to see the miraculous in the common.'[25] In this kind of visual relationship between the eye and the world, the eye stands completely passive and unselective while the surrounding world flows unbroken into it. Something like this was envisaged by Emerson when he described himself in the following way:

> Standing on the bare ground—my head bathed by the blithe air and uplifted into infinite space—all mean egotism vanishes. I am become a

transparent eyeball; I am nothing; I see all; the currents of the Universal
Being circulate through me; I am part or parcel of God.[26]

The notable aspect of this visual stance is its complete passivity, its mood
of pious receptivity. Unfocusing, unselecting, the eye is porous to the 'currents of the Universal Being'. Rather similar is Emerson's description of
the delight he receives from a fine day which 'draws the cords of will out
of my thought and leaves me nothing but perpetual observation,
perpetual acquiescence, and perpetual thankfulness'.[27] Thus relieved of
the active will and conscious thought, Emerson could feel himself reab-
sorbed into the flowing continuum of unselfconscious nature.

Of course it was because of his optimistic mysticism that Emerson endorsed this mode of seeing, for he was convinced that if man could reat-
tain a primitive simplicity of vision the ubiquitous divinity of the world
would suddenly become clear to him. The wonder he advises is a form of
visual piety: to see naively is to see religiously. This explains his interest in
the animal eye and the child's eye—neither of which have been overlaid
with the dust and dirt of custom and second-hand perception, both of
which are free from the myopic interference of reason. The child sees better than the man. 'To speak truly, few adult persons can see nature. Most
persons do not see the sun. At least they have a very superficial seeing.
The sun illuminates only the eye of the man, but shines into the eye and
the heart of the child.'[28]

The desired point of view is one which allows nature unhindered,
uninterrupted access to the eye, thence to the heart. Because for Emerson
this meant capitulation to a superior source of virtue. 'Man is fallen;
nature is erect'[29] and 'all things are moral'.[30] It follows we must not try
and impose our will on nature but rather 'suffer nature to intrance us'[31]
for our own good. Man's fall is not into knowledge of evil—but into consciousness: for Emerson, as Yeats noted, has no 'vision of evil' and maintains, rather incredibly, that what we call evil would disappear if we acquired a new way of looking at things: 'the evils of the world are such only
to the evil eye.' How such evil finds its way into an intrinsically benign
and moral universe is not clear—but the extremity of Emerson's position
is. To be conscious is the curse, for to be conscious is to be alienated from
our original home or womb (and Emerson often uses words like 'cradle'
and 'nestle' and 'embosomed' to describe the proper quasi-infantile relationship with nature), it is to have lost the comfort of our primary ties.
The unselfconsciousness of animals is enviable. 'The squirrel hoards nuts
and the bee gathers honey, without knowing what they do, and they are
thus provided for without selfishness or disgrace.'[32] Man's dilemma is
based solely on his consciousness. 'Man owns the dignity of the life which
throbs around him, in chemistry, and tree, and animal, and in the involuntary functions of his own body; yet he is balked when he tries to fling
himself   into   this   enchanted   circle,   where   all   is   done   without

degradation.'[33] Only the *involuntary* actions of man have any dignity: we hear nothing of 'the dignity of judgment' in James's phrase, nothing of the enlightened will, of considered intent, of the disciplined pursuit of noble ends. Consciousness is seen only as an inhibitor—for what Emerson really wants is to get back into the enchanted circle, to regain what he calls 'the forfeit paradise'.

> And so, perchance, in Adam's race,
> Of Eden's bower some dream-like trace
> Survived the Flight and swam the Flood,
> And wakes the wish in youngest blood
> To tread the forfeit Paradise,
> And feed once more the exile's eyes:[34]

And he makes the point as strongly in prose: 'Infancy is the perpetual Messiah, which comes into the arms of fallen men, and pleads with them to return to paradise.'[35] Not a change of heart but a change of eye, a new mode of access into nature, is the burden of Emerson's lay sermons. As exemplars he cites 'children, babes, and even brutes' because 'their mind being whole, their eye is as yet unconquered; and when we look in their faces we are disconcerted'.[36] Man's eye has been conquered—that was the fall: man has been 'clapped into jail by his consciousness'.[37] This is why the child sees the sun properly and the adult does not. 'Infancy, youth, receptive, aspiring, with religious eye looking upward, counts itself nothing and abandons itself to the instruction flowing from all sides.'[38] This is the child's genius: the openness to sensations, the visual abandon he is capable of. We are at our best when we too can 'gaze like children'.[39] 'It is very unhappy, but too late to be helped, the discovery we have made that we exist. That discovery is called the Fall of Man. Ever afterwards we suspect our instruments. . . . Once we lived in what we saw; now the rapaciousness of this new power, which threatens to absorb all things, engages us.'[40] 'We suspect our instruments'—Emerson diagnoses a crisis of vision: we see, but we are not sure what we see and how correct is our seeing. There is perhaps something greedy and predatory about the conscious eye, which scans the panorama of creation with utilitarian intention, every glance of which is an act of visual spoliation. But the eye which seeks passively and humbly for true connection and orientation lacks confidence. However the child and the animal still seem to live in what they see with no subject-object dichotomy to haunt them, with none of the sense of severance which assaults the conscious eye. If the adult eye is glazed and dull and blind to the lessons of nature, still the naive eye—idiot, Indian, infant—seems to pay the most profitable kind of attention to things, to enjoy a lost intimacy with the world, to have the freshest, clearest perceptions. Thus Emerson seems to have seen the problem and located the salvation.

Whether or not Emerson felt he had any medical and anthropological evidence for his description of the naive eye of the child and native is not important: for ultimately he was using the notion as a metaphor. His conception of the naive eye is not scientific so much as religious. It was a prelude to worship rather than a preparation for action. It is in this light that such curious passages as the following should be read:

> The child with his sweet pranks, the fool of his senses, commanded by every sight and sound, without any power to compare and rank his sensations, abandoned to a whistle or a painted chip, to a lead dragoon or a ginger-bread dog, *individualising everything, generalising nothing*, delighted with every new thing, lies down at night overpowered by the fatigue which this day of continual pretty madness has incurred. *But nature has answered her purpose with the curly dimpled lunatic.* . . . This glitter, this opaline lustre plays around the top of every toy to his eye to insure his fidelity, and he is deceived to his good. *We are made alive and kept alive by the same arts.*[41] [my italics]

It is the intellectual (not the mystical) generalization, so detrimental to a proper habit of awe, which Emerson is writing against; it is a new sort of naive wondering individualizing he is anxious to inculcate. And although he indulgently calls the child a 'dimpled lunatic' he elsewhere talks more seriously of 'the wisdom of children'.[42] Although he sometimes asserts a superior mode of vision which sees through all particulars to the Over-Soul, although he sometimes warns against the rapt attention to detail with which he credited the child, the savage and the animal; nevertheless he often returns to the superiority of the naive eye precisely because of the generous attentive wonder it displays in front of nature's multiple particulars.

Perhaps the child was ultimately Emerson's image for his own best intentions. 'The first questions are always to be asked, and the wisest doctor is gravelled by the inquisitiveness of the child.'[43] Adult maturity is no real maturity since we have lost the right approach to nature, the knack of correct penetration: in fact we no longer ask the right questions. The child in his unencrusted innocence does. There is a dangerous form of extremism here: Emerson's rejection of the past includes not only a denial of the accumulated wisdom of the race but also the lessons of experience. The inquiry ideally should commence afresh each day. Nothing accrues, everything is always to be asked: such is the extreme implication of the Emersonian stance. And certainly since his time the habit of renewed wonder, the ever-novel interrogation of experience has become a recurring theme in American literature, a temperamental predisposition and a literary strategy. Naivety has become an important form of wisdom.

*   *   *

> If we cannot make voluntary and conscious steps in the admirable science of universals, let us see the parts wisely, and infer the genius of nature from the best particulars with a becoming charity.[44]

(Emerson)

I have already suggested that although Emerson's vision alternated between detail and generalization, the 'mud pies' and the 'celestial influences', the overall effect of his work is to secure a new respect for close vision. What I want to point out in this section is how Emerson, despite his own preference for 'the admirable science of universals', focused unusual and exciting attention on 'the best particulars'. More remarkably he often equated the best particulars with low and commonplace objects and continually suggested that the need for 'a langue of facts'[45] could best be answered by turning to the vernacular. These emphases alone make him a major figure in American literature and they merit special attention here. Only rarely does Emerson give the impression that it might be disconcerting if one could not make the pieces of the mosaic add up to one flowing, binding picture. We just have some hints. 'But all is sour if seen as experience. Details are melancholy; the plan is seemly and noble.'[46] Having lost all sense of the 'seemly and noble' plan Henry Adams, for one, found the remaining heaps of particulars not only sour and melancholy but terrifying. Emerson, to whom mystical generalizations came all too easily, could tie up the world in a sentence. 'Our globe seen by God is a transparent law, not a mass of facts.'[47] Facts on their own were indeed 'heavy, prosaic' and 'dull strange despised things': but Emerson maintained that simply by wondering at them man would find 'that the day of facts is a rock of diamonds; that a fact is an epiphany of God'.[48] With such experience open to him Emerson could well afford to stress the value of a close regard for facts.

If you believe that the universe is *basically* such a perfect continuous whole then certain things follow. For a start every detail will be equally significant. 'A leaf, a drop, a crystal, a moment of time, is related to the whole, and partakes of the perfection of the whole. Each particle is a microcosm, and faithfully renders the likeness of the world.'[49] 'There is no fact in nature which does not carry the whole sense of nature.'[50] 'The world globes itself in a drop of dew. The microscope cannot find the animalcule which is less perfect for being little.'[51]

Now the interesting aspect of this belief that 'the universe is represented in every one of its particles'[52] is that it can easily lead, not to the mystical generalization, but to an extreme of particularization, a devoted preoccupation with the minutiae of existence. It can encourage a prose devoted to ensnaring the crystalline fragments of momentary experience. Emerson works against his own intentions here by giving a tremendous prestige to the smallest details of the material world: his mystical enthusiasm is, as it were, diffused among all the details he sees. There is no hierarchy of value or significance operative: *all* details are worthy of the most reverent attention because all are equally perfect and equally meaningful. If Thoreau, as Emerson said, was 'equally interested in every natural fact',[53] then he was only putting into practice an Emersonian prescription. The implications of this attitude are worth pondering. If every fact is equally interesting where does one find a criteria of exclusion, a principle of abridgement without which art cannot start to be art for it cannot leave off being nature? Emerson is endorsing an eye which refuses to distinguish and classify, which denies priorities of importance and significance, which refuses to admit of any sort of difference in import and value. From one point of view one could call this the egalitarian eye: an eye which affirms the equality of all facts. All facts are born equal and have an equal claim on man's attention. Yet in most art there is what we might call an aristocratic tendency: a claimed prerogative to exercise a lordly right of selection, omission, evaluation, and rearrangement. The aristocratic eye tyrannizes its facts: the egalitarian eye is tyrannized by them. This is not to say that the egalitarian or naive eye cannot discover things to which the aristocratic eye remains blind: it can, for it has that humility which makes new insights possible. It needed the naive eye as described by Emerson and adopted by Thoreau and Whitman, for America to be seen at all in its own right. But it is worth pointing out at this stage that there are distinct problems of organization and evaluation inherent in Emerson's concept of vision. What is completely absent is any sense of a scale of relative complexity, any feeling that small clusters of selected facts can yield a restricted amount of wisdom, any notion of a gradual increase of intelligence, any awareness of various modes of classification, any reference to the accumulating density of experience. There is the leaf—and there are the hidden laws of the universe: and nothing in between. Certainly not society, the notable omission in Emerson. For Emerson is a man talking metaphysics with his eye glued to the microscope, and plenty of American writers have taken their turn at the microscope after Emerson and his disciple Thoreau. This notion of Emerson's had far-reaching repercussions. For if the meaning of the world is to be found in a drop of dew, then the meaning of a given situation may be contained in the contingent objects which surround the participants. The lesson could be drawn from Emerson's thought that if the writer looks after the details the significances will look after themselves. A writer might construe his task to be a scrupulous itemizing of particulars, from the smallest to the largest with no accompanying distribution of significance, no perspective with its recession of priorities, no 'comparison and ranking of sensations'. Indeed he gives a clear warrant for such an attitude. Thus: 'the truth-speaker may dismiss all solicitude as to the proportion and congruency of the aggregate of his thoughts, so long as he is a faithful reporter of particular impressions.'[54] This means that a work of art depends for its form on the individual notation; no larger unit of meaning need be constructed. As he very revealingly wrote—'ask the fact for the form':[55] an attitude far removed from that which relies on the form to assign meaning to the fact. Although Emerson talked of the importance of the 'Intellect Constructive', the major emphasis of his work falls on the 'Intellect Receptive'.[56]

Emerson's belief that the part contained the whole—by implication, or in shorthand as it were—leads quite naturally to his mystique of facts. We remember his instructions to 'see the miraculous in the common': he goes on to arraign our blindness to the worth and significance of small everyday facts. 'To the wise, therefore, a fact is true poetry, and the most beautiful of fables.'[57] Facts contain their own story if we will simply look at them afresh. 'Pleads for itself the fact'[58] he says in one of his poems and he means just that: things will 'sing themselves'[59] if we learn to listen in the right way. Again, we note that the prescribed attitude is passive. We do not impose a meaning on facts, rather we try and make 'facts yield their secret sense'.[60] 'Every moment instructs and every object; for wisdom is infused into every form.'[61] Genius, then, will consist of 'the habit of fronting the fact';[62] the intellect is ravished 'by coming nearer to the fact'.[63]

Emerson's emphasis was most important for American writers of the time: because among other things he was continually dragging eyes back to the worth and status of American facts. He scorned artists who could only discern beauty through the conventions of the old 'sublime'. 'They reject life as prosaic, and create a death which they call poetic.'[64] Emerson was constantly canvassing for an artistic acceptance of prosaic everyday life. It is the instinct of genius, he affirmed,

> to find beauty and holiness in new and necessary facts, in the field and road-side, in the shop and mill. Proceeding from a religious heart it will raise to a divine use the railroad, the insurance office, the joint-stock company; our law, our primary assemblies, our commerce, the galvanic battery, the electric jar, the prism, and the chemist's retort; in which we seek now only an economical use. . . . The boat at St. Petersburg which plies along the Lena by magnetism, needs little to make it sublime.[65]

We can hear prophetic echoes of Whitman's enthusiastic listing of things here. It may sound naive to us but at the time this opinion of Emerson's rendered American literature a real service: his influence helped to make available whole areas of contemporary American life which had hitherto been considered all but ineligible for serious treatment. It was Emerson's insistence on 'the worth of the vulgar' which made Whitman's work possible. He himself chooses the simplest of objects as carriers of sublime revelations. His prose often seems to create a still-life of separately attended-to particulars. It conveys a sense of the radiance of things seen. Emerson succeeded in vivifying the 'common, the familiar, the low':[66] he dignified the details of 'the earnest experience of the common day'.[67] He invokes a new respect for contingent, mundane particulars.

But in order to see details properly man has to separate one thing from another. So although Emerson believes that there are no walls or separating barriers in the flowing tide of nature he yet talks of 'the cool disengaged air of natural objects'[68] and affirms that 'things are not huddled and lumped, but sundered and individual'.[69] Emerson the mystic talked on and on about the fluid inter-relatedness of all things, the transparency of nature to the ONE: but the Emerson whose influence is most marked in American literature was the man who asserted that 'the virtue of art lies in detachment, in sequestering one object from the embarrassing variety',[70] who approved 'the power to fix the momentary eminency of an object'.[71] And if it be asked what connection this particular virtue has with the naive eye we should recall that Emerson said: 'To the young mind everything is individual, stands by itself'.[72] The naive eye, as he depicted it, was likely above all others to be alert to the unique significance of the isolated random details of the material world.

In encouraging a new way of 'seeing' Emerson also made some comments on 'saying', on 'the language of facts' which we must now examine.

First, the indictment: 'The corruption of man is followed by the corruption of language . . . new imagery ceases to be created, and old words are perverted to stand for things which are not; a paper currency is employed, when there is no bullion in the vaults . . . But wise men pierce this rotten diction and fasten words again to visible things.'[73] Secondly, the precedent from which we should learn. 'Children and savages use only nouns or names of things, which they convert into verbs, and apply to analogous acts.'[74] As well as the child and the savage, Emerson cites the 'strong-natured farmer or backwoodsman'[75] as exemplifying the proper use of language. This equating of the child, the savage, and the vernacular type is questionable if a serious attempt to analyse speech-habits is being offered. But they occur more as exemplars in a sermon. Emerson wants to communicate the notion of some sort of verbal intimacy with the stuff of nature, a state in which words and things are at their closest. We should see like children: we should also speak like children and vernacular types, or at least with the simple, specifying concreteness that Emerson imputes to them. Just as Emerson wanted the eye to concentrate on concrete facts, so he wishes langue to be full of concrete factualness, and for the same reasons: a new or renewed intimacy with these facts affords us our quickest means of contact with the unifying sublime presence which runs through all things. So the concentration is always on the simplest forms of speech, on the speech which arises from physical involvement with nature rather than the subtle refined concepts used by those who meditate on life through the mind's eye. 'Life lies behind us as the quarry from whence we get tiles and copestones for the masonry of to-day. This is the way to learn grammar. Colleges and books only copy the language which the field and work-yard made.'[76]

An important by-product of this contention of Emerson's is his complete rejection of the classification of facts, things, and words into 'high' and 'low', a classification based on the dualism of spirit and body which was then still a major influence on New England thought. 'The vocabulary of an omniscient man would embrace words and images excluded from polite conversation. What would be base, or even obscene, to the obscene, becomes illustrious, spoken in a new connection of thought.'[77] The effect of this enlightened passage is to offer a card of eligibility to a whole range of experience and vocabulary which had hitherto been considered inherently unfit for literature.

More central to Emerson's theory of language is his assertion that 'It does not need that a poem should be long. Every word was once a poem', and the related idea that 'bare lists of words are found suggestive to an imaginative and excited mind'.[78] Every word was once a poem because every word was once a thing, or at least a 'brilliant picture' of a thing. ('Language is fossil poetry'[79] wrote Emerson, thus anticipating Fenellosa's notion of language as a pyramid with an apex of generality and a base composed of 'stunned' things.) Since every thing equally displays or hints at the divine plan of the universe, a list of words becomes a list of revelations, each noted fact an encountered epiphany. The influence of this belief on Emerson's own style can be discerned. His style, most characteristically, is composed of an effortless shifting from the suggestive list of facts and things to what he revealingly calls 'casual'[80] abstraction and generalization. In his own words: 'There is the bucket of cold water from the spring, the wood-fire to which the chilled traveller rushes for safety—and there is the sublime moral of autumn and noon.'[81] The philosophy is revealed in the style: he ascends direct from 'a crystal' to the 'Universal Spirit'.[82] Clusters of unrelated facts occur continually, embedded in his discursive sentences, pegging them to the ground. Examples can be proliferated. 'There is nothing but is related to us, nothing that does not interest us—kingdom, college, tree, horse, or iron shoe—the roots of all things are in man.'[83] His prose asserts but never analyses these relationships. We could recall the famous passage on the 'worth of the vulgar' which employs a similar method of assembling 'things', but things left separate and static: 'The meal in the firkin; the milk in the pan; the ballad in the street; the news of the boat; the glance of the eye; the form and gait of the body;'[84]—details which reveal not any one of man's world but God's world. Such passages in Emerson serve as the spring-boards for his sublime leaps: and obviously even as he is enumerating these 'things', telling his beads of facts as we might say, they seem to reveal universal laws to him. As in Whitman, they 'sing' to him. The more successful passages in Emerson are weighed down with concrete facts, laced with particulars which alert the mental eye. What has gone from his writing is almost all purposive complexity of syntax: his style is extremely paratactic and his sentences often start with an unintroduced enumeration of things, things held up for our beholding in the belief that they will 'plead for themselves'. One final example must suffice:

The fall of snowflakes in a still air, preserving to each crystal its perfect form; the blowing of sleet over a wide sheet of water, and over plains; the

waving rye field; the mimic waving of acres of houstonia, whose innumerable florets whiten and ripple before the eye; the reflections of trees
and flowers in glassy lakes; the musical, steaming, odorous south wind,
which converts all trees to wind-harps; the crackling and spurting of hem-
lock in the flames, or of pine logs, which yield glory to the walls and faces
in the sitting-room—these are the music and pictures of the most ancient
religion.[85]

This is writing of considerable visual sensitivity but which has no
sense whatever of the relation and inter-relation of things and things,
things and people, people and other people. It is a prose that stops before
society and the problems of human behaviour start. His idea that 'bare
lists of words are suggestive' is crucial here. They are suggestive if the
words are what he thought words should be—concrete facts, pictures of
things—but even so such bare lists help us not at all in the problems of living among those facts and things. Emerson's prose feels its way over the
surfaces and round the contours of parts of the empirical world but has no
means of discussing the problems of action and interruption in that world.
By way of meaning he can only produce the mystical generalization, but
as faith in such generalizations has diminished it is the former aspect of his
prose, the respect for details, which seems to have had most influence in
American literature.

Of the duality of his own vision he writes very clearly. 'We are am-
phibious creatures, weaponed for two elements, having two sets of
faculties, the particular and the catholic. We adjust our instruments for
general observation, and sweep the heavens as easily as we pick out a
single figure in the terrestrial landscape.'[86] Emerson found it easy to
'sweep the heavens' but subsequent writers have found it less so. The
heavens have changed for one thing—or rather man's relationship with
them has. They now seem to mock, whereas to Emerson they seemed to
smile on, the 'casual' all-explaining generalization. But there remains the
'faculty' for particulars, and the ability to isolate 'single figures in the terrestrial landscape' and this faculty has perhaps been cultivated as the
other faculty has increasingly come under suspicion—though it has by no
means disappeared (see the Afterword). Not surprisingly Emerson admired Plato above all others, and in his essay on him he manages to tell us
a good deal about himself. This is Emerson's Plato: 'If he made
transcendental distinctions, he fortified himself by drawing all his illustrations from sources disdained by orators and polite conversers; from
mares and puppies; from pitchers and soup-ladles; from cooks and criers;
the shops of potters, horse-doctors, butchers and fishmongers.'[87] Plato,
that is, obeyed Emerson and 'embraced the common, explored and sat at
the feet of the familiar, the low'. Perhaps the most revealing thing that
Emerson says about Plato is this: 'Plato keeps the two vases, one of ether
and one of pigment, at his side, and invariably uses both.'[88] The pigment
of low concrete facts and the ether of mystical generalization—they are

both to be found in Emerson. And it is worth repeating that for him peculiar prestige attaches itself to the 'low' in language and in facts and in people. 'The poor and the low have their way of expressing the last facts of philosophy as well as you.'[89] As well as, and by veiled implication, perhaps better. There is actually a preference for those minds which 'have not been subdued by the drill of school education'.[90] Do you think the porter and the cook have no anecdotes, no experiences, no wonders for you? Everybody knows as much as the savant. The walls of crude minds are scrawled over with facts, with thoughts.'[91] This is an attitude which could endorse the vernacular as a literary mode; which could encourage the belief in the superior wisdom of the backwoodsman, the rural inhabitant, the person living outside any urban-civilized field of force. It is difficult to assess the influence of one writer. Emerson is perhaps as much symptom as cause. The point is that certain novel attitudes and predilections which recur in many American writers seem to emerge articulated in Emerson's work for the first time. Some of these might be summed up as follows: the emphasis on 'seeing' things freshly; the prescription for the innocent non-generalizing eye; the concomitant preference for simple people and simple speech; whether that of the uneducated labourer, the savage or the child; the exhortation to accept *all* facts, the vulgar trivia of the world, as being potential harbingers of meaning; the celebration of the details of the concrete world and the (more than intended, perhaps) prestige accorded to the particularizing faculty, that faculty which develops the closest relationships between man and the natural world. 'We penetrate bodily this incredible beauty; we dip our hands in this painted element; our eyes are bathed in these lights and forms.'[92] Mysticism, yes: but a mysticism which encouraged a scrupulous yet wondering rediscovery of material appearances, which attached maximum importance to a new intimacy with the basic undistorted 'pigment' of 'this painted element', the world. In encouraging men to 'wonder at the usual' Emerson bestowed perhaps the greatest benefit on American literature.

Notes

1. Henry Nash Smith, "Emerson's Problem of Vocation: A Note on 'The American Scholar,'" *New England Quarterly*, 12 (March 1939): 52–67.

2. For a more sympathetic treatment of Emerson's handling of the problem of pain and evil see "The House of Pain: Emerson and the Tragic Sense" by Newton Arvin (*Hudson Review*, 12 [Spring 1959]: 37–53) and "Emerson's Tragic Sense" by Stephen E. Whicher (*American Scholar*, 22 [Summer 1953]: 285–292).

3. *The Complete Works of Ralph Waldo Emerson*, ed. Edward Waldo Emerson, 12 vols. (Boston: Houghton, Mifflin, 1903–1904), XII, 10.

4. *Journals of Ralph Waldo Emerson*, ed. Edward Waldo Emerson and Waldo Emerson Forbes, 10 vols. (Boston: Houghton Mifflin, 1909–1914), VIII, 550.

5. *Works*, I, 73–74.

6. *Works*, II, 147.

7. *Works*, I, 3.

8. *Works*, I, 4.

9. *Works*, III, 92.

10. *Works*, I, 127–128.

11. *Works*, I, 330.

12. *Works*, II, 269.

13. *Journals*, X, 238.

14. Sherman Paul, *Emerson's Angle of Vision* (Cambridge: Harvard University Press, 1952), p. 73.

15. *Journals*, V, 310–311.

16. Paul, *Emerson's Angle of Vision*, p. 75.

17. *Young Emerson Speaks*, ed. Arthur Cushman McGiffert, Jr. (Boston: Houghton Mifflin, 1938), p. 48.

18. Quoted by Leo Marx in his edition of Thoreau's *Excursions* (New York: Corinth Books, 1962), p. xiii.

19. *Works*, III, 59.

20. *Works*, III, 236.

21. *Works*, I, 63.

22. *Works*, IX, 181.

23. *Works*, II, 354.

24. *Works*, III, 285.

25. *Works*, I, 74.

26. *Works*, I, 10.

27. Quoted by F. O. Matthiessen, *American Renaissance: Style and Vision in the Age of Emerson and Whitman* (New York: Oxford University Press, 1941), p. 62.

28. *Works*, I, 8.

29. *Works*, III, 178.

30. *Works*, I, 40.

31. *Works*, III, 170.

32. *Works*, I, 338.

33. *Works*, I, 339.

34. *Works*, IX, 166.

35. *Works*, I, 139.

36. *Works*, II, 48.

37. *Works*, II, 49.

38. *Works*, II, 319.

39. *Works*, II, 329.

40. *Works*, III, 75–76.

41. *Works*, III, 185–186.

42. *Works*, I, 73.

43. *Works*, II, 325.

44. *Works*, III, 244.

45. *Works*, II, 335.

46. *Works*, II, 171.

47. *Works*, II, 302.

48. Quoted in Matthiessen, *American Renaissance*, p. 58.

49. *Works*, I, 43.

50. *Works*, III, 17.

51. *Works*, II, 101.

52. *Works*, II, 101.

53. *Works*, X, 474.

54. Quoted in Charles Feidelson, Jr., *Symbolism and American Literature* (Chicago: University of Chicago Press, 1953), p. 150.

55. Quoted in Norman Foerster, "Emerson on the Organic Principle in Art," *PMLA*, 41 (March 1926): 193–208.

56. *Works*, II, 334.

57. *Works*, I, 75.

58. *Works*, III, 88.

59. *Works*, I, 82.

60. *Works*, I, 9.

61. *Works*, III, 196.

62. *Works*, III, 92.

63. *Works*, III, 28.

64. *Works*, II, 367.

65. *Works*, II, 369.

66. *Works*, I, 111–112.

67. *Works*, II, 290.

68. *Works*, III, 183.

69. *Works*, I, 38.

70. *Works*, II, 354.

71. *Works*, II, 355.

72. *Works*, I, 85.

73. *Works*, I, 29–30.

74. *Works*, I, 26.

75. *Works*, I, 31.

76. *Works*, I, 98.

77. *Works*, III, 17.

78. *Works*, III, 17–18.

79. *Works*, III, 22.

80. *Works*, III, 237.

81. *Works*, III, 171.

82. *Works*, I, 43–44.

83. *Works*, II, 17.

84. *Works*, I, 111–112.

85. *Works*, III, 172.

86. *Works*, III, 229.

87. *Works*, IV, 55.

88. *Works*, IV, 56.

89. *Works*, II, 315.

90. *Works*, II, 350.
91. *Works*, II, 330.
92. *Works*, III, 173.

"Emerson and the Doctrine of Sympathy"

Carl F. Strauch*

I.

It is a commonplace that toward the close of the eighteenth century the Romantic order of dynamic unfolding superseded the static order of Platonic entities. Hence, in the new, mobile, ever-changing universe, relations assumed paramount importance, whether in nature or society. Terms like *sympathy*, *identity*, and *harmony*, as well as *Reason* and *Understanding*, *Genius* and *Talent*, *Becoming* and *Being*, were vital concepts in the Romantic consciousness, and in the new century the doctrine of sympathy, which the Romantic literature of Europe and America exploited so fully, encouraged the writer to search out polarities, correspondences, and affinities at every level of the Platonic scale of existence.[1] Eduard, in Goethe's *Elective Affinities*, succinctly expressed the Romantic view: "Man is a true Narcissus; he delights to see his own image everywhere; he spreads himself underneath the universe like the amalgam behind the glass." In 1833, studying the inexhaustible riches of nature in the Jardin des Plantes, the young and receptive Emerson echoed the idea, while giving it his own Swedenborgian shading: "Not a form so grotesque, so savage, nor so beautiful but is an expression of some property inherent in man the observer,—an occult relation between the very scorpions and man. I feel the centipede in me—cayman, carp, eagle, & fox. I am moved by strange sympathies, I say continually 'I will be a naturalist.' "[2]

In the present paper I shall deal with Emerson's treatment of sympathy in man's relations to nature, and I shall reserve for a subsequent paper his treatment of the doctrine in the relations of individuals to one another and to society.

Emerson's dualism or polarity made him oscillate between affirmation, growing out of his radical faith, and skepticism, reflecting his awareness of the illusory conditions of life; and these responses to the metaphysical frame of things become clear in his sensitive use of the doctrine of sympathy. But Emerson's oscillation was not indecisive wavering, for he gave full value to each record of each mood, at either extreme or at any point on the arc of his swinging pendulum. Thus in the spring of

*Reprinted from *Studies in Romanticism*, 6 (Spring 1967), 152–74.

1839, in a boldly affirmative mood, he made a journal entry on the poet's correspondence with nature, and what he said here constitutes the heart of his poetic consciousness:

> The perception of identity is a good mercury of the progress of the mind. I talk with very accomplished persons who betray instantly that they are strangers in nature. The cloud, the tree, the sod, the cat are not theirs, having nothing of them. They are visitors in the world, and all the proceedings and events are alien, immeasurable, and across a great gulf. The poet, the true naturalist, for example, domesticates himself in nature with a sense of strict consanguinity. His own blood is in the rose and the apple-tree. The Cause of him is Cause of all. The volcano has its analogies in him. He is in the chain of magnetic, electric, geologic, meteorologic phenomena, and so he comes to live in nature and extend his being through all: then is true science.[3]

Because of his spiritual affinities man may enter nature at the physical level and step by upward step, in an initiation of mystical import, realize his identity with the spirit informing the cosmos, as we shall see in a number of Emerson's poems, especially his much neglected masterpiece, "Woodnotes." In Part I of this poem man identifies himself in "strict consanguinity" with phenomenological nature, and thereby perceives the metaphysical reality lurking beneath; and at the close he is prepared for the further initiation into arcane lore revealed in "Woodnotes II." Part I is devoted entirely to a poetical exposition of the doctrine of sympathy, but since Part II ranges far beyond we shall dip into it only for necessary light in explicating Part I. We shall want especially to refer to the close of the entire poem, where Emerson rhapsodically affirms man's divine identity, the culminating expression of man's sympathy with the cosmos.

For the present generation of students Emerson's handling of the doctrine may be more fascinating as we descend on the scale. Man increasingly seeks out the physical or materialistic in nature corresponding to this excess in his own make-up. When Emerson delineates this attraction in "Guy" he is shrewd, witty, and ironic. When he discloses Daniel Webster's equivalence with "things" in "Ode to W. H. Channing" he is scornful in contrasting the statesman's immense pretensions with his ethical coarseness. But Emerson descends to a level even below the materialistic attraction between man and nature; in "Hamatreya" he explores the chilling horror of absolute, universal nothingness, and in so doing he anticipates by a good many years E. M. Forster's ugly "boum" in *Passage to India*.

II

Emerson's *Poems* (1847) centers upon the problem of man's falling away from an inherent cosmic harmony. With few and unimportant exceptions, poem after poem deals with this problem in one way or another, and Emerson placed "The Sphinx" (first printed in *The Dial,* January 1841) at the head of the collection because this poem constituted the most formal statement of the disjunction between man and nature, just as farther on in the book both parts of "Woodnotes" explicate the sympathetic quest and mystical reunion. It is within the framework of a harmonious universe that Emerson manipulates the doctrine of sympathy, and we must, therefore, acknowledge the prior role of harmony as he discovered this ancient Greek doctrine in both Gérando and Cudworth and as he subsequently set it forth in "The Sphinx."[4]

Throughout the poem we are told that there is a "Daedalian plan," that all things are enchanted by one music and stirred by one deity, that "Deep love" lies under the phenomenological world, and that this love "works at the centre." This harmony is not a simple thing, however, for it is the result of an underlying polarity, a constant attraction and repulsion beginning in the atomic structure of the universe:

> The journeying atoms,
>   Primordial wholes,
> Family draw, firmly drive,
>   By their animate poles.

All creation rests upon a balanced conflict, an attraction (atoms drawn to one another) and repulsion (atoms driving one another apart), which at the sentient surface of life evens out and produces not discord, but harmony among the diverse phenomena. In the following two examples of this harmony it will be noted that Emerson depicts a conscious enjoyment of the sympathetic relation. First, wind and water:

> The waves, unashamèd,
>   In difference sweet,
> Play glad with the breezes,
>   Old playfellows meet.

In the second example the relation of bird and leaves is deftly suggested, for if the leaves offer protection to the bird, the bird gives expression to the silent existence of plants:

> In beautiful motion
>   The thrush plies his wings;
> Kind leaves of his covert,
>   Your silence he sings.

The further argument of the poem suggests reasons why man has fallen out of his proper role in the scheme of nature and has, in consequence, failed to perceive his own cosmic "meaning." First, he has been drugged by "the Lethe of Nature," and it is to this opiate condition that "the great mother" refers when she asks, "Who has drugged my boy's cup?" In the essay "Experience" Emerson discourses at length on this topic, but in "The Sphinx" his references to it are projected, necessarily, in abrupt images. There is, however, a profounder cause, namely, man's aspirations, his desire to discover "new heavens"; hence, like the proud, rebellious angels, many may err and, paradoxically, fall "through love of the best." In "Circles" Emerson said, "The same law of eternal procession ranges all that we call the virtues, and extinguishes each in the light of a better." Man is a mixed creature, part spiritual and eternal, part physical and mortal, a "clothed eternity," and his falling represents, therefore, the inevitable disproportion between his spiritual insight and his physical limitation:

> Whose soul sees the perfect,
>   Which his eyes seek in vain.

Whatever the risks, man must, nonetheless, continue his upward striving, for it represents a three-fold effort—to return to the harmony of nature, to discover his true identity, and to transcend time. This is the full meaning conveyed by the climactic stanza:

> Thou art the unanswered question;
>   Couldst see thy proper eye,
> Always it asketh, asketh;
>   And each answer is a lie.
> So take thy quest through nature,
>   It through thousand natures ply:
> Ask on, thou clothed eternity;
>   Time is the false reply.

Man does but repeat at the level of conscious thought and action the ceaseless movement of "the journeying atoms." In Emerson's source reading or in his own essays and poems this movement is hit off in terms like polarity, attraction and repulsion, sympathy and antipathy, "eternal procession" (as we have just noted in "Circles") and "eterne alternation," in the following lines in "The Sphinx":

> Eterne alternation
>   Now follows, now flies;
> And under pain, pleasure,—
>   Under pleasure, pain lies.

These terms variously indicate the profound impression made upon Emerson by the dictum of Heraclitus that "le mouvement est la vie, et le repos est la mort,"[5] a dictum to which, in his practice, Emerson gave a peculiarly modern intensity, a dynamic quality, as a result of his reading in Schelling and Oken. Hence, the urgent, pulsating movement in "Woodnotes II" when at the climax man enters into the fullness of creative life in mystical union with the divine. Hence, also, at the opposite extreme, the identification, in "Hamatreya," between the land, "the sitfast acres," and the owner, "a lump of mould the more," in the eternal repose of death. In the elective affinities that dominate life one may have consciousness at the intensest pitch or extinction; and sympathy is the indicator of one's cosmic preferences.

III

For a sense of the pervasiveness of the doctrine of sympathy—Emerson's idealistic vision, it will be serviceable to preface the treatment of "Woodnotes I" with a look at a cluster of short poems, some well known, some not, all written from 1834 to about 1841.

Since man has fallen, the perception of harmony or of the ideal structure of the universe may come only in favorable moments of insight, aesthetic encounters that reveal a purposive cosmic order—in short, epiphanies. Elsewhere, in another connection, I have dealt with "The Rhodora," and I shall, therefore, merely note once again the teleological argument derived from Cudworth in the passage, "if eyes were made for seeing." Eyes are for beauty, so runs the argument; and the purposive order makes for a necessary attraction between man and flora: "The self-same Power that brought me there brought you."[6] Universal sympathy springs from the very constitution of the world man inhabits; and, as we shall see, this note of sympathy was to sound again in "Woodnotes I."

If "The Rhodora," in affirming metaphysical order, mounts to a sympathetic union, "Each and All" rises to a clairvoyant submission to the aesthetic order through a series of renunciations—birds, shells, and maid, which, divorced from their background, are symbols of a partial, individual beauty selfishly clutched at. Man must resist his selfish impulses so as to leave the harmony of nature undisturbed. "Beauty is unripe childhood's cheat," says Emerson, and he will "leave it behind with the games of youth" as he rises above such limited aesthetics. There follows a clairvoyant vision in which he is assimilated into the landscape:

> Beauty through my senses stole;
> I yielded myself to the perfect whole.

The conscious manipulation of the word "beauty" on two levels is as neat an instance of Emersonian Platonizing as one could ask for. When man rejects beauty at a lower level his reward is that he may have it at a higher level; and thus, Platonically, a higher insight extinguishes a lower one. But apart from this, what gives "Each and All" its grateful and graceful sense of an accomplished process is the fulfillment of an entirely satisfying sympathy between man and nature.

This assimilation of the creature attains its height in "The Humble-Bee," in which the bee is the symbol for man's happy, unreflecting epicureanism:

> Seeing only what is fair,
> Sipping only what is sweet.

At the close Emerson reverses the moralism of Aesopian fable by having the bee survive in hibernation "the fierce northwestern blast." But the gayety of the poem and the triumph of the bee are firmly supported by the purposive order and harmony of the universe that takes care of such a creature. Once again, in "Berrying," a delightful little poem that should be better known, Emerson enjoys the same sympathetic epicurean encounter when, as he is "strolling through the pastures," "feeding on the Ethiops sweet," he muses on his good fortune:

> I said, "What influence me preferred,
> Elect, to dreams thus beautiful?"
> The vines replied, "And didst thou deem
> No wisdom from our berries went?"

As we have already noted, there is evidently a power that "elects" those who are ready for these beautiful moments. But Emerson's use of the word "elect" is another and breath-taking instance of his bold wit—his detaching the word from its Calvinistic theological associations and applying it to an aesthetics of natural hedonism.

Admittedly, the hedonism is never far removed from ethics, since it is implicit, as an element of beauty, in the structure of the cosmos. All things are inextricably and Platonically good, true, and beautiful, as we may observe in another short and undeservedly neglected poem, "Forbearance," which we shall interpret both in the light of the preceding exposition of the doctrine of sympathy and also in the light of its Platonic structure. The poem follows:

> Hast thou named all the birds without a gun?
> Loved the wood-rose, and left it on its stalk?
> At rich men's tables eaten bread and pulse?
> Unarmed, faced danger with a heart of trust?
> And loved so well a high behavior,
> In man or maid, that thou from speech refrained,
> Nobility more nobly to repay?
> O, be my friend, and teach me to be thine!

If the long "Woodnotes," printed in *The Dial* in two installments, October 1840 and October 1841, is the culmination of Emerson's use of the doctrine in an expanding and rising succession of ecstatic affirmations, the short "Forbearance," printed in *The Dial* for January 1842, is, at the other extreme, the hard-packed statement in eight lines. The expansiveness of Romantics like Emerson and Whitman became a metaphysical and psychological necessity, for the unfolding vision must, in the creative act, recapitulate the processes of an unfolding universe; at the same time they were capable of recording their vision in sharp, bold strokes, in sparse form, to suggest the thematic germ.

The poem introduces us to Emerson's Platonic world in an ascension from the level of phenomenal nature (ll. 1–2) to that of man or human society (ll. 3–4) and thence to spiritual friendship and the divine (ll. 5–8). The poem does not, however, readily yield its meaning, for at each level the meaning is not stated but implied, if that; and hence for a clear perception of the ideas we must go to less occult poems and to Emerson's source reading. The first two lines hit off the encounter with nature that in "Each and All" leaves the harmony of the universe undisturbed. Man must go to nature neither aggressively, gun in hand, nor with a partial aesthetics that would despoil the cosmos. Lines 3–4 reject the materialism of society and the cowardice of the individual at variance with nature. The phrase "a heart of trust" reflects Emerson's Platonic, Stoic, and Romantic idealism in the dependence on the metaphysical framework, the divine ideal, the purposiveness of the universe, as we have already noted it in "The Rhodora."

If explicit statement of doctrine is withheld at each level, the omission is most perplexing in the second half of the poem; a reader might work out the ideas for the first half by referring to other poems, as we have just done, but for lines 5–8 one must, for clarity's sake, revert to a source in Plutarch and Cudworth and to a parallel passage in "Celestial Love," which itself, however, cannot be understood without the source. The argument in "Forbearance" is that the recognition of high and noble behavior provides a bond of sympathy among human beings at the highest level, where silence is the only adequate acknowledgment. But the expression is so cryptic that no reader could be expected to realize that silence ("that thou from speech refrained") is the key to the engrossing idea—viz., that silence is a symbol of the divine. The more elaborate passage in "Celestial Love" is possibly more understandable from the title but even so it too will benefit from source elucidation:

> Plain and cold is their address,
> Power have they for tenderness;
> And, so thoroughly is known
> Each other's counsel by his own,
> They can parley without meeting;
> Need is none of forms of greeting;
> They can well communicate
> In their innermost estate;
> When each the other shall avoid,
> Shall each by each be most enjoyed.

The silence in both poems comes directly out of Plutarch's "Of Isis and Osiris" and possibly Cudworth's summary as well, since Emerson knew both. Here I shall reproduce the argument from Plutarch. In speaking of the arcane lore of the Egyptians, Plutarch said that they worshipped the crocodile because it had no tongue and that it was, therefore, a symbol of the divine, "For the *Divine Discourse* hath no need of Voice."

For the same reason the young god Harpocrats (Horus, the sun-god, child of Osiris) is represented with "his finger upon his Mouth, as a Symbol of talking little and keeping Silence."[7] In the light of this source both passages in "Forbearance" and "Celestial Love" may be seen as referring to the silence man will observe when his behavior or development has reached up to the divine.

The second half of the poem grows directly out of the first half in the admonition of high behavior in all circumstances. Thus the Stoic title "Forbearance" is appropriate, since the Stoic philosophy emphasizes the organic relation of the parts of the cosmos to the whole in a scheme in which all things work together for good according to the divine ideal. There is, furthermore, an organic relation imparted by the single personality at all levels, exploring a "thousand natures," in the phrase of "The Sphinx," to achieve self-awareness.

It is apparent that "Forbearance" is a cryptic condensation, a kind of poetic shorthand, that only Emerson himself or some initiate would understand, for ideas exhibited at large in "Each and All," "The Rhodora," and "Celestial Love." As early as 1835 Emerson impatiently asked, "Why must always the philosopher mince his words & fatigue us with explanation? . . . Fable avoids the difficulty, is at once exoteric & esoteric, & is clapped by both sides. Plato & Jesus used it. And History is such a fable." In 1845, commenting on Chambers' *Vestiges of Creation*, he boldy observed, "These things which the author so well collates ought to be known only to few, and those, masters and poets." In the journal *NO* for 1855 he spoke of "esoteric metaphysics" and "that oblivion which accompanies any mind raised above the comprehension of his contemporaries (for he speaks as a man among oxen)." Such journal entries punctuating an entire career might seem excessive background commentary for eight lines; but "Forbearance" incorporates an occult habit that is a powerful motivation in Emerson, very like that in Yeats, and the creative result is a ritual of initiation into cosmic mysteries. It follows that sympathies are occult. We are at the threshold of "Woodnotes."

IV

In "The Rhodora" and "Berrying" Emerson employed symbolical experience and philosophical statement as vehicle for the elective affinities between man and nature; but "Woodnotes" contains an even more striking portrayal of the occult moment as the "forest seer" explores:

> It seemed that Nature could not raise
> A plant in any secret place,
>
> . . . .
>
> But he would come in the very hour
> It opened in its virgin bower,

>   As if a sunbeam showed the place,
>   And tell its long-descended race.

In "Woodnotes I" this moment, which on the smaller scale of "The Rhodora" constitutes the entire poem, is fitted into an elaborate setting as one of several significant points of illumination. True to his Platonic and Romantic heritage, Emerson regarded "bare lists of words," symbols, and symbolic moments as poems in themselves and as the germinal source of poetic activity. The sunbeam passage is by itself a poem or represents poetic activity that may be expanded in the fructifying light of the imagination. We must, therefore, explore the relation of this passage on sympathy to others and to the poetic continuum of "Woodnotes" if we are to arrive at a just notion of the fullness and depth of Emerson's treatment of the doctrine under discussion.

"Woodnotes," which has two complementary parts, confronts the reader in Part I with immediate, personal, and physical experiences in phenomenal nature, the *natura naturata* which, as Emerson said in his essay "Nature," is passive, lending itself to the spiritual cognitive insight of the beholder. Part II deals with the *natura naturans*, the "Efficient Nature," as Emerson put it in the same essay, "the quick cause before which all forms flee as the driven snows." In Part II, therefore, Emerson declares lofty doctrines of the organic unfolding of nature, its universality and harmony. The two parts are thematically and symbolically linked. The pine tree is the archetypal symbol for man's sympathetic cognition of nature, and the service the pine tree renders the active, penetrating mind is disclosed in the quatrain that stands as epigraph to Part II:

>   As sunbeams stream through liberal space
>   And nothing jostle or displace,
>   So waved the pine-tree through my thought
>   And fanned the dreams it never brought.

The dream, the intuitive capacity, this belongs to man, and it must somehow link up with the spiritual reality of Nature concealed and revealed by natural objects. The pine tree makes this metaphysical connection and at the same time effectually secures the unity of the poem.

The unity is further helped by parallel statements toward the close of each Part on man's identity with nature. In Part I man's relation is chiefly with *natura naturata*, the passive nature, physical objects that serve man's spiritual quest "by secret sympathy." But at the close of Part I when the identity is sealed in man's death it is *natura naturans* that provides for the burial in "her greenest field."

In Part II there is a similar identity, on a mystical level, between man and *natura naturans*, as the eternal Pan, the Traveller that "halteth never in one shape," saturates and permeates phenomenal nature and man's inquiring spirit with its own divinity. In both Parts, then, and on both levels of insight, there is a union of man and Nature, and the sympathy that drew the "forest seer" to the plant in its "secret place" grows throughout the poem until it is taken up to a high and rarefied plane of the abstract where it is transmuted into Platonic universals. As one masters this rich and complex poem one begins to understand that the doctrine of sympathy is at the heart of the ramifying whole. Sympathy is the synergistic and creative process by which man, ranging through the cosmos, perceives and identifies himself with the inhering harmony. Midway through Part II Emerson portrays this harmony as a kind of rhyme embracing all time and space—the entire creation:

> For Nature beats in perfect tune,
> And rounds with rhyme her every rune.

Man has fallen away from this harmony (the theme of "The Sphinx") and is, therefore, "unrhymed"; to understand "the fatal song" of harmony he must "leave [his] peacock wit behind" and enter upon an initiation into the secret places of nature.

No one aware of his poetic effort from 1834 onward can fail to realize that Emerson intended that Part I, though doctrinally inferior to Part II, should be his richest and most elaborate statement of the initiation into nature. The successive masks of personae throughout the four sections—the poet, forest seer, and peasant—are primary symbolic figures to show man's ever profounder involvement, for the first of them, the poet, has just abandoned society, and "the musing peasant, lowly great," the culminating figure, represents man under the unceasing sway of nature.

The poet, "Caesar of his leafy Rome," in Section I, leaves society to enter the harmonious setting of "woodland walks," and he approaches nature without fishing rod, gun, or scythe, which are emblems of hostility or commodity. He displays a receptive, childlike submission that prepares him for the initiation. Enchantment, knowledge, pondering, love, and wonder are, as we shall observe, names for closely allied stages of insight—or better, a flowing progression toward the secrets of nature. According to the usages of Romantic psychology, the initiation begins with a mood, a feeling. Emerson says, "Sure some god his eye enchants," and this state, altered, one must suppose, from the poet's condition in society, endures to the end of Part I, embracing all succeeding stages in the flowing progression. The immediate consequence of enchantment is that the poet "knows," but his knowledge, which "seems fantastic to the rest," is Romantic intuitive affirmation, at the opposite pole from Lockean empiricism. Emerson swiftly offers the word "pondering" as an equivalent of "knowledge," and the poet ponders not only a random selection from the phenomenal world—shadows, colors, clouds, grass-buds, caterpillar-shrouds, and the like—but also, in the same mood of enchantment, the compositional order of the universe:

> Why Nature loves the number five,
> And why the star-form she repeats.

The culmination of enchantment, knowledge, and pondering is the vitalistic concept of love embracing the cosmos, for the poet is "Lover of all things alive"; but love is, in turn, the preparation of a new and higher level of insight, for "knowledge" is now succeeded by a sense of wonder in a realm of mysteries. If, in Fichtean terms, Nature or the Not-Me is readily penetrated by man's intuition, the Me or personality is an inscrutable enigma:

> Wonderer at all he meets,
> Wonderer chiefly at himself,
> Who can tell him what he is?
> Or how meet in human elf
> Coming and past eternities?

The last two lines remind us of the phrase "clothed eternity" in "The Sphinx"; and the entire passage, suggesting the mysteriously dual nature of man, comes right out of Carlyle's "Signs of the Times" and *Sartor Resartus* and anticipates similar passages in Whitman's "Song of Myself." The intimation is that the poet goes to nature to discover his identity, which, as the poem develops, is co-extensive with the universe, a concept rendered in prose early in 1839 at about the time Emerson was working on "Woodnotes I"; and the reader will recall the journal entry quoted at the head of this paper. Finally, in its portrayal of an enchanted transformation and enlargement of insight the first section of Part I merits close comparison with the famous Section 5 of "Song of Myself," in which a like mystical rapture alters Whitman's comprehension.

In Section 2 the forest seer takes us into the secret hiding-places of nature, and the note of wonder, on which Section I closed, receives its fulfillment here in the sunbeam passage, quoted earlier, on the intuitive rapport between the forest seer and nature. But this moment of sympathy must not be taken out of context; it is a highly charged and dramatic symbol for a secret world that is disclosed progressively throughout Section 2 on increasingly higher levels, from phenomenal nature to the seer's own insight and finally up to Nature, the inhering principle of all creation.

Emerson, wishes to convey a sense of the magical quality of this secret world and also to characterize the initiation of the forest seer, and he accomplishes his double purpose by employing the key expression, or variants of it. "It seemed as if." Thus the seer's discoveries partake of magic, "As if a sunbeam showed the place," and

> It seemed as if the breezes brought him,
> It seemed as if the sparrows taught him.

Phenomenal nature, *natura naturata*, instinctively responds to the spiritual purposes of the forest seer and willingly serves him in a manifestation of magical sympathy.

On a higher level the forest seer has another aid, his own "secret sight" that permits him to know "Where, in far fields, the orchis grew." The culmination is reached in the second half of the section when Nature, the great inhering principle, *natura naturans*, yields all to this "lover true," so that he is inducted into the most sensitive intimacy and knowledge, for all things "at his bidding seemed to come." His penetration into the innermost recesses of nature is perfectly stated in the line, "And the shy hawk did wait for him." Most people are, by contrast, shut out from this secret world, and they cannot see these magical operations though they stand in the very midst of nature and though they have "wishful eyes." They can only hear "at a distance" and "guess."

Section 3 develops contrasting attitudes toward nature familiar to the reader from the first two sections, but here for the first time clearly set forth in an Aristotelian distinction of the mean, the excess, and the defect. In the wildest nature of "unploughed Maine" the "lumberers' gang" represents the materialistic and destructive purposes of man as "the aged pine-tree falls" under the ax, and the lumberers are to be regarded, therefore, as the savage excess. The defect is represented by those whose spiritual shortcomings are exposed by the contact with primeval nature, for they are timid and fearful. In the three sections Emerson noticeably sharpens his portrayal of the defective attitude toward nature as it emerges in much the same type of personality. In Section I, as we have seen, such people regard the poet's "knowledge" as "fantastic," for they are quite certain of the common-sense Lockean world they inhabit; but in Section 2 they are shut out from nature's secrets even though they might wish to know; and now in Section 3, confronted by the wild, they are utterly lost. The forest seer is, of course, the golden mean, for he roams "content alike with man and beast."[8] Throughout the three sections the sympathetic relation to nature receives ever stronger affirmation as we observe, first, the poet's sense of wonder, then the forest seer's rapport with phenomenal nature, and finally, the response of man to God in the closing couplet of Section 3:

> Where his clear spirit leads him, there's his road
> By God's own light illumined and foreshowed.

Section 4 presents the culminating figure of "the musing peasant, lowly great," sitting on his throne of "pine-roots crosswise grown," and in this manner, as the initiation ends with the acknowledgment that the human being is "the heart of all the scene," Emerson makes his own contribution to the Romantic hagiography of the peasant. In Section 2 the forest seer had "secret sight," and though Nature yielded all to him, he is nonetheless portrayed as vigorously penetrating nature's most secret life.

In Section 4 this pursuit is reversed, and as the peasant occupies his throne, hill and cloud are said to know him "by secret sympathy" as "the public child of earth and sky." The note of sympathy is sounded not only in the "likeness" between the peasant and hill and cloud, but also in the aid that the water-courses offer him as he makes his way from "thick-stemmed woodlands" downward to the "ocean sand." The affirmative moral is Wordsworthian:

> For Nature ever faithful is
> To such as trust her faithfulness.

Once again we have sympathy or like-to-like, and in the entire passage delineating the peasant's trust we have a sharp contrast with the lack of trust of the altogether different type that we have noted.

The effect of the water imagery is to suggest the liberation of man's spirit, and therefore the concluding passage on death comes appropriately hard upon the suggestions contained in the imagery of the ocean. Death is the liberation of man, for it returns him to nature, to the elements from which he sprang; hence, in another metaphor, Nature will yield, like a mother, "A pillow in her greenest field" for the "departed lover" of all nature.

The discourse of Part I is largely set in terms of *natura naturata*, the world of physical objects that, in Wordsworthian fashion, endear themselves to us for their own sake as well as for the spiritual meaning they convey. This initiation prepares us for the Plotinian ecstasy in the conclusion of Part II, where sympathetic attraction toward the divine is fulfilled as man reaches perfect enlightenment. The eternal Pan, expressing his creative urge in "a divine improvisation" and moving swiftly from shape to shape, cannot be contained. The god intoxicates:

> He is free and libertine,
> Pouring of his power the wine
> To every age, to every race;
> . . . .
> As he giveth to all to drink,
> Thus or thus they are and think.

The metamorphosis of life is, therefore, a spiritual inebriation. The tone of rhapsodic abandonment here at the close of Part II has been prepared for by the mood of enchantment at the start of I, where, speaking of the poet, Emerson says, "Sure some god his eye enchants." The poet's sense of wonder ("chiefly at himself") and his inquiring spirit are now brought home to a cosmic terminus in identity with the divine:

> Thou askest in fountains and in fires,
> He is the essence that inquires.

When the sphinx told the poet that he was "the unanswered question" and encouraged him to take his "quest through nature," the poet, though escaping time, did not achieve the mystical union with the divine; but "The Sphinx" prepares us for that consummation in "Woodnotes."

V

In the Emersonian scheme the insight that pierces through appearances to the spiritual reality and finally achieves union with the divine has many avatars. In "Woodnotes" the poet, forest seer, and peasant represent three related levels. With the "peasant, lowly great," this insight is an unreflecting and spontaneous awareness of man's place in the cosmos; with the forest seer it is practically an instinct directed toward an occult sympathy with phenomenal nature; and with the poet it is a mystical apprehension of "conscious Law." In other poems and journal entries, Osman, Saadi, Merlin, and Uriel represent significant aspects of the poetic experience—Osman, the assimilation to nature after rejection by society; Saadi, poetic cheerfulness in withdrawal from society; Merlin, the poetic magic of the universe; and Uriel, poetic insight and rebellion. The connection among all those Platonic expressions of ascending levels is man's sympathetic closeness to Nature.

In recreating the mythical world of Platonism and Neo-Platonism, Emerson contrasted the spiritual man ("God's darling," as he called the type in "Experience") with the materialist, who mastered Nature's physical secrets and hence achieved a corresponding power. In "Experience" Emerson acknowledged a Nature that came "eating and drinking and sinning," and he also acknowledged the sympathy between this Nature and a like humanity: "Her darlings, the great, the strong, the beautiful, are not children of our law; do not come out of the Sunday School, nor weigh their food, nor punctually keep the commandments." In spite of its aggressive power this type is nonetheless for Emerson an example of Fate or limitation hinted at in the midst of the rhapsody we have just examined:

> As he [Pan] giveth to all to drink,
> Thus or thus they are and think.

This limitation confines man to circumscribed and ultimately degrading sympathies, and if in the ascending order, the avatars we have named reveal more and more spiritual insight, then Guy, in the poem bearing that name, Webster, in "Ode to W. H. Channing," and the Yankee landlord, in "Hamatreya," show in descending order a limitation that ends not only in physical death but also in spiritual death and extinction.

"Guy" is a shrewd and witty portrait of one of Nature's "darlings" who has "caught Nature in his snares" for his own materialistic gain. Emerson always had a realistic respect for the entrepreneurs of life who, as he said in

"Experience," know that "power keeps quite another road than the turn-pikes of choice and will; namely the subterranean and invisible tunnels and channels of life." Both on the spiritual and physical levels there is a secret in mastering life, and in "Guy" Emerson gave the appearance of celebrating the materialistic exploiter of that secret; but under the surface there is an ironic rejection, as we shall see, in the very terms of approval.

The poem is nearly divided into two almost equal parts by the couplet,

> It seemed his Genius discreet
> Worked on the Maker's own receipt.

The first part deals with the qualities and capacities of the man as he came from his Maker's hand:

> Mortal mixed of middle clay,
> Attempered to the night and day.

On the Neo-Platonic scale man is midway between the divine and the lower forms of existence, and Guy is intended to exemplify the midpoint. But Guy is more than average humanity, for he has intimations of cosmic sympathy and power:

> Guy possessed the talisman
> That all things from him began
>
> . . . .
>
> In strange junctures, felt with awe,
> His own symmetry with law.

In his intuition that he is the source of all things, he requires "no amulets nor rings," merely artificial aids, for his lucky charm-piece is his cosmic self-confidence.

Guy is in sympathetic rapport with the magic inherent in the very constitution of life, and he is magically assisted by Nature to master circumstance in several ways: first, in his own defensive invulnerability; secondly, in his possession of occult power in attack; third, in his exploitive successes with a readily obedient nature. In the first instance, no element of the universe, like the iron in a sword, will harm Guy, but rather will heal, on the principle of homeopathic sympathy:

> Aimed at him, the blushing blade
> Healed as fast the wounds it made.

Again, physical and magical Nature equips its "darling" with the formidable powers of the "evil eye":

> If on the foeman fell his gaze,
> Him it would straightway blind or craze.

Finally, with such magical powers, Guy could not possibly fail in turning all nature to his advantage, as even disasters unaccountably helped him:

> There was no frost but welcome came,
> Nor freshet, nor midsummer flame.

Perhaps the wittiest couplet celebrating Guy's exploitive genius is this in which nature vainly attempts to escape "his snares":

> Stream could not so perversely wind
> But corn of Guy's was there to grind.

The poem ends on a note highly satisfactory to Guy:

> Belonged to wind and world the toil
> And venture, and to Guy the oil.

Of course, the poem must be seen in the framework of Emerson's evocation of a living universe that responds, "like-to-like," at whatever level man wishes. Guy's level is that of materialistic gain, physical power, and occult magic. There are unmistakable suggestions that the level on which Guy operates is a low one and that he is a cosmic dupe. If he is "interchangeable with things" then he is essentially and ultimately only a thing himself. If he works "on the Maker's own receipt," Emerson is hinting at limitation, not universality, for the Maker or artificer of the universe, the Platonic demi-urge, is only the second or third hypostasis of the divine trinity; and hence Guy's insight into magical power, though a true insight, is nonetheless on an inferior level.

The title "Guy" suggests a further irony, for although Guy appears to have his way, there is a sting in the portrayal deriving from the definition of the word "guy"—a person who is "guyed" or made a butt for ridicule; in this instance Emerson's wit lies in deftly undercutting the praise while heaping it on. It would appear that in this abstract portrait Emerson is not invoking moral censure but inviting enjoyment of the way in which both Guy and Nature have over-reached themselves.

The "Ode to W. H. Channing" is, on the other hand, specific, and the portrait of Daniel Webster in it is not intended for witty enjoyment but for moral censure and contempt. Like Guy, Webster is one of Nature's "darlings," but in Emerson's view his failure to assume leadership of the anti-slavery interests—indeed, his appeasement of the South—shows the tragic defects of the materialistic type he exemplifies.

Elsewhere I have dealt with Emerson's study throughout his journals of Webster as a supreme embodiment of the extroverted, power-seeking, daemonic type. For my purposes here of delineating Webster as the symbolic center of a national obsession with things, I shall omit both the entire background of Emerson's interest in Webster during more than two decades and also the comprehensive explication of the "Ode."[9] I wish to concentrate on the portrayal of Webster as an instance of the fatal attraction of things.

Emerson concedes the importance of the materialistic side of life in stanza nine, where he catalogues the national preoccupation with industry, commerce, transportation, agriculture, and settling the frontier; but he fears that in excess they "unking" the man. Hence the famous pronouncement of the "two laws discrete"—"law for man and law for thing"; and Emerson's unmistakable intention is to suggest restraints that must be imposed upon the realm of "things." Emerson sees slavery as a manifestation of the materialistic side of life, and in the portion of the poem concentrating on Webster's appeasement of the South, we do, indeed, observe how a man may be "unkinged."

Emerson starts with a rhetorical question and moral censure that reflect his contempt for the "statesman's rant," as he put it in stanza one. Emerson has in mind Webster's speech on June 17, 1843, at the dedication of the Bunker Hill monument. Webster had complacently contrasted the freedom-loving Anglo-Saxon in North America, improving life by commerce, the practical arts, and knowledge, with the oppressive, power-seeking Spaniard in Latin America. Stanza three is a rebuke aimed directly at his grandiloquent patriotism:

> But who is he that prates
> Of the culture of mankind,
> Of better arts and life?
> Go, blindworm, go,
> Behold the famous States
> Harrying Mexico
> With rifle and with knife!

There is rapport between Guy and Nature, but a measure of Emerson's altered purpose in the "Ode" is the alienation between Webster and Nature, deftly suggested in imagery contrasting great and small:

> The God who made New Hampshire
> Taunted the lofty land
> With little men;
> Small bat and wren
> House in the oak.

The dominant imagery, however, is reptilian, first presented on the miniature scale in "blindworm" and subsequently enlarged in a dramatization of Emerson's outrage with a repulsive national dilemma for which Webster stands in his consciousness as the central symbolic figure. In his oration, with President Tyler on the platform, Webster made flattering references to Virginia; and neither in his journal entries nor in the "Ode" did this kind of thing sit well on Emerson. The South did not respect Webster's appeasement, nor that of any other Northern politician, but held it in contempt as a sign of weakness. This is the simple, unambiguous prose that undergirds that staccato imagery in which, omitting all prose, Emerson expressed his anger against Webster:

> If earth-fire cleave
> The upheaved land, and bury the folk,
> The southern crocodile would grieve.

Stanzas six and seven are the climax of Emerson's censure and of the imagery in which he couches it. Not only the South, but the North also is involved in the dilemma:

> Boston Bay and Bunker Hill
> Would serve things still;
> Things are of the snake.

The culminating image follows rapidly:

> Things are in the saddle,
> And ride mankind.

In folk superstition the hag rides the human being as though he were but a horse; and Emerson conveys his sense of the quality of the dilemma by figuratively comparing it to a nightmare. But in the context of his imagery he makes us think of the snake rather than the hag and thus heightens the repulsive. In this manner Emerson includes the great statesman and the entire nation in his indictment and portrayal of the "thing" *malaise* in man, the result of sympathies gone mad. There remains something more to say about the doctrine of sympathy in the "Ode," but since it involves the figure of the poet, who also appears in "Hamatreya," it will be best to postpone the matter for the discussion of that poem.

The final exhibit on the scale downward to extinction is "Hamatreya." This poem is Emerson's most sharply accentuated commentary on the physical sympathies between man and nature, and the moment of horrified insight that it provides effectively annihilates the easy victories of Guy. The picture of the Yankee farmland is bathed in a sinister atmosphere of Hindu illusion.[10] There are three speakers, two of them paired in the fatal connection of like-to-like. The first of the pair is the Yankee landlord, materialistic and earth-bound, and the second is Earth, a sub-divinity—darkly primitive and universal. There is an astringent contrast between the blind ignorance of the landlord, unaware of ancient wisdom, and the freshly gained insight of the poet, who, as the third speaker, narrates the experience.

The poem is constructed in a pattern of ironies. When the landlord says that his property knows him, as does his dog, and adds, "we sympathize," he is, in his unwitting boast, preparing for the inexorable truth of the doctrine of like-to-like, for in the sequel death "adds him to his land, a lump of mould the more." Irony extends to the contrast between the flowing blank verse of the landlord's monologue and the cramped runic verse of the Earth-Song as well as the short verses of poetic insight at the close. It also includes the punning statement that the landlords can "steer the plough, but cannot steer their feet/Clear of the grave," in which the abrupt second line deserves comment, for after the expansive boasts and desires, this line imaginatively projects the width of a coffin and offers its own grim commentary on fatal sympathies. Irony is implicit in a pattern of verbal paradoxes: since the "hot owner sees not Death," the poet, in his moral reflection, says, "My avarice cooled/Like lust in the chill of the grave"; and the moment of insight ends without typical Emersonian affirmations.

In both the "Ode" and "Hamatreya" Emerson makes the figure of the poet the middle term between polar opposites—in the "Ode" Webster and Channing, in "Hamatreya" the landlord and Earth. The poet offers a vantage point shared by the reader, who, in an act of what Emerson would have called "creative reading," must help in the process of completing the poem. The "Ode," which mentions the Muse at the beginning, comes full circle with the Muse at the end. In stanza two the Muse is identified with the poet in his study, and in the final stanza with the people in their struggle for liberty. Emerson has dismissed the "priest's cant" and "statesman's rant" as "trick," and in the circular movement of the poem the argument becomes established that the same Muse inspires the poet and the people and binds them in a universal sympathy of true feeling that stands in sharp contrast to the sympathy that Webster has for "things."

In "Hamatreya" there is a similar circular return. The poet's insight at the end, offered in the image of the grave, directs the reader to the list of landlords in the first line: "Bulkeley, Hunt, Willard, Hosmer, Meriam, Flint." When the poem has been completed in an act of "creative reading," these names are, indeed, a roll-call of the dead, and no reader will overlook Emerson's ironic gesture in placing the name of his own ancestor at the head.

In both the "Ode" and "Hamatreya" the poet has a complex vision that balances conflicting polar opposites. He is the interpreter and reconciler for both man and nature, and this essential harmony, as we are now aware, is the subject not only of Emerson's most significant poems but also of highly imaginative prose in the journals like the entry of 1839 quoted at the head of this paper.

When we relate the poems on man's lower sympathies to "Woodnotes" we observe that in the figure of the poet Emerson is leading us to the affirmations in "Woodnotes." If this is a victory for the spirit, it is not an easy optimism, not a flabby acquiescence, but a hard-won struggle in time and space. On this score "Hamatreya" offers the last word, because death is definitive, a terminus. Understanding Emerson's total vision in terms of sympathy, we are now able to see that the optimism is essentially an affirmation of a living universe; and the mystical rapport, in this scheme, is the highest expression of consciousness, the intensest degree of life. It is this consciousness, elicited by the full range of man's affinities and sympathies, that became the Romantic *donnée* to subsequent schools of writers. It is this enlargement of sensitivity that has shaped our literature of a hundred years and more; and in this continuum Emerson, no less than Goethe, Wordsworth, and Carlyle, played a formative role.

Notes

1. In the present paper I am not interested in tracing the far ranging source reading that forms the background for Emerson's *sympathy*. The list of names in such a study would, for example, include, among others, Heraclitus, Plato, Plotinus, Cudworth, Swedenborg, Goethe, Gérando, and Coleridge. My sole aim is to disclose and interpret the function of the term and the doctrine in a number of Emerson's poems, though not all. I may observe in passing, however, that for each writer one must seek the source of an idea in his reading as well as in the general intellectual influences of his own and the preceding age. Thus the provenience of *sympathy* for Emerson is radically different than that established for Hawthorne in Roy Male's excellent article, "Hawthorne and the Concept of Sympathy," *PMLA*, 68 (March 1953): 138–149. Emersonian *sympathy* was in large part, if not exclusively, metaphysical and thus escaped the sentimentalism of the ethical social principle as found in eighteenth-century works on "the handkerchiefly feeling."

2. *The Journals and Miscellaneous Notebook of Ralph Waldo Emerson*, ed. William H. Gilman et al. (Cambridge: Harvard University Press, 1960–), IV, 199–200. All journal entries up to 1838 are taken from this edition.

3. *Journals of Ralph Waldo Emerson*, ed. Edward Waldo Emerson and Waldo Emerson Forbes, 10 vols. (Boston: Houghton Mifflin, 1909–1914), V, 179. All journal entries beyond 1838 are from this edition. For the poetry and essays I have used the standard Centenary Edition, *The Complete Works of Ralph Waldo Emerson*, ed. Edward Waldo Emerson, 12 vols. (Boston: Houghton, Mifflin, 1903–1904). Quotations from Emerson will no longer be annotated.

4. Joseph Marie, Baron de Gérando, *Histoire Comparée Des Systèmes De Philosophie*, 4 vols. (Paris, 1822–1823), I, 482–485. My reference is to the discussion of Heraclitus, which Emerson marked in his own copy of this edition. See also Ralph Cudworth, *The True Intellectual System of the Universe*, 4 vols. (London, 1820), I, 468; II, 268–269. Emerson owned this edition of the work by the seventeenth-century Cambridge Platonist.

5. Gérando, *Histoire*, I, 485.

6. See my article, "The Year of Emerson's Poetic Maturity: 1834," *Philological Quarterly*, 34 (October 1955): 363–364.

7. Plutarch, *Morals. Translated from the Greek by Several Hands*, 5 vols. (London, 1718), IV, 138, 131. Emerson owned this edition.

8. Thoreau may have been the original of the "forest seer," but such biographical background is not relevant to this study.

9. See my article, "Emerson's 'Unwilling Senator': The Background and Meaning of the 'Ode Inscribed to W. H. Channing,' " *Emerson Society Quarterly*, no. 42 (1st Quarter 1966): supplement, 4–14.

10. For a discussion of the relation of "Hamatreya" to its source in the *Vishnu Purana* see Arthur Christy, *The Orient in American Transcendentalism* (New York: Columbia University Press, 1932), pp. 170–175. For Christy, apparently, "Hamatreya" does not exist as a poem; it "possesses the virtue of being the most intelligible to those uninitiated in Oriental idealism" (p. 175). Christy's view is something other than seeing a Hindu element in the poem dramatically rendered to enhance the entire structure. Incidentally, there is no Hindu source for the word "Hamatreya," nor is it, as Christy suggests (p. 356), a variant for "Maitreya," the name of a character in the *Vishnu Purana*.

Emerson's "Each and All" Concept: A Reexamination

Norman Miller*

Ralph Waldo Emerson, by his own admission, was not a system-builder, at least not in the ordinary sense of the word "system"—a unified and internally consistent set of tenets built upon a basic premise or fact. And it is probably unfair for the twentieth-century American to judge Emerson's eclectic philosophy—born as it was out of such diverse roots as Platonism, Eastern mysticism, and German romanticism—by strictly logical criteria. For Emerson's philosophy, if it is informed by a logic at all, is informed by the logic of the spider web rather than that of the skyscraper; it is circular rather than linear, intuitional rather than syllogistic. Given this nature, it resists penetration and probing. Tear it at one point and the whole construct falls. It is this difficulty which has rendered much Emersonian criticism nebulous and highly metaphorical, and kept its exponents on the defensive.

On the other hand, it seems that only by a process of painful abstraction, however this violates the whole, might one get at the undercurrents at work in Emerson's thought and illuminate the essential nature and implications of his philosophy. It is with this aim in mind that a reinspection of Emerson's "each and all" doctrine is here undertaken. This doctrine, incorporating Emerson's idealism and mysticism alike, seems to explain, and is explained by, his concept of nature in general and his doctrine of correspondence in particular. Striking thus at the center of his philosophy, it furnishes us with a convenient springboard into Emerson's work.

Even a superficial reading of the essays and journal entries relevant to Emerson's concept of "each and all" reveals a serious inconsistency, if not contradiction. The doctrine purports to explain and illuminate the essential relationship between the part and the whole, between the particular and the universal. It seemed Emerson's ardent conviction that a fundamental essence runs through all things, and that the rule of the universe, the law by which all nature is governed, could be found in every particular—the pebble, the drop, the spark—no matter how seemingly incidental. To perceive this common denominator in all things should properly be the ultimate object of each man. At the same time, and paradoxically, he seemed to maintain that the particular, in and of itself, offered little; rather its essence can be realized only in its context.

That Emerson conceived of the particular as a microcosm of the universal is readily documented. In a journal entry dated March 11, 1836, we find:

> All is in Each. Xenophanes complained in his old age that all things hastened back to unity, Identity. . . . Every primal truth is alone an ex-

*Reprinted from *New England Quarterly*, 41 (September 1968), 381–92.

pression of all nature. It is the absolute Ens seen from one side, and any other truths shall only seem altered expressions of this. A leaf is a compend of nature, and nature is a colossal leaf. An animal is a compend of the world, and the world is an enlargement of an animal.[1]

Shortly thereafter, we find Emerson calling a day, an hour, and a moment miniature eternities. (IV, 26) But these two entries betray a curious ambiguity. While the essential thrust of the two passages seems clearly to point to the belief that the particular incorporates the essence, the sense and substance of the whole, the difference being one only of magnitude, each passage is subtly qualified. While maintaining the absolute position that "*every* primal truth *is alone* an expression of all nature" [italics mine], Emerson hedges the point with the qualifying "seen from one side." Similarly, the other passage is followed by the statement: "A child's game *hints* [italics mine] to an intelligent beholder all the attributes of the Supreme Being." (IV, 26) The juxtaposition of strong, positive assertion with subtle qualification seems to suggest that Emerson wants a bit of elbow room.

But in later entries, Emerson takes no such license. In entry dated April 11, 1839, we find:

> . . . I believe in Omnipresence; that is, that the All is in each particle; that entire nature reappears in every leaf and moss. (V, 184)

Still later, we find Emerson asserting that "every thing in nature should represent total nature." (VI, 186) These two entries put the matter beyond doubt. Clearly Emerson thinks of the part, the particle as an embodiment in miniature of the whole, the All.

But there is, as I noted earlier, another side to Emerson—and one which jars with his notion of the part as microcosm of the whole. It finds explicit expression most notably in a journal entry dated October 12, 1838:

> Succession, division, parts, particles—this is the condition, this the tragedy of man. All things cohere and unite. Man studies the parts, strives to tear the part from its connexion, to magnify it, and make it a whole. (V, 83)

Now the difficulty is exposed. If, as Emerson has contended elsewhere, the part is indeed a miniature representation or abbreviation of the whole, if it contains all essential nature within itself, why not study the part? Emerson continues:

> Meantime within him is the soul of the whole . . . the Universal Beauty to which every part and particle is equally related, the eternal one. . . . An ignorant man thinks the divine wisdom is conspicuously shown in some fact or creation: a wise man sees that every fact contains the same. (V, 83–84)

I shall have recourse later to the subtle but significant distinction made between the ignorant man and the wise man in the latter part of this entry. Let it suffice for now to point out that Emerson here seems to imply that the isolated particular cannot offer the kernel of wisdom and insight other aspects of his philosophy suggest it could.

Nor is this the only place that Emerson seems to emphasize the importance of the All in contradistinction to the Each. The poem "Each and All," for instance, is an explicit elaboration of this idea. After stressing the need to recognize men's mutual dependence upon one another, the poem moves through a series of three "cases" in which particulars—a sparrow, sea shells, a virgin—are removed from their proper setting and "brought home." Each loses its charm and beauty when isolated from its natural environment. The observer then rebukes beauty as "unripe childhood's cheat" and distinguishes it from truth. But as he speaks he is consumed by the composition of the total surrounding—flowers, trees, and sky—and he at last yields himself to the "perfect whole."

Emerson may have felt, of course, that a poem had to reach some sort of narrative or dramatic climax that brought its details into focus if it were to satisfy the formal demands of the genre. Or he may be using the poem to record a sudden revelation. Both these positions seem untenable, however, in the light of a series of journal entries, some preceding the composition of the poem by as much as ten years, which approximate, even to the wording, the poem's final form. Indeed, Emerson had been advocating this doctrine for many years, and his ultimate philosophy depended heavily upon it. Another look at the journals will bear out this point.

In an entry dated May 16, 1834, Emerson speaks of a boyhood experience which ultimately became part of the poem. Having taken home a few sea shells, only to find them to be "dry, ugly mussel and snail shells," he concludes that he "learned that composition was more important than the beauty of individual forms to effect." (III, 298) In another such entry, he states that "the movement and forms of all beings in nature, except man, are beautiful from their consonance to the whole" (IV, 101) and that "everything to be appreciated must be seen from the point where its rays converge to a focus." (III, 73) In both of these cases Emerson seems to be arguing for the more comprehensive perspective as an antidote for the study of isolated fragments.

Nor is this view limited to his poetry and journals. In "The American Scholar" address, even while pleading for individuality and self-reliance, he pleads as well for a larger and more social conception of man. Emerson prefaces his major remarks with a reference to an old fable which sees men related to their society as so many fingers are related to the hand, and he berates his contemporaries for being isolated from their fellow-men: "The state of society is one in which the members have suffered amputation from the trunk, and strut about so many walking monsters—a good finger, a neck, a stomach, an elbow, but never a man." He adds shortly thereafter that "there is One Man—present to all particular men only partially and through one faculty; and that you must take the whole society to find the whole man." Admittedly he is talking here about man, not nature, but it is interesting to note the striking similarity between the doctrine here expressed and one that comes, once again, out of a journal entry titled, revealingly, "To Know One you must know All," an entry which seems to indicate Emerson's awareness of the difficulty he had created:

> Nature hates finites and cripples. It is no use to say, because the world is represented in each particle as in a moss or an apple, Come, I will dedicate myself to the study of botany, in one thing; I will explore the dandelions. A dandelion will be my meat and drink, house and home, and through that alone will I achieve nature. It is all in vain, for the way Nature tells her secrets is by exposing one function in one flower, and another function in a different plant. If the spiral vessels are seen in bulbs, the vesicles are seen in others, *stómata* in another, *pila* in another, and *chromules* in a fifth; and to show you all the parts of the one plant, she leads you all around the garden. (V, 191)

It appears that we have now come full circle. That "nature exposes one function in one flower, and another function in a different plant" certainly seems the other side of the coin from "entire nature reappears in every leaf and moss."

On the surface, then, the doctrine appears to embody a contradiction, certainly an inconsistency. Certain immediate responses suggest themselves. First, of course, the matter can be left right there. The thinker who has become identified with one of his own phrases, "Damn Consistency," can be seen as simply practicing what he preaches. Only with great reluctance can one shrug off as merely confused the ideas of a man of Emerson's stature, perhaps only after all other avenues have been closed. Less superficial, but hardly fully satisfying, would be the explanation that the whole must be conceived *before* the part can be fully appreciated or apprehended as an essence—an explanation based on a temporal priority which the whole enjoys over the part. Such an explanation would necessitate the assumption of a finished, unchanging universal order, a concept which, as we shall see later, is manifestly inconsistent with Emerson's thought.

But another line of approach seems to beg attention. The clue to this hypothesis lies in a statement cited earlier that "an ignorant man thinks the divine wisdom is conspicuously shown in some fact or creation: a wise man sees that every fact contains the same." (V, 84) Emerson here clearly implies that he conceives of his "each and all" doctrine as an epistemology as well as a metaphysic. Juxtaposed as it is in context to the discussion of part and whole, the statement associates a fact with a part, and implies that divine wisdom inheres in a common denominator among all facts. The resemblance between the fact-wisdom relationship and the part-whole relationship is too great to ignore. Indeed, if one carries on an examination of Emerson's position regarding facts, he finds the same kind of inconsistency as that pointed out in the first part of this discussion. Wildly disparate positions are again in evidence. At one point in his journals, Emerson says: "Ah, a fact is a great thing; the soul passed into nature." (IV, 473) Elsewhere facts become "the genius of God," (IV, 499) even epiphanies of God. (IV, 488) Yet despite its divine nature, a fact, in order to be useful, must be seen in combination with other facts: "A fact detached is ugly. Replace it in its series of cause and effect, and it is beautiful." (V, 54) An almost identical position is asserted only a short time later: "Any single fact considered by itself confounds, misleads us. Let it lie awhile. It will find its place, by and bye, in God's chain." (V, 79) The curious paradox, then, appears once more. Facts must be received collectively if they are to yield all the wisdom and divine insight that they bear.

But in regard to this latter problem, Emerson furnishes us with ample material for possible resolutions. One such resolution is based upon Emerson's conception of nature as vital, plastic, and ever-changing rather than static and fixed. Note the imagery as well as the substance of an entry dated to 1840:

> Nature ever flows; stands never still. Motion or change is her mode of existence. The poetic eye sees in Man the Brother of the River, and in Woman the Sister of the River. Their life is always transition. Hard blockheads only drive nails all the time; forever remember; which is fixing. Heroes do not fix but flow, bend forward ever and invent a resonance for every moment. (V, 494)

In a similar vein, but even more revealing, is another entry:

> Metamorphosis is the law of the Universe. All forms are fluent, and as the bird alights on the bough and pauses for rest, then plunges into the air again on its way, so the thoughts of God pause but for a moment in any form, but pass into a new form, as if by touching the earth again in burial, to acquire new energy. A wise man is not deceived by the pause: he knows that it is momentary: he already foresees the new departure, and departure after departure, in long series. Dull people think they have traced the matter far enough if they have reached the history of one of these temporary forms, which they describe as fixed and final. (VII, 117)

The passages are interesting for several reasons. First, we can see Emerson insisting upon the dynamic nature of the material world. He couches his statements in images of movement—flight and flow, the bird and the river. Again we find the distinction between the wise man and the dull, the difference again being that the latter stops with a single fact, while the former carries on the probe in series. But by now the rationale for the distinction is clear. Facts are not to be taken in isolation simply because they are but fleeting, temporary manifestations of an eternal spirit. They are, as it were, like so many puddles on a beach which, however varied in size and shape, are nevertheless part and parcel of the waves that produced them and, further, subject to change with each ebb and flow. The wise man is alive to this ever-changing environment; the dull man conceives of his surroundings as static.

Implicit throughout the above passages, too, is a conception of nature as a symbol, a material though dynamic representation of a spiritual world, corresponding to that other, at any moment, part for part.

> The secret of the scholar or intellectual man is that all nature is only the foliage, the flowering and fruit of the soul, and that every part therefore exists as emblem and sign of some fact in the soul. . . . (IV, 281)

Having enlarged our notion of nature, Emerson returns to a discussion of facts and their significance. Facts, though they contain glimpses of the ultimate, are not ultimate themselves. They are merely symbols whose spiritual referents must be perceived. Emerson expresses it this way:

> Let me once go beyond any material fact and see its cause in an affection, an idea, and the fact assumes at once a scientific value. Facts are disagreeable or loathsome to me so long as I have no clue to them; . . . But give me the chain that connects them to the Universal consciousness, and I shall see them to be necessary, and see them to be convenient, and enlarge my charity one circle more and let them in. (IV, 281–282)

The fact, then, that still moment in the spiritual drama, does not so much present truth as circumscribe it. Indeed, the geometric figure suggested in the latter part of the citation, the circle, plays a prominent role throughout the entire canon of Emerson. Facts can be seen as points on the circumference of an all-encompassing circle which emanate from, and within which resides, the universal law, the soul. Facts are man's tools, his only means to truth, however fleeting and fickle. Emerson compares the philosopher to the surveyor who "selects points whence he can look on his subject from different sides, and by means of many proximate results . . . at last obtains an accurate expression of truth." (II, 523) Emerson tells us this much explicitly in a later entry:

> To the wise therefore a fact is true poetry. . . . We think it frivolous to record them [facts], but a wise man records them, and they agree with the experience and feelings of others. They no doubt are points on this curve of this great circle. (IV, 69–70)

The conception of nature is now complete. At the center of all being is a vital universal law which manifests itself in the material world in a dynamic succession of natural forms. Man stands, as it were, on the bridge between the two worlds. (V, 512) He must begin with the fragments, the particulars, the facts of nature which he sees around him. But aware that these forms are not fixed and final, he must make himself sensitive to the slightest fluctuations of nature. He must realize that "a fact is only the fulcrum of the spirit . . . the terminus of a past thought, but only a means now to new sallies of the imagination and new progress of wisdom." (IV, 71) Man must strive to find correspondence between the changing material and spiritual worlds. In short, he must be an analogist.

Emerson, thus, is setting up a dialectical conception of the universe. And man is able to "tune in," so to speak, on the universe by virtue of the peculiarity of his mind which, like the world he strives to understand, is dual, urged as it is by two opposite but complementary tendencies. His essay, "Plato," seems to furnish the clearest statement of this concept.

> The mind is urged to ask for one cause of many effects; then for the cause of that, and again the cause, diving still into the profound; self-assured that it shall arrive at an absolute and sufficient one—a one that shall be all. . . . Urged by an opposite necessity, the mind returns from the one to that which is not one, but other or many; from cause to effect; and affirms the necessary existence of variety, the self-existence of both, as each is involved in the other.

Man, then, as "transparent eyeball," must look both ways, both inside and outside, employing deduction and induction, Understanding and Reason. Even while eulogizing Plato, Emerson makes it clear that he is not the Idealist that Plato was. Emerson insists upon granting the material world a dignity it could not have for Plato. Plato's line of vision was one-directional, from material to spiritual; Emerson's was two-directional, urging a reciprocal relationship between the Ideal and the real. Clearly, Emerson asks for a balance of the two impulses of the mind: "a rapid unification, and an excessive appliance to parts and particulars, are the twin dangers of speculation." Two journal entries amply support this contention. In an entry dated April 4, 1841, Emerson says:

> The balance must be kept—the power to generalize and the power to individualize must co-exist to make a poet: Will and Abandonment, the social and the solitary humour, man and opportunity. (V, 537).

In another entry, he quotes, and apparently grants his assent to, a statement from Goethe:

> Every existing thing is an analogon of all existing things. Thence appears to us Being ever at once sundered and connected. If we follow the analogy too far, all things confound themselves in identity. If we avoid it, then all things scatter into infinity. (IV, 28)

The two worlds, then, are interdependent, and both are real. Man, in his quest for truth, cannot ignore either. Neither his Understanding nor his Reason alone will suffice; he must use all his faculties, for "all successful study is the marriage of thoughts and things: a continual reaction of the thought classifying the facts, and the facts suggesting the thought." (III, 519)

The doctrines of "unity-in-variety" and "each and all," if they are separate doctrines at all, are at least closely related and mutually illuminating. Just how closely they were associated in Emerson's mind is revealed by an entry alluded to in part earlier, an entry which, on close examination, seems now to offer us at least a partial resolution of our original problem:

> A fact, we said, was the terminus of spirit. A man, I, am the remote circumference, the skirt, the thing suburb, or frontier post of God, but go inward and find the ocean; I lost my individuality in its waves. God is unity, but always works in variety. I go inward until I find unity universal, that is before the World was, I come outward to this body, a point of variety.
>
> The drop is a small ocean, the ocean a large drop. A leaf is a simplified world, the world a compound leaf. (IV, 71)

In the light of the now deepened conception of Nature, of man and his mind, of facts and the Universal Idea, God himself, we can attempt to explain the seemingly paradoxical relationship which Emerson advocated between the part and the whole. That "all nature is repeated in every leaf and moss" is true in the sense that every leaf and moss represents, at the moment of its creation, the "terminus of a past thought." It is the cumulative result of the emanation of the spiritual law up to that point in time. It represents a stage in the progression of nature toward perfection in accordance with its informing spirit. But it must not be seen as an end in itself. Rather, it is "only a means now to new sallies of the imagination and new progress of wisdom." What is crucial to man's achievement of wisdom is not merely his perception of the law of the particular itself—the each—but his realization that *all* particulars, all facts, are governed by the same law. Hence, the significance of the more comprehensive view, the perception of the total composition.

Emerson's philosophy, then, is very much like the croquet game in *Alice in Wonderland* in which the rules keep changing and living creatures take the place of mallets, balls, and wickets. And the reader of Emerson who demands a finished, immutable order becomes as confused and frustrated as Alice herself. Emerson's tenets, like those of other philosophers who seek to build systems, do ultimately lead back to a central, fundamental essence. But what distinguishes his philosophy from the others is that this center is not a static assumption or premise. Rather it is a vital dynamic, living essence. And man, in order to achieve wisdom, must be vital and dynamic and living himself. Whatever of truth is accessible to man is within him, his to perceive or to miss. If he persists in seeing fragments and particulars as final truths, he is doomed to eternal myopia. If he sees only generalizations, only unity, he suffers from farsightedness. Both are aberrations. Only by the proper balance of his mental faculties, only by making himself a finely tuned instrument recording facts, generalizing, deducing, can man find that clarity of vision for which God has provided the potential. It is in offering this vital conception of man and this dynamic theory of nature as a fluid manifestation of

God's will that Emerson presented the greatest challenge to those religions and philosophies which preceded his.

Note

1. *Journals of Ralph Waldo Emerson*, ed. Edward Waldo Emerson and Waldo Emerson Forbes (Boston: Houghton, Mifflin, 1909–1914), IV, 21. All subsequent references to the *Journals* will be to this edition, and will be incorporated into the text in parentheses.

"Emerson's Dialectic"

R. A. Yoder[*]

We have put aside Emerson the figurehead and Emerson the philosopher, and we look now at the man—a "man thinking," admired most of all for the absorbing process of his inner life.[1] To see this process is of course to emphasize the conflicts and changes in his thinking; we are forced to take at face value Emerson's own statement, "I have no System,"[2] and we are more than ever conscious of a second crisis in his life or a later Emerson who shows us, much like Wordsworth in England, how quickly the Romantic lamp is dimmed.[3]

The inner process tells something important about the outward product, the works Emerson published during his life. It is easier, now, to understand why the essays do not submit to paraphrase or summary: the vitality of the inner life shows more clearly that ordinary logic would not serve Emerson's purpose; that purpose and the method it implies have been defined by John Holloway, who was writing about Carlyle, Newman, and Arnold but knew that Emerson belongs to the company of these Victorian sages:

> . . . the sage has a special problem in expounding or in proving what he wants to say. He does not and probably cannot rely on logical and formal argument alone or even much at all. His main task is to quicken his reader's perceptiveness; and he does this by making a far wider appeal than the exclusively rational appeal. He draws upon resources cognate, at least, with those of the artist in words. He gives expression to his outlook imaginatively. What he has to say is not a matter of 'content' or narrow paraphrasable meaning, but is transfused by the whole texture of his writing as it constitutes an experience for the reader.[4]

So we must attend, not to the logical argument, but to the rhetoric of the work if we are to understand fully the experience of Emerson's essays. By "rhetoric" I mean the chiefly literary effects—the telling ways of using phrases or images, or conveying a tone or personality, or organizing one's

*Reprinted from *Criticism*, 11 (Fall 1969), 313–28.

subject—insofar as they can be distinguished from subject, argument, and conclusion.

These two insights, then, direct our contemporary approach to Emerson: first, that he experienced a second crisis and change of view in the 1840s; and second, that his work must be analyzed as the special art of the sage. Putting them together, I want to consider just how the inward change in Emerson's life and thought is revealed in the outward product, and to do this I will examine one aspect of the sage's rhetoric, the shape or structure of his essays.

I

Most interpreters of Emerson have agreed that dialectic, in one sense or another, describes the structure of his essays; they have not agreed on the sense.[5] They claim too much, I believe, when they insist that Emerson employed a dialectical logic. True, Emerson did set apart "Dialectic" as "the science of sciences . . . the Intellect discriminating the false and the true. It rests on the observation of identity and diversity."[6] And an earlier statement from this same essay on Plato suggests that for Emerson dialectic and philosophy were practically synonymous:

> Philosophy is the account which the human mind gives to itself of the constitution of the world. Two cardinal facts lie forever at the base; the one, and the two.—1. Unity, or Identity; and, 2. Variety. We unite all things by perceiving the law which pervades them; by perceiving the superficial differences and the profound resemblances. But every mental act,—this very perception of identity or oneness, recognizes the difference of things. Oneness and otherness. It is impossible to speak or to think without embracing both.
>
> (IV, 47–48)

But Emerson never defined more precisely this philosophy or its method, and none of the intricate explanations of his dialectical logic has been persuasive enough to gain general assent—for good reason, it seems to me, because if they fit one essay they irreparably strain another. Take, for example, one version of Emerson's method, the "twice-bisected line" proposed by Walter Blair and Clarence Faust some twenty years ago.[7] Although Emerson called the twice-bisected line "a key to the method and completeness of Plato" (IV, 68), he would have been the first to agree that completeness is not necessarily the mark of greatness. In fact, what made Plato great, according to Emerson, was that he "apprehended the cardinal facts." "No man ever more fully acknowledged the Ineffable," but at the same time Plato could affirm, "And yet things are knowable" (IV, 61–62). To see the world as knowable and yet a mystery, to see both identity and diversity, this "double consciousness"[8] is both the art and the achievement of the sage. An awareness of the "two sides" reaches to the heart of every philosophical problem, Emerson wrote in his journal for the autumn of 1841:

> The whole game at which the philosopher busies himself every day, year in, year out, is to find the upper and the under side of every block in his way. Nothing so large and nothing so thin but it has two sides, and when he has seen the outside, he turns it over to see the other face. We never tire of this game, because ever a slight shudder of astonishment pervades us at the exhibition of the other side of the button,—at the contrast of the two sides. The head and the tail are called in the language of philosophy *Finite* and *Infinite*. Visible and Spiritual, Relative and Absolute, Apparent and Eternal, and many more fine names. (*J*, VI, 60–61)

This idea, that everything is two-sided, and that its polarity can be defined by a string of analogies based on the antithesis of identity and diversity, is the essence of Emerson's method. It is simple, but it fits most of the essays.

What Emerson practiced, then, was no rigorous and schematic organization but a mere habit of mind. His habit from youth was to divide any subject into two opposite or contrary sides and to examine the subject from each side, much as a formal debater is required to argue both sides of the question.[9] And it is constantly his technique to dichotomize within an essay, and even to arrange his essays in antithetical pairs.[10] In this loose sense of setting opposing concepts against each other, dialectic was Emerson's device for organizing what he had to say, and he used it at every stage of his career. There is an important difference, however, between the way Emerson's dialectic shapes an early essay like "The Over-Soul" and the structure it gives to the essays he wrote during the 1840s. The difference, briefly, is that in "The Over-Soul" the opposed pairs are arranged in a series of parallel paragraphs; in later essays the paragraphs themselves become units dialectically opposed and thus form contrastive, not parallel, series.

II

"The Over-Soul" is representative of Emerson's unwavering Romanticism during the 1830s. In it, as Holloway said of Carlyle, "the nerve of proof simply cannot be traced."[11] Emerson summons not argument or proof, but rather wave after wave of assertion, all striking from the same direction so that a tremendous cumulative force is built up and the rock of opposition finally shattered—the metaphor is Emerson's favorite, of course, and one of his finer quatrains epitomizes the rhetorical strategy and effect of "The Over-Soul":

> All day the waves assailed the rock,
> I heard no church-bell chime,
> The sea-beat scorns the minster clock
> And breaks the glass of Time.   (IX, 345)

Scoring the clock-logic of systematic thought, Emerson assails doubt with all the repeated power of a central, oceanic awareness, for which every paragraph of "The Over-Soul" is an analogy or variation.

That central awareness is the experience of revelation (II, 281). Cast in dialectical or polar terms, it is the awareness of identity in the midst of diversity, or it is using Reason in place of the Understanding. These generalized polarities, identity and diversity, Reason and Understanding, are in fact never mentioned in the essay, but the key terms in every paragraph are surrogates for them, and most important the dialectical relationship between the terms is always the same. In the first paragraph, for example, the "reality" we experience in "brief moments" is set against our "habitual" awareness (II, 267). Then the "incalculable" balks the "calculator" (II, 268). We live in "parts" for the sake of calculation, but in reality we are "ONE," integral with the single spiritual principle of the universe (II, 269). The soul is "indefinable, unmeasurable" (II, 271), triumphant over things bound in time and space (II, 272). The "soul's advances" can be represented only by "metamorphosis" as distinct from linear or arithmetic gradations (II, 274). And this growth involves a detachment from persons (II, 277). The soul, because it is general and linked to the Over-Soul, can never cross another man's soul the way one man's will can set itself against another's (II, 279). Thus we have still another set of opposed terms, impersonal soul against personal will. Moreover, the expression of one's soul is not a matter of personal or voluntary control. We are told not to "interfere with our thought" but to accept the "tide of being which floats us into the secret of nature" (II, 284). When "private will is overpowered," its limited and partial effects may be replaced by involuntary genius (II, 286). Thus, in another dichotomy, revelation is distinguished from "low curiosity" (II, 283).

The next variation distinguishes those who speak from within from those who speak from without, and this is illustrated by such opposites as the poets Herbert and Pope and the common Romantic antithesis of Kant and Locke (II, 287). From these specific illustrations Emerson generalizes again to separate the Coleridgean terms genius and talent. Talent is merely the "knack and skill" by which the scholar turns his morbid, monomaniac tendencies into some kind of virtue; talent lessens the man, while genius is the quality of intellect that broadens and makes him more humane (II, 288). The last polarity sets off the "lowly and simple" from the vain, ambitious, and cultivated (II, 289–90); since revelation demands "entire possession," it excludes sophisticated men, who are so intent upon dividing and refining distinctions that they can never give themselves to a momentary enthusiasm.

Pair after pair, this dialectical momentum continues through Emerson's summary and peroration where the key terms and images of the essay reappear. The central theme of unity is neatly recapitulated in a characteristic metaphor of flowing: The Over-Soul works like blood circulating, and that blood is indivisible like the sea.

> . . . the heart in thee is the heart of all; not a valve, not a wall, not an intersection is there anywhere in nature, but one blood rolls uninterruptedly an endless circulation through all men, as the water of the globe is all one sea, and, truly seen, its tide is one. (II, 294)

And the peroration recalls (from II, 269) how a man awakens to ONEness and lives no longer in parts: "He will weave no longer a spotted life of shreds and patches, but he will live with a divine unity" (II, 297).

There should be no doubt that the rhetorical structure of this essay is a series of parallel dichotomies. The point can best be summarized graphically:

IDENTITY	DIVERSITY
REASON	UNDERSTANDING
brief	habitual
incalculable	calculable
ONE	parts
unmeasurable	bounded
metamorphosis	linear gradation
impersonal	personal
spontaneous	voluntary
soul	will
Revelation	low curiosity
speakers from within	speakers from without
Herbert	Pope
Kant	Locke
genius	talent
simple	sophisticated
unity	"shreds and patches"

There is no let-up in this series; its steady flow is never broken by a turn or counter-assertion, and there is hardly a contrastive transition in the whole essay. The only one, in fact, begins a brief paragraph in the middle ("But beyond this recognition . . . ," II, 280) where Emerson seems to distinguish between the self-trust inspired by the soul (a theme closer to "Self-Reliance") and the soul's revelation of truth. This point might have been an important turn or bisection in the essay, but actually it is subdued and hardly affects the tide that sweeps through the whole. The harmony and unity implied by Emerson's use of parallel series in "The Over-Soul" reinforces not only the theme of this essay but also the broad assumption of his early faith—the assumption of a correspondence between nature and the mind, and its corollary that "there are no questions to ask which are unanswerable" (I, 3).

III

In 1836 Emerson had been positive and assured, speaking almost *ex cathedra* about nature. His Orphic poet had pierced easily through appearances to the central law, and the questions were all answered. How different things are five years later. When Emerson delivered "The Method of Nature" in the summer of 1841, the poet was unable to pierce an inch (I, 196): "the method of nature: who could ever analyze it? That rushing stream will not stop to be observed" (I, 199). The old question of 1836, "To what end is Nature?" (I, 4), can no longer even be posed—Nature "does not exist to any one or any number of particular ends, but to numberless and endless benefit" (I, 203–204). At this point the relationship between man and Nature ceases to be straightforward:

> I conceive a man as always spoken to from behind, and unable to turn his head and see the speaker. In all the millions who have heard the voice, none ever saw the face. . . . That well known voice speaks in all languages, governs all men, and none ever caught a glimpse of its form. (I, 209)

In "The Sphinx," "To Rhea," "Woodnotes," and "Monadnoc," all poems of this period, a remote, unembodied voice speaks for nature as a whole, lecturing the poet from nearby rocks, trees, and mountains.

Thus for Emerson in the early 1840s Nature has changed her personality, if not her principles. If the conclusions of his essays represent her principles, they are substantially what they were in the first *Nature* or in "The Over-Soul."[12] But in emphasis, in tone and imagery, and above all in their rhetorical shape, essays like "Circles," "Nature" (in *Essays: Second Series*), "Experience," or "Montaigne" differ markedly from the earlier ones. The old ideas are like unanalyzable counters arranged in a new way—before they overwhelmed the reader with nature's unity, now they dazzle him with nature's unpredictability. In 1839 Emerson decided that the philosopher must become a poet in order to express "fluxional quantities and values" (*J*, V, 189), and the keynote of these later essays comes appropriately from one of the poet's gnomic utterances: "Mount to paradise/ By the stairway of surprise" ("Merlin," IX, 121). The shape of art imitates the shape of life, and (Emerson repeats in "Circles" and "Experience") "Life is a series of surprises" (II, 320; III, 67). It is our continual "astonishment" that makes the game interesting (*J*, VI, 60–61, quoted above). Thus the later essays astonish us with an assortment of surprises, ambiguities, conclusions pulled out of a hat. To this end, the parallelisms of "The Over-Soul" offer no advantage, since change and contrast are the essentials of surprise.

A structure of contrastive divisions characterizes the essays written by Emerson after 1840. In fact, it can be seen already in "Compensation," probably written a short time after "The Over-Soul."[13] "Compensation" is perhaps Emerson's classic statement of polarity or a dialectic process operating in nature. At the same time, there is a real dialectical conflict, unobtrusive at first but erupting in the end, that gives "Compensation" a more dramatic structure than its major theme suggests. The essay begins with a series of assertions about polarity, or the balance of opposites, in nature—here are the lead sentences that link a group of paragraphs: "Polarity, or action and reaction, we meet in every part of nature . . ." (II, 96); "The same dualism underlies the nature and condition of man. Every excess causes a defect; every defect an excess" (II, 98); "Every act rewards itself, or in other words integrates itself, in a twofold manner . . ." (II, 102); "All things are double, one against another . . ." (II, 109). What Emerson seems to be saying, what is implied or hinted at by this doctrine of compensation, is that Nature is a sort of Manichean balance where good and evil cancel each other out. If he does not say this precisely, he comes very close—for example, the maxim "Every sweet hath its sour; every evil its good" strongly suggests that every good has its evil, too (II, 98). And Emerson depends on the reader's assimilating this implied amorality of nature, so that in the middle of the essay he can suddenly turn on the idea apparently established and end the essay on compensation with a counter-assertion. Here is the major turning point:

THESIS: Thus do all things preach the indifferency of circum-
                 stances. The man is all. Everything has two sides, a good
                 and an evil. Every advantage has its tax. I learn to be
                 content.

ANTITHESIS: But the doctrine of compensation is not the doctrine of
                 indifferency.

THESIS: The thoughtless say, on hearing these representations,—
                 What boots it to do well? there is one event to good and
                 evil; if I gain any good I must pay for it; if I lose any
                 good I gain some other; all actions are indifferent.

ANTITHESIS: There is a deeper fact in the soul than compensation,
                 to wit, its own nature. The soul is not a compensation,
                 but a life. (II, 120)

The balance in nature with its corollary of moral indifference is a fact of appearance only, and we must understand that beyond appearance is the reality of the soul. Thus the concept of the soul, the same idea as in "The Over-Soul," becomes the antithesis of this essay and the means by which apparent evil and "calamity" (II, 124–27) can be understood as ultimate good.

    "Circles," which immediately follows "The Over-Soul" in *Essays:*

First Series, must have been written in the fall of 1840.[14] Its rhetorical structure is exactly that of "Compensation," as an allusion in the opening paragraph suggests: "One moral we have already deduced in considering the circular or compensatory character of every human action" (II, 301). The action and reaction of compensation are represented here by two 180-degree arcs of a circle, "this first of forms" that returns upon itself. But if the figure of a circle symbolizes the compensation that works in every human action, it also symbolizes the deeper fact that no action is ever fixed or completed, that no single viewpoint or summary of events is ever final: "The life of a man is a self-evolving circle, which, from a ring imperceptibly small, rushes on all sides outwards to new and larger circles, and that without end" (II, 304). "There are no fixtures in nature" (II, 302), that is the dominant theme of the essay. With it Emerson is able to work the same effect as in "Compensation": he plays upon the moral ambiguity that inheres in this idea—is the change in nature and man a change for better or for worse? Or is it simply indifferent, and the world mere change? Some paragraphs in "Circles" imply mere flux: "Our moods do not believe in each other" (II, 306); "There is no virtue which is final . . ." (II, 316). Others suggest progress through a synthesis of opposites, as in this passage that calls to mind the dialectical method of the Socratic dialogues and then the doctrine of the Over-Soul: "By going one step farther back in thought, discordant opinions are reconciled by being seen to be two extremes of one principle, and we can never go so far back as to preclude a still higher vision. . . . Generalization is always a new influx of the divinity into the mind" (II, 308–309). Toward the end of the essay, however, Emerson assumes that the reader, as in "Compensation," has been led to view the process as merely flux and indifference:

> And thus, O circular philosopher, I hear some reader exclaim, you have arrived at a fine Pyrrhonism, at an equivalence and indifferency of all actions, . . .
> . . . But lest I should mislead any when I have my own head and obey my whims, let me remind the reader that I am only an experimenter. Do not set the least value on what I do, or the least discredit on what I do not, as if I pretended to settle any thing as true or false. I unsettle all things. No facts are to me sacred; none are profane; I simply experiment, an endless seeker with no past at my back. (II, 317–18)

And this leads him into the last and crucial turn of the essay where the whole thesis of fluidity and impermanence is countered by the antithesis of the soul:

> Yet this incessant movement and progression which all things partake could never become sensible to us but by contrast to some principle of fixture or stability in the soul. Whilst the eternal generation of circles proceeds, the eternal generator abides. That central life is somewhat superior to creation, superior to knowledge and thought, and contains all its circles. (II, 318)

Actually, these ideas of unity and the soul, which usually dominate Emerson's perorations, are overshadowed in the conclusion of "Circles" by themes of newness and change. Yet the turn of thought is placed and introduced so as to receive emphasis; Emerson gives it prominence, even if it is not required for his conclusion.

When Emerson came to write his "new chapter on Nature,"[15] he abandoned the form of the old. *Nature* of 1836 moved serenely from the level of material and practical apprehension to spiritual insight; its transitions are smooth, as in "The Over-Soul," without turns or hesitations. In contrast to such uninterrupted ascension, "Nature," as it appears in *Essays: Second Series* is organized, not from bottom to top, so to speak, but from side to side, in terms of polarities. First Emerson distinguishes *natura naturata* and *natura naturans*, the passive landscape on the one hand and the active or creative principle on the other. Both of these he treats with a slight indirectness or ambiguity, the same quality we observed in "Compensation" and "Circles." Nature as landscape "must always seem unreal and mocking" (III, 178), and there is something untrustworthy or exaggerated in men's descriptions of nature. Nature as principle or cause is secret—an unfathomable, slippery Proteus who can never be pinned down (III, 179; cf. IV, 121, 157). Then, quite out of the air, Emerson proposes a second dichotomy: "Motion or change and identity or rest are the first and second secrets of nature: Motion and Rest" (III, 180). Identity, which under the doctrine of correspondence was the guiding principle of *Nature* (1836), is briefly explained (III, 181–84), and then Emerson turns to the opposite principle of motion ("If the identity expresses organized rest, the counter action also runs into organization," III, 184). At this stage, motion is more important to him because it is motion and change that give nature its dominant personality in this essay—nature is Proteus who constantly changes shape, or the Sphinx who befuddles mankind (III, 194). The theme of mockery and deceit, muted in its introduction, now returns with full force: the "overfaith" of man in himself (III, 187) is mirrored in nature where there is "something mocking, something that leads us on and on, but arrives nowhere" (III, 190). If this sense of nature that urges us toward vague goals is the active principle or *natura naturans*, the same deceitfulness is evidenced in the *natura naturata*.

> Quite analogous to the deceits in life, there is, as might be expected, a similar effect on the eye from the face of external nature. There is in woods and waters a certain enticement and flattery, together with a failure to yield a present satisfaction. This disappointment is felt in every landscape. . . . The pinetree, the river, the bank of flowers before him [the poet] does not seem to be nature. Nature is still elsewhere. . . . It is the same among the men and women as among the silent trees; always a referred existence, an absence, never a presence and satisfaction. (III, 192–93)

At this point, clearly, the deceitfulness of nature has become Emerson's dominant theme or thesis, and the reader should be feeling appropriately uncomfortable, "encamped" but "not domesticated" in this alien world (III, 190). To assure that he does, Emerson adds one last rhetorical question—"Must we not suppose somewhere in the universe a slight treachery and derision?" (III, 193) And then Emerson reverses himself in a now familiar final turn to the essay:

THESIS: We cannot bandy words with Nature, or deal with her
               as we deal with persons. If we measure our individual
               forces against hers we may easily feel as if we were the
               sport of an insuperable destiny.

ANTITHESIS: But if, instead of identifying ourselves with the work,
               we feel that the soul of the Workman streams through
               us, we shall find the peace of the morning dwelling first
               in our hearts, and the fathomless powers of gravity and
               chemistry, and over them, of life, pre-existing within us
               in their highest form.
                  The uneasiness which the thought of our helplessness
               in the chain of causes occasions us, results from looking
               too much at one condition of nature, namely, Motion.
               But the drag is never taken from the wheel. Wherever
               the impulse exceeds, the Rest OR Identity insinuates its
               compensation. (III, 194–95)

The thesis that rose out of a consideration of motion is thwarted by the antithesis of rest—Emerson is into his last paragraph, into the peroration that urges us to heed universal law, to forget "our servitude to particulars"; and thus our uneasiness is dispelled.

I think now we can summarize the rhetorical structure or strategy that these essays have in common. They all assert a basic dichotomy and develop a balance between its opposite or extreme terms. This equilibrium gradually disintegrates, and a single theme or thesis emerges, often indirectly by image and suggestion rather than by direct statement. The theme or thesis expresses doubt or moral ambiguity in nature. It builds up assertive power until suddenly it is dashed away by a climactic turn in the essay, almost always indicated by a contrastive conjunction ("But," "yet," "whilst"). The antithesis introduced by the turn is an expression of unity and hope, and leads into Emerson's peroration.

A glance at several other essays of the same decade, the 1840s, should show that this structure is more than accidental. "Experience," for example, is a set of variations based on the idea that "life is a train of moods like a string of beads" (III, 50).[16] The crucial turn comes in a long paragraph about two-thirds through the essay (III, 70–72), the gist of which is that the seeming unrelatedness of the parts or moods of our lives is no proof that they are not or will not be related. And it moves to this sentence, which should be compared with the turning sentences of "Compensation" and "Circles":

> If I have described life as a flux of moods, I must now add that there is that in us which changes not and which ranks all sensations and states of mind. (III, 72; cf. II, 120 and II, 318)

Or to take another example, the essay "Montaigne; Or, the Skeptic" from *Representative Men*. The dualism by which it is constructed is obvious in the first paragraph (IV, 149), and out of the opposition between abstractionist and materialist arises the third party, the skeptic, who represents the thesis of the essay (IV, 154–55) and is the type for whom Montaigne is representative. In the course of the essay, however, the concept of a skeptic is stipulatively limited until skepticism is identified with self-reliance, hence with "belief" (in the "affirmations of the soul," IV, 180) and "faith" (presumably faith in oneself, IV, 181, 182, 183). The thesis is modified so that skepticism with regard to custom or dogma is approved, while skepticism or disbelief in man's power to apprehend the ultimate unity of nature is impossible. Thus Emerson can bring off this surprising climax, in which the apparent thesis of the essay is overturned.

> The final solution in which skepticism is lost, is in the moral sentiment, which never forfeits its supremacy. All moods may be safely tried, and their weight allowed to all objections: the moral sentiment as easily outweighs them all, as any one. This is the drop which balances the sea. I play with the miscellany of facts, and take those superficial views which we call skepticism; but I know that they will presently appear to me in that order which makes skepticism impossible. A man of thought must feel the thought that is parent of the universe; that the masses of nature do undulate and flow. (IV, 183)

In still later essays, the conflict and surprise generated by Emerson's dialectic is discernible though muted. More than ever he would depend on an antithesis, usually some version of Motion and Rest,[17] to establish a working balance. But, as if he now began to accept a universe of flux and ambiguity as a commonplace unworthy of emphasis, he does not build rhetorically in that direction—that thesis is underplayed; and nor then does he give so much prominence to a surprising reversal of direction in the end. "Fate," despite the limitations it places on man, never overwhelms us. Balance returns again and again as power and fate (VI, 14–15, 22), or intellect and fate (VI, 23), or thought and nature (VI, 43), terms that stand roughly for the individual consciousness and the external world—so we are back where Emerson began twenty years before, pondering the relation between ME and NOT-ME (I, 4). And the only answer, now, to this mystery is to trust compensation, "the cunning copresence" of limit and liberty in nature that assures us damages will be paid when nature is liable (VI, 47–48). Given a balance maintained throughout, there is little surprise in Emerson's peroration, despite its suddenness; there is no transition, no emphatic change of direction, but only the simple, hortative beginning—"Let us build altars . . ." (VI, 48–49)—that signifies Emerson's final movement.

Emerson always experienced difficulty in organizing his fine phrases, more than ever as years went by. Lecturing at Harvard in 1870, he seemed indifferent to the problems of organizing and dramatizing his thoughts: "What I am now to attempt is simply some sketches or studies . . . ," (XII, 14), he said in the introduction to *Natural History of Intellect*. The series of dichotomies that follows is loose and casually related, even for Emerson (one paragraph begins: "Well, having accepted this law of identity pervading the universe, we must next perceive that whilst every creature represents and obeys it, there is diversity, there is more or less of power," XII, 21). At the end, Emerson makes no attempt at his former rhetorical magic by which the whole thrust of the essay is reversed or contraries are suddenly reconciled. There is only a humble conclusion, pathetic almost, for a once great master of the dramatic peroration:

> We wish to sum up the conflicting impressions by saying that all point at last to a unity which inspires all. . . . (XII, 64)

Thin and transparent this sentence is, and it should remind us that if logic or argument counted for everything, then all of Emerson's conclusions could be adequately summarized this way. It should remind us that Emerson at his best is Merlin weaving a spell upon us—whether the spell is magic or rhetorical sleight-of-hand makes no difference, the point is we are caught up in a dramatic presentation the way we are not in a philosopical argument.

IV

Dialectic is an essential element in Emerson's dramatic presentation, as I have tried to show. Emerson fashions it into a device or structure that reflects his view of life, and it changes as he changes. In the essays of the early 1840s he adopts a strategy of dramatic reversal that can surprise and awaken and finally relieve his audience, both listeners and readers. This strategy enables him to keep his early ideal of a knowable nature and yet to take full account of the unknowable that lurks beyond reason and faith.[18]

To acknowledge the ineffable and yet affirm that things are knowable, is a greatness beyond consistency. The ability, temperamentally and then artistically, to face this paradox is what I take Emerson to mean by a "double consciousness."[19] Facing it and making it central to his art in the 1840s brings Emerson closer to Hawthorne and Melville, who are often at odds with Romantic enthusiasm and the Transcendental mysteries. But Emerson's Romanticism is complex and dynamic, and this rhetoric of contrast leads his art toward the ambiguity of Hawthorne—Saadi (IX, 130) can be just as inscrutable as Hawthorne telling what had been witnessed on the scaffold or as Miles Coverdale. Moreover, if Melville shields Ishmael from the fate of the arch-Transcendentalist Ahab, it is because Ishmael has learned a lesson along the way:

> Doubts of all things earthly, and intuitions of some things heavenly; this combination makes neither believer nor infidel, but makes a man who regards them both with equal eye.
>
> *(Moby Dick,* Chapter 85)

This "equal eye" is the fine-tempered balance yielded by Emerson's dialectic and the wisdom in his later essays.

Notes

1. Stephen E. Whicher, *Freedom and Fate: An Inner Life of Ralph Waldo Emerson* (Philadelphia: University of Pennsylvania Press, 1953), pp. 172–173. Whicher concluded, ". . . my hope has been to bring to light the drama of the inner life that lay concealed, too successfully, behind the unruffled mien which he presented to the world."

2. *Journals of Ralph Waldo Emerson,* ed. Edward Waldo Emerson and Waldo Emerson Forbes, 10 vols. (Boston: Houghton Mifflin, 1909–1914), V, 326–327 (hereafter abbreviated as *J* with volume and page-number).

3. In at least one sense, Wordsworth and Emerson move in opposite directions: Wordsworth from a naturalistic to a more religious pantheism, and finally to orthodoxy; Emerson from orthodoxy to the highly religious pantheism of *Nature* (1836), then to a diminished, more skeptical pantheism. But in general both represent the transition from Romanticism to Victorianism; cf. Jonathan Bishop, *Emerson on the Soul* (Cambridge: Harvard University Press, 1964), p. 205, "Emerson the Romantic has become Emerson the Victorian." Whicher stressed this shift *(Freedom and Fate,* Chapters 5 and 6), and Carl F. Strauch has contributed detailed studies of Emerson's thought during the period, "The Importance of Emerson's Skeptical Mood," *Harvard Library Bulletin,* 11 (Winter 1957): 117–139, and "Emerson's Sacred Science," *PMLA,* 73 (June 1958): 237–250.

4. *The Victorian Sage: Studies in Argument* (New York: W. W. Norton, 1965), pp. 10–11. Holloway later quotes Arnold to reinforce his points:

> Arnold brings these points out in a comment on Emerson, who would certainly have been included among these writers had space allowed. 'Yes, truly his insight is admirable; his truth is precious. Yet the secret of his effect is not . . . in *these*; it is in his temper. It is in the hopeful, serene, beautiful temper wherewith those, in Emerson, are indissolubly joined; in which they work, and have their being.'

Paul Lauter, "Truth and Nature: Emerson's Use of Two Complex Words," *ELH,* 27 (March 1960): 66–85, has applied Holloway's method in part. Lauter's approach is to analyze the terms as they are used in Emerson's whole canon; my aim here is not to analyze the terms, but to show how they are related in individual essays.

5. See William T. Harris, "Ralph Waldo Emerson," *Atlantic Monthly,* 50 (August 1882): 238–250, and "The Dialectical Unity of Emerson's Prose," *Journal of Speculative Philosophy,* 18 (April 1884): 195–202; Walter Blair and Clarence Faust, "Emerson's Literary Method," *Modern Philology,* 42 (November 1944): 79–95; Stuart Gerry Brown, "Emerson's Platonism," *New England Quarterly,* 18 (September 1945): 325–345; Sherman Paul, *Emerson's Angle of Vision* (Cambridge: Harvard University Press, 1952), pp. 103–119; Charles Feidelson, Jr., *Symbolism and American Literature* (Chicago: University of Chicago Press,

1953), Chapter 4, especially pp. 157–161. Both Harris and Blair and Faust stress a dialectic based on Platonic epistemology. Brown takes a broader view, suggesting that Emerson and Plato shared the same inconsistency by asserting monism and dualism (pp. 336–339). Paul traces Emerson's method to Coleridge, at the same time corroborating Harris and Blair and Faust. Feidelson calls Emerson's dialectic "quasi-poetic" and regards it as a step toward modern symbolist theory in that dialectic focuses upon words or concepts and not their referents in the external world (pp. 68–69).

6. *The Complete Works of Ralph Waldo Emerson*, ed. Edward Waldo Emerson, Centenary Edition, 12 vols. (Boston: Houghton, Mifflin, 1903–1904), IV, 61 (hereafter abbreviated in the text as roman numeral and page-number).

7. See note 5. While Paul follows Blair and Faust, Whicher comments, ". . . the parallel is not obvious in detail" (p. 160). Dorothea Krook, *Three Traditions of Moral Thought* (Cambridge: Harvard University Press, 1959), Appendices A and B ("Some Principles of Socrates' Dialectic Method" and "Two Meanings of 'Dialectic' "), pp. 301–332, shows what the Socratic dialectic is in a way that sets it apart from Emerson's.

8. Emerson uses the phrase in "The Transcendentalist," I, 353; "Fate," VI, 47; and "Demonology," X, 7–8.

9. See Emerson's discussion of slavery (1826) in *The Journals and Miscellaneous Notebooks of Ralph Waldo Emerson*, ed. William H. Gilman et al. (Cambridge: Harvard University Press, 1960–), II, 42–44, 48–49, 57–58. Division into opposites is characteristic of a number of early sermons, for example, "Religious Liberalism and Rigidity" or "Self and Others" in *Young Emerson Speaks*, ed. Arthur Cushman McGiffert, Jr. (Boston: Houghton Mifflin, 1938).

10. See Paul, *Emerson's Angle of Vision*, p. 117.

11. Holloway, *The Victorian Sage*, p. 3.

12. Whicher, though stressing change, comments on this similarity, pp. 119–122.

13. Edward Waldo Emerson (II, 426–427) says "The Over-Soul" was drawn from early lectures, especially from "The Doctrine of the Soul," first delivered 5 December 1838. Parts of "Compensation" derive from lectures of 1838–1839 (II, 396–397); Whicher assigns it to 1841 (p. 34).

14. See Edward Waldo Emerson's note (II, 433) and journal passages (*J*, V, 460–461, 480–481) dated September and October 1840.

15. *J*, V, 420. See also *J*, V, 455–456, dated September 1840 which appears in "Nature."

16. Harris, "Dialectical Unity," pp. 196–199, sees this essay as exemplary of Emerson's dialectical logic. The procession from illusion to subjectiveness is a series of steps or *stadia* leading to the greatest insight, toward absolute unity. I do not see the logic of this procession, since there is no apparent necessity in the order (and even if one assumes that the items of the series are arranged in, say, an order of increasing generality, there is no logical transition from one item to the next). Emerson wrote, "I dare not assume to give their order, but I name them as I find them in my way" (III, 83). George Sebouhian, "Emerson's 'Experience': An Approach to Content and Method," *Emerson Society Quarterly*, no. 46 (2d Quarter 1967): 75–78, follows Harris but his description of the essay as "a thought pattern in process" seems to me more accurate than Harris' analysis.

17. See Whicher, *Freedom and Fate*, p. 165.

18. To this extent, I agree with Brown (see note 5 above).

19. See references, note 8, above. If this paradox represented the "cardinal facts" for Emerson and Plato, it is also the starting point for Camus in *The Myth of Sisyphus*, trans. Justin O'Brien (New York: Vintage, 1959), p. 38: "And these two certainties—my appetite for the absolute and for unity and the impossibility of reducing this world to a rational and reasonable principle—I also know that I cannot reconcile them. What other truth can I admit without lying . . . ?"

"Emerson on the Scholar, 1833–1837"

Merton M. Sealts, Jr.*

"I think I may undertake one of these days to write a chapter on Literary Ethics or the Duty & Discipline of a Scholar." So runs an entry of 6 August 1835 in Emerson's journal (*JMN*, v, 84)[1] written two years before his Phi Beta Kappa oration at Cambridge known as "The American Scholar" and nearly three years before the subsequent address at Dartmouth College on "Literary Ethics." The context of Emerson's thinking about the scholar and his duties extends even farther back in time, to his own college days at Harvard. As early as 1818 he had proposed to his brother Edward, among other possible compositions, "a long letter embellished with all the ornaments of Rhetorick on the Age of the American Scholar" (*L*, i, 64), and in November of 1821 he had opened a theme "On the advantages of knowledge" by declaring that "it is the office of the scholar to *write*" (*JMN*, i, 189). The habit of periodic writing that he regarded as essential to the scholar had already been established: in January of 1820 Emerson began keeping the journal that he was later to think of as his "Savings Bank" (*JMN*, iv, 250). In its successive volumes he alternately accumulated and withdrew literary capital for college essays, his sermons as a Unitarian minister that began in 1826, the public lecturing that he undertook in 1833 after resigning his Boston pulpit, and his occasional addresses such as "The American Scholar" itself. More specifically, the oration on the scholar grew organically out of thinking recorded in the journal during the middle 1830's, when the young man who had preached a sermon with the title "Find Your Calling" was wrestling with his own problem of vocation.[2] "Emerson was variously Priest, Poet, and Philosopher," as Rober E. Spiller remarks, "but, when he chose his own role, he defined himself as the 'American Scholar'."[3] The oration is an essay in definition of that role as it appeared to him in 1837.

Another man than Emerson, receiving an unexpected invitation to deliver a Phi Beta Kappa address, and to do so on relatively short notice as a substitute speaker, might have responded with a conventional speech on some time-honored theme. Even "the office of the scholar" was scarcely a new topic in 1837, for many an American orator and essayist, holding forth at college Commencement exercises, had already examined the state of scholarship and literature in a new country—often in a spirit of flamboyant cultural nationalism. Emerson himself had touched on the subject as early as a lecture read in May of 1834, though with little satisfaction in what he saw in contemporary American life. "Imitation," he had charged, is "the vice of overcivilized communities" and "the vice eminently of our times, of our literature, of our manners and social action. All

*Reprinted from *PMLA*, 85 (March 1970), 185–95, with revisions by the author.

American manners, language, and writing are derivative. We do not write from facts, but we wish to state facts after the English manner" (*EL*, I, 74–75). In January of 1836, concluding his course of lectures on English literature, he had acknowledged that "the American scholar" must feel a "degree of humiliation" in reckoning how little his countrymen had "added to the stock of truth for mankind" in comparison with the bards, the scholars, the philosophers of England (*EL*, I, 381). Though cast in negative terms, such passages unmistakably anticipate Emerson's ringing challenge to his countrymen in the peroration of "The American Scholar": American freemen have "listened too long to the courtly muses of Europe" (*W*, I, 114).

But the oration of 1837 is more than an exercise in literary nationalism, though it has been so described, as it is more than a conventional speech for Commencement-time; its roots lie too deep within Emerson's troubled thinking about his own role as scholar to justify fitting it so easily into any standard pattern. What he said in Cambridge was addressed as much to himself as to his Phi Beta Kappa audience, putting to both the fundamental issue of creativity and originality that he had already posed in *Nature* (1836): Why should not every generation, instead of imitating some past model, "enjoy an original relation to the universe?" (*W*, I, 3). As early as 1834 he had privately resolved never to "utter any speech, poem, or book that is not entirely & peculiarly my work," promising himself to say in public only "those things which I have meditated for their own sake & not for the first time with a view to that occasion." Any other practice, he continued, means only "lost time to you & lost time to your hearer. It is a parenthesis in your genuine life" (*JMN*, IV, 335). As a public speaker Emerson had charged himself to present not what his audience would expect to hear but what was fit for him to speak (*JMN*, IV, 372). Every mind, he was persuaded, "is given one word to say," and a man "should sacredly strive to utter that word & not another man's word; his own, without addition or abatement" (*JMN*, IV, 348–349). According to this principle of self-reliant originality his topics for discussion must not be determined by mere assignment, since in his view "the Scholar who takes his subject from dictation & not from his heart . . . has lost as much as he seems to have gained" (*JMN*, V, 46; *EL*, I, 381–382). As Phi Beta Kappa orator he found no difficulty, however, in addressing that "topic which not only usage but the nature of our association" prescribed to him (*W*, I, 82), since it coincided exactly with a subject he had long been meditating, both for its own sake and for his own, in public lectures as well as in the journal.

For Emerson in the mid-1830's, defining his self-appointed role of scholar meant working out in actual practice and in words the questions posed when he gave up his pastoral duties in 1832: Who is the scholar, and what does he do and say? For whom and to whom does he speak? At one period he had thought of scientific work, or at least of writing and speaking about science. During his travels of 1832–33, excited by the scientific exhibits in the Garden of Plants at Paris, he said to himself, "I will be a naturalist" (*JMN*, IV, 200), and on his return home, meditating a projected "book about nature" (*JMN*, IV, 237), he made "natural history" the subject of his first series of secular lectures in 1833–34. But neither temperament nor training fitted Emerson to be a scientist, and the first lectures reveal his growing impatience with the science of his day. His subsequent lectures on biography in 1835 and on English literature in 1835–36 allowed more scope for the originality he prized and encouraged him to begin formulating in positive terms his idea of the creative scholar, based on his current situation but voicing his hopes and ambitions for the future. The following sections of this essay examine relevant strands of his thinking from 1833 to 1837: in 1833 and 1834 Emerson sees the scholar as a "Watcher," preparing himself for still-undefined service to come; in 1835 he describes the scholar ideally as a writer of genius who sees, thinks, and speaks for and to other men; in 1836 he particularly emphasizes the scholar's relations with nature and society. By the summer of 1837, having already formulated most of the basic concepts underlying "The American Scholar," Emerson was prepared to write the oration itself during a relatively brief period of concentrated effort.

I. THE SCHOLAR AS WATCHER (1833–34)

Though he had lived a scholar's life since his youth, it was not until Emerson turned lecturer in 1833 that the term "scholar" began to take on special meaning for him, anticipating the ideal figure he was to characterize in the oration of 1837 as "*Man Thinking*" (*W*, I, 84). In earlier pages of his journal the term carries only its usual significations: a student, one who reads and writes, a member of some learned profession. Thus the scholar appears variously as a reader of books, a writer and teacher, a "studious man" (*JMN*, I, 189). Emerson, born into a ministerial family and educated virtually as a matter of course for the ministry, continued to regard the clergy as "always, more universally than any other class, the scholars of their day," as he observed in the oration, where he also added ruefully that clergymen suffer being "addressed as women; . . . are often virtually disfranchised; and indeed there are advocates for their celibacy" (*W*, I, 94). Very likely he was recalling his own discomfitures as a minister. In 1830, before leaving his pastorate in Boston, he had acknowledged another difficulty in the scholar's dealings with society: that "degree of uneasiness" he feels in the presence of the well-to-do, a "soreness" that even drives him into solitude, though only because "he is not scholar enough in his heart. He labours with the desire of worldly good & therefore owns in these who have it a superiority to himself" (*JMN*, III, 196). As the journal reveals, Emerson long continued to experience what Stephen Whicher described as "a painful conflict . . . between his wish for companionship and his 'doom' of solitude; a mingled revulsion at and devotion to the confined life of the 'scholar'."[4] His personal knowledge of the scholar's ambivalent relations with society repeatedly comes to the surface, even in the oration itself. For example, there is a revealing journal entry written late in December of 1834 while he was preparing his winter lectures. Obviously pondering his future vocational role, Emerson in this passage weighs the competing claims of solitude and society, contrasting a life of action and a scholar's work of study and meditation, as he unfolds, in halting sentences, what he called a "philosophy of *Waiting*": "Thus he who < acts > [5] is qualified to act upon the Public, if he does not act on many, may yet act intensely on a few; if he does not act much upon any[,] but from insulated condition & unfit companions seem[s] quite withdrawn into himself, still if he know & feel his obligations, he may be (unknown & unconsciously) hiving knowledge & concentrating powers to act well hereafter & a very remote hereafter" (*JMN*, IV, 368).

Following these words, so clearly applicable to his own situation in 1834, Emerson proceeds to an examination of the false relation he observed "betwixt the uneducated & the educated classes." In an extended discussion he introduces distinctions that would recur both in the journal and in public addresses, including the Phi Beta Kappa oration itself, between the scholar as he actually is, the scholar as he appears to others, and the scholar as he ideally ought to be. "I suppose the graduate underestimates the grocer," he remarks, "whilst the grocer far overestimates the graduate, & so the strong hand is kept in submission to what should be the < strong > ⏐wise⏐ head. The reason why Mr Graduate's secret is kept & never any accident . . . discovers his bankruptcy & produces a permanent revolution, is,ᐟ that there is a real object in Nature to which the grocer's reverence instinctively turns" (*JMN*, IV, 370). That "real object," he explains, is "the intellectual man"—what he was later to call "the Thinker" and, in 1937, *"Man Thinking."* Though the scholar in actual life may not exemplify so high an ideal, he is nevertheless "its representative, & is, with more or less symptoms of distrust, honored for that which he ought to be" (*JMN*, IV, 370).

Next in this formulation of 1834, in a further passage that Emerson was to draw upon for the thought and phrasing of his 1837 oration, comes a more positive statement of the "claims" of the scholar's office. He is a man who sees, a "Watcher," set on a tower "to observe & report of every new ray of light in what quarter soever of heaven it should appear," one whose findings society should receive "eagerly & reverently." Though the Watcher's office is open to all men, Emerson continues, and though all men "see their interest in it," very few are inclined "to adopt it as their vocation," for most men are called to other forms of the world's work (*JMN*, IV, 370–372)—or as he was to say in the oration, men in the social state function not only as scholars but as farmers, professors, engineers, priests, statesmen, producers, and soldiers (*W*, I, 82–83). "A small number of men," however,

> have a contemplative turn & voluntarily seek solitude & converse with themselves ↑a work↓ which to <many> most persons has a <sta[l]e prison savor> ↑jail-smell↓. This needs a <rare &> peculiar constitution, a dormancy of some qualities & a harmonious action in all, that is rare. It has its own immunities and also its own painful taxes like the rest of human works. But where it is possessed, let it work free & honoured, in God's name. It is our interest as much in the economical way as that the pin or the chaise maker should be free[,] & in a moral & intellectual view far far oh infinitely more. Every discovery he makes[,] every conclusion he announces is tidings to each of us from our own home. His office is to cheer our labor as with a song by highest hopes. (*JMN*, IV, 372; cf. *W*, I, 100)

As these meditations suggest, Emerson's emerging definition of the scholar's role already involved a sense of obligation to society in terms of some unspecified form of action "upon the Public." While "hiving knowledge & concentrating powers" in the present, the scholar as Watcher is preparing himself "to act well hereafter," however remote the time for action may ultimately be: thus he exemplifies, like Emerson himself in 1834, the "philosophy of *Waiting*." As representative to society of the intellectual man the scholar must be left free to make his own discoveries as an observer or see-er and to report his own conclusions as a thinker and a would-be actor.

When Emerson projected his own aspirations in the journal passage just examined he was planning his new course of six lectures on biography for the early months of 1835, dealing with Michel Angelo, Martin Luther, John Milton, George Fox, and Edmund Burke. None of these men, it will be noted, was a scientist. Despite the strong interest in natural history apparent during his European travels of 1832–33 and his lectures of the following year, all of them on scientific subjects, Emerson had not identified the naturalist as a scholar. Conversely, Luther, though his learning was admittedly antiquated and he lacked "fitness to receive scientific truths," was in Emerson's eyes "a scholar or spiritual man"—a significant apposition. Emerson saw in Luther a scholar-leader who "achieved a spiritual revolution by spiritual arms alone" (*EL*, I, 131, 127). Even in acting upon society, as Luther did, Emerson's true scholar thus deals with intangibles rather than material facts; his "treasures," according to the journal, are "poetry, religion, philosophy" (*JMN*, IV, 297). Ideally, Emerson argued, even the naturalist in his "severest analysis" ought to be a poet, or rather, ought to "make the Naturalist subordinate to the Man" (*EL*, I, 81). What the science of the day, preoccupied as it was with recording facts (*EL*, I, 225), or with their description and classification, failed in Emerson's judgment to perform was the very task he regarded as its "greatest office"—"to explain man to himself" and show him "his true place in the system of being" (*EL*, I, 23). To study science "humanly," as Emerson wanted to do (*JMN*, v, 169), meant effecting a marriage between natural history and human history (*JMN*, iv, 311); it required turning from observation of particular natural facts to perception of general scientific laws, as Newton had done (*EL*, i, 80); finally, in his view, it meant going on to show that natural laws "express also an ethical sense" (*JMN*, iv, 254). Properly speaking, this was to leave the province of the naturalist for that of the moral philosopher, as Emerson himself did after 1834. By June of 1835 he was thinking of announcing his own "discoveries" in a projected "book of Essays chiefly upon Natural Ethics" (*L*, i, 447), and it was very likely with the same work in mind that he mentioned in the following August his possible "chapter on Literary Ethics or the Duty & Discipline of a Scholar."

II. THE SCHOLAR AS READER AND MAKER OF LITERATURE (1835)

When Emerson said, with reference to his "chapter," that one of the scholar's emblems should be "the camel & his four stomachs" (*JMN*, v, 84), he was applying a remark about reading and digesting lawbooks that had come from his brother Charles: "what law he reads in the morning he puts into the first stomach till evening; then it slides into the second" (*JMN*, iv, 381). During the summer of 1835 Emerson himself was reading widely in English literature in preparation for his next series of winter lectures, a course that served incidentally to develop ideas for the piece of writing that he now termed variously the "Sermon to Literary Men which I propose to make," "the scholar's sermon," and "the scholar's Ethics" (*JMN*, v, 164, 167, 187). The world of literature and its makers was clearly more relevant to Emerson's ideal of scholarship than natural history could ever be. One of his personal models for many years was John Milton, whom he had praised in his lectures on biography for exemplifying as well as delineating a "heroic image of man" (*EL*, i, 150). Like Luther, Milton played the double role Emerson coveted for himself: that of "an accomplished scholar" who was also an influential public figure, a man able to act upon others "by an influence purely spiritual" (*EL*, i, 146, 149). Milton appeared to Emerson not only as a great poet but as a dedicated truth-seeker like himself, an idealist whose opinions were "formed for man as he ought to be," and "a consistent spiritualist, or believer in the omnipotence of spiritual laws" (*EL*, i, 159, 160). He was not only a writer; he was a teacher. "Better than any other," in the words of Emerson's lecture on Milton, he "discharged the office of every great man, namely, to raise the idea of Man in the minds of his contemporaries and of posterity,—to draw after nature a life of man, exhibiting such a composition of grace, of strength, and of virtue, as poet had not described nor hero lived. Human nature in these ages is indebted to him for its best portrait" (*EL* i, 149).

The admiring lecture on Milton, given in February of 1835, anticipated both in subject and in theme the series of discourses that Emerson began later in the year, moving from science and biography into the more congenial world of books and reading. The scholar as reader is his concern in an address of August 1835 that also looks forward to the ensuing lectures on English literature; its announced subject is the development of literary taste. No "mechanical means," he insisted, is likely to promote any such "spiritual end": physicians cannot manufacture one drop of blood, nor can "colleges make one scholar nor the best library a reader." Here Emerson recognizes as ordained by Providence that division of labor which "appoints sailors and soldiers as well as poets from the cradle and makes strong hands separate from strong heads" (*EL*, ɪ, 210), thus accepting the general conviction that "we cannot make scholars. They must be born." Then follows a characteristic separation of the real from the apparent as Emerson distinguishes those he calls "natural scholars" from a "much larger class" guided to literature only by "the custom of the day": men who would become soldiers if born during a military age; become speculators instead in a community given to trade; in "a reading community" they may even become "men of letters," though never true scholars. "Sciolists are never nearer scholars than hypocrites are to saints" (*EL*, ɪ, 210–211). "The main action of every lover of letters," he continues, "will of course be spent" on the class of natural scholars and not dilettantes or pedants. To develop scholars, he now holds, is to serve society, because the true scholar is meant for leadership: "In bringing a scholar into acquaintance with himself and his proper objects we render all men such a service as he does to an army who nominates Washington or Napoleon to the Command in chief" (*EL*, I, 211).

As this address of August 1835 distinguishes true scholars from ordinary readers, so the opening lecture of Emerson's course in English literature, delivered in November, sets forth his related conviction that there are two orders of writers. The true scholar, he had already observed, shows himself a philosopher in his plan of study, not merely a "trader in science & literature"[6] or a hired "workman for the booksellers" (*JMN*, v, 93). Now, in the concluding paragraphs of the first lecture of the new series, he was adapting an earlier journal entry of 10 October devoted to that "meek self reliance" he believed to be "the law & constitution of good writing." The journeyman writer, thinking only "to sing to the tune of the times, . . . to be the decorous sayer of smooth things, to lull the ear of society," must "lay aside all hope to wield or so much as to touch the bright thunderbolts of truth which it is given to the true scholar to launch & whose light flashes through ages without diminution" (*JMN*, v, 92–93). In the journal Emerson is voicing his own growing aspirations as a writer; in the lecture, however, the now-familiar figure of "the true scholar" gives way to another related idealization: those "august

geniuses" who "make up the body of English literature." To these writers
he applies the very phrases from the journal he had first written of the
scholar, with his "bright thunderbolts of truth," emphasizing their "instinctive belief that the office of a great genius was to guide the future, not
follow the past" (EL, 1, 231–232). As the natural scholar stands above
mere readers, so the true scholar stands forth here in the company of men
of genius as a modern Milton: a truth-teller, a Teacher, a leader pointing
to the future.

   In so beginning his lectures on literature Emerson was entering a new
phase of his search for a calling and his exploration of the role of American scholar. By 1835, with increasing confidence in his natural endowments, he saw himself as one destined to be enrolled in that order of
writers which guides and inspires mankind. Emerson's consideration of
the scholar in his alternative function as "maker of literature" returns to
his earlier conceptions of the true or ideal scholar as the "intellectual"
and "spiritual" man. The writer's aim, he now declares, is "nothing less
than to *give voice to the whole of spiritual nature* as events and ages unfold it, to record in words the whole life of the world." He then poses a
series of questions in which the maker of literature is specifically equated
with a new figure: "the Thinker." "What interest have men" in
literature? "Is it made for a few? Is it made only for the Makers? Who are
the Makers? and for whom do they work? What service is rendered us by
the Thinker, or man of letters, and in what manner?" (EL, 1, 226). His
answer, though cast in terms of the writer as poet, philosopher, and
historian rather than specifically as the scholar, directly anticipates his
later definition of the scholar himself, in the "right state," as "*Man Thinking*" rather than "a mere thinker, or still worse, the parrot of other men's
thinking" (W, 1, 84). The answer, moreover, begins with one of the first
public statements of an idea that became central to his lectures of 1836–37
on the philosophy of history and later to "The American Scholar": the
conception of one generic or universal Man comprising all particular or
individual men. Here is the lecturer's affirmation in 1835:

> It is in the nature not of any particular man but of universal man *to
> think*; though the action of reflexion is very rare. The relation between
> thought and the world, of which I have spoken, is not fancied by some
> poet, but stands in the will of God, and so is free to be known by all men.
> It appears to men, or it does not appear. But there it is. He who perceives
> it, and every man, whilst he perceives it, is a poet, is a philosopher. To
> perceive it, is to take one's stand in the absolute, and consider the passage
> of things and events purely as a spectacle and not as action in which we
> partake. This the poet, this the philosopher, this the historian does. The
> habit of men is to rest in the objects immediately around them, to go along
> with the tide, and take their impulse from external things. The Thinker
> takes them aside and makes them see what they did as *in dumb show*.
> (EL, 1, 226)

Emerson's "Thinker" is thus a see-er, or in his earlier figure, a "Watcher," but he is more than a detached observer. By perceiving, by reflecting, and by causing other men to see, he acts not merely for himself or men like himself but in the service of all mankind: in the words of the lecture, "the great Thinker thinks for all; and all have a property in his wisdom" (*EL*, I, 229).

III. "A TRUE THEORY OF NATURE & MAN"
(1836–37)

At Paris in 1832, at the height of his enthusiasm for natural history, Emerson had said to himself, "I will be a naturalist," but by 1834 he was saying in public that the naturalist should be "subordinate to the Man." The scholar, the writer, must be more than a specialist; he must be a man speaking for Man to men. By 1835 Emerson was thinking of himself as a writer; on 22 January 1836, only eight days after concluding his lectures on English literature, he was actively planning a book, making an extended entry in the journal that directly looks forward both to *Nature* and to "The American Scholar." From earlier passages dating as far back as 1834 he assembled a page of characteristic observations about the scholar and his view of nature[7] that suggests a possible outline for the projected book on "Natural Ethics"—evidently a shadowy ancestor of both compositions. The entry begins with some of the drawbacks to a scholar's life that Emerson had encountered as a minister or lecturer. Working "with invisible tools to invisible ends," the scholar passes with other classes of men "for an idler or worse," though in reality his distinctive character is "founded on natural gifts as specific & as rare as military genius; the power to stand *beside* his thoughts, or, to hold off his thoughts at arm's length & give them perspective." Here again is the idea that a scholar is appointed to his calling from birth by reason of his specific "natural gifts." Such a man, made different from his fellows and studying "the art of solitude" like Emerson himself in 1834, is consequently "gravelled in every discourse with common people." But on the positive side the scholar makes those contributions to society that Emerson had been enumerating both in the journal and in his recent lectures: he "shows thought to be infinite" which was supposedly exhausted; he is ideally "the intellectual man," or "the Thinker," who if he succeed in setting other men upon thinking shall be to them "a god." Elaborating at this point on his ideal of the scholar as Thinker, Emerson emphasizes his complementary gifts of seeing and saying. For him, "all history, is poetry"; with his unique power of perception he sees as precious the facts upon which lesser men trample; to his sight even "meanest life" reveals "a thread of empyrean light." Through his utterance, the "dishonored facts" which all men know are transformed; he converts them into "trees of life." By "suggesting the principle which classifies the facts" he makes of everyday existence "a garden of God." Finally, the scholar evidently answers in the affirmative the seminal question with which the passage concludes: "We <stand> build the sepulchers of our fathers: can we never behold the Universe as new and ｜feel｜ that we have a stake as much as our predecessors[?]" (*JMN*, v, 116–117).

In this concluding question will be recognized the germ of that characteristically Emersonian paragraph on originality standing at the beginning of *Nature*, the book Emerson completed and published some eight months later: "Our age is retrospective. It builds the sepulchres of the fathers. . . . The foregoing generations beheld God and nature face to face; we, through their eyes. Why should not we also enjoy an original relation to the universe? Why should not we have a poetry and philosophy of insight and not of tradition, and a religion by revelation to us, and not the history of theirs?" (*W*, i, 3). A "true theory of nature & man," Emerson wrote, in his journal and again in his first book (*JMN*, v, 182; *W*, i, 61), must have in it something "progressive"—something that looks to the future. In the oration of 1837 "the active soul" is likewise "progressive," not content to "stop with some past utterance of genius" (*W*, i, 90) but truly original and creative. The most conspicuous movement of Emerson's mind in the middle 1830's is away from primary concern with institutions and works of the past in favor of creation in the present with an eye to the future. Books, he was to say in "The American Scholar," are "the best type of the influence of the past" (*W*, i, 87)—but if the books he reads stand in the way of a scholar's creative utterance they become actually harmful.

Emerson's repeated insistence on originality and creativity is concurrent with his emergence as an independent thinker, writer, and public speaker known for his own distinctive style and voice, confident in his own insight. The publication of *Nature* in September of 1836 marks the end of his literary apprenticeship; the lectures of the following winter stand as the richest he had yet delivered. Throughout the momentous year 1836 he was engaged in rounding out what his friend Carlyle was to regard as "the Foundation and Ground-plan" of a philosophy of nature and history, examining the relation between the self and the external worlds of physical nature and human society in terms of what he liked to call "spiritualism"—the more usual label, then and now, is of course "Transcendentalism." Meanwhile the related "Sermon to Literary Men," as he had come to think of his proposed "chapter" on the Scholar, remained unwritten, though a significant amplification of his ideas about the social function of the writer can be found in a lecture on "Literature" read in January of 1837. The discussion develops out of an initial definition of literature as "the conversion of action into thought" (*EL*, ii, 55). Two years before, it will be recalled, Emerson had said that the poet or philosopher, drawing men aside from their daily round, "makes them see what they did as *in dumb show*"; here he describes the pleasure a man takes in seeing objectified, through literature, what he cannot otherwise behold except subjectively: himself, and what he is feeling and doing (*EL*, II, 56). The point is in harmony with his growing conviction that a man should seek to transcend the immediate, the personal, the particular in favor of the eternal, the impersonal, the universal, or the material in favor of the intellectual and spiritual. For Emerson, moreover, literature yields a higher value than pleasure: what he calls "its effect as power" (*EL*, II, 57). The great writer, by his act of transforming "a common incident in our history" into "an object of thought," thus making it timeless and eternal, reveals to other men "the worth of the present moment" and shows the individual that "[his] being is of more worth than [he] knew," because the temporal has been related to the timeless and the individual being to universal being (*EL*, II, 59). Implicit in Emerson's account of this process is his desire, in common with all men of a Transcendental persuasion, to bridge two worlds, the temporal and the eternal, *transcending* the realm of the here and now by viewing it in terms of an intellectual or spiritual world beyond it.[8]

Such is "the inherent dignity," in Emerson's phrase, "of all intellectual activity," which is destined "to the pursuit of truth and to the conversion of the world of events into ideas of the mind" (*EL*, II, 59). This notion of "transformation" or "conversion," already associated in his mind with the functions of the scholar, was to appear again in the oration as in other work of 1837 and after, providing an additional criterion for distinguishing genuine literature, the original creation of true genius, from the derivative products of mere talent. In this distinction between genius and talent, creative insight and ordinary understanding, Emerson reveals his kinship with Coleridge, though his own thinking had carried him beyond the immediate dependence upon Coleridgean formulas visible in his writing of the earlier 1830's. "The man of genius," it now seemed to him, "must occupy the whole space between God or pure mind, and the multitude of uneducated men"—a significant statement for one who only a year before had written of the solitary scholar as "gravelled in every discourse with common people," convinced though he was of the scholar's obligation to inspire and guide society. Such a writer, he continues in "Literature," has a double obligation; he

> must draw from the infinite Reason on the one side and he must penetrate into the heart and mind of the rabble on the other. From one he must draw his strength: to the other, he must owe his aim. The one yokes him to the real; the other to the apparent. . . . A defect on either side of this entire range immediately affects the success. Plotinus and many philosophers united with God, on one side, do not attain to a sympathy with the crowd on the other. On the contrary, great numbers of persons dwell in full understanding with common life like Falstaff, but with slender communion with the spiritual source. (*EL*, II, 61–62; cf. *JMN*, V, 249–250)

This statement, with its balanced recognition of the world of common life as well as the world of mind and spirit, is characteristic of the double vision of Emerson at his best. Since 1834 he had found greater rewards in the fruits of everyday experience, though without in any way lessening his commitment to the interior life of the scholar. "I embrace the common, I explore and sit at the feet of the familiar, the low," he was to write in "The American Scholar"—not common life simply for its own sake, however, but in his scholarly pursuit of "the ultimate reason of these matters," that "one design" which for him transcends the apparent dualism of immediate experience and so "unites and animates the farthest pinnacle and the lowest trench" (W, i, 111–112).

Running through the lectures of 1836–37, an address on education in the following June, and "The American Scholar" itself is Emerson's desire not only to transcend the world of common life but to transform it—not politically, but "by spiritual arms alone," as he had said of Luther's "revolution." He stood apart, moreover, from contemporary reformers who sought to remold society at large; his primary objective was to ennoble individual men. "Progress," he declared in his lectures on the philosophy of history, "is not for society. Progress belongs to the Individual" (EL, ii, 176). Working "with invisible tools to invisible ends," he held before the private man a vision of his highest potential, his spiritual "infinitude." In 1836 and 1837 this vision took its distinctive form in Emerson's conception of generic Man distinct from individual men—that Man of whom the scholar at his best is representative. Further implications of this idea are set forth in the opening lecture on the philosophy of history, where Emerson alludes to the "great discovery" that "there is one Mind common to all individual men; that what is individual is less than what is universal; that those properties by which you are man are more radical than those by which you are Adam or John; than the individual, nothing is less; than the universal, nothing is greater; that error, vice, and disease have their seat in the superficial or individual nature; that the common nature is whole" (EL, ii, 11). On the basis of this conception of One Man and One Mind—his "old thrum," as Emerson came to call it in 1837 (JMN, v, 376)—the aim of education should be "to sink what is individual or personal in us, to stimulate what is torpid of the human nature, and so to swell the individual to the outline of this Universal Man and bring out his original and majestic proportions" (EL, ii, 12).

But when Emerson surveyed the world about him in 1837, a year of hard times for many and of financial worries, poor health, and low spirits even for him, there was cause for discouragement. The modern age, he granted in his lectures, had brought a wider diffusion of knowledge, but at considerable social cost: for the populace, "what is gained in surface is lost in depth," while the shortcomings of "formal and pedantic scholarship" have discredited the reverence in which former ages held the scholar and his learning (*EL*, ii, 164, 165). Current literature, politics, and religion display only a "great hollowness," according to his address on education, in spite of the "immense vital energy" at work in contemporary England and America: "A desperate conservatism clings with boths hands to every dead form in the schools, in the state, in the church" (*EL*, ii, 197). He saw the world of actuality as lying sick of a disease, its symptoms "the degradation of Man" through inaction of his "higher faculties" and "usurpation by the senses of the entire practical energy of individuals, and the consequent prevalence of low and unworthy views of the manly character" (*EL*, ii, 197, 196). So Emerson had written less than three months before "The American Scholar." One searching, like Diogenes with his lantern, for "individuals who satisfy the idea of Man" as Emerson himself conceived it in 1837 finds "here a strong arm, and there, cunning fingers; he will find a stout soldier; a ready writer; a shrewd banker,—he will find parts and beginnings, but no whole" (*EL*, ii, 196).

Still, as the oration was soon to attest, Emerson did not rest easily in a mood of discouragement. "The true scholar" must be more than another specialist—more even than society's "delegated intellect," in the phrasing of "The American Scholar," for he is potentially its ideal figure of Man and its "only true master" (*W*, i, 84). The modern age in its sickness needs his illuminating power of Reason, as Emerson had said in his winter lectures of 1836–37, to emancipate the spirit and neutralize injurious influences (*EL*, ii, 182, 184). In the subsequent address on education, considering the scholar as teacher, he was sharper in both diagnosis and prescription. Education should not aim at making specialists—"accountants, attornies, engineers"—but must develop men, "heroes and saints" (*EL*, ii, 199). To this end society establishes its colleges, schools, and churches, appointing to them its learned men as a "priesthood" to foster "the superior nature of man." This class, the scholars, comprises "the clergy, the literary men, the colleges, the teachers of youth"; without their transforming vision a people will perish. Of all possible failure, Emerson declares, "the most deplorable" occurs "when the eye itself has become blind"—when a nation's teachers themselves "lose sight of the capital secret of their profession, namely, to convert life into truth, or to show the meaning of events."[9] As a cautionary example he describes a man appointed to lead the public, one who has "dwelt and acted with other men" and shared the experiences of common life, but who nevertheless falls short of his duty as scholar and teacher: all his experience remains "aloof from his intellect," not yet "converted into wisdom, and instead, he entertains the people with words. Herein he utterly fails in his office" (*EL*, ii, 202).

IV. MAN THINKING (1837)

Turning from the address on education, which seems preoccupied with failure, to "The American Scholar," with its air of exuberant confidence, is like examining the upper side of the same continuous pattern in cloth: the thought is of a piece but the colors are noticeably brighter. The invitation to speak in Cambridge reached Emerson late in June of 1837, when the persistent illness that had left its mark on the address was still keeping him from study and leading him to think of "a long journey or a voyage" to restore his health (*JMN*, v, 339; *L*, ii, 83). He accepted the engagement, and once his strength returned began an exploratory series of journal entries, dated from mid-July to mid-August, that were to lead him into the very center of the oration: on the scholar as creator, exemplifying what Emerson was to call "The one thing in the world, of value, . . . the active soul" (*W*, i, 90). Despite a passing remark to his brother that "we cannot get any word from Olympus" for Phi Beta Kappa (*L*, ii, 94), there is no suggestion that Emerson regarded the impending engagement as anything but an opportunity to fulfill his long-standing intention of writing on "the Duty & Discipline of a Scholar." "If the Allwise would give me light," he noted on 29 July, "I should write for the Cambridge men a theory of the Scholar's office" (*JMN*, v, 347); on 18 August he amplified his objective in now-familiar terms: "The hope to arouse young men at Cambridge to a worthier view of their literary duties <teach> prompts me to offer the theory of the Scholar's function. He has an office to perform in society. What is it? To arouse the intellect; to keep it erect & sound; to keep admiration in the hearts of the people; to keep the eye open upon its spiritual aims" (*JMN*, v, 364–365).

Although the manuscript from which Emerson read his oration on 31 August has not come down to us, examination of the printed text in relation to antecedent passages of the journal and lectures shows in broad outline how "The American Scholar" took form under his hand during the summer preceding its delivery. As we have seen, most of its basic ideas about the scholar and his relation to society had already been worked out in discernible stages over the preceding three years. The key Emersonian distinction between "being" and "seeming" had required a separation of the scholar as he actually is both from what others think him to be and also from what he ought to be ideally: "the true scholar." At first Emerson had viewed the scholar in society as a rather unsatisfactory representative of "the intellectual man"; later he conceived a nobler figure, the Thinker who "thinks for all"; finally the scholar, viewed "in the right state," emerges in the oration as the very image of Universal Man—in short, as *"Man Thinking."* On the level of experience, moreover, Emerson had moved from his self-projection of 1834—a solitary "Watcher," isolated from his fellows, quietly practicing his "philosophy of *Waiting*" while hopefully preparing to "act well hereafter"—to successive visualizations of the active thinker, the influential writer and teacher that he saw in Luther and Milton and that he himself was in fact becoming. Now in 1837, clearly sensing the close of a "long apprenticeship" in himself as well as in his countrymen (*W*, i, 81), he was expressing his ideal vision of the true scholar—the American scholar—as an influential spiritual mentor, speaking not in the accents of tradition but as prompted by his own insight and revelation, actively leading men out of bondage to the faded past into a new relation to their own world of the living present. The true scholar, though born to his calling, must learn through experience to link himself equally to the common life of mankind and to its ultimate spiritual source, doing full justice to both. He serves his contemporaries by exercising his innate gift, his "capital secret," of transforming or converting temporal life into timeless truth, thus showing the underlying meaning of present events. While dwelling in a society of many diverse individuals, he endeavors to realize for them and for himself, by example as well as by precept, the ideal of One Universal Man and the value of the active soul.

In composing his oration in terms of these guiding ideas Emerson quite clearly went back to their earlier formulation in his journals and lectures. More than a third of "The American Scholar" is directly traceable to journal and lecture passages taken over with relatively slight revision or rearrangement, some of them written as early as 1834 and others drafted during the summer of 1837 after acceptance of the invitation from Phi Beta Kappa. Expansion of some of this existing material and provision for necessary transitional phrasing accounts for a considerable part of the additional writing evidently done late in August of 1837, when journal entries first tapered off and then stopped until after the oration had been delivered. Some of the earlier entries concerning the scholar had been brought together in January of 1836, when *Nature* was beginning to take definite form; others could always be readily located through Emerson's systematic indexing of every manuscript journal. Reading what he had previously written obviously stimulated further thought, as a typical illustration suggests. The same long journal entry of 21 December 1834 that outlines Emerson's "philosophy of *Waiting*" includes both the image of the scholar as a lone "Watcher" scanning the heavens for light and a pronouncement that his "office is to cheer our labor as with a song by highest hopes" (*JMN*, iv, 368, 370–371, 372). So in the oration, by way of an intermediate draft of August 1837 (*JMN*, v, 359), Emerson wrote: "The office of the scholar is to cheer, to raise, and to guide men by showing them facts amidst appearances. He plies the slow, unhonored, and unpaid task of observation . . . in his private observatory, cataloguing . . . stars of the human mind" (*W*, i, 100–101).

Again, in the entry of 1834, and in close juxtaposition with the figure of the "Watcher," is this proverb: "Time & patience change a mulberry leaf into satin" (*JMN*, IV, 371); this too turns up in the oration during Emerson's discussion of the scholar's need for experience and action.[10] "The true scholar grudges every opportunity of action past by, as a loss of power. It is the raw material out of which the intellect moulds her splendid products. A strange process too, this by which experience is converted into thought, as a mulberry leaf is converted into satin. The manufacture goes forward at all hours" (*W*, I, 95–96). Here Emerson is once again adverting to the act of transformation or conversion that he repeatedly associated with the creative process; his true scholar, like "the true preacher" of his Divinity School Address (1838), "deals out to the people his life,—life passed through the fire of thought" and so transformed (*W*, I, 138).[11] In Emerson's own writing, as we have seen, the journals contributed to this necessary metamorphosis both by storing for later use the raw material yielded by experience and by helping him to refine and finish the products originally molded by his shaping intellect.

On a somewhat different scale, much of what Emerson had already said in *Nature* is epitomized in the section of "The American Scholar" treating the primary influence of man's natural environment (paragraphs 8–9, *W*, I, 84–87). The concluding section of the oration, where Emerson turns his attention "to the time and to this country" (paragraphs 36–38, *W*, I, 108–110), virtually recapitulates the analysis of the contemporary world he had advanced a few months before in his lectures on the philosophy of history—particularly "The Present Age" and "The Individual," of which there are close verbal echoes that suggest a recent rereading. It was of course in the same lecture series that he had developed the abstraction which underlies his account of the scholar as Man Thinking: the concept of a single Universal Man of whom individual men are only components. In the address on education Emerson had set his ideal of One Man against the actuality of narrow specialization; his dark references there to the unhappy results of the division of labor in modern society anticipate the three paragraphs of the oration in which Man is seen as "metamorphosed into a thing," "ridden by the routine of his craft," and with his soul made "subject to dollars." In actual life, that "degenerate state" in which he is but "the victim of society," instead of its "only true master," even the scholar "tends to become a mere thinker, or still worse, the parrot of other men's thinking" (*W*, I, 82–84).[12]

If *imitation* is the hallmark of the degenerate scholar, as this early passage of the oration implies, *originality*, the consciously formulated objective of Emerson's own utterance, is the unmistakable sign of Man Thinking. The persistent theme of originality, already addressed in *Nature*, dominates the series of extraordinary journal entries written between 17 and 29 July 1837, shortly after Emerson had accepted the Phi Beta Kappa invitation and resumed regular habits of study after his debilitating illness; these entries were to provide the substance of the long middle section of the oration treating books, as representing the mind of the past, and their influence on the scholar. Emerson's first response to a speaking invitation was usually to explore possible topics by writing in his journal; in this instance, one might well suppose, his initial impulse was to present his Phi Beta Kappa audience with a blistering attack on books, academies, and all institutions inherited from the past. Though books may indeed "provoke thoughts," as one entry rather grudgingly admits, "The office of reading is wholly subordinate. . . . I get thereby a vocabulary for my ideas. I get no ideas" (*JMN*, v, 343–344). Books "are but crutches," according to a later passage (*JMN*, v, 345). And finally, in the Emersonian words that every protesting schoolboy knows—though their full implication may elude him, "Books are for the scholar's idle times." For when a man "can read God directly, the hour is too precious to be wasted on other men's transcripts of their readings" (*JMN*, v, 347; *W*, ɪ, 91).

Put negatively, Emerson's is a case against books and the past; put positively, however, he is once again asserting the essential originality and timeliness of truly creative scholarship. The unifying theme of the journal entries became the central message of the oration: original creation is the true function of the scholar and the sure testament of his genius. "To create, to create" is ultimately "the proof of a Divine presence," Emerson had written in July of 1837. "Whoever creates is God, and whatever talents are, <exhibited> if the man create not, the pure efflux of Deity is not his" (*JMN*, v, 341). As this formulation in the journal makes clear, Emerson's view of the creative process has powerful religious overtones: "Whoever creates is God"; the corresponding passage of the oration (*W*, ɪ, 90) is not quite so daring.[13] "Creation," according to the journal, "is always the style & act" of men of genius, in whom "the good human soul speaks because it has something new to say" (*JMN*, v, 341–342). Here is the epitome of all Emerson had been seeking to do as a writer and teacher: to utter only what he could offer as his own work, the product of his own insight, the sign of his own original relation to the universe. His characteristic drive toward original utterance, his inspiration to create, is what animates the oration and gives it distinctive substance and form.

It is this same creative impulse that unmistakably identifies Emerson's "true scholar," his recurrent image for "the idea of Man" he was seeking to raise, as Milton had done, "in the minds of his contemporaries and of posterity." As *"Man Thinking"* the scholar must be neither traditional nor imitative nor merely nationalistic, but truly original. What Emerson asks of this ideal figure he had asked again and again of himself, first in his journals and lectures, then in *Nature*, and now in "The American Scholar," his long-projected essay in definition. "The one thing in the world, of value," in the words of the oration, "is the active soul," which first "sees" truth and then "utters truth, or creates. In this action it is genius" (*W*, ɪ, 90). By his very creativity the scholar thus defines himself, as Emerson did in writing "The American Scholar"; to function as Man's "active soul" is to carry out the essential "Duty & Discipline" of his inspired office.

Notes

1. Parenthetical references within the text are to the following publications: *EL* = *The Early Lectures of Ralph Waldo Emerson*, ed. Stephen E. Whicher, Robert E. Spiller, and Wallace E. Williams (Cambridge: Harvard University Press, 1959–); *JMN* = *The Journals and Miscellaneous Notebooks of Ralph Waldo Emerson*, ed. William H. Gilman et al. (Cambridge: Harvard University Press, 1960–); *L* = *The Letters of Ralph Waldo Emerson*, ed. Ralph L. Rusk, 6 vols. (New York: Columbia University Press, 1939); *W* = *The Complete Works of Ralph Waldo Emerson*, ed. Edward Waldo Emerson, 12 vols. (Boston: Houghton, Mifflin, 1903–1904).

The present essay is an outgrowth of editorial work with Emerson manuscripts in the Houghton Library when *JMN*, V, was in preparation. Completion of the study was assisted by a grant from the Research Committee of the Graduate School, The University of Wisconsin-Madison.

2. See Henry Nash Smith, "Emerson's Problem of Vocation: A Note on 'The American Scholar,' " *New England Quarterly*, 12 (March 1939): 52–67.

3. Robert E. Spiller, "From Lecture into Essay: Emerson's Method of Composition," *Literary Criterion*, 5 (Winter 1962): 28.

4. Stephen E. Whicher, Introduction to *Selections from Ralph Waldo Emerson: An Organic Anthology* (Boston: Houghton Mifflin, 1957), p. xviii.

5. Cancellations in the manuscript journals are indicated here, as in *JMN*, by angle brackets: <. . .>; insertions are indicated by paired arrows: ↑. . .↓.

6. The phrase comes from an extract that Emerson had copied in 1832 from a magazine report of one of Schiller's lectures (*JMN*, VI, 107). The content was evidently in his mind two years later when he referred to Schiller as "prescribing the ethics of the Scholar" (*JMN*, IV, 367).

7. Emerson's manuscript Journal B, p. 128 (*JMN*, V, 116–117), reproduced as Plate I in *Emerson's* Nature—*Origin, Growth, Meaning*, ed. Merton M. Sealts, Jr., and Alfred R. Ferguson (1969; 2d ed., enlarged, Carbondale: Southern Illinois University Press, 1979), p. 4.

8. See Kenneth Burke, "I, Eye, Ay—Emerson's Early Essay 'Nature': Thoughts on the Machinery of Transcendence," in *Transcendentalism and Its Legacy*, ed. Myron Simon and Thornton H. Parsons (Ann Arbor: University of Michigan Press, 1966), pp. 3–24. Transcendence, according to Burke, p. 23, "involves dialectical processed whereby something HERE is interpreted *in terms of* something THERE, something *beyond* itself."

9. Emerson had formulated the "secret" in a journal entry of 7 May 1837 describing the sermon of a young Concord minister who failed to convert "one joy" of experience into wisdom for his hearers (*JMN*, V, 324). The Divinity School Address of 1838, which also draws on this same passage, applies the phrasing specifically to the work of the ministry (*W*, I, 138).

10. Contrast Emerson's earlier words in *Nature*: the soul "is a watcher more than a doer, and it is a doer, only that it may the better watch" (*W*, I, 60).

11. In the journal version Emerson had written: ". . . his life, life metamorphosed" (*JMN*, V, 464).

12. On man's "degenerate state," or "degradation," see *Nature*, *W*, I, 70 ("In the cycle of the universal man, from whom the known individuals proceed . . . all history is but the epoch of one degradation"), and the Divinity School Address, *W*, I, 127.

13. Emerson had been more explicit in a passage of *Nature* that throws light on his understanding of creativity: "spirit creates; . . . spirit, that is, the Supreme Being, does not

build up nature around us, but puts it forth through us." Man, who "has access to the entire mind of the Creator, is himself the creator in the finite. This view . . . animates me to create my own world through the purification of my soul" (W, I, 63–64).

"Emerson's Search for Literary Form: The Early Journals"

Ralph C. LaRosa*

That Emerson's literary career was a "search for form" is confirmed by both his temperament and style. Henry James first noted that "Emerson had his message, but he was a good while looking for his form." Subsequent commentary on Emerson's life has put into perspective the social and biographical details which informed that search for a life-style and literary form commensurate with his ambitions and abilities.[1] It has not been fully appreciated, however, that the form, method, and thematic preoccupations of Emerson's earliest journals allowed for discovery of a literary technique which shaped the very substance of his later message. Inevitably, the practice of journal keeping lent itself to a private, preliminary, and experimental art. As a reflection of Emerson's growing ambition to be a moral writer, his journal experiments involved coming to terms with two issues he would formally reconcile in "Quotation and Originality" (1859). The journals from 1818 to 1824 clearly reveal his earliest investigation of the relationship of originality, quotation, and the ends of written art.

In his earliest attempts to coordinate "quotation" and "originality" Emerson pursued a twofold investigation: he analyzed the concept of original genius and its relation to the past, and he collected large numbers of commonplace sentences (sententiae) which he experimented with as a means of defining his own originality. The first line of inquiry brought him to an accommodation of art and morality which is largely dependent on his attitude toward the commonplace moral sentence. And his journal experiments in sentence manipulation and essay writing established habits of composition which eventually determined the moral basis of his own art. His search for moral form began in earnest when he decided to keep and justify his early journals.

I

As a young man, Emerson was a direct heir of the American practice of keeping journals and commonplace books for self-analysis and composition.[2] His rhetorical training at the Boston Latin School and at Har-

*Reprinted from Modern Philology, 69 (August 1971), 25–35.

vard reinforced this traditional habit of New England intellectuals by its emphasis on rhetorical "invention" and "amplification," categories of Renaissance rhetorics.[3] Emerson and his schoolfellows thus kept common-place books stocked with *sententiae* in order to arrive at ("invent") topics for their school essays and to draw from them to support ("amplify") their arguments. Emerson's personal reading in the essays of Bacon and Montaigne also provided him with exemplars of essayists obviously depen-dent on the use of brief, sententious statements drawn from commonplace books. From Bacon's praise and use of aphorisms Emerson learned that the utility of collected sentences was as "the seeds of several arguments . . . cast into some brief and acute sentence; not to be cited, but to be the skeins or bottoms of a thread, to be unwinded at large when they come to be used; supplying authorities and examples by reference."[4]

Numerous references to journal keeping in letters and journals reflect his response to rhetorical training and reading. An early letter to his brother Edward about a schoolfellow's commonplace books is light and ironic, but it finds "what a loss to the world if by any unforeseen unlucky accident the Annotations and Memoranda of a Paine never come to press!" (*L*, 1:30).[5] At thirteen years of age, Emerson's epistolary tone is adolescently satiric, but it is clear that he understands the utility of jour-nals for recording the details, ideas, and problems of daily life. His in-creasingly serious attitude toward journal keeping was again expressed when he began keeping his "College Theme Book" (1819) several years later. That same year he wrote to Edward and admonished him to "keep that journal of yours faithfully regularly & largely." Convinced that jour-nals are compulsory equipment for the young intellectual and traveler, he adds that he will send Edward "Lord Bacon's rules for a traveller; the first is to keep a journal" (*L*, 1:91).

It was as a junior at Harvard in 1820 that Emerson dedicated his first regular journal. The dedication to "Wide World I" indicates that he had indeed assimilated the Renaissance methods and objectives of keeping commonplace books: "Mixing with the thousand pursuits & passions & objects of the world as personified by Imagination is profitable & enter-taining. These pages are intended at this their commencement to contain a record of new thoughts (when they occur); for a receptacle of all the old ideas that partial but peculiar peepings at antiquity can furnish or fur-bish; for tablet to save wear and tear of weak Memory & in short for all the various purposes & utility real or imaginary which are usually com-prehended under that comprehensive title *Common Place book*" (*JMN*, 1:3–4).

The spirit of keeping such books was exemplified and dictated by the moral essayists Bacon and Montaigne; and his emphasis on the faculties of imagination and memory in this dedication is apparently Baconian. Vivian Hopkins has pointed out that Bacon, like Emerson and the Transcendentalists, was a "simplifier" of approaches to knowledge.

Bacon, for example, had reduced Ramus's six mental faculties to three: memory, reason, and imagination.[6] Emerson's conception of the commonplace book as a receptacle of new and old ideas which could "save wear and tear on weak Memory" parallels Bacon's first category and his championing of commonplace books in *The Advancement of Learning.* The second faculty, reason, and its relation to memory is defined in Emerson's epilogue to "Wide World I." This first commonplace book, he noted, "afforded seasonable aid at various times to enlarge or enliven scanty themes &c."; it has "perhaps enriched my stock of language for future exertions. Much of it has been written with a view to their preservation as hints for a peculiar pursuit at the distance of years" (*JMN,* 1:25). In the future his "imagination" would work on his stockpiled commonplaces for his present purposes.

The form of Emerson's early commonplace books indicates how his practice, like that of Bacon and other masters of the Renaissance essay, involved collecting lists of proverbs, similes, analogies, and examples; in short, sentences (*sententiae*) of moral import and universal wisdom (cf. *JMN,* 6:388–89). As he noted in an early "Wide World," his purpose was to collect a "store of organized verbs, nouns, & substantives, to wit sentences" (*JMN,* 1:33); and he consciously devoted a section of this same journal to the *"down-putting* of sentences, quoted or original" (*JMN,* 1:14). Indeed, he collected several hundred such sentences in his regular journals and his special quotation book, "The Universe," between 1819 and 1824.

In order to facilitate his "down-putting" of these sentences, Emerson had as possible models many of the loosely organized commonplace books which proliferated during the Renaissance. His final choice, however, was a method more systematic than that of the earlier models. The plan of his earliest "Wide World" journals was based on a system of indexing by alphabet and topic headings, as illustrated in *A Common Place Book, Upon the Plan Recommended and Practised by John Locke, Esq.* (Boston, 1821; *JMN,* 1: 26 n.). By utilizing this plan, Emerson would be able, "at the distance of years," to check his index and immediately locate a series of original statements, paraphrases, quotations, or proverbs listed under specific topics on which he wished to write a sermon, lecture, or essay.

II

It is clear that by the early 1820s Emerson had purposefully established his commonplace books as a framework within which to collect sentences and explore his artistic strengths and weaknesses. In tune with the critical climate of the early nineteenth century, one of his concurrent preoccupations was with "originality" in writing. This broad concern involved his definition of the metaphysical and aesthetic worth of sentences. In his Harvard "College Theme Book" (1819), the repository of his own initial efforts at original composition, he wrote: "It is generally the case in all works of literature and in Poetry in particular that we much oftener meet with works which we can immediately classify as additional productions of a well known school than those which bear the impress of originality. The moment however that a writer of genius has marked out a new path for himself there will be followers enough to enlarge & beautify what his invention has discovered" (*JMN*, 1:165). Emerson clearly has a negative attitude toward the artistic products of any "well known school," as opposed to those bearing the "impress of originality." Nonetheless, when a work of genius comes to light, he seems to think it appropriate that men of lesser talent "enlarge and beautify" the inventions of true geniuses. There is bound to be imitation of the form and content of original and successful works of art. But Emerson draws a sharp distinction between the artistic genius and the derivative artist. Within several years he was convinced that "God doubtless designed to form minds of different mould, and to create distinctions in intellect" (*JMN*, 1:101). Even in 1819 he sees that there are few men who have the coextensive gifts of genius and originality; destructive and damnable imitation results from an adulation of true genius which borders on a "mania for originality" among lesser talents (*JMN*, 1:165).

The concept of a genius working through "invention" later evolved from a rhetorical practice to a complex, metaphysical facet of Emerson's theory of quotation and originality. Here he seems to use the word in its Baconian sense of the writer's ability to uncover and synthesize extant words, phrases, and sentences. Emerson felt that this mode of invention approached true originality, as opposed to merely seeking a semblance of originality through self-conscious eccentricity of style and matter. Originality of style should naturally follow from the writer's originality of sentiment, as Emerson's comments on one of Edward Search's sentences suggests: "It is a fine idea which he either intends to convey or else the form of expression unintentionally did (pray let us believe the latter for the credit of Originality)" (*JMN*, 1:4). Originality, then, is best expressed through a natural wedding of matter and style.

That genuine originality is the product of a writer's natural gifts is most fully developed in an extended journal analysis of Lord Byron as man and writer. As opposed to imitative poetasters, Byron's originality is "not so much owing to this common desire to please as by the natural peculiarity of his own character" (*JMN*, 1:165). Character and not "schools" or imitation provides the source of true genius and originality; Byron's "own wild character as a man stamped the character of his poetry; it is every where saddened by that deep feeling of desolateness & privation which appear to mark his own mind." An independent genius of "haughty indifference" to literary tradition, Byron expresses his character in a simple and plain "scripture style & phrase" (*JMN*, 1:166). Emerson later lost his youthful enthusiasm for Byron, but he never departed from his early conviction that originality must be inherent in the individual, not imitated, and that a man's style should clearly reflect the essence of his experience.

In the 1820s Emerson could insist, on the one hand, that true genius and originality are the property of the individual who retains his integrity despite conservative "literary demagogues" who hold on to traditional forms of literature and tyrannically prescribe them for the age (*JMN*, 1:168). But on the other hand he was aware that the past provides a reference for formulating judgment and taste in the present.[7] By the 1830s his belief that an individual embodies all thought and activity of the past, present, and future was basic to Emerson's concept of "self-reliant" originality. The evolution of this belief and its importance for his aesthetic theory and practice began with journal investigations of the relationship of the artist to the stream of tradition.

For instance, a journal essay "On Genius" (1820) sets up for ridicule the over-emphasis contemporary scholars put upon "their own unassisted exertions" while undervaluing the wisdom of "the wonderful men of old" (*JMN*, 1:207). And anticipating his later belief that "every man is a quotation" is an 1821 notation that all moral philosophy "was known two thousand years ago to every sagacious and experienced man" (*JMN*, 1:342). With this point of view, he dedicated one of his "Wide World" journals of 1822 to "the dead," because "all that adorns this world are the gifts which they left in their passage through it" (*JMN*, 1:91). Only by establishing what is the proper relationship of the individual to the stream of tradition, without negating either, could Emerson reconcile an apparent contradiction in his thinking.

A journal essay of 1822 reveals a more precise formulation of the relationship of the individual artist and tradition. At one point in his essay he asks, "How is it we preserve so accurately the knowledge of events and minds coeval with the Pyramids? How know we the history of the causes of private ambition or public outrage?" His answer is that "it is because every man bears within him a record of other men's motives" (*JMN*, 1:113). Originality and self-reliance are vaguely coextensive in the young man's mind, and his confrontation of the relationship looks ahead to his statement in "The American Scholar" (1837) that "in going down into the secrets of his own mind he [the scholar] has descended into the secrets of all minds" (*W*, 1:103). In 1822 Emerson seems to be seeking a balance between self-reliant integrity and the past. Tradition is, he must admit, very important, for he agrees with "speculative men" who find that while the modes and forms of expression change, "the principle" of truth motivating the expression "remains substantially the same" (*JMN*, 1:124) and is expressed through individual genius. Even at this early stage Emerson is seeking a unified principle of truth underlying the variety of experience.

As a check against falling back on a comforting view of unity at the expense of variety, he insists that although the *principle* of truth is unchanging throughout history, "Each generation takes in trust from the preceding the care and guidance of the world and each is at free liberty to amend whatever falsehood the oversight of other ages may have admitted" (*JMN*, 1:151). He does not except even those truisms traditionally considered sacred: "There is a comparison to be made between the primitive & the subsequent importance of passages (chiefly sacred) of the lives or language of remarkable persons, at first suggested by accidents, & long afterwards applied by posterity with mighty force, e.g., 'He that is not against us is on our part'; (Mark 9:40) & the like; and the predictions concerning St. Peter" (*JMN*, 1:202–3). At this early stage originality is not, then, either wholly accepting or completely shucking off all tradition, but is more an amending process. Like T. S. Eliot nearly a century later, he was formulating for himself the relationship between "tradition" and the "individual talent."[8] For Emerson the relationship was not only aesthetic, but moral and philosophical.

Emerson saw the relationship between the past and the individual as one of philosophic necessity: "No event . . . in mind or matter starts up into an independent existence, but all have an immediate dependence upon what went before. This is the foundation of the doctrine of human necessity" (*JMN*, 2:53). In short, "The remotest periods of human history are fatally and forever connected" (*JMN*, 2:22); and, again using philosophic terminology, he argues that "the world changes its masters, but keeps its own identity, and entails upon each new family of the human race . . . certain indelible features and unchanging properties" (*JMN*, 2:187). Finally, by tracing causal relations up the chain of contingency, he finds that all events "are bound and ordered by an adamantine chain," the bond being "divine justice" (*JMN*, 2:51).

A journal essay of 1822 makes clear that what the past has given is a body of formulaic standards for moral conduct which derive from an appreciation of this "divine justice," or Providence. Emerson's essay on "the history of religion" reveals that his efforts to define originality directly involved his attempts to understand man's relationship to God. The essay as a whole establishes an intimate relation between an understanding of God and the persistence of basic truths through history. The proverb, his favorite type of quotable sentence, is the key to this understanding (*JMN*, 1:86–87).

His essay begins by defining "providence" as the "general silent course of the Divine Government, manifested in the tendencies of human institutions and the human mind,—in the perfectness & imperfection, and their results, of brute or vegetable nature, in the daily events which take place and change in the universe," as compared with the direct interventions of God in the affairs of Abraham or Israel. The way to discovering this truth was for men to note after much experience that "there is a tendency in all human things to decay" but that out of this decay society moves toward new life. "Now," he adds, "these proofs of the action of some single intelligent Principle are not offered to the Atheist from the Bible or from the priest but they are taken out from the *proverbs* and familiar sayings of all nations, which are the first generalizations of the mind and have been repeated by the mouth of the million."

He finds that "as the peculiar language of experience, altogether independent of other purposes than as tried guides to life, *proverbs* demand notice." Approaching his major point, he adds: "It was early found that there were a few principles which controuled society; that the mother of all the arts, the nurse of social feelings; the impeller of individual energies—was Necessity; . . . and this was embodied in a maxim which has circulated through the world." The saying Emerson paraphrases into a history of providential power is, of course, "Necessity is the mother of invention." Having derived this truth and having cast it in a proverbial sentence, men then found its implications operating in the universe as a system of "compensations"; finally, Emerson continues, discerning men noted that this system always resulted in the progress of society.

The truth of this system of compensation was "ascertained by the progress of society, and corroborated by the observation of each succeeding generation" which incorporated the truth into "short maxims as rules for youth which maturity would establish." By Emerson's reasoning, proverbs first remind us of power which in turn reminds us of Providence in a forcible way. Then, through each man's youth and maturity, they are a means by which our "own recorded observations," in the form of proverbs, reflect the "Divine Administration of the world." Emerson sees the whole system of moral law as a broad proverbial generalization, a body of other proverbs generated by the master proverb, "Necessity is the mother of invention." The generated proverbs complete the cycle of understanding by leading us back to the source of this system of law, God. What Emerson says specifically about the power of proverbs seems equally applicable to the other *sentences* whose various designations (aphorism, maxim, etc.) are used synonymously throughout his work. This early conception of the inclusive nature of proverbs pervaded Emerson's thinking and influenced his style from this point on.

Having established that the sentence had metaphysical and moral implications, it remained for Emerson to determine the extent to which the moral sentence could be aesthetically justified. He found justification in Archibald Alison's *Essays on the Nature and Principles of Taste* (Edinburgh, 1811), a book that he excerpted at length during the year after the "essay" was written. For Emerson, who was looking for a standard of writing, taste, and morality, Alison's book "has helped to settle whether there be an ultimate standard of Taste" (*JMN*, 2:190). Alison argued that taste is "a code of general principles capable of being so applied to every possible production of Nature or Art as to determine at once its beauty or deformity." Alison was looking for a set of universal and ever applicable principles; to explain how these could be discovered he drew a parallel between moral law and aesthetics.

For Alison there was an analogical relationship between the moral law in Nature, the "Bible given by heaven," and "the mass of moral maxims gradually accumulated, without any supernatural aid, by the force of reason & observation in Greece" (*JMN*, 2:190). If these moral laws, expressed in man's own idiom and derived from experience and observation, were collected into a volume, they would constitute a system of natural law. Tacitly accepted by later generations, these laws would serve as an "ultimate standard of morality." The same principle is by analogy applicable to standards of good and bad art; and the assumption is that the standard of quality is moral as well as aesthetic.

III

Concurrent with his theoretical formulation of originality and the importance of the proverbial sentence in conveying it, Emerson also collected and experimented with the sentence as a unit of original thought and style. That he saw his journals as a medium for testing his theory of originality is evident from his dedication of his 1820 journal to the "downputting of sentences quoted or original, which regard Greece, historical poetical & critical" (*JMN*, 1:14). His intent was to discriminate carefully between quoted sentences and his own original observations. To facilitate setting off his invented sentences from those quoted he soon devised a sign of authorship which he consistently used throughout later journals and quotation books: "From this place to 'Detached Sentences' the pages are to be improved by lines, or verses, containing anything remarkable, either in expression, or sentiment, or remote association, principally quoted, but likewise original ones. The original are distinguished by the letter 'O.' or Junio or [R.W.E.]" (*JMN*, 1:215; cf. pl. 7). It is clear that Emerson's attention is here directed to both the style and content of his invented or quoted sentences. But at times he attempted to exercise his originality on what he quoted, thus blurring the distinction between quotation and originality. That no distinction obtains when quotation and originality are properly viewed later became basic to his aesthetic theory; at this point he tentatively experimented with the possibility as he approached individual sentences and adapted them to his journal essays.

Including a few used in his letters up to 1824, Emerson had collected only about 200 "Detached Sentences" concise enough to be included under his definitions of "proverb" or "sentence." By 1822 he had characterized the proverb and sententious remark as the "peculiar language of experience," but only a small fraction of his early collection expressed immediate, felt experience. Later, the young man would be brought into more direct contact with the facts of experience and the concrete referents essential to expressing universal truths. Up to 1824 he was more attuned to wisdom derived from books, in the form of "learned" abstract proverbs: "short maxims as rules for youth which maturity would establish" and which would in some instances be verified by his "own recorded experience" (*JMN*, 1:87). Prior to his commitment to the ministry in 1824, sentences quoted by Emerson were mostly unverified by his own experience. They were primarily a priori assumptions which, when tested in later life, would at times be controverted by personal disagreement or stylistically modified to illustrate his belief in organicism or compensation. In the early 1820s, however, Emerson drew almost exclusively from literature for his generalized sentences and from a scarce collection of John Ray's proverbs (reissued by Henry G. Bohn as *A Handbook of Proverbs* [1813]) for his more concrete items.[9]

Although Emerson usually entered his commonplaces without comment or revision, his current interest in the possibilities of the sentence as a moral and stylistic unit led him to make occasional adaptations of common proverbs or sententious remarks. For example, he ironically assigns to his "amusing friend Aristotle" a modified version of Protagoras's "man is the measure of all things" by entering it in his journal as "man is the measure and jest of all things" (*JMN*, 1:178). This type of manipulation at times became more extensive, as when he adapted the common proverb, "To kill two birds with one stone," to his own sentiments and sentence rhythm: "We shall then verify the old proverb, by killing two birds with one stone" (*JMN*, 1:45).

This tendency toward revision or adaptation of his collected sentences was often more elaborate and accompanied by commentary suggesting the young man's greater awareness that the practice had artistic importance. An attempt to recast one of Isaac Barrow's sentences "in purer & more fashionable English" (*JMN*, 1:17) expresses Emerson's desire to impose originality on his quotations. This practice was exemplified by Hugh Blair's method of scrutinizing sermons and essays in his *Lectures on Rhetoric*. When approaching his example of Barrow's sentence, Emerson may have had as a reference Blair's comment that the least admirable quality in Barrow's sermons was "the felicity of execution, or his talent of composition."[10] Emerson himself sees Barrow's sentence as "good," but "impaired by a blundering collocation." Since Emerson does not set down the original version of Barrow's sentence we cannot appreciate the extent to which he changed it for better or worse. Nonetheless, the seventeen-year-old's comments on his revision of the "Barrowistical" sentence suggest the germ of his later theory of originality, foreshadow his editorial practices, and exemplify his method of adaptation and alteration of his collected sentences: "In looking over the sentence however the grand outline of the whole was originally Rev Isaac Barrow's yet we self complacently confess that great alterations have rendered it editorially Mr. Ralph Emerson's & I intend to make use of it hereafter after another new modelling for it is still very susceptible of improvement" (*JMN*, 1:18). Emerson's alterations would not always be so extensive, but with practice he was soon capable of condensing, rewording, and adapting a quoted item to make it both editorially and thematically his own. Moreover, as his repeated use of individual items indicates, he always found them "susceptible of improvement."

These practices are again exemplified in the same journal by an analysis of one of Bacon's sentences. Bacon, he finds, is "indeed a wonderful writer; he condenses an unrivalled degree of matter in one paragraph . . . & withal writes with much more melody & rich cadence than any writer (I had almost said, of England) on a similar subject" (*JMN*, 1:21). He adds as proof for this encomium "a little sentence of Bacon" from the *Novum Organum*: "But these instances may be reckoned of the singular heteroclite kind as being rare & extraordinary in the universe; yet for their dignity they ought to be separately placed & treated. For they excellently indicate the composition & structure of things; & suggest the causes of the number of the ordinary species in the universe; & lead the understanding from that which is, to that which may be" (*JMN*, 1:21). Bacon's "little sentence" is, in fact, a series of closely related clauses, barely interrupted by conjunctions; and it is one of the less concise examples of the inductive movement of the Senecan "loose" style. Emerson's later style is rarely inductive, in sentence, paragraph, or essay movement. Rather, his accumulations of precisely stated and compressed sentences serve as specific examples supporting an initially stated and often reiterated generality. Nonetheless, Bacon's sentence had its appeal to a young man searching for an adequate style; it taught him that frequent repetition and "deception," or hiding of manifold meanings, had merit. Suggestive indirection and not the Baconian "loose" style finally left its mark on Emerson's prose. And it is indirection that is essential to the proverbial essay style for which both Bacon and Emerson are best known.

IV

The individual sentences Emerson collected up to 1824 are for the most part from moral contexts or the moral essayists in keeping with his early conclusion that all art should be moral. This belief was certainly intensified by his persistent attention to the moral essayists, Bacon, Montaigne, and Plutarch, whom the young man hoped to emulate. Although he drew from Plutarch only slightly prior to 1825 (cf. *JMN*, 2:4, 54, 27), Bacon was often referred to by name and his essays quoted from; and Montaigne was quoted nearly as often. Since Emerson's college years and early days in the divinity school were devoted to writing essays on topics such as final causes, God's attributes, man's nature and place in the universe, the moral sense, moral beauty, greatness and fame, friendship, and knowledge (see his index pages), it is not unusual that the moral essayists are most frequently cited and his sentence collection correlative to their essay topics.[11]

Emerson aspired to be not only a moral essayist, but a *modern* moral essayist. This is clear as early as 1821 in his journal "essay" on the "Influence of Modern Essays as Tatler Spectator &c &c upon Morals" (*JMN*, 1:331-32). This interest in the periodical essayists is centered on the fact that they have "penetrated into society where treatises professedly moral would never have come"; this is accomplished by these authors "so artfully that they could not displease." The importance Emerson would later attach to quotation as a means of indirectly teaching morality is only slightly evident in this essay; but he does introduce one direct quotation from Dr. Johnson: " 'The good and the evil of eternity are too ponderous for the wings of wit' says Dr. Johnson but the unnecessary load and obstructions of depravity may be removed and the way prepared for science to soar" (*JMN*, 1:331). The use of this single quotation is for orthodox rhetorical "amplification" and is not organically essential to his prose. But the framework of the moral essay is established as a preferred literary form—a form he used when incorporating the passage on the periodical essayists into his Bowdoin Prize Dissertation, "The Present State of Ethical Philosophy."[12]

That Emerson's concern is with moral philosophy was evident a year earlier, 1820, when he drafted his first version of a Bowdoin Prize Dissertation on "The Character of Socrates" (*JMN*, 1:206-15, 234).[13] Emerson introduced into the journal draft many "sentences" (*JMN*, 1:209): from the "oracle" of Delphi, Diogenes Laertius, Plato, Aeschylus, Crito, Swift, and Pope. These sentences were not integrated into the journal draft but merely entered where they would naturally amplify a point about Socrates's character or life. In the final version of the essay the only sentence quoted which occurred in the journal draft is the declaration of the Oracle of Delphi; and it is used as an element of exposition, revealing no theoretical interest in the sentence per se. What is significant is that the genesis of the essay (we have only the first and final drafts) in his commonplace books provides evidence that Emerson was consciously employing rhetorical "invention" for the "amplification" of his essay. That is, he had sought out illustrative quotations, proverbs and examples to support generalizations about his subject. But as was his habit in later compositions, Emerson used most of the examples only for journal support, and the concrete nature of the journal passage was resolved into generalization for formal composition. Emerson's characteristic method of essay composition from scattered sentences and paragraphs was established prior to his graduation from Harvard. "The outlines of the later, formal essay-writing," as his editors remark, "are vividly clear" (*JMN*, 2:xi). He was attempting to resolve the thoughts of others into original statement directed toward moral ends, in keeping with the theory of quotation and originality he was currently formulating.

These earliest instances of Emerson's method of composition indicate the penchant for abstraction and generality for which his published works have long been noted. In *A Fable for Critics*, Lowell formulated Emerson's tendencies in a phrase—as a "Plotinus-Montaigne," a man attempting to root himself in the concrete while more often soaring into the abstract. In the 1820s he might just as well be seen as a "Plotinus-Franklin" since Emerson's interest in this most proverbial of American writers was nearly as strong as that for Montaigne.[14] Emerson's interest in a writer dedicated to the proverb and sententious remark as his major unit of style could only encourage his sense of the proverb's importance.[15] He found in Franklin's proverbs a practicality and forthrightness characteristic of the man (*JMN*, 2:197, 208), and appreciatively entered a number of Franklin's typically concrete proverbs into his journals (*JMN*, 2:208, 377). By 1824 Emerson was familiar with his works (cf. *JMN*, 1:399) and set him up as a "great man" worthy of a journal essay (*JMN*, 2:222–23).

Before he entered the Unitarian ministry, Emerson was convinced that the ends of art were moral, that the sentence was an essential means to expressing that morality, and that the essay was the proper vehicle for moral art. Throughout his later journals and essays there is a tension between his theoretical interest in the commonsense proverb that Franklin had mastered and his own tendency to process all of experience abstractly. If Emerson neither completely transcended common experience nor ever completely succumbed to it in his art, he had good reason.[16] His early journals were at once his "Savings Bank" (*JMN*, 4:250) of proverbialized experience and his ledger of nature's morality. "Franklin's man," he would soon write, "is a frugal, inoffensive, thrifty citizen, but he savours of nothing heroic."[17] By the 1840s Emerson embraced a form of moral accountancy higher and more heroic than Franklin's.

Emerson came to disdain the "proverbs of base prudence." In saying so, he meant not to deny proverbial wisdom but to discriminate between a merely profit-and-loss morality and a transcendental prudence. The last could be measured only by the divine accountant of "Compensation" (1841). Franklin, in contrast, settled on a secular and "narrow cost-analysis of experience."[18] Emerson soon rose above this moral ledgerism, but he never wholly transcended the historic, economic model of Franklin's ethical capitalism. Emerson's early search for personal originality had opened his understanding to the *origins* of all morality, the commonplace and proverbial sayings of prudential man. He must, therefore, constantly address his art to the material and measurable in experience, but not at the expense of a style expressing the moral economy of the universe.

Notes

1. Henry James, *Partial Portraits* (London: Macmillan, 1888), p. 6. The phrase "Search for Form" is from F. O. Matthiessen, *American Renaissance* (New York: Oxford University

Press, 1941), pp. 14–24. Also see Stephen Whicher, *Freedom and Fate: An Inner Life of Ralph Waldo Emerson* (Philadelphia: University of Pennsylvania Press, 1953), and Henry Nash Smith, "Emerson's Problem of Vocation," in *Emerson: A Collection of Critical Essays*, ed. Milton R. Konvitz and Stephen E. Whicher (Englewood Cliffs, N.J.: Prentice-Hall, 1962), pp. 60–71.

2. Kenneth Murdock, *Literature and Theology in Colonial New England* (Cambridge: Harvard University Press, 1949), pp. 99ff, 185.

3. For a comprehensive survey of Emerson's early training in rhetoric, see Ralph S. Pomeroy, "Emerson as a Public Speaker" (Ph.D. diss., Stanford University, 1960).

4. Francis Bacon, *The Advancement of Learning*, bk. 3, chap. 18, sec. 8. On the pervasive influence of Bacon on Emerson's thought and style, see Vivian C. Hopkins, "Emerson and Bacon," *American Literature*, 29 (January 1958): 404–430.

5. The *Letters* and other sources cited in the text and notes are abbreviated to the following short titles: *JMN: The Journals and Miscellaneous Notebooks of Ralph Waldo Emerson*, ed. William H. Gilman et al. (Cambridge: Harvard University Press, 1960–); *L: The Letters of Ralph Waldo Emerson*, ed. Ralph L. Rusk (New York: Columbia University Press, 1939); *W: The Complete Works of Ralph Waldo Emerson*, ed. Edward Waldo Emerson, Centenary ed. (Boston: Houghton, Mifflin, 1903–1904).

6. Hopkins, "Emerson and Bacon," p. 419.

7. See Sheldon W. Liebman, "Emerson's Transformation in the 1820's," *American Literature*, 40 (May 1968): 141–142.

8. See Harry Hayden Clark, "Conservative and Mediatory Emphases in Emerson's Thought," in *Transcendentalism and Its Legacy*, ed. Myron Simon and Thornton H. Parsons (Ann Arbor: University of Michigan Press, 1966), pp. 41–48, for a discussion of this tendency in Emerson's later works (1837–1871).

9. C. Grant Loomis, "Emerson's Proverbs," *Western Folklore*, 17 (October 1958): 258n1.

10. Hugh Blair, *Lectures on Rhetoric and Belles Lettres* (New York: Duyckinck, Collins, and Hunnay, 1824), p. 291; cf. p. 179. Blair's *Lectures* was very influential in the development of Emerson's rhetoric, according to Sheldon W. Liebman, "The Development of Emerson's Theory of Rhetoric, 1821–1836," *American Literature*, 41 (May 1969): 178–206.

11. See, e.g., God's attributes: *JMN*, I, 6, 128; II, 47. Man's nature: *JMN*, I, 177, 203, 276; II, 18, 46, 73, 237, 214. Knowledge: *JMN*, I, 192, 184, 202, 340; II, 3, 212, 223, 230, 340, 351.

12. Printed in Edward Everett Hale, *Ralph Waldo Emerson* (Boston: American Unitarian Association, 1902), pp. 124–126.

13. Printed in Hale, *Emerson*, pp. 57–93.

14. Emerson alludes to or quotes from Franklin at least fifteen times from 1819 to 1824: *JMN*, I, 193, 250, 399; II, 95, 108, 197, 207, 209, 222, 223, 227, 230, 231, 371, 377.

15. See Stuart A. Gallacher, "Franklin's *Way to Wealth*: A Florilegium of Proverbs and Wise Sayings," *Journal of English and Germanic Philology*, 48 (April 1949): 229–251; and Charles Meister, "Franklin as a Proverb Stylist," *American Literature*, 24 (May 1952): 157–166.

16. See Albert Gilman and Roger Brown, "Personality and Style in Concord," in *Transcendentalism and Its Legacy*, ed. Simon and Parsons, p. 91; Edmund G. Berry, *Emerson's Plutarch* (Cambridge: Harvard University Press, 1961), p. 242; and Matthiessen, *American Renaissance*, p. 66.

17. *The Early Lectures of Ralph Waldo Emerson*, ed. Stephen E. Whicher, Robert E. Spiller, and Wallace E. Williams (Cambridge: Harvard University Press, 1959–), I, 150.

18. See Jesse Bier, "Weberism, Franklin, and the Transcendental Style," *New England*

Quarterly, 43 (June 1970): 179–192. Bier's convincing thesis is that "certain elements of Transcendental style represent the last clear literary reflex of the Protestant ethic and the spirit of capitalism, as described by Max Weber." His examples from Emerson are "Self-Reliance," "Compensation," and "Experience."

"Reading Emerson for the Structures: The Coherence of the Essays"

Lawrence I. Buell*

Emerson has never been taken very seriously as an artist of wholes. Even some of his best friends, like Alcott, claimed that he could be read as well backwards as forwards, and the best recent critic of his style agrees that he was primarily "a worker in sentences and single verses."[1] Indeed, Emerson himself admitted that his essays lacked continuity. Nor did this disturb him greatly, for in his study of other authors he himself "read for the lustres";[2] and in his critical theory he made much of the importance of symbolism and analogy but had little to say about form. Likewise, as a lecturer he was apt to make up his discourse as he went along, shuffling and reshuffling his papers as he spoke. Even if he had wanted to compose an orderly lecture, his method of composition by patching together passages from his journals would seem to have been an almost insuperable handicap.

This weight of evidence, however, has not kept a growing minority of Emerson's readers from insisting that there is an authentic and sophisticated unity to at least some of his prose. "The Poet," "Self-Reliance," "Art," and especially *Nature* and "Experience" have all been defended as intricately-structured wholes.[3] Unfortunately, these defenses have labored under two sorts of disadvantages, which have kept their conclusions from carrying the weight they deserve. First, they have usually emphasized very general and abstract patterns in the essays: "dialectical unity," Plato's twice-bisected line, "upward" movement, and the like. *Nature* treats its topics on an ascending order in the scale of being; the chapters in *Essays, First Series* are organized on the principle of complimentary pairs—few would dispute such claims as these. What is at issue, rather, is Emerson's control over his subject from section to section, paragraph to paragraph, especially after *Nature*, which is much more explicitly blocked out and argued than the essays. A student of mine put the problem exactly when he said that it's easy enough to see Emerson clearly from a distance but as you get close everything becomes foggy.

Secondly, previous studies of Emersonian structure have not taken

*Reprinted from *Quarterly Journal of Speech*, 58 (February 1972), 58–69.

into account the process of composition from journal to lecture to essay. Therefore they have not been able to speak directly to the assumption that Emerson failed to synthesize his raw materials where Thoreau, in *Walden*, succeeded. To know where Emerson succeeds and fails in composition, one has to catch him in the act.

This paper, accordingly, will attempt to pin down the extent to which Emerson's essays have continuity, taking their genesis into account when it is useful, and disregarding for the moment the metaphysical implications of Emersonian structure (*Nature* as a scale of being, "Nominalist and Realist" as bi-polar unity, etc.), important as these implications are. I do not mean to argue that Emerson mastered form as he did the aphorism: but I would contend that he was far more in control than at first appears, and that the appearance of formlessness is to a large extent a strategy on Emerson's part calculated to render his thoughts more faithfully and forcefully than direct statement would permit. The same holds true, I suspect, for a number of other literary artists who also seem positively to cultivate haphazardness as a stylistic attribute: e.g., Montaigne, Hazlitt, and Robert Burton.

I

In Emerson's case it is certainly clear that the dense, obscure style for which he is best known was a deliberate choice. Most of his early sermons are plain and lucid, sometimes to the point of formula, and in later life he was quite capable of the same style when he pleased, as in the "Historical Discourse at Concord," a number of his printed lectures, and most of *English Traits*. Whereas there is a real doubt whether Walt Whitman could have written a decent poem in conventional metre, there is no question that Emerson knew, and could use, all the techniques of conventional prose style.

As to the organization of Emerson's mature essays, it is likewise fair to say: (1) that there is usually more order than we at first notice, and (2) that Emerson provides enough clues to ensure continuity, though in a studiously offhand, and sometimes downright misleading manner. We read the first nine pages of "Intellect" with a sense of wandering, when all at once appears the general proposition which snaps the essay into a degree of focus: "In the intellect constructive . . . we observe the same balance of two elements as in intellect receptive" (W, II, 334), and we see that Emerson has been developing this general distinction all the while. Or in "Self-Reliance" we come upon: "The other terror that scares us from self-trust is our consistency" (W, II, 56) The *other* terror? Oh yes—conformity. But it was introduced, six pages before, in simple antithesis to self-reliance, with no indication to the effect "now, reader, we shall discuss the two threats to self-reliance." But presently comes the conclusion: "I hope in these days we have heard the last of conformity and consistency" (*W*, II, 60), and the ten pages spring together as a unit—not clarifying all the vagaries therein, but reassuring us that the Ariadne's thread is still in hand. Emerson could easily have guided his reader somewhat more, but of course he could not spend the day in explanation.

These intimations of order, which are continually turning up in the essays, encourage us to search for more. "If you desire to arrest attention," Emerson writes in his journal, "do not give me facts in the order of cause & effect, but drop one or two links in the chain, & give me with a cause, an effect two or three times removed."[4] This is a far better description of his method, overall, than "infinitely repellent particles,"[5] for upon close examination of the essays one can find a number of recurring devices used by Emerson both to supply and to conceal continuity.

The one just illustrated might be called the "buried outline." The key is either withheld for several pages, as in the two essays above, or thrown out so offhandedly that one is likely to miss it, as in "The Poet," where the plan for the essay is tucked into a part of the last sentence in the long exordium. "Experience" is an especially provoking case. "Where do we find ourselves?" the essay begins (*W*, III, 45). Where indeed? Not until the beginning of the second section do we learn that the first has been about "Illusion"; indeed, a previous hint suggests that "Surface" is the subject (*W*, III, 48). And the final organization of the essay is not clarified until near the end, when Emerson draws up a list of the seven topics he has covered (*W*, III, 82).

Actually, the reader is most fortunate to get such an exact list from Emerson; not only do all the items apply, they are even given in the right order. Possibly he is atoning for the prefatory motto (*W*, III, 43), which also contains a sevenfold list, but one which corresponds only in the part to the essay's structure. The reader who approaches the essay with it as a guide is bound to be misled. This is a second typical Emersonian tactic for "providing" structure—the careless list. Along with his passion for drawing up rosters of great men, immortal books, natural facts, and the like, seems to have gone an abhorrence for following them up. "Self-Reliance," he predicts, will work revolutions in men's "religion," "education," "pursuits," "modes of living," "association," "property," and "speculative views" (*W*, II, 77), and he starts to go down the list. But he gets through only four items, of which the last three turn out to be "travel," "art," and "society." In "Culture" Emerson is a little more accurate: he lists four antidotes to "egotism" ("books," "travel," "society," "solitude") (*W*, VI, 139) and covers all of them. But they might just as well have been called "education," "travel," "city," and "country."

Even if one concedes the worst to Emerson's detractors, it is inconceivable that the sloppy way he uses lists could be accidental. The device is too simple. He could have done better as a school-boy. Surely Emerson is inexact on purpose, either to suggest that demonstration of his principle is endless (as in the long list in "Self-Reliance," which is only half followed up), or, more commonly, to give a tentativeness to his subject. "I dare not assume to give their order, but I name them as I find them in my way," he says of the lords of life in "Experience" (W, III, 83). The motto proves his point—there they simply occur to him in a different way. The inaccurate list gives Emerson the fluid framework he needs to suggest both that his ideas have a coherence and that they are in a state of flux. Even when he categorizes precisely, as in *Nature*, he likes to add a disclaimer. Nature's "multitude of uses," he says, "all admit of being thrown into one of the following classes . . ." (W, I, 12). As if the act of classification, though necessary, were distasteful to him.

A third way in which Emerson uses and conceals structure is to develop a point without ever stating it. Consider this progression from "Spiritual Laws." (Brackets indicate material adapted from lectures and journals.)

> [. . . 'A few strong instincts and a few plain rules' suffice us.]
> [My will never gave the images in my mind the rank they now take. The regular course of studies, the years of academical and professional education have not yielded me better facts than some idle books under the bench at the Latin School. What we do not call education is more precious than that which we call so. We form no guess, at the time of receiving a thought, of its comparative value. And education often wastes its effort in attempts to thwart and balk this natural magnetism, which is sure to select what belongs to it.]
> In like manner our moral nature is vitiated by any interference of our will. People represent virtue as a struggle, and take to themselves great airs upon their attainments, and the question is everywhere vexed when a noble nature is commended, whether the man is not better who strives with temptation. But there is no merit in the matter. [Either God is there or He is not there.] [We love characters in proportion as they are impulsive and spontaneous. The less a man thinks or knows about his virtues the better we like him. Timoleon's victories are the best victories, which ran and flowed like Homer's verses, Plutarch said. When we see a soul whose acts are all regal, graceful and pleasant as roses, we must thank God that such things can be and are, and not turn sourly on the angel and say 'Crump is a better man with his grunting resistance to all his native devils.']
> [Not less conspicuous is the preponderance of nature over will in all practical life.] (W, II, 132–134).[6]

Not until the end of this sequence, if at all, do we begin to see how well-controlled it is. At first the initial paragraph transition comes as a shock—seemingly one of those instances in which Emerson was unable to dovetail two blocs of thought taken from lectures. His argument, a defense of total spontaneity, reinforces this suspicion. So may the next transition ("In like manner . . ."), which is almost as baffling as the one before. It is not clear to what "moral nature" is being compared. Like what? Like education? Like the Latin School? But eventually one sees that Emerson is developing a familiar threefold sequence: never explicitly stated, as, e.g., "The mind grows by nature, not by will." Had Emerson written this, he would have been almost pedantically straightforward—which is probably why he didn't.

As it is, the clues in the opening sentence of the next paragraph probably will not suffice to enlighten the reader as to what Emerson is about, because he immediately goes off on another tack. Rather than develop his second point at once, he turns back to dispense with the popular view ("People represent . . ."), and his attack takes the form of a battery of aphorisms which are sufficiently oblique to the opening sentence and to each other as to force the reader to strain for the connection. The statement, "Our moral nature is vitiated by any interference of our will," is vague and self-contradictory, and the vatic pronouncement, "Either God is there or he is not there," hardly clarifies matters. Both the tactic of veering away from an initial statement and then working back to it, and the tactic of fanning out from a statement with a barrage of apothegms (to be brought back abruptly, often-times, at the start of a new paragraph) are also typical of Emerson. Since the first three sentences of the paragraph have no apparent antecedent in journal or lecture, it would seem that the former strategy was deliberately manufactured for the occasion.

But is the rest of the paragraph under control? To be sure, some of it is memorable, but is it any more than a bag of duckshot? Even where a connection may be traced from point to point there may be no real development. In much of the passage Emerson seems to repeat himself rather than move forward. But again a close look shows more sophistication than at first appears. Though the last five sentences *could* be rearranged, there is a logic to their order: from the divine to the homely and back again, from "God" to "characters" in general, to a representative man, to a specific historical example, to a contemporary example which is more earthy and concrete and yet at the same time, by contrasting Crump with a great "soul" or "angel," brings us back to God and clinches Emerson's point about the divine quality of spontaneity. The previous paragraph unfolds with equal delicacy in a reverse fashion. A sudden and particular perception of the speaker's is given perspective by a parallel from his schooldays, which in turn suggests a general theory of education.

Not all passages in the essays will serve my case as well as the one just discussed. On the other hand, there are passages far more intricately designed. Here is one from "Self-Reliance."

> [I suppose no man can violate his nature.] All the sallies of his will are rounded in by the law of his being, as the inequalities of Andes and Himmaleh are insignificant in the curve of the sphere. [Nor does it matter how you gauge and try him. A character is like an acrostic or Alexandrian stanza;—read it forward, backward, or across, it still spells the same thing.] In this pleasing contrite wood-life which God allows me, [let me record day by day my honest thought without prospect or retrospect, and, I can-

not doubt, it will be found symmetrical, though I mean it not and see it not.] My book should smell of pines and resound with the hum of insects. [The swallow over my window should interweave that thread or straw he carries in his bill into my web also.] We pass for what we are. [Character teaches above our wills.] Men imagine that they communicate their virtue or vice only by overt actions, and do not see that virtue or vice emit a breath every moment (W, II, 58).[7]

Upon first reading, this paragraph seems to consist simply of variations on the theme of the topic sentence. What it says about achieving formal unity without conscious intent sounds like wishful thinking; the speaker seems to be hoping that he built better than he knew. One is tempted to substitute "paragraph" for "character" and take Emerson as encouraging the reader to read him as Alcott suggested. And yet the passage will indeed "be found symmetrical," if we look closely, and the way to see this is by making that very substitution, by seeing a double meaning in "character." The paragraph turns on the pun "character" equals "writing." Every man is defined by his nature, as a landscape in nature is limited by the horizon; and that nature can be read in his "character," as a poem is read. The poet, too, is defined by his landscape (and here Emerson brings the senses of nature as character and nature as countryside together), which if he is true to himself will be found, down to the last straw, in what he writes. For "character," whatever our conscious intention, "communicates" itself in our every "breath" or utterance.

In order to create this impressive piece of double-entendre, Emerson, as my notations show, drew on two and perhaps three lectures, and two journal passages, adding several new aphorisms. And in none of those individual passages is the eventual design more than adumbrated. But surely in synthesizing them Emerson must have known what he was about, judging not only from the effect of the ensemble but the fact that he added the sentence about "my book" and went back to JMN, V, after using the same passage in abbreviated form twice previously, to retrieve the metaphor of character as poem.

2

I hope that by now I have succeeded in showing that at his best Emerson was capable of full control over his materials, even when they were very diverse. How consistent that control was throughout a given essay remains to be seen, however. Undoubtedly Emerson had some clear-cut failures, especially in his old age, when like Thoreau he lost the power to synthesize. "Books" is an obvious example; it is little more than a catalogue. Another instance is "Poetry and Imagination," for which manuscripts also survive. These suggest that except for the introductory section, no part of the essay has a fixed and authentic order. The "essay" cannot, for the most part, be considered as much more than a collection of sayings.

The last ten pages especially seem to have undergone a last-minute re-shuffle before publication, involving a dozen or so thought-units.

But it is unfair to pick on Emerson in his old age, when Cabot was beginning to take over his editorial work. All the texts arranged by Cabot and Edward Emerson are more or less corrupt anyway, and more than the footnotes of the Centenary Edition indicate, because of the amount of silent cutting and patching that was done to prepare Emerson's lecture notes for publication.[8] Of course, the fact that the unusual desultoriness of "Poetry and Imagination" and other late works does not seem to have bothered critics is a sign that this is what one expects from Emerson.

Nevertheless, close scrutiny of his earlier prose reveals that he did pay a considerable attention to organization, even in some essays which are usually assumed to be formless. A discussion of two such hard cases, "History" and "The Over-Soul," should support this statement.

"History" is Emerson's most ambitious essay. Its scope is wider even than *Nature*, inasmuch as it traces the operation of cosmic unity-in-diversity in man's past as well as in his present environment. The vastness of this subject leads Emerson to a diffuseness of illustration extraordinary even for him, and practically overwhelming for the reader. The first page or so is highly explicit; the rest seems a maze of redundancy. Still, it has a plan, though with characteristic nonchalance Emerson puts off a direct statement of it until near the close, and even then is misleadingly vague: ". . . in the light of these two facts, namely, that the mind is One, and that nature is its correlative, history is to be read and written" (*W*, II, 38). This indicates, hazily, the essay's structure. After a long prologue which treats his themes in miniature (paragraphs 1–6), Emerson shows first that to the perceiving mind, the diverse manifestations of nature and history are governed by the same laws as itself (pars. 7–18) and then the converse proposition, that everything in individual experience is writ large in history and nature (pars. 19–44). In somewhat more detail, the essay can be summarized as follows:

Prologue. The individual mind partakes of the universal mind common to all men (par. 1). Therefore, while in order to understand the mind one must know all of history, which is the record of the mind, the whole of history can be explained from individual experience (2–3). Every experience of ours is duplicated in history; every fact in history is applicable to us (3). This principle of universality in the particular explains our reverence for human life and the laws of property, our identification with what we read (4) and with the "condition" of the great and the "character" of the wise (5); let us then apply this principle to the theory of history as well and take it as a commentary on us, rather than the reverse (6).

First Proposition (Unity-in-Diversity). All history has its counterpart in individual experience (7). We must therefore go over the whole ground of history and internalize it to learn its lesson (8–9). All study of antiquity—e.g., ancient and medieval architecture—is the attempt to reduce "then" to "now" (11–12). Just as man (12) and external nature (13) manifest a unity amid diversity of temperaments and forms, so with history, as in the diversity of Greek culture (14). Further instances of the cosmic principle of unity-in-diversity are the resemblance between human and natural forms (15–16), the similarity of the creative process in diverse areas (17), and the similarity with which great souls and great art affect us (18).

Second Proposition (Diversity-in-Unity). Everything in and of us has its counterpart in the not-me (19). For instance, common experience sometimes takes on cosmic significance (20); everyday objects supply civilization with models for its great architecture (21–24); the conflict in human nature between love and adventure vs. repose has caused the dispute throughout history between nomads and settlers (25). Each individual experiences in himself the primeval world (27), a Grecian period—i.e., a state of natural innocence (28–29), an age of chivalry and an age of exploration (30). Likewise with religious history (30–31): Christianity (32), ancient religion (33), monasticism (34–35), the reformation and its aftermath (36) all express various intuitions and moods in the individual. The same is also true of literature from Greek fable (38) to Goethe (39), from medieval romance (40–41) to Sir Walter Scott (42). Finally, man has affinities with all of nature as well as history. Men like Napoleon need the whole of nature in which to operate (43); and the endeavors of geniuses, and even ordinary people as well, have universal implications (44).

Conclusion (45)—quoted above.

Peroration (46–48).

This précis hardly captures the greatness of Emerson, but it may be argued that an awareness of what it does convey is essential to a just appreciation of that greatness. Otherwise one must picture Emerson simply as a talented aphorist who ran wild for forty pages.

As the summary shows, Emerson did not have total control over his subject. Paragraphs 16–18 are anti-climactic. The peroration is too diffuse. More seriously, Emerson feels obliged to go over his whole ground twice; that at least is the impression created by the preface, whose first three paragraphs splice together the pivotal passages of his 1838 lecture on history, which contains all his essential thoughts on the subject (EL, II, 11–15 passim). The sense of redundancy is increased by Emerson's nonchalance in distinguishing between his two propositions (cf. pars. 7, 19, 24, 26), nor is it clear whether some parts of the essay are "about" history, or nature, or the principle of unity-in-diversity underlying both. Finally, need it be said that Emerson never really confronts the question of history's importance? On the one hand, it is all-important, as a clue to our nature; on the other, it is superfluous, since we contain all history within ourselves. One should be prepared for ambivalence on so abstract a point, but he may justly expect at least an explicit statement of the problem.

When all this is deducted, though, it remains that the essay has method. After the first three paragraphs of lecture-in-miniature, Emerson prepares for his first proposition, as he often does, by appeals to common

sense experience: the way we regard property, reading, etc., should prepare us for the philosophical view which he is about to outline. He begins
proposition two in the same manner, with four personal anecdotes which
bear witness to his point. The "argument" in both sections moves, roughly
speaking, from this existential level to a variety of limited examples (e.g.,
Gothic architecture) to something like a comprehensive statement (12–14;
27–44). The nature of that statement differs according to the point.
Proposition one, unity-in-diversity, can be stated more simply than
proposition two, diversity-in-unity, which necessitates short sketches of
the history of society, religion, literature, and science. If this portion of
the essay seems prolix it is because as in *Nature* Emerson is trying to apply
his principle to all main branches of his subject. Altogether, then, while
structure is not Emerson's strongest point in "History," the essay does
have a form distinct enough for the careful reader to perceive.

So too, I think, does "The Over-Soul," despite the fact that it has
been singled out as an arch-example of discombobulated afflatus. As I
shall explain later, I think that the essay does fall apart about three-
quarters of the way through, but until then Emerson has his materials
well in hand.

The essay begins with a long and stately exordium (pars. 1–2),
stitched together mainly from two passages from lectures and one directly
from the journals, which supply its three stages of movement: the initial
paradox, "our vice is habitual," yet we hope; the question, what is the
ground of this hope?; and the preliminary answer, "man is a stream
whose source is hidden."[9] The way in which the passage converges to a
focus on this metaphor is emphasized by the switch from the general "we"
and "man" to the personal "I": "*Man* is a stream whose source is hidden.
Our being is descending into us from *we* know not whence. The most exact *calculator* has no prescience that somewhat incalculable may not balk
the very next moment. *I* am constrained every moment to acknowledge a
higher origin for events than the will *I* call *mine*" (*W*, II, 268; italics
mine). Emerson's supposed reticence and Thoreau's greater self-
assertiveness have distracted us from the fact that Emerson too was adept
at the subjective mood, and this is a good instance. The device of funnel-
ing in from the abstract to the personal, used now and again in other
essays too, makes the passage fall somewhat as a leaf falls, circling,
zigzag, into one's hand. Then, as the first-person mood continues for
another paragraph, along with the metaphor, it adds a sense of urgency to
the previous questions, the urgency of a personal witness.

The essay now proceeds to identify the mysterious source of power
(par. 3). It is the Over-Soul, which inheres in everyone and everything
and is always accessible to us whether we sense it or not. Again the
speaker ends his definition on a personal note: "I dare not speak for it";
but he will try to give some hints.

In the next section, as I see it (pars. 4–13), Emerson tries to indicate the signs of the Soul's operation—how it feels, some of the ways we can identify it, and so forth. The orientation here is mainly empirical ("If we consider what happens in conversation . . ."; "Of this pure nature every man is at some time sensible," etc.) At first the discussion is carried on in very general terms: the Soul animates all the faculties (par. 4); it is ineffable but everyone has felt it (5). Then Emerson attempts to particularize: its onset is marked by a suspension of the sense of limitations of time, space, and nature (6–7); it comes not by gradation but in a sudden access of power (8), both in virtue (9) and in intellect (10); it reveals itself through other people, humble as well as lofty (11–12), young as well as old (13). Though Emerson's handling of continuity is not unexceptionable, altogether he manages successfully to co-ordinate the large blocs from three different lectures which furnished him with most of his text for this section. For instance, the paragraph sequences 4–5 and 12–13, each of which involves a juxtaposition of passages from different lectures, sustain the motif of affirmation followed by pietistic diffidence.[10]

After the second of these semi-withdrawals Emerson strikes out in a different direction: "The soul is the perceiver and revealer of truth." Here is another case of the buried outline (even more elusive than in "History," since it is defective as well as soft-pedaled—more of which in a moment). The statement announces a shift of emphasis in the next section (14–24) from the experience of the holy to analysis of the Soul's powers. The shift is by no means total, for at one point Emerson gives a glowing account of the emotion of the sublime (16) and later he describes how to identify the tone of an inspired person (22–23); still, the basic framework of discussion is an anatomy of the Soul's attributes. Emerson distinguishes four. The Soul enables us to perceive truth beneath appearance (14); it reveals Absolute Truth (15–19); it reveals our character to others and vice-versa (20–23); it inspires the acts of genius and, potentially, those of all other men as well (24).

Only the first two of these points, we note, are prefigured in the outline. It is hard to know whether to ascribe this to subtlety or incompetence. That Emerson held them distinctly in his own mind is suggested by the fact that points corresponding to one, three, and four are explicitly distinguished and spelled out in his lecture, "The Doctrine of the Soul" (1838), which is the chief source for this section, while the bulk of point two comes from one short sequence in "Religion" (1840). On the other hand, some of the material from the former work appears in support of a different point in the essay, and the last category in the lecture version, "action," bears but a partial resemblance to "genius." Other features of this section of the essay also suggest a loss of direction: the paragraphs are longer than before, the transitions are weaker (cf. 17–18, 21–22, 23–24), the lecture passages are less spliced.[11] And yet a distinguishable framework *is* still maintained, as is the former tactic of qualifying the grand claims for the Soul with the enjoinment of personal humility (19, 23).

Until the section's end, that is. At this point, in conclusion to his discussion on genius, Emerson rises to an unexpectedly insistent note: "Why then should I make account of Hamlet and Lear, as if we had not the soul from which they fell as syllables from the tongue?" As usual, pride goes before a fall, for at this point the essay definitely does fall apart, at least temporarily (25–28), under the rising tide of feeling. Beginning with the passage on enthusiasm (16), Emerson's prose has taken on an intoxication which now seems to carry it away. Perhaps this is inevitable, since the subject is now precisely the imperativeness of abandonment: "This energy does not descend into individual life on any other condition than entire possession." The soul must cast off all pretense and open itself humbly and totally to God. For several pages Emerson celebrates this point, reaching a crescendo in paragraph 28:

> Ineffable is the union of man and God in every act of the soul. The simplest person who in his integrity worships God, becomes God; yet for ever and ever the influx of this better and universal self is new and unsearchable. It inspires awe and astonishment. How dear, how soothing to man, arises the idea of God, peopling the lonely place, effacing the scars of our mistakes and disappointments! When we have broken our god of tradition and ceased from our god of rhetoric, then may God fire the heart with his presence. It is the doubling of the heart itself, nay, the infinite enlargement of the heart. . . .

And so on, for another page and a half. Much of the writing here is very fine, notably the next-to-last sentence, but the effect of the whole is chaotic: hyperbolic affirmation ("The simplest person . . . becomes God"), heightened by the sense of awe and ineffableness, but shot through also with a sense of longing ("How dear, how soothing . . ."; "may God fire the heart with his presence"), so that finally one is conscious both of an exuberance and a desperation in the passage. It is a doxology, but also a *de profundis*, a passionate prayer for the fulfillment of the soul's need. In suggesting, then, that pride led the speaker to a lapse of coherence, I was not being entirely facetious. Once he has swelled to the thought "Why shouldn't *I* come into my own?", "In what way am *I* inferior to Shakespeare?" it is quite understandable that he should fall victim to the dualism which he has been holding in check by the affirmation-resignation device previously described. To put the matter in the language of New England theology, Emerson wants to assert, in the Arminian tradition, that preparation (in this case, simplicity and sincerity) will ensure grace; but secretly he senses as well as Jonathan Edwards did that grace is of God and man has no control over its workings. And so the rhetoric of Emerson's hymn to the "entire possession" of the soul by the Soul becomes turbid with undercurrents of frustration.

In the conclusion, however, and the peroration which follows, the essay regains its composure (29–30). "Let man then learn the revelation of all nature and all thought to his heart; this, namely; that the Highest dwells with him"—the tone here is calm, and the problem of dualism is resolved by two sorts of backings-off. First, primary emphasis is placed on an uncontroversial (for Emerson) point: faith is to be determined by experience and not by authority. And second, the very real problem of how inspiration is to come to the soul is circumvented by resorting to generalizations about the process of spiritual growth. "I, the imperfect, adore my own Perfect. . . . More and more the surges of everlasting nature enter into me. . . . So come I to live in thoughts and act with energies which are immortal," etc. Logically this is inconsistent with what was said about the soul's onsets being sudden and unpredictable, but emotionally and structurally it provides a graceful conclusion to the essay, which in retrospect is seen to flow like this: exordium; statement of subject; signs of the Soul; attributes of the Soul; preparation for grace; prospects.

3

We have seen that Emerson's prose preserves at least the semblance of order even in many places where it seems aimless. But how much importance should we attach to this fact? After all, it is no compliment to regard the two essays just discussed as attempts at systematic thought, inasmuch as Emerson obscures the central issues of the relation of self to history and soul to Soul.[12] Emerson's vitality, especially for the modern reader, lies in the provocativeness of his *obiter dicta*, not in his powers of reasoning. Yet the impact of his orphic sayings, as I have already suggested, depends partly upon the structure which loosely sustains them. For one thing, the sense of totality enhances one's pleasure in the individual detail, as Emerson himself well knew. "Nothing is quite beautiful alone; nothing but is beautiful in the whole" (W, I, 24). Furthermore, the way in which structure appears in Emerson—faintly adumbrated, often concealed, rarely very explicit—happens to be an excellent representation of the peculiar sort of ambivalence Emerson maintained, all his life, toward the idea of totality. Mainly he held to the simple principle of the microcosm, which underlies his theory of symbolism and which is often blamed for aggravating his tendency toward formlessness.[13] But he also entertained at least three other models of universal order, all of which are more specific than the microcosmic principle: 1) nature as operating on a principle of polarity ("Compensation"); 2) nature as an upward flowing through "spires of form" ("Woodnotes," "Nature"); and 3) nature as a book of meanings ("Language"). In short, Emerson's thought ran the whole gamut from complete open-endedness ("In the transmission of the heavenly waters, every hose fits every hydrant" W, IV, 121) to complete schematicism ("Natural objects . . . are really parts of a symmetrical universe, like words of a sentence; and if their true order is found, the poet can read their divine significance orderly as in a Bible" W, VIII, 8).

He desires to claim the utmost liberty for the imagination, on the one hand, and to preserve the prospect of a coherent world-order on the other. Against this background, his use of structure is most significant and appropriate. It furnishes the essays with the same combination of abandonment and unity that he observed in nature.

Indeed many of the essays derive their structures from one or another of Emerson's models of universal order, such as the principle of polarity or the principle of upward flowing, as those who have defended his coherence have pointed out. The two propositions in "History," for instance, are in a sense polar, being opposite ways of viewing the same thing. But I would not want to claim that this pale abstraction is the "subject" of "History," nor, again, that the subject of Nature is the six-fold hierarchy of nature from commodity to spirit. Rather I take it that the subject is the process of discovering the method of history or nature as Emerson sees it. In reading him, one seems meant to feel as he himself felt in reading nature, that "every one of those remarkable effects in landscape which occasionally catch & delight the eye, as, for example, a long vista in woods, trees on the shore of a lake coming quite down to the water, a long reach in a river, a double or triple row of uplands or mountains seen one over the other . . . must be the rhetoric of some thought not yet detached for the conscious intellect" (JMN, VII, 405). Emerson's rhetoric gives off intimations of order, which the reader seeks to follow up without withering them into formulae.

Though it may be praising Emerson overmuch to compare his structures to those of nature, it remains that his achievement in the area of form has been underrated. In particular, more attention needs to be paid to his habits of composition. Thoreau scholarship is ahead in this respect, doubtless because of the currency of the half-truth that he was the more dedicated artist. As the volumes of Emerson's journals, miscellaneous notebooks, and lectures continue to appear, making the record of his revisions more available than it has been, we may expect a general reappraisal of Emerson as an artist of wholes as well as parts.

Such a reappraisal, however, should not be apologetic, should not make the mistake of seizing upon the ordering elements in Emerson's prose as if they were the sole thing which saves his essays from disaster. We must also accept the validity, at least for him, of the open-ended kind of discourse Emerson was attempting. It was his temperamental preference to be suggestive, rather than definitive; this was also what was expected in the lyceum; and the empirical fact is that his mode of communication succeeded. In retrospect it may seem a bit amazing that a man of such intellectual sophistication, speaking in such an elusive style, with virtually no attempt at crowdplay, should have been regularly received with "something close to veneration" in a forum where popular entertainment was the norm.[14] The paradox largely resolves itself when one realizes that Emerson's admirers were looking for stimulation and elevation rather than rigorous thought or hard data. The same spiritual malaise which led Emerson into skepticism and out of the church, in search of alternative ways to express religious sentiment, was widely shared by his audiences; indeed it was one of the main reasons for the rise of the whole lyceum movement. In such a spiritual climate, vague moral uplift seemed much more appropriate than rational precision, which was fast becoming discredited in matters of belief.

No man is totally a product of his times, least of all a genius. The prevailing reverence for Emerson did not mean universal understanding or approval, as this record of an 1857 lecture in Emerson's home town suggests: "Friday Eve Jany 2, 1857 R. W. Emerson lectured. Subject, *The times: politics, preaching, bad boys, clean shirts &c &c.*"[15] But the important point is that after some initial hesitation over Emerson's heresies, most of New England did accept him on his own terms, as a poet, whose proper role was not to explain but to inspire. Had Emerson descended more often to the former, much of the sense of the poetic and the mysterious which was responsible for his charisma would have been lost.

Notes

1. Jonathan Bishop, *Emerson on the Soul* (Cambridge: Harvard University Press, 1964), p. 106.

2. *The Complete Works of Ralph Waldo Emerson*, ed. Edward Waldo Emerson (Boston: Houghton, Mifflin, 1903–1904), III, 233. Abbreviated below as *W*.

3. See for instance W. T. Harris, "The Dialectic Unity in Emerson's Prose," *Journal of Speculative Philosophy*, 18 (April 1884): 195–202; Walter Blair and Clarence Faust, "Emerson's Literary Method," *Modern Philology*, 42 (November 1944): 79–95; Sherman Paul, *Emerson's Angle of Vision* (Cambridge: Harvard University Press, 1952), pp. 117–118; Richard Francis, "The Architectonics of Emerson's *Nature*," *American Quarterly*, 19 (Spring 1967): 39–53; Enno Klammer, "The Spiral Staircase in 'Self-Reliance,' " *Emerson Society Quarterly*, no. 47 (2d Quarter 1967): 81–83; Richard Tuerk, "Emerson's *Nature*—Miniature Universe," *American Transcendental Quarterly*, no. 1 (1st Quarter 1969): 110–113.

4. *The Journals and Miscellaneous Notebooks of Ralph Waldo Emerson*, ed. William H. Gilman et al. (Cambridge: Harvard University Press, 1960–), VII, 90. Abbreviated below as *JMN*.

5. *The Correspondence of Emerson and Carlyle*, ed. Joseph Slater (New York: Columbia University Press, 1964), p. 185.

6. The sources of the bracketed passages are, respectively, *The Early Lectures of Ralph Waldo Emerson*, ed. Robert E. Spiller et al. (Cambridge: Harvard University Press, 1959–), II, 145; "School" (unpublished 1838 lecture), p. 11; *JMN*, VII, 442; *JMN*, VII, 66–67; "School, " p. 10. "School" and all other unpublished Emerson lectures cited below are in Houghton Library, Harvard University. Emerson's *Early Lectures* hereafter cited as *EL*.

7. The sources of the bracketed passages are *EL*, II, 171 ("I suppose . . . sphere"); *JMN*, V, 184 ("I suppose . . . same thing"); "Tendencies" (unpublished 1840 lecture), p. 33 ("I suppose . . . nature"; "let me record . . . see it not"); *JMN*, VII, 364 ("The swallow . . . my web also"); "Religion" (unpublished 1840 lecture), p. 41 ("Character . . . wills").

8. Sometimes excerpts from many different lectures are brought together, as in "Powers and Laws of Thought" (*W*, XII, 3–64). When only one lecture is used in the text, as with "Instinct and Inspiration" (*W*, XII, 65–89), long passages are often excised (sometimes without

notice), usually because Emerson has used them in other essays. Some passages which in manuscript are little more than rough jottings are deceptively organized in neat paragraphs. And there are copying errors as well.

9. The three chief sources are *JMN*, VII, 505–506; "Doctrine of the Soul" (unpublished 1838 lecture), pp. 31–32; and *EL*, II, 343.

10. Emerson's sources in this section are "Doctrine of the Soul," pp. 37–38 (for par. 4 entire); *EL*, II, 85 (for par. 5 entire); "School," pp. 14–15 (for par. 7, "See how the deep divine thought . . . she is clothed"); "Tendencies," p. 42 (for par. 8, "The growths of genius . . . populations, of men"); *EL*, II, 84 (for par. 9, "The soul requires purity . . . becomes suddenly virtuous"); "School," p. 25 (for par. 11, "One mode of the divine teaching . . . cities and war") and pp. 27–28 (for par. 11, "Persons are supplementary . . . higher self-possession"); "Doctrine of the Soul," pp. 39–40 (for most of par. 11, "It shines for all . . . seek for it in each other") and p. 53 (for the rest of par. 11 and par. 12, entire); "Religion," p. 40 (for par. 13, entire).

11. "Doctrine of the Soul," p. 52, contains the three-part distinction of the Soul's powers, from which I have quoted by permission of the Ralph Waldo Emerson Memorial Association and the Harvard College Library. Emerson's sources in pars. 14–24 are "Doctrine of the Soul," pp. 40–41 (for par. 14, entire); *EL*, II, 87–92 (for most of par. 16); "Religion," pp. 19–22 (for most of pars. 18–19); "Doctrine of the Soul," pp. 49–50, 51 (for pars. 20–21, entire); *JMN*, VII, 217 (for par. 22, "That which we are . . . over our head"); "Doctrine of the Soul," pp. 56–57 (for the remainder of par. 22); *JMN*, VII, 157 (for par. 23, entire); "Doctrine of the Soul," pp. 43–45 (for par. 24, "There is in all great poets . . . syllables from the tongue").

12. Cf. Roland Lee, "Emerson's 'Compensation' as Argument and as Art," *New England Quarterly*, 37 (September 1964): 291–304, which argues that the essay fails as art because it is too much of an argument.

13. See Charles Feidelson, Jr., *Symbolism and American Literature* (Chicago: University of Chicago Press, 1953), pp. 119–161, and René Wellek's section on Emerson in *A History of Modern Criticism* (New Haven: Yale University Press, 1965), III, 163–175.

14. Quotation from Carl Bode, *The American Lyceum: Town Meeting of the Mind* (New York: Oxford University Press, 1956), p. 226. The best contemporary account of Emerson's aura as a lecturer is James Russell Lowell, "Emerson, the Lecturer," *My Study Windows* (Boston: Houghton, Mifflin, 1886), pp. 375–384. Lowell shared in the veneration of Emerson, at least in public, almost to the point of idolatry. For a modern and more balanced view, synthesizing a number of nineteenth-century reports of Emerson both favorable and adverse, see Herbert A. Wichelns, "Ralph Waldo Emerson," *A History and Criticism of American Public Address*, ed. William Norwood Brigance (New York: McGraw-Hill, 1943), II, 501–525.

15. Concord Lyceum minutes, quoted in Kenneth Walter Cameron, *Transcendental Climate* (Hartford: Transcendental Books, 1962), III, 712.

"Emerson and the Civil War"

Leonard Neufeldt*

Emerson's late essays have been pretty much ignored by critics largely because the problem of his life in the 1850's and 1860's has not been posed candidly. The writings of these years directly and indirectly

*Reprinted from *Journal of English and Germanic Philology*, 71 (October 1972), 502–13.

report the impact of the Civil War on his consciousness, and a diminishing output adds mute testimony. The abolition controversy caught Emerson in his middle years and, despite his resistance, ultimately drew him out from his private mental places as a scholar. For Emerson this shift required a sacrifice which prospectively he feared more than the War itself, and which retrospectively he regarded with considerable disillusionment. When he returned after the War to the vocation of the scholar and to his old subject, the intellect, he found the writing and lecturing a disagreeable and exhausting chore.

I

Emerson's writings of the 1850's and 1860's throw into intelligible relief three phases in his relation to slavery, abolitionism, and the War. Retrospectively one can say that each prepared for the next, although their order and distinctive features remind us that ultimately Emerson must be explained by himself.

The first phase is one of definition, but definition by the scholar, who reminds himself where his commitment lies. The inevitability of a civil war was not yet a reality to him; the issues of the North-South controversy over slavery were somewhat simplistically bound up with his general views of the possibilities of individual and cultural progress. His opinions on slavery were uncomplicated: the institution is a disgrace which should be removed immediately. In 1851 he noted in his journal, "There can never be peace whilst this devilish seed of war is in our soil. Root it out, burn it up, pay for the damage, and let us have done with it. . . . I would pay a little of my estate with joy; for this calamity darkens my days. It is a local, accidental distemper, and the vast interests of a continent cannot be sacrificed for it" (*J*, viii, 202).[1] The proposal is consistent with Emerson's attitudes: end slavery to avoid war, that is, foreclose the possibility of permitting perverse local institutions to generate national distempers. As it is, he insisted, "the vast multitude are almost on all fours; . . . all go for the quadruped interest, and it is against this coalition that the pathetically small minority of disengaged or thinking men stand for the ideal right, for man as he should be" (*L*, v, 17). Emerson's opposition is directed not only against slavery, but against a slavery controversy, national hysteria, and war (see his essay "Emancipation in the British West Indies"). If, in fact, "America is a vast know-nothing party," as he wrote in his journal, such developments would force the citizenry "to make the most . . . of ignorance" (*J*, ix, 89).

In all of these irritated comments one can still catch the solid allegiance to the vital mind, to the role of the American Scholar. "I cannot leave / My honied thought / For the priest's cant, / Or statesman's rant," reads one of the stanzas of the "Ode to W. H. Channing." The sweetness of the life of thought, like honey to the bee or ambergris to the whaler, has no rival for the scholar. "The angry Muse," on the contrary, "puts confusion in my brain." The "thinking man," Emerson points out, is "disengaged." His intellect constantly separates between him and the world of his horizons and makes him an intellectual being. Without this separation he will be mindlessly immersed in his environment.

One should really not be surprised, then, to discover in Emerson at once hatred of slavery and a dogged recalcitrance toward the abolitionists. At times he seemed to regard abolitionists little more kindly than he did Southern slaveowners. The unionists fared worse with him because he suspected them of moral cowardice in addition to the deficiencies of the anti-slavery organizers. Both groups appalled him with their contourless language. The view of language developed in *Nature*, "Intellect," and "The Poet" was hardly compatible with what he found to be the fixed, repetitive, wholly partisan terminology of these groups. Even the forceful and articulate abolitionist Wendell Phillips generated suspicion. At the end of 1853 Emerson wrote about him: "The first discovery I made of Phillips was, that while I admired his eloquence, I had not the faintest wish to meet the man. He had only a *platform*-existence, and no personality. Mere mouthpieces of a party" (*J*, VIII, 434). In January 1857, while speaking in Rochester, New York, on one of his many lecture circuits, Emerson shared the stage with Horace Greeley, although the lectern belonged to Emerson for the evening. When the crowd began to shout rhythmically, "Greeley, Greeley," Emerson was thoroughly annoyed with their political frenzy and antipathy toward a scholarly address. In the early fifties he admonished abolitionists to love their neighbors more and their black brethren in the South a little less.

Even after Emerson moved closer to the abolitionist position and won the high regard of many of their leaders, he still carefully guarded the separate self and held back from becoming actively involved in the political forays. In 1856 he was appointed alternate delegate to the first national nominating convention of the Republican Party, to be held at Philadelphia. When vacancies occurred Emerson was urged to go, but he refused. He was approached to sign petitions and contribute political speeches, in some instances by individuals he personally admired, but he almost invariably disappointed and bewildered his petitioners. He was even reluctant to sign a petition calling for a national convention in support of total emancipation of slaves with fair compensation to the owners, a plan he had advocated for several years. About this time he wrote to Oliver Wendell Holmes, "When masses . . . go for things as they are, we take no note of it. . . . We leave them to the laws of repression, to the checks nature puts on beasts of prey, as, mutual destruction, blind staggers, delerium tremens" (*L*, V, 17). In the same letter he proceeded to defend the abolitionists' position on slavery despite their "narrowness and ferocity of their virtue." But he persistently referred to "they" and "them." "In our corners," he declared in another letter, "we will speak plain truth & affirm the old laws, heard or not heard, secure that thus we acquit ourselves." His loyalty pledge was his own truth for "the poor betrayed imbruted America" (*L*, v, 67).

Yet in May 1851 Emerson delivered the first of two addresses on the fugitive slave provisions of the Compromise of 1850. The Fugitive Slave Act stuck in his throat. It was eight months after the enactment of the essential bills of the 1850 Compromise before Emerson completed his address—a reticence entirely in character. The new stance (the public orator on a political question) is to be explained, in this instance, by his gathering hatred for the Fugitive Slave Act. "This filthy enactment was made in the nineteenth century, by people who could read and write. I will not obey it, by God!" (*J*, viii, 236). Among the first to acknowledge that the political speech was unusual for him, Emerson explained his position by contending that there was "no option. The last year has forced us all into politics, and made it a paramount duty to seek what it is often a duty to shun" (*W*, xi, 179). It was impossible to forget about slavery when runaway and free slaves were hunted down in Northern streets. For Emerson the lingering "painful sensation" is, in his words, "a new experience." "I have lived all my life in this state, and never had any experience of personal inconvenience from the laws, until now" (*W*, xi, 179). There is uneasiness in the declaration to the large audience in Concord that the slavery controversy and legislation has discredited every liberal study— "literature and science appear effeminate and the hiding of the head" (*W*, xi, 182). The effective punning reminds us where Emerson's head is. Near the end of his address he poses the important question, "What must we do?" It is a concern expressed at the outset of his essay "Fate," which he was writing at the time: "To me . . . the question of the times resolved itself into a practical question of the conduct of life. How shall I live?" (*W*, vi, 3). The only way out for the scholar was to disregard the Fugitive Slave Law, to abrogate it in one's own life. And so Emerson encouraged civil disobedience as the intelligent and moral response to the statute. Several months later he wrote Carlyle, "the abomination of our Fugitive Slave-Bill drove me to some writing & speechmaking, without hope of effect, but to clear my own skirts."[2]

Early in 1854 Emerson delivered for the first time a second address on the Fugitive Slave Act. Once again he apologized for speaking to public questions. The temperamental reserve of the essay apparently carried over into the reading, which disappointed those New Yorkers who had come to hear a fire-breathing speech. Emerson admits that most contemporary public men aren't worth serious attention: "I have my own spirits in prison . . . whom no man visits if I do not" (*W*, xi, 217). But the essay is not without practical proposals, including the elimination of slavery in a manner similar to the British action in the West Indies. This was one of several plans Emerson proposed, the plans varying largely according to the extent of his fear of the South as a threat to healthy mental life in America.

Having made his point in these two slavery speeches, Emerson drew back, very much like the angel Uriel in his poem by that name. Uriel breaks into the monotonous angelic harmony with an opinion of his own and shakes the realm with his truth. But he withdraws with a recantation of silence, fading into heavenly anonymity, recognizing, it seems, that by pressing his words too hard he will probably be crushed or completely ignored. Moreover, by being placed on the defensive he will diminish in his own eyes. Although Uriel withdraws his personal force from the statement, the statement itself still stands and occasionally triumphs by censoring the heavenly host into a collective blushing. Pulling back is personally and strategically imperative for heaven's most beautiful angel.

II

Emerson's distance from the political and social controversies of the day sharply diminished in the late fifties. Several years earlier he had entered in his journal, "It is indeed a perilous adventure, this serious act of venturing into mortality, swimming in a sea strewn with wrecks, where none indeed go undamaged. It is as bad as going to Congress; none comes back innocent" (*J*, viii, 240). As it turned out, Emerson fulfilled his own prophecy. On the one hand, the literary life became disconcertingly vulnerable. On the other hand, by the beginning of the War he was identified by abolitionists in New England and the Mid-west as one of the worthies in their movement.

Undoubtedly the reasons for the shift are many. Several stand out, however. Just after he read his second Fugitive Slave Speech in New York in 1854, Anthony Burns, a fugitive slave detained in Boston for investigation, was identified by his owner and returned to his plantation. It cost the government about $100,000 to return Burns to his master; the furious spectators were kept back by twenty-two companies of Massachusetts militia while Burns was escorted out of Boston by a battalion of United States artillery, several platoons of marines, and the inevitable sheriff's posse. It was a scene that Emerson could not forget. Understandably, his cynicism toward the federal government deepened.

That cynicism, however, did not extend to all elected officials. About the time of the Burns affair Emerson began a fairly regular correspondence with Senator Charles Sumner of Massachusetts, who vigorously opposed the Fugitive Slave Law and the institution of slavery. Emerson's letters are filled with praise and respect for the Senator, to him a man of intelligence, scholarship, and integrity. Regardless of who Sumner really was, Emerson saw him as one of the few men whose measurements approached those of the American Scholar. In May 1856 Sumner delivered a speech on "The Crime Against Kansas," a mixture of truth and falsehood, although Emerson did not recognize the latter. Much of the speech was personal invective, for which Sumner was beaten unconscious at his Senate desk with a heavy gutta-percha cane several days later. In his 1854 Fugitive Slave Address Emerson observed, "My own habitual view is to the well-being of students as scholars. And it is only when the public event affects them, that it very seriously touches me" (W, XI, 217). When the news of Sumner's beating became known, Emerson responded as if he personally had been attacked. In his anger he placed the blame on the entire South. Whereas eight months elapsed between the passing of the Missouri Compromise and Emerson's lecture on the Fugitive Slave provision, Emerson was ready only a few days after the Sumner affair with a bristling speech, "The Assault on Mr. Sumner," which he delivered in Concord. The speech unequivocally defines the enemy of Sumner and, by extention, the scholar. The speaker senses a state of siege for the scholar.

A week later he wrote his brother William that leaving the country might be his only recourse: "what times are these, & how they make our studies impertinent, & even ourselves the same! I am looking into the map to see where I shall go with my children when Boston and Massachusetts surrender to the slave-trade" (L, v, 23). The government is now described in the journal as "an obstruction, and nothing but an obstruction" (J, ix, 51). The opposition to slavery dovetailed with a hostility toward a government which he saw as a monumental threat to the free, creative action of the mind. President Buchanan is treated only with contempt. The brooding omnipresence of sectional hatred and inept political compromise was affecting Emerson much more than he had expected.

Emerson was not alone in his anger over Sumner's injuries. According to Longfellow and Edward Waldo Emerson, the assault on Sumner welded the attitudes of the fledgling Saturday Club of Boston, Emerson's favorite social circle, in an unprecedented fashion. Emerson rarely missed a meeting of this select number of knights of learning. Club members were mostly friends and acquaintances who had distinguished themselves in the arts or sciences. Their aim, according to their own testimony, was good food, good wine and good intellectual fellowship. Edward Emerson describes the Club members of the late fifties as a sweet-tempered scholarly group who preferred not to extend membership to aggressive reformers—since the club did not want "Calvinist" abolitionists among them. Emerson concurred in this. At least three distincts points of view on the slavery controversy were represented in the club—abolitionist, unionist, and pro-slavery. The men, however, were scholars; no one was interested in political proselytizing. With the attack on Sumner the temperature of the Club and the sympathy toward abolitionism rose noticeably. Even C. C. Felton, hitherto an intransigent defender of slavery, changed his stand. By 1858 slavery was debated pointedly in the Club. In 1859 most members indicated sympathetic interest in John

Brown, some contributing substantially to his anti-slavery campaign. By 1860 nearly all the Club members had changed their political affiliation to the Republican Party and voted for Lincoln. As the Club increased its membership during the early years of the War, only anti-slavery people were added.

This information gathers importance as one discovers in Emerson's journals for these years a gradual shift which in most respects is paradigmatic of the Club. On one issue Emerson became more stridently partisan than the majority of the members—the question of John Brown.

Two days after the beating of Sumner, Brown, a self-appointed avenger of the pro-slavery outrages in Kansas which Sumner had attacked, began his divinely sanctioned campaign against slavery by murdering five pro-slavery settlers living on Pottawatomie Creek in Kansas. Emerson had been supporting the Kansas relief program and strongly endorsed Sumner's speech on Kansas. Three months after Brown began his Kansas crusade Emerson spoke in Cambridge at the Kansas Relief Meeting. His speech on Kansas does not mention Brown directly or indirectly. But the true "Saxon man" who can be a law to himself while linking himself to his brothers (W, xi, 262–63) is a model after which Brown is tailored in the John Brown speeches of 1859 and 1860. Emerson was tremendously impressed with Brown when the latter visited Concord the next winter on a speaking tour in the stronghold of abolitionism. Suspicion accompanied Brown's reputation throughout much of New England, but Concord and Emerson accepted Brown's denials of any criminal action in Kansas (the truth was revealed about twenty years later). The fiery crusader did not have to convince Emerson that slavery was evil. But from the time of Brown's first visit to Concord, Emerson changed his views on how to respond to evil. His old belief in compensation was replaced by a conviction that evil does, at times, triumph, and must be opposed. Sumner's failure to recover from his injuries confirmed this. Journal entries made after Brown's second visit with Emerson report both vigorous identification with the abolitionists and occasional disgust over their stock langauge.

The attack on Harpers Ferry and Brown's subsequent imprisonment and execution produced a response in Emerson that was possible only at this particular stage. A few years earlier he had been slating the abolitionists for their Puritan sternness. Yet in 1859 it is the Puritan toughness that he praises in Brown. The first reaction in his letters to Brown's attack on the Harpers Ferry arsenal is in a letter to his brother William. Brown "is a true hero, but lost his head there" (L, v, 178). One would like to think the pun was intentional. Yet a short time later Hawthorne was convinced it was Emerson who had lost his head. It was Brown's very fanaticism that now appealed to Emerson:

> He believes in two articles,—two instruments, shall I say?—the Golden
> Rule and the Declaration of Independence; and he used this expression in

conversation here concerning them, "Better that a whole generation of men, women and children should pass away by a violent death than that one word of either should be violated in this country." There is a Unionist,—there is a strict constructionist for you. (*W*, xi, 268)

Brown "is one of those on whom miracles wait" (*L*, v, 182). "He joins that perfect Puritan faith which brought his fifth ancestor to Plymouth Rock with his grandfather's ardor in the Revolution" (*W*, xi, 268). He recalls "the best stock of New England," the "orthodox calvinists" (*W*, xi, 279). Above all, he is "a pure idealist" (*W*, xi, 268). This apotheosis of Brown is based on his intransigence, unconcern over bloodshed, simplistic fervor and absolute commitment to his principles. It is the apotheosis of Brown, not the evidence Emerson cites, which is revealing. Even Hawthorne, entirely unimpressed by people like Brown, agreed with Emerson on the evidence. His conclusion, however, was that "Nobody was ever more justly hanged."[3]

Many New Englanders and Middlewesterners reflected Hawthorne's opinion on Brown; probably just as many were openly pro-slavery. Emerson's position on Brown became a matter of public record which preceded him on the lecture tours in 1860–61. Frequently he was interrupted and forced to withdraw by a noisy, antagonistic group in the audience. The political controversy that traveled with him and the frequently hostile statements in local newspapers seem merely to have confirmed him in his stand. At the same time abolitionists were his best listeners.

By the end of the decade Emerson was resigned to the prospect of civil war. Indeed, war was perhaps the only way to deal with a culture as contemptible as the South; at least "war is the safest terms" (*J*, ix, 121). His descriptions of the South (in the last thirty years he had not traveled further south than St. Louis) report lunatics and animals: "they can be dealt with as all fanged animals must be" (*J*, ix, 121). Or more mercifully, "The insanity of the South. I acquit them of guilt on that plea" (*J*, ix, 211). In short, the South became a metaphor for mindlessness, lack of education, uncreativeness, pointless frivolity, and beastliness. During the War his language was rarely receptive to kinder terms.

The War itself took on the nature of an apocalyptic moment. It would vindicate his beliefs and do so quickly. The thought of a protracted bloodletting simply was not entertained. The range of problems that he hoped would be solved by the conflict is staggering. There was, of course, the problem of the scholar, which Emerson refers to in both general and personal terms. "The war . . . threatens to engulf us all—no preoccupation can exclude it, & no hermitage hide us." His response indicates relief, not dismay: "But one thing I hope,—that 'scholar' & 'hermit' will no longer be exempts, neither by the country's permission nor their own, from the public duty" (*L*, v, 253). This enthusiasm for the public duty shows itself in the journals, where he meticulously records all the details of a trip to Washington, D.C., in 1862 to lecture at the Smithsonian, an occasion he utilized to strike up an acquaintance with the Secretaries of War, Navy, and Treasury and the Attorney General. He also arranged for two interviews with President Lincoln. Back in New England he threw himself into various organizing activities and fundraising projects. The number of his lecture appearances declined. His platform style gradually drifted to a terser, more expository presentation. The content of the lectures, too, changed. In April 1861 he had planned to give a series of lectures which ultimately exfoliated into the *Natural History of the Intellect.* During a national war against slavery, however, the subject was an insult. Consequently he lectured instead on "Civilization at a Pinch." The "brute noise of cannon" intruded upon his lecture "The Celebration of Intellect" (*W*, xii, 113). He did not return to the subject of the intellect for the remainder of the War.

Not only would the War pull private scholars into public affairs for their own and the common good, but it would call out the greatness in all the citizens. The conflict was a moral tutor of the nation, particularly of the North. The North has been "driven into principles" by the South's "abnegation of them." These shaky principles of moral transformation were easily subsumed into the politics of war: "Our success is sure. Its roots are in our poverty, our Calvinism, our schools, our thrifty habitual industry, in our snow, east wind, and farm life, and sea life" (*J*, ix, 428). A new-found Calvinist firmness would inform and promote national morality in the cause of justice. And so he sought to console a mother grieving for her son killed in battle by affirming that tragedies such as this "teach self-renouncement, and raise us to the force they require" (*L*, v, 32). Even in the worst slaughters, especially of Northern troops, he was able to find virtue. It was the terrible beginning of a new salvation blessed by enthusiastic hope quite absent in a somewhat similar vision, Yeats's "The Second Coming." The ease with which Emerson accepted the bloodshed is at least as remarkable as the reasons for accepting it: "one whole generation might well consent to perish, if, by their fall, political liberty & clean & just life could be made to the generations that follow" (*L*, v, 332).

In part the optimism about the war must also be associated with Emerson's pessimism about political leaders. The Whigs and Democrats, he was convinced, were hopelessly corrupt. War and the political ascendancy of morally bound abolitionists would purify the government. The public event of war would make political affairs truly public. Despite his condescension to Lincoln, whom he considered a somewhat boorish man (he would much have preferred a New Englander in the Presidency), he was enthusiastic over Lincoln's election because it signified, to him, the triumph of principle in the political arena.

Although slavery remained the basic issue to fan Emerson's war-righteousness, obviously the War was seen in a larger context—nothing less than the thoroughgoing moral and intellectual regeneration of

America. Such a rationale for the War extended beyond most of the abolitionists, who aimed at specific political targets. In his speech on the
Emancipation Proclamation, Emerson declared that Lincoln's order sig-
naled the beginning of a new age: "A day which most of us dared not hope
to see . . . seems now to be close before us" (W, xi, 319).

III

The year 1863 was Emerson's moment of supreme optimism. His vision for the future did not labor under the burden of referenceless
generality because the age itself was making tangible and graspable his
goals in the immediate present. His journal was meager, he completed
very few essays in the war years, and he complained that he was able to
visit with few intellectual persons. But it was only as events failed to bear
out his hopes that he felt the strain of relating his hopes to the times and
began to have second thoughts about his personal sacrifice.

There are signs in 1863 and 1864 that his war fever was being replaced by a dubiousness about the times along with a renewed interest in
scholarship and the arts. The most obvious indication is "Fortune of the
Republic," which he wrote toward the end of 1863. In the essay, enthusiasm over the new age is checked by a pervasive ambivalence toward
America as a culture. The same year he returned to Thoreau's journal
manuscripts and was impressed anew by their excellence. He helped to
edit a selection from the manuscripts for publication, but it was his rediscovery of Thoreau's artistry which explains his absorption in the writing.
The journal for 1864 records his enthusiasm for the Saturday Club's com-
memoration of Shakespeare's birthday, an evening he helped to plan. He
also wrote at length about Shakespeare in the journal. Even more noteworthy, there are journal entries on artists and philosophers in America,
England, Germany, France, and Italy. With the death of Hawthorne, he
expressed sadness that Hawthorne's politics increased the distance between them in recent years. In late 1864 he zealously supported the creation of a "National Academy of Literature and Art."

Another sign of change in Emerson was his growing reliance on a
benevolent necessity quite removed from the motive and actions of individuals. The purposes of the War would be accomplished despite the
poor credentials of many of the participants: "This war has been conducted over the heads of all the actors in it" (J, x, 63).

In July 1865, he still claimed the permanent laudable change resulting from the War. And he favored the postwar programs of Sumner and
Stevens, both radical reconstructionists. Lincoln had been too lenient in
the War, and Grant's terms of surrender were too easy. On the systematic
destruction of Southern centers in the late stages of the War his attitude
was unequivocal: " 'T is far the best that the rebels have been pounded instead of negociated into a peace" (J, x, 93). Abolitionist leaders had not

lost any of their greatness. Of Garrison he wrote: "Round him Legis-
latures revolve" (J, x, 18).

Yet by November 1865, Emerson admitted for the first time that the
War may have meant the exhaustion and not the regeneration of national
life:

> We hoped that in the peace, after such a war, a great expansion would
> follow in the mind of the Country; grand views in every direction,—true
> freedom in politics, in religion, in social science, in thought. But the
> energy of the nation seems to have expended itself in the war, and every
> interest is found as sectional and timorous as before. (J, x, 116)

The tiredness evoked by the language extends to the speaker. In 1867
Emerson was still waiting for the new age. A journal entry, for instance,
reads, "It is not a question whether we shall be a nation . . . but whether
we shall be the new nation, the leading Guide and Lawgiver of the
world" (J, x, 195). But the entry has a history. He quotes the comment
verbatim from his 1864 journal. Three years later the question was not
closer to being answered.

By this time Emerson's old pessimism about politics seems to have returned in full force. He feared that Johnson's government was merely a
regression to prewar policies of conscienceless compromise. In 1866, he
referred to Johnson as "our mad President" (L, v, 477). Understandably,
he sought signs quite apart from politics to vindicate the faith he had
placed in the anti-slavery campaign and the War itself. Industrial
growth, technology, and science seemed to recommend themselves, yet
the strain of doubt crept into the observations he recorded in his journal
and letters. Basing his hopes on signs, he never seems to have gotten
beyond the quest for signs after 1865. In "Fortune of the Republic" the
speaker is forced to ask, "How soon?"

With the War, chattel slavery, and northern solidarity irrevocably
past, Emerson turned close to home, to old friends and old themes. "The
body politic was rarely cited as proving his ideals; usually a few close
friends embodied them. The few stout and sincere persons, whom each
one of us knows, recommend the country and the planet to us. . . . Is it
the thirty millions of America, or is it your ten or twelve units that encourage your heart from day to day?" (J, x, 278). Thoreau and Emerson's
Aunt Mary are paid special tribute in the journal. Ironically, both had
died during the War and lay buried in Sleepy Hollow Cemetery.

His return to the theme of the intellect was another answer to the
quandary set up by the experience of the War. He could, for instance,
concede public failure without accepting private defeat. Moreover, he
could re-establish his own life on a broader base than just the constricting
present moment. Ostensibly his new project seems out of keeping with the
War experience. In the larger scheme, however, it forms part of a continuity from his earliest essays, the writings of the War years representing

an aberration of sorts. And so he rallied mind and will to round out a series of essays finally published as *Natural History of the Intellect*. Drawing on material from a series of lectures he delivered in London in 1848 and another series at Harvard in 1858, he prepared six lectures which he read at Harvard in 1866. It would appear that he was indebted particularly to the 1858 lectures, too tired, perhaps, to work up anything new. At least four of these essays were subsequently reworked and expanded to become part of a series of lectures he presented at Harvard in 1870 and in a revised form in 1871. The tone and rhythms of his language recall in many ways his early writings. Yet the journals report how labored this effort was for him, that he lacked both inspiration and discipline. These essays, which hopefully were to be his chief consolation and confirmation after the War as artist and writer, convinced him instead that he was exhausted.

One can perceive a tragedy here. More instructive, however, is the recognition of a poignant irony: when Emerson sought, after the whirlwind of abolitionism and the War, to return to his old subject, the vital mind, he discovered that his own mind was failing him.

Notes

1. I use throughout the following abbreviations: *J* = *Journals of Ralph Waldo Emerson*, ed. Edward Waldo Emerson and Waldo Emerson Forbes, 10 vols. (Boston: Houghton, Mifflin, 1909–1914); *L* = *The Letters of Ralph Waldo Emerson*, ed. Ralph L. Rusk, 6 vols. (New York: Columbia University Press, 1939); *W* = *The Complete Works of Ralph Waldo Emerson*, ed. Edward Waldo Emerson, Centenary Edition, 12 vols. (Boston: Houghton, Mifflin, 1903–1904).

2. *The Correspondence of Emerson and Carlyle*, ed. Joseph Slater (New York: Columbia University Press, 1964), p. 470.

3. See Ralph L. Rusk, *The Life of Ralph Waldo Emerson* (New York: Scribners, 1949), p. 402.

"Emerson and the Loneliness of the Gods"

Joseph F. Doherty*

That Emerson's writings are in some sense seminal for the subsequent development of American literature enjoys universal agreement among commentators; it has become a critical cliché. Richard Poirier speaks for an entire community of scholars: "Indeed, so powerful has Emerson been that his works now constitute a compendium of iconographies that have gotten into American writers who may never have liked or even read him."[1] Few would quarrel with this view. It is no less true, however, that

*Reprinted from *Texas Studies in Literature and Language*, 16 (Spring 1974), 65–75.

recent generations of critics have shown a marked preference for the al-
lures of tortured vision. Consequently, because Emerson is judged deficient in his awareness of tragedy and is said to lack a "dark side," his stock
sells at a discount on the literary market. His Buddhist calm (his complacency?) appears out of step with an official modern sensibility rooted in
agitated perceptions of the emptiness at the core of human affairs. We are
drawn to Poe, Hawthorne, and Melville, whose "power of blackness"
makes them contemporary with our present anguish; we tabulate all those
traits in a benign Emersonian view of life that strike us as hopelessly
beside the point in their existential innocence. Inevitably, the elder Henry
James's reference to Emerson as his "fair unfallen friend" terminates discussion—a lethal benediction. This putative naivete, however, may owe
more to stereotyped expectations we bring to his pages than to Emerson's
actual temperament.

There runs through Emerson's work a submerged, troubled stream
of ideas which empties into a pool of desperation lightless and deep
enough for any current apocalyptic diver. Emerson's encounter with the
Awful has not been sufficiently recognized, because he refused to allow it
to overwhelm the rest of his writing. Precisely because he manages to
wrestle his horrors back under control at those moments when they erupt
into full consciousness, readers lulled by his confident tones have missed
the precariousness by which he maintains his apparent equilibrium. We
have mistaken equilibrium for equanimity. The threat of these perturba-
tions is there nonetheless, and it exerts a constant pressure on that composure which is so often criticized as too easily won. The performance by
which his concluding affirmations are achieved is a daring balancing act
dramatized against a background of ominous psychological and metaphysical forces always present just below the surface and threatening to
annihilate him at every false move of the pen. His writing is at its most
exciting when these subversive powers intrude into the center of his
awareness, so that all his energies must be marshalled against the
triumph of chaos. Emerson is one acquainted with the night, and his
mind is at its most muscular flex under the conditions of greatest psychic
duress. The crucial test he must expose himself to, over and over again, is
whether he can bear the isolated loneliness implicit in the solipsism back
to which his vision constantly leads.

During the 1840s and '50s American literature burgeons with an
unexpectedly large number of works focusing on the crisis of solipsistic
isolation that attacks the mind when it is no longer able to distinguish
clearly between its own projections and an external world. Obsessive self-
absorption haunts Hawthorne's Dimmesdale, Goodman Brown, and
Roderick Elliston until all three feel themselves entirely cut off from external reality; the same madness bedevils Poe's Roderick Usher and the
narrator of "Ligeia"; Melville identifies both Ahab and Pierre as locked
within the "desolation of solitude." All are fascinated by the destruction

visited upon consciousness when it is wholly self-enclosed. Out of these fictions develops a tradition of concern with the dilemmas of solipsistic consciousness that persists into the literature ("lost in the funhouse") of our own day. It is Emerson, however, in the process of analyzing some of the perceptual difficulties inherent in his idealism, who first defines this problem for America, and his is the most articulate and probing exploration of the *cul de sac* of loneliness into which the solipsistically isolated imagination works itself.

In tracking down the implications of an epistemological problem first posed in *Nature* (1836), Emerson inaugurates a revolutionary way of viewing consciousness in radical isolation from all other existence. This view of the self *in extremis* becomes an expressive model for the vision of the imprisoned imagination's chilling solitude.

I

The rhetorical appeal of *Nature* to a great extent lies in the ingenuity with which Emerson subtly and almost imperceptibly inverts his audience's traditional commonsense conception of nature as defined in terms of an extra-mental material substantiality. He begins by speaking of nature as the NOT ME of "essences unchanged by man; space, the air, the river, the leaf" (W,I,5).[2] Then, *mirabile dictu*, matter itself becomes what Jonathan Edwards had earlier called the "images or shadows of divine things." When he finally has subverted his reader's habitual material realism, Emerson can write that "Nature is the raw material which man may mold into whatever is useful. . . . One after another his victorious thought comes up with and reduces all things, until the world becomes at last only a realized will,—the double of the man" (W,I,40). Contrary to the initial expectations that Emerson himself invites the reader to adopt, nature is not substantially material at all, but rather willed thought. Nature becomes a reification of the idea of the self—"the double of the man."

Despite the heady enthusiasm of this, his first published work, Emerson was aware that his idealism posed a threat: it "leaves me in the splendid labyrinth of my perceptions, to wander without end" (W,I,63). By the essay's end, however, and without actually solving this epistemological impasse, he conjures the danger away with his famous optimistic exhortation: "Every spirit builds itself a house, and beyond its house a world, and beyond its world a heaven. Know then that the world exists for you. For you is the phenomenon perfect. What we are, that only can we see" (W,I,76). Sixteen years later Emerson would have to concede, "Every spirit makes its house; but afterwards the house confines the spirit" (W,VI,9). These early years in his career, however, were a time of almost total self-confidence, a feeling that reached its highest expression in an absolute identification between himself and God.

In *Nature* Emerson had announced his central doctrine of the self's divinity in a somewhat tentative form. "We apprehend the absolute. As it were, for the first time, we exist. We become immortal" (W,I,57). Although this statement might easily have been mistaken for only an analogy between the self and deity, his journal entry of 1837 leaves little room for qualification. He writes with a deliberate assertiveness emphasized by his own underlinings, "Who shall define to me an individual? . . . I can even with a mountainous aspiring say, *I am God*" (J,IV, 247). And again he set down, "Empedocles said bravely, 'I am God; I am immortal; I contemn human affairs'; and all men hated him. Yet every one of the same men had had his religious hour when he said the same thing" (J,III, 467–68). Such statements have led to a near unanimous agreement among his commentators that the keystone in the development of Emerson's thought is this total identification of the private self with the Godhead.[3] It is possible, however, to push beyond this perception in order to discover the unique logic that couples Emerson's identification with deity and those intrusions into his work of fearful loneliness—the olympian solitude of one who would be a god.

One clue to the connecting link we seek lies in Perry Miller's still crucial essay, "From Edwards to Emerson": that the barrier preventing Edwards from completely identifying his own being with that of God—or the Ground of all Being—was Edwards' belief in original sin whose stain ultimately kept man at an infinite distance from God; and that once faith in the doctrine of universal depravity disappeared, Emerson was able to fuse his own mind with that of God or the Over-Soul. But Miller fails to carry his insight far enough when he claims that this melting together of being with Being culminates in pantheism for Emerson.[4] Actually, the door has now been opened for a passage beyond pantheism into the more extreme position of solipsism itself. God, hitherto viewed as the independently existing Ground of Being, is so thoroughly absorbed by Emerson into individual consciousness that the theoretic possibility is now available for each private intellect to expropriate totally the scene of all existence, rather than to locate its identity by reference to an external, metaphysically objective geography. The final disappearance of God in American literature can be dated from the moment He is engulfed in Emerson's interior. When the scene of all existence, the ultimate substratum or medium in which all else inheres, becomes located in the private self, then the mind must necessarily be left suspended in a vacuum, unable to make contact with anything outside itself. Beyond the self-as-Ground-of-Being, logically there can only be Nothing. The limits of each person's now inevitably private universe come to be defined by the reach of the individual mind in which that universe is totally contained. This internalization of the Ground of Being is the critical maneuver in the development of Emerson's thought which ultimately leads to his encounter with solipsistic isolation. The moment an Emersonian individual abrogates the independent existence of the Deity as the scene of all Being, and instead establishes his own consciousness as ultimate, he has irrevocably enclosed himself in "the splendid labyrinth of [his own] perceptions, to wander without end," because all that *is* can only exist as a function or projection of his own intellect. The self becomes All: and then, as Emerson would eventually come to write in his journal, "for every seeing soul there are two absorbing facts—*I and the Abyss*" (J,X,171—emphasis Emerson's).

When the self has swallowed the ocean of Being and internalized the scene in which all action takes place, thus obliterating all discriminations between the Me and the Not-Me, we enter the realm of nihilistic solipsism. In the words of J. Hillis Miller:

> When man drinks up the sea he also drinks up God, the creator of the sea. In this way man is the murderer of God. Man once was a created being among other created beings, existing in an objective world sustained by its creator, and oriented by that creator as to high and low, right and wrong. Now, to borrow the passage from Bradley which Eliot quotes in the notes to "The Waste Land," "regarded as an existence which appears in a soul, the whole world for each is peculiar and private to that soul."[5]

For the true solipsist, the self can know only the self, and there is no existence outside the self. The ultimate terror of solipsism, of course, is the realization it brings that he who lives in a world unto himself is finally but an isolated island of consciousness adrift in the immensities of Void. "Nihilism is the nothingness of consciousness when consciousness becomes the foundation of everything. Man the murderer of God and drinker of the sea of creation wanders through the infinite nothingness of his own ego."[6] Emerson's internalization of the Ground of Being opened a window for American literature upon that emptiness into which numbers of its practitioners still bleakly stare. And in this discovery of the self encapsulated in absolute Nothingness, Emerson anticipates the conditions of such loneliness as innumerable critics claim obsesses a great part of our literature to the present time.

II

By 1844, without actually surrendering his initial position, Emerson had somewhat tempered the euphoria of his earlier claims to divinity. He came to realize in "Experience" that the consequence for an individual in arrogating to himself the prerogatives of God is to exist in the prison of his own heaven, the self-made prison of his own perceptions. "All things swim and glitter," he writes. "Our life is not so much threatened as our perception" (W,III,45). The singular privacy of each individual's vision leads him to lament a system of illusions that "shuts us in a prison of glass which we cannot see. There is an optical illusion about every man we meet" (W,III,52). And thus, each is driven to trust only the world he alone sees, with no guarantee that his vision is compatible with any others that may, or may not, exist. "We believe in ourselves as we do not believe in others" (W,III,78). This trust in the absolute self, however, leaves small room for consolation; elsewhere in the same essay he adds, "Dream delivers us to dream, and there is no end to illusion" (W,III, 50). The decisive text for my argument is Emerson's acknowledgment that, in transferring the Ground of Being from its exterior identification with the mind of God into the interior of the self's own consciousness, the individual loses all access to external references and becomes trapped within the confines of his own dreams:

> It is very unhappy, but too late to be helped, the discovery we have made that we exist. That discovery is called the Fall of Man. Ever afterwards we suspect our instruments. We have learned that we do not see directly, but mediately, and that we have no means of correcting these colored and distorting lenses which we are, or of computing the amount of their errors. Perhaps these subject-lenses have a creative power; perhaps there are no objects. Once we lived in what we saw; now the rapaciousness of this new power, which threatens to absorb all things, engages us. Nature, art, persons, letters, religions, objects, successively tumble in, and God is but one of its ideas. Nature and literature are subjective phenomena; every evil and every good thing is a shadow we cast.   (W,III,75–76)

"Once we lived *in* what we saw"; now this new power of the self-as-scene-of-Being absorbs into itself even God who is "but one of its ideas."

In writing "Experience" Emerson had resolved to face the worst. In this passage we see him grappling with the crux of his thought. Notice, it is not existence that he finds so demoralizing, but rather self-awareness. He comes to realize that consciousness itself can represent a threatening form of enclosure when it is able to collapse God, who has been the divine guarantee of all external existence, into the being of the self, so that "Nature, art, persons, letters, religions, objects, successively tumble in, and God is but one of its ideas." The enisled intellect awash in an ocean of Nothingness finds itself ruled by a stifling power—the power of the self possessed by the self. Demonic possession would seem welcome by comparison. Thus, a special irony attaches itself to Emerson's forays into the empty terrain of solipsistic Void. He chose to step out of geographical space, because he found its ground of being too restrictive. Physically immense though it might be, the landscape of the great American wilderness-garden was simply too imaginatively cramped for the total freedom Emerson envisioned—a freedom beyond the claims of nature, culture, economics, society, or even biology itself. By interiorizing the Ground of Being, he aimed at an absolute liberation beyond any and all constraints imposed from the outside upon the self's imperium. He discovered within himself, however, a confinement more oppressive than he ever experienced in the smothering presence of external things. There comes a moment in his self-conception as a limitless hero in infinitely expanding space—an interiorized space—when the vision instead of moving towards immensity begins to collapse upon itself. The godlike hero feels his identity diminished by comparison with the measureless scale of Nothingness, and now Emerson's images becomes increasingly ones of closure.

Along with the discovery that man's "subject-lenses" have a creative power, Emerson encounters the Cartesian doubt that "there are no objects." And so, the real meaning of the "Fall of Man" is, ironically, a deification of the self which leaves the individual captive within the confines of his own exclusive perceptions. To become conscious is to find oneself condemned to a privately made universe that no one else may enter, nor the self ever leave. "Thus inevitably does the universe wear our color, and every object falls successively into the subject itself. The subject exists, the subject enlarges; all things sooner or later fall into place. *As I am so I see*; use what language we will, we can never say anything but what we are" (W,III,79—italics mine). With the realization that all of an individual's perceptions may finally be nothing more than self-projected fantasies, Emerson now sees his divine man reduced to the stature of a foolish kitten chasing its own tail. "If you could look with her eyes," he writes of the cat, "you might see her surrounded with hundreds of figures performing complex dramas, with tragic and comic issues, long conversations, many characters, many ups and downs of fate,—and meantime it is only puss and her tail. How long before our masquerade will end its noise of tambourines, laughter and shouting, and we shall find it was a solitary performance?" (W,III,80).

Those who read "Experience" as Emerson's melancholy compromise of his idealism upon encountering the intransigence of an outer world are wide of the mark.[7] The desperation he experiences in 1844 does not stem from griefs suffered at the hands of an irrefragable external reality principle—such griefs he would welcome if only because they might provide a bridge out of himself, as his numbing remarks on the death of his son Waldo suggest; his fear is that pursuing his idealism to its logical conclusion would sink him in such depths of self he would become, to use Hawthorne's phrase, "the Outcast of the Universe." The relevant passage is the most naked Emerson was ever to write:

> There are moods in which we court suffering, in the hope that here at least we shall find reality, sharp peaks and edges of truth. But it turns out to be scene-painting and counterfeit. The only thing grief has taught me is to know how shallow it is. That, like all the rest, plays about the surface, and never introduces me into the reality, for contact with which we would even pay the costly price of sons and lovers. Was it Boscovich who found out that bodies never come in contact? Well, souls never touch their objects. An innavigable sea washes with silent waves between us and the things we aim at and converse with. Grief too will make us idealists. In the death of my son, now more than two years ago, I seem to have lost a beautiful estate,—no more. *I cannot get it nearer to me . . . it does not*

touch me; something which I fancied was a part of me, which could not be torn away without tearing me nor enlarged without enriching me, falls off from me and leaves no scar. It was caducous. *I grieve that grief can teach me nothing, nor carry me one step into real nature.* The Indian who was laid under a curse that the wind should not blow on him, nor water flow to him, nor fire burn him, is a type of us all. The dearest events are summer-rain, and we the Para coats that shed every drop. *Nothing is left us now but death. We look to that with a grim satisfaction, saying, There at least is reality that will not dodge us.* (W,III,47–48—italics mine)

Patior ergo sum! Like Melville's Pierre, Emerson hungers for a pain from the outside that will touch him with a reality beyond the desolate abyss of self into which his idealism has carried him. All that redeems him as human is the fact that he is able to grieve that grief can teach him nothing. Just as Ahab drops one tear into the ocean, Emerson can still feel a need for the external world which drives him to speak aloud the vacancy he experiences within. And again like both Ahab and Pierre, Emerson turns to death as the only hope for relief from his isolation. Herein lies that special bitter irony at the core of his thought. He had entered the universe of his ideal world in order to find relief from the constrictions and rigidity of a material reality he found too oppressive. The anguish of "Experience" is not that this external world has reasserted itself in vengeance, but that the dream of perfect liberation in the deeps of self turns out to be a lonely nightmare.

This epistemological estrangement from all other selves, and the loneliness this estrangement entailed, engenders in Emerson a Melvillian rhetoric of frustration. Emerson's voice—the voice of deprived access—carries unmistakable anticipations of the exclamatory and lamentational tonalities to be met with in *Pierre*. "Baulked soul!" he cries, "man is insular and cannot be touched. Every man is an infinitely repellent orb, and holds his individual being on that condition" (J,IV,238). Each man's individual being provided shaky ground upon which to erect the metaphysics of the world Emerson planned to build at the end of *Nature*. Amid the shifting surfaces of illusory perceptions he must finally confess, "Gladly we would anchor but the anchorage is quicksand" (W,III,55). By 1845 the full measure of each person's essential isolation in a dream world of his own manufacture appears in a journal entry which oddly anticipates such later models of self-enclosure in American literature as the predicament of Dreiser's Carrie Meeber at the end of her book: "In your rocking chair, by your window dreaming, shall you long, alone. In your rocking chair, by your window, shall you dream such happiness as you may never feel."[8] With an awareness of a bleak isolation far wider in its dimensions than Carrie's, Emerson writes:

Men go through the world each musing on a great fable, dramatically pictured and rehearsed before him. If you speak to the man, he turns his eyes from his own scene, and slower or faster endeavors to comprehend what you say. When you have done speaking, he returns to his private music. Men generally attempt early in life to make their brothers first, afterwards their wives, acquainted with what is going forward in their private theatre, but they desist from the attempt, on finding that they also have some farce, or perhaps some ear and heart-rending tragedy forward on their secret boards, on which they are intent, and all parties acquiesce at last in a private box with the whole play performed before himself, *solus*. (J,VII,71)

The ultimate, knowable realities with which an individual must deal are the self and its fantasies enclosed in hermetic privacy, in the box of the solipsistic mind—"*I and the Abyss*." Most readers will recognize how disturbingly close Emerson, the critically sanctioned spokesman for the American vision at its most optimistic, comes at this point to the desperate conclusions of Pierre, when that pathetic man speaks from the depths of his own solipsism, "It is all a dream—we dream that we dreamed we dream."[9] Seven years before the writing of *Pierre*, Emerson had already descended into the bottomless pit of self that Melville would describe in these terms: "Appalling is the soul of man! Better might one be pushed off into the material spaces beyond the outermost orbit of our sun, than once feel himself fairly afloat in himself."[10] Fairly afloat in himself in this, his 1845 journal entry, Emerson had already reached the grim conclusion of Twain's *The Mysterious Stranger*: "there is no God, no human race, no earthly life, no heaven, no hell. It is all a dream—a grotesque and foolish dream. Nothing exists but you. And you are but a thought—a vagrant thought, a useless thought, a homeless thought wandering forlornly among the empty eternities."[11] Emerson intended his speleological descent into the caverns of self as a journey into immensities, an excursion into space as spaciousness, which at once aimed to enlarge upon and displace his countrymen's expansive continental westerings in the name of manifest destiny. He aimed at taking visionary possession of an imperial terrain identified with himself, what Quentin Anderson has aptly identified as an "imperial self." This interior landscape, however, gave access to no Promised Land: it opened *the* exploratory passage into the geography of Void for American literature—a North-West passage of the mind into chilly territory indeed.

III

With his habitual prescience Tocqueville wrote that the extreme individualism of the American's mind "throws him back forever upon himself alone and threatens in the end to confine him entirely within the solitude of his own heart."[12] No better confirmation of this remark can be found than Emerson's discovery and elaboration of the uncharted wastes of the solipsistic imagination, where he anatomizes the loneliness that has preoccupied American literature down to the present. Emerson's encounter with solipsism grows out of his attempt to form a radical redefinition of the hero in space. In his effort to liberate consciousness from any and all external restrictions, he categorically transposes the concept of space from the usual notion of external scene to an interiorized Ground of Being, so that the self now becomes the author of all it perceives. Diffusing its being through space to create and sustain the world, the self grows to such dimensions that it is felt to underwrite all other existence. Perry Miller's description of the seventeeth-century Puritan's conception of the attributes of God applies with equal force to Emerson's new description of the self's potential. "The omnipotent Being fills all space, controls all actions, directs all destinies; out of Him comes all life, and without the constant play of His sustaining power physical being would disintegrate into nothing. He fills heaven and earth with His presence."[13] Here, however, lies the Emersonian self's solipsistic entrapment. Emerson learns that gods can only know themselves, and in the solpisism of divinity lies the isolation of a god. A central discovery he bequeaths to American literature is that men who would be gods, or Platonic conceptions of themselves—and what American hero has not dreamed this dream?—must abide the loneliness of the gods.

Notes

1. *A World Elsewhere* (New York: Oxford University Press, 1966), p. 56.

2. Subsequent Emerson references in parentheses are taken from *The Complete Works of Ralph Waldo Emerson*, Centenary Edition, ed. Edward Waldo Emerson (Boston: Houghton, Mifflin, 1903–1904), 12 vols., and from *The Journals of Ralph Waldo Emerson*, ed. Edward Waldo Emerson and Waldo Emerson Forbes (Boston: Houghton, Mifflin, 1909–1914), 10 vols.

3. For example, Stephen Whicher, *Freedom and Fate* (Philadelphia: University of Pennsylvania Press, 1953), p. 187; Randall Stewart, *American Literature and Christian Doctrine* (Baton Rouge: Louisiana State University Press, 1958), pp. 50, 55; Floyd Stovall, *American Idealism* (Port Washington, N.Y.: Kennikat Press, 1965 [1943]), p. 6; and Howard Mumford Jones, *Belief and Disbelief in American Literature* (Chicago: University of Chicago Press, 1967), p. 63.

4. *Errand into the Wilderness* (New York: Harper and Row, 1956), pp. 195–197.

5. *Poets of Reality* (Cambridge: Harvard University Press, 1965), p. 3.

6. *Poets of Reality*, p. 3.

7. See, for example, Stephen Whicher, "Emerson's Tragic Sense," *American Scholar*, 22 (Summer 1953): 285–292; and Newton Arvin, "The House of Pain: Emerson and the Tragic Sense," *Hudson Review*, 12 (Spring 1959): 39–53. Both these essays have since been collected in *Emerson: A Collection of Critical Essays*, ed. Stephen Whicher and Milton Konvitz (Englewood Cliffs, N.J.: Prentice-Hall, 1962).

These two articles are rarities in Emerson studies in that they do address themselves to those troubled and somewhat somber aspects of Emerson's mind which concern me in my own analysis. Both Whicher and Arvin, however, argue that Emerson's "tragic sense" arises out of the distance existing between his ideal image of perfection and his realization of the compromises imposed upon this perfect vision by an inexorable external necessity. My argument is the exact opposite since I maintain that Emerson's vision collapses from within under the weight of its own internal metaphysical logic, not because it is imposed upon by external forces that shatter it.

8. Theodore Dreiser, *Sister Carrie*, intro. by Louis Auchinloss (Columbus, Ohio: Charles E. Merrill, 1969 [standard facsimile edition made from Doubleday 1900 edition]), p. 557.

9. Herman Melville, *Pierre*, vol. 9 of *The Works of Herman Melville* (New York: Russell and Russell, 1963), p. 382.

10. *Pierre*, p. 396.

11. Mark Twain, *The Mysterious Stranger and Other Stories* (New York: Harper & Brothers, 1922), p. 140.

12. Alexis de Tocqueville, *Democracy in America*, trans. Henry Reeves, ed. Phillips Bradley (New York: Knopf, 1960 [1945]), II, 99.

13. *The New England Mind: The Seventeenth-Century* (Boston: Beacon, 1965 [1939]), p. 33.

"A New Look at Emerson and Science"

Gay Wilson Allen*

Professor Harry Hayden Clark's important study of "Emerson and Science," published in 1931,[1] has not been adequately assimilated in Emerson scholarship, though it has been widely cited and praised. In a detailed survey of the 1909 edition of Emerson's *Journals* and the "Centenary" Edition of his *Works*, Professor Clark traced the poet's interest in science though 1838, the "formative years," during which he read extensively in contemporary science and was most influenced by scientific theories and discoveries.

Emerson himself, in summing up the early influences on him, declared:

> I think the paramount source of the religious revolution was Modern Science; beginning with Copernicus who destroyed the pagan fictions of the Church, . . . Astronomy . . . showed that our sacred as [well as] our profane history had been written in gross ignorance of the laws [of science], which were far grander than we knew; and compelled a certain extension and uplifting of our views of the Deity and his Providence. . . .[2]

Professor Clark suggested that science, and especially astronomy, emancipated Emerson from anthropomorphic religion, and probably had a great deal to do with his resigning his Unitarian pulpit in 1832. This influence, Professor Clark demonstrated in his essay, also extended beyond Emerson's intellectual crisis in 1832, and may be seen in many of his early writings, including *Nature* (1836).

Late in my own teaching career I discovered that Emerson's first professional lectures (i.e., his first public lectures after he resigned from the

*Reprinted from *Literature and Ideas in America: Essays in Memory of Harry Hayden Clark*, ed. Robert Falk (Athens: Ohio University Press, 1975), pp. 58–78.

Second Church in Boston) can serve as a remarkably helpful approach to *Nature*, which my students had nearly always found difficult. *The Early Lectures of Ralph Waldo Emerson* were not published until 1959-66,[3] and Professor Clark did not have access to the manuscripts at the time of his writing "Emerson and Science." Although his exposition might have been strengthened by inclusion of these lectures, especially the first four, which were specifically on science, his conclusions need not be modified in light of this new evidence.

Emerson had been reading works on science, as Professor Clark showed, before he made his trip to Europe in 1832–33, and it was the scientific lectures which he attended in Italy, France, and England, and the museums of natural history which he examined that made the deepest impression on him[4]—much deeper, apparently, than the art galleries and cathedrals which he dutifully visited. The high point of his experiences in Europe was a visit to the Cabinet [Museum] of Natural History in the Garden of Plants in Paris on July 13, 1833. After describing in his *Journal* the Ornithological Chambers, which he thought finer than anything in the Louvre, and passing through several other collections, he recorded his state of mind:

> The Universe is a more amazing puzzle than ever as you glance along this bewildering series of animated forms,—the hazy butterflies, the carved shells, the birds, beasts, fishes, insects, snakes,—& the upheaving principle of life everywhere incipient to the very rock aping organized forms. Not a form so grotesque, so savage, nor so beautiful but is an expression of some property inherent in man the observer,—an occult relation between the very scorpions and man. I feel the centipede in me—cayman, carp, eagle, & fox. I am moved by strange sympathies, I say continually "I will be a naturalist."[5]

How seriously Emerson intended to become "a naturalist" one can only guess, but soon after his return to Boston on October 9, 1833, he accepted an invitation from the Natural History Society to give a series of lectures in the Masonic Temple.[6] The first, given on November 5, was on "The Uses of Natural History." Both this lecture and the second "On the Relation of Man to the Globe," were preliminary sketches for *Nature* (1836), which Emerson was planning during his travels in Europe. A third on "Water" was more factual than speculative, but in the fourth lecture, "The Naturalist," he made a strong plea for a recognition of the importance of science in education.[7]

In his first lecture Emerson recounted his experiences in the Cabinet of Natural History in Paris and elaborated the impressions he had recorded in his *Journal* about the "occult relation" he had felt between man and other forms of life. But as in the beginning of his future book called *Nature*[8] he stressed especially the practical *uses* of nature, the first being that "conversation with nature" promotes health, confirming the truth of the Greek fable of the giant Antaeus wrestling with Hercules. "Man is the broken giant, and in all his weakness he is invigorated by touching his mother earth. . . ."[9] Alexander Wilson, the celebrated American ornithologist, had taken up his specialty "for the benefit of his enfeebled health, and in his enthusiastic rambles in the wilderness his constitution was established whilst he enlarged the domain of science." Botany, Emerson said, could be no less beneficial as a health restorer.

In the second place, the uses of nature have made possible what we know as "civilization":

> It is the earth itself and its natural bodies that make the raw material out of which we construct our food, clothing, fuel, furniture, and arms. And it is the Naturalist who discovers the virtues of these bodies and the mode of converting them to use. In the most refined state of society, these are most accumulated; but these are now so numerous and the subdivision of labor has removed each process so far out of sight, that a man who by pulling a bell can command any luxury the world contains, is in danger of forgetting that iron came out of a mine, and perfume out of a cat.[10]

Here is Emerson's first warning that technology may interfere with man's healthy adjustment to nature. He did not at that point in his thinking consider the possible relationship between the "broken giant" and his misuses of natural resources, but Emerson saw that labor-saving inventions were undermining men's appreciation of nature. At the moment, however, he was more interested in the contributions of single men, chemists particularly, to the extension of commerce and the increase of mechanical power in modern society, without foreseeable limits. Yet he valued these contributions more for their "general truth" than the "riches which they have acquired."

In fact, Emerson's "third reason for the cultivation of natural history" was the *delight which springs from the contemplation of . . . truth* [Emerson's italics], "for every fact that is disclosed to us in natural history removes one scale more from the eye; makes the face of nature around us so much more significant."[11]

Various scholars have stressed the influence of astronomy on Emerson, but in 1833–34 he seems to have been more influenced by geology.[12] The new knowledge of the vast age of the earth preserved in the rocks had convinced him that the world was more than six thousand years old, and that it had been created not by a sudden Divine command but through countless ages of slow evolution. Coal, for instance, was "the relic of forests which existed at an unknown antiquity before the era of the creation of mankind, and by the overflowing of the sea and other changes of the surface had been buried below the surface at too great a depth to be reached by man."[13] But fortunately earthquakes brought the coal near enough to the surface in some places to be mined and used by mankind. Emerson held in reserve the implication of a Divine purpose in this fact, but he emphasized that "the informed eye" would see in all natural phenomena an ingenious fitness, order, and beauty. Linnaeus, Buffon,

Cuvier, Humboldt, and Galileo "used their senses to such good purpose, led on by the mere pleasure of observation," that their "high delight" has become the possession of mankind. This "high delight" also has a "salutary effect upon the mind and character of those who cultivate it. It makes the intellect exact, quick to discriminate between the similar and the same, and greedy of truth."[14]

The fifth use of nature, Emerson said, was to help man understand himself. "The knowledge of all the facts of all the laws of nature will give man his true place in the system of being."[15] Such knowledge will not only enable man to correct his errors and throw off his superstitions, but, most important of all, it will enable him to comprehend the relation of external nature to his "inward world of thoughts and emotions. . . ." This was the beginning of Emerson's theory of nature as a language, which was, first, a means of communicating to the human mind the nature of nature and how it operates; and, second, the power of expression itself, enabling men to share with each other their thoughts and feelings in words. Without words men could not themselves understand their own experiences, and of course not communicate them to other men. Words symbolize aspects of the external world, and metaphors (which embody the very origin of human language) are images of the material world:

> The strongest distinction of which we have an idea is that between thought and matter. The very existence of thought and speech supposes and is a new nature totally distinct from the material world; yet we find it impossible to speak of it and its laws in any other language than that borrowed from our experience in the material world. . . . And this, because the whole of Nature is a metaphor or image of the human Mind.[16]

This theory of language might have been developed in either of two directions: phenomenologically[17] or mystically (in a Neoplatonic sense).[18] "Where," Emerson asked, "is it these fair creatures (in whom an order and series is so distinctly discernible,) find their link, their cement, their key-stone, but in the Mind of Man? It is he who marries the visible to the Invisible by uniting thought to Animal Organization."[19] This statement could mean that all knowledge is empirical, and that nature can only be experienced in the mind as phenomena.[20] The "laws" discovered to govern nature would, therefore, be the laws of appearances. Emerson almost seems to say this in his assertion that "The very existence of thought and speech supposes and *is a new nature* [italics supplied] totally distinct from the material world. . . ."[21] And in a later lecture on "The Humanity of Science" he came even nearer to spelling out phenomenology: "Science is the arrangement of the phenomena of the world after their essential relations. It is the reconstruction of nature in the mind. This is at once its ideal and its historical aspect."[22] But the extent of Emerson's anticipation of twentieth-century phenomenology is his conviction that thought (consciousness) cannot exist without the world's body; thought and nature are co-related.[23]

Emerson did not say that consciousness is "a metaphor or image" of Nature, but exactly the reverse. He quoted a passage from Coleridge's "The Destiny of Nations: A Vision":

> For all that meets the bodily sense I deem
> Symbolical, one mighty alphabet
> For infant minds.[24]

Thus nature is the language that God speaks to men, and natural scientists learn the syntax of the language. It is not strange, therefore, that Emerson should deduce that "the axioms of geometry and of mechanics only translate the laws of ethics."[25] Such axioms as "A straight line is the shortest distance between two points" and "Reaction is equal to action . . . are true not only in geometry but in life. . . ." Consequently, "A man should feel that the time is not lost and the efforts not misspent that are devoted to the elucidation of these laws [of nature]; for herein is writ by the Creator his own history."[26] Robert Chambers expressed the same thought ten years later in *Vestiges of Creation*,[27] and in general contemporary geologists[28] agreed that in fossils men had a record not only of the evolution of life in the changing ages of the globe, but also a history of Divine creativity. In his closing thought, however, Emerson's imagination soared beyond the teleology of early nineteenth-century science when he speculated that maybe "all this outward universe shall one day disappear, when its whole sense hath been comprehended and engraved forever in the eternal thoughts of the human mind."[29] But however visionary such comprehension may appear to a twentieth-century mind, Emerson did not under-value scientific knowledge.

In his second lecture on science, 'The Relation of Man to the Globe," given on January 6, 1834,[30] Emerson drew heavily on his readings in geology, along with some biology and chemistry, and attempted to demonstrate how marvelously the world is adapted for human life. Man, he said, had "been prophesied in nature for a thousand thousand ages before he appeared." This "progressive preparation" was a kind of evolution, more like Lamarck's[31] than Darwin's later theory, for Emerson saw nature adapted to man, not man to nature. Though "the brother of his hand is even now cleaving the Arctic Sea in the fin of the whale, and, innumerable ages since, was pawing the marsh in the flipper of the saurus,"[32] these were merely preparations for "the finish of the rudimental forms" in Man.

According to Laplace, Mitscherlich, and Cuvier, Emerson's chief sources,[33] the whole globe was once in a state of vapor, then a solid mostly covered by water; internal heat threw up mountains and broke the surface of continents, though not necessarily the present ones. Lord Bacon pointed out that the shapes of the coasts of Africa and America so neatly fitted together on a map that they must have once been joined in one huge land-mass.[34] For ages after the globe was habitable to reptiles, palaeotheria, mammoths and mastodons, it was not suitable for man and his domestic animals. But finally, "Man is made; and really when you come to see the minuteness of the adaptation in him to the present earth, it suggests forcibly the familiar fact of a father setting up his children at housekeeping, building them a house, laying out the grounds, curing the chimneys, and stocking the cellar."[35] This domestic parable indicates Emerson's faith in a guiding purpose at work. In every way the globe is exactly fitted to man's structure and needs: the air he breathes, the foods that nourish him, the sounds, sights and forms which delight his senses, and even his difficulties are nicely proportioned to his strength. In all these observations there are echoes of eighteenth-century Deism and Bishop Paley's argument from "design."[36]

There seemed to be a design, too, in the geographical distribution of animals, plants, and minerals, forcing men to travel, explore, and trade to satisfy their wants. Thus nature "acquaints her children with each other, and contrives to impart whatever invention one man makes, to millions."[37] Different parts of the globe also contain a wide variety of beauties, "that the shows of nature might attract so imaginative a creature [as man] from his native spot." Although Emerson thought that natural beauty always surpassed the products of human ingenuity, he did think men had in some ways improved nature, by dredging rivers, draining swamps, planting trees in barren places, thereby sometimes even ameliorating the climate.[38] "Yet," as Shakespeare wrote, "nature is made better by no mean/ But nature makes that mean."[39] Then man's improvements were only repairs.

Emerson believed that the love of nature was innate in all human beings:

> The same organization which creates in the Chayma Indian such thirst and hunger for his boundless woods, which makes a sunny meadow spotted with flowers and visited by birds such a paradise to a child, is the cause in cultivated men of that interest in natural objects and processes which expresses itself in the sciences of botany, of zoology, of chemistry, and astronomy. The pursuit of these sciences has gradually disclosed a new and noble view of man's relation to the globe.[40]

Near the end of his lecture Emerson mentioned two principles which would become primary ideas in his future thinking and writing. The chemist by separating compounds into their separate elements appeared to anticipate "the resolving all created things into a few gases, perhaps two, perhaps one."[41] Emerson's own search for the underlying unity in all natural phenomena would carry him away from physical science into an attempted science of spirit, but he started from theories about the unity of variety in the material world. The second principle was less ambiguous, and would become one of the most basic parallels which he would henceforth find between matter and spirit: "we seem to be approaching the elemental secrets of nature in finding the principle of Polarity in all the laws of matter, in light, heat, magnetism, and electricity."[42]

But Emerson's conclusion in this lecture could have come as much from Paley as from contemporary scientists:

> I conclude . . . that the snail is not more accurately adjusted to his shell than man to the globe he inhabits; that not only a perfect symmetry is discoverable in his limbs and senses between the head and foot, between the hand and the eye, the heart and the lungs,—but an equal symmetry and proportion is discoverable between him and the air, the mountains, the tides, the moon, and the sun. I am not impressed by solitary marks of designing wisdom; I am thrilled with delight by the choral harmony of the whole. Design! It is all design. It is all beauty. It is all astonishment.[43]

Emerson's third lecture on science was on "Water," given January 17, 1834, before the Mechanic's Institute at the Athenaeum Library in Boston. This was his most technical lecture. He had read up on the geological effects of water, the laws of thermodynamics, the hydrostatic press, and related subjects. In his conclusion he permitted himself to generalize:

> It may serve to enlarge our perception of the boundless resources of the Creator, when we learn that in a bucket of water resides a latent force sufficient to counterbalance mountains, or to rend the planet, and when we trace the manifold offices which one [sic] atom of hydrogen and one of oxygen united in a particle of water may perform in the pulse, in the brain, in the eye, in a plant, in mist, in crystal, in a volcano, and it may exalt our highest sentiments to see the same particle in every step of this ceaseless revolution serving the life, the order, the happiness of the Universe.[44]

On May 7, 1834, Emerson addressed the Natural History Society of Boston for the third time.[45] This was the annual meeting and his lecture on "The Naturalist" was more eloquent and imaginative than the one he gave the Mechanic's Institute on "Water." His avowed purpose was to show "the place of Natural History in Education," and he emphasized particularly the study of nature to promote esthetic and moral growth:

> It is fit that man should look upon Nature with the eye of the Artist, to learn from the great Artist whose blood beats in our veins, whose taste is upspringing in our own perception of beauty, the laws by which our hands should work that we may build St. Peter'ses or paint Transfigurations or sing Iliads in worthy continuation of the architecture of the Andes, the colors of the sky and the poem of life.[46]

Nature also taught a lesson in "Composition," constructing innumerable forms of inconceivable varieties out of a few ingredients, illustrating "that rule of arithmetic called Permutation and Combination."[47] But the special beauty derives from the individual form in combination with other forms, which is "composition." The seashell is most beautiful on the seashore, the flower in the meadow, the tree on the hillside.[48] Among the "intellectual influences" of nature study, Emerson mentioned the restraint of "Imitation, the vice of overcivilized communities," and disci-

plined discrimination, learning "by observing and recording the properties of every individual specie and determining its place in the Universe
by its properties."[49]

Emerson thought that the discipline of scientific study might be
especially good for the poet, who "loses himself in imaginations and for
want of accuracy is a mere fabulist. . . ."[50] On the other hand, the "savant" runs the danger of losing sight of the end of his inquiries in the perfection of his "manipulations" and becoming a pedant. As for himself, "I
fully believe in both, in the poetry and in the dissection." And his journals
for this period show, as the editors of the *Early Lectures* note, that, "He
was checking his own observation of birds, shells, flowers, and other
natural objects against their Latin names and classifications in Gray and
other technical sources at the same time that he continued to read in such
favorite philosophers of science as Coleridge and Goethe."[51]

But what was such activity a *means to*? The great scientists knew
their ultimate goal:

> It was the ever present aim of Newton, of Linnaeus, of Davy, of Cuvier,
> to ascend from nomenclature to classification; from arbitrary to natural
> classes; from natural classes, to primary laws; from these, in an ever nar-
> rowing circle, to approach the elementary law, the *causa causans*, the
> supernatural force.[52]

To Emerson and many scientists and philosophers of his period, who
hoped to find the *causa causans*, studying nature was also a means of worshipping the Creator. Knowledge of creatures gave "intimations of the inward Law of Nature."[53]

Emerson's lectures on science were not actually trial versions of his
book on *Nature*; their value is that they reveal his reading and thinking
about science before he had fused his ideas thus derived with the
Neoplatonic and "transcendental" ideas of Plotinus, Swedenborg, Wordsworth, Coleridge, Carlyle, and seventeenth-century English Platonists.[54]
In his journals he made outlines and wrote down trial passages. These
show that his progress was erratic and that he had to struggle for clarity.
On May 6, 1834, he was not entirely sure of his reason for studying plants
and animals. Perhaps it would console him during times of disappointment, or cheer him in solitude. "Or again say that I am ever haunted by
the conviction that I have an interest in all that goes on around
me. . . ."[55] He could learn from nature "the laws by which I live." But
the strongest motive, to be frank, was "love," meaning personal interest.
He was fascinated by the "mysteries" of nature, and believed that "by patient contemplation & docile experiment" he could learn them.

A year later (May 14, 1835) Emerson was thinking of writing a book
on "spiritual things," and was contemplating "the parable of geometry &
matter."[56] By June 24 his future book was to be "essays chiefly upon
Natural Ethics." On January 22–23, 1836, he recorded, "All history is
poetry; the globe of facts whereon they [mankind] trample is bullion to

the scientific eye."[57] The "scholar" could convey these facts "into a garden of God by suggesting the principle which classifies the fact." This is very ambiguous, but the implications are that he was searching for the *causa causans* of natural phenomena. By March 27 he was outlining Chapters 2–5 of *Nature* and finding that "through Nature is there a striving upward"—a spiral evolution.[58]

On August 8, 1836, Emerson wrote his brother William that his book was nearly finished, but, "There is, as always, one crack in it not easy to be soldered or welded. . . ."[59] In a previous letter (June 28, 1836) to William he had expressed the intention of writing a companion essay on "Spirit."[60] This would seem to indicate that he was not yet satisfied with his explanation of the "correspondence" between spirit and matter, the "noble doubt" in Chapter 6 of the "absolute existence of nature."

In his Introduction to *Nature* Emerson says: "The fore-going generations beheld God and nature face to face; we, through their eyes."[61] But a true "theory of nature" may help men once again to see nature "face to face." The evangelical tone of the Introduction also indicates that he is really trying to bring about what William James would call a "religious experience"[62]—to *feel* the presence of the Divine in the observation of its visible creations. In Chapter 1 he follows up this purpose: the stars at night awaken "a certain reverence," and "all natural objects make a kindred impression, when the mind is open to their influence."[63] In the famous "transparent eye-ball" passage Emerson describes the sensations produced by such "open" receptivity of the mind. This passage has often been called a description of a personal mystical experience, but it is more likely an imaginative illustration of the "occult relation" which Emerson had felt to exist between man and the objective world.[64] The emotional delight, so intense as to border on pain (awe, fear), gave him an intuition of the creative spirit sustaining nature.

The "theory of nature" which Emerson attempted to express in *Nature* derived far more from Neoplatonism than modern scientific knowledge, but Emerson was not turning his back on science; he wanted instead to *spiritualize* science, to base science on the theory that the physical world is an emanation of spirit, "the apparition of God" (Chapter 6), or "a projection of God in the unconscious." Here the "unconscious" is the life-force in all existing things except man, who has *consciousness*, which is, as it were, a fragment of the Divine Reason. By cherishing and cultivating his Reason man can intuit the secrets of nature and the laws of his own existence. Thus Emerson's method of gaining knowledge of nature is now not by patient observation, but by epiphanies—sudden flashes of insight into the Divine mystery. "If the Reason be stimulated to more earnest vision, outlines and surfaces become transparent, and are no longer seen [for themselves]; causes and spirits are seen through them" (Chap. 6). And yet these "higher laws" are curiously paralleled by the laws of physics and physiology: "The axioms of physics translate the laws of ethics." Nature in serving man as "Commodity" (practical use), "Beauty," "Language" (symbol), and "Discipline" teaches him "the will of God."

It is not possible to test these Emersonian hypotheses by the methods of physical science. And yet in defending "Idealism" (Chap. 6) as a pragmatic way of handling the phenomenal appearances of the physical world to the mind, Emerson was attempting to construct a "Natural History of the Intellect," the *magnum opus* he planned for years to write, but got no further than some disconnected lectures which he gave at Harvard in 1870–71, published posthumously (in 1893) as *The Natural History of the Intellect.*[65] What he wanted was "the exhaustive accuracy of distribution which chemists use in their nomenclature and anatomists in their descriptions, applied to a higher class of facts: "laws" for the "intellect" comparable to the laws of science. In this ambition he plainly anticipated Phenomenology:

> In all sciences the student is discovering that nature, as he calls it, is always working, in wholes and in every detail, after the laws of the human mind. Every creation, in parts or in particles, is on the method and by the means which our mind approves as soon as it is thoroughly acquainted with the facts; hence the delight. No matter how far or how high science explores, it adopts the method of the universe as fast as it appears; and this discloses that the mind as it opens, the mind as it shall be, comprehends and works thus; that is to say, the Intellect builds the universe and is the key to all it contains. It is not then cities or mountains, or animals, or globes that any longer command us, but only man; not the fact, but so much of man as is in the fact.[66]

In *Nature* Emerson defended "Idealism" (Chap. 6) as a phenomenological psychology—and ethics also:

> The advantage of the ideal theory over the popular faith, is this, that it presents the world in precisely that view which is most desirable to the mind. It is, in fact, the view which Reason, both speculative and practical, that is, philosophy and virtue, take. For, seen in the light of thought, the world always is phenomenal; and virtue subordinates it to the mind. . . .[67]

Idealism says that "matter is a phenomenon, not a substance." For this reason Emerson remarks in "Prospects" (Chap. 8) that "Empirical science is apt to cloud the sight, and, by the very knowledge of functions and processes, to bereave the student of the manly contemplation of the whole." This is to say, that the deepest secrets of nature are learned by intuition, not by empirical observation. And unless the scientist himself understands this, his science will not have "sufficient humanity, so long as the naturalist overlooks that wonderful congruity which subsists between man and the world. . . ."[68] When the mind is prepared for this fact, the most common objects will be seen to be "miraculous," for "each phenomenon hath its roots in the faculties and affections of the mind. Whilst the abstract question occupies your intellect, nature brings it in the concrete to be solved by your hands." To illustrate his point Emerson creates a fabulous "Orphic poet" (somewhat resembling Bronson Alcott, partly Emerson himself, but suggested to him by Proclus,[69] the Greek Neoplatonist of the fifth century), who tells him:

> "Nature is not fixed but fluid. Spirit alters, moulds, makes it. The immobility or bruteness of nature, is the absence of spirit; to pure spirit, it is fluid, it is volatile, it is obedient. Every spirit builds itself a house; and beyond its house, a world; and beyond its world, a heaven. Known then, that the world exists for you. For you is the phenomenon perfect. . . ."[70]

Now of course the basic doctrine here is that, "The foundations of man are not in matter, but in spirit," and that by a *redemption* of his soul (accomplished through *love*, and a new awareness of the nature of the soul) man can transform the "bruteness of nature" into beauty and ideal virtue. Such bold leaping to conclusions based more on faith than objective proof (or at least proof extremely difficult to come by) opens Emerson to the charge of being himself "a mere fabulist," a danger from which he had said in his lecture on "The Naturalist" the poet needed the discipline of science to save him. Such proof is not found in *Nature*.

However, the psychology which Emerson assumed in *Nature* to underlie his theory of the relation of mind to matter, and of matter to the Creative Mind of all nature, including the human mind, he outlined with simple clarity at the end of 1836, three months after the publication of *Nature*, in a lecture on "Humanity of Science."[71] There he said that, "Science is the arrangement of the phenomena of the world after their essential relations. *It is the reconstruction of nature in the mind* [italics supplied]. This is at once its ideal and its historical aspect."[72] The ease with which the human mind can classify the phenomena of nature and by analysis discover the laws of their operation convinced him that "nature proceeds from a mind analogous to our own." Even if one insists on eliminating the transcendental "mind," he would still have to agree on analogies between his own experiences and natural phenomena. For example, man seems to have an instinct for putting things in a row.[73] "This methodizing mind meets no resistance in its attempts." The uniformity of nature makes it possible for the mind to extend one observation to a series in the same class: "as falls the apple, so falls the moon . . . ,"[74] etc. Fossils preserve stages of development of animals which today no longer exist, but those stages of development may still be found in an egg (cf. the "recapitulation theory"[75] in physiology).

Emerson saw "one grand idea" in nature's operation in the formation of the vertebral column in animals, in the shape of leaves, petals, and stems in plants, in the radiation of sound, light and heat, perhaps in the primary cause of electrical and chemical effects.[76] Maybe *one cause* effected all these results. He could not believe that "cause" operated blindly by chance, though it was still a mystery to science. In fact, this seemed to be the place where spiritual assumptions became necessary:

> Behind all the processes which the lens can detect, there is a *Life* in a seed, which predominates over all brute matter, and which irresistibly forces carbon, hydrogen, and water, to take shape in a shaft, in leaves, in colors of a lily, which they could never take themselves. More wonderful is it in animal nature. Above every being, over every organ, floats this pre-determining law, whose inscrutable secret defies the microscope and the alembic. The naturalist must presuppose it, or his results are foolish and offensive. As the proverb says, "he counts without his host who leaves God out of his reckoning," so science is bankrupt which attempts to cut the knot which always spirit must untie.[77]

Emerson believed, however, that, "The presence and antecedence of Spirit are impressively taught by modern science." He did not document this assertion, but his personal friend Louis Agassiz[78] would have agreed, and also Sir Charles Bell, whose recently published book on *The Hand, Its Mechanism and Vital Endowments, as Evincing Design* (1835) had been read by Emerson, with other works on comparative anatomy. "Step by step with these facts," Emerson continued, "we are apprised of another, namely, the Humanity of that Spirit; or, that, nature proceeds from a mind analogous to our own." Later, "Indeed, man may well be of the same mind as nature, for he too is a part of nature, and is inundated with the same genius or spirit. He lives by some pulsations of her life."[79]

Darwin would also agree that the human mind is "a part of nature," but there was a vast difference in this agreement. To Darwin the mind had been produced by "natural selection," retaining those aspects of consciousness which had "survival" value, though they had come into being by pure chance. To Emerson no chance was involved, but an undeviating Divine intention and design, inexorably unfolding—a teleological evolution, if that is not a contradiction. Because the unfolding was consistent and predictable, it could be said to have its "laws" and it was these laws that Emerson sought to discover. That was why Emerson called his hoped-for definitive work on consciousness "The Natural History of the Intellect." In spite of the theological bias in this fragmentary work, science cause Emerson to emphasize *Natural* and to search for innate laws. Since he continued to work on this treatise—or at least to think and worry about it—until his mental decay made it impossible to continue, it is incorrect to say that science did not influence him after 1836.[80] Indeed, the two most basic concepts in his philosophy, which he never doubted, were "compensation" and "polarity," both derived from scientific "laws," i.e., for every action there is a reaction, and the phenomena of negative and positive poles in electrodynamics. To these might also be added "circularity," which translated into poetic metaphors the principle of "conservation of energy." In fact, a nearly-complete interpretation of Emerson's thought could be based on these three concepts, but such a study goes beyond the scope of this essay.

Notes

1. Harry Hayden Clark, "Emerson and Science," *Philological Quarterly*, 10 (July 1931): 225–260.

2. *The Complete Works of Ralph Waldo Emerson*, ed. Edward Waldo Emerson, 12 vols. (Boston: Houghton, Mifflin, 1903–1904), X, 335–336.

3. *The Early Lectures of Ralph Waldo Emerson*, ed. Stephen E. Whicher, Robert E. Spiller, and Wallace E. Williams (Cambridge: Harvard University Press, 1959–).

4. *Early Lectures*, I, 2.

5. *The Journals and Miscellaneous Notebooks of Ralph Waldo Emerson*, ed. William H. Gilman et al. (Cambridge: Harvard University Press, 1960–), IV, 199–200.

6. *Early Lectures*, I, 5–26.

7. *Early Lectures*, I, 50–83.

8. *Nature* (a facsimile of the first edition), ed. Warner Berthoff (San Francisco: Chandler, 1968); all references are to this edition. Pagination is the same as the original 1836 edition.

9. *Early Lectures*, I, 11.

10. *Early Lectures*, I, 11.

11. *Early Lectures*, I, 14–15.

12. Although Emerson frequently mentioned or alluded to astronomy or astronomers, as Clark noted, in his four lectures on science his geological references are usually more concrete. Clark noted also (p. 248) that "In 1835 Emerson read Sir Charles Lyell's *Principles of Geology*." Before this work was published (1830–1833), Emerson's sources (see *Early Lectures*, I, 1) were primarily Baron G. Cuvier, *A Discourse on the Revolutions of the Surface of the Globe* (Philadelphia, 1831); R. Lee [Mrs. Sarah], *Memoirs of Baron Cuvier* (London, 1833); and John Playfair, "Illustrations of the Huttonian Theory of the Earth," *Works* (Edinburgh, 1822), vol. I.

13. *Early Lectures*, I, 16

14. *Early Lectures*, I, 19.

15. *Early Lectures*, I, 23.

16. *Early Lectures*, I, 24.

17. A philosophical movement started by Edmund Husserl in 1905. Bruce Wilshire, in *William James and Phenomenology* . . . (Bloomington: Indiana University Press, 1968), defines the term: "the central thesis of phenomenology is that the world is comprehensible only in terms of its modes of appearance to mind, . . . the relationship of mind to world is necessary and internal."

18. Neoplatonically, nature symbolizes Divine Reason. See John S. Harrison, *The Teachers of Emerson* (New York: Sturgis & Walton, 1910), and "neoplatonism" in Frederic Ives Carpenter, *Emerson and Asia* (Cambridge: Harvard University Press, 1930), chap. 4.

19. *Early Lectures*, I, 24.

20. The phenomenologist would say that such a view makes no assumptions about ultimate reality, or what may support "appearances."

21. *Early Lectures*, I, 24.

22. *Early Lectures*, II, 27.

23. See note 17, above.

24. *Early Lectures*, I, 25.

25. *Early Lectures*, I, 25.

26. *Early Lectures*, I, 26.

27. Robert Chambers, *Vestiges of the Natural History of Creation* (Edinburgh, 1844), which Emerson read in 1845. The idea was evidently not original with Chambers.

28. See note 12, above.

29. *Early Lectures*, I, 26.

30. *Early Lectures*, I, 27.

31. Chevalier de Lamarck (Jean Baptiste Pierre Antoine Monet), *Recherches sur L'Organization des Corps Vivants* (1802), *Philosophie Zoologique* (1809), and other works proposed that changes in environment caused structural, inheritable changes in animals and plants—greater or less use of organs resulted in growth or atrophy.

32. *Early Lectures*, I, 32. On 2 January 1834, Emerson quoted (*Journals*, IV, 254) Sir Charles Bell, *The Hand, Its Mechanism and Vital Endowments as Evincing Design* (Philadelphia, 1833).

33. *Early Lectures*, I, 31.

34. *Early Lectures*, I, 31. Lord Bacon's theory is accepted by modern science; see *Continental Drift: A Study of the Earth's Moving Surface* by D. H. Tarling and M. P. Tarling (London: G. Bell, 1971).

35. *Early Lectures*, I, 32.

36. William Paley, *Natural Theology* (1802).

37. *Early Lectures*, I, 41.

38. *Early Lectures*, I, 43–44.

39. *Winter's Tale*, IV, 4:89–90; Ferguson, *Early Lectures*, I, 44n25.

40. *Early Lectures*, I, 46.

41. *Early Lectures*, I, 48.

42. *Early Lectures*, I, 48.

43. *Early Lectures*, I, 48–49.

44. *Early Lectures*, I, 68.

45. *Early Lectures*, I, 69.

46. *Early Lectures*, I, 73.

47. *Early Lectures*, I, 73.

48. *Early Lectures*, I, 73. See also the poem "Each and All" (1834?) and the entry for 16 May 1834, *Journals*, IV, 291.

49. *Early Lectures*, I, 79.

50. *Early Lectures*, I, 79.

51. *Early Lectures*, I, 69.

52. *Early Lectures*, I, 80.

53. *Early Lectures*, I, 81.

54. See note 18, above.

55. *Journals*, IV, 291.

56. *Journals*, V, 40.

57. *Journals*, V, 117.

58. *Journals*, V, 146.

59. *The Letters of Ralph Waldo Emerson*, ed. Ralph L. Rusk, 6 vols. (New York: Columbia University Press, 1939), II, 32.

60. *Letters*, II, 26.

61. *Nature* (see note 8, above), p. [5].

62. William James, *Varieties of Religious Experience* (1902), especially chap. 3.

63. *Nature*, p. 10.

64. Cf. Berthoff, Introduction to *Nature*, pp. lxi ff. For a different view, see Jonathan Bishop, *Emerson on the Soul* (Cambridge: Harvard University Press, 1964), pp. 10–15.

65. *Works*, XII, 1–110.

66. *Works*, XII, 4–5.

67. *Nature*, p. 74.

68. *Nature*, p. 84.

69. Cf. Harrison, *The Teachers of Emerson*, p. 246.

70. *Nature*, pp. 93–94.

71. *Early Lectures*, II, 22–40.

72. *Early Lectures*, II, 27.

73. *Early Lectures*, II, 25.

74. *Early Lectures*, II, 25.

75. The embryo apparently develops through the evolutionary stages of its species.

76. *Early Lectures*, I, 29.

77. *Early Lectures*, II, 30.

78. Louis Agassiz refused to accept the Darwinian theory of the origin of the species, continuing to believe in the special creation of the different species.

79. *Early Lectures*, II, 35.

80. Whicher and Spiller, *Early Lectures*, I, 3: "To a considerable extent, as *Nature* (1836) makes evident, his interest in science was absorbed into his interest in moral philosophy and by 1836 no longer served a special function in his thought." While science may not have continued to serve "a special function," it continued to have a pervasive influence, as I have shown in *Waldo Emerson: A Biography* (New York: Viking, 1981), which also supports George Woodberry's observation in 1907, largely ignored, that "Nature as an element" in Emerson's poetry often takes on the form of the atom, "The mazy dance and Bacchanalia of Nature . . ." (see *The Recognition of Ralph Waldo Emerson*, ed. Milton R. Konvitz [Ann Arbor: University of Michigan Press, 1972], p. 132). [The last sentence is revised from the original footnote by Gay Wilson Allen (Ed.).]

"Emerson, England, and Fate"

Phyllis Cole*

The years after Emerson's second trip to England presented him more than ever with the need for social engagment as a writer and lecturer. With the English crisis of 1848 fresh in mind, he turned his attention back to America during a decade of westward expansion and accelerating conflict over slavery. Now, Emerson thought, was indeed the moment when the scholar must address "the Times." Conducting simultaneous and often comparative studies of England and America, Emerson worked throughout the 1850s toward an understanding of modern society. The results are evident in his two published books of that decade, *English Traits* (1856) and *The Conduct of Life* (1860); but the theme finds important expression in his lectures and journal writings as well.

Emerson saw himself as an unlikely participant in the social forum. A decade earlier he had suggested that the Transcendentalist would pro-

*Reprinted from *Emerson: Prophecy, Metamorphosis, and Influence*, ed. David Levin (New York: Columbia University Press, 1975), pp. 83–105.

claim truth to his society more often by silence than by speech, would perform actions only if they were "necessary" and "adequate."[1] By the 1850s,
however, closer involvement seemed a necessity. An 1851 journal passage
suggests the dilemma:

> The ancients most truly and poetically represented the incarnation or
> descent into Nature of Pythagoras, his condescension to be born, as his
> first virtue.
>   It is indeed a perilous adventure, this serious act of venturing into mor-
> tality, swimming in a sea strewn with wrecks, where none indeed go un-
> damaged. It is as bad as going to Congress; none comes back innocent.

Clearly, Emerson-as-Pythagoras still does not see the descent to Nature
and Congress as an easy accomplishment. As a present reality it is a struggle amidst wreckage, perhaps even a drowning. But "incarnation" has
become a primary virtue as well. "Those who conquer," Emerson concludes, ". . . announce this success in every syllable."[2] A new strength of
voice and vision will be the result.

   This double theme—the individual's need for incarnation into the
world and the danger of being engulfed or entrapped by it—significantly
informed all of Emerson's social thinking during these years. He characterized aspects of English and American society in metaphors of material
obstruction and enclosure; and he expanded a similar sense of oppression
into a cosmic principle, manifested both in nature and in society, when he
described "Fate" at the beginning of *The Conduct of Life*. As the Pythagoras passage indicates, Emerson himself felt the oppression he described.
But in addition this idea offered to him an important measure of larger
social vitality: a nation or circumstance could be judged according to its
deadening or enlivening effect upon that incarnated individual. I would
like to follow these various characterizations of the social world as they
mutually inform each other in Emerson's thought throughout the fifties.

   England provided Emerson with both a significant experience in the
development of a social theory and a crucial theme within it, and it is
with his English experience of 1847–48 that I will begin. Like so many of
his American contemporaries—Hawthorne and Melville, most notably—
Emerson approached travel in England as an exercise in self-definition,
responding positively to the source of his own native culture but looking
with some nationalistic contentment upon signs of the parent nation's
decline. In fact before his 1847 tour Emerson had already worked out in a
lecture series the theory about the relationship of England and America
that would later form the backbone of *English Traits*; in 1843 he had
characterized New England as the heir to England's vital Anglo-Saxon
materialism, possessing at the same time a spiritual vitality now waning
in England.[3] America, he felt, was both a new England and an anti-
England. His trip to England in 1847 was not, then, just another lecture
tour and certainly not, as some have said, an admission that his creative
work in America was over. It provided for a study of society from the

perspective of the potentiality and limitations of modern materialism, and America was only one thought away at all times. Emerson wanted to lecture to British audiences; but, as he wrote home to his wife, his real business there was not speaking in itself but "the faithful seeing of England."[4] For a man committed to the act of "seeing" in its fullest sense, this was important business.

The aspect of Emerson's English experience most important here is the society that appeared later as one of his strong images of the world's limitation on the active visionary capacity of the individual: a machine, a phalanstery, a universal Birmingham of the mind. The base in concrete experience is quite clear: Emerson spent the winter of 1847–48 lecturing in the world's capitals of mechanical power, first in Liverpool and Manchester, then in other cities of the industrial north. As a guest of the Free Trade Liberals, he was in a fine position to meet this society's most eminent men, its political leaders, manufacturers, and intellectuals. And it was their mental and moral qualities that most fascinated him in his journal observations. Emerson did express interest in the financial crisis of that winter and in the social arrangements proposed by these men; he did in fact register moral indignation at English industrial poverty the same decade that men as different as Carlyle, Melville, and Engels did;[5] but his particular question was the quality of mind elicited by such circumstances, the nature of the vision by which the leaders of government and culture would solve problems. Richard Cobden, the leader of the Anti-Corn Law movement, especially fascinated him, for instance, as "the *cor cordis*, the object of honor and belief, to risen and rising England." But soon Emerson realized that for Cobden Free Trade led nowhere, was only a limited practical device and not a principle. Using a simile that would take on some importance later in *English Traits*, he wrote in his journal, "Cobden was the better leader for what he did not see; like a horse with blinders." What Emerson was looking for was a British engineer, a master of machines and arrangements, who was not mastered by them—a man of vision as well as utility. George Stephenson, who built one of the first locomotives in England, seemed to possess that vision; and his ability to harness power became a chief metaphor for understanding the needs of the time. Emerson saw society itself as the ultimate object of such genius; and he wrote, "Stephenson executed the idea of the age in iron. Who will do it in the social problem? We want a moral engineer."[6]

That phrase "moral engineer" is crucial, because it is one of Emerson's first suggestions that English society itself is a kind of machine, a locomotive or a mill that might be reconstructed. We certainly see Emerson at his most utilitarian here. But, as one might expect, reservations arise quickly about the possibility or desirability of a new class of "social engineers." In Birmingham that winter Emerson wrote that the cities of industrial England were growing together to form a new kind of urban society bigger than London, and that such "mechanical might" was "oppressive to behold." Going on to London for the spring of 1848, he arrived in time to witness the Chartist uprising of April, and he saw that the "machine" of urban England was seriously malfunctioning both in its basic operations and in its proposed readjustments:

> Pauperism always accrues in English arrangements. Like sediment from brackish water incrusting the locomotive and choking it. Prisons breed prisons, workhouses workhouses, Army, Government, Church all have their pauperism and the means of remedy directly are found to have theirs.[7]

The remarkable thing about this journal passage is the extent of its fatalism. Emerson's more characteristic thought was that the reform impulse could animate the machine, provide spiritual vision. But here the "means of remedy" are prone to the same malfunction; social engineers are necessarily a part of the machine themselves. A few pages later Emerson comments further on the enclosure of the British mind by describing the "patent lustre" that "Birmingham" puts on all the nation's products.[8] He believes England's potentiality both for reform and for cultural achievement to be adversely affected by the "machine" its own power has produced.

   This image of England as an imprisoning technological society constituted only one element, of course, in the analysis of national character that Emerson offered in *English Traits*. My purpose here, however, is not to describe the broader assessment, but to trace the ramifications of this one strain of thought throughout Emerson's reflections on society in the 1850s. "Emerson on England" is too often taken as an anomalous subject within his total development: Philip Nicoloff analyzes the subject insightfully, but he does not make it his business to integrate that analysis into a wider view of Emerson; whereas general students of Emerson—Whicher, Paul, Bishop, Anderson—quite literally do not mention this aspect of his work. I believe that the image of technological England remained with Emerson and provided an essential element in the last major formulation of his thought.

   Emerson himself never thought of England as a topic unrelated to other concerns. In fact while still in England in 1848 he began already to assimilate his responses into a broader social analysis, composing for English audiences a new lecture called "The Spirit of the Times." The title should suggest his central question in his lecture: do the Times in fact have a spirit, a spiritual capacity, bent as they are upon material accomplishment? His age would be known, he said, for its devotion to commerce, to tools, and to natural science. And his message about "tools" drew immediately from his observations in Birmingham and Manchester: "Mechanism mechanizes." Just a few months earlier he had called for a "moral engineer" like George Stephenson. Now he repeated the phrase, but used it as illustration of the "very natural but somewhat alarming extension of this age of tools into the social relations." Such engineers wish to "employ men with the same precision and despotism with which they have used shovels and wheels." The mathematical minds of the socialists, he went on, try to apply a "vast arithmetic to society" and turn it into one large machine, a phalanstery. And what they urge on society is coming to pass without their help, because "the large cities are phalansteries."⁹ Speaking to an English audience, Emerson was already converting English experience into metaphor for a modern tendency that, by implication, encompassed his own nation as well.

For the two winters after his return to America, Emerson continued to reflect upon this kind of mechanized society in both of his major lecture series, one called "England" and the other, again, "The Spirit of the Times."¹⁰ Meanwhile, as he began to rework his notes on England into a book, his vocabulary for this kind of social limitation increased. It was about 1852 that he first characterized the English as "factitious" and declared as a general principle that "Birmingham birminghamizes all." "Political economy" joined "phalanstery" as a metaphor for the totally engineered society. And by the time that he composed *English Traits* in the middle of the decade, Emerson was capable of remarkably compressed and eloquent statements of his theme:

> Man in England submits to be a product of political economy. On a bleak moor a mill is built, a banking house is opened, and men come in as water in a sluice-way, and towns and cities rise. Man is made as a Birmingham button.¹¹

Here Emerson portrays the circumstances of modern England as a condition before which man is passive, a condition which could "make" him rather than dissolve into a self-made universe. Emerson still holds out the possibility that an individual consciousness can, as he put it in a letter from England, "outweigh all Birmingham."¹² The remedy to tyrannous circumstances remains the same: individual assertion of visionary power. But the terms of this assertion have indeed changed. One cannot become a transparent eyeball in Birmingham as easily as on a bare common. The individual consciousness must move mountains, must outweigh Birmingham, in order to be self-reliant. Such metaphors of oppression and engulfment suggest a new kind of conflict for the soul, a conflict at least potentially tragic.

This sense of spiritual obstruction reached its most forceful statement, however, not in *English Traits* but in Emerson's most remarkable late essay, "Fate," the first essay in *The Conduct of Life.* "In our first steps to gain our wishes," Emerson wrote there, "we come upon immovable limitations," upon "laws of the world."¹³ "Fate" was in fact Emerson's most characteristic idea throughout the fifties, beginning as a lecture title in 1851 and reaching published form in 1860. As such, it was closely interwoven with his reflections on English and American society; in fact Emerson thought out both subjects in the same few years, especially in the year he described himself as Pythagoras, 1851. As a result of this interweaving, Fate became among other things a crucial tool of *social* analysis for Emerson. It was the generic term for the social limitation that Emerson had first perceived as Birmingham. Let me point out the growth of this idea in some detail.

Emerson began reflecting on the cosmic principle "Fate" as he read Oriental literature during the forties, and to him the word meant particularly the defeat of character by earthly circumstance. "It is a sign of our impotence and that we are not yet ourselves."[14] The circumstances he had in mind were often biological; especially after the English trip and in response to contact with English scientists, the journals were filled with reflections about the limits placed on the freedom of men and animals by nature. His fatalism was never absolute. The scientists had also suggested a process by which nature itself overcame Fate: Emerson began reflecting on evolution as the means by which material circumstances constantly transcended their own limitations.[15] Evolution, Emerson believed, was the principle that insured ultimate victory of character over circumstance. The word Fate itself, however, was shorthand for his most pessimistic series of thoughts.

Fate did not suggest oppressing *social* circumstances to Emerson until early in the 1850s. I have not found any use of the term in his writing from the late forties about machine-like England. The concepts of Fate and of social mechanization seem to have had their beginning in separate, though parallel, reflections. Soon, however, Emerson did begin to analyze social situations from the perspective of Fate. He did so first in response to American rather than English events. What I take to be a crucial equation occurs in his journal in 1850: "*The Times.* That is to say, there is Fate; Laws of the world; what then?" The Times, the social circumstances in which one lives, are now perceived as a product of the same tyranny that governs the animal. And "the Times" that spring meant one thing to Emerson: the failure of spiritual values in America revealed in the passage of the Fugitive Slave Law. Men, he concluded, have no opinions, no virtue, no sense of principle higher than expediency; "the badness of the Times is making death attractive."[16] Emerson saw the Times as a force, like Fate and like Birmingham, spelling death to the soul unless it was willing to struggle. The Fugitive Slave crisis, and the fatalistic materialism it revealed, oppressed Emerson as the more distant circumstances of England could not have.

But all of these images of resistance—naturalistic Fate, English machine, godless Times—came to bear upon each other in 1851. The journals for this year include entries pages long on two subjects, the limitations of Fate and the immorality of political compromise. Meanwhile, important lectures took shape. The year started with Emerson giving isolated lectures from the series that would be called "The Conduct of Life"; and then, in March, he gave the whole series under that title in Pittsburgh. Interestingly enough, though, the first lecture in the series was not "Fate." The ideas for that were still being worked out in journal form. Instead the series began with his three-year-old lecture "England." Discussion of England must have served as a declaration of the material laws of the world. From this he could move on, in order, to "Laws of Success," "Wealth," "Economy"—and then ascending the scale of values, "Culture" and "Worship."[17] Nowhere is there better evidence of the parallel between these two metaphors for the world's realities; both England and Fate serve to represent what tyrannizes the passive self and converts to power for the visionary self.

A month after this series was completed, Emerson gave the most enraged and most partisan address of his career, "The Fugitive Slave Law," to the residents of Concord. Again he spoke in terms of a weight falling upon the individual self, but this time the ascent to victory was less certain than in the lecture series. An "ignominy" has fallen over Massachusetts, he proclaimed, an "infamy" is in the air, which "has forced us all into politics." Like Pythagoras as described two months later, Emerson felt both the necessity of descending into this realm and the pain, the struggle, of doing so. It is here for the first time that Emerson enunciated his own rationale for civil disobedience; and we feel the personal effort of the choice for him in his likening of action against slavery to digging away a mountain of sorrow. Emerson also used images of weight, enclosure, and degradation to characterize Daniel Webster's compromise of principle for material good in supporting the Fugitive Slave Law. "All the drops of his blood have eyes that look downward." In Webster's obedience to a "powerful animal nature," Emerson said in his journal, "Fate has been too strong for him."[18]

The rather desperate hope of the address was that Fate and animal nature would not prove equally strong to Emerson himself and to Massachusetts. "We are examples of Fate," he wrote that summer. "Toss up a pebble and it falls. And the soaring of your mind and the magnanimity you indulge will fall. But cannot we ride the horse that now throws us?"[19] Again the possibility of victory is held out here, the possibility of converting conditions that oppress into enabling circumstances. But only through resistance—this time by training wild horses. The problem is suggested by the title of the lectures: "The *Conduct* of Life." "Conduct" suggests temporal duration, not momentary soaring; and it implies the need to steer a path through difficulties. When Emerson repeated this series in December of 1851, beginning now with the lecture "Fate,"[20] he did affirm the possibility of conducting life through Fate to Freedom. But the unique emphasis of this address fell on the need to overcome obstacles prior to such a victory. Emerson's awareness of these obstacles, both personal and social, had certainly coalesced in the course of the year.

The concerns of 1851 could be taken as a microcosm for the whole decade. In a period when Emerson's most characteristic thoughts were the manifestations and the means of overcoming Fate, his focused topic of study was the nature of English and American society. I have tried to show here how cross-fertilization took place in one way between these concerns during the first year or two of the 1850s: lecturing frequently on technological England and reflecting on slave-holding America, Emerson began to think of society itself as a manifestation of Fate. But I have also said that Fate in turn became a useful tool of social analysis. If this is so, we might expect Emerson to put the concept to work explicitly in his comparative analysis of England and America during the years that followed. And in fact he did just this, asking of each society whether the material circumstances of nature and technology would entrap it or provide power for intellectual and spiritual accomplishment.

In *English Traits* Emerson concluded tactfully but firmly that the British nation had become a victim of Fate. The word Fate emerges in the journal passages about England that Emerson started recording about 1852 in preparation for his book, and it is linked immediately to the metaphors of mechanistic limitation already worked out in his mind. "What Englishman," Emerson asked in 1853, "has idealism enough to lift the horizon of brass which shuts down like an umbrella close around his body?" This horizon of brass, he concluded, illustrates "the power of Fate, the dynastic oppression of submind."[21] In *English Traits* England's wealth is seen as a product of this same "submind" in that it has never taken "the step beyond" its own sufficiency either to remedy the wrongs it has produced or to create a genuine culture. Both in its capacity for social management and in the life of the mind, Emerson concluded, England "is in the stream of Fate, one victim more in the common catastrophe." It would be possible to view Emerson's celebration of Saxon racial strength as a case study in positive, productive response to Fate, to biological and geographical determinism. But this perspective condemns England's present condition all the more. Even Carlyle, with whom Emerson visits Stonehenge and Winchester, scenes of past Saxon achievement, has been "driven by his disgust at the pettiness and the cant into the preaching of Fate." At Winchester the two men read that the body of Alfred—whom Emerson had earlier extolled as "the type of the race"—now lies covered by modern buildings and by ruins of the old. Again the individual is literally buried by a mountain of oppressions. England, Emerson asserted in his chapter on "Literature," has become "a roaring volcano of Fate."[22] England represented to him a society thoroughly imprisoned by "the laws of the world," a society where the individual soul is impotent.

His view of America's relation to Fate was more complex. There was a strong nationalistic aspect to this analysis; Emerson wished to assert that the good of England was now in America and would thrive without the calamities visited upon the parent nation. This is the Emerson speaking at the end of *English Traits*, telling Carlyle at Stonehenge about the fanatic dreams still possible on his own "great sloven continent," telling his bourgeois hosts in Manchester that if they do not solve their crises there will still be "elasticity and hope" for mankind on the Allegheny ranges.[23] This Emerson is also evident in his lecture "The Anglo-American," given many times in the years from 1853 to 1855 and in effect a final chapter to *English Traits* not included in the published book. "Anglo-American" reflects Emerson's experiences in the early fifties lecturing west of the Alleghenies and along the Mississippi River. And on the Mississippi Fate was crude natural power—not Birmingham, not a horizon of brass. There, he said, men "followed the river" quite literally; their lives assumed its gigantic form. There "the American . . . appears passively to yield to this superincumbent Fate. His task is to educe the capabilities of the continent, to make the most of it." Emerson's faith in evolution as growth out of material circumstances reaches one of its strongest formulations here. Fate, it would seem, is on the side of America; it leads directly, Emerson asserted in one of his most imperialistic statements, to "the natural growth of the republic."[24]

But if we conclude that Emerson is entirely an apologist for imperial America, we are reckoning without the allusions to Fate during those same years in which he characterizes a materialistic and slaveholding society's moral bankruptcy. When he spoke of these matters, America fared no better than England. If Emerson saw English society as a mill that Birminghamized men, he observed in his second address on the Fugitive Slave Law that American slavery was a mill for turning men into monkeys.[25] The machine that symbolized England's death was at work in America too. Even the natural power of the American West Emerson could affirm only if men used it to advance beyond material good to moral affirmation. And he saw a new kind of materialism taking over in America: not the metallic precision of Birmingham, but the "counterfeit" of mindless growth. America, he said even in the optimistic "Anglo-American" lecture, had so far built only "shingle palaces."[26] Emerson the advocate of American growth was always chastened by Emerson the critic of whatever was shoddy, immoral, or self-serving. In the long run he knew that Fate could catch up with America as it had with England.

It was in the published book *Conduct of Life* that Emerson interpreted the relationship of England and America to Fate most broadly; he assimilated his description of England's limitation and America's potential into more general possibilities open to individuals in both societies. He no longer tried at all to exempt America from the more tyrannous aspects of Fate. The essay "Fate" begins with the problem of "The Times," and Emerson speaks of articles on the subject in both Boston and London journals. Indeed he seems to be addressing his whole Anglo-American audience, an audience coping with shared modern experience. Instead of speaking about the "mill" of English industrialism or the "mill" of American slavery, he characterizes Fate, "the terms by which our lives are walled up," as possessing "the mechanical exactness . . . of a loom or mill." Emerson has brought Birmingham home to America by recharacterizing it as Fate. The distrust of spiritual values resulting from such a mill, Emerson implies in "Worship," manifests itself equally on both sides of the Atlantic. The English suspected Cobden was advocating free trade for his own profit, and American slavery propagandists have tried to make the idea of "higher law" a laughing matter. Finally, the kind of obedience to Fate that Emerson had attributed to the western American, the obedience that offers a means of getting beyond it to Freedom, is also presented now as a possibility in either nation. Stephenson proved himself to be England's best engineer, Emerson says, by laying out his railroad alongside a river, whereas his colleague Brunel wanted to go in a straight line from city to city.[27] "Following the river," following the necessities of nature, becomes a means of transforming potential tyranny into power for any modern man of vision.

What resulted from Emerson's encounter with England and Fate in this last decade before the Civil War, then, was the first substantial American study of a culture formed by modern technological power. If the primary source of insight into such a technological world was England, the resulting focus of insight included America. And this, I would like to suggest, was a remarkable achievement on Emerson's part. Industrial England had stood facing America for many decades, but Americans were slow to apply its lessons to themselves. If on the one hand they approached England with Irving's Anglophile reverence, as the masses of travel writers did, they managed quite well to pretend that Manchester and Birmingham did not exist at all. The England that mattered lay elsewhere. And if on the other hand they wrote nationalistic attacks on England, in the tradition of the *Inichquin* controversy, they seized upon the troubles of industrial England only as fault-finders; their basic rationale was to locate themselves in opposition to the world observed. Both American sensibilities presented obstacles to a self-implicating analysis of England's machine-made society.

The nationalistic impulse was strong in Emerson, of course, and in much of his Anglo-American writing it prevails. But on the deeper level, where experience was assimilated into primary concept and metaphor, his pessimistic reflections about England informed a larger view of man and society. He was, after all, no polemicist in his defense of America, but a student of all human consciousness. England might provide a continuing metaphor for the entrapment of men in society's mechanical structures; but while the place could serve to represent a human condition, the condition did not have to exist only and literally in that place.

A few contemporary American writers did approach England with an equally complex and probing imagination. Cooper certainly combined nationalistic fault-finding with a desire to analyze America's own deficiencies. But the world of "Birmingham," of modern city and technology, was far from his mind; very much a child of the eighteenth century, he analyzed the implications of aristocratic privilege and did not enter upon the ground which so interested Emerson. Hawthorne was closer to Emerson both in time and in preoccupation. He spent four years during the

1850s as a resident of Liverpool, and his *English Notebooks* include, if not any thoughts about the mechanism of industrial England, long and indignant descriptions of the Liverpool poor. But his central impulse was that of the Anglophile: to find his own "old home" in picturesque England. And that was the central theme of his writing about England both in the essays called *Our Old Home* and in the abortive romance *Dr. Grimshawe's Secret*. Hawthorne always sought for a fictional pattern that would allow for both reverential and critical description of England from an American's perspective, but he never found one. His "Outside Glimpses of English Poverty" never led anywhere, as Emerson's encounter with Birmingham did.

Only one of Emerson's American contemporaries pursued the implications of English technology as far, and that was Melville, the Melville of *Redburn* and *Israel Potter*. In *Israel Potter*, published just a year before *English Traits*, Melville too portrayed a modern life enclosed and crippled by mechanistic society, he too associated such enclosure with life in England, and he too explored the relationship between this England, and his own America. The differences are, of course, striking. Melville focused on the American nationalistic theme by making his hero a Revolutionary War soldier, and he did so in order to deflate such nationalism. His method was that of an ironist: after depicting an American hero trapped in an England rendered satanic by war, technology and poverty, he brought Israel Potter back home not to freedom, but to near-collision with a patriotic wagon careening through the streets of Boston. American nationalism itself takes on the relentless mechanical qualities of England. And, of course, Israel Potter's defeat is total: certainly no means of transcending "Fate" is offered him. Now Emerson did not share either this sense of ironic discrepancy or this tragic vision. He brought Birmingham home to America by assimilation, not by deflation of myth; and he reconciled it to growth and evolution, seeing transcendence rather than defeat as a possible end to the struggle. But the two writers stood on common ground in their sense of what the obstacles to a full human life might be. We are used to thinking of Emerson as a man with a deficient sense of evil, and Melville—most of all, perhaps, Melville in *Israel Potter*—as a man nearly paralyzed by his awareness of suffering. But these two documents of the 1850s share both a sense of the individual's struggle against deadening mechanization and an explicit denial of America's exemption from that struggle. No other American writer equally felt the impact of the mechanized English world upon his own until Henry Adams wrote about his trip through the Black District.

To make such a claim assumes the possibility of taking Emerson's social insights seriously, and indeed I wish to do so. Throughout his career, but especially in this decade of considering the Conduct of Life in a modern Anglo-American culture, social questions enter significantly into his dialectic of soul and world. Images of society can occur on either side of this dialectic: they can represent either an expanded identity for the soul or a barrier to the soul's assertion. I have been emphasizing barriers here: Pythagoras' sea of wreckage, the Times, Birmingham, the mill, Fate all represent the world of "not me," the world into which the self is incarnated or against which the self contends. The recognition of these counterforces to self-reliance itself constitutes an important kind of social vision, because it makes necessary an engagement of the individual self in its surrounding world.

In addition, however, Emerson's contention with Fate led him to consider society in another sense, that is, on the other side of the dialectic. It is not always the individual soul that must outweigh Birmingham or navigate its sea of troubles; Emerson increasingly makes room for a collective cultural enterprise of resistance to materialism. *English Traits* and "The Anglo-American" are centrally occupied with questions of total cultural vitality; and in *The Conduct of Life* Emerson speaks again and again of cultural questions despite his opening admission that he is "incompetent to solve the times." "Worship," the crucial essay in the book in terms of transition from Fate to Freedom, ends with the vision not of a new man, but of a "new church" for the society as a whole, a culturally shared sense of spirituality.[28]

Emerson aimed for the "melioration" or evolutionary growth of the society as a whole, but increasingly in the 1850s he recognized the role of a minority culture in affecting the direction of the whole. In *English Traits* he wrote that if the British still contained "retrieving power" it lay among a "minority of profound minds" which, though vastly outweighed, might by its discord yield new power. This minority constituted one of "two nations" in England, a class of perception and genius alongside a larger, materially oriented class.[29]

In this sense America too contained "two nations." The same year that he was working out this idea about the English, Emerson spoke on his favorite subject, the scholar in America, to the students of Williams College. His address offers a good indication of the distance he had come since he first described the "American Scholar" to Harvard students in 1837. At that time "Man Thinking" was to be a complete individual, "self-relying and self-directed." In 1854 Emerson proclaimed that "the Scholars are an organic caste or class" in an "Anglo-Saxon society" resembling "a great industrial corporation." The society in which scholars dwell, in other words, is a mechanistic and fatalistic Birmingham, a society immersed, Emerson said, in a "vulgarity" which "came to us, with commerce, out of England." Here is a fine example of Emerson's perception in the mid-1850s of society as an oppressive collectivity. But resistance is not simply his own personal business. The scholars, he went on to assert, are "accountable for this materialism"; they as another collectivity must understand it and resist its tyranny.[30] The obstructions set in the way of the scholar by modern Anglo-Saxon society demand engagement both of the individual and of the class.

Emerson has perhaps seemed aloof from social questions partly because he refused to be a reformer in an age of reform; he never followed the Abolitionists in America or Carlyle in England in their direct proposal of remedies for perceived ills. But his concern for a society's capacity to encourage the full development of the human soul involves, after all, the question of culture in its broadest sense—the question of an Arnold much more than a Carlyle. And indeed his appeal for a class of scholars or a new church does point toward the issues that Arnold would make central a decade later in *Culture and Anarchy*. The similarities are strong: Arnold portrayed a majority culture beset with the danger of too much "faith in machinery," in wealth and in mere bodily prosperity; he argued that a minority of men professing different values—the Oxford movement, for instance—could create new currents of life and feeling in a society despite short-term defeat; and he concluded that such apparent elitists were indeed "the true apostles of equality," because they worked for the creation of a genuine *national* vitality and intelligence. But I don't wish to move Emerson from his own center and convert him into a Victorian critic of culture. The issues of cultural materialism and idealism, of majority and minority values, are surely present in his thought, but they are present as corollaries to the central drama of individual vision. Arnold argued that "perfection . . . is not possible while the individual remains isolated"; he saw the end of culture as the creation of a *communal* "perfect man." Even in his passage about the "new church," on the other hand, Emerson characterized it as a form of worship which "shall send man home to his central solitude." Even in his description of an American scholar accountable for the nation's materialism, he went on from such "secular and outward benefit" to the quality of the individual's own soul.

What we have here, then, is not Arnold's cultural criticism any more than it is Melville's tragic portrayal of a man's destruction. It is, as ever with Emerson, an essentially affirmative vision of the individual's emergence into full consciousness. But it is an affirmative vision that takes fully into account the difficulties and responsibilities of existence in a modern technological society. This society provides both the world in which the soul must necessarily exist as it reaches for vision, and a significant object of the soul's action or vocation once vision has been reached. "Melioration" of the whole society will take place only through the "incarnation" of many individuals.

In fact personal vocation in a Birminghamized world cannot always *proceed from* vision; much more often Man Thinking must work on an ambiguous middle ground that partakes of both matter and spirit, Fate and Freedom, uncertain at any given moment what the results will be. Thus on the one hand the sense of struggle and obstruction is often dominant. But on the other, the possibility of imminent transformation is there too, the possibility that the actual conditions of Fate might produce power. The water that drowns one man, Emerson says, buoys up the other who knows how to swim; an iron bar that seems an obstacle can become a conductor. The point is, though, that the individual or society engaged in this process of transformation feels no assurance of victory. One is asked to exercise an attitude of trust and acceptance rather than require fully adequate forms of vision and action in the present.

This balance between a sense of limitation and a promise of fulfillment best characterizes Emerson's later thinking on his relation to the Times. Though the conditions of Fate and the Times are often perceived in adversarial terms, as a beast or a machine to conquer, they can also of themselves become a means to vision. Emerson ends *The Conduct of Life* not with Pythagoras still floundering in his sea, but with the story of Thor, who was set three tasks to do and only later found that he had been drinking the sea, and wrestling Time, and racing Thought. Almost parodying his earlier and more lofty Transcendentalist, Emerson imagines us demanding, " 'Set me some great task, ye gods! and I will show my spirit.' " But we are required instead to contend with "seeming trifles," with "bad company and squalid conditions." And he concludes, "If we weave a yard of tape in all humility, and as well as we can, long hereafter we shall see that it was no cotton tape at all, but some galaxy which we braided, and that the threads were Time and Nature."[31] It is this need to "work and affirm" that is Emerson's final response to the obstacles he perceives as Fate. He presents the need for such affirmation both to the individual soul and to a modern Anglo-American culture seeking for faith and value amidst its own materialism.

Notes

1. *The Complete Works of Ralph Waldo Emerson*, ed. Edward Waldo Emerson, 12 vols. (Boston: Houghton, Mifflin, 1903–1904), I, 350. Quotations from Emerson's lecture manuscripts are made with the permission of William H. Bond of Houghton Library and the Ralph Waldo Emerson Memorial Association.

2. *Journals of Ralph Waldo Emerson*, ed. Edward Waldo Emerson and Waldo Emerson Forbes, 10 vols. (Boston: Houghton Mifflin, 1909–1914), VIII, 239–240.

3. "New England" lecture series; Houghton Library mss., Lectures and Sermons of Ralph Waldo Emerson, 199 (1–5).

4. *The Letters of Ralph Waldo Emerson*, ed. Ralph L. Rusk, 6 vols. (New York: Columbia University Press, 1939), III, 461.

5. See, for instance, *Letters*, III, 442; *The Journals and Miscellaneous Notebooks of Ralph Waldo Emerson*, ed. William H. Gilman et al. (Cambridge: Harvard University Press, 1960-), X, 245; Houghton Library ms. lectures "England" and "London," 201 (1–2).

6. "The Emerson-Thoreau Correspondence," *Atlantic Monthly*, 69 (June 1892): 745, *Journals and Notebooks*, X, 221, 300.

7. *Letters*, III, 452–453; *Journals and Notebooks*, X, 258–259.

8. *Journals and Notebooks*, X, 260.

9. Houghton Library lecture ms., 200 (8), leaves 20, 36.

10. William Charvat, *Emerson's American Lecture Engagements: A Chronological List* (New York: New York Public Library, 1961).

11. *Journals and Notebooks*, X, 501; *Works*, V, 98.

12. *Letters*, III, 455.

13. *Works*, VI, 3–4.

14. *Journals and Notebooks*, VIII, 228.

15. See *Journals*, VIII, 8–9, 16, 50–51, etc.

16. *Journals*, VIII, 88, 112.

17. Charvat, *Emerson's American Lecture Engagements*, p. 26.

18. *Works*, XI, 179, 209, 204; *Journals*, VIII, 231.

19. *Journals*, VIII, 239.

20. Charvat, *Emerson's American Lecture Engagements*, p. 26.

21. *Journals*, VIII, 239.

22. *Works*, V, 169, 170, 249, 290, 255.

23. *Works*, V, 314.

24. Houghton Library lecture ms., 202 (2), leaves 24, 42, 46.

25. *Works*, XI, 227.

26. Houghton Library lecture ms., 202 (2), leaf 12.

27. *Works*, VI, 19, 209–211, 121–122.

28. *Works*, VI, 3, 241.

29. *Works*, V, 259.

30. *Journals*, VIII, 471–473.

31. *Works*, VI, 320–321.

"From Franklin to Emerson"

William L. Hedges*

1. Perry Miller and Connections in American Literature

To reread Perry Miller's well-known essay "From Edwards to Emerson" is to enter a half-forgotten world in which reputations, connections, and meanings in American literature were more nebulous than they have become for many scholars and critics since 1940.[1] Miller was surprisingly defensive in regard to Emerson, doubtful in his own mind, quite clearly, of the lasting value of so blithe a sage in an era of depression and world war, and well aware of pragmatic America's limited tolerance for mysticism and pantheism. In his essay, however, he unearthed native "roots" for transcendentalism, and his ironic innuendo managed to suggest a con-

*Reprinted from *The Oldest Revolutionary: Essays on Benjamin Franklin*, ed. J. A. Leo Lemay (Philadelphia: University of Pennsylvania Press, 1976), pp. 139–56.

temporary relevance for Emerson which foreshadowed a somewhat strained significance that students seem increasingly to find in American literature generally or in what is taken to be the dominant literary tradition in America.

The hackneyed metaphor of roots and soil justified itself by being part of a snide reference to Van Wyck Brooks, who had obviously failed in Miller's eyes to account satisfactorily for the "particular blossom" of Emerson "in the flowering of New England." Later in his essay the author of *The New England Mind* grumbled that the popular volume by Brooks, which had appeared four years earlier, although ostensibly a search for a usable American past, was based on insufficient knowledge of Emerson's period and of "the nature of social change in general." It is true that Brooks had done little to dispel the prevalent notion that Emerson was basically an amalgam of Kant, Coleridge, Swedenborg, the *Bhagvad-gita* and other assorted foreign influences. Brooks's explanation of Emerson was probably, for Miller, too close to that of Emerson himself, which Miller described sarcastically as seeing in transcendentalism "one more expression of the benign gentleman who previously had spoken in the persons of Socrates and Zoroaster, Mohammed and Buddha, Shakespeare and St. Paul."[2] Going to William James as an authority on religious experience, Brooks had argued that Emerson's doctrine of self-reliance was simply the reiteration of a fundamental idea or attitude implicit in "all the periods of revival, the early Christian age and Luther's age, Rousseau's, Kant's and Goethe's."[3]

Although Emerson identified transcendental idealism with a sequence of antiauthoritarian moments in philosophy and religion reaching back as far as the Stoics, Miller largely scoffed at his antihistoricism: it was part or parcel of transcendentalism's alarming eclecticism, its tendency to lump things together indiscriminately, its declaring "all ideas to be one idea, all religions the same religion, all poets singers of the same music." For Perry Miller in 1940 in the wake of the Nazi *Blitzkreig* it was imperative to be able to distinguish between the slayer and the slain, whatever their ultimate merger in the Over-Soul. So too it was necessary to insist "that ideas are born in time and place, that they spring from specific environments, that they express the force of societies and classes, that they are generated by power relations."[4]

And yet ironically Miller's own accounting for Emerson is in one sense not very different from that of Emerson or Brooks. Fundamental for all three is the notion of a periodic revival of religious enthusiasm. The difference is that Miller locates Emerson within the framework of a recurrent New England impulse in the direction of mystical piety, whereas for Emerson and Brooks the framework is much more vast. The two views, however, might well be made to coexist.

The heart of "From Edwards to Emerson" is the outline which Miller offers of the intellectual history of New England from 1630 to 1830. It emphasizes the polarity in Puritan thought, its intense piety and spirituality on the one hand and its diligent attention to the practical world on the other. As he put it, "At the core of the theology there was an indestructible element which was mystical, and a feeling for the universe which was almost pantheistic; but there was also a social code demanding obedience to external law, a code to which good people voluntarily conformed and to which bad people should be made to conform." This contradiction produced or characterized the conflicts between the Antinomians and John Winthrop and John Cotton and between Edwards and Charles Chauncy. In the nineteenth century Miller saw a recurrence of the same tension in the opposition between Emerson and the Unitarians. Passing over the terror in Edwards at the wrath of the Omnipotent, Miller stressed the revivalist's sense of the world as "dynamic . . . , filled with the presence of God, quickened with divine life, pervaded with joy and ecstasy."[5] Edwards thus became an incipient transcendentalist, held in check only by the bonds of Calvinist theology. Emerson, Miller noted, was fortunate enough to have had Chauncy and Unitarianism liberate New England (or at least Boston and Cambridge) before the mystical pantheistic urge made its presence felt in himself.

Thus was transcendentalism given native roots, and mysticism and pantheism Americanized. I hope I have made the reader a bit uneasy by my glib use of "mysticism" and "pantheism." I deliberately echo Miller, who I think is also uneasy with these words but who seems determined to make the reader swallow them as representing the essential Emerson. What is amazing about the essay is that Miller largely rejects a traditional view of Emerson that could easily have been made to mesh with his interpretation of Puritanism. The view goes back at least as far as James Russell Lowell, who laid it out very obviously in his deft caricature of Emerson in "A Fable for Critics." The personality was polarized: "Plotinus-Montaigne," Lowell called him, or "Greek head on right Yankee shoulders." Why did Miller not look at Emerson as himself an embodiment of the tension between the two pronounced tendencies in New England thought, especially in view of Emerson's own fascination with polarities, his sense of experience as oscillation?

The answer is that to concede that Emerson had much of the shrewd Yankee in him would have meant weakening what Miller obviously saw as Emerson's strongest claim for sympathy in 1940. Although he specifically disclaims any interest in having the higher metaphysics of transcendentalism taken "seriously" by his own contemporaries, Miller does stress Emerson's sense of transcendentalism as a reaction against the evils of the "commercial times" of Jacksonian America—as well as against Unitarianism.[6] In Miller's mind, perhaps more than in Emerson's, the "commercial times" are intimately connected with the social and political conservatism of the worldly-minded commonsensical Unitarians. Miller's depression-sharpened liberalism makes itself clearly felt. Call Emerson a "mystagogue," as Lowell did, if you like, Miller seems to say, but first and last there has been a lot of mystagoguery in America and it has something to do with the dominance in this culture of the State Street mentality and the failures of industrial capitalism.

The trouble is that for many the sharp distinction between Emerson and Yankee industry, frugality, and finance has been hard to maintain. Lowell was quite specific: Emerson's "range" was from the "pole" of "Olympus" to that of "the Exchange." Bliss Perry began his *Emerson Today* in 1931 by noting the "open parable in the very lines of his face. . . . Seen from one side, it was the face of a Yankee of the old school, shrewd, serious, practical; the sort of face that may still be observed in the quiet country churches of New England or at the village store. Seen from the other side, it was the face of a dreamer, a seer, a soul brooding on things to come, things as yet very far away."[7] While Miller in the lead article of the December 1940 issue of *The New England Quarterly* was relating transcendental pantheism to puritan piety, Alexander C. Kern in "Emerson and Economics," the final article, was suggesting that the "influence of Emerson's puritan New England background" on the "crass portion of his thought" was much stronger than had generally been noticed. Emphasizing the conflict in Emerson between materialism and idealism, Kern argued the fundamental domination of the latter but admitted that the Emersonian concern with practical endeavor sometimes amounted to almost overt advocacy of "rugged individualism."[8] The next year Miller's colleague F. O. Matthiessen was to suggest that Emerson's "most balanced' assessment of his own position "was that which placed him between the transcendentalists and Franklin."[9] And Miller himself was later in speaking of Emerson to praise his "levelheadedness" as "his most precious bequest to a posterity which is understandably exasperated by his unction."[10]

Miller would have been the first to recognize that his own thought, as much as Emerson's, was a product of a particular time and place. It is well, however, for those of us who utilize his ideas to develop an equal awareness. I propose therefore an inquiry into Emerson's relation to Benjamin Franklin to balance Miller's study of Emerson and Edwards. My primary purposes concern the two classic American sages themselves: if, as I believe, they are closer to each other than Miller would have admitted, then we are missing something important in both of them if we ignore the affinity.

True, nothing is more commonplace in Emerson scholarship than recognition of the tension between his practicality and his piety.[11] But "From Edwards to Emerson" has given comfort to those who would rather forget Emerson's pragmatic side. These days Emerson's detractors—of whom there are still a fair number, especially among devotees of Thoreau, Hawthorne, and Melville—are apt to be the ones who make the most of his interest in wealth, power, and success. It is not uncommon to find him at least briefly compared to Franklin, but the Franklin who is invoked in the most detailed and extended comparison that I know of is a one-dimensional figure, a flat abstraction out of Max Weber.[12]

In the back of my mind also is a sense that Miller's widely reprinted essay serves as keystone in an overarching framework of general concepts which for many people greatly affect the ways in which American literature is seen and interpreted.[13] What, one wonders, is the strength of the whole structure if the keystone is loose or out of line? This is a question I propose only to raise, not answer, except to say generally that I believe there is cause for concern. But let me, before getting on with Franklin and Emerson, briefly explain what I take to be the larger significance of "From Edwards to Emerson."

These days Emerson is much less apologized for than he was in 1940. If Thoreau seems to many to have given a more thoroughly satisfying literary expression to basic Emersonian insights and awareness than the master himself, the seminal power of Emerson in the development of a central tradition in American literature is now not only recognized but much more fully understood. The year after Miller's essay Matthiessen in *American Renaissance* demonstrated the fundamental modernity of the sensibility of Emerson and his illustrious contemporaries Thoreau, Hawthorne, Melville, and Whitman. And once the significance of Emerson's theory of language and poetics was more clearly discerned, the temptation to dismiss transcendentalism as moonshine diminished. Matthiessen paid less attention to the early native roots of the American renaissance than to its affinities with some of the baroque and metaphysical literature which the taste of T. S. Eliot and other moderns had resuscitated. But the net effect was very much the same, especially after Edward Taylor became better known and after Edward's *Images or Shadows of Divine Things* was published by Miller and the Puritan interest in symbolism came to be more and more fully explored.

Something like what Miller called Puritan "piety, a religious passion, the sense of an inward communication and of the divine symbolism of nature" came to seem the motive being realized most powerfully in a great deal of American literature.[14] Indeed it may not be too much to say that there gradually emerged out of the conjunction of implications in the works of the two Harvard professors—one focusing primarily on the seventeenth and the other on the nineteenth centuries—a theory or ideology of American literature which has won wide acceptance. It is a theory which sees the main tradition leaping from early Puritanism into the mid-nineteenth century and which tends to ignore much that came between. Miller made the vital connection between Puritan piety and transcendentalism with an enthusiasm and a flair for irony which have a lot to do with his essay's continuing appeal. What he suggests is what has been said over and over again since 1940 in discussions of major tendencies and developments in American literature: in essence that literature is not what we should expect it to be. It is not primarily a body of open straightforward, realistic, practical-minded, commonsensical expression, the embodiment of progressive dreams, but rather something private, cryptic, symbolic, mysterious, sometimes mystic, often nightmarishly fantastic. Obviously the irony implicit in what I am calling the ideology of American literature is congenial to the modern (and post-modern) sensibility and its dionysian distrust of the pragmatic and the merely rational. An inquiry into Franklin and Emerson therefore is to some extent an exercise in distrust of that distrust.

2. Franklin to Emerson

We may begin by noting that in 1962 Miller published an essay on Edwards and Franklin. Perhaps had he lived longer he would himself have completed what I hope to make clear ought to be seen as a natural or logical triangulation. As was to be expected, he found in Franklin the perfect foil for Edwards that so many others have seen and, in the contrast between the two "massively symbolic characters," a made-to-order representation of the split in Puritanism which he had posted two decades earlier. That the split still lived on in the mid-twentieth century he implicitly demonstrated by showing his own admiration for Edwardsean piety coupling snugly with an inherent skepticism and irreverence. He responded with gusto to Franklin's independent-mindedness, his shrewd wit, his down-to-earth style and his ribaldry. He saw an understanding of Franklin as an important part of an understanding of America. And finally he saw a crucial connection: underneath the surface Edwards was "Franklin's brother."[15]

Why? Because of what Carl Becker had called Franklin's "disinterestedness." Miller observed that in the "most perceptive sentence yet written about Franklin," Becker had said "that it was no wonder he sought for his ultimate satisfaction in natural science, because only in the physical universe could he find a 'disinterestedness' equal to his own." Going on, Miller wrote that "one learns to appreciate that the actual charm of [Franklin's] writing is his disengagement from all the multifarious activities of his career. He could never have . . . written about them . . . in exactly the quizzical spirit he unfailingly maintains, unless he had somewhere in his intricate constitution an ultimate sense that all . . . local aims were subordinate to a larger one, in relation to which they were indeed trivial." In the end Miller sensed that Franklin the "master worldly-wiseman," like Edwards the "archspiritualist," somehow felt himself a "negligible finite in the face of a glorious incomprehensibility."[16] Thus piety and practicality merge.

Emerson, I shall maintain, felt and responded to this same quality in Franklin which Becker and Miller tried to define as disinterestedness or disengagement. The terminology may not be quite adequate to the elusiveness of the attitude in question. Were it not for the fact that no one shows less indication of having gone through a dark night of the soul than Franklin, Eliot's prayer from "Ash-Wednesday," "Teach us to care and not to care," might serve as appropriate text for the peculiar equilibrium one senses in Franklin. But let us put it this way, that Franklin's empiricism was something more than a commitment to scientific method; it was a receptivity to experience and its complex possibilities that *practically* speaking amounted to reverence—or to what Emerson might have called absolute trust, the self-reliance that is ultimately reliance on Nature. One thinks of the third paragraph of "Self-Reliance," with its paradoxical movement from the "iron-string" of "Trust thyself" to what seems a contradictory imperative, "Accept the place the divine providence has found for you, the society of your contemporaries, the connection of events. Great men have always done so, and confided themselves childlike to the genius of their age, betraying their perception that the absolutely trustworthy was seated at their heart, working through their hands, predominating in all their being." We shall be reminded of this reference to heart and hands a bit later.

To the author of "Self-Reliance," Franklin was quite clearly a great man. His name appears frequently on the lists of great men which Emerson compiled in his notebooks and journals.[17] And part of the greatness obviously was his capacity for feeling perfectly at home in the world. Emerson comments explicitly on the "extraordinary ease" with which Franklin's mind worked; he was "unconscious of any mental effort in detailing the profoundest solutions of phenomena & therefore [made] no parade" (*Journals*, II, 208). And in 1841 he wrote, "When the great man comes, he will have that social strength which Dr. Kirkland or Dr. Franklin or Robert Burns had & so will engage us to the moment that we shall not suspect his greatness until late afterward[;] in some dull hour we shall say I am enlarged. . . . This man! this man! whence came he?" (*Journals*, VIII, 126–27).

Franklin's early "Articles of Belief and Acts of Religion" are a clear indication of the coexistence in him of impulses that, for all their connection with the early Enlightenment, suggest Edwards and traditional Puritanism on the one hand and on the other Emerson and transcendentalism. He acknowledges himself as "less than nothing" in the face of the supreme perfection of the "INFINITE." And yet he conceives human happiness and pleasure to be part of the system created by that Infinite Being, who in Himself can have no regard for man. As elsewhere in Franklin, virtue and happiness are conceived of as bound together, though the logic of the relationship is quite unclear. Superficially this may seem to point toward the total secularization and hence vulgarization of the Protestant ethic and the notion that material success is demonstration of moral virtue. Or he may seem simply shallow in equating virtue with happiness rather than suffering. There certainly is a material dimension to the pleasure which this religious confession is so much concerned with: it involves awareness of a world in which "many Things . . . seem purely design'd for the Delight of Man"—though this emphasis, it is worth observing, represents a welcome awakening out of Puritan inhibition. But one suspects a kernel of deep awareness in the assertion that "without Virtue Man can have no Happiness in this World."[18]

The absoluteness of the statement is what startles: "*no* happiness" except with virtue. This goes farther than routine neoclassical couplings of happiness and virtue such as the one in the excerpt from Addison's *Cato* which Franklin uses as an inscription to the "Articles of Belief." It suggests the surprising intensity of his personification of virtue a few weeks later in the third of the "Busy-Body" papers—the idealized figure of an American "Cato," a compound of "Innocence and Wisdom" dressed in "plainest Country Garb," whose moral force, apparent in "the Air of his Face" and "every Part of his Behavior," compels "Respect from every Person in the Room." And one thinks ahead also from "without Virtue . . . no Happiness" to Emerson's "All things are moral" and Thoreau's pronouncement from the tranquility of *Walden*, "Our whole life is startlingly moral. There is never an instant's truce between virtue and vice. Goodness is the only investment that never fails."[19] Franklin is obviously active rather than meditative, more interested in *doing* good than in contemplating the nature of goodness. And yet when he talks of the "inward Joy" of "ADORATION," one wonders for an instant who was the incipient transcendentalist, he or Edwards.[20] In any case his "Articles of Belief" represent the man of reason in effect throwing up his hands, confiding himself to the genius of the world, which is ultimately irrational or incomprehensible. This is the larger context of his empiricism.

In some passages Emerson sees Franklin as we would expect a transcendentalist to see him. In the lecture on Milton we hear, "Franklin's man is a frugal, inoffensive, thrifty citizen, but savours of nothing heroic." On another occasion he associates Franklin with the "vulgar Utilitarianism" of the late eighteenth century, content with "Common Sense" and incapable of transcendental "Reason."[21] But on the whole Emerson's response to Franklin is surprisingly positive. While most of his references to him in the journals occur in the 1820s and 1830s—and we may speculate that Franklin came to mean less to him in his later years—the frugal man of common sense also figured earlier as a "moral philosopher" and revolutionary (*Journals*, II, 208) and was clearly involved in the original formulation of some key Emersonian ideas.

To begin with, the American Revolution was a crucial event in Emerson's sense of his heritage. It marked for him an epoch of mental and moral as well as political liberation. In the same entry in which he marveled at Franklin's intellectual brilliance, he declared, "That age abounded in greatness," and he compared it with his own, in which "men . . . do not produce new works but admire old ones" (II, 208). In another early entry he wrote of "the cowed benevolence of" his own "dismal time" (*Journals*, IV, 37). His dim view of the present, so crucial to *Nature*, "Self-Reliance," and especially "The American Scholar," clearly formed itself against a strong sense of the preceding age as nonretrospective. "Where is the master that could have instructed Franklin or Washington," he wrote in 1832, going on to add, "or Bacon or Newton?"(*Journals*, IV, 50). He reiterated the question in "Self-Reliance." He also transcribed in his journal the Latin inscription (by Turgot) from Houdon's bust of Franklin, which in English reads, "He snatched the thunderbolt from heaven, then the scepter from tyrants" (*Journals*, VI, 208).

At the same time, one sees that Emerson's conception of the Revolutionary period is intimately tied to his sense of himself as a New Englander. It is not Jefferson or Patrick Henry he looks back to, but James Otis, John Hancock, Samuel Adams, and in that context Franklin, born only a few doors away from the Emerson house in Boston. And the Revolutionary group relate to Bradford, Winthrop, Mather, and Edwards. If there is any division in this heritage for Emerson, it is between the overzealousness of the seventeenth-century Puritans and the comparative moderation of their eighteenth-century descendants—a view, by the way, which Otis and Sam Adams make difficult to substantiate. The earlier period had seen lamentable excesses of bigotry and persecution; it was well that the original Puritan ardor had cooled down into the "*Good Sense*" which he at first thought Franklin, but then realized Gibbon, had called "as rare as genius." All in all Emerson valued his "Puritan stock" for its "vigorous sense, or practical genius" (*Journals*, II, 197, 227). Its piety he seems to have taken for granted. He was at one point, very early, disturbed by Franklin's reputation for skepticism, but before long let himself be persuaded—rather too easily, one is tempted to conclude—that the philosopher who stole the thunderbolt from heaven believed in immortality (*Journals*, II, 108, 208).

Franklin, it may be argued, was for Emerson a model of the American scholar. His life obviously taught the greater importance of "observation of men & things" over books as a source of knowledge. He and, intriguingly, Edwards were the early American writers who Emerson thought showed most clearly the stamp of a native American genius (*Journals*, II, 230, 197). As one would expect, he clearly admired Franklin's delight in proverbial wisdom. In Franklin's style, one suspects, Emerson felt himself in touch with one thing he was looking for in poetry—"the common": the "meal in the firkin; the milk in the pan; the ballad in the street; the news of the boat."[22] In a journal passage which must offend those who see Franklin primarily as the embodiment of smugness, Emerson observed that the "greatest men have been most thoughtful for the humblest. Socrates, . . . Alfred, Franklin, Jesus Christ, & all the Pauls and Fenelons he has made. . . . And, so keep me, heaven, I will love the race in general if I cannot in any particular" (*Journals*, IV, 315). So

Emerson apparently was not one of the readers put off by the addition of "Humility," with its attendant exhortation, "Imitate Jesus and Socrates," to Franklin's list of virtues.[23]

At times in talking about Franklin, Emerson balances him against an opposing tendency in a polar relationship, thus seeming to sever practical ingenuity completely from morality or spirituality. "Transcendentalism says, the Man is all," he observes, whereas "Franklin says, the tools. . . ." And in another passage he substitutes for the conventional head/heart dichotomy one between hand and heart, "the hand of Franklin & the heart of Paul." Yet even as he makes the distinctions there is a sense of an ultimate relationship, as is implied in the passage from "Self-Reliance" quoted above that "the absolutely trustworthy" being "seated" at the "heart" and working through the "hands." Both Franklin and Paul are examples of trust in oneself, secure "among gluttons & sycophants." And, "A master *and* tools,—is the lesson I read in every shop and farm and library" (*Journals*, III, 249; X, 53–54).

What Franklin represents for Emerson is the practical side of Puritanism, which for the most part he found it impossible to repudiate, however much he may have wanted to, because Nature is real as well as ideal, fact as well as spirit. The soul, at least in this life, is nothing without the body. The body has to be cared for, and taking care of the body or learning to cope with the physical demands of Nature is the beginning of the cultivation of the mind or spirit. Franklin, the journals suggest, belongs as much with the "Discipline" chapter of *Nature* as with "Commodity." As early as 1830 Emerson associates him with the phrase "the conduct of life" and calls him one of the "astonishing instances" of it. And the very next entry in the journal deals with the subject of virtue in a way strongly reminiscent of Franklin (*Journals*, III, 200).[24]

First comes an insistence on virtue as action, *doing* good, not just talking about it. The problem, as in Franklin, is method, how to produce virtue. And the answer is surprisingly similar to Franklin's. It is astounding to discover that Emerson may have taken seriously just that part of Franklin which most tempts the modern reader's laughter or derision, that "bold and arduous Project of arriving at moral Perfection."[25] Instead of talking about all the virtues being "comprehended" in "self-trust" he specifies individual virtues that are worth acquiring, starting with "Early Spartan rising," then "Temperance" and "fasting," after which he calls for "attention to . . . personal habits."[26] The habits that Emerson is most concerned to cultivate tend, it is true, to reveal his predilection for contemplation over action. If he has Franklin's list of virtues in mind, he seems to get stalled on "Silence," as he notes the value of the "habit of being sometimes alone, the habit of reading, the habit of abstraction in order to find out what his own opinion is, the habit of controlling his conversation, the habit of praying, or referring himself always to God." For Emerson, of course, piety ultimately transcends practicality. But the respect for a discipline which recognizes the close relationship of body and mind, appetite and morality, remains somewhat Franklinesque. He ends the passage with a sentence which sounds like something Franklin might have written had he tried to get transcendental resonances into Poor Richard's maxims: "Order has a good name in the world for getting the most sweetness out of time" (*Journals*, III, 200).

Thirty years later the phrase "the conduct of life" surfaced as the title of a book by Emerson in which the essay "Wealth" holds a position somewhat comparable to that of "Discipline" in *Nature*. Or, more accurately, "Wealth" is like an expanded merger of "Commodity" and "Discipline." It is crucial because it makes clear that the Emersonian ethic was the Protestant ethic in a highly exalted form, an effort, like the one implicit in Franklin's life and writings, to fuse piety and practicality, to maintain that work, virtue, salvation, and enjoyment of the world are functions of one another.[27] As the first two paragraphs quickly demonstrate, "Wealth" is an elaboration of the basic Puritan idea of the calling:

> As soon as a stranger is introduced . . . , one of the first questions which all wish to have answered is, How does that man get his living? And with reason. He is no whole man until he knows how to earn a blameless livelihood. Society is barbarous until every industrious man can get his living without dishonest customs.
>
> Every man is a consumer, and ought to be a producer. He fails to make his place good in the world unless he not only pays his debt but also adds something to the common wealth. Nor can he do justice to his genius without making some larger demand on the world than a bare subsistence. He is by constitution expensive, and needs to be rich.

Already Emerson's conception of the calling has become exorbitant and implies an openness to enjoyment which, like Franklin's, we do not ordinarily associate with Puritanism. With an expansiveness that suggests Whitman, he is soon saying that man "is born to be rich. He . . . is tempted out by his appetites and fancies to the conquest of this and that piece of nature, until he finds his well-being in the use of his planet, and of more planets than his own. . . . The same correspondence that is between thirst in the stomach and water in the spring, exists between the whole of man and the whole of nature." But the connection betwen wealth and virtue or discipline is never laid by. "The subject of economy mixes itself with morals, inasmuch, as it is a peremptory point of virtue that a man's independence be secured. Poverty demoralizes."

To find the way to wealth—what Emerson would consider "true" wealth—is to acquire transcendental discipline. Character is formed by honest labor in a calling, since "wealth is in applications of mind to nature" and respect for the laws of nature. It necessitates the formulation of rules, the creation of "a better order." Emerson's observation in "Wealth" that the "counting-room maxims liberally expounded are laws of the universe" is an updating of his famous Aunt Mary's declaration, "I respect in a rich man the order of Providence."[28] In sum Emerson sees a legitimate pursuit of wealth as consistent with the natural order, part of Nature's functioning to fully humanize man. The concept of economy ultimately involves the satisfaction of moral and spiritual as well as material wants. Dishonest gain is thus not true wealth. To the charge that dishonesty pays, Emerson would reply, it is an illusion; in the long run fraud produces material and moral waste, which touches everyone.

Emerson is close here to a central perception in Franklin, which develops with his realization that he could dispense with revelation as far as morality is concerned. Both men assume an ultimate connection between self-interest and cosmic well-being. Franklin's secularization of morality begins with his daring to think, as he tells us in the *Autobiography*, that "vicious Actions are not hurtful because they are forbidden, but forbidden because they are hurtful, the Nature of Man alone consider'd." Applied only to success in business, his belief that "*Truth, Sincerity and Integrity* in Dealings between Man and Man" are "good" for one may seem naive. But when that belief expands suddenly to the far-reaching hypothesis that, "all the Circumstances of things considered," moral actions are beneficial to one, he brings us to the wisdom of a world in which if everyone behaved decently to one another, everyone would prosper.[29]

3. Franklin and Emerson:
The Nature of the Game

What tries the patience of the twentieth-century mind is the way in which Emerson and Franklin sometimes seem to take the connection between wealth and virtue too much for granted or interpret "wealth" too literally. We are skeptical when Franklin says that "no Qualities" are "so likely to make a poor Man's Fortune as those of Probity and Integrity."[30] *The Great Gatsby* is more real to us than *Poor Richard*. The pursuit of success demoralizes—as much as poverty: that is our fear. Commercialism distracts attention from the higher values in Emerson's economics and virtually guarantees waste and exploitation. Emerson's daring is apt to startle us more than he intended when in "Wealth" he says, "I have never seen a rich man. I have never seen a man as rich as all men ought to be." For metaphor most of us would probably prefer Thoreau's curiously parallel observation, "I have never yet met a man who was quite awake. How could I have looked him in the face?"[31] Disinterestedness has its limitations, its proximity, through indifference, to callousness.

While Franklin and Emerson are polar figures, each is polarized within himself between the attractions of practicality and contemplation. There is a certain remoteness or splendid isolation—some call it complacency—in both, Franklin's gregariousness notwithstanding. He is much more involved in the day-to-day world than Emerson, but, as Miller and Becker maintained, not completely so. There is a casualness about him that sometimes disappoints us. Promising as the *Autobiography* is, for instance, as a record of self-education and self-liberation in a society moving toward self-government, he shows no signs of wanting to push his awareness, particularly his self-awareness, any further than circumstances seem to require. There is a point in the consideration of moral issues beyond which he apparently does not want to get involved, perhaps on the assumption that in the long run the practical differences are negligible. Openmindedness, his greatest virtue, comes to seem at times an evasion of the responsibility of being serious down to the deepest level. Thus his mistakes remain mere "errata," typographical errors in the little book of his life.

The happy side of this failing, if such it should be called, is that he is a less somber, less pompous wise man, seer, or lay preacher than he is often taken to be—which is to acknowledge the depth of his sense of humor, its inextricable tie with his wisdom. The complex and subtle Franklin who emerges from recent scholarship and criticism has more in common with Emerson than did Franklin the plain-style Puritan or nononsense apostle of reason and utility.[32] We see his irony looking askance at his own moralizing out of a wry awareness of human (including his own) limitations lodged within a broad vision of human possibility. He preached as much as any Puritan, but no one was more aware than he that he was not better than he should be—as he shows at the beginning of the *Autobiography* by the pains he takes to call attention to his vanity: he is writing basically to please himself. When we see him in effect thanking God for his vanity "with all humility," we begin to see the man in his humor.[33]

Like Emerson, he is sententious in both the good and bad senses. Both lay down rules of conduct in aphoristic rather than legalistic language, aiming not so much for precision as for provocation, to startle the reader or listener into sudden awareness. Franklin's interest in rules, law, and order was perhaps fundamentally, though he scarcely realized it himself, a function of an aesthetic, awareness, of his recognition that the way something is said determines what is said, that admonition or prohibition, effectively conceived or formulated, is liberating, not restrictive, illuminating, not stupefying.

A sage with a high sense of drama, he may be as much artist as scientist. It is true that as a man of affairs he generally took a practical view of the arts, in theory writing to inform, instruct, and persuade, putting a high premium on the most directly communicative qualities in style. "*Heavenly Father*," he argues, "is more concise, equally expressive, and better modern English" than "*Our Father which art in Heaven*."[34] His devastating criticism of a song by Handel[35] puts so much stress on the words coming through clearly that one may wonder what, if anything, he heard in the music, whether he conceived of artistic expression as anything more than the direct transference from one brain to another of a few simple ideas—the utilitarian aesthetic, essentially, of the *Bay Psalm Book*. Yet obviously Franklin did not always mean business when he wrote. One finds him too often taking a delight in forms and formality that quite belies the virtual philistinism of his insistence on the purely didactic function of literature.

Consider, for instance, the artfulness with which he contrives a letter of condolence:

> We have lost a most dear and valuable relation, but it is the will of God and nature that these mortal bodies be laid aside, when the soul is to enter into real life; 'tis rather an embrio state, a preparation for living; a man is not completely born until he be dead: Why then should we grieve that a new child is born among the immortals? A new member added to their happy society?

One may doubt the strength of Franklin's faith in death as a new birth, but something in him rises to the occasion. Having decided to use a conventional form of commiseration, he works the whole letter out with neat precision. The elegance of his final image of death—an invitation to an eternal "party of pleasure"—has the authentic ring of something he would have liked to believe.[36]

He uses standard flourishes like the letter of condolence or congratulations to help him define himself in various social roles, personalizing the gestures, of course, often giving new life to shopworn sentiments. On happy occasions, he sometimes mocks rituals that threaten to turn into empty formalities. Standard forms and models, neoclassic formality, rather than a sense of organic form, moved him. Yet he could tell when a form did not fit a subject and could play on the discovery, often making fun of himself in the process. Gallantry was his forte, especially with women much younger than himself in whom his interest was supposed to be more or less paternal. In response to a letter received during a winter storm he writes, "Your Favours come mixed with the Snowy Fleeces which are pure as your Virgin Innocence, white as your lovely Bosom, and—as cold:—But let it warm toward some worthy young Man."[37] Another time the "fatherly Advice" he offers this lady becomes not only slightly risqué self-mockery, but also a parody of the advice-giving routine on which *The Way to Wealth* was later to be based. "Be a good Girl," he writes.

> Go constantly to Meeting . . . till you get a good Husband. . . . You must practice *Addition* to your Husband's Estate, by Industry and Frugality; *Substraction* of all unnecessary Expenses; *Multiplication* (I would gladly have taught you that myself, but you thought it was time enough, and wou'dn't learn) he will soon make you a Mistress of it. As to *Division*, I say with Brother Paul, *Let there be no Divisions among ye*.[38]

For Franklin the conduct of life, as commentators are fond of noting, seems to have involved his self-dramatization in appropriate roles as much as it did the daily discipline of forming steady habits. We may see "cosmetic" image-making in his acting out the diligent tradesman for all Philadelphia to see or his playing the homespun American in Paris. Perhaps Emerson would have scented hypocrisy or self-deception in his shifting roles, or at any rate interpreted concessions to public opinion as inconsistent with a self-reliant nonconformity. But Emerson's conception of self-reliance was not withdrawal into a narrow privacy. He knew about complicated selves from personal experience. Given his sense of the self as so much of the time shifting, oscillating in a world of illusion, self-reliance becomes for him something more than a routine discipline. The Franklin who self-consciously plays social roles, who "loves," as Benjamin DeMott says, "to stage virtues,"[39] and who as a writer speaks through numerous personae seems ultimately a compatriot in cunning of the philosopher who in "Self-Reliance" warns against a "foolish consistency," who in the same essay admits his willingness, if need be, to speak from the devil and who alternately identifies with representative men of such radically different persuasions as Montaigne and Swedenborg, the democrat and the aristocrat, the slayer and the slain.

From the immediate or existential point of view both Emerson and Franklin see chaos in experience almost as often as order and harmony. In theory, however, they regard the world from another viewpoint as well—from the aspect of eternity. And the two views blending together at times transform confusion into mystery and surprise. The world becomes an infinitely intricate and entrancing work of art. Or to shift to, and at the same time recast, Carl Becker's image of Franklin looking at public affairs as a game,[40] life in general becomes for both of these shrewd observers a game, in which the object is to discover the rules—and they are infinitely complex. It is a game in which one does the best one can on proverbial wisdom and fresh observations of nature—a parcel of partial, relative insights—and with some part of the mind enjoys watching oneself play, surprised by the tricks life plays and excited by sudden discoveries and occasional tricks of one's own. In this game fair play and trickery are assumed to be ultimately compatible.

Trial-and-error is the name of the game. Both Emerson and Franklin are empiricists, trying to learn from an experience which has its endless complications. In the *Autobiography* Franklin observes himself making his picaresque way through life, sometimes in control of himself and the situation, sometimes simply running in luck, sometimes being victimized or remaining largely passive—though willing—lacking a sure sense of direction, having to respond to events he has scarcely anticipated. And this life, even with all its spectacular success, has more than a little in common with the experience which Emerson analyzes in terms of fate, polarities, and illusions.

Given the nature of this experience, both men take refuge in cosmic optimism. The serenity or tranquility of Franklin seems more actual,

Emerson's more theoretical. In both, however, there is an oft-commented-on coldness. Too much has probably been made of it in both cases, yet the coldness still seems an important link between the two. For if, as Miller maintains, Franklin's "boredom with humanity" is what makes him Jonathan Edwards' brother,[41] then it must make him Emerson's great-uncle as well. And Yankee reticence will perhaps come to be seen as an indication that the split in Puritanism divides the individual within himself as much as it divides man from man. While the outward eye is alert to the practical, the would-be "transparent eyeball" of the inner self, alone with what circulates as "currents of the Universal Being,"[42] winks. On the verge of becoming nothing while seeing everything, the Yankee knows enough to smile—as Becker sensed Franklin smiling at the signing of the Declaration of Independence—and hold his peace.[43]

Notes

1. The essay, originally called "Jonathan Edwards to Emerson," was first published in *New England Quarterly*, 13 (December 1940): 589–617. Miller reprinted it under the title "From Edwards to Emerson" in *Errand into the Wilderness* (Cambridge: Harvard University Press, 1956), the version cited in this essay.

2. *Errand into the Wilderness*, pp. 187, 200, 188.

3. Van Wyck Brooks, *The Flowering of New England 1815–1865* (New York: E. P. Dutton, 1936), p. 207.

4. *Errand into the Wilderness*, p. 187.

5. *Errand into the Wilderness*, pp. 192, 195.

6. *Errand into the Wilderness*, pp. 186–187, 188. The phrase "commercial times" Miller takes from *The Complete Works of Ralph Waldo Emerson*, ed. Edward Waldo Emerson (Boston: Houghton, Mifflin, 1903–1904), I, 339.

7. Bliss Perry, *Emerson Today* (Princeton: Princeton University Press, 1931), p. 1.

8. Alexander C. Kern, "Emerson and Economics," *New England Quarterly*, 13 (December 1940): 683, 681.

9. F. O. Matthiessen, *American Renaissance* (New York: Oxford University Press, 1941), p. 66.

10. Perry Miller, "Emersonian Genius and the American Democracy," *New England Quarterly*, 26 (March 1953): 43.

11. In his *Emerson Handbook* (New York: Hendricks House, 1953), Frederic Ives Carpenter lists "*The Two Sides of the Face*" as the first major problem in Emerson's biography and maintains, "There are not only two sides of Emerson's face and philosophy, but also two (or more) interpretations of each side. The best biographies are those which recognize and describe this dualism without falsely simplifying its complexity" (pp. 1, 3).

12. See Jesse Bier, "Weberism, Franklin, and the Transcendental Style," *New England Quarterly*, 43 (June 1970): 179–192. Contrasting Emerson unfavorably with Thoreau, Bier reads the opposition of poety and practicality in the older transcendentalist as hypocrisy, self-deception, or confusion. Interestingly he ridicules Kern for having put a more favorable construction on Emerson's "ambivalence," charging him with having written a "simple apologia" (p. 191).

13. I have made no systematic investigation of the reprinting of "From Edwards to Emerson," but its popularity in books of essays designed to supplement college and university

courses in American literature is obvious. It is included in *Interpretations of American Literature*, ed. Charles Feidelson and Paul Brodtkorb (New York: Oxford University Press, 1959); *American Literature: A Critical Survey*, ed. T. D. Young and R. E. Fine (New York: American Book Co., 1968); and *Theories of American Literature*, ed. D. M. Kartinager and M. A. Griffith (New York: Macmillan, 1972).

14. *Errand into the Wilderness*, p. 192.

15. Miller, "Benjamin Franklin, 1706–1790, Jonathan Edwards, 1703–1758," in *Major Writers of America*, gen. ed. Perry Miller (New York: Harcourt, Brace & World, 1962), I, 97, 95.

16. *Major Writers of America*, I, 95, 96.

17. *The Journals and Miscellaneous Notebooks of Ralph Waldo Emerson*, ed. William H. Gilman et al. (Cambridge: Harvard University Press, 1960–), I, 193, 250; II, 227; III, 200, 357; IV, 36, 50, 315. (This work is subsequently referred to by volume and page numbers in parentheses in the text.) Franklin's greatness was the subject of a draft of an early composition in the *Journals* (II, 223–224).

18. *The Papers of Benjamin Franklin*, ed. Leonard W. Labaree et al. (New Haven: Yale University Press, 1959–), I, 102–103.

19. For the "Busy-Body," see *Papers*, I, 119. Emerson's statement occurs in the "Discipline" chapter of *Nature*, which speaks of the "ethical character" penetrating "the bone and marrow of nature." Thoreau's statement is from "Higher Laws" in *Walden*.

20. *Papers*, I, 104.

21. *The Early Lectures of Ralph Waldo Emerson*, ed. Stephen E. Whicher et al. (Cambridge: Harvard University Press, 1959, 1964), I, 150; II, 67. Even so, in the latter passage Franklin remains for Emerson "the clearest name" of his period, in contrast to "Rousseau and Voltaire, Diderot and the other unclean democrats." For other less flattering references to Franklin, see *Journals*, V, 202; VI, 232; VIII, 398.

22. Emerson, "The American Scholar." He makes note of aphorisms, epigrams, and fables by Franklin in *Journals*, II, 208, 237, 377; IV, 132; VI, 170.

23. *The Autobiography of Benjamin Franklin*, ed. Leonard W. Labaree et al. (New Haven: Yale University Press, 1964), p. 150. Emerson elsewhere links Franklin and Socrates for their humility (*Journals*, X, 298) and also speaks of the latter's "Franklin-like wisdom" ("Plato; or, the Philosoper" in *Representative Men*; cf. *Journals*, X, 482).

24. The two entries were made three weeks apart but are closely enough linked in subject matter to suggest that Emerson probably reread the first just before or while writing the second.

25. *Autobiography*, p. 148.

26. As in "The American Scholar."

27. Kern suggests the connection between Emerson and the Protestant ethic in "Emerson and Economics," p. 683.

28. Quoted by Miller, *Errand into the Wilderness*, p. 201.

29. *Autobiography*, pp. 114–115, 158.

30. *Autobiography*, p. 158.

31. Henry David Thoreau, *Walden* ("Where I Lived, and What I Lived For").

32. J. A. Leo Lemay's "Franklin and the *Autobiography*: An Essay on Recent Scholarship," *Eighteenth-Century Studies*, 1 (1967–1968): 185–211, gives some sense of the emerging Franklin. The essay calls particular attention to Franklin's virtues as a humorist (p. 195). In a more recent article, "Benjamin Franklin," in *Major Writers of Early American Literature*, ed. Everett Emerson (Madison: University of Wisconsin Press, 1972), pp. 205–243, Lemay depicts a writer of great artfulness and subtlety, thoroughly accustomed to directing and controlling the attitudes and emotions of his readers through sophisticated fictional contrivances

which frequently obscure or mask his real identity or motive. Other recent works which stress the contradictions and complexities of Franklin and his writings are John W. Ward, "Who Was Benjamin Franklin?" *American Scholar*, 32 (Autumn 1963): 541–553; David Levin, "*The Autobiography of Benjamin Franklin*: The Puritan Experimenter in Life and Art," *Yale Review*, 53 (December 1963): 258–275; Robert F. Sayre, *The Examined Self: Benjamin Franklin, Henry Adams, Henry James* (Princeton: Princeton University Press, 1964).

33. *Autobiography*, pp. 44–45.

34. *Benjamin Franklin: Representative Selections, with Introduction, Bibliography, and Notes*, ed. Frank L. Mott and Chester E. Jorgenson (New York: American Book Co., 1936), p. 415.

35. *Benjamin Franklin: Representative Selections*, pp. 351–354.

36. *Papers*, VI, 406–407.

37. *Papers*, V, 503.

38. *Papers*, VI, 225.

39. Benjamin DeMott, *New York Times Book Review*, 5 July 1964, p. 19.

40. Carl Becker, in *Dictionary of American Biography*, VI (1931), 597.

41. Perry Miller, *Major Writers of America*, I, 97.

42. Emerson, *Nature* ("Nature").

43. Becker, *Dictionary of American Biography*, VI, 597.

"Emerson"

Robert D. Richardson, Jr.[*]

1. The Quality of Mythic Experience

Emerson once noted it would be "a good subject for book or lecture . . . to read the riddle of ancient Mythology." He saw clearly and said quite simply that "we need a theory or interpretation of Mythology." But it was not only ancient mythology and myth theory that interested him. In the middle of one of Margaret Fuller's Conversations when she was defending the ancient myths, Margaret said: "the age of the Greeks was the age of Poetry; ours was the age of Analysis. *We* could not create a Mythology," and Emerson had broken in to ask "Why not? We had still better material."[1] Much of Emerson's best work is just such an attempt to fashion a new mythology out of new materials, a new mythology which would be an important part of that "original relation to the universe" he wanted for his own generation. Though he wrote no essay called "Myth," the subject is thus central to his thought. His conception of history is fundamentally mythic, his understanding of the process of change, especially organic change, is most forcefully expressed in the myth-derived concept of metamorphosis, and his book of modern heroes, *Representative Men*, is

[*]Reprinted from *Myth and Literature in the American Renaissance* (Bloomington: Indiana University Press, 1978), pp. 65–89, 245–49.

in part the result of his efforts to create a worthy mythology for the America of his day.

Emerson was remarkably well read in myth and mythological scholarship, and from his college days on he was thoroughly familiar with both skeptical and affirmative views of myth.[2] The side of Emerson accepting myth as something deeply and importantly true is the side that can be traced back through Taylor, Creuzer, Goethe, K. O. Müller, and Herder to Lowth and Blackwell. Emerson had read all of these writers and many more, but however Emerson's sympathetic interest in myth may have evolved, the form it took was characteristically concerned with the relation of the individual to history. Over and over, Emerson strove to enter imaginatively into the myth-creating mind, to recover for himself the kind of empathic openness to experience that his reading told him had marked the early mythopoetic ages. From the beginning, then, Emerson was interested in mythic thought as an imaginative means of projecting oneself into the past, of participating in the process of history, to understand what was important about the past for any given individual.

In an interesting and unusual early effort to determine whether man can exist in solitude, Emerson tried to recreate, imaginatively, the condition of utter solitude which must have existed at the beginning of things, projecting himself and his reader backward into Adam, prototype of the solitary man.

> We must quit the city, the house, the cleared road, the simplest improvement of civilization, and stand up on the banks of the river which no dams have confined, amid woods which no axe hath felled, in a solitude which none partakes but the invisible Being who hath just now made it. I think that person who stands there alone among the trees with his eye on the waters and his hand upon his lips—is an object of interest. His name is Adam.[3]

Emerson was nineteen when he wrote that; it shows clearly a sympathetic willingness to understand the past by entering into it in imagination and trying to relive it. Emerson is not usually conceded to have had much interest in the past, but his repeated efforts to grasp the presentness of some past event suggest that he was indeed interested in historical process, in how certain religious attitudes had arisen, how gods and myths originated. His imagination ran to both Christian and pagan examples. In the same year as the description of Adam on the riverbank, Emerson also noted that he "who wanders in the woods perceives how natural it was to pagan imagination to find gods in every deep grove & by each fountain head." Such statements are not surprising perhaps in one who believes that myth arose from early perception of nature. What is a little surprising, though, are the turns of phrase and the unmistakable tone of delighted discovery suggesting that such moments of insight were not just academic exercises but intimately meaningful for Emerson in a most personal way. In another early notebook entry he writes, "Joy comes, but is

Speedily Supplanted by grief & we tremble at the approach of transient adversities like the mists of the morning fearful indeed & many, but fairies are in them & White Ladies beckoning."[4]

Emerson obviously had precociously grasped the idea that any serious understanding of the past would have to reanimate what seemed dead, regarding as present and unfinished what one had previously thought of as past and done. "It is pleasant when you hear in autumn the song of the reaper which is a spontaneous expression of joy springing directly from the heart, to revert to former ages and to find in the earliest gathering of the harvest the same pleasant music from those whose bones have slept for ages and whose song hath been echoed back at every annual labour for thousands of years and is echoed back today."[5] Only in this way does the past become alive. Only through this imaginative habit of sympathetic participation can myth cease to be old curious folktales and come to be immediate personal experience. Emerson knew this so well that he could both describe and experience the process at the same time. And where some saw mythic religious conceptions springing from fear, Emerson saw something quite different. He could imagine that in primitive times "some fortunate youth bounding over the mountains & enlivened by the splendour of a summer morn, may occasionally feel the expansion of social thoughts within him which for want of other objects will fix upon inanimate objects—upon the mountains or the clouds & endow them with life & thought, or on the Sun & call him God of Day." He could suggest such congenial conditions for the creation of myth, and he himself tried to write a bit of Arthurian legend in which "Arthur wandered in the wood of Cornwall as the day dawned and, by the better vision of his eye, he discerned, as he passed among the trees, the dauncing fayries in companies, that had not yet departed before the face of the sun."[6]

He did the same thing also in modern terms: "How does Nature deify us with a few cheap elements. Give me health and a Day & I possess more magnificence than emperors covet. The Morning sky before sunrise is my Assyria; the sunset my Paphos & unimaginable realms of Faerie; the night is my Germany."[7] This is a complex state of mind, one that could easily be interpreted as mystical—or even just misty. But this and other passages reflect experiences which are deliberately put in a context of myth, and are understandable if thought of as a deliberate effort at imaginative or sympathetic participation in the creating of myth. These passages all have an excited sense of being present at the creation. Emerson was also conscious of such moments in the lives of others. Shortly after the death of his brother Charles, Emerson wrote:

> He sympathized wonderfully with all objects & natures, & as by a spiritual ventriloquism threw his mind into them, which appeared in the warm & genial traits by which he again pictured them to the eye. I find him saying to E. H. [Elizabeth Hoar] 3 April 1834 "I do not know but one of the ancient metamorphoses will some day happen to me, & I shall shoot

> into a tree, or flow in a stream. I do so lose my human nature & join
> myself to that which is without. Today even Goethe would have been sat-
> isfied with the temper in which I became identified with what I saw, a
> part of what was around me."[8]

The image of a respectable New Englander shooting up into a tree or
flowing off in a stream is delightfully silly, but of course the point, as
Charles and his brother both saw, is one's sympathetic identification with
the world around one. Difficult to express, it is often experienced as a
mystical trance, as in Yeats's "Vacillation," for example. Emerson usually
turned to myth—or the mythic experience or mood—to record such
moments:

> Come out of your warm angular house resounding with few voices into
> the chill grand instantaneous night, with such a Presence as a full moon in
> the clouds, & you are struck with poetic wonder. In the instant you leave
> behind all human relations, wife, mother, & child, & live only with the
> savages—water, air, light, carbon, lime, & granite. I think of Kuhleborn.
> I become a moist cold element. "Nature grows over me." Frogs pipe;
> waters far off tinkle; dry leaves hiss; grass bends & rustles, & I have died
> out of the human world & come to feel a strange cold, aqueous, terra-
> queous, aerial, ethereal sympathy & existence. I sow the sun & moon for
> seeds.[9]

It is scarcely necessary to know that Kuhleborn is the water spirit uncle of
Undine in La Motte-Fouqué's story in order to grasp the experience Emerson is describing. Indeed, the reference to Kuhleborn could be deleted
and the passage would lose nothing. At any rate, it is the experience and
not the label that matters most. Myth matters because it provides or suggests a form, a language for expressing those remarkable moments when
we feel somehow greater or other than our everyday selves. Emerson's
personal acquaintance with the internal working, the "feel," of the
mythmaking mood helped him to use myth in his writing in a creative
way. For Emerson as for Wordsworth, myth was "authentic tidings of invisible things."

Myth was for Emerson an almost direct expression of that great original power or energy that lay behind and created all appearances. As
early as 1822, Emerson noted that "the idea of *power* seems to have been
every where at the bottom of the theology." The kind of power he had in
mind was present in mythology as well as theology, and could be seen, for
example, in the terrific disparity between ordinary mortals and gods.
Commenting on a drawing by Flaxman, Emerson noted that

> Orestes supplicates Apollo whilst the Furies sleep on the threshold in Flax-
> man's drawing. The face of the God expresses a shade of regret & compas-
> sion for the sufferer, but is filled with the calm conviction of disparity &
> irreconcileableness of the two spheres. He is born into other politics, into
> the eternal & beautiful; the man at his feet asks for his interest in turmoils
> of the earth, into which his nature cannot enter. And the Eumenides there

lying express pictorially this disparity. The god is surcharged with his divine destiny.[10]

Emerson sees in Apollo a calm superiority of power so great it needn't be demonstrated. It is typical of the way myth affected Emerson's imagination that he should apply the myth to himself. Accordingly, a short time after the above, we find Emerson trying to encourage the Apollo in himself. "A preoccupied attention is the only answer to the importunate frivolity of other people. An attention, & to an aim which makes their wants frivolous. This is a god's answer, & leaves no appeal & no hard thoughts."[11]

2. The Verdict of Reason

Balancing this natural sympathy for myth in Emerson's mind was a streak of cool skepticism. At various times in his career, Emerson was dubious about the religious origins of myth, disturbed by the misuses of myth, and uncertain as to whether myth really was a vehicle for truth. In a comment probably written around 1820, we find the young Emerson grinding away like a good Christian polemicist at heathen superstition. "Examine the gods of all barbarous nations, and you will find that their characters offend against every article of Moral law; you will find thieves, murderers, adulterers, & liars, enshrined in heaven by the zeal of ignorance; and these motley deities form the best illustration of the religious influence which a savage life promotes." Five or six years later Emerson was debunking a wide range of mythological figures with the supercilious swagger of a Yankee *philosophe*. "If Hercules & Ajax & many a Templar & knight & titled brigand of the middle ages were to be born again it is plain that they must descend from the dignified condition the ignorance & fear of men assigned them & be content to take up the cudgels in a common street with the lowest of mankind for their competitors & the applause of alehouses for their reward."[12] These are cheap shots; the easy sneer gives them away. But such comments at least show that from an early point in his career Emerson was sometimes inclined to dismiss myth, just as he was sometimes moved to try to relive or re-create it. He could also use myth as a tool for social criticism. Assuming that a people's heaven in their mythology represents their idea of perfection, Emerson compares Greek, Teutonic, and Persian heavens for what they reveal about those peoples. Here the negative view of myth is more subtle. It is assumed that each mythology is a limited, culture-bound reflection of the humdrum aspirations of a group of people. After reviewing the Greek and Roman views of heaven, Emerson turns to the Teutonic, about which he remarks:

> They too had a mythology, they had a *war*like heaven; a paradise of the strong, a glorified gymnasium, fresh air, fine horses, robust good health & good game—filled up to the brim all their conceptions of wellbeing; blood

& thunder in the background of Valhalla. Then go a little further Southeast, & you shall find the vestiges of the Persian & Turkish idea of perfection. They saw in the clouds all voluptuous forms; they asked for nothing but women; away with the trumpet, away with virtue, enough of that in the earth. They wanted nothing but coffee, tobacco, opium & sensual love.[13]

This is a sociological view of myth, an intellectual tool for discussing a society. It is notable that most of Emerson's appreciative comments on myth concern its effect on the individual, his negative comments generally applying to groups.

Emerson did not use mythic and theological terminology carelessly. For example, he once bluntly wrote: "the words 'I am on the eve of a revelation,' & such like, when applied to the influx of truth in ordinary life, sound sad & insane in my ear." This may have been a comment wrung from him in his exasperation over some of Alcott's writing, but whatever the cause, it shows him to have had a clear critical sense of when one should use such terms and when one should not. Emerson accepted mythology no more uncritically than he did revelation. A good example is his discussion of demonology. The problem is that if the invisible world is accepted as real, as it must be in any thoroughgoing Platonism or idealism, then how can one avoid accepting as real the "underside of theology," which is demonology. Emerson's compact answer to this problem occurs in a journal passage written in 1839 and incorporated into his lecture on "Demonology" later.

Demonology seems to me to be the intensation of the individual nature, the extension of this beyond its due bounds & into the domain of the infinite & universal. The faith in a Genius; in a family Destiny; in a ghost; in an amulet; is the projection of that instinctive care which the individual takes of his individuality beyond what is meet & into the region where the individuality is forever bounded by generic, cosmic, & universal laws. . . . The divine will, or, *the eternal tendency to the good of the whole, active in every atom, every moment,*—is the only will that can be supposed predominant a single hairbreadth beyond the lines of individual action & influence as known to experience; by a ghost, a Jupiter, a fairy, a devil, and not less a saint, an angel & the God of popular religion, as of Calvinism, & Romanism is an aggrandized and monstrous individual will. The divine will, such as I describe it, is spiritual. These other things, though called spiritual, are not so, but only demonological; & fictions.[14]

Mythology is here included among those things that are sometimes mistakenly thought to be spiritual. This is, in fact, a sweeping attack on mythology and demonology together as emanating from the individual will though posing as a divine or at least as a non-human will. From this point of view mythology, like demonology, misrepresents the way things really are. Mythology if not a distortion is a veil. In another place Emerson puts it more simply, saying, "the Father is a convenient name & image to the affections; but drop all images if you wish to come to the elements of your thoughts, & use as mathematical words as you can. . . ." From about 1838 through the mid-1840s there runs through Emerson's thought a persistent streak of this sort of distrust of myth as a falsifying veil over nature, while during these same years Emerson was elaborating, in other notes and essays, a view of myth as the necessary language of nature, as the only means by which to express certain kinds of elusive experiences and complex truths. Much of the skeptical attitude of these years was directed at what Emerson now habitually referred to as "Christian mythology." He would for example note down that "Christianity must quickly take a niche that waits for it in the Pantheon of the Past, and figure as Mythology henceforward." But it goes deeper than mere anti-Christian sentiment. It seems clear from such comments as the following that Emerson had moments when he simply distrusted the adequacy of mythology to express anything important. "Does it not seem imperative that the Soul should find an articulate utterance in these days on man and religion? All or almost all that I hear at Church is mythological."

But Emerson was far too aware of the many possible ways to look at myth to resort to such a flat, uncompromising negation. In a mood of less sweeping condemnation, he sometimes considered mythologies as systems that were once but are not longer believed, and he included Christianity as just one example.

> In talking with William Ellery Channing on Greek mythology as it was believed in Athens, I could not help feeling how fast the key to such possibilities is lost, the key to the faith of men perishes with the faith. A thousand years hence it will seem less monstrous that those acute Greeks believed in the fables of Mercury & Pan, than that these learned & practical nations of modern Europe & America, these physicians, metaphysicians, mathematicians, critics, & merchants, believed this Jewish apologue of the poor Jewish boy, & how they contrived to attach that accidental history to the religious idea.[15]

This comment is unusual for Emerson. It sounds very much as though he had been reading D. F. Strauss or Theodore Parker. Whatever the immediate spur, he rarely allowed this sharp edge of rationalist criticism into his published work. It is interesting to see that virtually all the disparaging things he said about myth are embedded in context where Emerson affirms the historical school, rather than his own characteristic view of the past as unimportant except as it is still a felt pressure on the individual. In other words, Emerson's disparagement of myth coincides with untypical moments of enthusiasm for the conventional view of history. In 1846 Emerson still entertained such moments, and when he spoke of an essay he was projecting having as one of its merits a "resolute rejection of the faded or regnant superstitions, as of the Christian mythology, of the agricultural, commercial, and social delusions which pass current in men's mouths, but have long lost all reality," he meant it as an exercise in debunking.

But in general, Emerson called popular delusions "superstitions" and reserved the word "mythology" for something more complex. In a list of the "Superstitions of our Age" drawn up in 1847, he included "the fear of Catholicism; the fear of pauperism; the fear of immigration; the fear of manufacturing interests; the fear of radicalism or democracy; And faith in the steam engine." Superstition usually involved fear; mythology was, even to Emerson in his skeptical moods, a phenomenon that involved belief. The most perceptive of Emerson's skeptical estimates of myth is a brilliant prefiguring of Marx and also of the particularly twentieth-century meaning of myth as reigning ideology. "History," he wrote in his journal in 1848,

> . . . is the group of the types or representative men of any age at only the distance of convenient vision. We can see the arrangement of masses, and distinguish the forms of the leaders. Mythology is the same group at another remove, now at a pictorial distance. . . . The forms and faces can no longer be read, but only the direction of the march, and the result; so that the names of the leaders are now mixed with the ends for which they strove. Distance is essential. Therefore we cannot say what is our mythology. We can only see that the industrial, mechanical, the parliamentary, commercial, constitute it, with socialism; and Astor, Watt, Fulton, Arkwright, Peel, Russell, Rothschild, George Stephenson, Fourier are our mythological names.

Emerson is here using myth as a way to frame a critique of the invisible assumptions of his own times. From this viewpoint, myth is not so much a term of praise or disparagement as it is a way of describing pervasive social and cultural ideas and beliefs.[16]

It cannot be too strongly emphasized, as we turn to Emerson's more imaginative uses of myth, that his willingness upon occasion to doubt, to look on the other side of the question, did not prevent him from valuing myth. Far from it. His skeptical and critical analyses helped balance out his frequent enthusiasm for myth, and his acceptance of myth for some purposes and in some contexts deserves more careful attention precisely because it was a tested, not an unthinking, acceptance. In fact, Emerson usually avoided dealing with myth as flatly true or false. There is an obvious sense of the word "myth" which then as now carried unavoidable overtones of "false," and there was a general sense then as now that "myth" along with "fiction" and "poetry" was a word you could not usefully apply to things which were expected to be historically "true"—yet myth, like fiction and poetry, had uses, values, and a reality of its own. Emerson's greatest achievements vis-à-vis myth all stemmed from his persistent efforts to utilize his understanding of mythic processes to lead the individual to fresh ways of thinking about history, about change, and about great men.

3. Myth and History

Emersonian thought is usually understood to have a strong an-tihistorical bias. This is true only in a limited sense. Emerson did indeed distrust the flat-footed historical literalism that accompanied biblical literalism in such writers as Humphrey Prideaus or Sharon Turner, and he distrusted any view of history that tended to praise the past at the expense of the present or to intimidate living men by magnifying dead ones. In these attitudes Emerson is very close to Alfred North Whitehead's insis-tence that "no more deadly harm can be done to young minds than by depreciation of the present," or in Whitehead's urging that we try to gain a *sense* of the past rather than an inert knowledge of it. Instead of memorizing the fact that Caesar died in 44 B.C., we should try to imagine that the cry "Caesar is murdered" was once still an unsubstantiated rumor flying the streets of Rome.[17] Sharply aware of what W. J. Bate has called "the burden of the past," Emerson was, for example, oppressed by the 420,000 volumes on the twelve miles of shelves in the British Museum when he visited that library in 1848; he was moved to complain that "it is impossible to read from the glut of books." It was precisely because Emer-son had read so much history that he reacted strongly against any ap-proach to history which extolled the golden past while looking down on the present as a degenerate time. For such a point of view he had only scorn, and he borrowed a phrase from Byron to describe these seekers-after "the unreached paradise of our despair." Emerson was against any view of history that did not emphasize its usefulness. As he viewed every-thing else, so he saw history as valuable only if it helped the individual to self-realization and self-reliance.

Emerson's own notebooks and journals and his early lectures, especially those he delivered under the general heading "Philosophy of History," bear ample witness to his extensive historical reading and to the overriding interest early in his career in establishing a right view of history. In such passages as the following one can see him working toward his characteristic position by studying rather than by rejecting history:

> I think it will be the effect of insight to show nearer relations than are yet known between remote periods of history & the present moment. . . . Homer, Greece, Rome, & Egypt certainly have come nearer to us for Bentley, Wolf, Niebuhr, Müller, Winckelmann & Champollion.[18]

By the time of Emerson's first series of essays (1841), the problem of history had become paramount. His journal notes show that the essay on "History" was planned all along as the crucial first essay. And indeed, the much more famous second essay, "Self-Reliance," cannot be properly understood without the first essay's preparation of the ground. The two essays are on the same theme, that of the relation between the individual and society or history. The emphasis is different in each essay, of course, but an understanding of one's relation to history was a necessary first step to self-reliance. The main purpose of the essay on history is to undercut the ordinary, overly respectful, and, Emerson thought, disheartening view of history and to suggest a more useful approach. Emerson was trying to persuade his readers to turn to nature rather than to the past, to ask for historical insight rather than historical details, and to trust myth and biography instead of chronological accounts of battles and leaders.

Emerson's reason for wanting to dislodge the customary deferential view of history is always perfectly apparent. "The Centuries are Conspirators against the saintly & majesty of the soul. The greatness of Greece consists in this, that no Greece preceded it." If we understand the real lesson of Greek history, we will not tell over again the Greek's exploits, but we will seek to re-create for ourselves the conditions which made possible the exploits of the Greeks, so that we can get on with our own exploits.[19]

Emerson argued for nature over history, on grounds of superior antiquity and prior influence, pointing out that "the knowledge of nature is *most permanent*, clouds & grass are older antiquities than pyramids or Athens. . . . Goethe's plant a genuine creation." Emerson prefers the organic principle illustrated in Goethe's concept of the *Urpglanz* to the monumental principle represented by the pyramids. Just as the past needs to be replaced by nature in our thinking, so the dry recital of facts must give way to myth and biography. Thus Emerson could say of Aeschylus' *Prometheus Bound*, "it is a part of the history of Europe. The Mythology thinly veils authentic history & there is the story of the invention of the mechanic Arts."[20]

The great thing was to replace a sense of pastness with a sense of presentness. "All inquiry into antiquity . . . is simply & at last the desire to do away with this wild, savage, preposterous *Then*, & introduce in its place the *Now*: it is to banish the *Not Me* & supply the *Me*." As he talks about the change, his examples show why he thought either myth or biography was the right medium for such a change. "We say Paradise was; Adam fell; the Golden Age; & the like. We mean man is not as he ought to be; but our way of painting this is on Time, and we say *Was*."[21]

Just as he insisted that "our admiration of the Antique is not admiration of the Old but of the Natural," so he argued that history properly understood is not chronicle but myth, and he made the point in several different ways. First he argued (and here Emerson's reading of Müller lies back of the argument) that earliest history is known to us chiefly through myth.

> Time dissipates to shining ether the solid angularity of facts. No anchor, no cable, no fences avail to keep a fact. Babylon and Troy and Tyre and even early Rome are passing already into fiction. The Garden of Eden, the Sun standing still in Gibeon, is poetry thenceforward to all nations.

> Who cares what the fact was when we have thus made a constellation of
> it. . . .?[22]

The facts behind these stories, whatever they were, are now lost, but
Emerson's point is that it does not matter. The story and its point are more
significant to us than any bit of local history could ever be. Emerson
argued a similar case for the story of Prometheus. "Besides its primary
value as the first chapter of the history of Europe, (the mythology thinly
veiling authentic facts, the invention of the mechanic arts, and the migra-
tion of colonies) it gives the history of religion with some closeness to the
faith of later ages. Prometheus is the Jesus of the old mythology." Myth
provides the meaning of history. "Look then at history as the illustration
by facts of all the spiritual elements. Stand before each of its tablets with
the faith, Here is one of my coverings: Under this heavy & odious mask
did my Proteus nature hide itself."[23] The full force of this is apparent only
when it is read in the context of the opening argument of "History."
Emerson starts by saying: "There is one mind common to all individual
men. . . . Of the works of this mind history is the record." Furthermore,
as each man participates in the common mind, so "the whole history is in
[each] man," and "it is all to be explained from individual experience."
Myth makes history from bare chronicles, and turns lists into story; it
renders history in terms of persons and actions, brings out what is human
in history, and provides each reader with his "own secret biography" as he
finds that "one after another he comes up in his private adventures with
every fable of Aesop, of Homer, of Hafiz, of Ariosto, of Chaucer, of
Scott." Not chronicle but myth contains the truth we need. "The beautiful fables of the Greeks," says Emerson, "are universal verities," and he
then gives a long illustration, starting with Prometheus, working through
two pages of examples and ending with an analysis of Proteus in which
Emerson epitomizes the art of reading history through the glass of myth.

> The philosophical perception of identity through endless mutations of
> form, makes him [man] know the Proteus. What else am I who laughed or
> wept yesterday, who slept last night like a corpse and this morning stood
> and ran? And what see I on any side but the transmigrations of Proteus? I
> can symbolize my thought by using the name of any creature, of any fact,
> because every creature is man agent or patient.[24]

Emerson learned from classicists that myth, including religious
myth, contained all that was left of prehistory. "First nations were
remembered by their religion," he wrote in his journal in the early
1820s.[25] Emerson came to perceive that myth generalized historical data
into a comprehensible and, above all, a usable form. Through myth, the
individual saw himself in history. Only when he had achieved this viewpoint, which freed him from subservience to the past, could he live his
own life, realizing in the present the latent pattern that myth told him
was there if only he could see it.

History must thus be reworked and understood as myth, according to Emerson, in order to see the past as an extended present, to understand the "identity of human character in all ages" and myth as the key to that character. We are to admire the Greeks, not because they are old but because they are natural. Above all we are to live in the present without always looking over our shoulder. Why should the kind of man "who looked Apollos into the landscape with every glance he threw" spend his time carving statues of Apollo?[26]

4. Metamorphosis, Metaphor for Organic Process

Myth, then, reveals human character. And therefore myth can be found in literature as well as in history. Emerson was emphatic in his recognition of the creative writer's mythmaking function.

> The point of praise of Shakespeare is, the pure poetic power: he is the chosen closest companion, who can, at any moment, by incessant surprises, work the miracle of mythologizing every fact of the common life; as snow, or moonlight, or the level rays of sunrise—lend a momentary glory to every pump and woodpile.

What Emerson means here by "mythologizing" is a process of creative transforming. The idea of creation as a transforming process runs all through Emerson; in one way it is linked to his interest in organic form, and in another it led him, via Ovid, to a lifelong fascination with metamorphosis. Once when he was planning a book or a lecture on mythology, Emerson had noted that "an obscure & slender thread of truth runs through all mythologies & this might lead often to highest regions of philosophy." His interest in metamorphosis is a perfect example of how a single aspect of ancient myth served as the touchstone for one of Emerson's leading ideas.[27]

In 1843 Emerson put "metamorphosis" at the head of a list of "the capital lessons of life." The idea of metamorphosis had appealed to Emerson rather early; in 1829 he noted, apropros of an unnamed person he thought had changed for the worse, "we must beware of the nature of the spiritual world. It has this terrible power of self change, self accommodation to whatsoever we do [and thus] Ovid's Metamorphoses take place continually. The nymph who wept became a fountain; the nymph who pined became an echo. They who do good become angels. They who do deformities become deformed. We are not immoveably moored as we are apt to think to any bottom." Most of Emerson's early comments on metamorphosis are warnings; he is most keenly aware of the degradation that can overtake and transform us for the worse. The passage above continues: "that part of us which we don't use dries up & perishes. Perhaps thus (I shudder whilst I write) a good spirit may become a bad spirit by insensible departures & whilst yet my acquaintance is praised for the former amiableness of his character he is rapidly declining on the road to malignity & lowest sensuality." In 1834 Emerson used the image of Proteus (a favorite with him, found all through his journals and in virtually every essay in *Representative Men*) to suggest much milder transformations, but here, too, the direction of change is unfortunate. "One of the forms the Proteus takes is that of civil self-depreciation. 'You quite mistake, sir; I am not that you took me for. A poor evanescent topic not really worth your consideration.' " And some time later, around 1840, Emerson was concerned with the same general idea, but set now in terms of transmigration; "*Transmigration* of souls: that too is no fable. I would wish it were; but look around you at the men & women, & do you not see that they are already only half human. . . ."

As long as Emerson thought of metamorphosis principally as change for the worse, as a process of deterioration, the idea was of no great consequence to his thought, but when he began to see it as a process that operated in the opposite direction as well, it gathered all sorts of associations around it and took on great importance for him. In the late 1830s, he noted that "Goethe says the mind & the endeavor of the Greeks is to deify man not to humanize the Godhead. Here is a theomorphism not anthropomorphism." From this time forward, metamorphosis, with the stress on morphology, began to have a developmental or even an evolutionary aspect for Emerson. "We fable to conform things better to our higher laws," he had noted in his journal, while in "The Poet" he links the idea of metamorphosis with ascension: "But nature had a higher end, in the production of new individuals, than security, namely *ascension*, or, the passage of the soul into higher forms." From this linking of ideas of change, including metamorphosis, transmigration of souls, evolution, and ascension (with the inevitable overtones, respectively, of Greek, Hindu, scientific, and Christian thought), Emerson soon came to refer simply to "the metamorphosis" as a central aspect of nature itself.[28]

He noted how "the different ages of man, in Hesiod's *Works and Days*, signify the mutations of human lives. . . ." These and other observations were subsumed into a general rule. "The method of advance in nature is perpetually transformation . . . ," he wrote in 1840. "Nature ever flows, stands never still. Motion or change is her mode of existence. The poetic eye sees in Man the Brother of the River, and in Woman the Sister of the River. Their life is always transition." Metamorphosis is the method of nature, but so deeply is that method ingrained that Emerson at times describes metamorphosis as nature itself. "What we call nature," he wrote in "The Poet," "is a certain self-regulated motion, or change; and nature does all things by her own hands, and does not leave another to baptize her, but baptizes herself; and this through the metamorphosis again." Elsewhere, thinking of metamorphosis not just as change but as "the necessity of progression or onwardness in each creature," he proclaims that "metamorphosis is the law of the Universe." Metamorphosis became Emerson's symbol or shorthand for his version of evolutionary idealism, or the belief that idea or spirit progressively evolves and reveals itself through a series of concrete mutations or morphological changes.[29]

This concept is central to Emerson's view of things, and the language of metamorphosis is part of his effort to domesticate the vague and abstract language that usually went with philosophical discussions of idealism, whether evolutionary, Christian, or transcendental. The problem of adequate expression was very real. Sometimes Emerson fell back on Ovidian stories, and often he invoked the figure of Proteus. Sometimes he borrowed expressions from Hindu or Pythagorean concepts of the transmigration of souls. Sometimes he used Heraclitean or Neoplatonic abstractions, and often he combined several of these. In "History" it is expressed this way:

> Genius watches the monad through all his marks as he performs the metempsychosis of nature. . . . Nature is a mutable cloud, which is always and never the same. She casts the same thought into troops of forms, as a poet makes twenty fables with one moral.[30]

The problem, how to express the metamorphosis that Emerson saw at the heart of nature, leads always to the poet, for it is he that must perform that second metamorphosis, transforming nature into thought and adequate expression. First, of course, the poet must perceive the perpetual change in the nature of things. It was for this reason that Swedenborg struck Emerson as "a right poet. Every thing Protean to his eye." Indeed Swedenborg was, for a time, Emerson's ideal of "the person who of all men in the recent ages stands eminently for the translation of Nature into thought. I do not know a man in history to whom things stood so uniformly for words. Before him the Metamorphosis continually plays." The poet's means for expressing metamorphosis is the symbol. And of course Emerson would claim that this is fitting because nature itself is symbolic. "The Metamorphosis of nature shows itself in nothing more than this that there is no word in our language that cannot become typical to us of nature by giving it emphasis. The world is a Dancer, it is a Rosary; it is a Torrent. . . ."

The language and the idea of metamorphosis are Emerson's way of talking about organic form. This is clear from a passage in his notebooks for 1847.

> The interest of the gardener and the pomologist has the same foundation as that of the Poet,—namely in the metamorphosis: these also behold the miracle, the guided change, the change conspicuous, the guide invisible; a bare stick studs itself over with green buds, which become again leaves, flowers, and at length, delicious fruit.[31]

The Ovidian concept of metamorphosis as a story or myth in which characters change their outward appearance but retain their inner or essential identity was validated for Emerson and given an exciting new meaning by his reading of Goethe's *Metamorphosis of Plants*, a book Emerson summarized as follows: "Thus Goethe suggests the leading idea of modern botany, that a leaf or the eye of a leaf is the unit of botany, and that every part of a plant is only a transformed leaf to meet a new condition, and by varying the condition, a leaf may be converted into any other organ, and any other organ into a leaf."[32] Emerson's interest in organic form—in literature and in nature—and in the process of change itself found its best expression in his constantly reiterated image of metamorphosis, an image that expressed Emerson's lifelong conviction that changes in external form are directed by inner purposes, needs, and forces.

5. The Heroic Life and the Uses of Myth

Emerson looked at everything as potentially present now or as usuable for present purposes. He energized or activated every idea he touched, and his best writing still evokes an answering energetic self-assertion in the reader. What Emerson said of Goethe is equally true of himself. He "teaches courage, and the equivalence of all times; that the disadvantages of any epoch exist only to the faint-hearted." Emerson considered the past as only a version of the present extended backward in time, and he perceived a metamorphosing or transmutation of form at the heart of reality. Mythology not only expressed these things, it showed how such knowledge might be used. Perhaps following Goethe, or perhaps merely reinforced by him, Emerson came to believe that mythmaking, when it was a serious business and not just a matter of superimposed imagery or arbitrary apologue, was theomorphic rather than anthropomorphic. This put a whole new face on the mythmaking process. Where Christianity had started with an idea of God, his revelation to men, and his incarnation as a man, and where Enlightenment skeptics had refused to accept the idea that there was anything at all beyond the human, Emerson (and other romantic writers) sought the meaning of myth and also of religion by starting with man and seeking the spark of divinity in man himself. Emerson's theism sought "the great God far within." By reversing its polarity, so to speak, Emerson made myth vital again, both as explanation of certain appearances in nature and as the expression of genuine religious impulses. It was of course not myth itself that Emerson cared about, but how it could help men lead heroic lives. If Emerson played a part—many would insist it was a founding part—in creating a heroic literature for America, it is mainly because he saw clearly that unless Americans undertook to live heroic lives there would be no heroic literature.[33]

Heroism and greatness had appealed to Emerson's imagination as early as he began to keep journals, and as he said of Napoleon, "whatever appeals to the imagination, by transcending the ordinary limits of human ability, wonderfully encourages and liberates us." In 1822 he was making notes for an essay on "Greatness" which show him aware not only of "the stupendous greatness which men rather believe than behold," but of another, lesser, more useful impulse toward greatness that could warm "each ordinary day of common life." By the mid 1830s he was inclining toward a rather aristocratic view of greatness. "The great man should occupy the whole space between God and the mob." A notebook passage which also shows up in "The American Scholar" (1837) says "Men behold in the hero or the poet their own being ripened and are content to be less so that [other] may attain to its full stature. . . ." This is the principle of aristocracy in history. Ultimately, in *Representative Men*, Emerson was to make a serious effort at reconciling his recognition of greatness with his fervent democratic idealism. Indeed, he saw this as part of the promise of America. He thought that "when all feudal straps & bandages were taken off an unfolding of the Titans had followed & they had laughed & leaped young giants along the continent & ran up the mountains of the West with the errand of Genius & of love." Sometimes he felt himself part of such an adventure. "We early men," he wrote in 1843, "at least have an advantage; we are up at four o'clock in the morning and have the whole market,—We Enniuses and Venerable Bedes of the empty American Parnassus." Here, as elsewhere, he was sure that there would one day be a literature which "will describe the new heroic life of man, the now unbelieved possibility of simple living." Heroism was always associated in Emerson's mind with the grand simplicities of life, with clear perceptions and basic religious feeling. One day in 1838 he wrote "I woke this morning saying or thinking in my dreams that every truth appealed to a heroic character." A year later Emerson commented that the live religious feeling of his day was not finding expression in institutionalized religion. As he put it, "Religion runs now not to cultus, but to heroic life."[34]

More and more, though, Emerson's ideas about greatness and heroism were drawn together over the problem of the uses of great men for the people of a democratic republic. The germ of *Representative Men*, the idea that the greatest men are representative or typical or symbolic of all men, goes back clearly at least to 1841 and the remark in his journal that "the history of Jesus is only the history of every man written large." Emerson came to believe that all men had more in them then they commonly realized; the use of *great* men was, simply, to awaken *all* men to their own possibilities. Emerson's method in *Representative Men* reflects this. The book consists of seven sketches, each sketch beginning with a biographical view of a single great man. This is followed in each sketch by a section on that man's meaning for the present written from a generalized or "mythological" point of view. Emerson clearly expects the reader to be attuned to both approaches. The opening paragraph strikes the mythological tone clearly:

> It is natural to believe in great men. If the companions of our childhood should turn out to be heroes, and their condition regal, it would not surprise us. All mythology opens with demigods, and the circumstance is high and poetic; that is, their genius is paramount. In the legends of the Gautama, the first men are the earth, and found it deliciously sweet.

By association, Emerson links great men, heroes, kings, and demigods in an explicitly mythological context. He is concerned that we find ourselves mirrored in the great men whose lives he is about to present. He is not interested in the great men as historical specimens, nor as entertainment. Emerson is the American Plutarch, expecting us to take these "lives" seriously as models. *Representative Men* illustrates Emerson's conviction, phrased with a directness rare among writers on myth, that "the gods of fable are the shining moments of great men." This approach amounts to nothing less than a modern Euhemerism; it became Emerson's most frequent and I think his most deeply held conviction on the subject. Emerson's originality turned this theory, often used to debunk, to positive uses. Mythology becomes the best means of expressing the essential—and repeatable—qualities of human character. "Our colossal theologies of Judaism, Christism, Buddhism, Mahometism, are the necessary and structural action of the human mind." Mythology and theology both result from theism, and, Emerson goes on, "theism is the purification of the human mind. Man can paint, or make, or think nothing but man."

Emerson presents the reader with seven great men, each representative or symbolic of some one human quality. Emerson calls them heroes, demigods (he sometimes tries to freshen up this phrase by calling them half-gods), or types. They are epitomes, deliberately drawn archetypes. Plato, the philosopher, is the archetypal thinker who can perceive multiplicity in Unity. Swedenborg, the mystic, stands for the perception of the world as symbol and the primary relation of mind to matter. Montaigne, the skeptic, is the archetype of the reasonable man, the man of cool, witty mental equilibrium. Shakespeare, the poet, stands for "the translation of things into song." Napoleon, the man of the world, is the prophet of commerce, money, and material power, epitome of the common man and worshipped by him. Lastly, Emerson chooses Goethe as the archetypal hero of that group to which Emerson himself belongs, "the class of scholars or writers, who see connection where the multitudes see fragments, and who are impelled to exhibit the facts in order, and so to supply the axis on which the frame of things turns."

Representative Men is part mythology, part theology, and part hagiography. Emerson proposes saints and heroes for the self-reliant. It is remarkable that none of his demigods or types are American, none are biblical, none are Christian. If Emerson is trying to set up a canon of heroes, it is very different indeed from most. First, all but Napoleon are heroes of thought or art. Secondly, the only founder of a religion included is Swedenborg. Third, and most important, Emerson does not intend to work up his audience into a servile adulation or stunned admiration. Each sketch ends with a thorough critique of the figure's weak points and failures. Emerson as much as says that we are not to be intimidated by great men, but encouraged, and if he learned from myth how to magnify man, he had also learned how to approach a magnified figure skeptically. As Emerson treats his seven men, his Seven against Conformity, we are made to see that the great heroes of the past have not exhausted all possibilities, that they all have shortcomings, and that there is plenty of room for us. "Great men exist that there may be greater men."

Emerson thus accomplishes something quite unusual. He simultaneously cuts down the greatest of men to ordinary human size and then builds them up into representative figures, symbolic heroes in whom we recognize ourselves. Emerson makes the reader believe in their representativeness. In theological jargon, he was both mythologizing and demythologizing. He was in fact doing with his seven modern wise men just what he describes Goethe doing in *Faust*. Goethe, says Emerson, was one of those "who found himself master of histories, mythologies, philosophies . . . ," and he exclaimed "what new mythologies sail through his head! . . . in the solidest kingdom of routine and the senses, he showed the lurking daemonic power; that, in actions of routine, a thread of mythology and fable spins itself; and this, by tracing the pedigree of every usage and practice, every institution, utensil, and means, home to its origin in the structure of man."[35] Sometimes in his pursuit of the proper form in which to express "the structure of man," Goethe must demythologize. So with the Devil, who "had played an important part in mythology in all times." In order to make him seem real and believable, Emerson says, Goethe "stripped him of mythologic gear, of horns, cloven foot, harpoon tail, brimstone, and blue-fire, and, instead of looking in books and pictures, looked for him in his own mind." So well did Goethe succeed that his new figure becomes a permanent addition to our stock of images. We would call it a new mythological figure. Emerson says simply that Goethe "flung into literature, in his Mephistopheles, the first organic figure that has been added for some ages, and which will remain as long as the Prometheus." The *process* of mythmaking is valid, though sometimes the old results of the process become fixed and dated and have to be replaced or reformed. But just as the process of forming myth is valid, so the process of demythologizing is not just simple debunking, nor is it essentially antimythic in outlook. It is a matter of being able to discard old mythological forms from which the vitality has departed, in order to let the informing idea reemerge in a new and currently believable form. It is here, as always with Emerson, the idea, or the spirit, or the power behind the form and compelling the form that he was most deeply interested in. His philosophical, literary, and religious views all converged on the idea that there was a great informing energy or creating power animating our words, our symbols, and our myths.

Myth was, for Emerson, a medium for important wisdom. It was one of the many ways in which Spirit manifested itself in form—to use the familiar terms of the German idealism which so closely resembles New England Transcendentalism—but (unlike Hegel, for example) there is no indication in Emerson's writing that he assigned myth a place lower than any other mode of expression. If anything, the opposite is true. Mythology comes up, as a subject, a process, a touchstone to some vital emotion or idea, over and over, all through his career. Myth was evidently real enough to him, if by real we mean what is persistently valued. He could write after a walk in the storm, "I love the wood god. I love the mighty PAN." He sought ceaselessly to find and explain what it was in nature that was so well expressed in what he called "mythology and the Undersong of Epics." Myth seemed to have a vitality and a truth of its own, independent of its creator. Emerson called Greek mythology "a wonderful example . . . of profound sense overmastering the finite speakers & writers of the fables."[36] Emerson thought it the office of his age "to annul that adulterous divorce which the superstition of many ages has effected between the intellect & holiness." Myth was one of the things that tended to unite the two, partly because myth was both necessary and useful, and partly because it lay behind both literature and religion as a symbolical form of communication. "There are always a few heads, and out of these come the mythology and the machinery of the world," he remarked. To be useful, myth needed only to be read aright. "The poet writes fable, but I read truth in it."

Throughout Emerson's work myth served well as one of his habitual resources. Often enough myth itself revealed something or was the best possible explanation of a thought or a feeling. Often, his theomorphic humanism found its characteristic expression in mythic rather than in strictly theological (or in Christian) terms. There is some evidence that he believed in the American Adam; there is equally good evidence that he believed in the American Proteus. But he did not rest his case on these external images, which are, after all, no more than what he called "modern antiques." It was only typical, but typically briliant, that he borrowed an idea from myth to argue that the human soul will never have peace while it seeks an external god, but will when "it sees the Great God far within its own nature."[37] In Emerson's perception of the nature of the divine or sacred, in his view of history as present time, in his understanding of the metamorphosing principle in nature and his urging the possibility of our living lives of intellectual or spiritual heroism, myth was indispensable to his heroic vision.

Notes

1. *The Journals and Miscellaneous Notebooks of Ralph Waldo Emerson*, ed. William H. Gilman et al. (Cambridge: Harvard University Press, 1960–), IV, 374, V, 7. Emerson's lively participation in Margaret Fuller's Conversations is recorded in Caroline W. Healey Dall, *Margaret and her Friends, or Ten Conversations with Margaret Fuller upon the Mythology of the Greeks* (Boston: Robert Brothers, 1895), esp. p. 45.

2. Emerson's reading in mythology and myth scholarship and criticism was prodigious. His library included John Lempriere, *A Classical Dictionary* (London, 1788; 6th ed., 1806), and Alexander Adam, *Roman Antiquities* (Glasgow, 6th ed., 1835). According to Walter Harding (*Emerson's Library* [Charlottesville: University Press of Virginia, 1967]), Emerson knew the second of these as early as 1821. He had ten editions of Homer in various languages, including two of Pope's Homer and one with Flaxman's drawings. He had three versions of Aeschylus and three of Ovid. For Emerson's knowledge of Indic myth, see Kenneth Walter Cameron's exhaustive annotation in his edition of Emerson's poem *Indian Superstition* (Hanover, N.H.: Friends of the Dartmouth Library, 1954). Cameron's book lists an enormous number of works that touched on India and were available in and around Emerson's Harvard; indeed, there are many more things listed than Emerson's poems and journals show him to have known. The collection of books on the Orient, which Cholmondely gave Thoreau, and Thoreau in turn gave Emerson, is conveniently listed in Frederic Ives Carpenter, *Emerson and Asia* (Cambridge: Harvard University Press, 1930). Emerson's acquaintance with the life and work of Sir William Jones goes back to his senior year at Harvard when he read Teignmouth's *Life of Sir William Jones* (London: J. Hatchard, 1804). The volumes on Nordic myth in Emerson's library include Amos Cottle's *Icelandic Poetry* (Bristol, 1797), G. W. Dasent's *The Prose or Younger Edda* (London, 1842), and P. H. Mallet's *Northern Antiquities* (London, 1847). Carlyle's opening lecture on Odin in *Heroes and Hero Worship*, published in 1841, is important for Emerson's attitude toward Nordic myth. Emerson's copy of Ossian is a Boston edition of 1857. From the piece on "Stonehenge" in *English Traits*, it is clear that Emerson had some knowledge of William Stukeley's *Stonehenge, a Temple restor'd to the British Druids* (London, 1740) and Edward Davies, *The Mythology and Rites of the British Druids* (London: J. Booth, 1809).

Emerson owned Ralph Cudworth's *The True Intellectual System of the Universe* (a seventeenth-century work) in an edition edited by Thomas Birsh, 4 vols. (London, 1820). For his knowledge of Bayle, see John Clendenning, "Emerson and Bayle," *Philological Quarterly*, 43 (January 1964): 79–86. Emerson withdrew Volney's *Ruins* from the Harvard College Library in 1828. References to John Gillies, *The History of Ancient Greece . . .* , 4 vols. (London, 1786), occur all through his early journals. He withdrew William Mitford's *History of Greece* from the Boston Library Society in 1822. Emerson owned an edition of George Bancroft's translation of Arnold Heeren's general history of Greece somewhat oddly titled *Reflections of the Politics of Ancient Greece* (Boston: Cummings, Hilliard & Co., 1824), which insists that Greek myth and religion constitute the starting point for Greek culture. Emerson's acquaintance with K. O. Müller's *The Dorians* dates from 1831, when he took it out of the Boston Athenaeum. *Selected Writings of Thomas Taylor*, edited by Kathleen Raine and George Mills Harper, contains an excellent essay on Taylor's influence on Alcott and Emerson. Emerson owned Taylor's five-volume *Works of Plato* (London, 1804), Taylor's *Select Works of Plotinus* (London, 1817), Taylor's five-volume edition of Plutarch's *Morals*, Taylor's *Iamblichus on the Mysteries of the Egyptians, Chaldeans, and Assyrians* (Chiswick, 1821), and Taylor's two-volume *Commentaries of Proclus on the Timaeus of Plato* (London, 1820), as well as various other editions of books of these writers. Emerson owned August Schlegel's *Lectures on Dramatic Art and Literature*, translated by John Black and published in Philadelphia in 1833, as well as Friedrich Schlegel's *The Philosophy of History*, tr. J. B. Robertson (London, 1835). He also owned Novalis's *Henry of Ofterdingen*, tr. J. Owen (Cambridge, Mass., 1842). Emerson withdrew Herder's *Outlines of a Philosphy of the*

History of Man from the Harvard Library in 1829 and later from the Boston Athenaeum in 1831. Emerson owned the *Deutsches Wörterbuch*, published in 1854 by Jacob and Wilhelm Grimm, and had withdrawn the famous *Kinder- und Hausmärchen* from the Athenaeum in 1836. For Emerson's anecdote about Strauss see *Journals of Ralph Waldo Emerson*, ed. Edward Waldo Emerson and Waldo Emerson Forbes, 10 vols. (Boston: Houghton Mifflin, 1909–1914), VII, 396, and his correspondence with Parker in spring and summer of 1842. Emerson's knowledge of Creuzer's ideas comes mainly from two books explicitly indebted to Creuzer: Joseph Marie de Gérando, *Histoire comparée des systèmes de philosophie* (2d ed., Paris, 1822–23), 4 vols., and J. G. E. Oegger, *The True Messiah*, tr. and pub. E. P. Peabody (Boston, 1842).

Thomas Blackwell's *An Enquiry into the Life and Writings of Homer* (1735) and Robert Lowth's *The Sacred Poetry of the Hebrews* (1753; Eng. tr., 1787) both appear in Emerson's "Catalogue of Books Read" between 1819 and 1824, printed in *Journals and Miscellaneous Notebooks*, 1, 396.

Emerson owned a copy of Newton's *The Chronology of the Ancient Kingdoms Amended* (London and Dublin, 1728). Emerson's knowledge of Humphrey Prideaux's *The Old and New Testaments connected* (London, 1716–18) is attested by entries in his journal in 1824. See *Journals and Miscellaneous Notebooks*, II, 307, 402. Emerson's knowledge of Hegel and Schelling is discussed by Prof. Wellek in his "Emerson and German Philosophy," *New England Quarterly*, 16 (March 1943): 41–62. Emerson owned George Eliot's translation of L. A. Feuerbach's *The Essence of Christianity* (New York: C. Blanchard, 1855). Emerson was withdrawing books by F. Max Müller starting in 1861. He took out Müller's *History of ancient Sanskrit Literature* (London, 1859) in 1861, and at least part of the famous *Chips from a German Workshop* (London: 1867–75), in 1868. He also owned copies of the book Müller dedicated to him, the *Introduction to the Science of Religion* (London, 1873).

F. O. Matthiessen's *American Renaissance* (New York: Oxford University Press, 1941) contains a brilliant and suggestive discussion of Emerson's awareness of the possibilities of myth. I am greatly indebted to this book. J. Russell Reaver's *Emerson as Mythmaker* (Gainesville: University of Florida Press, 1954) approaches Emerson from the vantage of modern ideas about myth, particularly those of depth psychology. Some of Reaver's findings are sound, but he neglects almost entirely Emerson's own thoughts and comments on myth and mythmaking: Reaver's later article, "Mythology in Emerson's Poems," *Emerson Society Quarterly*, no. 39 (2d Quarter 1965): pt. 2, 56–63, is much more satisfactory in this respect. John S. Harrison's *The Teachers of Emerson* (New York: Sturgis & Walton, 1910) has an excellent chapter on Emerson's mythology and its debt to Plato. Sherman Paul's brilliant *Emerson's Angle of Vision* (Cambridge: Harvard University Press, 1952) also takes up Emerson's mythology. Among recent studies must be singled out Sacvan Bercovitch's *The Puritan Origins of the American Self* (New Haven: Yale University Press, 1975), which ends with an excellent section on how Emerson "expressed himself by expressing the myth of America" in essentially Puritan terms, and Harold Bloom's *Figures of Capable Imagination* (New York: Seabury Press, 1976), which contains a brightly suggestive treatment of what Bloom calls Emerson's American Orphism.

3. *Journals and Miscellaneous Notebooks*, I, 98.

4. *Journals and Miscellaneous Notebooks*, I, 138, 174.

5. *Journals and Miscellaneous Notebooks*, I, 200.

6. *Journals and Miscellaneous Notebooks*, I, 327, II, 63.

7. *Journals and Miscellaneous Notebooks*, V, 13

8. *Journals and Miscellaneous Notebooks*, V, 155.

9. *Journals and Miscellaneous Notebooks*, V, 496–497.

10. *Journals and Miscellaneous Notebooks*, I, 76, VIII, 389–390. See also Emerson's essay "Experience."

11. *Journals and Miscellaneous Notebooks*, VIII, 401.

12. *Journals and Miscellaneous Notebooks*, I, 314, III, 17.

13. *Journals and Miscellaneous Notebooks*, III, 148.

14. *Journals and Miscellaneous Notebooks*, V, 322, VII, 167–168.

15. *Journals and Miscellaneous Notebooks*, V, 468, VII, 403, 194, VIII, 196.

16. *Journals*, VII, 233, 317–318, 383.

17. Alfred North Whitehead, *The Aims of Education* (New York: Macmillan, 1967 [1929]), p. 4, and "Historical Changes, " in *Science and Philosophy* (New York: Philosophical Library, 1948), p. 213.

18. *Journals*, VII, 434; *Journals and Miscellaneous Notebooks*, III, 26, V, 443.

19. *Journals and Miscellaneous Notebooks*, VII, 280. See also "Self-Reliance."

20. *Journals and Miscellaneous Notebooks*, IV, 282, VII, 506–507.

21. *Journals and Miscellaneous Notebooks*, VII, 111, V, 371.

22. *Journals and Miscellaneous Notebooks*, V, 198–199; "History" in *Essays* (1841).

23. "History," in *Essays* (Boston: James Munroe, 1841), p. 25; Introductory lecture on "Philosophy of History," in *The Early Lectures of Ralph Waldo Emerson*, ed. Stephen E. Whicher, Robert E. Spiller, and Wallace E. Williams, 3 vols. (Cambridge: Harvard University Press, 1959–1972), II, 8; *Journals and Miscellaneous Notebooks*, V, 262.

24. "History," in *Essays* (1841), pp. 1–2, 25–26.

25. *Journals and Miscellaneous Notebooks*, I, 71.

26. *Journals and Miscellaneous Notebooks*, VII, 144.

27. *Journals*, X, 27; *Journals and Miscellaneous Notebooks*, IV, 375. For a general discussion see Daniel B. Shea's excellent "Emerson and the American Metamorphosis," in *Emerson: Prophecy, Metamorphosis, and Influence*, ed. David Levin (New York: Columbia University Press, 1975).

28. *Journals and Miscellaneous Notebooks*, VIII, 411, III, 167–168, IV, 323, VII, 385, V, 417, 175; "The Poet," in *Essays: Second Series* (Boston: James Munroe, 1844), p. 66.

29. *Journals*, VII, 120–121, VI, 477; *Journals and Miscellaneous Notebooks*, VII, 524, 539; "The Poet," in *Essays: Second Series* (1844), p. 24; *Journals*, VII, 177.

30. "History," in *Essays* (1841), p. 11.

31. *Journals and Miscellaneous Notebooks*, VIII, 221, 223, 23; *Journals*, VII, 313–314.

32. *Representative Men*, in *The Complete Works of Ralph Waldo Emerson*, ed. Edward Waldo Emerson, 12 vols. (Boston: Houghton, Mifflin, 1903–1904), "Goethe," p. 275.

33. *Representative Men*, "Goethe," p. 284; *Journals and Miscellaneous Notebooks*, V, 417.

34. *Representative Men*, "Napoleon," p. 241; *Journals and Miscellaneous Notebooks*, II, 70, V, 249, 354, VII, 24; *Journals*, VI, 472; *Journals and Miscellaneous Notebooks*, VII, 45, 217.

35. *Journals and Miscellaneous Notebooks*, VII, 519; *Representative Men*, pp. 9–11, 260, 35, 267–269, 271–272.

36. *Journals and Miscellaneous Notebooks*, V, 179, 295, VII, 277.

37. *Journals and Miscellaneous Notebooks*, VII, 438–439; *Journals*, VII, 552; *Journals and Miscellaneous Notebooks*, VIII, 26, V, 223.

"Emerson's Natural Theology and the Paris Naturalists: Toward a Theory of Animated Nature"

David Robinson*

I. To Emerson, who was making his first visit to Europe after the resignation of his pulpit in 1832, Paris could not compare with Italy. "Well, what of Paris?" he wrote his brother William some ten days after his arrival there in 1833: "Why it leads me twice to brag of Italy, for once that I see anything to admire here" (*L*, I, 387).[1] Although his attitude toward the city was not to change substantially during his visit of four weeks, he did find in Paris one experience which, important though it was at the time, would loom increasingly more important in his intellectual development in the period immediately following the journey, as he launched his career as a lecturer and essayist. That experience was Emerson's direct exposure to the flourishing school of natural historians, botanists, and zoologists centered around Paris's Muséum d'Histoire Naturelle. Even though his letters and journals are filled with evidence of the impact of the Muséum's Jardin des Plantes and its other exhibits, his most eloquent testimony to its impact on him comes in his first public lecture after his return from Europe in November 1833. After telling his audience of his "opportunity of visiting that celebrated repository of natural curiosities the Garden of Plants in Paris," he goes on to say that "except perhaps to naturalists only I ought [not] to speak of the feelings it excited in me" (*EL*, I, 7). Nevertheless, he does speak of those feelings in the most intense and personal way.

> The limits of the possible are enlarged, and the real is stranger than the imaginary. The universe is a more amazing puzzle than ever, as you look along this bewildering series of animated forms, the hazy butterflies, the carved shells, the birds, beasts, insects, snakes, fish, and the upheaving principle of life everywhere incipient, in the very rock aping organized forms. Whilst I stand there I am impressed with a singular conviction that not a form so grotesque, so savage, or so beautiful but is an expression of something in man the observer. We feel that there is an occult relation between the very worm, the crawling scorpions, and man. I am moved by strange sympathies. I say I will listen to this invitation. I will be a naturalist. (*EL*, I, 10.)

Emerson's involvement with science in this period and his apparent inclination to study it with some seriousness as this passage indicates, are well known to students of his early development.[2] But the prevailing view of Emerson's relation with science has been established by Harry Hayden Clark's cautionary reminder that Emerson was not "an inductive

*Reprinted from Journal of the History of Ideas, 41 (January–March 1980), 69–88.

scientist" but instead "approache[d] natural history with a method essentially *a priori*, ethical and deductive, like that of Plato, Schelling, Goethe, Kant, and Coleridge."[3] Clark's point is well taken, and a reading of Emerson's writings on science certainly shows him to be no more than a dabbler in astronomy, geology, and natural history. But such necessary caution about approaching Emerson as a scientist should not obscure the impact of science on his thought. If Goethe and Coleridge were finally more influential (as they were), and if Emerson more nearly resembles them in his pursuits than the actual scientists of his day, there is still much to be said about the contribution of pure science to the pattern of his development. His experience at the Paris Museum is the clearest example of such influence in his early writings, and stands, I will argue, as a significant turning point in his thought, culminating one phase of his thinking and initiating another. The impact of the experience lay in its forceful presentation of the implications of botanical and zoological classification to Emerson's mind, emphasizing both the appeal of scientific procedure itself, and its potential philosophical uses. While Emerson's final attitude toward science has received most of the critical analysis, sufficient attention has yet to be given to the place of science in the historical pattern of Emerson's developing moral philosophy. In short, Emerson was not entirely ready to abandon revealed theology until his experience at Paris, and he had no clear vision of how nature might support the moral sense until he had worked through this experience. The basis of such a claim is the analysis which follows of the essential problem of a basis for moral philosophy confronting him before his trip to Paris, the nature of his experience there, and the contribution of that experience to his continuing thought on moral philosophy.

II. As Clark has pointed out, Emerson's mind was made receptive to the influences of science in large part by his reading in the works of the eighteenth-century natural theologians such as William Paley and Joseph Butler, a standard part of his Harvard undergraduate curriculum.[4] The work of these natural theologians centered around the attempt to infer the existence and character of God from the design of nature, a form of work based upon the observation of nature and the ability to relate those natural observations to the God revealed in the Bible. Their work was therefore a blend of rationalism and faith, two intellectual tendencies which are much in evidence in Emerson's early journals and sermons. Although we tend to look back on Emerson as one who championed truth as a form of intuition, it is important to remember that his early rationalistic tendencies were significant in his development, helping to free him from a Biblically based religion, and sustaining his interest in close scientific observation. "Is anything gained by depreciating our reason[?]" he asked his congregation in 1830. "Is not one God the author of reason & of revelation? The best the indispensable evidence of revelation is its entire agreement with reason."[5] Even though Emerson could assert this "entire agreement" of reason and revelation in 1830, his commitment to revelation would become more and more qualified in the period that immediately followed.

One clue to the nature of his interest in science can be found in an early journal entry, a long passage in which he pauses to take stock of himself before entering on ministerial studies, after some hesitation, in 1824. He begins by noting his "keen relish for the beauties of poetry," and admitting a corresponding distaste for the drier forms of intellectual endeavor. It is a curious admission for one to make who would later seriously consider scientific classification of plants and animals as a vocation.

> My reasoning faculty is proportionately weak, nor can I ever hope to write a Butler's Analogy or an essay of Hume. Nor is it strange that with this confession I should choose theology, which is from everlasting to everlasting 'debateable Ground.' For, the highest species of reasoning upon divine subjects is rather the fruit of a sort of moral imagination, than of 'Reasoning Machines' such as Locke & Clarke & David Hume. Dr Channing's Dudleian Lecture is the model of what I mean, and the faculty which produced this is akin to the higher flights of the fancy. I may add that the preaching most in vogue at the present day depends chiefly on imagination for its success, and asks those accomplishments which I believe are most within my grasp. (*JMN*, II, 238.)

The passage clearly displays what can, on a first impression, be taken as a young poet's contempt for rationalism, and seems to establish a clear path for the young Emerson in expressive and imaginative oratory rather than theological or philosophical reasoning or natural science. Emerson's exemplary theologian in the passage, Channing, is not a surprising one, given Channing's enormous popularity as a preacher at the time. But the modern reader who actually goes to the Dudleian lecture will, I think, be surprised at the nature of the "higher flights of the fancy" to which Emerson refers.[6] The lecture's form is closer to a Thomistic theological argument than an inspirational oration or poem. Channing begins with a careful and systematic refutation of the objections to a belief in the possibility of the Biblical miracles, including a direct refutation of Hume. He goes on to offer a point by point listing of the reasons that give a rational foundation to a belief in miracles. The lecture thus serves as an example of the theological synthesis of rationalism and credence in supernatural miracles that Channing and his associates inherited from the theologians of the eighteenth century.[7] Rationalism was not, it should be remembered, exclusively a method of the deists in the eighteenth and early nineteenth centuries, those who held that reason alone could reveal God to man. As Conrad Wright has noted, the New England Unitarians, a far more dominant group of rationalists, "agreed with the deist that there was such a thing as Natural Religion, but denied its adequacy, insisting that it must be supplemented with additional doctrines which come to us by a special revelation of God's will."[8]

The distinction between these forms of rationalism in religion is relevant to Emerson's development of a natural theology because his intellectual disaffection with Unitarian theology was not a rejection of the entire tradition that used nature and reason as evidence of divinity. Emerson's eventual departure from his tradition was due in part to his rejection of the idea that reasoning about nature had to be supplemented by belief in miracles as revealed in Scriptures. The fact is that despite his own doubts about his reasoning powers and his growing self-conception as a poet, Emerson exhibits a persistent rationalism in his early years which suggests the extent of his immersion in the rationalism of his Harvard teachers and Unitarian colleagues. In his early work, Emerson's rationalism can be seen most clearly in his growing preference for a natural theology based on reason rather than a revealed theology which relies upon miracles. Thus, while there is much truth in Perry Miller's argument that transcendentalism is best defined as "an expression of religious radicalism in revolt against rational conservatism,"[9] there is corresponding truth in the fact that the transcendentalists' "religious radicalism" was itself nurtured in rationalism. In Emerson's case, rationalism undermined the historicism of revealed religion, preparing the way for a faith based in the immediate perceptions of the self.

One appeal of Channing's Dudleian lecture to the young Emerson, therefore, must have been the fact that Channing rather ingeniously argued that miracles have a rational basis. Stressing that God's creation of an orderly universe was a means for Him to prove His power and benevolence, and not an end in itself, Channing concluded that "Nature clearly shows to us a power about itself, so that it proves miracles possible."[10] The argument is a curiously circuitous one on close examination: reason tells us that an orderly universe establishes a creator; the existence of such a creator tells us that an orderly universe is not necessary. For Channing, there was no problem in belief in miracles, but rather the opposite: "To a man who cherishes a sense of God, the great difficulty is, not to account for miracles, but to account for their rare occurrence."[11]

Emerson himself was preaching virtually the same doctrine a decade later. In his sermon "Miracles," first preached January 23, 1831, he declares that "The existence of God is necessarily suggested to the reasoning man by what he now beholds and a miracle suggests no more." Emerson's elaboration of the argument, however, is interesting as an indication of his future development:

> The ordinary course of nature indicates an intelligence capable of alleged works, for it can require no greater power to suspend than to originate the operations of nature. In other words, I can believe a miracle, because I can raise my own arm. I can believe a miracle because I can remember. I can believe it because I can speak and be understood by you. I can believe

in a manifestation of power beyond my own, because I am such a manifestation. (*YES*, 122.)

Emerson's equation of miracles with the normal processes of nature in this passage marks the beginning of his eventual rejection of any belief in miracles, stated most emphatically in the Divinity School Address, where he argued that Jesus spoke of miracles "for he felt man's life was a miracle," adding that "the very word Miracle, as pronounced by Christian churches, gives a false impression; it is Monster" (*CW*, I, 81). Even though the sermon "Miracles" was an attempt to lay a rational basis for the supernatural in Christian revelation, the eventual result of this attempt, as his stand in the Divinity School Address confirms, was to make such a belief irrelevant to true religion.

Emerson's refusal of his assent to the reality of miracles is the clearest evidence that he embraced the more purely rationalistic side of his rationalist inheritance. He affirmed the human ability to recognize God through nature, adopting in his preaching a position quite close to the more deistic natural theologians of the eighteenth century. But his unqualified acceptance of these arguments from the design of nature was not confirmed and supplemented by revealed religion as it was for many other Unitarians. The problem created for Emerson by this growing impatience with revealed religion was one he struggled to solve throughout the early 1830's, a struggle which culminated in *Nature*. While arguments from the design of nature could easily establish the existence of God, they could not so easily serve as the foundation for moral action. Nature clearly indicated a creator, but to derive an elaborate moral code from it, or even the moral principles necessary for the conduct of life, was much more problematic. Channing commented upon the difficulty in his Dudleian lecture, noting that "The laws of nature, operating as they do with an inflexible steadiness, . . . give the idea of a distant, reserved sovereign much more than a tender parent."[12] In Channing's view, the result of the use of natural reasoning alone has historically been a failure to accept "the doctrine of one God and Father, on which all piety rests."[13] To Emerson, for whom moral perception was the essence of religion, the moral gap created when revealed religion was rejected posed a serious problem.

His concern about the moral problem left by natural theology is clearly revealed in an unpublished sermon, first preached July 11, 1829. Emerson begins by explaining the assumption that the world indicates a creator, just as a watch indicates a maker, an argument used with great effect in Paley's *Natural Theology*.[14] Even though he is glad to accept the argument as proof of God's existence, he is clearly worried about the assumption that naturally follows from it, that God is a withdrawn and uncaring technician, unrelated vitally to his creation. To counter this idea, Emerson revives the claim of "the pious Bishop Berkeley" that the *"material world exists only as it is perceived."* If we accept the assumptions of Berkeley, Emerson argues, we must conclude that we do not perceive independently existing things, but only their impressions stamped upon our mind by an act of God. Since these impressions are continually before us, God must sustain them continually, in which case he cannot be withdrawn. He thus concludes:

> The artist who constructs a watch avails himself of powers perpetually afforded him by nature that is by God—as the force of gravity or the elasticity of the steel. If these powers shd. be withdrawn his machine wd. stop—But God has not such powers out of himself—[15]

Emerson's argument may not be entirely convincing, though we can see some of its elements emerging more persuasively later in the "Idealism" chapter of *Nature*. But it is an interesting early instance of his attempt to extricate himself by rational means from what he considered a possible dilemma of natural theology.

This dilemma became increasingly problematic as Emerson's reluctance to accept the Biblical revelation grew. He had largely identified Christianity with morality in his early years, and his growing doubts about the supernatural foundations of Christianity thus robbed his "moral sense" of one important support. Even though he noted in 1826, for example, that Christianity had made the human mind "a solemn instrument of truth & goodness" (*JMN*, III, 14), he remarked a few months later that he looked forward to a time when "the true character of God & man's relations to him shall cease to be partially communicated shrouded up in absurd and monstrous errors" (*JMN*, III, 61), those errors being the myths and miracles of the Bible. Nature increasingly became the factor to which he turned for confirmation of his own moral sense: if it could, with the aid of reason, establish God's existence, could it not, with close observation and enlightened perception, be transformed into a moral guide as well? In a journal entry late in 1826, Emerson notes that "The changes of external nature are continually suggesting to us the changes in the condition of man" (*JMN*, III, 50–51), a prelude, at least, to the position that nature leads to moral perception. Later in 1830, he is more explicit about man's ability to use nature morally:

> Man is the interpreter of all the works[;] he draws the audible moral from all. His tongue should tell the ethics of the creation. (*JMN*, III, 186)

If, in fact, man could discern "the ethics of the creation," then moral philosophy as well as cosmology could be based upon speculation about nature.

III. The fact that Emerson was rendered receptive to a natural basis for moral truth by his background in natural theology and his growing rational doubts about the truth of revealed religion accounts in large part for the impact of the experience at the Paris Muséum.[1] But it is also important to note that his exposure to science in Paris, which consisted essentially of a face-to-face introduction to the most current system of botanical and zoological classification, was new only in one important respect: it was a first hand exposure to classification rather than an exposure through books. What Emerson was most impressed by, and most eager to tell his lecture audience upon his return, was the physical arrangement of the actual plants and animals in a system of classification. His remark, in "The Uses of Natural History," on the botanical cabinet in the Muséum reveals the profound impact of that arrangement.

> Moving along these pleasant walks, you come to the botanical cabinet, an inclosed garden plot, where grows a grammar of botany—where the plants rise, each in its class, its order, and its genus, (as nearly as their habits in reference to soils will permit,) arranged by the hand of Jussieu himself. If you have read Decandolle with engravings, or with a *hortus siccus*, conceive how much more exciting and intelligible is this natural alphabet, this green and yellow and crimson dictionary, on which the sun shines, and the winds blow. (*EL*, I, 8)

The cabinet Emerson describes here is the product of the enlargement and rearrangement of the Jardin du Roi in Paris in 1773, under the supervision of Antoine-Laurent de Jussieu, the central member of an established family of French scientists, and an important member of the faculty associated with the Muséum d'Histoire Naturelle. Jussieu's arrangement of the garden was intended to reflect his own "natural" system of plant classification, one which would demonstrate a natural order and unity in the plant kingdom, what Jussieu labelled "une chaine contînue, dont les deux extrêmes sont l'herbe la plus petite & l'arbre le plus élevé."[16] Jussieu's classification system therefore, was a tool for discovering and reflecting "l'ordre de la Nature,"[17] a presupposed harmony of nature from the lowest to the highest, which, as Frans Stafleu has noted, has close affinities with what A. O. Lovejoy has described as the concept of the "Great Chain of Being."[18] Jussieu insists on a "natural" order of classification over an artificial one, which he feels is typified in the system of Linnaeus, thus characterizing his own commitment, and that of several of his colleagues at the Muséum d'Histoire Naturelle, to pursue the idea of an essential unity of nature. The concept was easily lost sight of in the pressure to classify the overwhelming numbers of new plant specimens discovered in the late eighteenth and early nineteenth centuries.[19] This commitment to search for a natural order which would explain all nature is a concept which lends itself well to the purposes of natural theology, for order and unity can be taken as a suggestion of design in nature. Although Jussieu himself does not draw theological conclusions in explaining his system, he does end his description of it with a ringing call for botanists and zoologists to work together in search of "cet ordre, dont l'existence est démontrée & quel est fondé sur des principes invariables."[20] Such a search for a unified system revealed in nature parallels the theological search for an understanding of the design of nature profound enough to reveal moral truth in a way that Emerson himself would surely recognize. Writing almost a year after seeing the botanical cabinet, in the last of his lectures on science, "The Naturalist," Emerson is able to put into perspective the hints he gained at the Muséum.

> So no intelligent person can come into a well arranged cabinet of natural productions without being excited to unusual reveries, without being conscious by instinctive perception of relations which he can only feel without being able to comprehend or define. (*EL*, I, 81–82)

The philosophical basis of Jussieu's work on botanical classification was shared by several of his colleagues at the Paris Museum, notably Jean-Baptiste Lamarck and Etienne Geoffroy Saint-Hilaire. There was not, however, a complete unanimity of views among the group, as indicated by the debate between two of its leading members, Geoffroy Saint-Hilaire and Georges Cuvier, which simmered for some years before it became dramatically public in 1830. The debate centered around the interpretation of a paleontological discovery, but the underlying issues were the closely related questions of the existence of a unified natural order as conceived in the chain of being idea, and the possibility of the mutation of species. Cuvier insisted on the fixity of species, and denied the idea of a natural order arranged in a chain of being, while Geoffroy Saint-Hilaire argued that the natural order suggested a chain of being, whose gradual changes established the fact that lower forms of life do change to higher ones over time.[21] In this debate, Geoffroy Saint-Hilaire had the support of his older colleague Lamarck, who had previously proposed the idea of the mutation of species, and even drew support from Goethe, who saw important scientific principles for which he had fought at stake in the debate.[22] In his discussion of Emerson's visit to the paleontological exhibitions at the Muséum, Rusk wonders whether Emerson realized the irony of catching a glimpse of evolutionary thought through the exhibit of Cuvier, who had himself opposed the theory so vigorously (*Life*, 188). But as the debate between Cuvier and Geoffroy Saint-Hilaire suggests, Emerson was not the only one to draw a differing opinion about the order of nature from the exhibit of Cuvier, and the reverberations of that debate were still in the air in 1833, at the time of Emerson's visit to Paris. Emerson was, we might conclude, being exposed to the cutting edge of advancing scientific thought at a time which found him in almost perfect readiness for such an exposure.

Emerson's initial description of the botanical cabinet quoted above, with his references to Jussieu and De Candolle, reveals both his excitement with the arrangement of the Paris gardens, and his familiarity with the literature of scientific classification. But the literature of classification he now sees as a second-hand substitute for the actual plants arranged in the garden, a bookish and abstract knowledge which only dimly reflects the emotional and intellectual impact of the garden itself. Kenneth W. Cameron puts the point well in noting that it was "an experience which opened his eyes to the wonders in the 'book of nature'."[23] It was not the idea of scientific classification itself which was so impressive to Emerson, but the physical evidence of its power to reflect truth, that truth being the unity and dynamism of nature.

By way of analogy, we might say that the difference between seeing the plants arranged in Jussieu's garden and reading about plant classification is similar to the difference between personally seeing the beauties of a natural landscape and reading a book of landscape description. The pictorial quality, the visual evidence of kinship among plants, is not as forcefully evident in illustrative plates as in personal vision. Moreover, the ability to note structural kinships between plants through the use of books may not lead readily to the perception of the complex harmony of all parts of nature. But this simultaneous sense of nature's complexity and underlying unity, underscored by Jussieu's gathering and arrangement of the variety of plants, seems to have been the most moving part of the experience for Emerson.

The experience itself cuts across the usual categories of description, merging the distinctions between the intellectual, the aesthetic, and the religious in a way that is characteristic of Emerson's sensibility. On an intellectual plane, Emerson seems here to have achieved a fuller comprehension of the significance of scientific classification, moving from a stance of comprehending it with what he would call the understanding to comprehending it on a higher level of the reason.[24] The fact that the visual impact of the garden seems to have triggered this intellectual movement suggests that the basis of the movement is closely akin to aesthetic perception. But finally, the abiding consequence of the experience, incorporating both its intellectual and aesthetic aspects, is religious, a fact that becomes clear when we follow Emerson's lecturing on science later in the year when he returns to America. The moral and philosophical conclusions that Emerson drew from the Paris Muséum reflect his own habit of mind, but it should be noted that these same concerns were not compatible with the motivations of the French naturalists associated with it. They were men of science, but in most cases they felt that their commitment to natural description and classification was not incompatible with larger philosophical and religious speculations. In this sense, their underlying assumptions about the relation of nature and God have similarities with those of the natural theologians with whom Emerson was familiar.

The resulting intellectual consequences of Emerson's introduction to the accomplishments of the Paris naturalists were twofold. In the first place, he gained new insight into a developing theory of nature itself, which he would begin to express in the scientific lectures and bring to completion in *Nature*. Emerson sensed the fact that "Nature is not fixed but fluid" (*CW*, I, 44), indicating his movement to what we might call a dynamic concept of nature rather than a static one. To use Emerson's phrase, he began to formulate a "Theory of Animated Nature" (*EL*, I, 83), in which he saw the possibility of the fulfillment of his earlier search for the "ethics of the creation." Rusk refers to this theory as "a hazy vision of evolution" (*Life*, 189), but the word "evolution," with all its post-Darwinian associations, has to be used guardedly to measure the nature of Emerson's new insight. Beach is right to argue against Clark (and Rusk who later follows Clark) that "evolution" is not the best expression for the nature of Emerson's vision, if that phrase is taken in too strict a sense.[25]

In addition to his theory of animated nature, Emerson also acquired a new respect for the scientific method of classification which revealed it to him. The intellectual procedure of classification clearly fascinated him epistemologically; in his later attempt to write a *Natural History of Intellect* he intended to apply the tools of scientific classification to mental processes, thus indicating his lifelong fascination with the methodology of classification. Yet it is also important to note that classification appealed to Emerson vocationally as well, if only for a brief period. It posed to him an alternative which he rejected only after a serious weighing of its potential to foster his expanding search for his proper intellectual work. His declaration "I will be a naturalist" (*EL*, I, 10) was a serious proposition, and should not be regarded merely as the poetic effusion of an impressionable young man. Emerson may not have known fully the implications of such an ambition, but he would soon set about finding them out.

IV. Circumstances favored Emerson's continuing exploration of science upon his return to America, for there were available audiences for lectures of a scientific nature, not only spurring his scientific reading, but laying the groundwork for his move from preaching to lecturing. From November 4, 1833 to May 7, 1834, Emerson lectured on science four times, finding his first audience at the Natural History Society of Boston and another at the Boston Mechanic's Institution. Over the course of that winter, Emerson began his formulation of the moral implications of a theory of animated, or dynamic, nature, which was influenced by his Paris experience, while working through his attitude toward the method of scientific classification he had experienced there as well.

The first of the lectures, "The Uses of Natural History," begins, as noted earlier, with a description of the Muséum, and the entire lecture is permeated with a quality of intellectual exhilaration originating in the description of the Muséum, but carrying over into Emerson's entire attitude toward science. The lecture itself is a prolonged argument for the usefulness of scientific study, which Emerson depicts as a series of rising benefits similar to the rising ladder of uses of nature in *Nature* (*EL*, I,

23n). Emerson's growing absorption with science is most clearly depicted in two major emphases of the lecture: his portrayal of the scientific pursuit in heroic terms, and his insistence that such a pursuit will indeed have moral implications.

Emerson's conception of the pursuit of science is most clearly established in his assertion that "Every fact that is disclosed to us in natural history removes one scale more from the eye" (*EL*, I, 15). The scientist is thus portrayed as a seer, and Emerson's association of images of vision and of the eye with the scientist, significant terms in his philosophical vocabulary, confirm his importance. The lecture is filled with biographical examples from the history of science: Duhamel, Linnaeus, Buffon, Cuvier, Humboldt, Galileo, Réaumur, Huber, Newton, and Kepler are all referred to as representatives of extraordinary vision and achievement. And, for Emerson, their pursuit itself, not only the results it obtains, is crucial. The life of the scientist, he says, "abounds in sleepless nights, laborious days and dangerous journeyings." It is "this high unconditional devotion to their cause" (*EL*, I, 22–23) which is valuable enough of itself to be worth all their actual discoveries.

The results of the scientific pursuit do, however, have great importance, in that "the greatest office of natural science (and one which as yet is only begun to be discharged) is to explain man to himself" (*EL*, I, 23). This idea of science explaining man to himself is extended in Emerson's assertion that "knowledge of all the facts of all the laws of nature will give man his true place in the system of being" (*EL*, I, 23). Emerson was certainly not blind to the implications of the search for a natural order, such as Jussieu's, for a theory of man, and it was here that he saw the moral ramifications of natural science. In a way that prefigures *Nature* strikingly, he notes "the power of *expression* which belongs to external nature" based on "the correspondence of the outward world to the inward world of thought" (*EL*, I, 24). The result of this correspondence is the realization that "The laws of moral nature answer to those of matter as face to face in a glass" (*EL*, I, 24). He thus concludes the lecture on a note of expectancy: "I look then to the progress of Natural Science as to that which is to develop new and great lessons of which good men shall understand the moral" (*EL*, I, 26). It is clear at this point that Emerson has incorporated the study of science as a key tool in his search for "the ethics of the creation."

Emerson only hints in this lecture of the most impressive and useful fact that science was providing him, that of the dynamism or flux of nature. He appeals to geology to substantiate his assertion that "before the period when God created man upon the earth very considerable changes have taken place in the planet" (*EL*, I, 15). Emerson is, of course, still bound to the teleological assumption of the primacy of man in creation, but we see here that his assumption of the design of nature is beginning to incorporate ideas of change and mutation. Natural forms, he realizes, must be seen from the perspective of their changes over time, or, as he puts it, "every form is a history of the thing" (*EL*, I, 17).

Expanding on this idea in his next lecture, "The Relation of Man to the Globe," Emerson argues that the history of the development of nature is a progressive series of changes in preparation for the advent of man who "is no upstart in the creation, but has been prophesied in nature for a thousand ages before he appeared" (*EL*, I, 29). Emerson uses the evidence of these changes to argue for the perfect adaptation of the earth for man's uses, suggesting a developing perfection of nature and a developing perfection of man's uses of nature: "With the progress of the cultivation of the species the globe itself both in the mass and in its minutest part, becomes to man a school of science" (*EL*, I, 46). As an example of this use of nature as a school, he cites

> the fact that the savans [*sic*] of France have detected more than eight hundred species of shells, almost all unknown in the existing seas, in the limestone of Paris; that Cuvier has determined and classed the remains of more than one hundred and fifty mammiferous and oviparous animals, ninety of which are wholly unknown at present among living species. (*EL*, I, 47.)

Emerson's point is that the development of nature puts man in the position, finally, of realizing the process of that development, and therefore of putting nature to use for his own further development. His enraptured conclusion to the lecture suggests that his exposure to science is indeed strengthening his sense that nature has a potential moral use: "I am thrilled with delight by the choral harmony of the whole. Design! It is all design. It is all beauty. It is all astonishment" (*EL*, I, 49).

Emerson's third lecture, "Water," differs from the first two in the restricted range of its subject matter, but it is an extended example of the dynamic quality of nature and its potential moral uses. The lecture, which is superficially a rather puzzling treatment of an equally curious topic, has elicited little comment from Emerson's critics, perhaps because, as Whicher and Spiller note, it is the "most factual and least personal of his scientific talks" (*EL*, I, 50); it may even strike us as the driest of his lectures. The clue to understanding the lecture, however, is Emerson's quotation from Playfair that "Water everywhere 'appears as the most active enemy of hard and solid bodies' " (*EL*, I, 53). Emerson devotes an entire lecture to this single element because he sees it as a central illustration of the fact that nature is a process, not a static substance. The qualities of water demonstrate "how mighty a benefactor is this most flexible and active of created things" (*EL*, I, 68). As the medium which dissolves the solider substances of the earth, such as the minerals, it acts as a constant unifier of the earth, changing otherwise solid and separate substances into fluid and unified ones. But because "the same power that destroys in different circumstances is made to reproduce" (*EL*, I, 55), this dissolving action of water nourishes the plant and animal life of the planet. As he concludes, "we cannot help returning with new interest to the beautiful phenomenon of its eternal circulation through nature" (*EL*, I, 63).

Water, therefore, most nearly exemplifies Emerson's contention that "the axioms of geometry and of mechanics only translate the laws of ethics" (*EL*, I, 25). In its fluid and ever changing state, it exemplifies the ideal state of both nature and of the soul. In its ability to dissolve and rearrange the elements it contacts, it exemplifies the ideal of unity in diversity, which was a central moral axiom for Emerson. And in the sustenance of the organic life which is its product, it metaphorically demonstrates the organic growth of the soul. Emerson's concluding remark in the lecture is well founded when all of these symbolic properties of water are taken into account: "it may exalt our highest sentiments to see the same particle in every step of this ceaseless revolution serving the life, the order, the happiness of the Universe" (*EL*, I, 68). It is not surprising, in fact, to hear him describe an experience of God, some two years later, by saying that "The currents of the Universal Being circulate through me" (*CW*, I, 10).

The moral lesson that Emerson is beginning to see emerge from nature is one that he does not explicitly state until the end of *Nature*. When we correctly perceive that the creation is "fluid," we then know that its dynamic quality reflects the dynamic quality of the soul. The admonition, "Build, therefore, your own world" (*CW*, I, 45), not only stresses the quality of self-reliance, but that of ongoing spiritual growth and expansion, of self-culture, as well. If the truth of nature is her progressive development for the culture of man, the moral truth to be drawn from that is the use of nature for the willed continuance of that process of self-cultivation.

V. The reader of the first three of Emerson's science lectures will be struck by the significant change of tone in the fourth and last lecture, "The Naturalist," read before the Boston Natural History Society on May 7, 1834. There are, of course, many obvious similarities with the first lecture—the same emphasis on the levels of usefulness of the study of nature, and the same quality of awed devotion to natural beauty—but there is a new note of skepticism about science which is not apparent in the earlier lectures. Quite early in the discourse, Emerson voices this skepticism in the following terms:

> But the question occurs to a man mainly engaged in far different pursuits whether it is wise to embark at all in a pursuit in which it is plain he must content himself with quite superficial knowledge; whether it is no waste of time to study a new and tedious classification. (*EL*, I, 70)

Although the passage is in the third person, there is little doubt that the "man mainly engaged in far different pursuits" is Emerson himself, who, now almost a year after his visit to Paris, is coming to a recognition that his command of science will remain "superficial," and that further pursuit of the "tedious classification" could well be a "waste of time."

It should be remembered that the year 1834 is a significant one in relation to Emerson's development of another calling, that of the poet, and the pursuit of that calling, broadly defined, is surely the "far different pursuit" in which he now finds himself engaged.[26] But while the competing demands of this other calling can explain in part Emerson's change in attitude toward science, it cannot fully explain the note of warning sounded in the essay, best expressed in his remark: "We are not only to have the aids of Science but we are to recur to Nature to guard us from the evils of Science" (EL, I, 76). What lies behind such a statement is Emerson's personal investigation not only of scientific results, but of the method of scientific classification. His rejection of that method as a mode of work for himself is a revealing episode in his search for vocation and marks his emergence from his yearlong flirtation with the exact sciences as a chosen form of intellectual work.

Several of the entries in Emerson's "Journal A" for early 1834 provide the personal background behind the note of skepticism about science he expresses in "The Naturalist." His first journal entry for 1834, dated January 2, expresses his supposition that "a selection of natural laws might be easily made from botany, hydraulics, natural philosophy, &c. which should at once express also an ethical sense" (JMN, IV, 254), a point which he elaborated in "The Relation of Man to the Globe," probably delivered a few days later. But by April of that year, influenced by the coming of Spring, Emerson is beginning to note in his journal actual observations of plants, much in the manner of Thoreau. On April 26, he notes a number of plants by their scientific names, and adds, apparently in an afterthought, that "Nat. Hist. gives *body* to our knowledge. No man can spare a fact he knows" (JMN, IV, 282). Two days later he is again noting his observations with some care, but adding that the spring air "invites man with provoking indifference to total indolence & to immortal actions" (JMN, IV, 283). His comment seems to indicate that he was finding the discipline of detailed natural observation difficult, that a walk in the woods was more conducive to poetry, or even to indolence, than to scientific nomenclature. But it also indicates his sense of a need to find appropriate channels for his intellectual energies. Thus he adds that "A day is a rich abyss of means yet mute and void" (JMN, IV, 283), a perceptive comment on his own situation as a thinker who has become his own taskmaster.

The next day, April 29, Emerson records an anecdote which humorously reveals his growing frustration with his dabbling in scientific classification. The story is of a "boy learning his alphabet" who, when told by the teacher " 'That letter is W'," only responds " 'The Devil! Is that W?' " Emerson asks whether the story is not "exquisite ridicule upon our learned Linnaean classifications?" and concludes with his own version of it: "What shell is this? 'It is a strombus.' 'The Devil! Is that a strombus?' " (*JMN*, IV, 285). The anecdote gives us an inkling of what Emerson calls in "The Naturalist" the "evils of Science." When natural science becomes mere naming, or dead classification, it loses its vital connection to larger philosophical truths. The right use of classification is a question of means and ends, and Emerson realizes the danger of the means, classification, becoming an end in itself.

As Emerson worked toward the completion of "The Naturalist," the limitations of scientific classification became more and more apparent to him. On May 3 he notes that all classification is "arbitrary" but that one system someday might find a combination "which should flash on us the very thought," a remark which he clarifies in these terms: "All our classifications are introductory & very convenient but must be looked on as temporary & the eye always watching for the glimmering of that pure plastic idea" (*JMN*, IV, 288). The "Idea" here, which is similar to Jussieu's notion of a "natural order," is the overriding goal for which classification strives, an intellectual perception that binds the universe into a unity. The problem is that the idea itself is "plastic," meaning both that our comprehension of it is fleeting, according to Emerson, and more importantly, that the result of that comprehension is a realization of the mutable or fluid essence of nature.

Thus on May 5, two days before he delivers "The Naturalist," he notes what he calls a "black spot" at the center of the "subject of Classification." He then concludes:

> The true classification will not present itself to us in a catalogue of a hundred classes, but as an idea of which the flying wasp & the grazing ox are developments. Natural History is to be studied not with any pretention that its theory is attained, that its classification is permanent, but merely as full of tendency. (*JMN*, IV, 290.)

The significant word in the passage is "tendency" because of its suggestion of the animated or dynamic quality of nature. No system of classification, therefore, can pretend to final truth because of this fluidity of nature.

Yet the next day, after asking himself "Well, my friend, are you not yet convinced to study plants and animals?" Emerson answers yes: "say that you love nature, & would know her mysteries, & that you believe in your power by patient contemplation & docile experiment to learn them" (*JMN*, IV, 289-90). It is an answer that affirms the study of nature, but it seems to be a poet's answer, not that of a scientist. A month later, on June 18, Emerson makes it clear that he has pushed both his scientific interests and capabilities to the point at which he can close the case on the life of science. He sees his interests and capabilities for what they are, those of a dilettante, but seems to draw a moral from the admission:

Every thing teaches, even dilettantism. The dilettante does not, to be sure, learn anything of botany by playing with his microscope & with the terminology of plants but he learns what dilettantism is; he distinguishes between what he knows & what he affects to know & through some pain and self accusation he is attaining to things themselves[.] (*JMN*, IV, 297.)

Again, Emerson is putting frank self-analysis in impersonal terms indicating that he has gained enough distance from the "pain and self accusation" of his superficial career as a natural scientist to see its place in his own development. "The Naturalist," which was delivered to the same group that heard his first excited lecture after his return from Europe, is the public testimony that corresponds to this private admission that his abilities and inclinations are not suited for the life of a scientist.

That Emerson was able to abandon the pursuit of science yet maintain his commitment to natural philosophy is in part attributable to the influence of Goethe at this period, who offered him a somewhat more poetic example of the natural scientist than that of the Paris naturalists.[27] "The Naturalist" is filled with references to Goethe, whom Emerson sees as a figure of great enough vision to know and use the tools of science as a means to the larger pursuit of truth.[28] Goethe's influence is best understood from a continuation of the May 3 journal entry quoted above. After noting that science rightly pursues a "pure plastic Idea" of nature, Emerson notes: "This was what Goethe sought in his Metamorphosis of plants" (*JMN*, IV, 288), drawing analogies between Goethe's search for the ideal plant which would explain the structure of all other plants, and other theories of Pythagoras and Swedenborg.[29] The moral drawn from Goethe's example is that the student's mind should be "in a natural, healthful, & progressive state" so that "in the midst of his most minute dissection" he will "not lose sight of the place and relations of the subject" (*JMN*, IV, 288). Again the emphasis is on progress and perspective, and the two ideas are clearly related: if one loses the larger perspective, the study of nature loses its progressive quality, becoming dead and confining. In "The Naturalist," this notion becomes a plea for the proper proportion of means and ends:

The necessity of nomenclature, of minute physiological research, of the retort, the scalpel, and the scales is incontestable. But there is no danger of its being underestimated. We only wish to insist on their being considered as *Means*. (*EL*, I, 80.)

The larger end toward which those means should be directed is again indicated in the May 3 journal entry: "We have no theory of animated Nature. When we have, it will be itself the true Classification" (*JMN*, IV, 288–89). Emerson's "theory of animated Nature" is the clearest statement of his sense that "the ethics of the creation" is to be found in the dynamic quality of nature—a quality which classification pursues, but which is finally available through a unified vision which transcends the divisions pursued by science. "Integrate the particulars" (*JMN*, IV, 288) is his advice to the naturalist, for the act of integration will serve as a progressive act as well, since the notions of unity and progress are inseparable in the larger view of nature. Emerson's realization of the moral possibilities of his theory of animated nature is underscored in the concluding words of "The Naturalist":[30]

> No truth can be more self-evident than that the highest state of man, physical, intellectual, and moral, can only exist with a perfect Theory of Animated Nature. (*EL*, I, 83).

Without a vision of nature's dynamism, we lose our vision of the dynamism of the soul, and thus our sense of human potential. Nature's ability to reflect man's moral nature "as face to face in a glass" has its most important implications in the shared progressive quality of both. By the time Emerson had worked through the last of his lectures on science, this idea was clear to him. Its origin we have seen in the search for fundamental ethical lessons available in nature, whose roots were in the questions posed by natural theology, and whose development was fundamentally altered by the visit to Paris. Emerson would not fully formulate his own theory of animated nature until the final chapter of *Nature*, when his Orphic poet would sing of nature's fluidity, and apply the lesson to a vision of the growth of the soul. But the story of Emerson's experience in Paris, and his emergence from that experience, explains why an Orphic poet, and not a natural scientist, is the hero of *Nature*.

Notes

1. The following abbreviations will be used through this paper in parenthetical documentation: *CW* = *The Collected Works of Ralph Waldo Emerson*, ed. Alfred R. Ferguson et al. (Cambridge: Harvard University Press, 1971–); *EL* = *The Early Lectures of Ralph Waldo Emerson*, ed. Stephen E. Whicher, Robert E. Spiller, and Wallace E. Williams, 3 vols. (Cambridge: Harvard University Press, 1959–1972); *JMN* = *The Journals and Miscellaneous Notebooks of Ralph Waldo Emerson*, ed. William H. Gilman et al. (Cambridge: Harvard University Press, 1960–); *L* = *The Letters of Ralph Waldo Emerson*, ed. Ralph L. Rusk, 6 vols. (New York: Columbia University Press, 1939); *Life* = Ralph L. Rusk, *The Life of Ralph Waldo Emerson* (New York: Scribners, 1949); *YES* = *Young Emerson Speaks*, ed. Arthur Cushman McGiffert, Jr. (Boston: Houghton, Mifflin, 1938). Except where their retention seemed appropriate, I have omitted the editorial symbols of the new edition of the *Journals and Miscellaneous Notebooks* and the cancelled portions they include, for ease of reading. The reader may wish to refer to the passages in full to follow more closely Emerson's movement of thought. I would like to acknowledge research support from the College of Liberal Arts Research Program and the General Research Program at Oregon State University in preparing this essay.

2. For the major study of science in Emerson's thought in the period before *Nature* see Harry Hayden Clark, "Emerson and Science," *Philological Quarterly*, 10 (July 1931): 225–260. Clark's views are reconfirmed in the light of the publication of *Early Lectures* in Gay Wilson Allen, "A New Look at Emerson and Science," in *Literature and Ideas in America: Essays in Honor of Harry Hayden Clark*, ed. Robert Falk (Athens: Ohio University Press, 1975), pp. 58–78. Other important commentaries on Emerson's view of science in the

period can be found in the following: Joseph Warren Beach, *The Concept of Nature in Nineteenth Century English Poetry* (New York: Macmillan, 1936); *Life*, pp. 187–189; Kenneth Walter Cameron, *Emerson the Essayist* (Raleigh, N.C.: Thistle Press, 1945), I, 224–227; Sherman Paul, *Emerson's Angle of Vision* (Cambridge: Harvard University Press, 1952), pp. 208–220; and Jonathan Bishop, *Emerson on the Soul* (Cambridge: Harvard University Press, 1964), pp. 45–59. Rusk (*Life*) and Bishop particularly note the importance of Emerson's observations in Paris. Joel Porte's discussion of Emerson's use of nature for moral purposes is also relevant to this discussion: see *Emerson and Thoreau: Transcendentalists in Conflict* (Middletown: Wesleyan University Press, 1965).

3. Clark, "Emerson and Science," p. 228.

4. Clark, "Emerson and Science," pp. 226–227.

5. Emerson, "[Reason and Revelation]," manuscript sermon bMS Am 1280.215 (92), Houghton Library, Harvard University. Quoted by permission of the Houghton Library.

6. The lecture, entitled "The Evidences of Revealed Religion," was delivered by Channing in 1821 as part of the lecture series endowed by Paul Dudley, the oldest endowed lectureship in America. Emerson had mentioned the lecture earlier in the fall of 1823 as a model of eloquent preaching; see *JMN*, II, 160. The oration is published in *The Works of William Ellery Channing, D.D.* (Boston: American Unitarian Association, 1899), pp. 220–232.

7. The case for seeing Channing as less a transcendentalist than a "supernatural rationalist" of the eighteenth-century mold is made by Conrad Wright, *The Liberal Christians* (Boston: Beacon, 1970), pp. 22–40.

8. Wright, *The Liberal Christians*, p. 5. The group which Wright describes, the "supernatural rationalists," attempted to use the deists' own weapon, rationalism, to undermine the deist position by demonstrating that the Biblical revelation is rationally defensible.

9. *The Transcendentalists: An Anthology*, ed. Perry Miller (Cambridge: Harvard University Press, 1950), p. 8.

10. Channing, *Works*, p. 224.

11. Channing, *Works*, p. 226.

12. Channing, *Works*, p. 224.

13. Channing, *Works*, p. 223.

14. William Paley, *Natural Theology* (New York: Sheldon, 1875), Chapter I, "State of the Argument," pp. 5–8. The work was first published in 1802.

15. Emerson, "[Christianity Confirms Natural Religion]," manuscript sermon bMS Am 1280.215 (43), Houghton Library, Harvard University. Quoted by permission of Houghton Library.

16. Antoine-Laurent de Jussieu, "Exposition d'un Nouvel Ordre de Plantes adopté dans les Demonstrations du Jardin Royal," *Mémoires de l'Académie Royale des Sciences*, 76 (1774): 175. In this and another essay (see note 17 below) Jussieu discusses the philosophical basis for his arrangement of plants, and describes in some detail the system of classification which Emerson saw exemplified in the botanical cabinet.

17. Antoine-Laurent de Jussieu, "Examen de la Famille des Renoncules," *Mémoires de l'Académie Royale des Sciences*, 75 (1773): 214.

18. Frans A. Stafleu, "Introduction to Jussieu's *Genera Plan tarum*," in Antoine-Laurent de Jussieu, *Genera Plantarum*, Historiae Naturalis Classica, vol. 35, ed. J. Cramer and H. K. Swann (New York: Stechert-Hafner, 1964), p. xxii. Stafleu refers to A. O. Lovejoy, *The Great Chain of Being: A Study in the History of an Idea* (Cambridge: Harvard University Press, 1936). Lovejoy's chapter "The Chain of Being and Some Aspects of Eighteenth Century Biology" (pp. 227–241) is partially relevant to Jussieu's work.

19. William Coleman notes the overwhelming numbers of new species discovered in the late eighteenth and early nineteenth centuries: "The number of Linnaean genera almost

doubled between 1757 and 1797 and the number of species rose from 20,000 in 1805 to 50,000 in 1824 (De Candolle)" (see Coleman, *Georges Cuvier: Zoologist* [Cambridge: Harvard University Press, 1964], p. 18).

20. Jussieu, "Exposition d'un Nouvel Ordre des Plantes," p. 194.

21. For discussions of this debate, see Isidore Geoffroy St. Hilaire, *Vie, Travuax et Doctrine Scientifique d'Étienne Geoffroy Saint-Hilaire* (Paris, 1847; rpt. Brussels, *Culture et Civilisation*, 1968), pp. 366–396; Théophile Cahn, *La Vie et l'Oeuvre d'Étienne Geoffroy Saint-Hilaire* (Paris, 1962), pp. 194–210; and Frank Boudier, "Geoffroy Saint-Hilaire Versus Cuvier: The Campaign for Paleontological Evolution (1825–1838)," in *Toward a History of Geology*, ed. Cecil J. Schneer (Cambridge: MIT Press, 1969), pp. 36–61.

22. Cahn, *Saint-Hilaire*, pp. 211–220. See also one of Goethe's conversations recorded on 2 August 1820 concerning the debate, in which he calls Geoffroy Saint-Hilaire "a powerful and permanent ally" whose "synthetic manner of treating nature . . . cannot be kept back any more." He had, earlier, said of Cuvier that "No one expounds a fact better than he; but he has scarcely any philosophy" (*Conversations of Goethe with Eckermann and Soret*, trans. John Oxenford [London: George Bell, 1874], pp. 479–481, 432).

23. Kenneth Walter Cameron, "Emerson, Thoreau, and the Society of Natural History," *American Literature*, 24 (March 1952): 22.

24. See Emerson's letter to his brother Edward, 31 May 1834 (*L*, I, 412–413) for a discussion of the reason-understanding distinction.

25. Beach argues that what Emerson accepted in the late 1820s and early 1830s was a version of the "scale of being" philosophy, not a version of evolutionary theory in what came to be known as the Darwinian sense (see *The Concept of Nature*, pp. 330–333).

26. See Carl F. Strauch, "The Year of Emerson's Poetic Maturity: 1834," *Philological Quarterly*, 34 (October 1955): 353–377. Both "poet" and "naturalist," and several other vocational terms can be subsumed under the larger label of "scholar" as discussed in Merton M. Sealts, Jr., "Emerson on the Scholar, 1833–1837," *PMLA*, 85 (March 1970): 185–195.

27. There is, of course, the great influence of Coleridge's *The Friend* as well, discussed in Beach, *The Concept of Nature*, pp. 319–320. Coleridge, like Goethe, influenced Emerson in other profound ways besides his discussion of science, notably in terms of method. On this point, see Barry Wood's recent essay, "The Growth of the Soul: Coleridge's Dialectical Method and the Strategy of Emerson's *Nature*," *PMLA*, 91 (May 1976): 385–397. See also Emerson's direct reference to this reading of Coleridge on classification in the 3 May 1834 journal entry discussed above (*JMN*, IV, 288–289). One might also note the lesser influence of Charles Bell, whose Bridgewater Treatise, *The Hand, Its Mechanism and Vital Endowments as Evincing Design* (London: W. Pickering, 1833), Emerson read in the winter of 1833–1834 (*JMN*, IV, 236, 254), citing it with approval in "The Relation of Man to the Globe" (*EL*, I, 40). Bell's work at this time apparently reinforced Emerson's commitment to the argument from design. Later, however, during the completion of *Nature*, Emerson borrowed Bell's earlier work, *Essays on the Anatomy of Expression* (London: Longman, Hurst, Rees, and Orme, 1806), from the Boston Athenaeum, 7 July to 26 August 1836 (Kenneth Walter Cameron, *Ralph Waldo Emerson's Reading* [Raleigh, N.C.: Thistle Press, 1941], p. 23). This work, which explores the close connection between art and anatomical study, apparently had greater relevance for Emerson as his concerns changed from the purely scientific to the relation of natural science to aesthetics.

28. One important immediate source of the influence is Sarah Austin's translation, *Characteristics of Goethe*, a long work which attempts to portray the many-sided nature of Goethe, and discusses his work in botany and in the theory of color (Sarah Austin, *Characteristics of Goethe, from the German of Falk, Von Müller, &c.*, 3 vols. [London: E. Wilson, 1833]).

29. Emerson would have found a discussion of Goethe's *Metamorphosis of Plants* in Austin, I, 171–173.

30. As Whicher and Spiller note, the arrangement of this lecture from the manuscript leaves is to an extent conjectural.

INDEX